Bridge Engineering

About the Authors

DEMETRIOS E. TONIAS, P.E., is a leading design engineer and software developer who has worked on a wide range of bridge rehabilitation, site development, and public works projects. An award-winning author of numerous civil engineering titles, Mr. Tonias is a former member of the Adjunct Engineering Faculty at Union College.

JIM J. ZHAO, P.E., is president with Frederick Engineering Consultants, LLC, where he is in charge of bridge design and overall project management. The author of distinguished books on bridge design and risk management, Mr. Zhao is also president of the Structural Engineering Institute, ASCE Maryland chapter.

Bridge Engineering

Demetrios E. Tonias, P.E.
President
HMC Group Ltd.

Jim J. Zhao, P.E.
President
Frederick Engineering Consultants, LLC

Second Edition

New York · Chicago · San Francisco · Lisbon · London · Madrid
Mexico City · Milan · New Delhi · San Juan · Seoul
Singapore · Sydney · Toronto

The **McGraw·Hill** Companies

Cataloging-in-Publication Data is on file with the Library of Congress.

Copyright © 2007, 1995 by The McGraw-Hill Companies, Inc. All rights reserved. Printed in the United States of America. Except as permitted under the United States Copyright Act of 1976, no part of this publication may be reproduced or distributed in any form or by any means, or stored in a data base or retrieval system, without the prior written permission of the publisher.

2 3 4 5 6 7 8 9 0   QPD/QPD   0 1 3 2 1 0 9 8 7

ISBN-13: 978-0-07-145903-7
ISBN-10: 0-07-145903-0

The sponsoring editor for this book was Larry S. Hager, the editing supervisor was David E. Fogarty, and the production supervisor was Richard C. Ruzycka. It was set in Garamond by International Typesetting and Composition. The art director for the cover was Margaret Webster-Shapiro.

Printed and bound by Quebecor/Dubuque.

This book was printed on acid-free paper.

McGraw-Hill books are available at special quantity discounts to use as premiums and sales promotions, or for use in corporate training programs. For more information, please write to the Director of Special Sales, McGraw-Hill Professional, Two Penn Plaza, New York, NY 10121-2298. Or contact your local bookstore.

Contents

Design Examples

Design Perspectives

Preface

This, the second edition of *Bridge Engineering*, preserves most of the text and style of the previous one. At the same time, it presents a number of significant changes and additions.

A book of this nature is by definition an ever-evolving project. In the period since this book was first written there has been a major change in bridge design methods. Twelve years ago, allowable stress design (ASD), and to some less extend, load factor design (LFD), dominated bridge engineering profession in this county. Now, we are in the transition of implementing load and resistance factor design (LRFD) as a uniformed design method.

In reflecting the reality that both LRFD and LFD are currently being used by various state transportation agencies, I am mindful that both methods are covered by this new edition. It is my belief that young engineers, especially college students, should study and understand both AASHTO Standard Specifications and AASHTO LRFD Specifications, so that they will be well prepared to face the challenges of becoming bridge engineers in this exciting and quite rewarding job market.

By introducing young engineers not only to the theory of bridge design, but also to the complete tasks of bridge design, maintenance, inspection, rehabilitation and management, I hope to enlist talents and new enthusiasm in working toward improving our aging transportation infrastructure on which the nation's future economy and growth depend.

JIM J. ZHAO, P.E.
Germantown, Maryland

Preface to First Edition

Highway bridges dot our landscape by the hundreds of thousands. We pass over and under them, paying no more attention to these structures than we would a tree or a hill. Indeed, the highway bridge has become part of our environment. From an historical perspective, the modern highway bridge was born in the depression years of the 1930's, came of age in the 1950's to 1970's, and is entering its golden years in the 1980's and 1990's. These structures have performed so well, they have been so durable, that most of us, engineers or not, tend to take the highway bridge for granted. We simply cannot envision a time when the life of these structures will reach the stage when they will no longer be so durable; when we will no longer be able to take the highway bridge for granted. We have, however, reached that time.

The majority of bridges in our infrastructure were constructed in an era when the growth of our transportation networks was less of an expansion and more of an explosion. The engineers of this era were faced with the daunting task of designing and erecting structures at a pace that many engineers in the present, litigiously active, society have difficulty imagining. Because those individuals charged with the design and maintenance of these bridges did such a good job, the work of today's bridge engineers is tightly interwoven with those of their predecessors.

Old bridges don't die or fade away; they deteriorate. The concrete spalls, the steel corrodes, the piers settle. Still, traffic passes over them. The snow plows come and the deicing agents spray against exposed concrete surfaces causing an electrochemical reaction that accelerates the deterioration of concrete. And still the traffic comes. The trucking industry, as much a beneficiary of the highway bridge as any other industry, pushes the design of structures to the outside of the envelope. Taller trailers barely squeak through minimum vertical clearances, heavier trucks test the load-carrying capacity of primary members. Through it all, the traffic still comes and, remarkably, the bridges still stand.

How and why these highway bridges perform in such a remarkable fashion is what this book is about. Civil engineering, by definition, is a diverse, multifaceted profession. As civil engineering projects go, the design, rehabilitation, and maintenance of modern highway bridges requires the incorporation of just about every discipline in the civil engineer's repertoire. In this respect, integration, rather than specialization, is the key to the performance of a highway bridge.

> The majority of bridges in our infrastructure were constructed in an era when the growth of our transportation networks was less of an expansion and more of an explosion.

xxii BRIDGE ENGINEERING

Bridge Engineering Encompasses More Than Design
How the Text Is Organized
Design, Rehabilitation, and Maintenance Discussed Concurrently

The reader, when using this text, should always keep in mind that this book is about bridge *engineering*; a subject which is much broader than bridge *design* alone.

There are many ways to write a book about highway bridges. The reader, when using this text, should always keep in mind that this book is about bridge *engineering,* a subject which is much broader than bridge *design* alone. In the past, it may have been possible for designers to ignore the important subjects of maintenance and rehabilitation when designing bridges. Today, however, there is a heightened awareness of the important roles these subjects play, even in the design of a completely new structure. Engineers are also increasingly being called upon to retrofit and strengthen existing structures which still can offer several years, if not decades, of additional service.

This text is intended to serve as an overview of the bridge engineering process: from the origins of a bridge project through its design and the eventual maintenance and rehabilitation of a structure. Due to the wide variety of structure types currently being used, it would be impossible for any single volume to cover each specific type of highway bridge in intimate detail. An attempt has been made, however, to provide a description of all of the major forms of highway bridges used, with an *emphasis* placed on the types of structures which are most prevalent. The book is divided into five major sections which provide an examination of

- ❑ The structure as a whole
- ❑ How a bridge project begins
- ❑ Superstructure elements
- ❑ Substructure elements
- ❑ The implementation and management of a bridge in a highway network

The reader will notice that there is no specific section for design, rehabilitation, or maintenance. All three subjects are discussed concurrently for any given topic. For example, the design of a concrete deck is followed immediately by a discussion of rehabilitation and maintenance techniques. The material is organized in such a fashion, in part, because it is functional and beneficial to the reader. The organization of the material, however, is also meant to serve as a symbol of the importance of integrating these three project phases. One cannot design a structure in today's environment without planning for its future maintenance. Similarly, it is impossible to maintain a bridge without understanding the nature of its design. The rehabilitation design of a structure offers a whole new set of circumstances which confront an engineer. All of these subjects play off one another in such an intimate fashion, that an engineer engaged in the design of a bridge must be constantly aware of how each part of the design-rehabilitate-maintain process works in relationship to another.

This text is intended to be more practical than theoretical. In terms of analytical techniques, there is no new ground broken in this book. Rather, the book is meant to synthesize and coalesce the broad range of material into a coherent document describing the entire bridge engineering process. The reader will notice this when perusing through the sections on such diverse, yet important, topics as project funding, inspection of bridges, preparation of contract documents, and the development of a Bridge Management System (BMS).

The presentation of the material in this book is also somewhat different from the engineering texts we have become accustomed to. Although the graphical presentation of the subject matter may seem like a new approach, it is

Discussion of Presentation of Material
Design Examples Presented as Calculation Sheets
Sidebars Highlight Material in the Text

PREFACE **xxiii**

really a throwback to a style of text which was more prevalent 40 years ago. Design examples, for instance, are presented in a calculation sheet format, just as a designer would write them up in an actual bridge project. This technique has previously been used by authors like George Large in his excellent treatise on reinforced concrete design, which was first published in 1950 [Ref. 3.46]. Since the design examples have been separated from the text, they do not break the continuity of the discussion. This approach also has the benefit of not confusing the reader when perusing through the design sections, as can be the case when a calculation step is mistaken for an equation and vice versa. To the immediate right of each calculation sheet is an in-depth discussion of the steps taken on the particular sheet. Contained within each *step outline* are references to pertinent specifications and equations located within the text proper.

The large physical dimensions of the text are specifically used to allow for the incorporation of *sidebars* to the left and right side of each facing page. The use of large margins, such as these, dates back even further than George Large's book. In what has euphemistically (and somewhat erroneously) become known as the dark ages, monks and scholars provided large margins around their text so that the author, or the people reading the document, could *gloss* the text. A "gloss" was a comment, explanation, or translation of the material located within the accompanying manuscript. In this vein, a variety of information is provided in each page's sidebars. Almost always there is a direct quote from the accompanying text which has been pulled out to act as a highlight of the information provided on the page and draw the reader's attention to an especially important fact or issue.

Also included in the sidebars are design specifications which are relevant to the material being discussed on the page. This saves the reader from the task of constantly having to flip back and forth between pages. The structure of the design examples follows a similar logic. Within the sidebars, the reader will also find quotes from some of the reference material. These quotes are intended to act as an accent on the topics currently being discussed. It is hoped that the readers, like the reviewers of medieval manuscripts, will gloss the text with their own notes, commentary, and thoughts.

No matter how important bridge engineering is, the subject matter can become a little dry sometimes. To break the monotony which will inevitably occur in any engineering text, *Did You Know?* sidebars are provided which offer relevant historical data, statistics, or other information about the subject matter currently being discussed, which the reader may or may not be aware of. To provide a real world slant on the information being covered, several separate discussion pieces have been included under the *Design Perspective* header. These discussions offer some current thinking on a variety of interesting and controversial issues such as the hazards of lead bridge paint and steel vs. concrete bridges.

At the top of each page, three lines are provided which give a synopsis of the major topics discussed on a given page. This synopsis acts as a sort of *on-the-fly outline*. It is realized that engineering books are not so much *read* as they are *referenced*. Because of this, the information located in the margins of the document are intended to act as pointers, directing the reader's attention to the material contained within. Hopefully, as the reader flips back and forth, looking for the desired information, he or she will use the sidebars as tools in identifying pertinent information.

> In what has euphemistically ... become known as the dark ages, monks and scholars provided large margins around their text so that the author, or the people reading the document, could *gloss* the text.

xxiv **BRIDGE ENGINEERING**

Engineering Books Are Referenced More Than Read
Lexicon Acts as a Dictionary of Bridge Terms
Importance of Bridge Engineering

Included at the end of the first section is a *Bridge Engineering Lexicon.* This lexicon acts as a glossary of pertinent bridge engineering terms. For the reader who is new to bridge design, it is important to spend time reviewing this list. Since most civil engineers possess a common background in structural design (at least from college experience), one of the first major hurdles that must be overcome is the development of a familiarity with the nomenclature used on a daily basis by bridge designers. For the most part, the definitions provided in the lexicon reappear throughout the course of the text. The lexicon should serve as a quick lookup table for readers so that they do not have to consult the index, flip to a page in the book, and then try to track down the definition they are looking for.

The design, rehabilitation, and maintenance of highway bridges is, at least for this author, an exciting subject. More than that, however, the engineering of highway bridges is an important subject. From a distance, it is difficult to appreciate our dependence on highway bridges and the important role they, along with the highways they carry, play in our modern economy. The individuals charged with the responsibility of keeping these structures operational are faced with a daunting task. With limited resources and imposing constraints, somehow the job manages to get done. It is hoped that, in some small way, this text will help in the effort to design, rehabilitate, and maintain highway bridges, into the next century and beyond.

DEMETRIOS E. TONIAS, P.E.
Schenectady, New York

The design, rehabilitation, and maintenance of highway bridges is, at least for this author, an exciting subject. More than that, however, the engineering of highway bridges is an important subject.

1

Highway Bridge Structures

Section Overview

In this section we will present a short history of bridge design and construction with an emphasis on the bridge as part of the modern highway network. The reader will also be given an overview of the various bridge structure components. This overview of bridge components will be presented in the form of a guide to bridge nomenclature and terminology to be used throughout the course of the text.

Section 1
The Structure

When the average individual is asked to think of a bridge, some pretty impressive images usually come to mind. The Golden Gate and Brooklyn bridges might strike you if you are an American. Perhaps one would think of the Firth of Forth Bridge if you hailed from the United Kingdom. For the historically minded, Pont du Gard is almost always a favorite choice.

Without a doubt, these are magnificent structures and volumes have been written on their history and the engineering behind them; but what of the *common* highway bridge structure? Although you probably feel a bump every time your automobile hits an expansion joint, most people and even many engineers take these average highway bridges for granted. The common highway bridge struc-

Figure 1.1 The type of bridge we *won't* be talking about in this text.

ture, however, is one of the most integral components in any transportation network. It is also one of the most exciting design projects a civil engineer can be engaged in.

By common highway bridges, we imply structures which typically consist of a slab-on-stringer configuration crossing relatively short span lengths. The deck is usually a concrete slab which rests on a set of girders composed of one of the following types:

- ❑ Steel rolled sections or plate girders
- ❑ Prestressed concrete beams
- ❑ Timber beams

There are a wide variety of other forms of bridge structures in use (suspension, cable-stayed, arch, truss, concrete, or steel box girder, etc.), however, the backbone of the modern transportation network is the slab-on-stringer type structure. The Golden Gate, and other major bridges like it, also carry traffic, and can quite rightly be called highway bridge structures.

However, the design and construction of the slab-on-stringer bridge is the focus of this text, not only because of its continued popularity as a structure in new design projects, but also due to the pressing issues of maintaining and rehabilitating existing slab-on-stringer bridges in an aging infrastructure. With regard to rehabilitation, today's civil engineers are presented with a situation that their forerunners were, for the most part, unfamiliar with. Throughout the text we will see that rehabilitation design offers its own set of unique challenges. As young engineers, when we think of bridge design, we all dream of a magnificent project like the George Washington or Sydney Harbor bridges; but these are few and far between. In the trenches, so to speak, we are faced with the slab-on-stringer bridge which, while maybe not as glamorous, can prove every bit as challenging as its larger cousins.

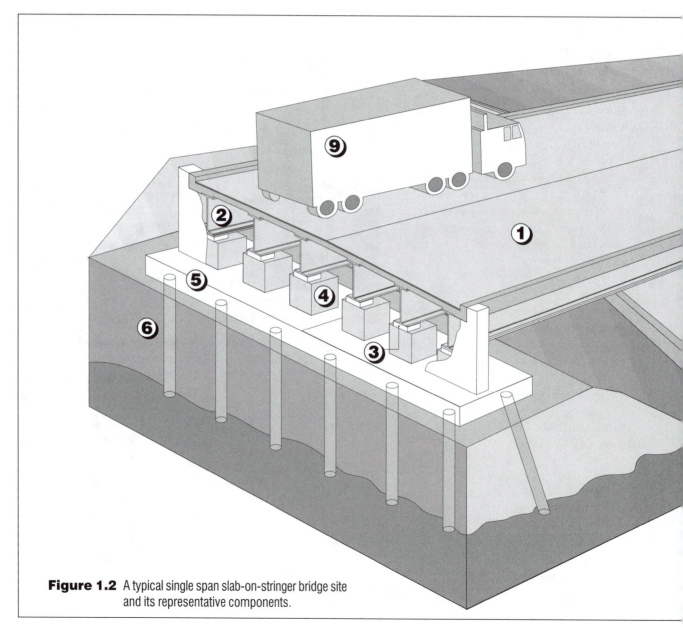

Figure 1.2 A typical single span slab-on-stringer bridge site and its representative components.

1.1   USE AND FUNCTIONALITY

Quite obviously, any integrated transportation network requires bridge structures to carry traffic over a variety of crossings. A crossing, which we will call an *underpass*, could be man-made (other highways, rail lines, canals) or natural (water courses, ravines). As facile as this point may seem, it should bring home the magnitude of the number of bridges currently in use and being maintained by various agencies throughout the world. It is very rare, indeed, when a highway or road of sizeable length can proceed from start to finish without encountering some obstacle which must be bridged. In the United States alone there are over 590,000 structures [Ref. 1.1] currently in service and that number grows every year as new highway projects come off the boards and into construction.

I n the United States alone there are over 590,000 structures currently in service and that number grows every year as new highway projects come off the boards and into construction.

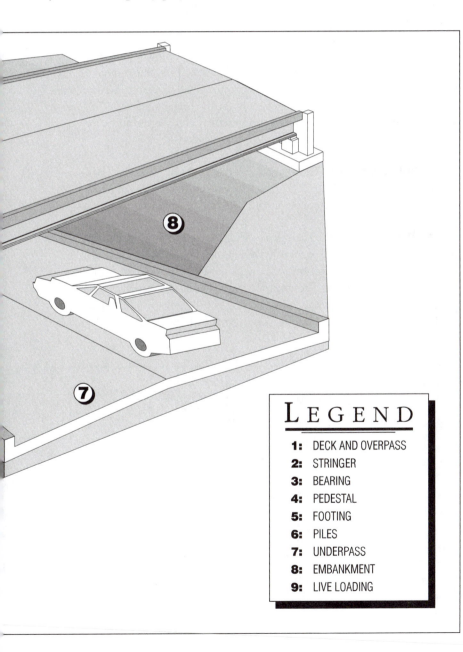

L E G E N D

1: DECK AND OVERPASS
2: STRINGER
3: BEARING
4: PEDESTAL
5: FOOTING
6: PILES
7: UNDERPASS
8: EMBANKMENT
9: LIVE LOADING

A HIGHWAY BRIDGE SITE is a complicated place and a point where a suite of civil engineering disciplines converge to form one of the most exciting challenges in the profession. A scan of the associated figure shows that a bridge designer must be concerned with:

Highway Design for the overpass and underpass alignment and geometry.
Structural Design for the superstructure and substructure elements.
Geotechnical Engineering for the pier and abutment foundations.
Hydraulic Engineering for proper bridge span length and drainage of bridge site.
Surveying and Mapping for the layout and grading of a proposed site.

Yet even with such a breadth of engineering topics to concern ourselves with, the modern highway bridge remains an intriguing project because of the elegant simplicity of its design and the ease with which its system can be grasped. For the new or experienced bridge designer one of the most helpful aids is continual observation. Bridge engineers have constant exposure to highway bridges as they travel the expanses of our transportation networks. By looking for different forms of elements, the reader will gain a better understanding of the variety of components in use in bridge design and possess a more well defined physical appreciation of the structure and design process.

The 1950's through early 1970's saw an explosion in the number of highway bridges being designed and built in this country. According to U.S. Department of Transportation, by 2003 over 27% of U.S. bridges were deemed structurally deficient and functionally obsolete [Ref. 1.1]. This situation means that in this century we will see a major push toward the repair and eventual replacement of many of these structures. It is with this in mind that we must identify the basic use and functionality of highway bridge structures.

1.1.1 Terminology and Nomenclature

As is the case with any profession, bridge engineering possesses its own unique language which must first be understood by the designer in order to create a uniform basis for discussion. Figure 1.2 shows a typical, slab-on-stringer structure which carries an *overpass* roadway over another road. This particular structure, shown in the figure, consists of a single *span*. A span is defined as a segment of bridge from support to support. The following offers a brief overview of some of the major bridge terms we will be using throughout the text. At the end of this section, the reader is provided with a comprehensive *Bridge Engineering Lexicon* which acts as a dictionary for the bridge designer. The lexicon contains many of the most common bridge engineering terms and expressions used on a day-to-day basis by bridge design professionals.

1. **Superstructure.** The *superstructure* comprises all the components of a bridge above the supports. Figure 1.3 shows a typical superstructure. The basic superstructure components consist of the following:

   ■ **Wearing Surface.** The *wearing surface (course)* is that portion of the deck cross section which resists traffic wear. In some instances this is a separate layer made of bituminous material, while in some other cases it is a integral part of concrete deck. The integral wearing surface is typically 1/2 to 2 in (13 to 51 mm). The bituminous wearing course usually varies in thickness from 2 to 4 in (51 to 102 mm). The thickness, however, can sometimes be

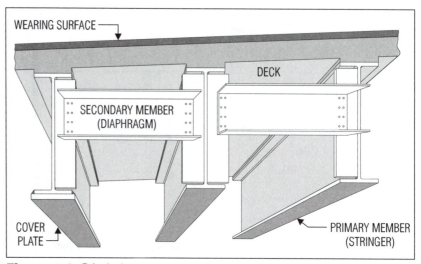

Figure 1.3 Principal components of a slab-on-stringer superstructure.

LATERAL BRACING is a type of secondary member used to resist lateral deformation caused by loads acting perpendicularly to a bridge's longitudinal axis. Wind forces are an example of this type of loading. In horizontally curved steel bridges, like the one shown in Figure 1.4, lateral bracing enhances the ability of the superstructure to resist torsion (i.e., twisting about the longitudinal axis of the bridge). This torsional rigidity emulates the performance of a box beam super-structure (see Section 3.1.1, Part 4). In addition to these inherit structural benefits, lateral bracing also simplifies the construction process by allowing girders to be connected prior to erection and installed as a unit.

Figure 1.4 Lateral bracing on a horizontally curved steel girder bridge.

larger due to resurfacing of the overpass roadway, which occurs throughout the life cycle of a bridge.

■ **Deck.** The *deck* is the physical extension of the roadway across the obstruction to be bridged. In this example, the deck is a reinforced concrete slab. In an *orthotropic bridge*, the deck is a stiffened steel plate. The main function of the deck is to distribute loads *transversely* along the bridge cross section. The deck either rests on or is integrated with a frame or other structural system designed to distribute loads *longitudinally* along the length of the bridge.

■ **Primary Members.** *Primary members* distribute loads longitudinally and are usually designed principally to resist flexure and shear. In Figure 1.3, the primary members consist of rolled, wide flange beams. In some instances, the outside or *fascia* primary members possess a larger depth and may have a cover plate welded to the bottom of them to carry heavier loads.

Beam type primary members such as this are also called *stringers* or *girders*. These stringers could be steel wide flange stringers, steel plate girders (i.e., steel plates welded together to form an I section), prestressed concrete, glued laminated timber, or some other type of beam. Rather than have the slab rest directly on the primary member, a small fillet or *haunch* can be placed between the deck slab and the top flange of the stringer. The primary function for the haunch is to adjust the geometry between the stringer and the finished deck. It is also possible for the bridge superstructure to be formed in the shape of a box (either rectangular or trapezoidal). Box girder bridges can be constructed out of steel or prestressed concrete and are used in situations where large span lengths are required and for horizontally curved bridges. A more detailed discussion of the different types of primary members used in bridge construction is presented in Section 3.1.1.

> The deck either rests on or is integrated with a frame or other structural system designed to distribute loads longitudinally along the length of the bridge.

PIERS, like abutments, come in a variety of shapes and sizes which depend on the specific application. The schematic figures below show some of the more basic types of piers which are popular in highway bridges.

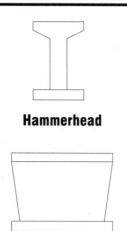

Hammerhead

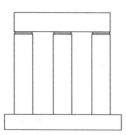

Solid Wall or Gravity

Column Bent

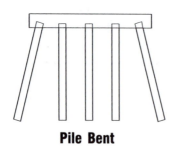

Pile Bent

The physical conditions of the bridge site play an important role in deciding which type of pier to use. For example, to provide a large clearance makes a hammerhead attractive, while pile bents are well suited for shallow water crossings.

Figure 1.5 A hammerhead pier supports a slab-on-stringer superstructure.

■ **Secondary Members.** *Secondary members* are bracing between primary members designed to resist cross-sectional deformation of the superstructure frame and help distribute part of the vertical load between stringers. They are also used for the stability of the structure during construction. In Figure 1.3 a detailed view of a bridge superstructure shows channel-type *diaphragms* used between rolled section stringers. The channels are bolted to steel *connection plates,* which are in turn welded to the wide flange stringers shown. Other types of diaphragms are short depth, wide flange beams or crossed steel angles. Secondary members, composed of crossed frames at the top or bottom flange of a stringer, are used to resist lateral deformation. This type of secondary member is called *lateral bracing* (see Figure 1.4 and sidebar). See Section 3.1.4 for more information on the different types of secondary members.

2. **Substructure.** The *substructure* consists of all elements required to support the superstructure and overpass roadway. In Figure 1.2 this would be Items 3 to 6. The basic substructure components consist of the following:

■ **Abutments.** *Abutments* are earth-retaining structures which support the superstructure and overpass roadway at the beginning and end of a bridge. Like a retaining wall, the abutments resist the longitudinal forces of the earth underneath the overpass roadway. In Figure 1.2 the abutments are cantilever-type retaining walls. Abutments come in many sizes and shapes, which will, like all elements described in this section, be discussed in detail later.

■ **Piers.** *Piers* are structures which support the superstructure at intermediate points between the end supports (abutments). Since the structure shown in Figure 1.2 consists of only one span, it logically does not require a pier. Like abutments, piers come in a variety of forms, some of which are illustrated in the sidebar. From an aesthetic standpoint, piers are one of the most visible components of a highway bridge and can make the difference between a visually pleasing structure and an unattractive one. Figure 1.5 shows a hammerhead-type pier.

■ **Bearings.** *Bearings* are mechanical systems which transmit the vertical and horizontal loads of the superstructure to the substructure, and accommodate movements between the superstructure and the substructure. Examples of bearings are mechanical systems made of steel rollers acting on large steel plates or rectangular pads made of neoprene. The use and functionality of bearings vary greatly depending on the size and configuration of the bridge. Bearings allowing both rotation and longitudinal translation are called *expansion bearings,* and those which allow rotation only are called *fixed bearings.*

■ **Pedestals.** A *pedestal* is a short column on an abutment or pier under a bearing which directly supports a superstructure primary member. As can be seen in Figure 1.2 at the left abutment cutaway, the wide flange stringer is attached to the bearing which in turn is attached to the pedestal. The term *bridge seat* is also used to refer to the elevation at the top surface of the pedestal. Normally pedestals are designed with different heights to obtain the required bearing elevations.

■ **Backwall.** A *backwall,* sometimes called the *stem,* is the primary component of the abutment acting as a retaining structure at each approach. Figure 1.6 shows a backwall integrated with a wingwall in a concrete abutment.

> From an aesthetic standpoint, piers are one of the most visible components of a highway bridge and can make the difference between a visually pleasing structure and an unattractive one.

Figure 1.6 Wingwall of a two-span bridge crossing the Interstate.

A WINGWALL can be poured monolithically with the abutment backwall to form a single, integrated structure. An alternative method is to place a joint between the backwall, or stem, and the wingwall, thus creating the effect of the wingwall acting as a cantilever retaining wall by itself. A wingwall poured monolithically is difficult to analyze, and the design of the reinforcing steel connecting the wingwall to the backwall is relatively empirical. Because of this, many wingwalls erected in this fashion have been known to crack at this connection. The presence of a joint at the interface between the two walls provides for a movement which often results from extreme temperature changes.

■ **Wingwall.** A *wingwall* is a side wall to the abutment backwall or stem designed to assist in confining earth behind the abutment. On many structures, wingwalls are designed quite conservatively, which leads to a rather large wall on many bridges [Figure 1.6].

■ **Footing.** As bearings transfer the superstructure loads to the substructure, so in turn do the abutment and pier *footings* transfer loads from the substructure to the subsoil or piles. A footing supported by soil without piles is called *a spread footing*. A footing supported by piles, like the one in Figure 1.2, is known as a *pile cap*.

■ **Piles.** When the soil under a footing cannot provide adequate support for the substructure (in terms of bearing capacity, overall stability, or settlement), support is obtained through the use of *piles,* which extend down from the footing to a stronger soil layer or to bedrock. There are a variety of types of piles ranging from concrete, which is cast in place (also called *drilled shafts* or *caissons)* or precast, to steel H-sections driven to sound rock. Figure 1.7 shows piles being driven for the replacement of an abutment during a bridge rehabilitation project.

ANYONE WHO HAS ever been next to a pile driver will remember it, for they tend to make a great deal of noise. As shown in this photograph, piles are typically driven into the earth using a hammer which falls between two guides suspended from a crane boom. Rails guide the hammer into place, which is located using a *spotter* extending out from the base of the crane boom. The driver can either drive the piles vertically or be adjusted to allow for an inclined or *battered* pile.

It is interesting to note that, in the photograph, the piles are being driven to replace an existing abutment, which could imply that there was a problem with the footing or the footing design for the original structure. Replacement structures, though, will often require a new foundation to accommodate a larger structure. In many instances, the footing and piles are in adequate condition so that only modifications of bearing seats are required to accommodate the superstructure replacement.

Figure 1.7 Driving piles for a new abutment in a bridge replacement project.

Figure 1.8 Steel sheeting can also be used as an economical abutment material.

■ **Sheeting.** In cofferdams or shallow excavation, the vertical planks which are driven into the ground to act as temporary retaining walls permitting excavation are known as *sheeting*. Steel *sheet piles* are one of the most common forms of sheeting in use and can even be used as abutments for smaller structures. In Figure 1.8 a two-lane, single-span bridge is supported at each end by *arch web* sheet piling abutments providing an attractive and economical solution for this small structure.

3. Appurtenances and Site-Related Features. An appurtenance, in the context of this discussion, is any part of the bridge or bridge site which is not a major structural component yet serves some purpose in the overall functionality of the structure (e.g., guardrail). The bridge site, as an entity, possesses many different components which, in one way or another, integrates with the structure. Do not make the mistake of underrating these appurtenances and site features, for, as we shall see throughout the course of this text, a bridge is a detail-intensive project and, in defining its complexity, a highway bridge is truly the sum of its parts. The major appurtenances and site-related features are as follows:

■ **Embankment and Slope Protection.** The slope that tapers from the abutment to the underpass (embankment) is covered with a material called *slope protection,* which should be both aesthetically pleasing and provide for proper drainage and erosion control (Item 8 in Figure 1.2). Slope protection could be made of dry stone or even block pavement material. Figure 1.9 shows an abutment embankment being prepared with *select granular fill.* This type of slope protection consists of broken rocks which vary in size and shape. The form of slope protection varies greatly from region to region and is mostly dependent on specific environmental concerns and the types of material readily available. For water way crossings, large stones (*rip rap)* are usually used for foundation scour protection.

> S teel sheet piles are one of the most common forms of sheeting in use and can even be used as abutments for smaller structures.

> D o not make the mistake of underrating these appurtenances and site features, for ... a bridge is a detail-intensive project and, in defining its complexity, a highway bridge is truly the sum of its parts.

THE ABUTMENT under construction in Figure 1.9 has a few interesting features to mention. First, this abutment has a backwall and breastwall. The backwall, or stem, is the wall behind the pedestals, and the breastwall is the wall under the pedestals in the foreground. In instances where a breastwall is not used (as shown in Figure 1.2), the pedestals are free-standing columns. Second, the reader will notice several drainage holes located in the abutment backwall and breastwall. These holes provide subsurface drainage protecting the backfill soil from excessive moisture, which can result in a buildup of hydrostatic pressure and cause deterioration in concrete elements.

Figure 1.9 Broken rocks, varying in size, can be used as slope protection.

> The approach slab helps to evenly distribute traffic loads on the soil behind the abutment, and minimizes impact to the abutment which can result from differential settlement between the abutment and the approach.

■ **Underdrain.** In order to provide for proper drainage of a major substructure element, such as an abutment, it is often necessary to install an *underdrain,* which is a drainage system made of perforated pipe or other suitable conduit that transports runoff away from the structure and into appropriate drainage channels (either natural or man-made).

■ **Approach.** The section of overpass roadway which leads up to and away from the bridge abutments is called the *approach* or *approach roadway.* In cross section the approach roadway is defined by the American Association of State Highway and Transportation Officials (AASHTO) as the "traveled way plus shoulders" [Ref. 1.3]. The approach roadway typically maintains a similar cross section to that of the standard roadway. To compensate for potential differential settlement at the approaches, a reinforced concrete slab or *approach slab* is sometimes used for a given distance back from the abutment. The approach slab helps to evenly distribute traffic loads on the soil behind the abutment, and minimizes impact to the abutment which can result from differential settlement between the abutment and the approach. An approach slab is typically supported by the abutment at one end, and supported by the soil along its length.

■ **Traffic Barriers.** A traffic barrier is a protective device "used to shield motorists from obstacles or slope located along either side of roadway" [Ref. 1.3]. Traffic barriers can range from a *guard rail* made of corrugated steel to reinforced concrete *parapets.* On bridges, they are usually called *bridge railings.*

4. **Miscellaneous Terms.** Some of the more basic expressions and terms that we will use throughout the course of the text are as follows:

■ **Vertical Clearance.** *Vertical clearance* is the minimum distance between the structure and the underpass. AASHTO specifies an absolute minimum of 14 ft (4.27 m) and a design clearance of 16 ft (4.88 m). The location of the structure (i.e., urbanized area vs. expressway) has a great deal to do with how this is enforced by the governing agency.

■ **Load Rating.** An analysis of a structure to compute the maximum allowable loads that can be carried across a bridge is called a *load rating*. The guidelines for load ratings are set forth in AASHTO's *Manual for Condition Evaluation of Bridges*. [Ref. 1.4] Two ratings are usually prepared: the inventory rating corresponds to the customary design level of capacity, while operating rating describes the maximum permissible live load to which the structure may be subjected. Therefore, operating rating always yields a higher load rating than inventory rating.

■ **Dead Loads.** Permanent loads placed on a structure before the concrete slab hardens are called *dead loads*. For example, in a slab-on-stringer bridge the stringers, diaphragms, connection plates, and concrete slab itself (including stay-in-place forms) would be considered as dead loads.

■ **Superimposed Dead Loads.** *Superimposed dead loads* are permanent loads placed on the structure after the concrete has hardened (e.g., bridge railing, sidewalks, wearing surface, etc.). Superimposed dead loads are generally considered part of total dead loads.

■ **Live Loads.** Temporary loads placed on the structure, such as vehicles, wind, pedestrians, etc., are called *live loads*. In Figure 1.2 the truck traveling over the structure (Item 9) represents live load on the bridge. As we will see later in Section 3.5.3, the vehicles used to compute live loads are not duplicate models of a tractor trailer seen on the highway but rather hypothetical design vehicles developed by AASHTO in the 1940's and 1990's.

> **V**ehicles used to compute live loads are not duplicate models of a tractor trailer seen on the highway but rather hypothetical design vehicles developed by AASHTO...

■ **Sheeted Pit.** A temporary box structure with only four sides (i.e., no top or bottom) which can be used as an earth support system in excavation for substructure foundations is called a *sheeted pit*. The bracing elements used inside a sheeted pit to keep all four sides rigid are called *wales* (which run along the inside walls of the sheet piling) and *struts* (which run between the walls). When this type of structure is used where the ground level is below water, the sheeted pit is designed to be watertight (as much as possible) and is called a *cofferdam*. In Figure 1.10 a sheeted pit used for excavation at the center pier can be seen.

■ **Staged Construction.** Construction that occurs in phases, usually to permit the flow of traffic through a construction site, is called *staged construction*. An example would be a bridge replacement project where half of the structure is removed and replaced while traffic continues over the remaining portion of the structure. Once the first half has been removed and reconstructed, traffic is then diverted over to the new side while work begins on the rest of the structure. This is an aspect of rehabilitation design which offers some interesting challenges to engineers (see also Section 5.1.2). A bridge rehabilitation under staged construction is shown in Figure 1.10.

THE SHEETED PIT being used for excavation is located at the center pier. At this location, the pier columns have been removed and temporary steel supports have been installed under the pier cap. Staged construction, such as this, presents many design challenges not only in replacement of elements but also in their removal.

The reader will also notice traffic barriers placed in front of the piers. While this is definitely a need during construction to protect workers, barriers are required during normal operation as well to protect piers from vehicle impact. Barrier, railing, or a combination thereof placed in front of a pier is often referred to as *pier protection*.

Figure 1.10 A bridge undergoing staged construction for a rehabilitation.

B y physical applications we imply man-made, natural, or climatological conditions which dictate the type of structure to be used at a given crossing.

1.1.2 Structure Types and Applications

As has been previously mentioned, the majority of bridges present in our infrastructure are of the slab-on-stringer configuration. There are, however, a wide variety of structures in use for a variety of different *physical applications*. By physical applications we imply man-made, natural, or climatological conditions which dictate the type of structure to be used at a given crossing. These could be in the form of

- ❏ Length to be bridged from the start to the end of the structure
- ❏ Depth of channel or ravine to be crossed
- ❏ Underpass clearance required
- ❏ Extreme temperature conditions
- ❏ Precipitation or snowfall
- ❏ Curvature of overpass alignment
- ❏ Aesthetics of the surrounding environment

Any or all of these criteria could play a critical role in the ultimate decision reached as to what type of structure is to be used in general, and what type of components in particular (i.e., wide-flange prestressed concrete girders vs. steel stringers). While it is not within the scope of this text to present a detailed investigation into all different forms of structures, it is important for the reader to have an understanding of some of the major structure types in use and the conditions which make them more attractive than competitive solutions.

1. Slab-on-Stringer. In Figures 1.2 and 1.3 the bridge superstructure consists of a concrete slab resting on a set of stringers, which are connected together by diaphragms to form a frame. The stringers could be steel beams, precast-prestressed concrete girders, or of other suitable materials. Traffic passes over the top of the slab, which can be covered with a wearing surface, although sometimes the slab itself is made thicker to create an *integrated wearing surface* (i.e., using a portion of the slab rather than a separate layer to resist the wear of traffic). The principal advantages of this system are:

❑ Simplicity of design. It should be understood that simplicity is a relative term. From an engineering perspective, slab-on-stringer structures don't break much new ground theoretically, but the complexity they offer from a total project perspective presents a challenge for any designer (see sidebar with Figure 1.2). Indeed, because of all the aspects involved in any highway bridge project, the need of providing a straightforward design is essential toward ensuring that costs be kept at a reasonable level for the engineering services portion of a bridge contract.

❑ The slab-on-stringer bridge lends itself well to a uniform design which can be standardized easily. This is an advantage because standardization and uniformity are critical for maintaining bridges in large transportation networks. Standardization minimizes the need for creating a plethora of codes and specifications for designers to follow, especially when many owners of bridges rely on private consultants to assist in the design of new bridges and rehabilitation of existing bridges. Uniformity means that consistent, and therefore economical, methods can be employed in repairing deteriorated structures. Imagine if a highway network had hundreds of *unique* designs with customized components for each structure!

❑ Construction is relatively straightforward and makes use of readily available materials. Prefabricated primary members like steel wide-flange stringers or prestressed concrete beams allow for quick erection and a clean appearance while at the same time provide for an economy of materials that is a benefit to the contractor as well as the owner.

Slab-on-stringer structures, however, are primarily for short span lengths and average clearance requirements (we will quantify *short* and *average* a little bit later). When span lengths become excessive and the geometry and physical constraints of a site become excessive, other forms of structures must be investigated.

2. **One-Way Slab.** For a very short span [less than 30 ft (9 m)] a one-way concrete slab supported on either end by small abutments is an economical structure. Such a short span structure often gains the tag of *puddle crosser* because of the diminutive size of the structure. For short to median spans, [30 to 80 ft (9 to 24 m)] prestressing steel is typically used. Circular voids in the slab are sometimes used to reduce the dead load.

3. **Steel and Concrete Box Girder.** When bending and torsion are major concerns, a box girder type structure offers an aesthetically pleasing, albeit expensive, solution. Since these types of structures do not make use of standardized or prefabricated components, their role is usually restricted to

> **U**niformity also means that consistent, and therefore economical, methods can be employed in repairing deteriorated structures. Imagine if a highway network had hundreds of unique designs with customized components for each structure!

[1.1.2, Part 3]

CONCRETE BOX GIRDER BRIDGES can be precast or cast-in-place. Most of these bridges are posttensioned. For large span bridges, the balanced cantilever construction method is typically used to build the bridge superstructure.

Figure 1.11 KCRC West Rail Viaducts, Hong Kong.

major highway bridges that can take advantage of their ability to meet relatively long span requirements. Figure 1.11 shows the KCRC West Rail Viaducts in Hong Kong.

4. **Cable-Stayed.** Although box girder bridges with span lengths of 760 feet (232 m) have been built, a significant number of modern bridges with span lengths from 500 feet to 2800 feet (153 to 853 m) have been constructed as cable-stayed bridges. These types of bridges have begun to be built in the United States only 40 years ago, but the response has been overwhelming. Low cost, ease of construction, and aesthetics are the major reasons why this type of structure is now a popular choice for medium and long span bridges. Figure 1.12 shows the William Dargan Bridge in Dublin, Ireland.

5. **Suspension.** Everyone immediately recognizes the suspension bridge as one of the consummate marvels of civil engineering. When presented with spans of significant length over impressive physical obstacles (e.g. the Mississippi River), the suspension bridge offers an elegant answer to a monumental engineering task. For the majority of structures in use, however, their application is relatively limited and their design relegated to the domain of a small group of engineers. Oddly enough, despite this limited role, numerous quality texts are available on the subject and the reader is referred to them for further discussion on these types of structures.

6. **Steel and Concrete Arch.** Like the cable stayed and suspension bridges described above, the arch is most often used for major crossings like the Hell Gate and Sydney Harbor bridges. Figure 1.13 shows a picture of the

Figure 1.12 William Dargan Bridge, Dublin, Ireland.

Figure 1.13 Twin steel through arches cross the Mohawk River in upstate New York.

THE DESIGN OF ARCH bridges is beyond the scope of this text. There are, however, several terms concerning arch bridges which every bridge engineer should be familiar with. The highest point on an arch is known as the *crown*. In a through arch, the vertical cables from which the deck is suspended are called *hangers*. In deck arches, like the one shown in the Bridge Engineering Lexicon (Section 1.4), the area between the bridge deck and the arch is known as the *spandrel*. Deck arch bridges with open areas between supporting columns are known as *open spandrel* arches, while those that are solid between the arch and deck are called *filled spandrel* arches. The *springing line* is the extension of the arch from the abutment or pier support. The surface that the arch is supported on is inclined at an angle. This surface is called the *skewback*. The lower surface of an arch is the *soffit,* and the upper surface is the *back* [Ref. 1.6].

twin Thaddeus Kosciuzko bridges crossing the Mohawk River in upstate New York. In this particular site, the steel arches provide for an attractive-looking structure while also eliminating the need for a pier in the river. When the deck, as is the case with the structures in Figure 1.13, is suspended from the steel arch, the structure is called a *through arch*. When the deck is supported on top of the arch, this is called a *deck arch*. An arch bridge generates large reaction forces at its end supports. The horizontal component of these reaction forces is either resisted by abutment foundations, or in the case of a *tied arch*, resisted by a tie between arch supports. Other elements of an arch bridge are described in the sidebar accompanying Figure 1.13.

7. **Truss.** The truss bridge is encountered most often in historical engineering projects that require preservation or rehabilitation of an existing structure. For the most part, the day of the truss as a new bridge structure in and of itself is over, because truss members are typically fracture critical members (i.e., there is no redundancy in the load path, so should one member fail, the whole structure would collapse). Another major reason it becomes unpopular is that the construction and maintenance costs of truss bridges are very high. However, the use of trusses as bridge components in large structures is still prevalent. Trusses are also used as temporary bridges. Figure 1.14 shows a picture of American River Bridge near Sacramento, California.

While there are countless variations on the structures listed above, these seven types represent the major forms in use today. Our focus will be on the most common structures, with reference made to specialty bridges when the topic warrants discussion of them. In reality, although their forms vary, all highway bridges have one task: to get traffic from one approach to the other.

TRUSS BRIDGES were the most popular bridge type a century ago. Due to their high construction and maintenance costs, and also due to the lack of structural redundancy, very few truss bridges have been built in the past 50 years.

Figure 1.14 American River Bridge near Sacramento, California.

1.2 ORIGINS OF THE MODERN HIGHWAY BRIDGE

Today's highway bridge is an offspring of the rapid development of the modern transportation network. In the United States, this development took the form of what is known as the U.S. Interstate system, a highway system composed of over 46,500 miles (74,800 km) of roadway. The history of the Interstate system is germane to our discussion of bridge design because its development parallels the growth of bridge engineering in the second half of the twentieth century. The evolution from the design of new structures in almost assembly-line like fashion, to the detailed design of a bridge rehabilitation, did not occur overnight. Indeed, the creation of modern standards and specifications in place today, central to the design sections of this book, are an outgrowth of the efforts of an entire generation of civil engineers who grew up professionally during the formative years of what was, and still is, the largest public works project in the U.S. history.

The Interstate system was funded as a response to the growing U.S. economy after World War II. Although the plan to build some major form of highway system that would link the major U.S. metropolitan areas existed before World War II, the impetus for the plan did not gain strength until 1956. One of the principal impacts of the Interstate system on highway bridges is in its servicing of long-distance trucking. It is this function that would serve as one of the overriding design constraints in all highway bridge structures. At a variety of levels, the construction of the Interstate highway system affected the way we build bridges today. Whether it is the width of the structure set to allow multilane travel over a bridge or its clearance, defined to accommodate the passage of large military vehicles under it, the Interstate was the primary influence on the functionality of the modern highway bridge.

Before the Interstate took hold, most small bridge structures were designed to handle low-level vehicular traffic. The advent of the Interstate greatly impacted the need for structures to carry heavier and heavier loads. It was also the construction of the Interstate on a national level that led to the adoption of uniform design standards across the states, bringing about the many advantages of standardization enumerated in our discussion of the slab-on-stringer structure [Sec. 1.1.2]. In short, the development of the Interstate system has had the following effects on highway bridges:

❑ Through federal funding, the Interstate system financed the construction of a large number of the highway bridges in use today.

❑ The Interstate system spurred the research and development of highway bridge design and construction which has led directly to many of today's common design and construction practices.

❑ Because of the national concept of the Interstate system, a refined and common design standard was developed. The detailed design standard, which was once a reality for a few major states like New York, California, and Ohio, now became accessible throughout the United States (and even to other countries throughout the world) that could not afford to finance the high level of research and effort required to produce such specifications.

> Indeed, the creation of modern standards and specifications in place today ... are an outgrowth of the efforts of an entire generation of civil engineers that grew up professionally during the formative years of what was, and still is, the largest public works project in the U.S. history.

All of these factors have coalesced to form the science of bridge engineering as we know it today and make it unique from any other type of structural design. If we make an analogy to building design, it can be recognized that the design of highway bridge structures could never be facilitated in the same fashion as one would engineer a building. Although buildings and their associated sites incorporate many, if not all, of the same concepts and design principles as bridges, they are often unique with specific solutions designed on a site-by-site basis with code and specifications varying dramatically from municipality to municipality. Imagine a highway network populated with bridges in this same fashion with its thousands upon thousands of structures. The Interstate system, as a result of its magnitude, *forced the issue*, if you will, by making the various state and local agencies adopt a uniform approach to the engineering of highway bridges. While some may argue that this has depleted bridge design of its flare and creativity, the reality is that construction of such a large number of structures in so short a time frame could never have been undertaken any other way.

Many engineers, both new and experienced, view the heyday of the Interstate in the late 1950's and 1960's as the golden age for civil engineering. It is difficult, in today's litigious environment, for civil engineers to fully appreciate the velocity with which Interstate development took place and, with this growth, the number of bridges constructed in so few years. In truth, many of today's rigorous rules were born out of the problems associated with moving so quickly in the early days. The alacrity with which new standards were created, as engineers began to more fully understand the impact which the new level of traffic would have on their designs, was so great that plans would literally have to be changed from the time design was completed to the time the project was let for construction. For the bridge designer, it is almost amusing to note that it only took 10 or 11 plan sheets to build a new structure in the 1950's and today it takes almost 40 just to repair it! The early years of Interstate development, however, also represented a time when there was considerable public approval for the building of roads and bridges, which facilitated the speed with which projects came off the boards and into the field. The environmental movement in the mid 1960's followed by public apathy (if not downright disapproval) toward new highway projects effectively ended this *heyday* and ushered in the era of maintaining what our predecessors have built.

Yet make no doubt about it, rehabilitation is neither trivial nor mundane. An engineer at the Kansas Department of Transportation was quoted as saying about rehabilitation work that "It's a lot more fun to build something new than it is to try to refurbish something that is already there." Where there is certainly nothing exciting about performing surface concrete patching on deteriorated pier columns, the scope and magnitude of a rehabilitation design can often exceed that of the design of a new structure. Bill Cosby once noted in a monologue that having only one child does not constitute being a parent because "too many things are left out" [Ref. 1.7]. In a similar fashion, we can say the same thing about the modern bridge designer because, like having only one child to blame when a vase is broken, not having to worry about staged construction, maintaining traffic through a project site, dealing with lead paint and other hazardous materials put in the initial design, etc., just leaves too many things out of the experience of being involved in bridge design today.

It is difficult, in today's litigious environment, for civil engineers to fully appreciate the velocity with which Interstate development took place and, with this growth, the number of bridges constructed in so few years.

Bill Cosby once noted in a monologue that having only one child does not constitute being a parent because "too many things are left out." In a similar fashion, we can say the same thing about the modern bridge designer ...

In reality, today's bridge designers should be envious of their predecessors for the relative ease with which they could throw a bridge up. Modern design requires a higher level of details than the engineers of the 1950's and 1960's would have ever imagined. Many states require that details, like the design of temporary earth support systems and reinforcing steel bar schedules, which were once left to the contractor at the site, be rigorously detailed by the design engineer. Indeed, the number of managers and agency personnel involved in any one bridge design project today most likely exceeds the number of people it took to make high-level decisions on where to locate whole sections of the Interstate.

As with the Germans, who owe a great deal to the building of the Autobahn, we owe much in the United States to the development of the Interstate system, for it was major public works projects like these that created a workable and efficient method of erecting bridges in a manner that was both consistent and manageable. It is also important to always keep in mind that the highway bridge and its many components is but itself one piece in an entire transportation network. The importance of the role the bridge plays in this network was never so vividly demonstrated than when the bridge carrying the New York State Thruway over the Schoharie Creek collapsed in the rushing waters of a near record flood. The earth beneath the piers washed away *(scoured)*, the footings became undermined, careening out of place, and, in an instant, this tragic failure effectively cut the state's transportation trunk in half and in the process cost 10 people their lives.

1.3 BRIDGE DESIGNERS AND THEIR PROJECTS

In his excellent treatise *Bridges and their Builders*, D. B. Steinman closes his text with a section called "The Bridge Builder in Contemporary Civilization." In this final chapter, he defines the role of the modern bridge engineer (circa 1957) as a metallurgist, mathematician, foundation expert, steel erector, artist, and leader of mankind [Ref. 1.2]. While *leader of mankind* may be stretching the point a bit, the breadth of scientific and engineering knowledge involved in bridge design is formidable, yet as we shall see, quite definable.

Through the efforts of bridge engineers involved in projects such as those described in Sec. 1.2, the past 40 years have yielded a set of design standards that allows today's engineer the luxury of not having to *reinvent the wheel* for each project. However, do well-defined standards and sets of details stifle creativity? Perhaps on a more fundamental level, the proper question is: Who are today's bridge designers anyway? In the United States, highway bridge design is typically undertaken by two principal groups:

❑ Municipal Agencies. These could be local agencies, but for the most part they are design groups for a state or county transportation agency or autonomous agency in charge of a specific branch of highway.

❑ Private Consultants. The majority of private civil engineering consulting firms that engage in bridge design are medium (15 to 100 person) to large (100 plus persons) size firms specializing in highway design work in general and highway bridge design in particular.

> "Thoughtful owners might better loosen some of the artificial bonds they impose on their designers ... and seek to restore what was once a design team, or once, even a design and construction team."
>
> THOMAS R. KUESEL
> [Ref. 1.8]

In the United States a highway bridge project is usually slated for construction by the owner (the agency), after which design is either undertaken by an outside consulting firm or the in-house design department of the owner. Once the appropriate reviews are completed, the project is then listed in an advertisement in response to which several contractors will bid on the job. The contract is then awarded to the lowest bidder, although this is not always the case.

An intriguing alternative to this process is under the term *design-build* (sometimes called *value engineering*) under which approach, a consultant or the owner prepares a preliminary plan of the bridge to be constructed which includes only basic information such as physical location, basic dimensions, design loading and specifications, alignments, clearances, etc. Based on these preliminary plans and specifications, contractors then propose their own design and construction costs. The design is either completed by an in-house engineering department of the contractor or a hired consultant. Once the design and price proposals are submitted to the owner, a group of independent or *check engineers* review the plans and the costs, and along with the owner, decide which design and its contractor will construct the project. The decision is not based on cost alone but on the overall solution and its impact on everything from aesthetics to environmental concerns (so called *technical evaluation*). Design-build proponents believe that their approach creates a competitive atmosphere that stimulates the various parties to provide better solutions for the client, which leads to innovative and more economical designs for the owner [Ref. 1.8]. Since there is only a single party responsible for design and construction, the cost and schedule should be improved. Any problem, either from design or construction, can be resolved easily. From the owner's perspective, he or she only needs to deal with one party who takes responsibility of engineering, cost, schedule, and quality.

There are several problems which engineers in the United States have with this approach. First and foremost is the belief that competitive bidding for engineering services is considered

DESIGN PERSPECTIVE

A Predatory Attitude?

*I*n a discussion about the pros and cons of value engineering in bridge design [Ref. 1.8], Thomas R. Kuesel, former chairman of the board of Parsons Brinckerhoff Quade & Douglas, Inc., of New York, New York, talks about the "predatory attitude" many owners have toward "departures from precedent." Mr. Kuesel is not alone in his frustration that many private consulting engineers have in dealing with their counterparts at various agencies.

Even the most innocuous of deviations from an agency's standard details, like a new way of draining an abutment, can often be met with, at best, close scrutiny and, at worst, open hostility. In Mr. Kuesel's opinion, value engineering is a superficial attempt at solving what is a much deeper problem.

To understand the owner's perspective in all of this, it is important to recognize that years and years of research and development go into the development of department standards and practices. This development is sometimes analytical, many times empirical, and to stray from the course means changing the way department personnel have been building bridges for decades. To hold onto these standards as gospel, however, is to deny that there is "always room for improvement."

Successful agencies make a concerted effort to carve out a middle ground where both owner and consultant design personnel can work together in developing new methods and ideas.

The thing that all parties must keep in mind, however, is that there are many egos to bruise in any design situation, a fact which both sides of the fence seem to loose track of. Agencies almost reflexively deride anything but their practices as acceptable, and consultants take any rejection as an insult to their professional integrity.

If the owner recognizes that consultants aren't just thinking of new ways to make their life difficult and consultants understand that deviation means a lot of work on the owner's part, each can more objectively understand the other. The key to the whole process, as basic as it may sound, is civility, something a lot of civil engineers have difficulty with.

to be unethical. The thinking behind this belief is that, in trying to save costs to impress a panel on the design of a project, the engineer will be tempted to sacrifice safety of the structure in order to minimize construction expense. The other major problem U.S. engineers have is with the notion that the contract will not be based solely on price. Municipal agencies, who must ultimately report to the public, would have to make an extraordinary case for choosing a more expensive design just because it looks better or fulfills some abstract criterion of the panel. Under the design-build approach, contracts are awarded on a lump sum basis, which means that the owner and contractor must have an extraordinarily good working relationship for this type of arrangement to be successful. In many cases, an outside consulting firm is hired by the owner to supervise and to approve the contractor's design, and to oversee the construction for the owner.

The opponents argue that with respect to the contractors, having to submit design proposals (in most cases, 30% to 50% complete drawings) is a costly venture, especially when they may not be awarded the project. In some instances there are monies available to compensate all bidders for their design proposals, but if this is not the case, the costs that contractors incur preparing these proposals will just be passed along to the consumer on subsequent projects. In this instance the consumer is the owner and the public they serve. That also indicates that the future maintenance of any constructed project that is part of an overall infrastructure, be it a bridge or highway, cannot be so easily dismissed as to say that an independent design under the design-build approach will "meet the maintenance needs of the owner." To do so means following, to a certain degree, a set of standard details and specifications that in and of itself puts a constriction on creativity.

As with any argument, the answer most likely lies somewhere in the middle. Design-build does spur the participants on to more creative designs. It reduces the cost and overall project time. However, competitive engineering presents many dangers which cannot be ignored. Also, owners need to do more in the way of working with consultants and contractors within their present system to foster innovation in design, something they have not done well in the past (see *Design Perspective*, on facing page). If all parties involved recognize that the three fundamental goals of any highway bridge project are low costs, quality and safety, and longevity of the structure, then much has already been accomplished in securing the completion of a successful project, regardless of the way in which it is undertaken.

At present, only a few states in the U.S. have adopted the design-build approach as an alternative contract method for large or high profile projects. So far, their results seem to be positive, and as a result, more and more states are considering joining this group to have the design-build as an alternative contract method to save project costs, speed up the projects, or choose the best design for high profile projects.

> **U**nder the design-build approach ... the owner and contractor must have an extraordinarily good working relationship for this type of arrangement to be successful.

1.4 THE BRIDGE ENGINEERING LEXICON

So far, we have examined the major components of a highway bridge structure and, in the process, obtained a general understanding of the nomenclature employed by bridge engineers. Provided below is a more detailed lexicon of the bridge engineer's daily vernacular. To be sure, it would be impossible to compile a complete list of all the expressions and terms used in the profession. The items listed below, however, represent the common expressions used throughout this text. An attempt has been made to de-regionalize the terms used in this book. It should be understood by the reader that each geographic region maintains its own distinct flavor of design, and to a certain extent, the terminologies used for bridge elements. Complicating this situation is that many designers refer to elements by manufacturers' brand names. While there is nothing inherently bad about this except that we should not specify any brand name in our design, it does tend to confuse young engineers.

It may seem to the reader that a good many of the entries in the lexicon are repeated definitions from the preceding (and following) text. The lexicon is meant to act as a handy reference for the reader to flip back to while reading the text. While it is certainly hoped that the book is read from cover to cover, a measure of reality would suggest that many readers will be moving about the book in a somewhat nonlinear fashion. So, for example, if the term *weep tube* is used liberally in a section, the reader will not have to hunt down the exact point of definition in the text but rather can refer back to the entry below. It is recommended that newcomers to bridge design spend time familiarizing themselves with the definitions below before moving on to the subsequent sections. The definitions provided herein are within the context of bridge engineering in general and this text in particular.

The lexicon is meant to act as a handy reference for the reader to flip back to while reading the text.

AADT Average Annual Daily Traffic.

AASHO American Association of State Highway Officials. Founded in 1914 and renamed in 1973 to AASHTO (see below).

AASHTO American Association of State Highway and Transportation Officials. Name changed from AASHO in 1973 to include all modes of transportation.

Abrasion A weathering action causing a wearing away of a surface due to frictional or similar forces, as in the abrasive action of wind or water transporting sediments which grind against a surface.

Absorption The process where a liquid is taken into the permeable pores of a solid body (as in wetting of concrete). Absorption leads to an increase in the weight of the porous solid.

Abutment Earth-retaining structures supporting the superstructure at the beginning and end of the structure.

Acceleration Coefficient Dimensionless coefficient used to describe ground motion due to seismic forces.

ACI American Concrete Institute.

Acidity The measure of acids in a solution typically represented by a pH factor less than seven. In surface water, acidity is initiated by carbon dioxide in the air, which forms carbonic acid.

Acute An angle less than 90 degrees.

ADT Average Daily Traffic.

ADTT Average Daily Truck Traffic.

Adhesion The sticking together of two different materials (e.g., clay to a concrete pile).

ABUTMENT

Admixture A material other than portland cement, aggregates, or water which is added to a concrete batch prior to or during mixing (e.g., sand, clay, fly ash, hydrated lime).

Advanced Detail Design Project level of completion just before submission of final plans. At this stage all major portions of design should be complete. See also *Preliminary Design* and *PS&E*.

Aggradation A condition in a water channel where, over a long period of time, more sediment is added to a stream bed than removed.

Air Entrainment The process of adding air to concrete in order to increase durability while causing only a small decrease in strength. Used in bridge decks to offer resistance to freeze-thaw cycles.

AISC American Institute of Steel Construction.

Alkalinity The measure of negative ions in water typically represented by a pH factor greater than seven.

Alligator Cracking Cracks in a wearing surface or approach pavement which form interlocking, rectangular shapes (similar to an alligator's skin). Typically initiated by insufficient base support or concrete shrinkage.

Allowable Stress Design AISC designation for Working Stress Design.

Anchorage A tie embedded in concrete, rock, or other fixed material (e.g., an anchor for a post-tensioning tendon).

Approach Section of roadway immediately before and after the structure.

Approach Pavement Used to describe an approach with a cross section either consistent with or slightly wider than that of the overpass road.

Approach Slab Used to describe an approach with a reinforced concrete slab. An approach slab is used to prevent settlement of the approach pavement.

Appurtenance A feature that serves the overall functionality of the bridge site (e.g., railing, lighting, signing, etc.).

Apron A concrete slab located underwater at the base of culverts to prevent scour (erosion) at the inlet and outlet.

Arch A curved structure which transfers vertical loads through inclined reactions to its end supports.

Armored Joint A joint equipped with steel angles installed to protect the adjacent concrete edges.

As-Built Plans Plans issued after the construction of a structure reflecting any and all field changes made to the final design plans.

Asphalt A bituminous material, black in color, used in pavements and wearing courses. Typically made by distilling petroleum oil.

Auger Drill used to retrieve soil samples. See also *Boring*.

Axle Load The total load on a truck axle. For most design vehicles this is twice the wheel load.

Back See *Extrados*.

Backfill Retained fill as in the region behind an abutment backwall and beneath the approach.

Backwall The principal retaining component of an abutment above the bearing seat level.

Backwater The backing up of water in a water channel due to a downstream constriction or excess channel flow.

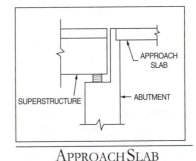

APPROACH SLAB

ARCH

Balustrade A railing system comprised of short columns called balusters which are connected together by a rail.

Bascule Bridge A moveable bridge in which the deck opens up like a set of doors in an upward direction.

Base Course A layer of compacted material directly under the wearing surface, typically consisting of mineral aggregates and additives which are compacted to support the pavement. See also *Subbase*.

Base Metal The existing steel material to which another member is welded using an electrode.

Batch Total weight of cement and aggregates which produces a given amount of concrete.

Batter Pile A pile which is inclined (e.g., 1 horizontal on 3 vertical) in order to resist large lateral loads.

Beam A horizontal member supporting vertical loads (e.g., pier cap beam, primary member).

Bearing Mechanical system which transmits loads from the superstructure to the substructure. Expansion bearings allow longitudinal movement, while fixed bearings do not.

Bearing Plate A steel plate which is used to transmit loads from the superstructure to the substructure.

Bearing Stiffener A steel plate which is welded to the web directly above a bearing to resist bearing force.

Bedrock Underlying layer of rock on top of which rest various other layers of soil.

Benchmark A point with a known elevation and coordinates from which other survey points are referenced.

Bent A basic structural configuration consisting of a rigid frame with two or more vertical supports connected by a horizontal member.

Berm See *Bench*. Also, an older expression for the median in a dual highway.

Binder Course A layer between the wearing surface and base course made of a bituminous material and aggregate. See also *Base Course*.

Bitumen The petroleum-based cementing component used in asphaltic binders.

Bituminous Concrete Bituminous cement mixed with aggregate and filler material.

Bleeding The flow of mixing water from within recently placed concrete.

BMS Acronym for Bridge Management System.

Bolster In reinforced concrete, a support used for horizontal steel. Also known as a chair.

Boring A soil sample taken by drilling a hole in the ground and retrieving a portion for testing.

Box Culvert A culvert made out of a reinforced concrete box structure. See also *Culvert*.

Box Girder A superstructure design which utilizes a box-shaped tube as primary load carrying member.

Brace A structural member which is usually placed diagonally in order to provide stiffness to a frame.

Bracket See *Corbel*.

Breastwall A continuous wall, typically in front of an abutment backwall, upon which the superstructure rests. Used in lieu of free-standing pedestals. See also *Pedestal*.

BATTER PILE

BENT

Bridge Seat Refers to the surface on which a bearing rests. Also known as beam seat. See also *Pedestal*.

Brittle Fracture A sudden failure of a steel element prior to plastic deformation typically occurring at a sharp change of section properties, or due to fatigue cracks.

Brush Curb A curb used in lieu of a sidewalk to provide wider travel lanes on a bridge deck.

BS 5400 The bridge design code used in the United Kingdom and issued by BSI Standards. The code comes in 10 parts.

Buckling Sudden large and irreversible deflection in an axially loaded member under compression.

Bulb T-Girder A concrete I girder with a bulb shape at the bottom of the girder cross section (e.g., AASHTO-PCI Type V and VI prestressed girders).

Built-Up Member A steel member composed of various standard AISC shapes in order to enhance section properties (used in many old bridges).

Butt Joint The joint between two pieces of metal in the same plane which have been bolted or welded together.

Cable Stayed Bridge A bridge in which the deck is suspended by straight, diagonal cables.

Caisson A hollow, watertight box which is used to construct pier foundations in water channels. The caisson is sunk where the pier is to be constructed and eventually becomes part of the pier itself.

Camber The arching or bending of a beam upward to compensate for the dead load deflections that occur when a load (such as the bridge deck) is placed on it.

Cap Beam The top beam in a bent which ties together the supporting columns or piles.

Cast-in-Place Refers to concrete which is poured and cured in its final location in the field.

Catch Basin A box-type structure, located within pipe segments of a storm water collection system which is used to collect storm water and prevent debris from entering the storm water system.

Cathodic Protection An electrochemical method of inhibiting the deterioration of concrete through introduction of a metal anode which allows reinforcing steel to become cathodic and thus stop corrosion.

Causeway An elevated roadway used to cross long expanses of water, swamps, or wetlands.

Chamfer A notched or angled edge or corner typically formed in concrete at a 45 degree angle.

Channel See Channel Shape and Water Channel.

Channel Shape An AISC rolled section in the shape of a "C" or channel.

Cheekwall A concrete wall, typically joined to an abutment wingwall used to shield pedestals, bearings, and stringer ends.

Chloride Component in deicing agents which has adverse effects on concrete and steel bridge elements.

Chord Longitudinal members located at either the top or bottom plane of a truss.

Clearance Used to indicate the distance between two elements (e.g., vertical clearance is the distance between the bottom of the superstructure and the top of the underpass surface).

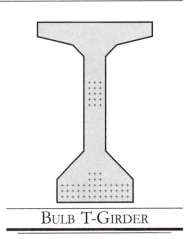

BULB T-GIRDER

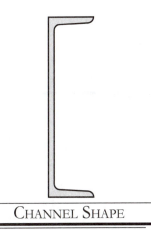

CHANNEL SHAPE

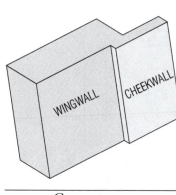

CHEEKWALL

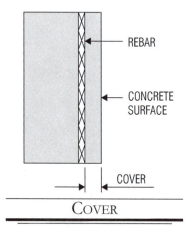

REBAR

CONCRETE
SURFACE

COVER

COVER

Cofferdam A watertight sheeted pit used for construction of foundations at locations where the ground level is below water. See also *Sheeted Pit*.

Cold Joint Joint between old or hardened concrete and new concrete.

Column Bent A bent shaped pier using columns integrated with a cap beam. See also *Bent* and *Cap Beam*.

Composite Construction Type of design where the bridge deck works together with primary members in resisting loads.

Compression Seal Joint A joint assembly typically consisting of an extruded neoprene elastic seal squeezed into a joint opening.

Concentrated Load A point load at a specific location (e.g., 18 kips at 14 ft from the left support).

Connection Plate A steel plate which connects two elements (e.g., a connection plate which joins a diaphragm to a rolled girder).

Construction Joint A point where two concrete pours meet (e.g., the face between an abutment backwall and footing).

Continuous Footing A footing beneath a wall. Also known as a wall footing. See also *Footing*.

Continuous Span A span with primary members extending across a pier uninterrupted.

Corbel A ledge projecting from a column or wall used to support a beam or other element such as an approach slab. Also known as a bracket.

Core A cylindrical specimen taken from either concrete, rock, or timber elements which is used to determine the condition of the element.

Corrugated A material (usually metal) with alternating ridges and valleys used for elements such as guard railing.

Couplant A jelly-like substance used with ultrasonic gages in determining steel thickness.

Coupon A portion of steel taken from an element used to determine the condition of the element.

Cover The distance between the exposed surface of a concrete element and the topmost surface of the reinforcing steel.

Cover Plate A steel plate attached to the bottom flange of a steel girder used to increase the overall section properties of the member.

Creep Deformation of concrete under loads over a period of time. This deformation will stop after a certain amount of time. Also known as plastic flow.

Crest Used to describe a vertical curve formed by an upward tangent followed by a downward tangent (i.e., curve crests upward like a hill).

Cross Frame Steel elements, comprised of crossing, steel angles, which are placed in an "X" configuration to act as diaphragms.

Cross Section A section taken transverse to an element's centerline (e.g., a roadway cross section, deck cross section, etc.).

Crown The high point on a road which may or may not be located on the road centerline. Also the high point of a rib or barrel of an arch.

Culvert A structure through which runoff flows (e.g., a corrugated metal pipe under a roadway discharging into an open ditch).

Curb A raised element used to denote the edge of pavement. Curbs can be made of concrete, granite, or other material.

Curved Girder A girder which is curved in the horizontal plane to accommodate the overpass horizontal alignment.

Cut A term used to define a region of excavation, as in cut and fill.

Cutwater The pointed portion of a pier facing the water channel current. Also known as an ice breaker. See also *Nosing*.

Dead Man An object buried with an anchor. See also *Anchorage*.

Dead Load The aggregate weight of all permanent, non-moving superstructure elements resting on the substructure.

Deck The physical extension of the roadway across the obstruction to be bridged. The deck transfers vehicle loads to the supporting superstructure primary members.

Deck Arch An arch bridge in which the deck rests on top of the arch.

Deck Joint A gap between two spans, or the approach and a span, which allows for some rotation and/or translation.

Degradation A condition in a water channel where, over a long period of time, more sediment is removed from a stream bed than deposited.

Deflection The vertical displacement of a member subjected to loading.

Deformed Bar A reinforcing bar with raised rib-shaped surface deformations that enhance the bond between steel bar and concrete.

Delamination Cracks or voids in a concrete element below the exposed surface which cause the concrete to peel off in layers.

Diagonal A member placed at an angle to provide stiffness.

Diaphragm A transverse secondary member which is attached between stringers acting to stiffen primary members and help distribute vertical loads.

Drainage The removal of storm water runoff from the bridge and site.

Drop Hammer A piece of metal acting as a hammer in a pile driver.

Drop Inlet A box-type structure within pipe segments of a storm water collection system into which storm water enters from the top.

Drop Line A line extended from the bridge deck to a water crossing underneath used to generate channel cross sections.

Dowel A reinforcing bar embedded in two concrete sections which transfers stresses and holds the sections together.

Duct The void in a prestressed concrete girder in which the prestressing tendon is placed.

Effective Width In composite construction, the width of a concrete slab which functions as the top flange of a composite T-shaped section.

Efflorescence A white substance which forms on the surface of concrete due to water seeping into cracks.

Elastic Deformation Deformation which takes place when stress is proportional to strain (elastic), allowing the recovery of the original shape after loads have been removed.

Elastomeric Pad A pad made of a synthetic rubber which compresses under loads and is used in bearings. See also *Bearing* and *Neoprene*.

Electrode A material which, when combined with the base metal, helps form the weld between two pieces of metal. See also *Base Metal*.

Elevation A vertical distance from an arbitrary reference (datum). Also used to denote a view along the length of an element (e.g., a view of the bridge from abutment to abutment).

Embankment A raised area of fill surrounding a structural component (e.g., abutment).

DECK ARCH

DIAPHRAGM

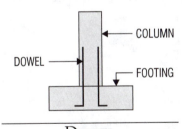

DOWEL

FLOOR BEAM

FORMWORK

Expansion Support A support designed to accommodate both rotation and longitudinal translation.

Epoxy-Coated Reinforcing steel Reinforcing steel with a protective coating placed to prevent corrosion.

Extrados The intersection of the upper surface of an arch with the vertical plane through the crown and springing lines.

Eye Bar Used in certain suspension bridges as links forming a chain.

Facial Referring to the surface of an element. As in, "Facial repairs to a concrete column."

Falsework A temporary support structure made of steel or wood. Typically used for formwork or erection of a structural member.

Fascia The exterior face of the deck.

Fascia Girder The outside or exterior girder in a set of beams.

Fatigue Cracking The propagation of localized cracks through repetitive loading and unloading.

Faulting A differential movement of concrete sections at a joint.

Fill A term used to define a region where additional earth is needed to raise the elevation of a constructed project, as in cut and fill.

Fixed Support A support designed to accommodate rotation only.

Flange The top and bottom horizontal component in an "I" girder cross section or top horizontal component in a "T" girder cross section.

Flexural Rigidity The ability of a beam to resist bending.

Flood Plain A region of land adjacent to a water channel which is susceptible to flooding.

Floor Beam A transverse member supporting longitudinal primary members.

Footing The base to a column or wall which transfers loads from the substructure to the subsoil.

Form A temporary structure which acts as a mold for a concrete element until the element has the required strength to support itself.

Formwork An entire system of forms, supports, and related elements.

Fracture See *Brittle Fracture*.

Fracture Critical A member whose failure due to fracture could result in the failure of the entire structure.

Framing Plan A plan view of the bridge used to show the layout, geometry, and properties of superstructure primary and secondary members.

Friction Pile A pile which derives its principal support from shear resistance between the pile and surrounding earth.

Gabion A galvanized or PVC-coated wire basket filled with stones and stacked with other baskets to form an earth-retaining structure.

Ganged Forms Reusable forms which are prefabricated and assembled to make a complete unit.

Geometrics Concerning the layout, orientation, and spatial properties of an element, group of elements, or component.

Girder Commonly used to refer to a primary member placed along the longitudinal axis of a bridge. Used interchangeably with the term stringer.

Glued Laminated A timber member created by gluing together two or more pieces of lumber no more than 2 in (50.8 mm) in thickness.

Grillage Footing A footing comprised of horizontal members which distribute loads over the footing.

Group Loading Combinations of loads and forces (e.g., dead load with live load, wind, stream flow pressure, etc.) that a structure must be able to withstand.

Grout A cement-based filler material used to fill in voids, cracks, cavities, and other openings in concrete elements. Usually a thin mix of cement, water, and sometimes sand.

Grouting The process of filling cracks and voids with grout.

Gunite Portland cement mortar which is blown onto a surface using compressed air.

Gusset Plate A steel plate used to connect steel members to each other (e.g., as in a cross frame assembly).

H Loading A hypothetical design truck developed by AASHTO that comes in two types, H20-44 and H15-44.

Hairline Cracks Extremely fine cracks which are formed on the surface of new concrete. Typically occurs at high temperatures which causes a rapid loss of moisture.

Hammerhead Used to describe the geometry of a pier with a cap similar in shape to a hammer.

Hanger An assembly utilizing a pin connection designed to allow for expansion between a cantilevered and suspended span at a point between supports.

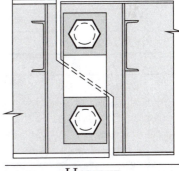

Haunch A small [roughly 2 to 4 in ± (50.8 to 101.6 mm)] layer of concrete between a superstructure member and a concrete deck.

Haunched Girder A member whose cross-sectional depth varies from support to support.

Heave The upward movement of soil which can be caused by moisture, excavation, pile driving, etc.

HANGER

Heel The rear face of a footing. See also *Toe*.

Horizontal Alignment The mathematical description of a roadway's centerline or baseline alignment in the horizontal plane (i.e., plan view).

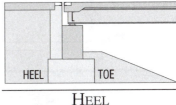

HEEL

Horizontal Curve A curve in a horizontal alignment altering the direction of two tangents.

HS Loading A hypothetical design truck developed by AASHTO that comes in two types, HS20-44 and HS15-44 (although HS-25 is used in many states recently).

Hybrid Girder A girder with load-bearing plates of varying steel types (e.g., high-strength steel used for flanges and lower strength for webs).

I-Girder A girder whose cross section resembles the letter "I".

Impact A factor used to describe the dynamic effect of a vehicle moving across a bridge.

Individual Column Footing A footing which supports a single column. See also *Footing*.

Integral Abutment An abutment which is integrated with an approach slab, thereby eliminating a joint at that location.

Interstate The United States Interstate and Defense Highway system, which encompasses 46,500 miles (74,800 km) of roadway.

Intrados The intersection of the lower surface of an arch with the vertical plane through the crown and springing lines.

Inventory Rating The load capacity of a bridge under normal service conditions (same as design strength).

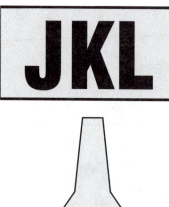

JERSEY BARRIER

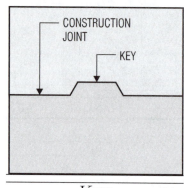

KEY

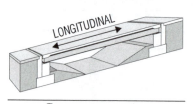

LONGITUDINAL

Invert Elevation The elevation of the lowest point of a catch basic, drop inlet, culvert, or streambed.

Item Number A number assigned by a transportation department to reference a specific material, element, or construction operation.

Jack Arch An arch-type bridge constructed with steel beams encased in concrete. The concrete is typically formed using stay-in-place forms.

Jacket A surrounding encasement of an element such as a pier column or pile which can be made of concrete, fabric, or other material.

Jacking The lifting of an element or group of elements using hydraulic or other types of jacks and, if needed, a temporary support system.

Jersey Barrier A concrete barrier named after the New Jersey Department of Transportation, which first developed it. Also known as traffic barrier, median barrier, shape barrier, and concrete barrier.

Joint See *Cold Joint* and *Deck Joint*.

Keeper Plate A plate which is bolted or welded to a sole plate to prohibit a beam from being disconnected from the bearing.

Key A notched or raised protrusion of concrete located on one face of a construction joint which fits into a recess on the other face.

Lateral A member which is placed roughly perpendicular to a primary member.

Laminate Two or more pieces of wood which are joined together, typically with adhesive or nails. See also *Glued Laminated* and *Nail Laminated*.

Lane Loading A hypothetical design loading used to simulate a train of trucks moving across a bridge.

Lateral Bracing Bracing located at either the top flange or bottom flange of a stringer to prevent lateral deformation induced by forces normal to the bridge centerline (e.g., wind).

Leveling Course A layer of asphalt or binder used to smooth together two sections of pavement.

Lighting Standard The main supporting pole for a lighting fixture. See also *Luminaire*.

Limit States Design A method of design based on the ability of a structure to fulfill its function. This ability is defined by limit states defining safety and serviceability.

Live Load A temporary, moving load such as vehicular traffic.

Load Factor Design A form of limit states design used by AASHTO standard specifications as an alternative to Working Stress Design.

Load Rating A value indicating the load capacity of a bridge. See also *Inventory Rating* and *Operating Rating*.

Load and Resistance Factor Design A form of limit states design used by AASHTO LRFD specifications.

Local Buckling Localized buckling of one of a beam's plate elements which can potentially lead to failure of the member.

Longitudinal Used to describe the axis of a bridge which proceeds from abutment to abutment

Luminaire A lighting fixture located at the top of a lighting standard.

Maintenance Basic remedial operations performed on a bridge which allow the structure to maintain an adequate level of service.

Mandrel A thin steel shell used in the placement of cast-in-place concrete piles.

Maintenance of Traffic The control of traffic through a project site that ensures safety to both vehicles and construction personnel.

Masonry Plate The bottom steel plate of a bearing which is anchored to a concrete bridge seat.

Military Loading A loading configuration used to simulate heavy military vehicles passing over a bridge. Also known as Alternative Military Loading.

Modular Joint A joint used to accommodate very large movements consisting of multiple strip or compression seals.

Movable Bridge A bridge, typically located over water, which allows spans over the crossing to be raised and lowered. Also known as a drawbridge. See also *Bascule Bridge*.

Nail Laminated A timber member created by nailing two or more pieces of lumber together.

NCHRP National Cooperative Highway Research Program.

Negative Moment Bending moment which causes tension in the top fiber and compression in the bottom fiber of a beam.

Neoprene A popular material for seal-type expansion joints made of polychloroprene.

Nosing A facing placed on the portion of a pier facing the water current. Usually made of steel.

OHBDC Ontario Highway Bridge Design Code published by the Ontario Ministry of Transportation, Province of Ontario, Canada.

Operating Rating The load capacity of a bridge under special service conditions (maximum permissible load to which the structure may be subjected).

Orthotropic Deck A steel deck which is stiffened both longitudinally and transversely using open or closed ribs and floor beams, respectively.

Overdriving The continued driving of piles after they have reached an obstruction or impenetrable layer (e.g., rock), which can cause severe damage to the pile.

Overlay See *Wearing Surface*. Also known as Deck Overlay.

Overpass The feature carried by the bridge over an obstruction.

P Loading A hypothetical design vehicle developed by the California Department of Transportation for special Permit Loading.

Parapet A concrete barrier. Typically refers to a barrier placed on the outside face of the bridge deck over the fascia girder.

PC Point of Curvature. The location on a horizontal alignment which represents the first point of tangency of a specific horizontal curve.

PI Point of Intersection. The point of intersection of two tangents of a horizontal curve.

Pedestal A short column on an abutment or pier which directly supports a superstructure primary member. See also *Bridge Seat*.

Physical Testing Field or laboratory testing of bridge component materials and/or members.

Pier Structures which support the superstructure at intermediate points between end supports (abutments).

Pier Cap See *Cap Beam*.

MOVABLE BRIDGE

MODULAR JOINT

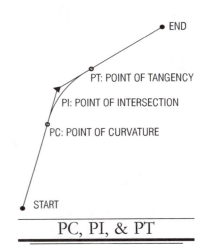

PC, PI, & PT

PEDESTAL

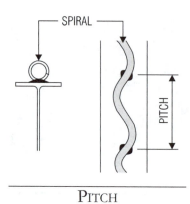

PITCH

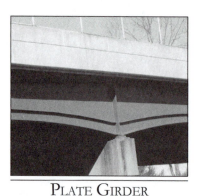

PLATE GIRDER

Pile A member with a small cross-sectional area (in comparison to its length) used to provide adequate support for a column or wall resting on soil which is too weak or compressible to support the structure using a spread footer.

Pile Bent A pier comprised of a cap beam and a set of piles. See also *Bent*, *Pier*, and *Pile*.

Pin and Hanger See *Hanger*.

Pitch A grade or slope given to a surface, usually to provide for adequate drainage. Also the distance between rows of shear studs or complete revolutions in a spiral shear connector.

Plan Used to denote a view of an element, component, or the site from a viewpoint directly above the object looking down.

Plan and Profile A drawing which presents both the roadway plan view along with its profile on the same sheet and at equal horizontal scales. See also *Profile* and *Vertical Alignment*.

Planimetry Topographic information detailing the location and/or elevation of non-terrain related features (e.g., vegetation, fences, catch basins, etc.)

Plastic Deformation A permanent deformation of a member due to loads that have been placed on a member for a given period of time.

Plate Girder A girder with an "I" cross section composed of steel plate elements which are connected together by welds, bolts, or rivets.

Plinth A projecting base of a wall.

Positive Moment A bending moment which induces compression in the top fiber of a beam and tension in the bottom fiber.

Post-tensioned Girder A prestressed concrete girder where the prestressing force is applied to the reinforcing tendons after the concrete has cured.

Precast A concrete element which has been formed and cured prior to placement in the field.

Preliminary Design An initial design which outlines the major scope of work to be done in a project.

Prestressed Girder A concrete girder which utilizes steel tendons that have a tensile force placed on them, thereby increasing internal compression and reducing or eliminating stresses due to tension once the beam is loaded.

Pretensioned Girder A prestressed concrete girder where the prestressing force is applied to the reinforcing tendons before the concrete has been poured.

Primary Member A load-bearing member which distributes loads longitudinally and is principally designed to resist flexure.

Profile A graphical depiction of the vertical alignment of a roadway.

PS&E Plans, Specifications, and Estimate. A term used to identify the final submission package of the design team to be given to the owner.

PT Point of Tangency. The location on a horizontal alignment which represents the last point of tangency of a specific horizontal curve.

PVC Point of Vertical Curvature. The location on a vertical alignment which represents the first point of tangency of a specific vertical curve.

PVI Point of Vertical Intersection. The point of intersection of two tangents of a vertical curve.

PVT Point of Vertical Tangency. The location on a vertical alignment which represents the last point of tangency of a specific vertical curve.

Railing Traffic barrier system made of longitudinal rails attached to vertical posts. Also known as guard railing and guide railing.

Raveling Cumulative loss of aggregate from a pavement made of bituminous material, which results in a poor riding surface.

Rebar Shortened name for reinforcing steel.

Redundancy The presence of multiple load paths so that, if a structural member fails, another element or group of elements can sustain the load. See also *Fracture Critical*.

Rehabilitation Repair work of a significant nature that calls for the engineering design of remedial measures.

Reinforced Earth The registered trademark name for a type of earth retaining structure that utilizes galvanized steel strips placed in granular backfill and connected to interlocking concrete facing units.

Relaxation A decrease in stress due to creep.

Relief Topographic information pertaining to the surface of the terrain. Relief is typically presented with annotated spot elevations, contours, or a combination thereof.

Residual Camber Camber which results from a prestressing force minus a girder's dead load deflection. See also *Camber*.

Residual Stress Stress locked into a member after it has been formed to its final shape.

Resurfacing The overlay of wearing surface material on top of an existing approach and/or deck overlay to create a more uniform and smooth riding surface.

Rib A longitudinal stiffener used in orthotropic decks.

Rigid Frame A set of columns supporting a transverse member. See also *Bent*.

Rim Elevation The elevation at a catch basin, manhole, or drop inlet grate.

Rip Rap Broken rock placed around piers and abutments to prevent erosion and scour.

Rivet A cylindrical metal fastener which is used to connect multiple pieces of metal.

Rolled Beam A steel girder which is formed by hot-rolling.

Sag Used to describe a vertical curve formed by a downward tangent followed by an upward tangent (i.e., the curve sags downward like a valley).

Scour The washing away of stream bed material by water channel flow.

Scour, General Scour which occurs as a result of a constriction in the water channel openings.

Scour, Local Scour which occurs as a result of local flow changes in a channel due to constrictions caused by the presence of bridge piers, abutments, etc.

Screed A long section of metal or wood which is dragged across freshly placed concrete to both smooth the surface and consolidate the concrete.

Scuppers A drainage system used to drain storm water runoff from a bridge deck.

Seal A closure material. Typically used in reference to deck joints and made out of neoprene. Used in strip seal and compression seal assemblies.

Secondary Member Bracing between primary members designed to resist cross-sectional deformation of the superstructure frame and help distribute part of the vertical load between stringers.

RAILING

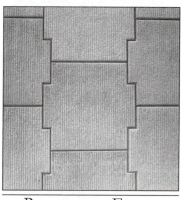

REINFORCED EARTH

SECONDARY MEMBER

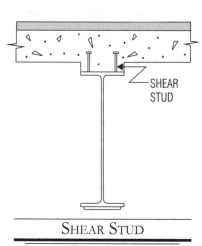

SHEAR STUD

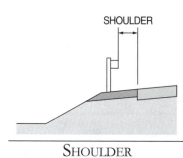

SHOULDER

SIGNING

Section Used to denote a view of an element taken in section (i.e., a slice of an element or component at a given location).

Segmental Concrete Girder A girder composed of concrete units, which are generally precast and post-tensioned to form an integrated unit.

Seismic Relating to earthquakes as in *seismic forces*.

Select Granular Fill Broken rocks, varying in size [typically less than 24 in (610 mm)] consisting of rock, stone, slag, cobbles, or gravel.

Service Load Design AASHTO designation for Working Stress Design.

Settlement The movement of foundations or footings due to deformations and/or changes in soil properties.

Shear Connector Devices used in composite construction which extend from the top flange of a girder and are embedded in the concrete slab, allowing the slab and girder to act as a unit.

Shear Hinge Similar to a hanger assembly but with no horizontal movement allowed.

Shear Spiral A type of shear connector found in older structures which consists of a coil-like assembly welded to the top flange of a girder.

Shear Stud A common form of shear connector which is bolt-shaped and attached to the top flange of a girder with an automatic welding stud gun.

Sheeted Pit A temporary box structure with only four sides (i.e., no top or bottom) which can be used as an earth support system in excavation.

Sheeting Vertical planks which are driven into the ground to act as temporary retaining walls permitting excavation.

Shim A thin metal plate placed under bearing assemblies usually to adjust bridge seat elevation discrepancies.

Shore An inclined supporting member for formwork and the enclosed concrete. See also *Form*.

Shoulder The section of roadway on either side of the travel lane.

Shrinkage The natural (i.e., not load-related) change in volume of concrete. This change in volume is typically decreasing (shrinking) and caused by moisture loss when drying.

Side Slope The slope on the side of an embankment.

Sight Distance The length of visible roadway in front of a vehicle. The distance is determined as that which is required to allow a vehicle to safely stop prior to reaching a stationary object (*stopping sight distance*).

Sight Triangle A triangle formed at intersecting streets used to define a region which must be free from obstructions (e.g., vegetation, signs, buildings, etc.) in order to ensure the safe operation of vehicles.

Signing Traffic or construction signs and their related support structures located at or near the project site.

Simple Span A span in which primary members begin and end at supports. See also *Continuous Span*.

Site The bridge and area surrounding the structure which either affects the bridge or is affected by the bridge.

Skew The angle between a line projected orthogonally or radially from the overpass alignment and the centerline of bearings.

Slab-on-Stringer A type of bridge composed of a deck resting on a set of primary members. Also known as Slab-on-Girder.

Slipform Forms which are moved in a regulated fashion along a concrete element. The form is moved as the section it leaves has reached sufficient strength.

Slope Protection Material covering the slope which tapers from an abutment to the underpass. See also *Embankment*.

Slump A measurement used to define the workability of concrete which is taken by determining the loss in height of wet concrete after a cone-shaped mold is removed. The smaller the slump, the stiffer the mix.

Soffit See *Intrados*.

Sole Plate The top steel plate of a bearing which is attached to the bottom flange of a stringer.

Sounding A method of checking for voids in a concrete or timber member by banging with a hammer on the element and listening for hollow spots.

Spalling The breaking away of surface concrete from an element.

Spandrel In a deck arch, the area between the deck and the top surface of the arch.

Spillway A paved channel used to carry water from the top of a slope to an adjacent outlet.

Splice The joining of two elements through a connection device (e.g., two steel girders joined by a plate bolted to each).

Spread Footing A footing that is not supported by piles.

Springing Line The intersection of the lower surface of an arch with a pier or abutment.

Staged Construction Construction that occurs in phases, usually to permit the flow of traffic through a construction site.

Station A term used to denote location on a roadway alignment. A 100 ft (30.5 m) section represents a full station.

Stay-in-Place Forms Forms, usually present at the underside of a deck slab, which remain in place after the deck has cured. Also known as permanent forms.

Stem A wall extending up from a footing as in a solid wall pier or cantilever abutment.

Stiffener A plate welded to a steel beam web to enhance section properties of the beam. Intermediate stiffeners are welded vertically and longitudinal stiffeners along the length of the beam.

Stirrup A U-shaped reinforcing bar used to resist shear or diagonal tension in concrete beams.

Strand A twisted group of wires.

Strength Design AASHTO and ACI designation for Load Factor Design.

Strengthening A method employed to enhance the capacity of a structural member.

Stringer See *Girder*.

Strip Seal Joint A joint assembly typically consisting of a preformed neoprene seal which is fitted to dual steel rails anchored to the faces of the joint opening.

Strut The transverse (i.e., non diagonal) member in a lateral bracing system (also known as lateral struts). Also, a member which runs between walls in a sheeted pit or a cofferdam.

Subbase A base course layer within a flexible pavement structure, placed between the base course and subgrade.

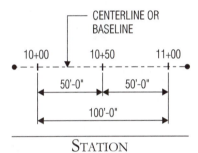

STATION

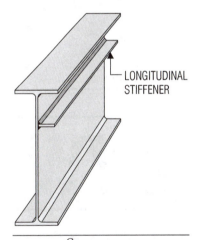

STIFFENER

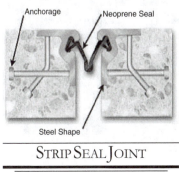

STRIP SEAL JOINT

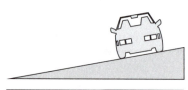

SUPERELEVATION

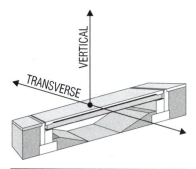

TRANSVERSE & VERTICAL

UNDERDRAIN

Substructure Structural components and all constituent elements designed to support the superstructure and overpass roadway.

Surcharge A load, in addition to soil loads, acting on a retaining wall.

Superelevation A banking of the roadway cross section.

Superimposed Dead Load Permanent loads that are placed on a structure after the concrete has hardened (e.g., bridge railing, sidewalks, etc.)

Superstructure Structural components and all constituent elements of a bridge above the supports.

Suspension Bridge A bridge in which the roadway is suspended from two or more cables hanging from tower structures.

Swale A shallow drainage channel used to carry runoff from the bridge and/or site. A swale can be made of earth, concrete, or other material.

T-Girder A girder whose cross section resembles the letter "T".

Tack Coat A thin layer of liquid bituminous material sprayed on a new or existing bituminous surface prior to placing another layer.

Tendon A steel strand stretching along the length of an element used in concrete prestressing.

Theoretical Grade Line The alignment along which the vertical alignment is set. Also referred to as the TGL.

Through Arch An arch bridge in which the deck passes through the arch.

Tip The bottom end of a pile.

Toe The front face of a footing. See also *Heel*.

Topography A representation of the bridge site composed of both relief and planimetric information. See also *Relief* and *Planimetry*.

Torsional Rigidity The ability of a beam to resist torsion (i.e., twisting about the longitudinal axis).

Transverse Used to describe the axis of a bridge which lies perpendicular or radial to the centerline of the structure.

TRB Transportation Research Board.

Tremie A pipe or funnel, used for placing concrete in water whose top and bottom are open, allowing for concrete to be poured into it.

Trestle Usually used in reference to timber structures consisting of a set of stringers resting on a pile or frame bent.

Truck Loading A hypothetical design loading used to simulate a single truck on a bridge.

Truss A set of members arranged vertically in a triangular fashion to form an integrated load-bearing unit.

Ultimate Strength Design Former ACI designation for Load Factor Design.

Ultrasonic Gage A device used to measure the thickness of steel elements which uses a probe placed in a couplant that is smeared on the surface of a steel member. See also *Couplant*.

Underdrain A drainage conduit, usually placed in backfill material and used to transport runoff away from substructure elements.

Underpass The feature crossed by a bridge.

Uniform Load A load distributed uniformly over the length of an element.

Uplift A combination of loads which causes the superstructure to lift up off the substructure.

Vertical Used to describe the axis of a bridge which proceeds upward, perpendicular to the underpass surface.

Vertical Alignment The mathematical description of a roadway's centerline or baseline alignment in the vertical plane.

Vertical Clearance The minimum distance between the structure and the underpass.

Voided Slab A bridge which uses a concrete slab with voids introduced to decrease the overall weight of the superstructure.

Wale Bracing inside a sheeted pit or a cofferdam which runs along the inside walls of the structure.

Water Cement Ratio The ratio between water and cement which controls the strength of concrete.

Water Channel A channel carrying a water course under a bridge. A water channel could refer to a stream, river, or other similar feature.

Waterproofing Membrane A protective sheet placed between a wearing surface and concrete deck to shield the concrete deck from water and corrosive chemicals which could cause delamination and spalling.

Wearing Surface A layer of asphalt or concrete based material placed on top of the bridge deck to protect the deck and substructure from traffic and chemicals and provide for a smooth riding surface.

Web The vertical component in an "I" or "T" girder cross section.

Web Crippling A localized yielding which occurs when high compressive stresses arise from a concentrated load.

Wedge A piece of metal with one edge much thicker than the other.

Weep Hole A hole in a concrete element (e.g., abutment backwall) used to drain the element.

Weep Tube A tube made of PVC or other material which is embedded in a concrete element (e.g., deck, abutment) and extends past the surface to drain the element.

Wheel Load The load due to one wheel in a design vehicle. Two wheel loads typically comprise a single axle load.

Wide Flange Shape An AISC rolled section in the shape if an "I". "W" is used for wide flange shape designation.

Wingwall A side wall to an abutment backwall designed to assist in the confining of earth behind the abutment.

Working Stress Design A method of design based on maximum allowable stresses which are defined by the yield stress of the material and a factor of safety.

Yield Point The stress at which a material begins to yield.

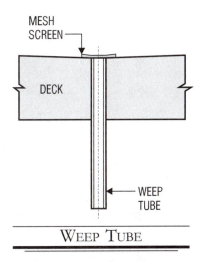

WEEP TUBE

REFERENCES

1.1 *State Transportation Statistics, Bureau of Transportation Statistics, US Department of Transportation, Table 1-1 and Table 1-7.*, Washington, D.C., 2004.

1.2 Steinman, D.B., and Watson, S.R., *Bridges and Their Builders*, 2nd Edition, Dover Publications Inc., New York, 1957.

1.3 *A Policy on Geometric Design of Highways and Streets*, 4th Edition, American Association of State Highway and Transportation Officials, Washington, D.C., 2001.

1.4 *Manual for Condition Evaluation of Bridges*, 2nd Edition, American Association of State Highway and Transportation Officials, Washington, D.C., 2003.

1.5 *National Transportation Statistics 2004.* Table 3-29a, Bureau of Transportation Statistics, US Department of Transportation, Washington, D.C. 2005.

1.6 Kavanagh, Thomas C., and Young, Robert C.Y., "Arches and Rigid Frames," pp. 17-1 to 17-2, *Structural Engineering Handbook*, Edited by Gaylord, Edwin H. Jr., and Gaylord, Charles N., McGraw-Hill, New York, 1990.

1.7 *Bill Cosby: Himself*, Jemmin, Inc., released by 20th Century Fox, 1982.

1.8 Heinen, Richard, "Who Should Build Bridges?" *Civil Engineering*, American Society of Civil Engineers, vol. 55, no. 7, pp. 63–66, July 1985.

2

Beginning the Project

Section Overview

In this section we will look at the major issues which face a bridge engineer prior to design. We begin with a discussion of how highway projects are funded. Following this is a look at some of the important reference material designers must consult. The section concludes with a detailed presentation of the important issue of bridge inspection and how it affects the design of new bridges and the rehabilitation of existing bridges.

There are several important issues which concern the bridge engineer prior to commencement of design. Before any design can begin, there is the issue of how bridge projects are selected and funded. Then there is the issue of which standards and references should be utilized by the engineer during design. Finally, when design actually begins in earnest, what field data, and, in the case of a rehabilitation project, record data, are required to commence, and eventually complete the work.

This section of the text is intended to provide the reader with an overview of the project inception phase of a highway bridge design. While many engineers tend to focus most intently on the nuts and bolts of the actual design, it is important to recognize the importance of the issues identified above and how they affect the underpinnings of any bridge design project. Quite often, design projects can go astray because of a failure to collect proper field data, a misunderstanding of the owner's wishes and intents, or even an improper use of reference material.

2.1 PROJECT FUNDING

The design and rehabilitation of highway bridges is an activity which has considerable financial demands. Rehabilitation of a medium size overpass structure can easily cost over a million dollars. When considering the vast number of structures in need of repair, it is easy to see why national infrastructure programs consistently weigh in with multi-billion dollar price tags. An example of the magnitude of these costs can be found in the Transportation Equity Act for the 21st Century [Ref. 2.1]. The U. S. federal government alone spent $218 billion on the surface transportation from 1998 to 2003. When states and local governments are included, the cost exceeded $100 billion per year [Ref. 2.2].

With such huge costs associated for bridges, the obvious question is: where does all this money come from? Funding for highway projects in general, and bridge projects in particular, comes from a variety of sources and varies from region to region. Fund sources, however, can be broken down into five principal categories: user fees, nonuser fees, special benefit fees, private financing, and debt financing [Ref. 2.3]. The following offers a brief description of these funding sources.

THE LONDON BRIDGE

2.1.1 User Fees

User fees (i.e., taxes imposed on the users of the highway system) imply funds generated through traditional, highway-related fees such as vehicle registration, gasoline taxes, and trucking fees. Of these, the gasoline tax provides one of the largest funding sources for highway programs. The gas tax, however, has never been popular with the public because of its direct, sometimes daily, impact on the taxpayer. This has led to a relatively slow growth in the gas tax rate with respect to inflation so that funds, as a result of this revenue source, have actually decreased since the late 1960's [Ref. 2.3]. Recently, the gas tax as a fund generator for infrastructure programs has become an issue once again.

Another form of user fee is the toll road. In the United States, toll roads are found predominantly in the northeast. A 2003 report listed 4,722 miles (7,600 km) of toll roads with 2,814 miles (4529 km) of those on the Interstate [Ref. 2.4]. Toll facility authorities have the advantage of a relatively precise form of user funding so they can afford a rapid and high level of maintenance compared to other transportation departments. However, toll roads are typically restricted access highways which results in limited availability to users. They are also encumbered by high toll collection costs, although electronic toll collection has significantly reduced the costs. Some organizations, like the Automobile Association of America, see tolls as a form of double taxation since users are already paying highway use taxes in the form of the gasoline tax [Ref. 2.5]. Another disadvantage is a federal law which states that any conversion of existing facilities to toll roads requires repayment of the federal portion of the construction cost. This law, associated with public disapproval of such a conversion, makes the toll road a difficult solution, even though most toll roads have paid for themselves. With the introduction of the electronic toll collection system, the public's acceptance of toll facilities has increased recently.

2.1.2 Nonuser Fees

Funds obtained from sales taxes, income taxes, or other general fund sources are known as nonuser fees. While many engineers know what it feels like to have highway funds go *into* the general fund, the money can flow the other way as well. It is because of this that many highway departments shy away from nonuser fees. Once general funds are accepted by a highway agency for use in highway programs, the impetus for other non-highway

Figure 2.1 Toll roads, such as the NYS Thruway, are principally found in the northeastern U.S.

agencies to dip into the highway budget increases many fold. This leads to a competition between state agencies for tax dollars, which engineers often have difficulty winning.

2.1.3 Special Benefit Fees

A special benefit fee is a tax placed on those individuals (usually developers) who benefit from a new or rehabilitated highway system. The special benefit fee provides a source of revenue for improving or expanding facilities to meet the needs of a growing community. Sometimes this takes the form of an impact fee which calls for developers to pay for part of a highway expansion or make a direct cash contribution to meet a new development's highway related needs. Any tax, however, is regressive and, in the case of communities with a depressed economy, can result in impeding development.

Another detriment to fund sources such as special benefit fees is that transportation projects are initiated outside of the context of an overall highway planning scheme. Such a situation can often lead to maintenance headaches in the future [Ref. 2.3].

2.1.4 Private Financing

Private financing, or funding from the private sector, has been found to be a good source of revenue in large states such as California, New York, and Texas [Ref. 2.3].

Typically, developers make a donation to the transportation department in return for changes in zoning, building codes, etc. The drawback to private donations is that they are usually a one-shot operation and therefore are difficult to incorporate into an overall transportation plan.

Privatization is another form of private financing which relies not only on private funding, but also private maintenance of constructed facilities (see *Design Perspective* this page). While the concept of privatization is nothing new, in economically difficult times,

DESIGN PERSPECTIVE

Is Privatization an Answer?

The idea of having private developers get involved in the building of new and rehabilitating of existing highways and bridges has many intriguing possibilities. The most obvious benefit would be in relieving financially strapped public agencies of some of their already huge financial burden. As privatization proponents put it, private funding and development of roads and bridges will greatly increase innovation in bridge design and other arenas. By putting bridge design into the marketplace, the standard of design and construction will increase due to the competitive influences of the market.

The other side of the coin, however, shows the downside to many of the advantages of privatization. While private funding will indeed lower the amount of money public agencies have to expend in building and maintaining the infrastructure, someone will still have to pay for the facility. Private groups will be recouping their costs for the facility through the most direct of user fees: the toll. Where private influence to bridge design standards would definitely add a

breath of fresh air to the practice, larger issues concerning bridge maintenance, inspection, and design uniformity come into play as well.

In the United States, though, there is a definite interest in privatization. Recent legislation has called for enticements designed to get private organizations involved in public facility development. One proposal called for making federal funds available to private developers involved in the construction of public transportation facilities (up to 80% for the cost of a bridge) [Ref. 2.5].

Recently, in Canada, an 8 mile (13 km) crossing of the Northumberland Strait from New Brunswick to Prince Edward Island called for private developers to finance the project and recoup investments through tolls to be collected over a 35 year ownership period. Even in this instance, however, the Canadian government was an implicit partner in the venture by subsidizing the project.

Privatization may not be a panacea, but it does offer agencies another option in funding projects.

Countries like Mexico and Pakistan are aggressively pursuing privatization initiatives to fund transportation projects.

the concept gains increased attention. At one end of the spectrum, privatization allows for a private organization to entirely fund, build, and maintain a public facility, such as a transportation project. Transportation projects, however, often require the developer to perform activities like right-of-way acquisition, environmental assessment, etc., that public agencies are better suited to handle. Due to these, and other issues, a privatization scheme which allows a private group to work in concert with a public agency can provide for more flexibility and a higher chance of success [Ref. 2.7]

Countries like Mexico and Pakistan are aggressively pursuing privatization initiatives to fund transportation projects. Mexico allows private groups to finance and build public toll roads. Ownership stays with the private group for 20 years after which the facility is turned over to the government. Acting in the public's interest, the Mexican government sets the toll prices [Ref. 2.8].

2.1.5 Debt Financing

Debt financing, usually through revenue bonds, offers a "pay-as-you-go" approach to financing highway projects. This method has the advantage of providing highway departments with immediate access to funds which can be used on major projects in a timely fashion. An obvious danger would be in an agency's overborrowing, leaving transportation departments with a shortfall in covering maintenance needs. Because of this danger, debt financing is avoided as a source of revenue for ongoing maintenance and construction requirements. For areas with a solid (and growing) tax base, debt financing is more of an option than for smaller communities [Ref. 2.3].

2.1.6 Conclusions

To many engineers, the process of funding projects is the domain of planners and highway department administrators. However, not only is the bridge engineer's livelihood directly linked to this funding, the magnitude and extent of design is quite often dictated by the way a transportation department receives and allocates monetary resources. To understand this, one only has to compare how bridges are designed and rehabilitated on a toll road with those in a rural county. The spending on surface transportation infrastructure in the United States alone encompasses over $100 billion every year [Ref. 2.2]. Bridge engineers not only need to understand the funding mechanisms that drive bridge design projects, but they must also become part of the process of more efficiently allocating these massive resources.

Bridge engineers not only need to understand the funding mechanisms that drive bridge design projects, but they must also become part of the process of more efficiently allocating these massive resources.

2.2 TYPES OF DESIGN STANDARDS

The design of a highway bridge, like most any other civil engineering project, is dependent on certain standards and criteria. Naturally, the critical importance of highway bridges in a modern transportation system would imply a set of rigorous design specifications to ensure the safety and overall quality of the constructed project. However, as Figure 2.2 may indicate, the volume of information which a bridge engineer must consult throughout the course of any given design can be somewhat formidable.

Figure 2.2 Just a few of the references in the bridge engineer's library.

"A specification containing a set of rules is intended to insure safety; however, the designer must understand the behavior for which the rule applies, otherwise an absurd, a grossly conservative, and sometimes unsafe design may result."

CHARLES G. SALMON
and
JOHN E. JOHNSON

Rather than trying to view the wealth of design information as a single entity, it is easier to think of the various references in discrete categories. In addition to this, very few of the reference texts need to be fully absorbed from start to finish. Even references such as this book are not read from cover to cover, but rather referred to on an as-needed basis. Presented below are the principal classes of design reference material which will be used throughout the text.

2.2.1 General Specifications

By general specifications, we imply an overall design code covering the majority of structures in a given transportation system. In the United States bridge engineers use AASHTO's *Standard Specifications for Highway Bridges* [Ref. 2.9] or AASHTO LRFD Bridge Design Specifications [Ref. 2.10], depending on which state the bridges are located. In a similar fashion, Canadian bridge engineers utilize the CSA or Ontario bridge design codes, and British designers use the BS 5400 code. In general, countries like Canada and the United Kingdom which have developed and maintained major highway systems for a great many years possess their own national or regional bridge standards. Like the BS code, the AASHTO bridge design codes have been accepted by many countries as the general code by which bridges are designed.

This does not mean that the AASHTO code is accepted in its entirety by all transportation agencies. Indeed, even within the United States itself, state transportation departments regularly issue amendments to the AASHTO code. These amendments can offer additional requirements to certain design criteria or even outright exceptions.

The need for a general set of specifications, as discussed in the previous section, is paramount. Without one, there would be no common basis for design in a transportation system. Deviation from design standards is acceptable, and quite often desirable depending on regional constraints. A unified transportation

Indeed, even within the United States itself, state transportation departments regularly issue amendments to the AASHTO code.

network, however, demands a consistent standard, and this is exactly what the AASHTO specifications offer.

Currently, both AASHTO Standard Specifications and AASHTO LRFD specifications are used by different states, but the trend is that more and more states are adopting LRFD method. The major advantage of using LRFD is to have a uniform and predictable reliability. To speed up the effort to unify the design standard across the nation, the U. S. Department of Transportation set up year 2007 as the deadline after which all bridges will have to be designed using AASHTO LRFD to qualify for federal funding.

2.2.2 Material-Related Design Codes

Material design codes are those standards which pertain to bridge components constructed out of various engineering materials such as steel, concrete, prestressed concrete, timber, etc. General material specifications are put forth by the American Society for Testing and Materials (ASTM). These specifications cover a wide range of materials and are contained within numerous volumes. For the application of specific materials in bridge design the following organizations offer material-related design information:

1. **Steel.** The American Institute of Steel Construction (AISC) offers structural steel related design and detailing manuals. Where AASHTO is comprised of professionals from member state transportation departments, AISC standards are developed by steel fabricators, design professionals, and manufacturing companies [Ref. 2.11]. The principal AISC reference to be used throughout this text is the *Manual of Steel Construction—LRFD* [Ref. 2.12]. AISC also publishes design information based on the Allowable Stress Design (ASD) method [Ref. 2.13], but it is being phased out because the advantage of LRFD over ASD has been recognized by most structural engineers. The organization was founded in 1921 and, like other similar organizations listed below, seeks to advance the use of its material (i.e., steel) in construction projects.

2. **Concrete.** The American Concrete Institute (ACI) offers bridge engineers a set of standards in the analysis and design of reinforced concrete structures. The principal design manual to be used throughout this text is the *Building Code and Commentary* [Ref. 2.14]. Like the AASHTO and AISC specifications, the ACI code covers almost all of the essential information a bridge engineer will need in the design of concrete elements. The *ACI Detailing Manual* [Ref. 2.15] is another important publication which provides the designer with guidelines on how to detail concrete structures and elements. As we will see later in the text, detailing and drafting the final contract documents is not a trivial effort to be treated lightly (see Section 5.2). In conjunction with these texts, ACI offers a wide variety of references covering various other material standards and specifications which the designer can refer to on an as-needed basis.

For prestressed concrete structures, the Prestressed Concrete Institute (PCI) publishes the *PCI Design Handbook* [Ref. 2.16].

3. **Timber.** For bridge structures or structural components constructed out of timber, designers can refer to the *Timber Construction Manual* [Ref. 2.17]

As we will see later in the text, detailing and drafting the final contract documents is not a trivial effort to be treated lightly.

published by the American Institute of Timber Construction (AITC) and the *National Design Specification for Wood Construction* [Ref. 2.18] issued by the American Wood Council (AWC).

It is important to note that, although these manuals offer information specific to various design materials, the AASHTO Specification still provides its own interpretation and guidelines for the use of the material in highway bridge structures. For example, an entire section of the AASHTO Standard Specifications discusses the use of timber in highway bridges. While this does not imply that bridge designers need only reference the AASHTO Specifications, it should alert the reader to make sure that all possible standards have been investigated and the most reasonable specifications applied to the design at hand. Normally, AASHTO specifications adopt the same design philosophies as those manuals, but AASHTO takes a more conservative approach so it may not necessarily use the identical equations as in these material design manuals.

One has to keep in mind that these material-related codes mostly deal with building structural design, therefore, they can only be used as references and background information. Bridge engineers should always apply AASHTO Code for the design.

2.2.3 Use of Design Standards

It does not take one long to reach the disclaimer in a set of design standards like those listed above. Sometimes this disclaimer can be found in the preface, where it says something like, "While these data have been prepared in accordance with recognized engineering principles and are based on the most accurate and reliable technical data available, they should not be used or relied upon for any general or specific application without competent professional examination and verification ..." [Ref. 2.17].

While, in a way, this may frustrate an engineer looking for *the answer* in a reference, it should also serve as a signal for the responsibility the engineer carries in any design. Salmon and Johnson's quote at the beginning of this section illustrates the point quite nicely. Design specifications are essential tools which the bridge engineer uses in cobbling together a design, but by no means do they offer a uniform template for punching out final contract documents.

In this text we will look at several basic design examples which act as an excellent guide through the design process. These examples, however, cannot possibly cover every aspect of design which an engineer will encounter. In one sense, this is what makes bridge engineering so challenging. Even a set of structures in the same contract submission will offer distinctly different design problems for each bridge.

One bridge may have footings on rock, while another requires piles. A structure on a straight alignment leading into another on a horizontal curve can make a world of difference between two apparently identical structures only a few hundred feet apart. The design should define the boundary conditions and the specifications should apply to those constraints, not the other way around.

The bridge engineer should also think to question and improve upon reference design material whenever possible. This does not mean that one should begin to question things like the HS20-44 design vehicle, but items like

> The design should define the boundary conditions and the specifications should apply to those constraints, not the other way around.

Figure 2.3 There is plenty room for improvement in the way bridges are designed.

standard details and the application of design specifications should be on the table for discussion and review. If we cannot blindly follow design specifications as gospel, it seems only natural that they can be improved upon to suit the needs of a specific design. This is something many engineers tend to forget. Partly because of everyone's desire to maintain statusquo and partly due to resistance from other designers, it becomes easier to avoid innovation rather than pursue it.

Although the design of the modern highway bridge is, at this point, several decades old, there is still considerable room for improvement (as evidenced by Figure 2.3). Anyone who has stood under a bridge and observed the effects that traffic and weather have on a structure can bear witness to the need for improved joints, substructure elements, and a host of related components and appurtenances. These are problems which have no solutions in the AASHTO Specifications or any other book for that matter. The answers lie only in the minds of today's and tomorrow's bridge engineers and will only come about if the question itself of "How do I improve this?" is asked in the first place.

These are problems which have no solutions in the AASHTO Specifications ... the answers lie only in the minds of today's and tomorrow's bridge engineers and will only come about if the question itself of "How do I improve this?" is asked in the first place.

2.3 SITE INSPECTION

When one uses the term *inspection*, especially in bridge design, it can mean many things. Within the scope of this text, we will be discussing inspection as it pertains to

- ❏ Inspection of a site for a new bridge structure
- ❏ Inspection of an existing bridge and site to ascertain its present condition
- ❏ Inspection of an existing bridge and site where the structure is to be rehabilitated

There is a great deal of overlap between the various forms of inspection, with the greatest degree of commonality existing between the latter two types listed above. The reader should be aware, however, that the level of detail in an inspection varies depending on what the intent is. With regard to new bridge structures, a great deal of time and effort will be focused on geologic conditions, highway alignment orientation, and underpass crossing features. In a rehabilitation design, the inspecting engineer will spend time focusing on the existing structure elements in an effort to determine which need simple maintenance and which need extensive rehabilitation or replacement. Maintenance inspections, conducted to rate a bridge structure and judge its performance, are more rapidly conducted than the other two forms. The principal intent of this type of inspection is to document the structure's condition and aid in deciding whether maintenance or rehabilitation is required.

This section is titled *Site Inspection*, because it is important to remember that a highway bridge exists within a defined environment. This environment is composed of many other features in addition to the bridge structure. A bridge inspection can fail if the inspector does not take into account important site features such as drainage channels, wetland, embankments, utility lines, etc., and how they function within the confines of the bridge site.

2.3.1 The Scoping Inspection

In the case of a new or rehabilitation design a thorough site inspection should be conducted by principal members of the design team prior to commencement of design. There are two levels of inspection which should be conducted. First, a cursory visit or *scoping inspection* should be made to determine any physical or natural constraints at the site. The design team project manager, the lead designer, and (if possible) a representative of the owner should attend this inspection. Prior to the site visit, any record documents concerning the site or an existing structure should be reviewed. These documents could be in the form of a base map, prior inspection reports, and as-built plans.

There are a variety of site characteristics which need to be investigated for the engineer to begin formulating the boundary conditions of the project. Some of the major site features which should be investigated are:

❑ Drainage conditions and potential wetland impacts
❑ Vertical clearance
❑ Soil condition
❑ Horizontal and vertical alignment constraints
❑ Underpass or channel constraints
❑ Potential utility impacts

Following the scoping inspection, a more detailed follow-up inspection should be made. In the *detailed site inspection*, actual physical measurements are recorded, photographs are taken, and a report prepared.

When dealing with a rehabilitation project or performing a maintenance inspection, however, the designer is also faced with having to evaluate an existing structure. The following section describes some of the major issues concerning the detailed site inspection for a rehabilitation design project.

> **A** bridge inspection can fail if the inspector does not take into account important site features such as drainage channels, wetland, embankments, utility lines, etc., and how they function within the confines of the bridge site.

THE FHWA RATING system is based on a scale from 0 to 9. An inspection manual is provided to bridge inspectors describing how various components should be rated and which ratings should be assigned for various levels of deterioration.

Rating 0-1:	Potentially hazardous.
Rating 2-4:	Poor condition.
Rating 5-6:	Fair condition.
Rating 7-9:	Good to excellent condition.

Rating N: Not inspected or unknown.

2.3.2 Recording the Inspection

As would be expected, the inspection of an existing structure is broken down by structural components. In Section 1.1.1, an overview of the major structural components for a typical slab-on-stringer bridge was presented. The inspection process is centered around these components and their associated elements. Summarizing from Section 1.1.1, an example of a structural *component* is an abutment, where a pedestal in that abutment is an *element*. Each element is assigned a rating value after which the entire component proper is given a rating. This procedure is repeated for all major structural components such as piers, the deck, superstructure, etc. A final, overall rating is then determined for the entire structure.

The Federal Highway Administration utilizes a rigorous inspection system based on a scale of 0 to 9 (see sidebar on this page) [Ref. 2.19]. Using predefined inspection forms, the inspection team rates the structural components, photographs key elements, and documents their findings for submission to the owner. Any component with a rating of 4 or less is documented in greater detail with notes and sketches.

For the owner, the inspection report offers a consistent method for tracking the condition of bridge structures in their transportation network and deciding which bridges require maintenance or rehabilitation. For the designer in a rehabilitation project, the inspection report acts as a reference document throughout the course of design. As a rule of thumb, it is only feasible for the engineer to visit a project site on certain occasions. Therefore, it is necessary, not only for record purposes but also for design purposes, to have a well-documented inspection of the structure.

When an inspection is being conducted for design purposes, the inspection team is not only concerned with rating the performance and functionality of various elements but must also take specific field measurements which detail the extent of deterioration in an element. These measurements will eventually be used to

- ❑ Prepare the preliminary design and scope of work for the project
- ❑ Analyze the adequacy of structural components to remain, be repaired, or replaced
- ❑ Develop rehabilitation alternatives
- ❑ Provide a basis for making an accurate cost estimate

Detailed field measurements are essential if a designer is to define a realistic scope of work for a project. It is one thing to say a pier column rates a 3 or a 4, but knowing that 20% to 30% of the column surface is deteriorated to a depth below the reinforcing steel provides the engineer with the ability to make a decision on whether to patch the column or replace it. Noting that a steel primary member shows evidence of rusting and paint loss is helpful in flagging a bridge for maintenance work, but also knowing that the stringer has lost 20% of its section properties allows for an accurate load rating analysis to be performed. Final costs are always more realistic when they can be backed up with documented field measurements. This is especially true when patching or superficial maintenance is being conducted on an element.

2.3.3 Rating Substructure Elements

When inspecting a major structural component, an engineer must not only investigate the *condition* of the component but must also determine the *causes* of any deterioration. Without adequately ascertaining the nature of the deterioration process, the potential exists for an incorrect specification of remedial measures to be performed. Figure 2.4 shows a typical abutment configuration. Noted on the figure are three major areas which an inspector will focus on when rating the component.

> **W**hen inspecting a major structural component, an engineer must not only investigate the condition of the component but must also determine the causes of any deterioration.

1. Joints. Deck joints are located between bridge decks on a pier or between the bridge deck and the abutment backwall. Joint elements are particularly critical because they:

❑ Prevent the leakage of runoff and deicing chemicals from rusting and corroding substructure elements below the deck
❑ Provide a smooth transition from approach to bridge deck
❑ Allow for longitudinal movement of the structure

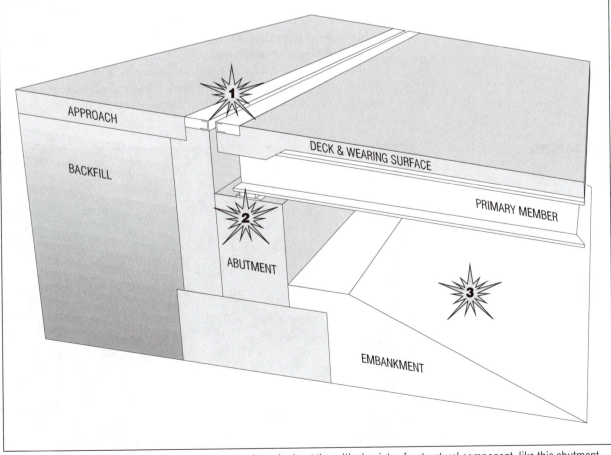

Figure 2.4 During the inspection process, an engineer looks at the critical points of a structural component, like this abutment.

When inspecting a joint, the engineer should first look to see if the joint is free of debris which, if present, may hinder movement.

Other potential hazards are joints which have been paved over during highway maintenance operations and become clogged.

Deck joints may take the form of a preformed elastomeric material or an assembly consisting of a metal mechanism integrated with elastomeric materials.

When inspecting a joint, the engineer should first look to see if the joint is free of debris which, if present, may hinder movement. Mechanical joints, with steel fingers or sliding plates which are bent or deformed, can also hinder movement and provide for a poor riding surface. Leaking joints, as mentioned above, can cause serious deterioration in bearings, pedestals, and other substructure elements. Other potential hazards are joints which have been paved over during highway maintenance operations and become clogged. It is important to keep in mind that any restriction to movement at the joint, when combined with thermal or other forces, can result in excessive stresses at the joint and other points in the structure.

2. Bearings, Bridge Seats, and Pedestals. By far, the substructure elements which suffer the most from leaking joints are the bearings, bridge seats, and pedestals. Bearings, like joints, must be free of debris to allow for adequate movement at the support.

The type of movement the bearing allows depends on the type of support. At an expansion support, rotation and longitudinal translation are allowed, while at a fixed support only rotation is permitted. Some transverse movement in both fixed and expansion bearings is also allowed to accommodate thermal expansion and contraction. Although the effect of temperature change is of great importance, bearings must also be designed to handle movement caused by concrete creep and shrinkage, especially for prestressed concrete structures.

Steel bearings should be inspected to ensure that they are oriented properly, not subjected to excessive rusting, and that all bolts and anchorages are secure. Excessive corrosion and accumulated debris inhibits the

A BEARING resting on a concrete substructure is typically comprised of four elements:

1. The sole plate which connects the bearing to the load bearing member.

2. The bearing mechanism itself which allows for the specified movement. Types of bearing mechanisms are bot bearings, rockers/rollers, and elastomeric material.

3. The masonry plate which acts as an interface between the bearing and the concrete substructure.

4. The anchor bolt which connects the masonry plate to the substructure.

Figure 2.5 This bearing and pedestal are in good condition.

bearing from functioning as it was designed. Elastomeric-type bearings should be checked for excessive deformation to the pad. Any distortion to an elastomeric bearing which exceeds 25% the height of the bearing is considered excessive. Another concern is hardening of the elastomeric material over time. Hardening of the material, evidenced by cracking and discoloration, inhibits the ability of the bearing to accommodate structure movement.

For bridge seats, a critical issue is whether or not the integrity of the bearing surface area has been corrupted. Such loss of bearing area will be illustrated in the bridge seat and pedestal by map cracking, spalling, and, in extreme cases, loss of concrete at the perimeter of the pedestal. This is a situation which can result from inadequate reinforcing steel in the pedestal. Any time an engineer sees a situation where there is space between the masonry plate of a bearing and the concrete bearing surface, immediate repair should be recommended. The affected girder may need to be temporarily supported if extensive repair is to be performed under the bearing.

Probably the most common culprit leading to the physical deterioration of a bearing and/or pedestal is leakage from a deck joint. Once the integrity of the joint has been compromised, the flow of deicing agents, water, and other potentially corrosive substances will begin to affect the performance of a bearing. Again, the situation which the inspector should look for is if the deterioration that has occurred is impeding the movement for which the bearing was designed.

Another danger at the bearing location is the effect of longitudinal movement at the approach/ abutment interface. The cumulative effect of vehicle impact and thermal expansion and contraction can lead to excessive bearing deformation or even collapse of the span. Since movement at the bridge deck joints is so critical, the combination of corrosion inhibiting

> **O**nce the integrity of the joint has been compromised, the flow of ... potentially corrosive substances will begin to affect the performance of a bearing.

DESIGN PERSPECTIVE

Who should inspect what and when?

*T*here are many schools of thought on the nature of bridge inspection and how it should be conducted. In the United States, the minimum requirement set forth by the Federal Highway Administration is a biennial inspection conducted by a certified bridge inspector who may or may not be a licensed professional engineer. There is, however, a good deal of debate over the type of person who should be inspecting a structure and the extent and level of detail of the inspection.

One thinking calls for bridge engineers to play a more active role in the inspection process. The idea is that bridge designers are better suited to identifying design failings such as fatigue, cracking, and other adverse structural conditions. By involving the design engineer in review of the structural design, the argument goes, many potentially hazardous situations can be avoided by pointing the inspection team in the right direction [Ref. 2.21].

Others argue that bridge inspection is essentially a visually oriented project that stands apart from the design of the structure itself. It is the inspector's role to identify how the structure is performing in its present environment and that any design considerations are, at this point, moot. Rather than spending funds on design review, they would be better spent on diagnostic tools and increased inspector education [Ref. 2.22].

As to who should be conducting the inspection, some states require that a licensed professional engineer be in charge of the inspection team. In states with thousands of structures requiring inspection every 2 years, however, the demand on personnel resources is severe.

A compromise solution is to supplement the current biennial routine inspection with a detailed in-depth inspection every 4 to 5 years, lead by a professional engineer. The biennial inspection would continue to serve in flagging bridges in extreme disrepair and rating component and element condition. The detailed in-depth inspection would allow for an intensive look at potential strengthening measures and review of component performance. Any expansion, however, will put a drain on already limited resources.

bearing movement with excessive span movement can lead to complete failure of the span at the bearing location. This was the case in 1988 when a 50-ft span on Interstate 678 literally fell off its bearings. The bearings had locked into place as a result of corrosion, and when thermal expansion set in, brackets above the bearing fractured at their welds, causing the entire span to drop 4 in [Ref. 2.20].

3. **Concrete Elements.** Like all concrete components, concrete substructure components need to be inspected for cracking, spalling, delamination, or exposed reinforcement as evidenced in Figure 2.6. Pier caps should be examined for a buildup of moisture and excessive spalling. If at all possible, the inspection engineer should seek to identify the *cause* of any deterioration to substructure elements. Outside of poor construction methods, a vehicle collision, or an error in design, advanced stages of deterioration in concrete substructures are caused by other components of the bridge. In addition to the consistently mentioned joint leakage could be settlement, excessive movement of the superstructure, or, in the case of water crossings, scour.

Inspection engineers should always keep in mind that they are the eyes for the managers and designers back in the office. In the case of a maintenance inspection, the inspection engineer's remarks and ratings will be critical in determining whether the structure is selected for rehabilitation or not. In a rehabilitation design project, the inspector's notes lay the framework for the entire design process to follow.

A picture is worth a hundred words. Always take as many photos as you practically can. With digital cameras, the cost of taking pictures is no longer an issue.

> **I**nspection engineers should always keep in mind that they are the eyes for the managers and designers back in the office.

SPALLING OCCURS when surface concrete breaks away from the structural element. Some of the situations which can lead to spalling are a poor concrete mix, reaction to chemicals which come in contact with the concrete, expansion due to reinforcing steel corrosion, and salts coming in contact with cracks. The design engineer can limit spalling by providing adequate cover for reinforcement, properly designing for drainage of the element, and accounting for creep. Spalls can even result from small cracks which widen as vehicles continually pass over the structure. As the cracks widen, chemicals, such as deicing agents, seep into the crack and begin to affect the reinforcing steel. When structural elements, like the pier column at right, reach an advanced stage of deterioration, the decision has to be made whether to attempt to repair the element or replace it.

Figure 2.6 Exposed reinforcing signals repair.

4. **Steel Elements.** Steel substructure elements should be closely inspected for section loss, fatigue cracks, or buckling of columns. All connections should also be checked for loosening. The inspector should differentiate between primary load-bearing members and bracing members in the inspection report. See Section 2.3.4, on primary and secondary members, for more information on inspecting steel elements.

5. **Timber Elements.** Although its use as a material in the construction of new bridges is somewhat limited, timber structures are prevalent throughout the United

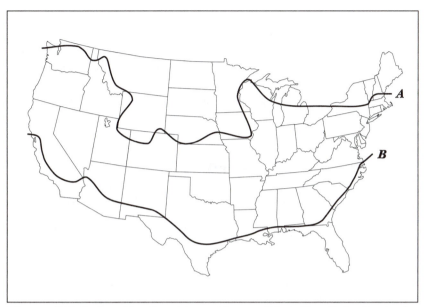

Figure 2.7 Regions of termite and drywood damage. *(Adapted from Timber Construction Manual, fifth edition, Ref. 2.17.)*

SUBTERRANEAN termites live underground and are found in areas below line A in the map at left. Line B shows the northern edge of nonsubterranean termite and drywood damage. Subterranean termites live underground and tunnel to get at the wood they need for food. These termites have wings and fly before they mate and begin to build the colonies that feed off of wood. An inspector can look for the telltale signs of so-called flying ants or shed wings to determine whether subterranean termites exist in the vicinity of a structure [Ref. 2.17].

States and are often the subject of inspection. When inspecting timber bridges the principal concern is to identify any and all decay. The inspection engineer should look for signs of moisture, moss, fungi, drywood, and insect attack. Figure 2.7 illustrates the regions of the continental United States affected by termite and drywood damage [Ref. 2.17]. The process of testing for decay in timber is similar to the method used for testing for delaminations in concrete. Sounding (i.e., pounding on the timber element with a hammer) and listening for a *hollow* sound is the best method for identifying decay beneath the surface. Small hole test drilling or coring is another useful way to detect and determine the extent of decay.

Unlike steel and concrete, however, timber elements are susceptible to attacks from fungi and insects that use the material as food. The inspection engineer should identify whether elements have been coated with a preservative treatment like creosote or an oil-borne or waterborne treatment [Ref. 2.17].

6. Embankment. Deteriorated embankment slope protection may seem to have more of an aesthetic impact than structural. At highway crossings, however, failure of embankment material can indicate larger site drainage problems. At water crossings, erosion or scour of embankment material can undermine footings and jeopardize the overall integrity of the structure. Particularly susceptible to this condition are abutments and piers on spread footings.

Footings on piles, however, can also be affected by extreme scour conditions. The inspection engineer must pay close attention to any exposed footing surface or pile. Particular regard should be given to horizontal loading of the substructure component. If scour has removed embankment

If scour has removed embankment material on one face of the footing and accumulated material on an opposing face, the component could become unbalanced and subsequently fail.

material on one face of the footing and accumulated material on an opposing face, the component could become unbalanced and subsequently fail [Ref. 2.24]. Highway bridges crossing water channels are now required to have underwater inspection. As a result of this new requirement, states are now hiring or contracting divers to inspect submerged footings and ensure that bridge footings are stable. The issue of inspecting for scour will be discussed in more detail in Section 2.3.6.

2.3.4 Rating Superstructure Elements

In Section 1 we mentioned that a bridge superstructure is composed of a deck, which carries the roadway over a crossing highway or waterway, and a frame, which supports the deck and transmits its loads to the substructure components.

> The constant wear of traffic over the deck surface, its total exposure to the elements, and the use of deicing agents all combine to put the deck under adverse conditions.

1. Deck and Wearing Surface. Of all the bridge components, the deck is the one which physically takes the most abuse. The constant wear of traffic over the deck surface, its total exposure to the elements, and the use of deicing agents all combine to put the deck under adverse conditions. By far the most prevalent material used in the construction of bridge decks is concrete, although steel decks and, to a lesser degree, timber decks are also used.

When inspecting a concrete deck, the engineer should give close attention to any cracking or spalling which may be present. Deterioration typically proceeds from the top of the deck down through the slab to the bottom. The presence of wet concrete, delaminations (cracks or voids below the surface of the deck) and cracks or efflorescence on deck soffit

STAY-IN-PLACE FORMS do not rest directly on the top flange of a stringer but are fastened to a form support which is connected to the flange. When the deck is newly poured, the field engineer asks the same question an inspecting engineer does many years afterward: *Is the concrete underneath sound?* New York State, for example, requires the field engineer to inspect each span of a bridge by having the contractor remove a section of the steel form and visually inspect that the concrete is in sound condition. In addition to this, the condition is further investigated by banging a hammer on the stay-in-place forms and listening for any voids or honeycomb areas [Ref. 2.24].

Figure 2.8 Stay-in-place forms can hide deterioration beneath them.

(bottom surface of a deck) can indicate more serious damage throughout the slab.

Engineers attempting to determine the condition of a concrete deck, however, can be hindered by the presence of a wearing surface and/or stay-in-place forms, both of which can hide damage existing beneath them (see Figure 2.8). Although methods such as infrared thermography allow for the testing of concrete decks for delaminations, such facilities may be out of reach for the average inspector.

Apart from visible signs of deterioration, the inspection engineer should always be on the lookout for excessive deflections and listen for abnormal sounds emanating from the structure. While these observations tend to be extremely subjective, the presence of a strange noise or odd motion in the structure can often lead to discovering problems which may otherwise have gone unnoticed. This general rule of thumb applies not only to the deck but also to all structural elements.

The most common and effective way of detecting deck delaminations is the chain drag over the deck. Any hollow sound is an indication of poor concrete underneath.

Wearing surfaces should be inspected for general forms of pavement distress, which range from cracking and potholing for asphalt surfaces to cracking and spalling for concrete. With regard to asphalt surfaces, the inspector should note whether resurfacing has been performed on the bridge wearing surface, as this will introduce additional dead loading on the structure, which could change the structure load rating value.

2. **Primary and Secondary Members.** The supporting structural frame represented by the bridge's primary and secondary members are typically inspected for deterioration which causes loss of section to a member. More serious deterioration can lead to a member being unable to resist the loading conditions it was designed for. Primary and secondary members are also susceptible to impact by vehicles passing under the structure.

Close attention should be given to areas where there is a distinct change in section properties, such as at the end of a cover plate, or where weld connections exist. These areas are especially susceptible to fatigue stress which can be induced by a concentrated stress at this location. Any debris which has accumulated at the end of a cover plate should be brushed away by the inspector to ascertain the true condition underneath. Fatigue stress can also be caused by excessive vibration and stress changes in the primary member. This is why, as we will see later in the text, the traffic loading of a structure plays a key role in a fatigue analysis for a bridge.

If the structure is being designed for rehabilitation, the engineer should pay a close attention to these members, and like other items discussed in this section, document all findings with measurements. Taking a steel, wide-flange girder as an example, field measurements which describe the current state of the member's cross-sectional properties (e.g. web and flange thickness, cover plate width and thickness, etc.) should be taken (see Section 2.5.4). These dimensions can then be used to perform an updated and accurate load rating analysis for the structure based on the present condition.

Close attention should be given to areas where there is a distinct change in section properties, such as at the end of a cover plate, or where weld connections exist. These areas are especially susceptible to fatigue stress...

It may also be necessary to determine the type of steel present in the field if it was not noted on the as-built plans for the bridge, or if plans are unavailable. In this case the designer has two options. One is to rely on the AASHTO *Manual for Condition Evaluation of Bridges* [Ref. 2.23], which presents a table for yield stresses to be used in analyzing steel members. This table gives minimum tensile strength and minimum yield point values for steel of various vintages. These age groups are, specifically as follows:

❑ Prior to 1905
❑ 1905 to 1936
❑ 1936 to 1963
❑ After 1963

Another option is to perform a coupon test on the steel. In this case, a portion of the steel is taken from a member in the field and tested in a laboratory to determine its properties.

For concrete primary and secondary members, an inspection similar to that performed for the concrete deck should be conducted. Concrete beams should be checked for cracking, the presence of efflorescence, and delaminations. Like steel members, concrete beams are also subject to vehicular impact and should be checked for any collisions. In prestressed concrete bridges, particular attention should be given to the prestressing tendons for any corrosion. Corrosion typically begins at the anchorages and travels along the tendon, or at voids where duct was not properly grouted. The structural adequacy of the concrete is tested by taking a core sample from the concrete member. For more information on coring, refer to Section 2.5.

> **I**n prestressed concrete bridges, particular attention should be given to the prestressing tendons for any corrosion. Corrosion typically begins at the anchorages and travels along the tendon, or at voids where duct was not properly grouted.

2.3.5 Rating Appurtenance and Site-Related Elements

Due to the diverse forms of structures in use, there are a wide variety of appurtenance elements to be considered. Discussed below are the major types of elements at a bridge site and what they should be investigated for.

1. **Railing.** A great many bridges that are 30 years, 40 years old, or even older still utilize the same bridge railing installed at the time of construction. With regard to inspection, AASHTO recommends that the inspector check to see if the railing is performing as originally designed [Ref. 2.23]. It is quite likely, however, that this will not meet present standards for many older structures. The greatest danger, with regard to bridge railings, is if the unit has been subjected to impact as a result of a traffic accident. Such impact could damage the rail itself or loosen its anchorages. If this has occurred, notification to the owner should be made at once to prevent a situation where the railing fails.

    If a railing shows signs of repeated impact, the engineer should note any site characteristics that could be leading to this condition and design the remedial measures to correct it. Poor sight triangles at an approach, a narrow transition from approach to bridge, an excessively curved overpass alignment, or a due east-west alignment are some of the site conditions which can lead to accidents on or near a structure. In some cases it may be possible to eliminate the cause of repeated impact (e.g., trimming back obstructing foliage); in others, a more rigorous railing/barrier system may be required. The designer should be aware, however, that existing fascia stringers may not be able to sustain the placement of a new barrier.

2. **Drainage Systems.** The drainage system of a highway bridge can be composed of a variety of elements. Deck swales, weep tubes, and scuppers can be used to carry water off the deck, while gutters and earth swales drain runoff from the site and structure proper. Even the composition of backfill material plays an important role in the effective drainage of the structure and its site.

The most common problem with any drainage system is the accumulation of debris in a pipe or channel. Another problem can arise from changes in the overpass or underpass roadway surface. Constant resurfacing can lead to a flattening of the roadway crown which, in turn, leads to ponding of water. If there has been a recent rainfall, the inspecting engineer should look for telltale ponding as well as the flow of runoff. However, if such a situation does not present itself, a close examination of any clogging to drainage elements should be made.

For prestressed concrete bridges, drainage facilities are not only required to drain storm water runoff but are needed to carry off corrosive deicing chemicals as well. The inspecting engineer should ensure that these drains function properly.

3. **Utilities.** Highway bridge structures quite often carry various utilities across an underpass feature. These utilities could be in the form of public services such as electric, gas, water, cable, or telephone lines among others. In addition to physically carrying a utility line across a road or channel, the presence of overhead and buried utilities may also affect various characteristics of the bridge and site.

With respect to lines carried by the bridge, the inspection engineer should determine the condition of both the conduit and its support system (should one exist). Obvious failures such as leaks, cracks, and failed support connections should be investigated. Utility lines should be checked to ensure that they do not adversely affect vertical clearance. Any foliage interfering with lines on or near the site should be cleared away to prevent possible fire hazards. Foliage close to utility lines may also cause downed lines during storms with high winds or ice.

For the most part, utilities that an inspection engineer finds at a bridge site have been granted a special permit by the owner. There are, however, instances when unauthorized utility lines encroach onto the bridge or site. Therefore, it is important to note the presence of all utilities so that a check can be made by the owner to determine any possible encroachments.

4. **Lighting and Signing.** Like railing, lighting and signing are safety-related appurtenances designed to offer protection to traffic over and under a bridge. They also offer a degree of protection to the structure itself. Lighting standards and sign structures are typically made of steel or aluminum. When placed in the vicinity of traffic, they are susceptible to

DID YOU KNOW

THAT the red, white, and blue shield on Interstate route signs is a registered trademark of AASHTO? In an effort to prevent signs similar to the Interstate sign from being erected close to highways, AASHTO filed for, and was granted, a registered trademark in 1967 [Ref. 2.26].

If lighting and sign standards are continually subjected to damage from collisions with vehicles, the installation of some form of fender/barrier system should be investigated by the owner.

collisions and damage to their anchorages and other structural members. If lighting and sign standards are continually subjected to damage from collisions with vehicles, the installation of some form of fender/barrier system should be investigated by the owner.

At the top of the lighting standard is a lighting fixture. The lighting fixture is comprised of the lamp, its housing, and a lens. At a basic level, the lamp or luminaire at the top of the light standard should be inspected to ensure that it still functions properly (i.e., illuminates). Dirt and other debris can limit the amount of roadway covered by the lamp. On a more serious level, damaged light housings and exposed electrical connections can create potential shock and fire hazards. Bridges may also be equipped with lighting on signing, aircraft warning lights, or navigation lights. They should be inspected in a manner similar to highway light fixtures.

One of the more common damages to signing is vandalism from graffiti which impairs visibility of the sign message or, in some cases, renders it illegible. The inspection engineer should also note any encroaching foliage which may also limit visibility of the sign.

2.3.6 Inspecting for Scour

Bridges that cross water channels require detailed inspection of channel characteristics and the condition of substructure elements in the channel. The need for a detailed and thorough scour inspection program is a result of the catastrophic effects which can be caused by excessive scour.

In order to properly inspect for scour, it is necessary to have a basic understanding of what causes it in the first place. Scour is the washing away of streambed material by water channel flow. Typically, scour occurs when the water channel becomes narrowed or constricted. From basic fluid dynamics, we know that a smaller opening leads to a greater velocity ($Q = Av$). If constrictions in the channel are significant, the velocity of the stream can increase such that the substructure footings and/or piles become undermined. Sharp bends or curves in the water channel also increase velocity which can create cross-currents and turbulence. Scour can either occur locally at specific substructure components (local scour) or over the entire structure crossing the channel (general scour). Discussed below are key issues concerning the inspection of water channels and bridge elements located in them.

Scour is the washing away of streambed material by water channel flow. Typically, scour occurs when the water channel becomes narrowed or constricted.

1. **The Channel.** A principal difficulty in anticipating the effects of scour lies in the amorphous nature of water channels. Put another way, the geometry of a channel changes periodically both horizontally and vertically. At any given point in time, a waterway's width can increase or decrease, its depth rise and fall. To adequately plan for the types of scour protection that should be incorporated at a bridge site, a channel cross section and profile record should be maintained.

The channel cross section is created by measuring the distance from the bridge deck to the top of the water surface at points along the deck fasciae. A drop line is used and measurements logged in the inspection report. The New York State Department of Transportation recommends

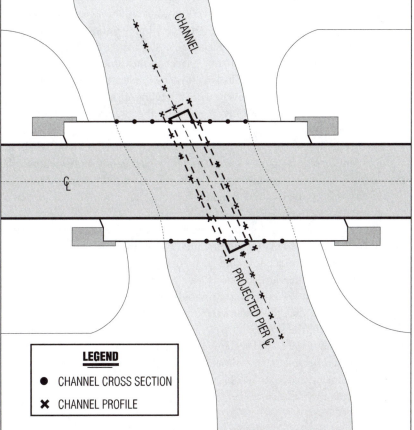

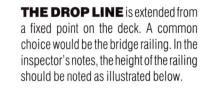

THE DROP LINE is extended from a fixed point on the deck. A common choice would be the bridge railing. In the inspector's notes, the height of the railing should be noted as illustrated below.

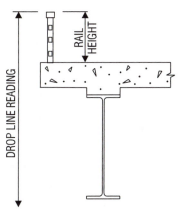

The New York State DOT recommends using the top of footing as the reference for all readings, however; readings referenced to the top of pier, bridge seat, or top of plinth are also acceptable [Ref. 2.25].

LEGEND

● CHANNEL CROSS SECTION

✖ CHANNEL PROFILE

Figure 2.9 Location of channel cross-section and profile measurements. *(Adapted from New York State Department of Transportation Bridge Inspection Manual, Ref. 2.25.)*

measurements be taken at 10-ft (3.05-m) intervals from the first substructure component in the water channel (either abutment or pier). Additional shots are required on each face of intermediate piers [Ref. 2.25].

Similarly, a channel profile is constructed at substructure components. The profile is constructed by taking measurements on each face of the substructure component and at intervals upstream and downstream of the component. The NYSDOT inspection manual recommends 30 ft (9.14 m) to each side [Ref. 2.25]. Figure 2.9 illustrates the position of cross-section and profile readings.

As discussed in Section 2.3.3, Part 6, the embankment around substructure components should be investigated for any effects brought on by changes in the water channel. The washing away of any scour protection material should be noted and, if severe, brought to the immediate attention of the owner. Another difficulty is accumulated debris, such as tree branches, deposited at substructure locations. In addition to inhibiting the channel flow, brush-type debris can be a potential fire hazard. Any obstruction in the channel itself, such as sand or gravel bars, which can alter the flow of water, should be noted [Ref. 2.23].

A nother difficulty is accumulated debris, such as tree branches, deposited at substructure locations. In addition to inhibiting the channel flow, brush-type debris can be a potential fire hazard.

2. The Substructure. Investigation of abutments and piers submerged in the water channel is an involved process, but an ultimately necessary one. It is required by the Federal Highway Administration when in-depth inspections are carried out. To make life easier for all involved, inspection of these components should take place at the time of year when the channel's water elevation is at its lowest point. Underwater inspection should be performed by certified divers with a training in bridge inspection. The major focus of the diver's investigation is the presence of scour at the footing location.

A red flag is always raised in the inspection team's mind when the abutment or pier rests on a spread footing which is not supported by solid bed rock. Footings resting on piles, while more secure than spread footings, are also susceptible to undermining. Particular attention should be placed on any exposed pile. This concern increases in saltwater environments, where corrosion of the piles can become severe. The condition is serious enough that AASHTO recommends a 4-year underwater inspection program for steel substructure elements in freshwater, and it requires biennial underwater inspections in salt water [Ref. 2.23].

In addition to checking for voids around the foundation for an indication of scour, the underwater inspector should also note any visible deterioration to the substructure element as would be the case if the element were not submerged. Any spalling of concrete, corrosion of steel members, decay in timber piles, etc., should be noted in the inspection report for possible maintenance or rehabilitation. Pictures should always be taken to document any deficiencies.

2.3.7 Conclusions

As the preceding text would illustrate, the inspection of a highway bridge structure is an involved undertaking. Its necessity, however, was born out of the failures of bridges and the public's demand to ensure that bridges in a highway network offer the maximum level of safety possible.

Bill Kallman of the New York State Department of Transportation wrote that, "I would not explain to an inspector that any particular bridge is better built or inherently safer or less risky than another, since the inspector, with his few tools, must be very sensitive to things that are going on at that bridge at which he is looking" [Ref. 2.22]. There is a great deal of truth in that statement, and the inspection engineer should understand that each bridge site represents an individual project.

Unlike the mechanical engineer, who can often construct numerous prototypes before the final design rolls off the assembly line, the civil engineer has only one opportunity to *get it right*. When an inspector goes into the field, he or she is witnessing the culmination, not only of a designer's work, but also of the effort of dozens of detailers, draftsmen, managers, agency review personnel, and the like. In all of that work the chance of a poor concrete mix, inadequate reinforcement, or blown elevation is great. No amount of analysis in the office will ever be able to give the level of accuracy and specificity that the inspector's report provides.

In a more macroscopic sense, the maintenance inspection's role in assisting an owner in project selection is critical to say the least. Agencies measure

> **U**nlike the mechanical engineer, who can often construct numerous prototypes before the final design rolls off the assembly line, the civil engineer has only one opportunity to get it right.

their performance based on the inspection ratings of their structures. If this measure is to be an accurate indicator of the overall quality of the bridges in a highway network, then the inspection report must offer as complete and accurate a portrayal of each structure as possible.

As a result of this importance, the quality of the inspector's end product is paramount. The reader should understand that many inspectors work at an extremely accelerated pace. The demands placed on an inspector by a biennial inspection are great. Where the inspector in a rehabilitation design project has the luxury of taking time in recording details and measurements, the maintenance inspection must be completed in a quick and dirty fashion. The industry as a whole needs to recognize the role each inspection type plays in the bridge design process and award it with appropriate levels of respect and resources.

> The industry as a whole needs to recognize the role each inspection type plays in the bridge design process and award it with appropriate levels of respect and resources.

2.4 SITE SURVEY

Before the actual design process can commence in full, a detailed site survey needs to be performed. The survey, led by an experienced land surveyor, is used to create a model of

❏ Topographic features which detail the surface of the overpass and underpass roadways as well as the surrounding site
❏ Delineate wetland if it exists at the vicinity of the bridge site
❏ Planimetric features which detail various natural and man-made items such as railing, edge of pavement lines, vegetation, drop inlets, etc.
❏ Water channel cross-sections if it is a waterway crossing bridge
❏ In the case of a rehabilitation design, structural features which detail location and elevation of bridge structure key points such as bridge seats, top of walls, pylons, etc.

Discussed below are these groupings and the essential data which needs to be obtained in the survey. As is the case with the bridge inspection, it is important to maximize the information taken while in the field to avoid repeated trips to the project site.

2.4.1 Topography

In the case of a new bridge design, a thorough survey of the site should include adequate coverage of proposed substructure component locations (i.e., abutments and piers). Since the final position of the abutment and pier footings (and piles if needed) are quite often subject to change due to geologic or hydrological conditions, the survey team should take care to provide maximum coverage of the general substructure locations.

When conducting a rehabilitation design, the establishment of accurate profiles for the overpass and underpass roadways is essential. Cross sections should be taken at an interval fine enough to accommodate the length of the structure and adequately establish a centerline profile (particularly if the bridge lies on a vertical curve).

Recent advancements in computer-aided design software allow engineers to construct a three-dimensional graphic model of overpass and underpass

[2.4.1]

COMPUTER SOFTWARE

does a great deal to aid bridge engineers in applications like profile generation. Care should be taken, though, when using software in any instance. As illustrated in Figure 2.10, the centerline points picked up in the field may or may not fall on the mathematical centerline or station line of the structure. Rather than blindly plotting the points as a profile, they should first be projected onto the horizontal alignment and then plotted. Some software packages may perform this operation automatically, while others may require some user inter-action. In a rehabilitation design, the surveyed profile can be compared against a profile from the as-built plans to deter-mine any changes in grade. Also, by referencing the two profiles, the designer will be able to approximate the amount of resurfacing on the structure.

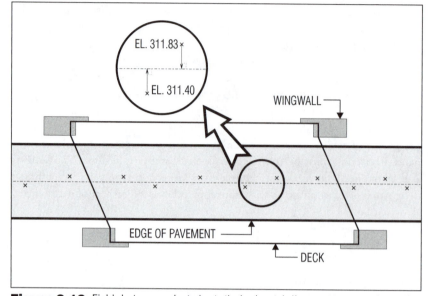

Figure 2.10 Field shots are projected onto the horizontal alignment to create the profile.

alignments, allowing designers to visualize the project site in the office. Care should be taken, however, by the engineer in using such models to construct the existing original ground profile. Profiles can be generated by *stripping* off of a triangulated network (TIN) or associated contour strings. Such a method, however, can lead to inaccurate results since the elevations will be calculated from the interpolated TIN. A better solution is to utilize hard centerline shots to depict the centerline profile. Since the location of the shot taken in the field will vary somewhat from the true mathematical centerline of the roadway, the field shots will need to be projected onto the roadway horizontal alignment. This is done by projecting the points perpendicular to a tangent or radial to a curve. It is very important to obtain the coordinates and elevations of the key points of the existing bridge, such as edges of abutments and wingwalls, bearing seat, edge of deck, center of bearings, etc.

An accurate original ground profile is the basis for establishing vertical clearance for the structure, bridge seat elevations, determination of resurfacing on an existing structure, haunch depths along a stringer, and a host of other key geometrics. The engineer needs to have a high level of confidence in the quality of the profile before design commences. When one considers that an error in the profile can affect the setting of every bearing, top of wall elevations, etc., it is easy to see the amount of time and money which such a mistake can cost a project. Incorrect profile data can easily lead to an entire pier being re-detailed and drafted by throwing off all the reinforcing steel measurements. If the designer is lucky, the error will be caught in the office, and if not so fortunate, the error will definitely be found in the field during construction.

2.4.2 Planimetry

A detailed planimetric map acts as the key for integrating a bridge into the site. The survey team should take care to document their notes extensively,

> **W**hen one considers that an error in the profile can affect the setting of every bearing ... it is easy to see the amount of time and money which such a mistake can cost a project.

both in terms of written notes and sketches. An example of how planimetric data play a role in the design process would be in the tying in of a new abutment underdrain to an existing storm water collection facility at the site. The survey team should not only physically locate various catch basins but also denote their size and type as well as rim and invert elevations (see Section 2.7.1). Prior to conducting the site inspection and site survey, team leaders from both groups should meet to identify which planimetric features (e.g., railings, inlets, etc.) will be the inspection team's responsibility and which items the survey team's.

Once again, computer-aided methods can be used to create a layer of planimetric information, complete with annotation and symbology to be incorporated in the final contract documents. The preparation of final drawings will be discussed in more detail later in Section 5.2.

2.4.3 Structure Features

Rehabilitation design projects, in particular, require detailed field documentation on the existing bridge components. It may be tempting for the design team to rely primarily on the record or as-built plans of an existing bridge. While such plans are indeed essential in creating the new design of the structure, they are no replacement for accurate field measurements (see Section 2.7).

> **R**ehabilitation design projects, in particular, require detailed field documentation on the existing bridge components.

To build a model of the bridge as it relates to the surrounding site, elevations at structure key points need to be determined. Prior to commencing work, the survey team, in conjunction with the design team, should identify the points on the bridge to be surveyed. Some of the basic features which should be picked up are

- ❑ Bridge seats
- ❑ Wingwall start and end locations
- ❑ Top of pier caps and abutment bearing seats
- ❑ Berm (bench) at the abutment embankment
- ❑ Deck elevations at bearing lines

It is also necessary to field measure the current vertical clearance. Contrary to what one may initially think, vertical clearance is a dynamic rather than static measurement. Resurfacing to the underpass roadway can significantly alter a bridge's vertical clearance. With many trucks pushing the clearance criteria to the limit, having hard clearance measurements on an existing structure can make the difference between a primary member being hit by a truck and not. If possible, vertical clearance measurements should be taken at the underpass crown or other high point at every stringer location. The effort may take a little longer in the field, but any anomalous resurfacing or changes in the underpass profile will be documented.

Like planimetric data, the survey team should thoroughly document all structure data with notes, sketches, and photographs. All sketches should clearly indicate the direction of north. If there are multiple bridges in the survey, the structure bridge identification number should also accompany any measurements being taken to remove any chance of confusion back in the office when the notes are being reduced. If as-built plans are available, it is extremely useful that all structure measurements are annotated in the survey notes using the identification nomenclature found in the as-built plans. Meaning that, if the

> One can easily imagine the confusion that can occur back in the office, if the survey team numbers the stringers from north to south and the as-built plans from south to north.

as-built plans call a certain stringer *S7*, the survey notes should reference any vertical clearance measurements at that stringer with the *S7* identifier. One can easily imagine the confusion that can occur back in the office, if the survey team numbers the stringers from north to south and the as-built plans from south to north.

2.5 PHYSICAL TESTING

While visual inspection provides the bulk of information in most biennial maintenance inspections, the rehabilitation inspection must also make use of various forms of physical testing to supply needed information concerning the adequacy of materials used in the construction of the bridge. The following offers a brief discussion of some of the methods used to accomplish this.

2.5.1 Coring

Physical testing, in the form of pavement and structure cores, should be performed for a rehabilitation design in which components of the bridge are to remain in place and become part of the new design. In the case of pavement, the cores serve the function of indicating

- ❏ The material composition of both the approach pavements and structural deck
- ❏ The amount of resurfacing on the structure

Structural cores should be taken at key points in certain concrete elements such as piers and abutments. Typical locations are in abutment stems as well as deck, pier caps, and columns. Compression tests are then performed at the testing laboratory to indicate the strength of the samples taken. The tests will also indicate the amount of voids and specific gravity of the sample. If existing components are to remain in place, it is essential that core testing be performed to ensure the adequacy of the concrete to remain. Conversely, if the component is to be completely removed and replaced, no cores should be taken at that location.

> If existing components are to remain in place, it is essential that core testing be performed to ensure the adequacy of the concrete to remain.

When the testing is complete, the testing laboratory should issue a report, complete with test results and color photographs of all cores taken. This report will become part of the engineer's final design report. In some instances, it may be necessary to depict the core results in table form on the final contract documents.

For timber structures, cores are taken to determine the moisture content and the extent of decay within the timber element.

2.5.2 Delamination Testing

As mentioned previously, delaminations are cracks that occur below the concrete surface, typically at the location of the upper reinforcing steel. The most basic method of testing is using a hammer and sounding for hollow spots. Obviously such a method is quite time consuming and, for large surfaces such as decks, can prove impractical. As an alternative, a chain can be dragged along the deck surface to cover more area, but surrounding noises may make it difficult to detect hollow sounds.

To facilitate delamination detection, machines based on this acoustic method are available. Typically they are walked by the inspector, like a lawn mower, along the bridge deck recording delaminations as it travels. Infrared thermography looks for voids beneath the surface by measuring the temperature differential that exists due to the presence of moisture at a void.

2.5.3 Testing for Cover

The chances for spalling greatly increase when there is insufficient cover between the concrete surface and the reinforcing steel. Devices, such as a pachometer, can be used to determine the amount of cover present in an element. While the pachometer determines the location of a reinforcing bar via a magnetic field, other methods are available which utilize ultrasound methods to locate the steel.

2.5.4 Measuring Steel Thickness

When calculating the load rating of a rehabilitated structure where the steel primary members are to remain in place, it is important to base the analysis on primary member cross-section properties which accurately reflect the current condition of the steel. While a micrometer and/or calipers can be used to determine flange and web thickness values at the ends of members, the problem of picking up web readings along a stringer requires another method. One approach is to use an ultrasonic gage. The ultrasonic gage, a hand-held device which is about the size of a calculator, has a probe connected to it which, when placed on the steel, determines the thickness by sending ultrasonic waves through the steel.

These devices require a relatively smooth surface in order to take an accurate reading. The inspector should bring a wire brush into the field to clean off any rust, dirt, or debris accumulated on the surface of the steel. Another option would be to use a battery-operated drill with a wire brush attachment. Once the surface has been cleaned, a jelly or couplant is smeared onto the steel to ensure proper contact with the probe. The ultrasonic gage then shows the measured value on a display.

When using an ultrasonic gage, the inspector should expect some fluctuations in the readings. Prior to going out to the bridge site, a schematic framing plan locating the primary members should be made which not only indicates the type of steel members present, but all pertinent cross-section dimensions. If possible, a two-person team should take the measurements. While one inspector uses the gauge, the other can record the measurements and check to see that the values are in line. It is very disheartening to spend a day in the field taking steel measurements, only to return to the office and find out the flange which shows deterioration has *increased* in thickness!

Some ultrasound devices allow for the measurements to be stored in the device and then uploaded to a personal computer where they can be tabulated by a spreadsheet program. Even if this functionality is present, the presence of a second inspector will still speed the recording process by allowing the

It is very disheartening to spend a day in the field taking steel measurements, only to return to the office and find out the flange which shows deterioration has increased in thickness!

inspector measuring the thickness to concentrate on taking the readings while the partner checks the validity of the measurements and assists in cleaning spots on the steel for measurements to be taken.

2.5.5 Detecting Fatigue Cracks

Unlike most structural failure mechanisms, fatigue failure offers almost no warning. A fatigue crack spends about 95% of its life as a dormant, barely visible hairline crack, so early detection is the key to prevent catastrophic structural failures. Once the crack passes the dormant period, it will develop rather rapidly, leaving little chance of being detected by bridge inspectors.

Fatigue cracks should be inspected where stress concentrations or weld connections exist. Because most fatigue cracks are hardly visible, special dye penetrant may be used to help visual inspections. If fatigue cracks are suspected, other advanced methods such as X-ray, magnetic field disturbance, and ultrasonic tests can be used to detect any discontinuity in steel, thus detect invisible fatigue cracks.

2.6 THE INSPECTION TEAM

The discussion above, on how steel measurements should be taken, makes a good point on how inspections, in general, should be conducted. Having two partners work on an inspection is a sound approach. The biennial maintenance inspection may not have the resources to commit two individuals for a single inspection, but the inspection for a rehabilitation project certainly demands it. As stated above, one inspector should be designated as the note taker, while the other can take measurements, photographs, and generally climb around the bridge and site. Two inspectors also means that the design team in the office will always have two sources of information and viewpoints concerning the condition of the bridge. Questions like, "Was there corrugated railing in the mall or box beam?" which may not have been documented in the inspection report (and as-built plans may not accurately show) always seem to come up. If there was only one inspector, he or she may be hard pressed to have the answer to all questions that come up. This does not mean that having two inspectors guarantees all design team questions will have an immediate answer. It does, however, tend to make life a little easier.

It is also strongly recommended that at least one of the individuals be a licensed professional engineer (see *Design Perspective*, in Section 2.3.3, Part 2) with an understanding of bridges. If personnel resources permit, it is also desirable that the people performing the inspection are also scheduled to work on the rehabilitation design. Preserving the continuity from field inspection to final design is an important issue. The bridge engineer gains a better understanding of the structure and site by being a part of the inspection process. Surgeons spend time with their patients before operating, and the bridge engineer should spend time in the field with the bridge prior to design.

When the team is out in the field, there are a few essential items which will be needed. Below is a checklist of some of these items.

> **S**urgeons spend time with their patients before operating, and the bridge engineer should spend time in the field with the bridge prior to design.

Figure 2.11 Three tools inspectors should always have.

WHEN AN INSPECTOR goes out to the bridge site, he or she should be equipped with three essential tools. At all times an inspector should wear a hard hat and a reflective safety vest. The vehicle parked at the site should have a warning light prominently displayed to provide added warning to traffic passing by the bridge (note that the light must be amber to signify a construction vehicle). If at all possible, the inspection team should have the owner place warning signs and traffic cones where needed to provide added protection and notice to motor vehicle operators.

❑   Hardhat, safety vest, rotating warning light.
❑   Mason's hammer for sounding and clearing off spalled concrete.
❑   Ladder. Some instances may require the need for a cherry picker or snooper-type vehicle to be brought to the site.
❑   A digital camera with sufficient battery.
❑   Measuring instruments such as a tape measure, scale, micrometer, and (if needed) ultrasonic gage.
❑   Orange spray paint for marking areas.
❑   Traffic cones.
❑   Flashlight.
❑   Clipboard, inspection forms, pencils, a calculator, and paper.

The team should always have *safety first* in mind. The traffic passing by a bridge site could care less whether there are inspectors at the site or not. As we will see later in the discussion on maintenance of traffic (Section 5.1.2), it is tough enough to get cars and trucks to slow down at a bridge under full reconstruction with numerous warning signs in place, much less during a bridge inspection. While the hardhat, safety vest, and warning light do not offer an impenetrable shield that protects an inspector, they represent the minimum requirement for safety. Safety is another sound reason for having two inspectors at the site. When one inspector is on a ladder, the other should be a spotter.

For reaching bridge elements that are inaccessible by conventional ladders due to height, mechanical aids such as a cherry picker, which elevates the inspector in a bucket from underneath the structure, can be used. When it is impossible to access superstructure elements from underneath the structure, either because the superstructure is too high to get at with a cherry picker or the bridge crosses a water channel, an access device like a snooper which extends from the top of the bridge and under the deck can be used (see Figure 3.57).

When taking notes, the inspector designated as the note taker may prefer to have a clipboard with a cover. The inspectors will be climbing around bridge abutments, onto pier caps, and other dust-filled areas. A cover on the clipboard may seem innocuous, but it helps a great deal in preserving the quality of the notes recorded in the field. This is important since the inspection notes are a legally binding document which reflect the inspector's observations.

A cover on the clipboard may seem innocuous, but it helps a great deal in preserving the quality of the notes recorded in the field.

2.7 AS-BUILT PLANS AND OTHER RECORD DATA

As-built plans are the design plans of a project which have been issued as a final revision reflecting any and all changes made in the field during construction. In a rehabilitation bridge design, the as-built plans reflect both the original intent of the designer and the condition of the structure at the completion of construction. Prior to beginning a rehabilitation design project, the design team should be provided with a complete set of as-built plans by the owner. The role these plans play throughout the course of design is an important one since it represents, along with the inspection report, one of the best sources of information concerning the existing structure. The following discusses some of the issues concerning use of as-built plans as well as other sources of record data.

2.7.1 Supplementing As-Built Plans

A common problem is to rely on as-built plans as a basis for all design. As-built plans, however, are not a gospel-like representation of what the bridge is presently like. By the time a structure requires rehabilitation, a good deal of maintenance work has already been performed on the bridge.

Items such as guard railing and drainage facilities can often change entirely from what is depicted on as-built plans. Dimensions can also vary. If a pier, for example, has a column which was jacketed because of excessive spalling, the diameter of the pier will have changed. Because of situations like this, the inspection and survey teams should attempt to take measurements as much as possible to either confirm or refute as-built plan information. This is not meant to imply that every last detail needs to be recorded. Key elements, however, should be identified prior to the field inspection, and recorded once there. If at all possible, a half-size reduction of the as-built plans should be brought to the field during inspection to aid the team during the inspection. The following are some of the elements that should be field verified.

t he inspection and survey ...**t** teams should attempt to take measurements as much as possible to either confirm or refute as-built plan information.

1. **Guard Railing.** It is important for either the inspection or survey team to record the type of railing present at various locations around the bridge. In addition to this, items such as the size and type of backup posts and lengths of railing segments should be recorded. The reason for this is that railing in the field may not conform to new specifications and will therefore require replacement. If an older type of railing on the bridge deck is to be replaced, it will have to tie into existing railing on the approaches, the length of which needs to be noted on the rehabilitation

plans. It may be the case that the railing measurements are never used, but the cost associated with a return trip to the field could outweigh the extra time spent recording them.

2. **Drainage Facilities.** Drainage-related appurtenances such as drop inlets and swales should be measured. Dimensions and type of drainage element should be noted. Again it is important to emphasize that the inspection team not rely on the as-built plans to have the information. The inlet may be entirely new or have been repaired since the bridge was constructed. The survey team should take care to record both rim and invert elevations as well. This will aid the design team in performing the drainage analysis of the site and, if necessary, tie into an existing drainage system.

3. **Traffic Barriers.** Jersey-type barriers should be measured in cross section and length of each segment. Measurements should also be taken to determine the taper used on end segments. If there is railing attached to the barrier and it requires replacement, the barrier measurements will be needed to attach the new railing.

4. **Miscellaneous Elements.** The need to record the cross-sectional properties of steel primary members has already been discussed. In addition to these measurements, *gross geometry* measurements should be taken in a quick and dirty fashion. By gross geometry it means items such as column circumference, pedestal depth, width and height, distance between the edge of pedestal and edge of bearing masonry plate, curb width, etc. The general rule of thumb is to think of elements which may have been repaired or replaced and to record them.

It does not take much time at all to write down *6" brush curb* in the inspection notebook. If this is not done, however, and the record plans show a 3"-6" sidewalk, serious problems could arise. The urge to rely solely on the as-built plans is great. The plans are always at the designer's side and easily accessible. It is the job of the inspection team to ensure that the designers are provided with as complete a representation of what is presently at the bridge site as possible.

2.7.2 Other Sources

In addition to as-built plans, the design team should request any other sources of information concerning the bridge. Most agencies maintain a detailed maintenance history log of work performed on the structure. If earlier design reports are available, they should also be provided. The most recent inspection prior to the bridge being designated for rehabilitation should be obtained to investigate any potential issues that were overlooked. Utility permits, indicating the location of any utilities at the site, are required by the design team to determine the effects the utilities may have on issues ranging from maintenance of traffic to staging operations. This is of particular concern when underground utilities are present at the bridge site.

Where most agencies make a good effort to provide the designers with all information possible, it does not hurt to ask for any of the items listed above

I t is the job of the inspection team to ensure that the designers are provided with as complete a representation of what is presently at the bridge site as possible.

if they have not been initially provided by the owner. The designers should understand that theirs is just one of many projects the owner has to manage and things sometimes fall through the cracks. A gentle reminder, however, could go a long way in securing needed information.

Conversely, owners need to realize that the design team is trying to design a rehabilitation based on various sources of information that are cobbled together by the designers. Any information that the agency can provide to the design team will not only speed the design process but also make for a better end product. An agency often takes for granted that they have the ability to walk across the hall to a filing cabinet or ask someone in another department about an issue. Where it is impossible to expect that every last shred of information be compiled and put into a box which is delivered to the design team, an earnest effort should be made by both parties, prior to design, to identify and secure the major sources of information.

> **A**ny information that the agency can provide to the design team will not only speed the design process but also make for a better end product.

2.8 CONCLUSIONS

As evidenced by the preceding dialog, there are many factors which the bridge engineer must be cognizant of before he or she ever lifts a pencil in anger at a design pad. If bridge engineering teaches us anything as civil engineers, it should serve to illustrate the dangers of excessive specialization. While there are solid arguments for professionals to seek a *vertical* arena of expertise, there are many compelling reasons for engineers in general, and bridge engineers in particular, to be well versed in all aspects of the engineering design *and management* processes.

Quite often, engineers find themselves in the position of drawing comparisons between themselves and their professional counterparts in the medical field. Specialization proponents suggest that engineers should be skilled in individual disciplines. As physicians have specialists in the care and treatment of everything from heart to foot ailments, so too should civil engineers be specialized in structural, geotechnical, hydraulic, and every other discipline.

Specialists, however, see with different eyes and varied vision that can lead to difficulties in engineering projects as involved as a highway bridge design. A hydraulic specialist may go to a bridge rehabilitation site and notice poor removal of surface water. A geotechnical engineer could go to the same site and notice foundation movement. The professional well versed in both fields, however, realizes that inadequate drainage facilities led to the foundation movement. While conceding that this example is somewhat cartoonish, it is, however, indicative of the broad range of engineering disciplines and the interrelationship we have discussed just in this section alone.

From project funding to inspecting for scour, the bridge engineer needs to be, if not an expert, at least knowledgeable of the varied aspects of the field in order to successfully complete his or her work. It should be reemphasized that while a bridge is composed of many components, it still behaves as a unit, interacts and affects its environment as a unit, and causes the most serious damage when it fails as a unit. It is all too easy for engineers to pass off certain aspects of the design and say that this or that issue is the responsibility of another specialist. Bridge engineering, like many civil engineering projects, is exciting because it demands integration rather than dissemination.

> **B**ridge engineering, like many civil engineering projects, is exciting because it demands integration rather than dissemination.

This section should also serve as a warning for the engineer new to bridge design to take their time prior to beginning design. The project inception phase is, for lack of a better term, an information-gathering period. At the end of this phase, the design team should have most, if not all, of the information necessary to perform a sound and professional design of the new or rehabilitated structure. In addition to this, they should also have an understanding of the owner's wishes and desires and how they impact the eventual design. As we will see later, errors at the project inception phase can lead to some of the most severe problems later in the design process.

REFERENCES

2.1 TEA-21, Transportation Equity Act for the 21st Century, U.S. Department of Transportation, Washington, D.C., July, 1998.

2.2 National Transportation Statistics 2004, Bureau of Transportation Statistics, U. S. Department of Transportation, Washington, D.C., Table 3-29a, January 2005.

2.3 *Understanding the Highway Finance Evolution/Revolution,* American Association of State Highway and Transportation Officials, pp. 7–23, Washington, D.C., 1987.

2.4 Toll Facilities in the United States, Bridges - Roads - Tunnels - Ferries, Office of Highway Policy, U. S. Department of Transportation, Washington, D.C., Table T-1 Part 3, and Table T-1 Part 4, January 2003.

2.5 Novack, Janet, "Toll Call," *Forbes*, p. 67, 17 February 1992.

2.6 Wuestefeld, Norman H., "Toll Roads," *Understanding the Highway Finance Evolution/Revolution,* American Association of State Highway and Transportation Officials, p. 63, Washington, D.C., 1987.

2.7 Tarricone, Paul, "What do you mean by that?" *Civil Engineering,* American Society of Civil Engineers, vol. 63, p. 62, April 1993.

2.8 Forbes, Jr., Malcom, "Alien Idea," *Forbes,* p. 26, 2 March 1992.

2.9 *Standard Specifications for Highway Bridges,* seventeenth edition, American Association of State Highway and Transportation Officials, Washington, D.C., 2002.

2.10 *AASHTO LRFD Bridge Design Specifications.* American Association of State Highway and Transportation Officials, Washington, D.C., 2004.

2.11 Salmon, Charles G., and Johnson, John E., *Steel Structures: Design and Behavior,* 2nd ed., p. 22, Harper & Row, New York, 1980.

2.12 *Manual of Steel Construction, LRFD,* 3rd Edition, American Institute of Steel Construction, Chicago, 2003.

2.13 *Manual of Steel Construction, Allowable Stress Design,* 9th Edition, American Institute of Steel Construction, Chicago, 1989.

2.14 *Building Code Requirements for Reinforced Concrete (ACI 318-05)* and *Commentary-ACI 318R-05,* American Concrete Institute, Detroit, 2005.

2.15 *ACI Detailing Manual,* SP-66(04), American Concrete Institute, Detroit, 2004.

2.16 *PCI Design Handbook-Precast and Prestressed Concrete,* 6th Edition, Precast/Prestressed Concrete Institute, Chicago, 2004.

2.17 *Timber Construction Manual,* 5th Edition, American Institute of Timber Construction, Wiley Publishers, New York, October, 2004.

2.18 *National Design Specification for Wood Construction,* American Forest & Paper Association, American Wood Council, Washington, D.C., 1997.

2.19 *Bridge Inspector's Training Manual/90,* U. S. Department of Transportation, Washington, D.C., March 1995.

2.20 Harris-Stewart, Charmaine, "Deck Fails a Month after Inspection," *Engineering News Record,* vol. 220, p. 15, March 1988.

2.21 Fox, Gerald, "Bridge Inspections: The Role of the design Engineer and Benefits of Research," *Civil Engineering,* American Society of Civil Engineers, vol. 54, p. 6, December 1983.

2.22 Kallman, Bill, "Bridge Inspection Proposals," *Civil Engineering,* American Society of Civil Engineers, vol. 55, pp. 22–24, April, 1984.

2.23 *Manual for Condition Evaluation of Bridges,* 2nd Edition, American Association of State Highway and Transportation Officials, Washington, D.C., 2003.

2.24 *Standard Specifications for Highway Bridges,* New York State Department of Transportation, Albany, N.Y., 2002.

2.25 *Bridge Inspection Manual,* New York State Department of Transportation, Albany, 1997.

2.26 *The States and the Interstates,* American Association of State Highway and Transportation Officials, p. 104, Washington, D.C., 1991.

3

Design of Superstructure Elements

Section Overview

This section provides a detailed look at the various elements that compose a highway bridge superstructure. Different types of superstructures are discussed along with many of the design, maintenance, and rehabilitation issues affecting them. Design examples for commonly used superstructure elements are provided to give the reader an understanding of principal superstructure design fundamentals.

A superstructure can be thought of as the conduit which carries a roadway over a crossing. Like any other bridge component, the superstructure is comprised of many elements. In the bridge design profession, no other component elicits so much discussion, and even downright controversy, as to the type of elements to be utilized in construction. The structural and geometric complexities of the superstructure component make it one of the most challenging design problems in a bridge engineering project.

In this section we will examine the various types of superstructures and the different elements which comprise them. While it would be impossible to cover every permutation of superstructure types that are in use, this section will attempt to provide the reader with fundamentals behind several of the common superstructure configurations presently being used in highway networks around the world.

3.1 SUPERSTRUCTURE TYPES

The type of superstructure chosen for a bridge can be based on a variety of factors ranging from maintenance considerations to personal preference. Specifically, some of the commonly used criteria in selecting the type of superstructure to be used are:

- ❑ Material function and availability
- ❑ Construction cost
- ❑ Speed of construction and constructability
- ❑ Design complexity
- ❑ Maintenance costs and life expectancy
- ❑ Environmental concerns
- ❑ Aesthetics

Where there are no steadfast rules governing which of the factors listed above is more important than the other, one certainty is that the use of

Section 3

The Superstructure

WIDE-FLANGE stringers vary from a standard I-beam cross section in several ways. As shown below, the I-beam has a tapered flange where the wide flange is orthogonal to the web, with the top face parallel to the bottom face. As the name would indicate, the flange width on a wide-flange stringer is greater than an I-beam. The I-beam, however, has a thicker web. The small flange width of the I-beam, combined with the inefficiency of material in its web, has made it unattractive to designers. In the AISC specifications, wide-flange stringers are referred to with the W designation and I-beam stringers with an S.

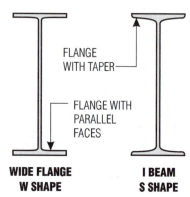

superstructure types varies geographically. Due to the way highway systems like the U.S. Interstate develop, bridges tend to come into an area en masse (see Section 1.2). Once a particular type of superstructure gains acceptance in a geographic region, it develops a certain critical mass that is difficult to alter in a different direction. Although no transportation system is homogenous, there will definitely exist a predominance of one type of superstructure system.

The types of superstructures also change with the bridge span lengths. Each type of superstructure has span limitations beyond which it will become uneconomical.

Superstructures generally vary by support type (simply supported or continuous), design type (slab-on-stringer, arch, rigid frame, etc.), and material type (steel, concrete, timber, etc.). Obviously there are a variety of combinations of the above. For example, a designer could choose to use a slab-on-stringer superstructure with either steel or concrete girders. This superstructure could be simply supported or continuous, and so on. Discussed below are the major types of superstructures and their principal advantages and disadvantages which affect their design, construction, and maintenance.

3.1.1 Steel Superstructures

The two principal materials utilized in superstructure construction are steel and concrete. Materials such as timber (see below) and aluminum are also utilized to a lesser extent. When compared to concrete, steel has the advantage of lighter weight and more rapid construction. Steel also lends itself well to prefabrication at the factory which reduces the amount of field labor for operations such as bolting, welding, etc. Recent advancements in fabrication methods and materials, especially with the introduction of weathering steel, has

HAUNCHED plate girders vary the depth of the girder cross section to reduce the amount of steel used. At what span length, though, does haunching a girder become attractive? Recent studies have indicated that for span lengths from 178 ft (54.3 m) to 420 ft (128 m) contractors have opted for conventional, parallel flange plate girders over a haunched alternative. In some instances, contractors have not even submitted bids on haunched designs. Although the intent of the haunched girder is to save on costs, the market seems to indicate that any span length under 400 ft (122 m) does not warrant the increased fabrication costs [Ref 3.1].

Figure 3.1 A haunched plate girder economizes the amount of steel used for *long spans*.

made steel much more competitive with concrete. Element assembly and welding automation and the use of stay-in-place forms are just two examples of how steel has improved to meet the challenge of the concrete bridge.

As discussed in Section 1.1.1, a superstructure frame is composed of primary and secondary members. Steel primary members come in a variety of types, some of which are listed below.

1. **Rolled Beam.** The rolled beam is a steel girder which has been formed by hot-rolling. The most common type of rolled beam used as a primary member in highway bridges is the wide-flange variety. The wide flange differs from its I-beam cousin in that its flanges are parallel rather than tapered (see figure and sidebar on accompanying page). When the term I-beam is used throughout the text, it implies a beam with an I-type cross section, not the American Standard I-beam (S shape) cross section discussed in the sidebar.

2. **Rolled Beam with Cover Plate.** To maintain an economy of material, rolled beams are sometimes equipped with a rectangular plate, or *cover plate*, at the bottom flange. The cover plate increases the ability of the stringer to resist flexure without having to use a larger size rolled beam or plate girder. As we will see, however, the cover plate also increases the potential for fatigue cracks by introducing welds and stress concentrations at the ends of the plate.

3. **Plate Girder.** A plate girder, like a rolled beam, has an I-type cross section. Rather than being hot-rolled, however, the girder is constructed from steel plate elements which are connected together with welds, bolts, or rivets. For modern highway bridges, shop welding is the most predominant method. Since the designer is specifying the section properties of the stringer (i.e., flange width and thickness, web depth, etc.) a greater economy of materials results. To further reduce the amount of steel used, plate girders can be varied in depth, or *haunched*, to accommodate regions of low and high moment and/or shear. Plate girders gain an advantage over rolled beams as span lengths become large (see sidebar with Figure 3.1).

4. **Box Girder.** The box girder was briefly discussed in Section 1.1.2. In reality, the box girder is a form of plate girder which combines two girders into a single unit. A box girder may be designed as a four-sided box (closed box), or it may be designed as an open-box where a relatively narrow top flange is welded on top of each web. Closed box girders possess excellent torsional stiffness, so they usually do not require secondary members to provide bracing. For open boxes, bracing is usually required to provide torsional stiffness. Although the box girder provides an aesthetically pleasing structure, the amount of steel required, especially for closed box girders, can sometimes exceed that for a standard I cross-section plate girder. Box girders usually have higher fabrication costs than plate girders.

5. **Steel Rigid Strut Frame.** A steel bridge with integral steel supporting legs is another form of structure which utilizes steel as its

To further reduce the amount of steel used, plate girders can be varied in depth, or haunched, to accommodate regions of low and high moment and/or shear.

BOX GIRDERS come with two different fashions. One is closed box (as illustrated below). The other (more common) way is open box which has two small top flanges on the webs. The top flanges and the concrete deck work together (composite) to resist loading.

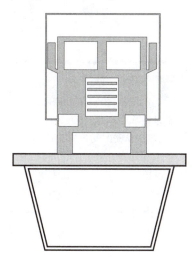

AASHTO STANDARD
DIVISION II
10.6 GROUT FOR PRESTRESSED CONCRETE BEAMS

AASHTO requires that the void between the tendon and duct be completely filled with a portland cement grout to create a permanent bond between the concrete and prestressing steel (10.6.1). The ducts are prepared for grouting by first flushing with water and then blowing air through them (10.6.2). Vent openings at high points and drains at low points should be provided for ducts in continuous structures to allow for the dissipation of entrapped air and water, respectively (10.4.1.1). With the vents open, grout is injected into the duct at a pressure of 250 psi maximum. Grout is allowed to come out of the first vent until remaining air or water trapped in the duct has been removed, at which time the vent is sealed. Subsequent vents are capped in a similar fashion (10.6.5) [Ref 3.3].

Before prestressed concrete was accepted by the design community, most highway bridge superstructures were constructed with ... steel elements.

To allow the beam to act as a transformed section in resisting loads ... the space or *ducts* between the tendons which exist after tensioning ... must be grouted before any live loads are placed on the girder.

---

principal component. In such a configuration, not only is the superstructure made of steel, but the substructure as well.

6. Large Structures. Steel is also an excellent material for large structures requiring spans of significant length. As discussed in Section 1, the arch, truss, and cable-stayed structures all provide solutions for this class of bridge. The design and rehabilitation of these structures, however, is beyond the scope of this text.

3.1.2 Concrete Superstructures

Before prestressed concrete was accepted by the design community, most highway bridge superstructures were constructed with the types of steel elements described in Section 3.1.1 above. Concrete bridges were generally relegated to short, single-span structures. By the middle of the last century, however, prestressed concrete structures began to gain acceptance and the number of highway bridges constructed with concrete superstructures increased dramatically. In 2003, 47% of all new bridges built in the U.S. are prestressed concrete bridges [Ref 3.2]. Like steel, concrete superstructure elements come in a variety of configurations, which are detailed below.

1. Prestressed Concrete Girder. A general axiom for concrete performance is that it handles compression very well but performs poorly under tension. For steel bars, the converse holds true. The combination of steel with concrete, with one material taking up the deficiencies of the other, is the basic principal behind reinforced concrete.

Prestressed concrete takes this characteristic feature one step further by application of a tensile force to reinforcing tendons. This has the effect of increasing internal compression in the concrete beam where tension is anticipated under loading, and thus reducing or eliminating stresses due to tension once the beam is loaded. The prestressing force may be applied after the concrete is cast *in situ* (i.e., poured in the field) or before the beam is precast.

When the force is applied to the reinforcing tendons *before* the concrete is poured, the beam is said to be *pretensioned*. If the force is applied *after* the concrete has cured, the beam is called *post-tensioned*. In post-tensioning, the tendons are encased in tubes to prevent bonding with the surrounding concrete. After curing, jacking devices are used to apply the tensile force. To allow the beam to act as a transformed section in resisting loads (i.e., transforming the concrete and steel into a single equivalent section) the space inside *ducts* where the tendons are placed (for post-tensioned beams) must be grouted before any live loads are placed on the girder (see *AASHTO Specification* sidebar). Prestressed concrete girders come in a variety of cross-section geometries (see Figures 3.2 and 3.3). The pretensioning strands are dependent on the length of span and type of loading the structure is subjected to.

In addition to the I-girder and bulb T-girder shown in Figures 3.2 and 3.3, prestressed girders can come in the form of a box girder (see also Part 2 below), conventional T-girder, voided slab or solid slab. Although exact span lengths vary, listed below are ranges for various types of prestressed

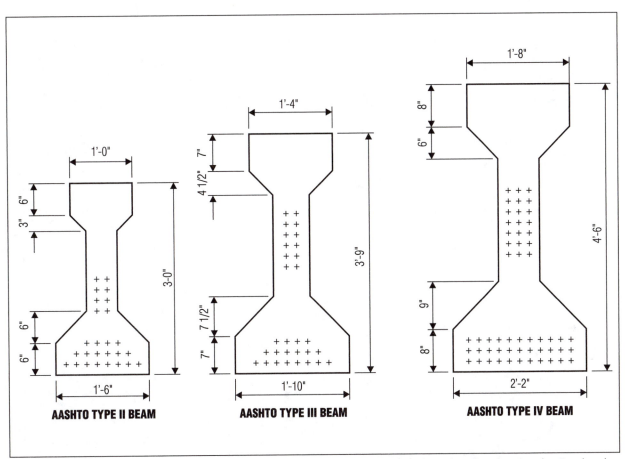

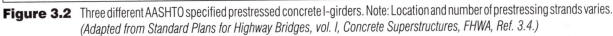

Figure 3.2 Three different AASHTO specified prestressed concrete I-girders. Note: Location and number of prestressing strands varies. *(Adapted from Standard Plans for Highway Bridges, vol. I, Concrete Superstructures, FHWA, Ref. 3.4.)*

girders for HS-20 loading. These span range should be reduced if higher live load is used for the design.

- ❏ AASHTO Type I girder: 35–55 ft (10.7–16.8 m)
- ❏ AASHTO Type II girder: 45–75 ft (13.7–22.9 m)
- ❏ AASHTO Type III girder: 65–95 ft (19.8–29.0 m)
- ❏ AASHTO Type IV girder: 85–120 ft (25.9–36.6 m)
- ❏ AASHTO Type V girder: 110–145 ft (33.5–44.2 m)
- ❏ AASHTO Type VI girder: 120–160 ft (36.6–48.8 m)
- ❏ Small box girder: 60–100 ft (18.3–30.5 m)
- ❏ Voided slab: 20–100 ft (6.1–30.5 m)
- ❏ Solid slab: 0–60 ft (0–18.3 m)

Each geometry has its own particular advantages, and, like steel, the goal is to economize material whenever possible without compromising the integrity of the design. As is the case with any design, a variety of factors influence the type of element selected. From an aesthetic standpoint, it is definitely more pleasing to the eye to have all girders be of a constant depth. A maintenance perspective almost always demands the elimination of as

> **F**rom an aesthetic standpoint, it is definitely more pleasing to the eye to have all girders be of a constant depth.

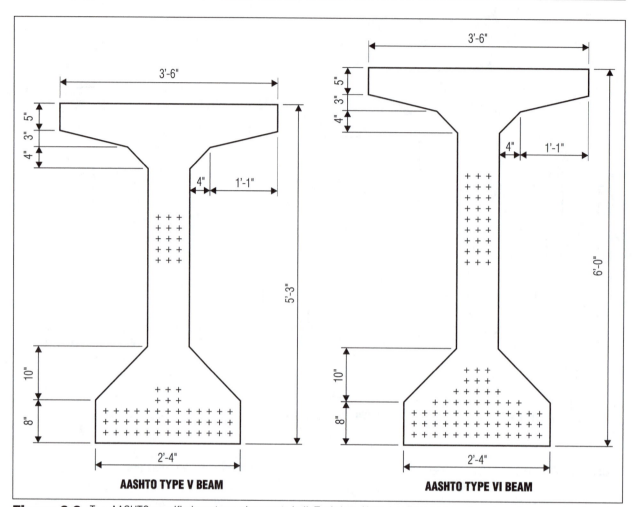

Figure 3.3 Two AASHTO specified prestressed concrete bulb T-girders. Note. Location and number of prestressing strands varies. *(Adapted from Standard Plans for Highway Bridges, vol. I, Concrete Superstructures, FHWA, Ref. 3.4.)*

many deck joints as possible to preserve the deck and substructure elements as well. Therefore, most bridges are designed using continuous spans to reduce the material usage, and to eliminate expansion joints over piers. It is up to the bridge engineer to synthesize the many opinions and needs into a single, cohesive design.

2. **Concrete Box Girder.** As mentioned in Part 1 above, box girders are a form of prestressed concrete girder. Like their steel cousins, box girders are good at resisting the effects of torsion and typically do not require the introduction of bracing elements. Compared with prestressed I-beams, box girders have less creep deformation and are easier to position tensile reinforcement. Because of these characteristics concrete box girders are well suited for large span lengths. A bridge with a box girder superstructure, near Tokyo, has a clear span of 787 ft (240 m) [Ref. 3.5].

Since, in terms of an overall transportation network, large prestressed box girders are relative newcomers, maintenance issues have recently come to the forefront. Deterioration of concrete box girders begins when the

> Since, in terms of an overall transportation network, large prestressed box girders are relative newcomers, maintenance issues have recently come to the forefront.

post-tensioning relaxes. If tension in the strands is reduced, the concrete will begin to lose compression causing existing cracks to widen and new cracks to form. Corrosion of post-tensioning strands is another major problem concrete box girder bridges are facing. As development of these types of superstructures has progressed, though, new design codes have begun to take into account the necessary criteria concerning the corrosion and relaxation of tendons, shrinkage, and other issues.

3. **Concrete Slab.** A slab bridge is one in which the structural deck slab itself represents the superstructure (i.e., there are no supporting primary and secondary members). Conventionally reinforced concrete slab bridges are common for short spans up to 40 ft (12 m) in span length.

When longer spans and correspondingly deeper slabs are required, voids in the slab are introduced to decrease the weight of the superstructure. Voids can be formed using any one of a variety of materials ranging from cardboard to polystyrene tubes. Most voided slab bridges are post-tensioned. The slab bridge has the advantage of being able to accommodate skew crossings. The advancement of prestressed concrete superstructure elements, along with the development of entire modular slab units has made this type of bridge unattractive to the modern bridge engineer.

> When longer spans and correspondingly deeper slabs are required, voids in the slab are introduced to decrease the weight of the superstructure...Most voided slab bridges are post-tensioned.

4. **Adjacent Prestressed Slab.** Adjacent prestressed concrete slab units can be used for short spans up to 60 ft (18 m). A 3 to 4 inch (75 to 100 mm) concrete overlay with reinforcement is usually cast over the slab units. Slab units are transversely post-tensioned prior to placement of overlay to form a single bridge deck. The advantage of this type of bridges is the rapid construction and low costs, which make it very popular for short span bridges.

> Adjacent prestressed concrete slab units ... are transversely post-tensioned prior to placement of overlay to form a single bridge deck.

5. **Concrete Rigid Frame.** A concrete rigid frame, like the steel rigid frame, incorporates the superstructure and substructure into a single integrated unit. A conventional rigid frame has a deck slab integrated with abutment walls. This type of structure is usually for very short spans. A box culvert can be considered as a concrete rigid frame structure.

6. **Concrete Strut Frame.** A strut-frame type has integrated legs or struts extending from the superstructure at angles. These structures are useful when underpass width is an important concern and placement of a substructure element in the middle of the underpass is impossible.

7. **Concrete Arch.** The different types of arches were discussed in Section 1.1.2. Since arches convert most loading into compressive forces, concrete, with its excellent compressive strength, is an ideal material for these types of structures. Concrete arches can range from short to long span bridges.

3.1.3 Timber Superstructures

While timber structures come nowhere near steel and concrete structures in terms of number of bridges in use, they still maintain a niche in the highway bridge arena. The use of *glulam* (glued laminated) members and the application of

THIS TIMBER BRIDGE,
located at the upper level of the Keystone Wye Interchange in South Dakota, is a composite concrete-timber design. The open spandrel arch spans a considerable 290 ft (88.5 m) crossing. The superstructure utilizes the composite concrete-glulam timber T cross section. Timber bridges, like this, have changed the way many designers think of wood construction in highway bridges [Ref 3.6].

Figure 3.4 Timber was used to construct this open spandrel arch bridge in South Dakota.

A common argument against timber structures is that they are exceedingly prone to deterioration from the elements. Covered bridge structures over 100 years old, however, are still in use today.

AASHTO STANDARD

DIVISION II

17.2 TREATMENT OF TIMBER ELEMENTS

AASHTO requires that timber railings and posts be treated with either pentachlorophenol with a Type C solvent or waterborne preservative (AASHTO 17.2.2). There are three basics types of treatments for timber structures: pentachlorophenol, creosote, and waterborne salts. Protective treatments like creosote should be avoided on any timber elements coming in contact with humans since creosote causes skin irritation [Ref 3.6].

advanced preservative coatings have made the use of timber in major structures feasible, such as modern highway bridges, like the one shown in Figure 3.4.

A common argument against timber structures is that they are exceedingly prone to deterioration from the elements (see Section 2.3.3, Part 5). Covered bridge structures over 100 years old, however, are still in use today. Conventional bridge materials, like concrete, may not be susceptible to insect and fungi attack, but even these accepted materials do not react that well when they come in contact with chlorides. Timber has the advantage of a high strength to weight ratio and a replenishable material source [Ref. 3.6]. An overview of glulam timber and the various forms of timber structures is provided below.

1. **Glulam Timber.** A glulam timber member is created by gluing together two or more pieces of lumber, no more than 2 in (50 mm) in thickness. In older timber structures, elements like bridge decks utilized a similar approach with nail-laminated lumber. As heavier loads were introduced on these bridges, however, nail-laminated assemblies would begin to loosen. Also, prior to the introduction of glulam timber, member sizes were somewhat limited due to the scarcity of large, individual timbers [Ref. 3.7].

2. **Stress-Laminated Timber Deck.** Stressed-laminated timber deck bridges are composed of 2 inch (50 mm) thick and 8 to 12 inch (200 to 305 mm) height strips which are transversely stressed with prestressing steel bars. This type of bridge is similar to concrete slab bridge where the deck is the primary load carrying member. The timber deck is normally

covered by a waterproofing membrane, and paved with asphalt pavement as a wearing surface.

3. **Trestle.** A trestle is a set of timber stringers integrated with a pile or frame bent. Stringers can have a rectangular cross section, although glulam I-beam stringers are also used. Previously, timber decking utilized the nail-laminated approach discussed earlier. Recently, prefabricated, glulam deck panels which are placed transverse to the primary members have been utilized [Ref. 3.6].

4. **Truss.** A timber truss bridge can be constructed with a timber truss and timber decking. It is also possible to utilize steel truss components in conjunction with a timber deck. One form of truss bridge, common to timber structures, is the pony truss. A pony truss bridge is a through truss (i.e., the deck passes through, not on top of, the truss) with no bracing on top. A problem with through trusses, like this, is that they are prone to impact damage from traffic [Ref. 3.8].

3.1.4 Secondary Members

Secondary members act as bracing for primary members. In general, secondary members are not load bearing elements but are designed to prevent cross-sectional deformation of the superstructure frame. In addition to this, secondary members provide for vertical load distribution between stringers by permitting the superstructure to work together as a unit.

Longitudinal spacing of secondary members varies depending on the type of primary member and the length of the span. Specific spacing values for various types of diaphragm type secondary members are listed below. The type of secondary members used varies depending on the type of structure and preference of the designer.

Secondary members come in three general classes: diaphragms, lateral bracing, and portal/sway bracing. Listed below are these three major classes of secondary members and their types and function.

1. **Diaphragms.** A diaphragm is a secondary member attached between stringers, in the vertical plane, which acts to stiffen the primary member and help distribute vertical loads. For steel superstructures comprised of rolled beam or plate girder primary members, a rolled beam diaphragm can be used. This rolled beam is usually of the channel or wide flange type cross-section. Channel type rolled sections are designated in the *AISC Steel Construction Manual* by either the C (American Standard Channels) or MC (Miscellaneous Channels) designations. For rolled beam primary members, the diaphragm should be at least one-third to one-half the depth of the primary member. Diaphragms for plate girders should be one-half to three-quarters the girder depth.

When the primary member in a steel superstructure is exceedingly deep [approximately 48 in (1.2 m) or larger] or when curved girders are used, a cross frame style diaphragm is desirable. Cross frames are typically composed of steel angles in a cross (X) or vee (V) configuration. In steel box

---

DID YOU KNOW

THAT in the 1960's research was conducted concerning the pre-stressing of glulam timber elements? The findings showed that by reinforcing a glulam beam with posttensioning steel, bending strength could be increased by roughly 30 percent and the modulus of rupture by 25 percent [Ref. 3.6].

When the primary member in a steel superstructure is exceedingly deep [approximately 48 in (1.2 m) or larger] or when curved girders are used, a cross frame style diaphragm is desirable.

AASHTO STANDARD

10.20.1 CROSS FRAMES ON CURVED GIRDER BRIDGES

For horizontally curved structures, cross frame type secondary members are required by AASHTO to be designed as main members which allow for the transfer of lateral forces from stringer flanges [Ref. 3.3]. Because of the geometry of a horizontally curved girder, the midspan location is eccentric to that of the supports. This eccentricity induces a twisting effect in addition to the normal vertical deflection. The role the cross frames play in resisting loading, therefore, becomes more predominate. Using computer-aided methods, the superstructure is analyzed as a system in order to model the response of the curved girders and cross frames to loading conditions.

Type of Span	Span Geometry	Diaphragm	Spec.
Rolled Beam and Plate Girder	All Spans	At each support and intermediate locations spaced not more than 25 ft (7.6 m) apart.	AASHTO 10.20.1
Orthotropic-Deck	All Spans	At each support and intermediate locations where required by the design.	AASHTO 10.41.4.7
Composite Steel Box Girder	All Spans	At each support within box girder. Intermediate diaphragms are not required.	AASHTO 10.39.6
Steel Deck Truss	All Spans	In the plane of each end post and all panel points for deck truss spans.	AASHTO 10.16.7
Prestressed Concrete T-Beam	Spans > 40 ft (12.2 m)	At span ends and points of maximum moment.	AASHTO 9.10.2
Prestressed Concrete Spread Box Beam	Spans > 80 ft (24.4 m)	At span ends and points of maximum moment.	AASHTO 9.10.3.1
Prestressed Concrete Box Multi-beam	All Spans	Only necessary for slab end support or to resist transverse tension ties.	AASHTO 9.10.3.2
Prestressed Concrete Cast-in-Place Box Girder	Inside Radius of Curvature > 800 ft (243.8 m)	At span ends only (Use diaphragm or other means).	AASHTO 9.10.3.3
Prestressed Concrete Segmental Box Girder	Inside Radius of Curvature > 800 ft	At span ends only.	AASHTO 9.10.3.4
Prestressed Concrete Box Girder (All Types)	Inside Radius Curvature < 800 ft	At span ends and intermediate locations where required.	AASHTO 9.10.3.5

Table 3.1 Diaphragm requirements for various superstructure types

girder structures, this type of bracing is used *inside* the box girder to increase the rigidity of the member.

Diaphragms are typically connected to stringers with a connection plate. The connection plate is either bolted or welded to the primary member and the diaphragm.

Structures with prestressed concrete primary members utilize concrete diaphragms which are cast as shapes like the C channel used in steel superstructures. The concrete diaphragms are then tied to the prestressed girders with rods. Another alternative is to have the diaphragms cast in place with the stringers themselves and tied together with reinforcing to form an integrated unit.

The longitudinal spacing values (i.e., along the length of a primary member, from support to support) for various types of steel and concrete structures are shown in Table 3.1. Basically, the diaphragm types vary depending on the span material (steel or concrete) and primary member type. For more information the reader should consult the AASHTO specification referenced in the table. Figure 3.5 shows a typical cross frame type secondary member for a steel, plate girder superstructure.

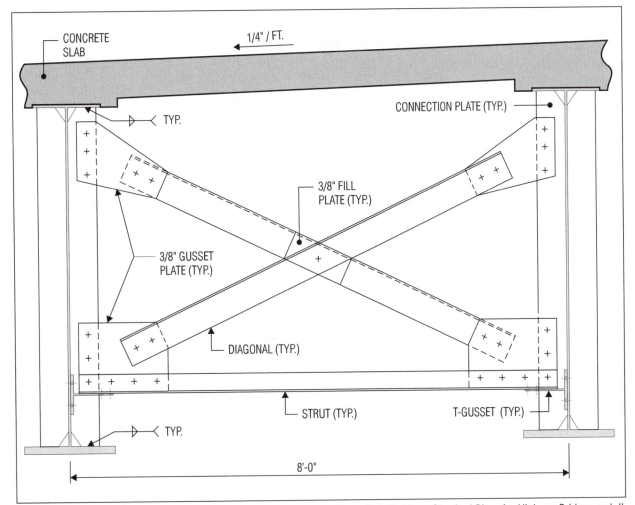

Figure 3.5 Cross-frame-type bracing for a plate girder superstructure. *(Adapted from Standard Plans for Highway Bridges, vol. II, Structural Steel Superstructures, FHWA, Ref. 3.9.)*

2. Lateral Bracing. Bracing located at either the top flange or bottom flange of a stringer to prevent lateral deformation is called lateral bracing. The bracing is similar in form to a cross-frame (i.e., laid out in an X-type configuration) but is laid out along the length of the stringer (in the horizontal plane), rather than its depth. Lateral bracing is not required at stringer flanges attached to a rigid element, such as a concrete deck or between box girders. In general, spans less than 125 ft (38.1 m) are not required to have lateral bracing, provided they have a system of diaphragms or cross-frames installed. Lateral bracing, however, can also add stability to the superstructure during construction and, for large spans, may be desirable from this standpoint.

3. Portal and Sway Bracing. Portal and sway bracing are transverse bracing elements used in truss bridges. Both portal and sway bracing are located at the top series of truss members called the top chord. Portal bracing differs from sway bracing in that it is located at the portal (i.e., entrance) of a through-truss. Portal bracing is designed to accommodate the total end reaction of the lateral system located at the top chord of the truss, and transfer it to the substructure components. Sway bracing is located at intermediate panel points of the top chord in either a cross or knee brace configuration to provide lateral support for the truss top chords. Deck trusses require sway bracing at the truss end and intermediate posts to ensure truss stability during construction.

> In general, spans less than 125 ft (38.1 m) are not required to have lateral bracing, provided they have a system of diaphragms or cross frames installed.

3.2 DECK TYPES

In Section 1, it was stated that the deck is the physical extension of the roadway over a crossing. In Section 3.1 we saw that, in certain instances, the deck can also serve as the bridge superstructure. Like their supporting systems, bridge decks can vary based on material and configuration. The following discussion concerns bridge decks which are supported by or work with a superstructure system.

3.2.1 Noncomposite and Composite Decks

When a deck is physically connected to and working with a superstructure load bearing member in resisting loads, it is said to be composite. If the deck is just resting on top of the superstructure and has no means of transferring longitudinal shear from primary members to the deck, then it cannot assist in the resistance of bending moments induced by vehicle loading and is said to be noncomposite.

From the above it is obvious why composite construction became the norm for concrete-steel bridge construction from the 1950's and onward. Composite construction offers:

❏ A more efficient use of materials since steel member size can be significantly reduced due to the incorporation of the deck into the resisting cross-section properties

❏ Greater vertical clearance by a reduction in stringer depth

❏ An ability to sustain greater vehicle loading and to reduce live load defection

Because of these significant advantages, composite construction is utilized whenever possible in an effort to maximize the performance and use of, not only different materials, but also different structural elements.

3.2.2 Cast-in-Place Concrete Slab

By far, the predominate form of deck in use is the cast-in-place, reinforced concrete deck slab. The conventional slab can work with either steel or concrete superstructures. If properly designed and maintained, a concrete slab will offer many years of service, even though it takes the most abuse out of any bridge component. As mentioned above, when working in composite action, the slab essentially becomes an element in the superstructure component. To protect the concrete slab, a deck overlay can be used or a portion of the deck reserved to resist the wear and tear of traffic (see Section 3.3 below).

3.2.3 Precast, Prestressed Concrete Panels

Decks can also be made of precast, prestressed concrete panels which are longitudinally post-tensioned after installation. The panels, which are 4 to 6 ft in width (1.2 to 1.8 m), are placed next to one another transverse to the stringers. A female-female keyway, filled with epoxy mortar, is used to join the panels together. Should the panels be used in conjunction with a steel superstructure, voids in the panels allow for stud shear connectors to be placed on primary members once the panels are in place. After installation of the studs, the voids, like the keyways, are filled with epoxy mortar [Ref. 3.9]. Precast panels are useful alternatives in rehabilitation projects because they allow for quick placement and are not susceptible to traffic vibrations, which may be a problem in projects undergoing staged construction. They cannot, however, be easily used on curved structures and have a higher cost than the traditional cast-in-place deck.

3.2.4 Steel Orthotropic Plate

An orthotropic deck is a steel plate with stiffeners attached underneath it. The plate is stiffened in two directions: longitudinally and transversely. Longitudinal to the bridge, open or closed rib systems are used (see sidebar) to stiffen the deck plate. Floor beams are used to provide stiffness in the transverse direction. Since the stiffness of the ribs vary from the floor beam, the system is said to be anisotropic. The term orthotropic is derived from the orthogonal (*ortho*) placement of the stiffeners and the anisotropic (*tropic*) behavior.

An orthotropic deck acts as the top flange of the primary members and, compared to a concrete deck, adds little dead load to the superstructure.

> **C**omposite construction is utilized whenever possible in an effort to maximize the performance and use of, not only different materials, but also different structural elements.

> **T**he term orthotropic is derived from the orthogonal (ortho) placement of the stiffeners and the anisotropic (tropic) behavior.

OPEN RIB SYSTEMS are used when issues like clearance are important. In general, however, closed rib systems are more popular because they are more economical and provide for better load distribution. When closed rib systems are used, they should be attached to the deck plate through a continuous weld to prevent moisture from entering into the stiffener. Any connections to splices or transverse beams should also be welded (AASHTO 10.41.4.10).

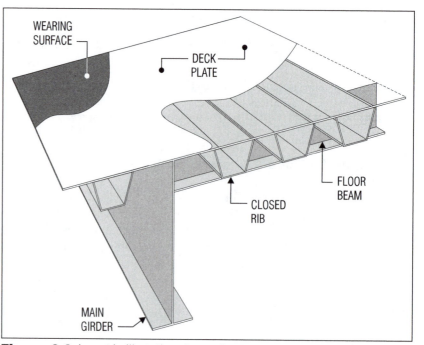

Figure 3.6 Isometric illustration of a steel orthotropic deck.

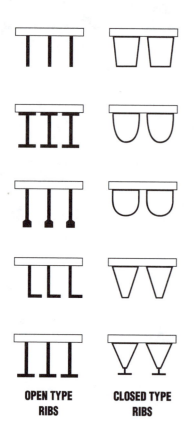

OPEN TYPE RIBS   **CLOSED TYPE RIBS**

Because of this reduced weight, a bridge equipped with an orthotropic deck can carry large live loads. This becomes a major advantage in large span bridges, since dead load represents a major part of the total loading. Since this is not the case with shorter span structures of less than 200 ft (61 m), they rarely are equipped with such decks since the benefit of reduced dead load is not offset by the increased fabrication costs.

Figure 3.6 shows a typical orthotropic deck superstructure cross section and its representative elements. Depicted in the illustration is a closed rib longitudinal stiffening rib.

3.2.5 Steel Grid

A steel grid deck, as its name would imply, utilizes a steel grid which can be left open or filled with concrete. This type of deck is especially useful when light decks are desired. A steel grid flooring system comes in panels which are welded to the supporting superstructure. While an open steel grid has less dead load than one filled with concrete, it does not offer as good a riding surface and can be prone to poor skid resistance. Like any other exposed steel element, an open steel grid deck system is also susceptible to corrosion from the elements and chemicals. Steel grids are extensively used in moveable bridges.

3.2.6 Timber

As mentioned in Section 3.1.3, glulam or stress-laminated timber planks can be used as bridge decking. This decking can be used with or without a wearing surface. Like open steel grids, when not equipped with a wearing surface, timber decks offer poor skid resistance. Glulam timber planks are placed transversely to the superstructure stringers, as in precast, prestressed concrete panels. Stress-laminated panels are placed longitudinally and no stringers are used.

3.2.7 Corrugated Metal

For bridges on local roads, a corrugated metal form filled with concrete or asphalt can also be used. Such a system, while reducing dead loads, requires close spacing of primary members and can suffer from corrosion.

3.2.8 Fiber Reinforced Polymer (FRP)

Although not widely used due to extremely high costs, fiber reinforced polymer (FRP) deck has drawn considerable worldwide attention. These decks are typically 5 to 8 inch (125 to 200 mm) thick, depending on the spacing of the supporting stringers. The major advantages of using FRP decks are light weight, rapid installation, and resistance to corrosion (maintenance free). Due to the high costs, FRP decks are currently mainly used on rehabilitation projects where light weight and rapid construction are key considerations.

3.3 WEARING SURFACE TYPES

The wearing surface (also called wearing course or deck overlay) for a structure is designed to resist traffic wear and, with periodic maintenance, provide for a smooth riding surface. The wearing surface serves the function of protecting the deck proper from traffic and the superstructure and substructure elements from associated deterioration. Without an adequate wearing surface, concrete decks in particular, will form delaminations more rapidly and initiate the top-down process of deterioration of a highway bridge (as discussed in Section 2). In a way, the wearing surface can be thought of as the first line of defense against deterioration for a bridge. Wearing surfaces can take one of the following forms.

> In a way, the wearing surface can be thought of as the first line of defense against deterioration for a bridge.

3.3.1 Asphalt Concrete

An asphalt concrete overlay rests on top of the deck. If the bridge deck is made of concrete, it should first be texturized by brooming or other methods to roughen its surface prior to placement of the asphalt concrete overlay. To protect the deck from moisture and chemical agents, a waterproofing membrane should be installed between the asphaltic wearing surface and the deck. A tack coat can be used to provide a more secure contact between the deck and membrane. For new structures, the New York State Department of Transportation recommends a 2.5 in (64 mm) thickness [Ref. 3.11], while Ontario Ministry of Transportation recommends a 90 mm (3.5 in) asphalt overlay. Older structures, subjected to several resurfacing operations, may have upward of 4 in (102 mm) of asphalt on them.

TYPES OF LATEX

There are a variety of latex types used as cement modifiers for Latex Modified Concrete (Section 3.3.2). Some of the more common forms and their abbreviations are listed below [Ref. 3.42].

ELASTOMERIC	
Natural Rubber	NR
Styrene-Butadiene	SB
Styrene-Butadiene Rubber	SBR
Polychloroprene (Neoprene)	CR
Acrylonitrile-Butadiene Rubber	NBR

THERMOPLASTIC	
Polyacrylic Ester	PAE
Styrene-Acrylic	SA
Ethylene Vinyl Acetate	EVA
Vinyl Acetate-Ethylene	VAE
Polyvinyl Acetate	PVAC
Polyvinylidene Chloride	PVDC
Vinyl Acetate-Acrylic Copolymer	VAC
Polyvinyl Propionate	
Polypropylene	
Pure Acrylics	

3.3.2 Latex Modified Concrete

Similar to the way an asphalt concrete overlay is placed, a wearing surface composed of latex modified concrete can be used. Latex modified concrete (also known as polymer modified concrete) is composed of cement, aggregate, and a latex emulsion admixture (such as styrene butadiene). With regard to wearing surfaces, latex modified concrete provides for a surface which is less porous, thereby limiting the intrusion of water and chlorides. Latex modified concrete wearing surfaces also enhance the ability of an overlay to adhere to an existing concrete slab and resist thermal forces caused by temperature fluctuations (see Section 3.5.4, Part 5). Because of its durability, a latex modified concrete overlay is usually specified at a depth less than for an asphalt concrete surface [1.5 in (38 mm)] [Ref. 3.10]. Prior to placement of the latex modified concrete, the concrete deck surface should be blast cleaned and wetted.

Latex modified concrete overlay is routinely used to replace the wearing surface of existing bridge decks.

3.3.3 High Density-Low Slump Concrete

Another wearing surface material, developed by the Iowa Department of Transportation, is high density-low slump concrete. Typically the slump should be no more than 1 in (25.4 mm) and water/cement ratio approximately 0.32. New York State specifies a minimum thickness of 2 in (50 mm) with an absolute minimum of around 1.75 in (45 mm) [Ref. 3.10]. Like latex modified concrete, the deck surface should be cleaned and wetted prior to placement.

3.3.4 Integrated Wearing Surface

An integrated wearing surface is part of the deck system itself. In the case of a monolithic concrete deck, the top portion of the concrete deck slab is taken as the wearing surface. From a design standpoint, this means that a portion of the top of the slab is neglected for section properties resisting loads. This amount of concrete, however, is still included as dead load on the structure. In the State of Maryland, 0.5 in (13 mm) of concrete on the top of slab is ignored when calculating the deck properties. When an integrated wearing surface is used, the surface should be grooved to ensure that hydroplaning does not occur during rain storms.

3.4 DECK JOINT TYPES

As we saw in Section 2, deck joints can play a critical role in the overall performance of a structure. The type of joint selected for a structure is generally dependent on the type and magnitude of motion the joint is required to accommodate. Deck joints can provide for longitudinal and transverse movement as well as rotation caused by thermal expansion/contraction and loading conditions. In addition to this, deck joints act as a sealant that protects substructure elements from deicing agents and excessive moisture.

3.4.1 Open Joints

Deck joints fall into two classes: open and closed. An open joint is nothing more than an opening between the concrete deck and an adjacent structure element (e.g., deck/deck, deck/abutment backwall). Sometimes, open joints are equipped with steel angles at the opening to create an armored open joint. An armored joint prevents some debris from entering the joint and will offer greater protection to the faces of concrete elements.

The obvious deficiency of any open joint, however, is its inability to prevent leakage and its susceptibility to deterioration. In addition to this, an open joint can only handle small longitudinal movements. Because of these inadequacies, open joints are rarely used in new structures and are predominately found in older, short span bridges.

Joints consisting of fitting plates, like finger plate joints, can also be considered to be open joints. These types of joints are more elaborate than the type of open joint discussed above and provide for greater longitudinal movement of the superstructure elements. Specific types of plate joints are discussed in greater detail later in the Section.

A closed joint covers the gap between the deck and associated structure element. A closed joint is typically comprised of a sealant and (if needed) mechanical system to provide for movement at the joint. Closed joints are available in a wide range of configurations from various manufacturers. Some of the more common forms of closed joints, as well as plate type joints, are detailed below.

3.4.2 Filled Joints

For short span bridges requiring small joint movement, a filled joint can be used as an alternative to the open joint discussed above. Filled joints are field formed and hot poured into the joint. A backer rod is usually inserted into joint gap prior to pouring the joint sealer material (typically silicon).

These types of joints are most often used in rehabilitation work, where upgrading an open joint or repair of a damaged joint is required. The advantages of this type joint are quick and easy installation, inexpensiveness, and ability to be preformed by owners' in-house maintenance teams. This type of joint normally last 5 to 10 years.

3.4.3 Compression Seal Joints

A compression seal consists of an elastic material which is squeezed into a joint opening coated with an adhesive lubricant. The most popular material for compression seals is extruded neoprene (polychloroprene) with an open cell cross section. The type of cross section used, combined with the material's elasticity, allows the seal to maintain compression and account for movement of the deck. For added durability, compression seals can also be combined with steel angles at the deck slab edge to form an armored joint (see Figure 3.7). Compression seal joints are typically used for decks experiencing movement in the range of 0.5 to 2.5 in (12 mm to 63 mm).

> **"It is probably safe to say that a completely satisfactory deck expansion joint has not yet been designed."**
>
> ### ARTHUR L. ELLIOT
> [Ref. 3.12]

> **The obvious deficiency of any open joint, however, is its inability to prevent leakage and its susceptibility to deterioration.**

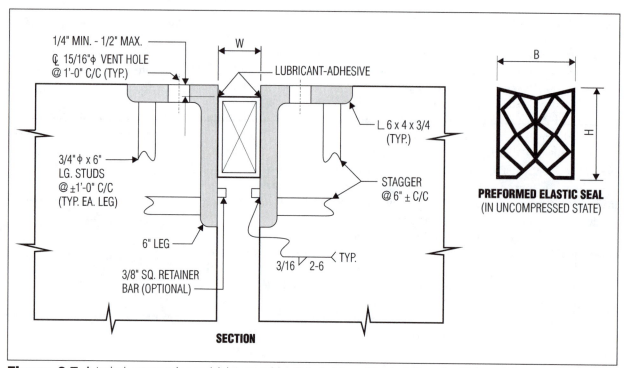

Figure 3.7 A typical compression seal joint assembly. *(Adapted from Standard Plans for Highway Bridges, vol. I, Concrete Superstructures, FHWA, Ref. 3.4.)*

When considering deck movement, it should be remembered that bridges on a skew must allow for both longitudinal and transverse movement. Since the bridge deck falls at an angle to the centerline of the roadway alignment, the resultant movement at the joint has two components which must be accounted for when choosing a deck joint.

Like all joints, compression seal joints can suffer from the constant wear of traffic and the accumulation of debris. A common problem is loosening of the bond between the seal and concrete surface. This loosening, combined with a loss in compression, can lead to the seal popping out of the joint. Another danger is of excessive joint compression which may make the seal inelastic, or it may force the seal above the deck surface where it can be damaged by traffic [Ref. 3.13].

Compression seal joints typically last for 10 to 15 years.

3.4.4 Strip Seal Joints

A strip seal uses a preformed strip of elastomeric material which is placed between dual steel rails that are anchored to the face of the joint opening. Most joints of this type utilize a neoprene gland as the sealant. Unlike a compression seal, which is squeezed into place, the strip seal is mechanically fitted to its steel rail assemblies (see Figure 3.8). Strip seals are also capable of larger movement than compression seals, with acceptable ranges going upward of 4 in (100 mm).

For strip seals, it is important that the gland chosen be made of a durable material. Sealants made from asphalt-based products, for example, are not

> A common problem is a loosening of the bond between the seal and concrete surface. This loosening ... may make the seal inelastic, or it may lead to the seal popping out of the joint.

> Strip seals are also capable of larger movement than compression seals, with acceptable ranges going upward of 4 in (100 mm).

Figure 3.8 Expansion joint rails and anchors. *(Photo courtesy of D.S. Brown Company, North Baltimore, Ohio.)*

JOINT RAILS used in strip seal joint assemblies are typically rolled or extruded to conform to the strip seal cross section. The rails restrain the seal so that it can accommodate both tension and compression at the deck joint. Like the steel angles that armor a compression seal joint assembly, the metal rails in a strip seal joint protect the concrete deck edges from debris and the impact of vehicles passing over the bridge. In the photograph shown in Figure 3.8, a pair of strip seal joint rails are shown. Also visible are the studs used to anchor the rail assemblies into the concrete deck.

resistive to the accumulation of debris found at bridge sites and can cause severe performance problems to the joint and deck [Ref. 3.13].

Strip seal joints typically last 10 to 20 years.

3.4.5 Modular Joints

A modular joint utilizes multiple (two or more) compression or strip seals to accommodate very large joint movements. The seals are fitted between rolled beams which run along the length of the joint. The seal/beam rests on support bars which are spaced along the length of the joint. These support bars rest on bearing devices located on each span the joint crosses (see Figure 3.9).

Two types of modular joints are available on the market. One is called multiple support system, in which each joint rolled beams is supported by individual support bars, as is shown in Figure 3.9. This type of modular joint is for relatively small joint openings (up to 4 strip seals). Another type of modular joint is called single support bar system in which all joint rolled beams are supported by the same supporting bars. The single support bar design greatly increased the movement capacity of the expansion joints.

Large modular joint systems can accommodate movements in ranges upward of 3 ft (0.9 m) and even 4 ft (1.2 m). Modular joint systems can also conform to structures which are excessively skewed or horizontally curved.

Many early modular joints suffered fatigue cracks due to the poor detailing and the dynamic nature of the loading. New designs have significantly improved the performance. Modular joints now normally last 15 to 25 years.

> **T**wo types of modular joints are available in the market. One is called multiple support system... Another type of modular joint is called single support bar system...

MODULAR JOINTS are typically used in large structures requiring a joint that can accommodate deck movements which are both large and complex. Modular joints, such as the one shown in Figure 3.9, essentially consist of multiple strip seal joints placed together and resting on support bars at a prescribed spacing [4 ft (1.2 m)]. The support bars ensure that sealer deformation occurs in a consistent and uniform fashion. Modular joints also represent an attractive solution for horizontally curved bridges which demand joints which can accommodate varied deck movement.

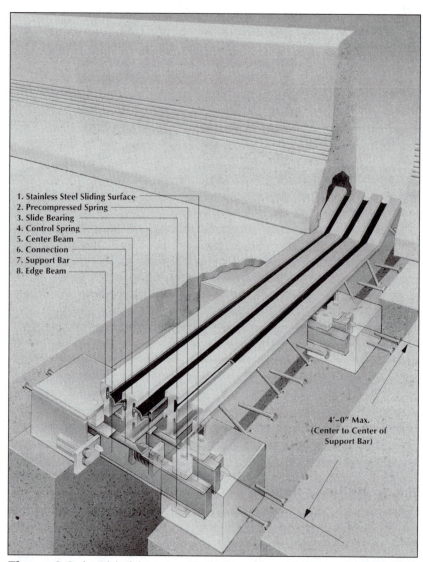

1. Stainless Steel Sliding Surface
2. Precompressed Spring
3. Slide Bearing
4. Control Spring
5. Center Beam
6. Connection
7. Support Bar
8. Edge Beam

4'-0" Max.
(Center to Center of Support Bar)

Figure 3.9 A modular joint system *(Illustration courtesy of D.S. Brown Company, North Baltimore, Ohio.)*

3.4.6 Finger Plate Joints

Finger plate type joints consist of steel plates which are married together through extending fingers. Finger plate type joints allow for movement up to 2 ft (609 mm). As mentioned previously, a finger plate joint can be considered an open joint. Therefore, it is necessary to protect substructure elements from leakage. This is accomplished through the use of a drainage trough, made of elastomeric material, which is installed underneath the finger plates and at the centerline of the joint. The trough should be placed at a slope sufficient to carry flow away from the bridge and into the site drainage system. A difficulty with this type of drainage system is that, if not properly maintained, the trough can easily become clogged with debris and fail to function.

A difficulty with this type of drainage system is that, if not properly maintained, the trough can easily become clogged with debris and fail to function.

Should the approach pavement or substructure settle, it is possible that the joint fingers can become locked making it impossible for the joint to function properly. Another problem with finger plate joints is that the joint surface can cause problems for motorcycles or bicycles passing over a bridge, especially if there is a rotation or differential settlement between the both sides of the joint. Fingers bent by snow plows can create hazards even to automobiles and trucks.

> **A**nother problem with finger plate joints is that the joint surface can cause problems for motor cycles or bicycles passing over a bridge.

3.4.7 Sliding Plate Joints

A sliding plate is similar to a finger plate joint, except that in place of meshing fingers is a single plate attached to one side of the joint. This plate spans the joint opening, with a gap maintained on the other span to permit movement of up to 4 in (101 mm). From a maintenance perspective, it is important to keep this gap free from debris, as this will inhibit the movement at the joint. Also, although the plate covers the joint, a drainage trough, like that described for finger plate joints in Section 3.4.6 above, is still required to drain runoff and protect substructure elements. Figure 3.10 shows a typical sliding plate joint and its representative components.

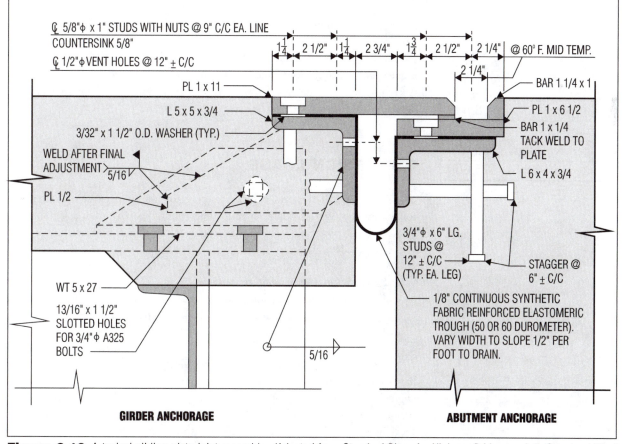

Figure 3.10 A typical sliding plate joint assembly. *(Adapted from Standard Plans for Highway Bridges, vol. II, Structural Steel Superstructures, FHWA, Ref. 3.9.)*

DID YOU KNOW

THAT the number of bridges in the United States dwarfs those of other nations? Listed below are the number of bridges in nations with developed infrastructures [Ref. 3.14].

Nation	Total
Australia	30,000
Belgium	5,300
Denmark	10,000
Finland	11,000
France	110,000
Germany	64,000
Italy	30,000
Japan	36,223
Netherlands	4,000
Norway	19,400
Spain	30,000
Sweden	12,000
Switzerland	8,500
Turkey	4,682
United Kingdom	155,000
United States	575,000

3.4.8 Conclusions

Opinions vary as much on deck joints as on the types of joints themselves. Like so many other details in a highway bridge, decisions on which type of joint to use are based, to a great deal, on subjective rather than on functional issues. For example, some technical literature is extremely laudatory of strip seal joints, while others decry them as a maintenance nightmare.

Yet everybody agrees that most expansion joint failures are caused by:

❏ Movement in excess of system capacity
❏ Chemical attack from gasoline, oil, and salts
❏ Snow plow damage
❏ Traffic pounding
❏ Structure deflections across the joint
❏ Poor design and installation

In the end, however, it is the owner and the design engineer who must decide which type of joint is best suited for the particular operation. Although they are often relegated to only part of a final drawing sheet, deck joints play an important role in the overall performance of a bridge. In making this decision, designers need to weigh heavily the maintainability of the selected joint and the costs associated therewith.

If possible, expansion joints should accommodate all movements of the structure (longitudinal, transverse, and rotation), withstand all applied loads, have a good riding quality without causing inconvenience or hazards to the road users, resist corrosion and withstand attack from grit and chemicals, require little maintenance, and allow easy inspection, repair or replacement. Currently, these demands seem to exceed what expansion joint industry can deliver.

3.5 DESIGN LOADS

The design of the bridge superstructure (or any other structural elements, for that matter) is based on a set of loading conditions which the component or element must withstand. The bridge engineer must take into account a wide variety of loads which vary based on:

❏ Duration (permanent or temporary)
❏ Direction (vertical, longitudinal, etc.)
❏ Deformation (concrete creep, thermal expansion, etc.)
❏ Effect (shear, bending, torsion, etc.)

In order to form a consistent basis for design, organizations like AASHTO have developed a set of standard loading conditions which are applied to the engineer's design model of the structure. As mentioned in Section 2, other nations maintain their own set of design loads like the BS 5400 loads utilized in the United Kingdom or the Ontario Highway Bridge Design Code (OHBDC) loads utilized in the Canadian province of Ontario and elsewhere in that nation.

Detailed below is a brief history of the AASHTO design loads and a discussion of various loading conditions based on the four classes listed above. While the values of the loads will vary from country to country, the laws of mechanics (fortunately) do not. An overview of the principal design methods used by designers is also provided.

3.5.1 Background and History

In general, the principal loading constraint which highway bridges are designed by is truck loading. Given the variety of trucks in use, it was determined that a standard set of design loading caused by truck traffic needed to be developed. This need led to the development, by AASHTO, of standard design trucks to be used by bridge engineers in modeling the performance and adequacy of their designs. In the early part of the last century, designers utilized a *train* of trucks as design loading for their bridges. As the highway trucking industry grew, and along with it truck loads, many bridges began to evidence overstressing in structural components. In 1944, a suite of hypothetical truck classes designated as H and HS class trucks were developed by AASHTO. These design vehicles were created with two and three axles, respectively, set at specified offsets. In 1975, however, the U.S. federal government upgraded the allowable gross weight for trucks from 73,280 lb (325.9 KN) to 80,000 lb (355.8 KN). This meant that the heaviest design vehicle was 8000 lb (35.6 KN) less than the allowable truck weight (i.e., 80,000 lb allowable minus 72,000 lb design vehicle). Some states responded by upgrading the standard AASHTO 1944 circa design vehicles from a 72,000 lb (320 KN) weight to a 90,000 lb (400 KN) weight (from HS-20 to HS-25).

The H and HS design trucks dominated the core standard in the United States until AASHTO LRFD specifications became widely accepted [Ref. 3.15].

In the AASHTO LRFD Specifications, which is gradually replacing the AASHTO Standard Specifications, HL-93 live load is used. The HL-93 is composed of a truck (identical to HS-20) or a tandem, combined with a lane load of 0.64 kip/ft (9.34 KN/m). HL-93 loading is significantly heavier than the HS-20 loading, especially for medium and long span bridges.

3.5.2 Permanent Loads

Permanent loads, as the name would imply, are those loads which always remain and act on a bridge throughout its life. Although the term dead load is often used synonymously with permanent loads, there are distinctions which need to be made. For this discussion, permanent loads are divided into the following three major categories.

1. Dead Load. The dead load on a superstructure is the aggregate weight of all superstructure elements (i.e., those elements above the bearings). This would include, but are not be limited to, the deck, wearing surface, stay-in-place forms, sidewalks and railings, parapets, primary members, secondary members (including all bracing, connection plates, etc.), stiffeners, signing, and utilities. As we will see later on, one of the first steps in any design of a superstructure is to compile a list of all the elements which contribute to

AASHTO STANDARD

3.3.6 UNIT WEIGHTS FOR COMPUTING DEAD LOAD

ITEM	lb/ft³
Steel or cast steel	490
Cast iron	450
Aluminum alloys	175
Timber (treated or untreated)	50
Concrete, plain or reinforced	150
Compacted sand, earth, gravel, or ballast	120
Loose sand, earth, and gravel	100
Macadam or gravel, rolled	140
Cinder filling	60
Pavement, other than wood block	150
Railway rails, guard rails, and fastenings (per linear ft of track)	200
Stone masonry	170
Asphalt plank, 1 in thick	9 lb sq. ft

AASHTO LRFD

Table 3.5.1-1   UNIT WEIGHTS

ITEM	kcf
Aluminum Alloys	0.175
Bituminous wearing surfaces	0.140
Cast iron	0.450
Cinder Filling	0.060
Compacted sand, silt or clay	0.120
Light weight concrete	0.110
Sand lightweight concrete	0.120
Normal weight concrete	0.145
Loose sand, silt gravel	0.100
Rolled gravel, macadam or ballast	0.140
Steel	0.490
Stone Masonry	0.170
Hard wood	0.060
Soft wood	0.050
Fresh water	0.0624
Salt water	0.0640

Given the variety of trucks in use, it was determined that a standard set of design loading caused by truck traffic needed to be developed.

I n AASHTO LRFD Specifications, which is gradually replacing the AASHTO Standard Specifications, HL-93 live load is used. The HL-93 is composed of a truck (identical to HS-20) or a tandem, combined with a lane load of 0.64 kip/ft (9.34 KN/m).

...S uperimposed dead loads are those loads placed on the superstructure after the deck has cured and begun to work with the primary members in resisting loads.

dead load. The sidebar provides a list of some dead load unit weights that are used in computing the overall superstructure value. In AASHTO Standard Specifications, all dead loads are treated as one group. In AASHTO LRFD Specifications, however, dead load for wearing surfaces and utilities are treated as a separate dead load group, which have higher load factors due to the fact that this group of dead loads have larger uncertainty than the other dead loads (See AASHTO LRFD Section 3.5.1). The purpose of load factors is to account for the uncertainty of the underlining loads.

2. **Superimposed Dead Load.** In composite construction (see Section 3.2.1) superimposed dead loads are those loads placed on the superstructure after the deck has cured and begun to work with the primary members in resisting loads. From the list of elements above, the designer would separate items such as sidewalks, railings, parapets, signing, utilities, and the wearing surface. With regard to the utility and wearing surface, it is important to anticipate future changes would add to these loads on a structure. One should keep in mind that superimposed dead load is part of the total dead load. It is separated from the rest of the dead loads because it is resisted by a composite section, therefore cause less deflection and stress in the stringer than other dead loads.

3. **Pressures.** Pressures due to earth or water are also considered permanent loads. While these loads primarily affect substructure elements, they have the potential of impacting superstructure elements as well at points where these two components interface (e.g., rigid frame or arch

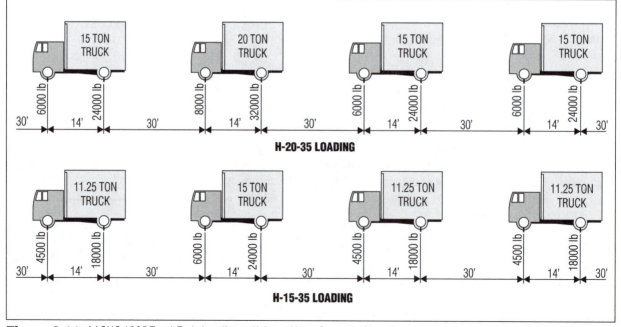

Figure 3.11 AASHO 1935 Truck Train Loadings. *(Adapted from Standard Specifications for Highway Bridges, 17th Ed., Appendix B, Ref. 3.3.)*

structures). This serves as a reminder that, while we are discussing the design of a highway bridge in terms of its individual components, we should not lose sight of the structure as a whole.

3.5.3 Temporary Loads

Temporary loads are those loads which are placed on a bridge for only a short period of time. Just as dead loads are the principal permanent loading condition, live loads represent the major temporary loading condition. There are, however, several other classes of temporary loads which the designer must consider. Discussed below are the major forms of temporary loading.

1. Vehicle Live Load. The term live load means a load that moves along the length of a span. Therefore, a person walking along the bridge can be considered live load. Obviously, however, a highway bridge has to be designed to withstand more than pedestrian loading. To give designers the ability to accurately model the live load on a structure, hypothetical design vehicles based on truck loading were developed. In Section 3.5.1 we discussed the origins of this system of loading.

In 1935, what was then called AASHO issued a loading scheme based on a train of trucks. These are identified as H-20-35 and H-15-35 in Figure 3.11. To meet the demands of heavier trucks, the introduction of five new truck classes was made in 1944. These classes have the following designations and gross vehicle weights:

- ❏ H10-44   (20,000 lb - 89 KN)
- ❏ H15-44   (30,000 lb - 133 KN)
- ❏ H20-44   (40,000 lb - 178 KN)
- ❏ HS15-44 (54,000 lb - 240 KN)
- ❏ HS20-44 (72,000 lb - 320 KN)

Today, all but the H10-44 vehicle are still included in the AASHTO standard specifications. Figure 3.12 illustrates these design trucks and their associated geometries. To load a structure one such truck per lane, per span is used (see sidebar on design traffic lanes). The truck is then moved along the length of the span to determine the point of maximum moment. Recently, to account for higher loading conditions, some states have begun using the so-called HS-25 design vehicle, which represents a 25 percent increase in loading over the standard HS20-44 truck for a total gross vehicle weight of 90,000 lb (400 KN). It is important to stress that the H and HS trucks do not represent an actual truck being used to transport goods and materials. They are approximations used to simulate the greatest bending and shear forces caused by actual trucks.

From Figure 3.12 we see that the HS trucks have a variable spacing between the two rear axles. This distance between axles, varying from 14 to 30 ft (4.27 to 9.14 m), is used to create a live loading situation which will induce maximum moment in a span. For simply supported bridges, this value will be the 14 ft minimum. In continuous spans, however, the distance between axles is varied to position the axles at adjacent supports in such a fashion as to create the maximum negative moment.

AASHTO STANDARD

3.6 PLACING TRUCK AND LANE LOADS IN TRAFFIC LANES

The AASHTO design trucks and lane loadings are meant to cover a 10 ft (3.05 m) width. These loads are then placed in 12 ft (3.66 m) lanes which are spaced across the bridge from curb to curb (AASHTO 3.6.2). If the curb-to-curb width is between 20 ft (6.10 m) and 24 ft (7.31 m), two design lanes are to be used, each of which is half the curb-to-curb distance (AASHTO 3.6.3). The table below shows the number of design lanes based on a bridge's curb-to-curb width.

DESIGN TRAFFIC LANES

Curb-to-Curb Width	No. of Lanes
20 to 30 ft	2
30 to 42 ft	3
42 to 54 ft	4
54 to 66 ft	5
66 to 78 ft	6
78 to 90 ft	7
90 to 102 ft	8
102 to 114 ft	9
114 to 126 ft	10

While we are discussing the design of a highway bridge in terms of its individual components, we should not lose sight of the structure as a whole.

In continuous spans, however, the distance between axles is varied to position the axles at adjacent supports in such a fashion as to create the maximum negative moment.

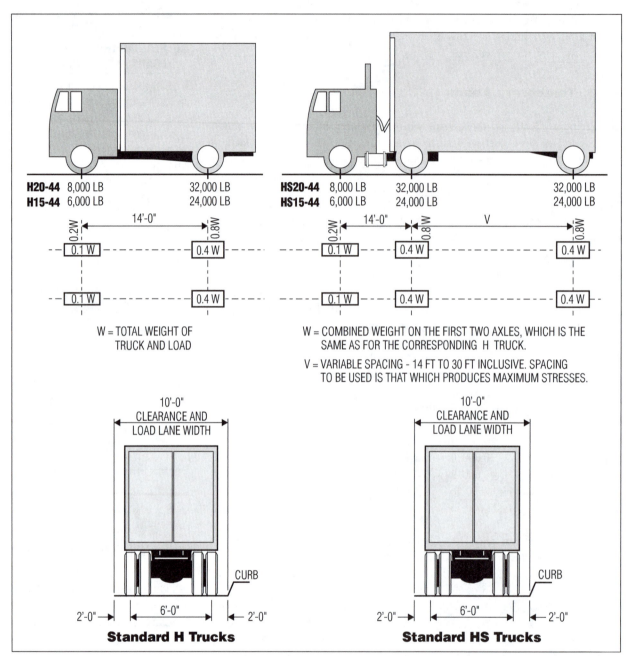

W = TOTAL WEIGHT OF
TRUCK AND LOAD

W = COMBINED WEIGHT ON THE FIRST TWO AXLES, WHICH IS THE
SAME AS FOR THE CORRESPONDING H TRUCK.

V = VARIABLE SPACING - 14 FT TO 30 FT INCLUSIVE. SPACING
TO BE USED IS THAT WHICH PRODUCES MAXIMUM STRESSES.

Standard H Trucks

Standard HS Trucks

Figure 3.12 AASHTO Standard H & HS Design Trucks. *(Adapted from Standard Specifications for Highway Bridges, Ref. 3.3.)*

Replacing the train of trucks in the 1935 circa design code are lane-loading configurations which approximate a 40,000 lb (178 KN) truck followed by a train of 30,000 lb (133 KN) trucks. To model this, a uniform distributed load is used combined with a concentrated force. This force varies for moment and shear computations. Where truck loading generally governs for short, simple spans, lane loading typically holds for long and continuous span bridges. Like truck loading, the concentrated load is moved along the span to determine the point of maximum moment.

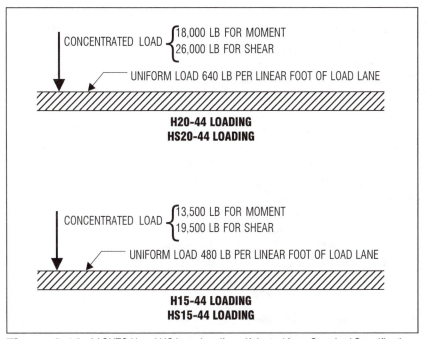

Figure 3.13 AASHTO H and HS Lane Loading. *(Adapted from Standard Specifications for Highway Bridges, Ref. 3.3.)*

FOR CONTINUOUS span bridges an additional concentrated load should be used in determining maximum negative moment only (AASHTO 3.11.3). The second load should be placed in another span of the series. For simple span bridges and for the computation of maximum positive moment in continuous span bridges, a single concentrated load is used as shown in Figure 3.13. The lane loading depicted in this figure approximates the train-of-trucks loading configuration developed in the 1935 AASHO specifications (see Figure 3.11).

For simple span bridges and for determining maximum positive moment in continuous spans, only one concentrated load is used in conjunction with the uniform load. To determine maximum negative moment in continuous spans, however, two concentrated loads are used. Figure 3.13 shows the standard H and HS lane loadings.

Another form of live loading, known as alternative military loading was developed in 1956 by the Federal Highway Administration. This loading consists of two axles separated by 4 ft (1.22 m) and each weighing 24,000 lb (107 KN). This loading is used to represent heavy military vehicles (AASHTO 3.7.4). Bridges designed on the U.S. Interstate system are required to compare the standard HS20-44 loading with the alternative military loading. The loading configuration causing the greatest forces is then used.

These H, HS, and military loading are used by AASHTO Standard Specifications. For AASHTO LRFD Specifications, HL-93 loading is used. HL-93 consists of a design truck or tandem (whichever produces the greater forces), combined with a design lane load. The design truck is identical to HS20-44. The design tandem consists of a pair of 25,000 lb (111 KN) axles spaced 4.0 ft (1.2 m) apart. The transverse spacing of wheels for both the design truck and the design tandem is 6.0 ft (1.8 m).

The design lane load in the AASHTO LRFD Specifications is 0.64 kip/ft (9.34 KN/m). This load is used in conjunction with the design truck or tandem. In the AASHTO Standard Specifications, no lane load is required to be added to an HS truck loading.

A reduction in the live load intensity is permitted for bridges with two or more lanes that have maximum stress caused by fully loading each lane.

> **A**lternative military loading was developed in 1956 by the Federal Highway Administration ... to represent heavy military vehicles.

In the AASHTO Standard Specifications, a 10 percent reduction of three lane structures and 25 percent reduction for bridges with four or more lanes is allowed (AASHTO 3.12). In the AASHTO LRFD Specifications, a 20 percent increase for a single lane, 15 percent deduction for 3 lanes, and a 35 percent deduction for four or more lanes loaded is required (AASHTO LRFD 3.6.1.1.2). This reduction is permitted given the decreased probability that worst loading in multiple lanes will occur.

While we have discussed the legal load limits for trucks, there is also the issue of providing for those trucks which are overweight. In an attempt to deal with extralegal loading conditions, the California Department of Transportation developed a live loading configuration known as the permit design loads or P loads. Like their H, HS, and HL cousins, P loads are hypothetical design vehicles. The P load design vehicle consists of a steering axle and between two to six pairs of tandems. The number of tandems used is based on the configuration that produces the maximum stress in a span [Ref. 3.16]. The abbreviation *LL* is used to reference live load in the text.

> **I**n an attempt to deal with extra-legal loading conditions, the California Department of Transportation developed a live loading configuration known as the permit design loads or P loads.

> **B**eginning with the 1971 San Fernando earthquake, the seismic design code has undergone extensive revision and expansion.

2. **Earthquake Loading.** Earthquake loading is a product of *natural forces* which are dependent on the geographic location of the bridge. In general, there are four major natural forces with which the bridge engineer must be concerned:

- ❑ Seismic forces
- ❑ Wind forces
- ❑ Channel forces
- ❑ Thermal forces

Like the vehicle live loads discussed above, seismic, wind, and channel forces are temporary loads on a structure which act for a short duration. Thermal forces fall in another group to be discussed later. Seismic forces primarily affect bridge substructure components and, therefore, will be covered in more detail in Section 4. Superstructure elements, though, are affected by seismic forces in many ways. We can, then, offer the following general overview concerning earthquake loading.

The seismic analysis of highway bridges has become an involved task over the years. Beginning with the 1971 San Fernando earthquake, the seismic design code has undergone extensive revision and expansion. Because of the complex nature of seismic activity (and the lack of any concrete methodology) the design provisions, as set forth in codes like the AASHTO Standard and LRFD specifications, are at best, simplifications of the actual physical effects of an earthquake, and, at worst, approximations of what might happen. As is the case with vehicular loading, the forces caused by seismic activity are described as an idealization of those actually exerted.

Although there are differences between AASHTO Standard Specifications and LRFD Specifications, the general procedures of estimating earthquake forces for bridges are similar. Hence only AASHTO Standard Specification procedures are discussed here.

AASHTO STANDARD
DIVISION I-A

3.3 IMPORTANCE CLASSIFICATION

3.4 SEISMIC PERFORMANCE CATEGORY

Essential bridges are assigned an importance classification (IC) of "I." All other structures have an IC of "II." An *essential* bridge is one that is determined to be critical to "social/survival and security/defense" needs (AASHTO, I-A, 3.3). Based on the IC and the acceleration coefficient at the bridge site, a seismic performance category (SPC) can be determined from the table below (AASHTO, I-A, 3.4).

Seismic Performance Categories		
Acceleration Coefficient	IC	
A	I	II
$A < 0.09$	A	A
$0.09 < A < 0.19$	B	B
$0.19 < A < 0.29$	C	C
$0.29 < A$	D	C

An earthquake force acting on a bridge is a function of the following factors:

- ❏ Dead weight of the structure
- ❏ Ground motion (acceleration)
- ❏ Period of vibration of the structure
- ❏ Type of soil present

These factors are used to determine the response of the bridge to an assumed uniform loading on the structure. This response takes the form of an equivalent static earthquake loading which is applied to the structure to calculate forces and displacements on bridge elements. The AASHTO Standard Specifications provides four methodologies for calculating this loading. The method used is dependent on whether the bridge is single span or multispan and the geometric characteristics of the structure. For single span structures, the connections between the bridge span and the abutment with fixed bearings should be designed to resist the superstructure weight multiplied by the acceleration coefficient and the site

AASHTO STANDARD

DIVISION I-A
4.2 CHOOSING THE APPROPRIATE SEISMIC ANALYSIS METHOD

Once a seismic performance category (SPC) has been assigned, the type of analysis required is identified based on the SPC and whether the bridge is regular or irregular. Regular bridges are those with an unchanging bridge cross section, similar supports, and a uniform mass and stiffness. Bridges which do not satisfy these criteria are irregular. Four methods are allowed to calculate the earthquake loads (AASHTO, I-A, 4.1).

Method 1 = Uniform Load Analysis
Method 2 = Single-Mode Spectral Analysis
Method 3 = Multimode Spectral Analysis
Method 4 = Time History Analysis

Analysis Procedure		
SPC	Regular Bridge	Irregular Bridge
A	–	–
B	1 or 2	3
C	1 or 2	3
D	1 or 2	3

Method 4 may be used for any bridges with owner's approval

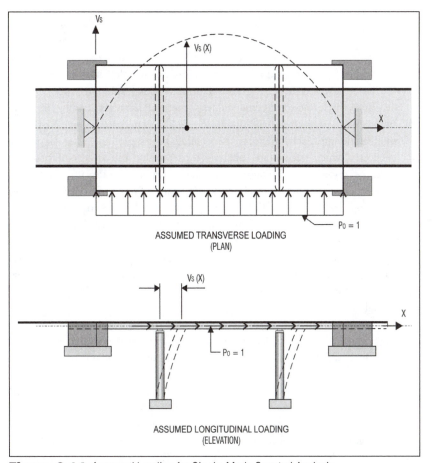

ASSUMED TRANSVERSE LOADING
(PLAN)

ASSUMED LONGITUDINAL LOADING
(ELEVATION)

Figure 3.14 Assumed Loading for Single-Mode Spectral Analysis.

A DISPLACEMENT is initially computed based on a unit load of 1. The dead weight of the superstructure and those elements of the substructure integrated with the superstructure also needs to be calculated. Then, based on the initial displacement and the dead weight value, three factors α, β, and γ are computed. These factors are used to calculate the fundamental period of the bridge and the resultant equivalent static earthquake loading [Ref. 3.3].

3.5 SITE COEFFICIENT

As stated at the beginning of this section, the type of soil present at the bridge site plays an important role in the forces an earthquake exerts on a structure. The site coefficient is determined by selecting one of four soil profile types that best fits the conditions at the site. (AASHTO, I-A, 3.5.).

SOIL PROFILE TYPE I: S = 1.0

If rock of any type is present, this profile type applies. Shalelike or crystalline types with a shear wave velocity greater than 2,500 ft/s (760 m/s). Stiff soil on top of rock with a depth less than 200 ft (60 m) consisting of stable deposits of sands, gravels, or stiff clays.

SOIL PROFILE TYPE II: S = 1.2

For stiff clay or deep cohesionless soil conditions along with sites where the soil depth on top of rock is greater than 200 ft (60 m) consisting of stable deposits of sands, gravels, or stiff clays.

SOIL PROFILE TYPE III: S = 1.5

Soft to medium-stiff clays and sands with a depth of 30 ft (9 m) or more of soft to medium-stiff clay with or without intervening layers of sand or other cohesionless soils.

SOIL PROFILE TYPE IV: S = 2.0

Soft clays or silts greater than 40 ft (12 m) in depth [shear wave velocity less than 500 ft/s (150 m/s)], and include nonengineered fill.

coefficient for the soil type (AASHTO Division I-A, 3.11). The acceleration coefficient is a dimensionless constant used to describe ground motion (see Figure 3.15).

The analysis of multispan bridges varies depending on the type of geometry present and the degree of seismic activity at the bridge site. The so-called *regular bridges* are those with consistent and similar superstructure cross sections and intermediate support structures (piers). Bridges with a varying cross section and different types of supports are considered *irregular* (AASHTO Division I-A, 4.2). The degree of seismic activity is based on the acceleration coefficient at the bridge site. Bridges with an acceleration coefficient greater than 0.19 are considered to be in an area of high seismic activity. This coefficient, along with whether the bridge is classified as essential or not (see sidebar), are used to assign the bridge a *seismic performance category* (SPC).

Based on the SPC and the number of spans, one of the four different analysis methods is chosen to calculate the loading on the bridge due to earthquake forces. The two most frequently used methods are:

❑ Single-mode spectral analysis
❑ Multimode spectral analysis

In general, regular bridges in areas of low seismic activity utilize the less involved single-mode analysis method, while irregular bridges in high seismic risk locations require the multimode spectral analysis approach. The former can be performed using conventional hand calculation methods, but the latter demands more rigorous computer-aided solutions.

The single-mode spectral analysis method assumes loading in basic transverse and longitudinal directions as illustrated in Figure 3.14. The multimode approach, however, is required because of the irregular bridge geometry which necessitates analysis to determine the effects of coupling in three coordinate directions for each vibration mode. Calculation of seismic effects using the multimode spectral analysis procedure is beyond the scope of this text. For regular, multispan bridges the single-mode spectral analysis method for calculating equivalent static earthquake loading is shown below.

Longitudinal and Transverse Earthquake Loading. The single-mode spectral analysis procedure uses the same method for calculating both longitudinal and transverse earthquake loading. This method utilizes the principle of virtual displacements to develop a mode shape model of the bridge. An arbitrary, uniform static loading p_o is applied to the length of the structure to produce an initial displacement v_s. This displacement, combined with the dead load weight of the superstructure (and part of the substructure), can be used to determine the resultant earthquake loading.

The first step is to calculate the initial displacement of our generalized model. Figure 3.14 shows the longitudinal loading of the structure. The initial displacement v_s is illustrated at the piers and at the end of the last span. This value varies depending on the type of piers in place (e.g., two column or three column piers, solid stem, etc.). The displacement is calculated assuming an arbitrary unit load of $p_o = 1$.

The next step is to calculate the dead weight value *w(x)*. This represents the dead load of the superstructure and contributing substructure elements (e.g., an integrated pier cap). It is even possible to include live load values for structures in high traffic urban areas where large numbers of vehicles may be present on the structure during an earthquake (AASHTO Division I-A, 4.4).

Once the values of v_s and *w(x)* are known, the following three factors can be calculated:

$$\alpha = \int_0^L v_s(x)dx \qquad (Eq. 3.1)$$

$$\beta = \int_0^L w(x)v_s(x)dx \qquad (Eq. 3.2)$$

$$\gamma = \int_0^L w(x)v_s(x)^2 dx \qquad (Eq. 3.3)$$

where L = length of bridge

AASHTO STANDARD
DIVISION I-A
3.7 RESPONSE MODIFICATION FACTORS (R FACTOR)

For bridges with a SPC = B, C, or D, the seismic design forces for individual members are calculated by dividing the elastic forces by the appropriate R factor.

Substructure	
Wall-Type Pier	2
Conc. Pile Bent (Vertical Piles)	3
Conc. Pile Bent (1 + Batter Piles)	2
Single Columns	3
Steel Pile Bent (Vertical Piles)	5
Steel Pile Bent (1 + Batter Piles)	3
Multiple Column Bent	5
Connections	
Superstructure to Abutment	0.8
Exp. Joints within Span of Super	0.8
Columns, Piers, or Pile Bents to	
Cap Beam or Superstructure	1.0
Colums or Piers to Foundations	1.0

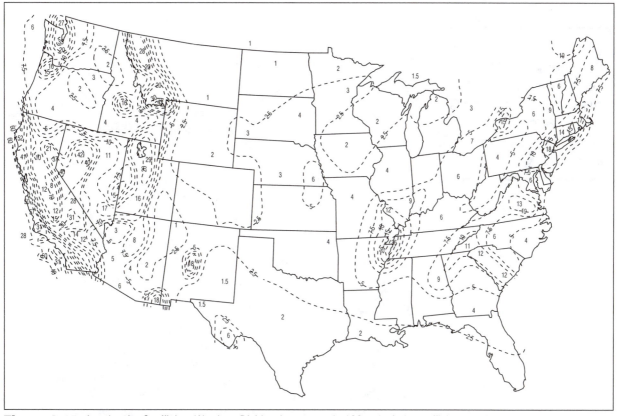

Figure 3.15 Acceleration Coefficient (A) values. Divide values on map by 100 to obtain the coefficient used in calculations. *(Adapted from Standard Specifications for Highway Bridges, 17th Ed., Ref. 3.3.)* Consult map in the AASHTO specifications for more detail.

DID YOU KNOW

DID YOU KNOW

THAT the Loma Prieta earthquake which struck on October 18, 1989, had a magnitude of 6.9, killed 62 people, and left over 12,000 homeless, all of this with only 10 seconds of strong motion [Ref. 3.17]? A drawback to the response spectrum approach taken in the AASHTO seismic specifications is that duration of shaking is not directly considered but rather accounted for by the spectrum. The duration accounted for in the current code is approximated to be between 20 to 30 seconds [Ref. 3.3].

I t is even possible to include live load values for structures in high traffic urban areas where large numbers of vehicles may be present on the structure during an earthquake.

With these factors known, the fundamental period of the bridge can be computed with the following:

$$T = 2\pi \sqrt{\frac{\gamma}{p_o g \alpha}} \qquad \text{(Eq. 3.4)}$$

where $p_o = 1$
g = acceleration of gravity (length/time^2)

We are almost ready to compute the resultant horizontal earthquake loading on the structure. This loading can be described as a function of

❑ The mass of structure
❑ The acceleration coefficient
❑ The soil type
❑ The fundamental period

AASHTO provides an elastic seismic response coefficient which quantifies these parameters into a dimensionless value. This single coefficient greatly simplifies the analysis since it does not require the designer to calculate an overall site period. The coefficient is described by

$$C_s = \frac{1.2 A S}{T^{2/3}} \qquad \text{(Eq. 3.5)}$$

where A = acceleration coefficient (see Figure 3.15)
S = site coefficient (see sidebar)

With the values from Equations 3.1 through 3.5 in place, the intensity of the earthquake loading can be computed. This loading is an approximation of the inertial effects resulting from the dynamic deflection of the structure and is defined as

$$p_e(x) = \frac{\beta C_s}{\gamma} w(x) v_s(x) \qquad \text{(Eq. 3.6)}$$

This load can now be applied to the structure in a fashion similar to the one in which the initial unit loading of $p_o = 1$ was at the beginning of the process. Now, though, the value of $p_e(x)$ is substituted to determine displacement, shears, and moments due to earthquake loading.

3. **Wind Loading.** Like earthquake loading, wind loading offers a complicated set of loading conditions which must be idealized in order to provide a workable design. Although the problem of modeling wind forces is a dynamic one, with winds acting over a given time interval, these forces can be approximated as a static load being uniformly distributed over the exposed regions of a bridge.

The exposed region of the bridge is taken as the aggregate surface areas of all elements (both superstructure and substructure) as seen in elevation (i.e., perpendicular to the longitudinal axis). The loading on a bridge due to wind forces is specified by AASHTO based on an assumed wind velocity of 100 miles per hour (160 km/h).

For conventional girder/beam type bridges this translates into an intensity of 50 lb/ft² (2.40 kN/m²) with the minimum total force being 300 lb/ft (4.38 KN/m). Trusses and arches require wind loads applied with an intensity of 75 lb/ft² (3.60 kN/m²) with the minimum total force of either 300 or 150 lb/ft (4.38 or 2.19 kN/m), depending on whether the affected member is a windward or leeward chord, respectively (AASHTO 3.15.1). The windward chord is that chord exposed to the prevailing wind and, conversely, the leeward chord is located away from the wind.

The design wind pressure on vehicles is based on a wind velocity of 55 mph (88.5 km/h), acting on a long row of randomly sequenced vehicles, which results a wind pressure of 100 lb/ft, acting normal to, and 6.0 ft (1.8 m) above the bridge deck. This load should be transmitted to the substructure.

With regard to the superstructure, wind forces are applied in a transverse and longitudinal direction at the center of gravity of the exposed region of the superstructure. AASHTO offers a set of wind loading values for truss and girder bridges based on the angle of attack (skew angle) of wind forces (AASHTO 3.15.2.1 or AASHTO LRFD 3.8.1). For conventional slab-on-stringer bridges, however, with span lengths less than or equal to 125 ft (38.1 m), AASHTO Standard Specifications allow the simplified wind loading (AASHTO 3.15.2.1.3):

❏ Wind Load on Structure:
  Transverse Loading = 50 lb/ft² (2.40 kN/m²)
  Longitudinal Loading = 12 lb/ft² (0.58 kN/m²)

❏ Wind Load on Live Load:
  Transverse Loading = 100 lb/ft (1.46 kN/m)
  Longitudinal Loading = 40 lb/ft (0.58 kN/m)

The transverse and longitudinal loads are to be placed simultaneously for both the structure and live load (AASHTO 3.15.2.1.3). Another loading consideration is the effect of overturning. To account for this, AASHTO specifies a 20 lb/ft² (0.96 kN/m²) upward force to be applied at windward quarter points of the transverse superstructure width. For AASHTO LRFD, this vertical wind pressure should be applied only for limit states that do not involve wind on live load, and only when wind direction is perpendicular to the longitudinal axis of the bridge.

4. Channel Forces. Channel forces are those loads imposed on a structure due to water course–related features. These forces include, but are not limited to stream flow, floating ice, and buoyancy. Channel forces, similar to seismic forces, primarily affect substructure elements. The following discussion is offered within the context of design loads in general and their relationship to the substructure.

Stream Flow. Structures with supports in water courses are at risk for having those supports slide or overturn due to stream flow forces. As discussed in Section 2.3.6 an excessive stream flow velocity can lead to

---

AASHTO STANDARD

3.18.1   PIER SHAPE CONSTANT

The equation for the pressure due to stream flows uses a constant to describe the geometry of the pier in a water channel. The three possible values are listed below:

PIERS SUBJECTED TO DRIFT BUILD-UP AND SQUARE ENDED PIERS: K = 1.4
CIRCULAR PIERS: K = 0.7
ANGLED ENDS: K = 0.5

Where the pier ends are angled at 30 degrees or less.

AASHTO LRFD

3.7.3.1   DRAG COEFFICIENT

Semicircular-nosed pier: $C_D = 0.7$
Square-ended pier: $C_D = 1.4$
Debris lodged pier: $C_D = 1.4$
Angled end at 90 degrees or less:
                        $C_D = 0.8$

[3.5.3, Part 4]

AASHTO LRFD

3.7.3.2 LATERAL DRAG COEFFICIENT

The coefficient C_L varies depending on the angle between the direction of flow and the longitudinal axis of the pier.

0 degrees:	$C_L = 0.00$
5 degrees:	$C_L = 0.50$
10 degrees:	$C_L = 0.70$
20 degrees:	$C_L = 0.90$
30 degrees or more:	$C_L = 1.00$

adverse scour conditions which can undermine footings and threaten the integrity of the structure. In general, the pressure due to stream forces is a result of the change in momentum of water as it impacts a pier and then travels away from it [Ref. 3.18].

AASHTO Standard Specifications defines the average pressure acting on a bridge pier due to flowing water as (AASHTO 3.18.1):

$$P_{avg} = K \cdot \left(V_{avg} \right)^2 \qquad \text{(Eq. 3.7)}$$

where P_{avg} = average stream pressure (lb/ft^2)
K = constant based on shape of pier (see sidebar)
V_{avg} = average velocity of water (ft/s)

The average velocity is computed by dividing the flow rate by the flow area. Flow values should be obtained from a thorough hydrologic/hydraulic study for conditions producing maximum velocities. Such a study may be carried out concurrently with the bridge design project or as a part of an independent study. The maximum stream flow pressure P_{max} is equal to twice the average stream pressure P_{avg}. A triangular distribution in used with P_{max} located at the top of water elevation and a pressure of zero at the flow line.

In the AASHTO LRFD Specifications, the pressure of flowing stream water acting in the longitudinal direction of substructure is (AASHTO LRFD 3.7.3.1):

$$p = \frac{C_D V^2}{1000} \qquad \text{(Eq. 3.8)}$$

where p = pressure of flowing water (ksf)
V = velocity of water (ft/s)
C_D = drag coefficient for piers (see sidebar)

AASHTO STANDARD

3.18.2.2.1 INCLINATION OF NOSE

The coefficient C_n varies depending on the inclination of the nose to vertical (i.e., the pier nose angle in the vertical plane). Pier noses are often equipped with a steel angle or similar device raked at an angle to act as an ice breaker.

0 to 15 degrees:	$C_n = 1.00$
15 to 30 degrees:	$C_n = 0.75$
30 to 45 degrees:	$C_n = 0.50$

When the stream flow and the pier have a skew angle θ, the lateral water pressure is (AASHTO LRFD 3.7.3.2):

$$p = \frac{C_L V^2}{1000} \qquad \text{(Eq. 3.9)}$$

where p = lateral water pressure of flowing (ksf)
V = velocity of water (ft/s)
C_L = lateral drag coefficient for piers (see sidebar)

Ice Load. In cold weather climates highway bridges can suffer severe damage from ice floes and ice sheets impacting substructure and from static pressure due to thermal movements of ice sheets. In the case of low clearance bridges, superstructure elements may also be subjected to the ice load. The magnitude of this loading condition is dependent on the characteristics of the ice mass and the exposed surface of the pier it comes in contact with.

In AASHTO Standard Specifications, the horizontal force due to moving ice is calculated as (AASHTO 3.18.2.2):

$$F = C_n p t_w \qquad \text{(Eq. 3.10)}$$

where F = horizontal ice force acting on pier, lb
C_n = nose inclination coefficient (see sidebar)
p = effective ice strength, lb/in^2 (see sidebar)
t = thickness of ice in contact with pier, in
w = width of pier or diameter of circular shaft pier at the level of ice action, in

In the AASHTO LRFD Specifications, the horizontal force F due to moving ice is taken as (AASHTO LRFD 3.9.2.2):

$$F = \text{smaller of } F_c \text{ and } F_b \qquad \text{if } \frac{w}{t} \le 6.0 \qquad \text{(Eq. 3.11a)}$$

$$F = F_c \qquad \text{if } \frac{w}{t} > 6.0 \qquad \text{(Eq. 3.11b)}$$

where F = horizontal ice force acting on pier, kip

$$F_c = C_a \cdot p t w \qquad \text{(Eq. 3.11c)}$$

$$F_b = C_n p t^2 \qquad \text{(Eq. 3.11d)}$$

$$C_a = \left(5 \frac{t}{w} + 1 \right)^{0.5} \qquad \text{(Eq. 3.11e)}$$

$$C_n = \frac{0.5}{\tan(\alpha - 15)} \qquad \text{(Eq. 3.11f)}$$

where p = effective ice crushing strength in ksf (see sidebar)
t = thickness of ice in feet
α = inclination of nose to the vertical in degrees
w = width of pier at level of ice action in feet
F_c = horizontal force caused ice flows that fail by crushing over the full width of the pier (kip)

ICE STRENGTH
AASHTO STANDARD 3.18.2.2.3
AASHTO LRFD 3.9.2.1

The effective ice strength is dependent on a variety of factors including the temperature of the ice mass at the time of movement and the size of moving ice pieces. Listed below are AASHTO's general guidelines on selecting the effective ice strength. In general, the lower the temperature the ice moves at, the more damage it can do to a pier or other bridge component it comes in contact with.

$p = 100$ lb/in^2 (AASHTO STANDARD)
$p = 8$ ksf (AASHTO LRFD)
Ice breaks apart at the melting temperature. Ice pieces are disintegrated and move as small cakes.

$p = 200$ lb/in^2 (AASHTO STANDARD)
$p = 16$ ksf (AASHTO LRFD)
Ice breaks apart at the melting temperature. Ice pieces are solid and move as large pieces.

$p = 300$ lb/in^2 (AASHTO STANDARD)
$p = 24$ ksf (AASHTO LRFD)
When breaking apart, the ice moves in large, solid sheets which may impact with the pier.

$p = 400$ lb/in^2 (AASHTO STANDARD)
$p = 32$ ksf (AASHTO LRFD)
Ice breaks apart or moves at a temperature well below the melting temperature.

F_b = horizontal force caused by ice floes that fail by flexure as they ride up the inclined pier nose (kip)

C_a = coefficient accounting for the effect of the pier width/ice thickness ratio where the floe fails by crushing

C_n = Coefficient accounting for the inclination of the pier nose with respect to a vertical

If α <15, ice failure by flexure is not possible. So $F = F_c$.

The thickness of the ice which is in contact with the pier must be determined from local records for the given water channel. On small streams where large ice floes are unlikely, up to a 50 percent reduction of forces F_b and F_c may be considered (AASHTO LRFD 3.9.2.3).

It is also possible for the entire pier to become frozen in ice. Sometimes the pier may be subjected to force due to significant thermal movement of the ice. This typically occurs in a large water body, and should warrant special attention by the designer.

The frazil accumulation in a hanging dam may cause a pressure of 0.2 to 2.0 ksf on piers. An ice jam may cause a pressure of 0.02 to 0.2 ksf on piers (AASHTO LRFD 3.9.4).

The vertical force due to ice adhesion (due to rapid water level fluctuation) can be taken as:

$$F_v = 80.0t^2\left(0.35 + 0.03\frac{R}{t^{0.75}}\right) \quad \text{for a circular pier} \quad \text{(Eq. 3.12)}$$

$$F_v = 0.2t^{1.25}L + 80.0t^2\left(0.35 + 0.03\frac{R}{t^{0.75}}\right) \quad \text{for an oblong pier} \quad \text{(Eq. 3.13)}$$

where F_v = vertical force due to ice adhesion, kips

R = radius of pier or circular ends of an oblong pier, ft

L = perimeter of pier, excluding half circles at ends of oblong pier, ft

Buoyancy. Bridges with components (e.g., piers) which are submerged underwater can sometimes suffer from the effects of buoyancy. This is generally a problem only for very large hollow structures. Buoyance may produce an uplifting force on pier footings and piles.

A s a truck brakes, the load of the vehicle is transferred from the truck wheels to the bridge deck.

5. Longitudinal Forces. Longitudinal forces is also called Braking Force in AASHTO LRFD Specifications. As a truck brakes, the load of the vehicle is transferred from the truck wheels to the bridge deck. AASHTO Standard Specifications specifies that 5 percent of the appropriate lane load along with the concentrated force for moment, as shown in Fig. 3.13, to be used as the resulting longitudinal force (AASHTO 3.9). AASHTO LRFD specifies the breaking force as the greater of 5 percent of design truck plus lane load, or 5 percent of design tandem plus lane load, or 25 percent of the axle weights of the design truck or design tandem (AASHTO LRFD 3.6.4).

This force is applied 6 ft (1.8 m) above the top of deck surface. All travel lanes are assumed going in the same direction. The effect of longitudinal forces (breaking force) on the superstructure is inconsequential. Substructure elements, however, are affected more significantly. Like longitudinal earthquake forces, the breaking force is resisted by the piers and/or abutments which support fixed bearings.

6. Centrifugal Forces. For structures on horizontal curves, the effect of centrifugal force must be calculated. Like longitudinal loading, centrifugal loading simulates a vehicle traveling along the bridge and, in this instance, following a curvilinear path. The force is applied 6 ft (1.8 m) above the top of deck surface and is defined as (AASHTO 3.10):

$$C = 0.00117 \cdot S^2 D = \frac{6.68 \cdot S^2}{R}$$ (Eq. 3.14)

where C = centrifugal force, percent of live load without impact
S = design speed, mph
D = degree of curve
R = radius of curve, ft

Rather than an actual force, the value C above is a percentage, similar to the 5 percent for longitudinal forces, which is applied to the live load on the structure. This percentage, multiplied by the live load, yields the force to be applied 6 ft over the deck surface. Unlike longitudinal forces, though, centrifugal forces are computed using the truck loading rather than the lane loading. One standard design truck is placed in each design traffic lane such that maximum forces in the bridge are generated.

Decks that are attached to the superstructure primary members (e.g., a composite concrete deck integrated with steel girders using shear connectors) transmit centrifugal forces to substructure elements through secondary members and bearings at piers and abutments.

7. Impact (Dynamic Load Allowance). In order to account for the dynamic effects of a vehicle riding over a structure, an impact factor is used as a multiplier for certain structural elements. From basic dynamics, we know that a load that moves across a member introduces larger stresses than one statically placed on it. While the actual modeling of this effect can be a complex affair, the impact factor used by AASHTO allows for a conservative idealization of the problem. AASHTO Standard Specification defines the impact factor as follows (AASHTO 3.8.2):

$$I = \frac{50}{L + 125}$$ (Eq. 3.15)

where I = impact fraction (not to exceed 30 percent)
L = length of span loaded to create maximum stress, ft (See side bar)

AASHTO STANDARD

3.8.1 WHERE IMPACT APPLIES

The impact factor is applied only to certain elements and components. Group A elements include the impact factor. Group B elements do not.

**GROUP A
IMPACT INCLUDED**

SUPERSTRUCTURE
PIERS
All features above the ground level.
MISCELLANEOUS SUPPORTS
Portion of concrete or steel piles above the ground level.

**GROUP B
IMPACT NOT INCLUDED**

ABUTMENTS
FOUNDATIONS
TIMBER STRUCTURES
SIDEWALK LOADS
CULVERTS
With 3 ft (0.9 m) or greater of cover.

> **U**nlike longitudinal forces, though, centrifugal forces are computed using the truck loading rather than the lane loading.

3.8.2.2 THE LOADED LENGTH

The loaded length L varies depending on the element being analyzed. When calculating the impact factor, the following lists AASHTO's specification for certain members and calculations.

ROADWAY FLOORS

Design span length.

TRANSVERSE MEMBERS

Span length of member from center to center of supports (e.g., a floor beam).

TRUCK LOAD MOMENT

Design span length. For cantilever arms use length from moment center to farthest axle.

TRUCK LOAD SHEAR

Length of loaded portion of span from point of analysis to farthest reaction. For cantilever arms use I = 0.30.

CONTINUOUS SPANS

Length of span being analyzed for positive moment and the average of two adjacent spans loaded for negative moment.

I t is possible that, during the erection of a structure, various members come under loading conditions which are induced by construction equipment or other types of loads.

Live load forces are then multiplied by this factor. The reader should note that this is a factor which *increases* live load values. So, for example, a span which is 55 ft long would yield an impact *fraction* of 0.28 and an impact *multiplier* of 1.28. As stated by AASHTO Standard Specification, the value cannot exceed 0.30. This means that, for any values of L less than or equal to 41.7 ft (12.7 m), I will always be 0.30. In addition to the dynamic response of the bridge as a whole to passing vehicles, the impact factor is also designed to take into account the effects of a vehicle vibrating and striking imperfections (e.g., pot holes) in the deck.

As mentioned above, the impact factor applies only for certain elements which AASHTO Standard Specifications classifies as Group A and Group B. A listing of the applicable components is provided in the sidebar of the facing page. The length of span loaded L also varies depending on the type of element being analyzed (see sidebar this page).

AASHTO LRFD specifies the impact as 15% for fatigue and fracture limit states, and 33% for all other limit states. For deck joints, a 75% impact shall be used for all limit states. For buried structures such as culverts with 8 ft or more soil on top, the impact is taken as zero. If a structure is buried with less than 8 feet soil, linear interpretation can be used to calculate the live load impact (AASHTO LRFD 3.6.2.2). The impact shall only apply to the truck or tandem portion of the live load. No impact should be applied to the lane load (AASHTO LRFD 3.6.2). Similar to the Standard Specifications, no impact should be applied to timber structures or foundations.

8. Construction Loads. It is possible that during the erection of a structure, various members will come under loading conditions which are induced by construction equipment or other types of loads. In situations where this is foreseen during the design process (as in a staged construction or a segmental construction), the designer should take such additional loads into account and present any necessary bracing or support structures on the plans. In other instances, loads are introduced by a method of construction preferred by the contractor. In this case, the contractor should provide for all necessary strengthening of members or support structures. These measures should be submitted by a licensed professional engineer working for the contractor, and reviewed and accepted by the owner.

3.5.4 Deformation and Response Loads

Deformation loads are those loads induced by the internal or external change in material properties or member geometry. Because many bridges have structural redundancies, the effects of deformations such as support settlement, creep and shrinkage in concrete induce stresses on a member outside of conventional dead and live loading. Response loads are those loads created by the response of the structure to a given loading condition. Uplift is an example of a response load. The following is a discussion of some of the principal deformation and response loads found in bridge construction.

1. **Creep.** Creep is the deformation of concrete caused by loads sustained over a period of time. When a concrete member is initially loaded, it undergoes an instantaneous strain and related deformation. If the load is sustained over a period of time (as in a deck resting on concrete girders), a creep strain, roughly 1.5 to 3 times the magnitude of the instantaneous strain, will be induced.

Figure 3.16 shows a comparison of instantaneous to creep strain in the form of a stress-strain diagram. When constructing a concrete element, rather than introducing loads instantaneously, they are instead placed gradually on the member. When this approach is taken, the creep and instantaneous deformations are introduced concurrently.

The major factor which affects creep is the maturity of the concrete when the loads are applied. The earlier the concrete is subjected to permanent loading, the larger the creep is. Therefore, it is preferable to wait until concrete reaches a certain strength before applying loads to it.

Other factors such as humidity of air and the water/cement ratio of the concrete also affect the magnitude of the creep.

With respect to highway bridges, creep can cause changes in the physical length of concrete members. This deformation can lead to problems with bearing alignment and superstructure stability. The ACI Code instructs designers to make a "realistic assessment" of the effects of creep [Ref. 3.19]. This *assessment* is taken into account when computing the ultimate deformation of a concrete structure.

2. **Shrinkage.** Although creep is related to shrinkage, the two types of deformation are separate phenomena. Shrinkage is the natural change in

> **I**f the load is sustained over a period of time ... a creep strain, roughly 1.5 to 3 times the magnitude of the instantaneous strain, will be induced.

CREEP DEFORMATIONS taking place in the elastic range are approximately proportional to the applied stress. Once any member is loaded, it deforms elastically. Concrete, however, will continue to deform over an extended period of time. One way of counteracting the effects of creep is to simply use a higher strength concrete with low water/cement ratio.

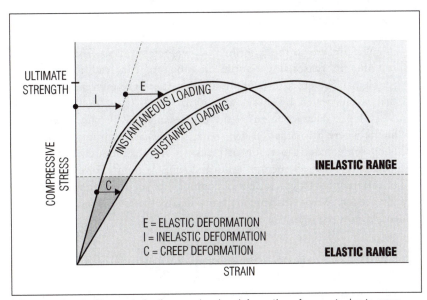

Figure 3.16 Stress-strain diagram showing deformation of concrete due to creep.

DID YOU KNOW

THAT because of the long time it takes for structures to settle, the settlement of structures was once considered to be a phenomenon of an unknown, if not, strange nature? The first successful attempt to define settlement was made in 1919 by the recognized father of modern soil mechanics, Karl Terzaghi (1883–1963) [Ref. 3.20].

volume of concrete. *Natural* implies a change which is not related to loading of a member. When shrinkage takes place, the concrete volume generally decreases (shrinks). This is usually caused by a moisture loss while drying. Therefore, like creep, shrinkage is sensitive to the water/cement ratio of the concrete, and the humidity condition of the air.

Shrinkage and creep take place at the same time and independently. They have similar effect to the structure. Reinforcement is added perpendicular to the main reinforcement to account for tensile stresses induced by shrinkage (see also Part 5, Thermal Forces). Another way of limiting the effects of shrinkage is for the contractor in the field to make sure that the concrete is properly cured. To ensure shrinkage is minimized during the curing process, the contractor must first use concrete that possesses a minimum amount of water necessary for workability and strength. The concrete should then be kept moist during curing, allowing for a slow cure that will minimize contraction of the concrete. There is no way of completely eliminating shrinkage, but proper attention will limit its effects.

If not properly controlled, shrinkage can lead to cracking in conventional concrete elements. In prestressed concrete, shrinkage can normally lead to a loss of prestress force in a member.

3. **Settlement.** The downward movement of a footing, approach pavement, or structure due to deformations of the supporting soil or piles is known as settlement. Settlement can be initiated by a number of factors which include, but are not limited to:

❏ Overloading the supporting soil or piles
❏ Lowering the water table for spread footings or friction piles
❏ Vibrations from live loads or seismic loads
❏ Loading embankments
❏ Changes in soil properties

With regard to the latter item above, the shrinkage and swelling of soil due to seasonal variations in moisture can lead to settlement problems. Therefore, it is important that footings be located at a depth that is unaffected by these fluctuations.

Of particular concern to the bridge engineer are *differential* settlements where a foundation will move downward in an uneven fashion. Such settlements can result in cracking of substructure elements and instability at superstructure joints and support points. In extreme cases of differential settlement, entire components such as abutments can be tilted over. When settlement occurs in a consistent or *uniform* fashion the effects are often less severe.

Of particular concern to the bridge engineer are differential settlements where a foundation will move downward in an uneven fashion. Such settlements can result in cracking of substructure elements and instability at ... support points.

4. **Uplift.** For a continuous span structure, different loads can combine in such a fashion that results in the superstructure being lifted upward from the substructure supports. Such a phenomenon is known as uplift. When uplift is possible, AASHTO requires that superstructures be designed with appropriate superstructure restraining measures (tension ties) (AASHTO 3.17). Uplift

typically occurs in continuous span bridges with widely varying adjacent span lengths (e.g., a long span next to a short end span).

5. Thermal Forces. The effects of thermal forces on a structure are significant and should not be underestimated by the designer. In general, thermal forces are caused by fluctuations in temperature (i.e., from hot to cold or cold to hot) and caused by the structural redundances or bearing failures. AASHTO Standard Specifications provides recommended temperature ranges for the design of metal and concrete structures (AASHTO 3.16). A table showing these values is presented in the sidebar on this page.

In AASHTO LRFD, the change in temperature is dependent on the location of the bridge site, as well as the superstructure material. The ranges of temperature may be obtained from the table in the sidebar. Once the construction temperature is assumed, the designer can determine maximum temperature rise and fall (AASHTO LRFD 3.12.2).

Like the adverse effects which result from uneven settlement, structures can suffer from uneven temperature distribution. This means that, if one side of a structure is continually exposed to the sun while the other side is shaded, the differential in temperature can cause high thermal forces. These forces generally have the most impact on bearings and deck joints.

Bridge engineers should pay close attention to the effects of thermal forces on bridges with a skew. As mentioned in Section 3.4.3, bridges on a skew must allow for both longitudinal and transverse movement. Excessive movement due to temperature changes should be accounted for in the design of all deck joints. Pin and hanger type connections are also susceptible to thermal forces. A design consideration for large concrete structures, such as segmental box girders, is the differential in temperature between the outside surface and enclosed, hollow interior of the structure.

A change in temperature can also affect concrete in a manner similar to shrinkage. When there is a decrease in temperature compared to the temperature when the concrete element was poured, a deformation similar to that found in shrinkage (discussed in Part 2 above) takes place. When the concrete contracts, *thermal stresses* are introduced into the element if the thermal movement is restricted (due to structural redundancy or bearing failure).

Temperature stresses may be tensile or compressive stresses depending on if the temperature is reducing or increasing. Since concrete is deficient in handling tension, tensile stresses are likely to cause cracks to form. To account for this, added reinforcement is provided in the concrete element. This reinforcement, known as temperature reinforcement, is laid orthogonally to the main reinforcement.

Extreme drops in temperature can also affect steel structures. A rapid change to extremely cold temperatures can lead to a phenomenon known as brittle fracture. Brittle fracture is the sudden failure of a steel member prior to plastic deformation. That is, instead of bending in a ductile fashion, as steel normally does, the member suffers an instantaneous, and often fatal, failure. While there are other factors such as fatigue which can lead to brittle fracture, the effects of sudden temperature fluctuations cannot be ignored.

GROUP	γ	β Factors													
		D	$(L+I)_n$	$(L+I)_p$	CF	E	B	SF	W	WL	LF	R+S+T	EQ	ICE	%
WORKING STRESS DESIGN															
I	1.0	1	1	0	1	β_E	1	1	0	0	0	0	0	0	100
IA	1.0	1	2	0	0	0	0	0	0	0	0	0	0	0	150
IB	1.0	1	0	1	1	β_E	1	1	0	0	0	0	0	0	**
II	1.0	1	0	0	0	1	1	1	1	0	0	0	0	0	125
III	1.0	1	1	0	1	β_E	1	1	0.3	1	1	0	0	0	125
IV	1.0	1	1	0	1	β_E	1	1	0	0	0	1	0	0	125
V	1.0	1	0	0	0	1	1	1	1	0	0	1	0	0	140
VI	1.0	1	1	0	1	β_E	1	1	0.3	1	1	1	0	0	140
VII	1.0	1	0	0	0	1	1	1	0	0	0	0	1	0	133
VIII	1.0	1	1	0	1	1	1	1	0	0	0	0	0	1	140
IX	1.0	1	0	0	0	1	1	1	1	0	0	0	0	1	150
X	1.0	1	1	0	0	β_E	0	0	0	0	0	0	0	0	100
LOAD FACTOR DESIGN															
I	1.3	β_D	1.67*	0	1.0	β_E	1	1	0	0	0	0	0	0	NOT APPLICABLE
IA	1.3	β_D	2.20	0	0	0	0	0	0	0	0	0	0	0	
IB	1.3	β_D	0	1	1.0	β_E	1	1	0	0	0	0	0	0	
II	1.3	β_D	0	0	0	β_E	1	1	1	0	0	0	0	0	
III	1.3	β_D	1	0	1	β_E	1	1	0.3	1	1	0	0	0	
IV	1.3	β_D	1	0	1	β_E	1	1	0	0	0	1	0	0	
V	1.25	β_D	0	0	0	β_E	1	1	1	0	0	1	0	0	
VI	1.25	β_D	1	0	1	β_E	1	1	0.3	1	1	1	0	0	
VII	1.3	β_D	0	0	0	β_E	1	1	0	0	0	0	1	0	
VIII	1.3	β_D	1	0	1	β_E	1	1	0	0	0	0	0	1	
IX	1.20	β_D	0	0	0	β_E	1	1	1	0	0	0	0	1	
X	1.30	1	1.67	0	0	β_E	0	0	0	0	0	0	0	0	

Table 3.2 Group Loading Coefficients and Load Factors (*AASHTO Standard Specifications*)

AASHTO STANDARD

3.22.1 NOTES ON TABLE OF COEFFICIENTS AND FACTORS

$(L+I)_n$: Live load plus impact for AASHTO H or HS loading.

$(L+I)_p$: Live load plus impact consistent with owner's overload criteria.

(CONTINUED ON NEXT PAGE)

3.5.5 Group Loading Combinations

Unlike an action movie where villains conveniently attack the hero one at a time, loads do not conveniently act individually but rather in various combinations. That is, vehicle live load could be on a bridge at the same time wind forces and stream forces are applied. The bridge engineer must design a bridge such that it can handle plausible groupings of loads which are placed on a bridge simultaneously. But on the other hand, the probability of all worst loads acting on the structure simultaneously is very small, so engineers should not simply add all the worst case loads together to design a bridge.

β	LOAD	VALUE	ELEMENT
β_E	Earth Pressure	1.15	Lateral at-rest earth pressure.
β_E	Earth Pressure	1.3	Lateral earth pressure for retaining walls and rigid frames excluding rigid culverts.
β_E	Earth Pressure	0.5	Lateral earth pressure when checking positive moments in rigid frames.
β_E	Earth Pressure	1.0	Rigid culverts.
β_E	Earth Pressure	1.5	Flexible culverts.
β_E	Dead Load	0.75	Columns, when checking member for minimum axial load and maximum moment or maximum eccentricity.
β_E	Dead Load	1.0	Columns, when checking member for maximum axial load and minimum moment.
β_E	Dead Load	1.0	Flexural and tension members.

Table 3.3 Earth Pressure and Dead Load Coefficients for Load Factor Design

3.22.1 NOTES ON TABLE OF COEFFICIENTS AND FACTORS (CONTINUED)

Group X:
Pertains to culverts.

Wind Load:
If member or connection carries only wind load, then no increase in allowable stress is allowed.

* NOTE:
For outside roadway girders, if the governing load combination is

Sidewalk Live Load + Traffic Live Load with Impact

use

$\beta = 1.25$

The capacity of the section *should not be less than*

Traffic Live Load with Impact

with

$\beta = 1.67$

** NOTE:
Compute the increase in the normal allowable stress to be

$$\% = \frac{\text{Maximum Unit Stress}}{\text{Allowable Basic Unit Stress}} \times 100$$

% COLUMN:
For working stress design method is the percent increase of the basic unit stress.

To account for this, AASHTO developed a set of loading combinations which are divided into various *groups*. These groups represent probable occurring combinations of loads on a structure. All structural components should be designed to withstand all load groups. Different expressions have been used by AASHTO Standard Specifications and AASHTO LRFD Specifications to reflect the difference in their design philosophies.

1. AASHTO Standard Specifications. The general equation used to define a group load is given by

$$Group_N = \gamma \cdot \begin{bmatrix} \beta_D \cdot D + \beta_L \cdot (L+I) + \beta_C \cdot CF + \beta_E \cdot E + \beta_B \cdot B \\ + \beta_S \cdot SF + \beta_W \cdot W + \beta_{WL} \cdot WL + \beta_L \cdot LF \\ + \beta_R \cdot (R+S+T) + \beta_{EQ} \cdot EQ + \beta_{ICE} \cdot ICE \end{bmatrix} \qquad \text{(Eq. 3.16)}$$

where N = group number
γ = load factor
β = coefficient

AASHTO STANDARD

3.22 GROUP LOAD VARIABLES

The AASHTO group loading combinations are broken down by types of loads. These load types have been detailed throughout Section 3.5. The following lists the coefficient subscript convention used in Equation 3.16 and Table 3.2.

D = Dead Load
L = Live Load
I = Live Load Impact
E = Earth Pressure
B = Buoyancy
W = Wind Load on Structure
WL = Wind Load on Live Load 100 lb/ft (1.46 kN/m)
LF = Longitudinal Force from Live Load
CF = Centrifugal Force
R = Rib Shortening for Arches or Frames
S = Shrinkage
T = Temperature
EQ = Earthquake
SF = Stream Flow Pressure
ICE = Ice Pressure

A ASHTO LRFD is a probability-based design method. The philosophy is to have a relative constant probability of structural failure for all structures and elements...

The subscript values in Equation 3.16 represent different types of loads. A listing of the various load variables is presented in the sidebar. AASHTO Standard Specifications presents values for γ and β based on the working stress (service load) and load factor (limit state) design methods (see Section 3.6). These values are illustrated in Table 3.2.

The coefficient β varies based on the type of load. The load factor γ is unity for all working stress groupings and varies, naturally, only for load factor design groupings. The last column of the Table 3.2 gives a specified increase of allowable stresses for the working stress design method. For example, the Group II allowable stress would be 125 percent, or 1.25 times the normal allowable stress. This increase is intended to take into account the improbability of peak values of each type of loading taking place at exactly the same time. Allowable stress values will vary depending on individual components and elements. The reader should consult the specific sections for these values.

From Table 3.2 it is clear that the β coefficients for earth pressure and dead load vary somewhat depending on the load group and design method. This variation results from different values being applicable for different types of elements or components (e.g., columns, rigid frames). Table 3.3 provides a description of the various coefficient values to be used for the design of different bridge elements.

The reader should note that the AASHTO specifications reference various load groups throughout the code. An example of this would be for overload provisions. The AASHTO code accounts for the infrequent overloading of a structure, for example, by a truck carrying excessively heavy equipment (AASHTO 3.5). In doing so certain load groups are identified for use to ensure appropriate loading conditions.

The sidebars on each of these facing pages contain notes and special considerations with regard to the group combinations. By inspection, it should be evident to the reader that it is not necessary to physically calculate every single load group. While the AASHTO specifications call for the structure to be able to withstand all loading combinations, in most structures only a few load groups will govern and therefore require calculation and incorporation into the final design report.

Another important item to note is that different load groups govern for different structural elements. Some members, in this respect, will require a closer investigation than others to determine the controlling load combination group.

The load factors given for the load factor design method represent values for the majority of highway bridges in use. Large or specialized structures may warrant the designer increasing the values to accommodate certain bridge specific design criteria which the conventional load factors were not structured to handle. In this instance, AASHTO leaves definition of the load factors to the "engineer's judgment" (AASHTO 3.22.4).

2. AASHTO LRFD Specifications. AASHTO LRFD is a probability-based design method. The philosophy is to have a relative constant probability of structural failure for all structures and elements during their design lives regardless of their types, geometry, materials, or construction

AASHTO LRFD LOAD COMBINATION AND LOAD FACTORS													
Load Combination Limit State	DC DD DW EH EV ES EL	LL IM CE BR PL LS	WA	WS	WL	FR	TU CR SH	TG	SE	EQ	IC	CT	CV
STRENGTH I (unless noted)	γ_P	1.75	1.00	--	--	1.00	0.50/1.20	γ_{TG}	γ_{SE}	--	--	--	--
STRENGTH II	γ_P	1.35	1.00	--	--	1.00	0.50/1.20	γ_{TG}	γ_{SE}	--	--	--	--
STRENGTH III	γ_P	--	1.00	1.40	--	1.00	0.50/1.20	γ_{TG}	γ_{SE}	--	--	--	--
STRENGTH IV EH, EV, ES, DW DC ONLY	γ_P 1.50	--	1.00	--	--	1	0.50/1.20	--	--	--	--	--	--
STRENGTH V	γ_P	1.35	1.00	0.40	1.00	1.00	0.50/1.20	γ_{TG}	γ_{SE}	--	--	--	--
EXTREME EVENT I	γ_P	γ_{EQ}	1.00	--	--	1.00	--	--	--	1.00	--	--	--
EXTREME EVENT II	γ_P	0.50	1.00	--	--	1.00	--	--	--	--	1.00	1.00	1.00
SERVICE I	1.00	1.00	1.00	0.30	1.00	1.00	1.00/1.20	γ_{TG}	γ_{SE}	--	--	--	--
SERVICE II	1.00	1.30	1.00	--	--	1.00	1.00/1.20	--	--	--	--	--	--
SERVICE III	1.00	0.80	1.00	--	--	1.00	1.00/1.20	γ_{TG}	γ_{SE}	--	--	--	--
SERVICE IV	1.00	--	1.00	0.70	--	1.00	1.00/1.20	--	1.00	--	--	--	--
FATIGUE - LL, IM & CE ONLY	--	0.75	--	--	--	--	--	--	--	--	--	--	--

Table 3.4 LRFD Load combinations and load factors.

Type of Load	Load Factor	
	Maximum	Minimum
DC	1.25	0.90
DD	1.80	0.45
DW	1.50	0.65
EH:		
Active	1.50	0.90
At-rest	1.35	0.90
EL	1.00	1.00
EV:		
Overall Stability	1.00	N/A
Retaining walls and abutments	1.35	1.00
Rigid buried structures	1.30	0.90
Rigid Frames	1.35	0.90
Flexible buried structures other than metal box culverts	1.95	0.90
Flexible metal box culverts	1.50	0.90
ES	1.50	0.75

Table 3.5 AASHTO LRFD Load factors for permanent loads γ_p.

methods. The measure of safety of any structure member is a function of variability of loads and resistance. The bigger the variation of a load, the larger the load factor should be (i.e. load factor for live load should be larger than that of dead load). Also, the more uncertainly of a material's load

AASHTO LRFD

3.3.2 LOAD DESIGNATION

The following load designations are used in Table 3.4 for AASHTO LRFD load combinations.

Permanent Loads:

DD = Downdrag
DC = Dead load
DW = Dead load of wearing surface and utilities
EH = Horizontal earth pressure
EL = Force effects resulting from construction process, including secondary forces from post-tensioning
ES = Earth surcharge load
EV = Vertical earth fill load

Transient Loads:

BR = Vehicular braking force
CE = Vehicular centrifugal force
CR = Creep
CT = Vehicular collision force
CV = Vessel collision force
EQ = Earthquake
FR = Friction
IC = Ice load
IM = Vehicular dynamic load allowance
LL = Vehicular live load
LS = Live load surcharge
PL = Pedestrian live load
SE = Settlement
SH = Shrinkage
TG = Temperature gradient
TU = Uniform temperature change
WA = Water load and stream pressure
WL = Wind on live load
WS = Wind load on structure

> **S**trength I - This is a basic load combination relating to normal vehicular use of superstructure... Most superstructure members are controlled by this load combination.

resistance, the smaller resistance factor it should have, so that all materials will have similar factor of safety.

To achieve that design objective, strength limit states, service limit states, and fatigue limit states are checked for every structure member. Strength limit states are intended to ensure that structures have sufficient strength and stability under various load conditions. Service limit states are used to control deflection, crack width, stress level, and in some cases, stability under normal service conditions to ensure the structure's serviceability during its design life. Fatigue limit states are restrictions on stress range under service loading to prevent fatigue failure during the design life of the bridge.

Under each load combination, the total factored force effect should be taken as:

$$Q = \Sigma \eta_i \cdot \gamma_i Q_i \qquad \text{(Eq. 3.17)}$$

where η_i = load modifier, a factor relating to the structure's ductility, redundancy, and operational importance. For most bridges, $\eta_i = 1.0$ (AASHTO LRFD 1.3).
  γ_i = load factor, a statistically based multiplier for specific force effects under specific load combinations.
  Q_i = force effect from specific loads.

Each member and connection of a structure should satisfy the following limit states:

Strength I. This is a basic load combination relating to the normal vehicular use of the structure without wind or any extreme event loads such as earthquake. Most superstructure members are controlled by this load combination.

Strength II. This load combination is used for owner-specified special design vehicles or permit vehicles. Like Strength I load combination, no wind or any extreme event load need to be considered. Most bridges are designed for HL-93 live load, so this load combination is not commonly used. Note that if the owner-specified load is very heavy and the bridge is not subjected to such load regularly, the bridge may be controlled by escorts so that only one such vehicle is loaded on the bridge, while other lanes are assumed unoccupied so the bridge will be able to carry the load, but without being too much overdesigned.

Strength III. This load combination relates to the bridge being exposed to maximum wind velocity. Under such event, no live load is assumed to be present on the bridge.

Strength IV. This load combination is used for structures with very high dead to live load force effect ratios. It may become controlling load combination for certain structural elements if the structure has a short span length and/or a large dead load. The purpose of this load combination is to make sure that various types of bridges have a similar probability of failure.

Strength V. This load combination relates to normal vehicular use of the bridge with wind velocity of 55 mph (90 km/h). When live load and wind loads are combined, both values are reduced because the probability is very low for a structure to experience a very heavy live load and extremely high wind load.

Extreme Event I. This is a load combination related to earthquake. Note that live load shall be considered based on daily traffic volume of the bridge. For normal bridges, a live load factor of 0.5 may be used, which indicates a low probability of the presence of maximum live load at the time when a large earthquake may occur.

Extreme Event II. This load combination is used for extreme events such as ice load, collision by vessels and vehicles. Only one of such events should be considered at a time. Like in an earthquake event, only reduced live load need to be considered at these extreme events.

Service I. This load combination is used for normal operational use of the bridge with a 55 mph (90 km/h) wind. All loads are taken at their nominal values and extreme loads are excluded. This load combination is used to control deflection, crack width in reinforced concrete structures, compressive stress in prestressed concrete members, and soil slope stability.

Service II. This load combination is for preventing yielding of steel structures due to vehicular live load. The live load used in this load combination is approximately halfway between that used for service I and Strength I limit states.

Service III. This load combination relates only to tension in prestressed concrete superstructure. Researchers have found that if nominal design live load is used, the superstructure will be overdesigned for concrete tensile stress. Therefore, a load factor of 0.80 is applied to the live load in this load combination.

Service IV. This load combination relates only to tension in prestressed concrete substructure to control cracks. The 0.70 factor on wind represents a wind velocity of 84 mph (135 km/h), which reflects the probability that the prestressed concrete substructure will be subjected to a tensile stress once in every 10 years.

Fatigue. Fatigue and fracture load combination relates to repetitive gravitational vehicular live load and dynamic responses. The live load factor of 0.75 reflects a load level that represents the majority of truck population. Note that only a single truck with a constant spacing of 30 feet (9.1 m) between the 32 kip (142 kN) axles should be applied for this load combination (AASHTO LRFD 3.6.1.4.1).

3.6 DESIGN METHODS

In bridge engineering, there are two principal methods of design in use today. The names used to define these design methods vary depending on the structural material being used, the design code being referenced, or even the era of a publication. For the purposes of this text, we will classify the two design methods as

> In bridge engineering, there are two principal methods of design in use today.

❏ Working stress design
❏ Limit states design

For the most part of the last century, the working stress design approach was the standard by which bridges and other structural engineering projects were designed. By the 1970's, however, limit states design began to gain acceptance by the general engineering community. What are these two approaches to design and how do they differ? Is one better than the other? To answer these questions, it is first necessary to understand the concepts behind each approach. The following offers both a background and overview of these two design methods and how they apply to the design of structures in general and bridges in particular.

3.6.1 Working Stress Design

> **W**orking stress design is an approach in which structural members are designed so that unit stresses do not exceed a predefined allowable stress.

Working stress design is an approach in which structural members are designed so that unit stresses do not exceed a predefined allowable stress. The allowable stress is defined by a limiting stress divided by a factor of safety, so that, in general, working stress is expressed in the form of

$$f_{actual} \leq f_{allowable}$$

For a beam in bending, this actual stress would be defined by

$$f_{actual} = \frac{Mc}{I}$$

STEEL IS KNOWN AS an elastic material. That is, stress to strain is relatively proportional up to the yield point. This means that in the elastic range there is no permanent (plastic) deformation. As long as the stress (i.e., loading) is kept below the yield point, the strain will return to zero if the load is removed. If the strain does not return to zero, this means that a plastic deformation has occurred. Plastic deformation is not just a function of the magnitude of the stress applied but also the duration for which the load is placed. The effect of the former is known as slip and the latter as creep. The effect of the creep in concrete was discussed in Section 3.5.4, Part 1.

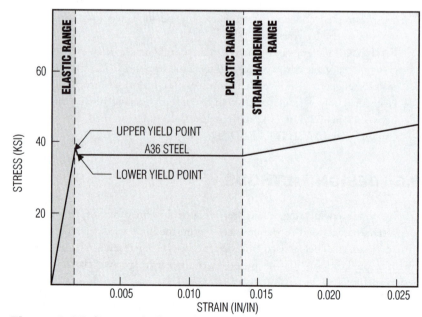

Figure 3.17 Stress-strain diagram for A36 steel in tension.

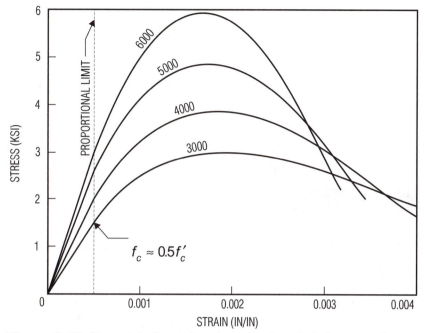

Figure 3.18 Stress-strain diagram for various concrete strengths in compression.

where M = maximum moment
c = distance to the neutral axis from the extreme fiber
I = moment of Inertia of the beam cross section

and the allowable stress could be given by:

$$f_{allowable} = \frac{f_y}{FS}$$

where f_y = minimum yield stress
FS = factor of safety

The allowable stress could also be defined by some other controlling criterion such as the buckling stress for steel, compressive strength of concrete, etc. Thus, the allowable stress can be thought of as a fraction of some failure stress for a given material like steel or concrete.

Under the working stress approach, the actual stresses are representative of stresses due to the service or working loads that a structure is supposed to carry. The entire structure is designed to fall well within the *elastic range* of the material the element or component is constructed with. When the strain, or deformation, of a material is proportional to the applied stress, the material is said to *behave elastically*. Figures 3.17 and 3.18 show stress-strain diagrams for steel and concrete, respectively. The point where a material ceases to behave elastically is defined as the *proportional limit* (i.e., stress and strain are no longer proportional and the stress-strain curve is no longer linear). Once stress and strain are no longer proportional, the material enters the *plastic range*.

> **U**nder the working stress approach, the actual stresses are representative of stresses due to the service or working loads that a structure is supposed to carry.

> This means that concrete elements, under the working stress approach, are designed at a level that is well below failure.

For elastic materials (i.e., materials that behave elastically up to their yield stress) such as steel, the working stress approach seemed to make a great deal of sense. Since, if a material is loaded passed the yield point, a permanent or *plastic deformation* will occur, the elastic range offers a known, safe region within which an engineer could confidently design structures. In addition to this, the load a member can carry prior to failure is easily measured. What of materials like concrete though? Figure 3.18 shows that, under compression, concrete only behaves elastically to a stress that is approximately one-half its compressive strength. That is, for concrete with a compressive strength of 3000 psi, the elastic range only goes up to about 1500 psi. This means that concrete elements, under the working stress approach, are designed at a level that is well below failure.

Another question mark for the working stress approach is the incorporation of factors of safety. While the allowable stress has, for all intents and purposes, a built in factor of safety, it is, however, fixed. This means that no matter how variable loads are, either in terms of frequency or magnitude, the factor of safety is always the same. These deficiencies led to the development of an alternative to the working stress design method based on the limit states of a material.

DESIGN PERSPECTIVE

Limit States Design— Concrete: Yes. Steel: Is Following.

What has taken so long to get engineers in the United States to move toward a limit states approach for the design of steel structures?

After all, since ACI released its 1971 edition of the concrete design code, the limit states approach has been the de facto norm for all concrete structures. Indeed, development and promulgation of the concrete limit states approach began in earnest as early as 1956. Steel, however, has been a relative new comer to the limit states arena.

The lack of a widely accepted limit states approach in steel can be attributed to a number of factors. First of all, it wasn't until 1986 when AISC first introduced the Load and Resistance Factor Design version of their *Manual for Steel Construction*. Even with this release, the code was tailored toward the design of building structures.

Another obstacle to overcome, for many engineers, was one that was not an issue when concrete design made the switch over to limit states in the 1970's. Computer software for steel design had already been tailored toward the working stress approach and, although LRFD versions were readily available, many designers seemed reluctant to upgrade, the school of thought being, "If it ain't broke, don't fix it" [Ref 3.23].

As time has progressed, however, the 1990's have seen a growth in the accepted use of limit states in steel bridges. The growing familiarity of designers with the nuances of limit states design, combined with the advent of such limit states approaches as the load factor design method and LRFD, have led to a growing use of this method in the design of steel highway bridges.

Perhaps the biggest factor which will spur the acceptance and use of a limit states approach, however, has been the instruction of it in civil engineering curriculums throughout the United States.

With the U.S. Federal Highway Administration's mandate to use LRFD to qualify federal funding, it will not take long before LRFD becomes the only bridge design code in the United States no matter what construction materials are used. That will also mean the end of the service load method anywhere in the world. It should be noted that both AISC and AASHTO have stopped providing revisions for the service load method design.

3.6.2 Limit States Design

The limit states design method was, in part, developed to address the drawbacks to the working stress approach mentioned above. This approach makes use of the plastic range for the design of structural members and incorporates load factors to take into account the inherit variability of loading configurations.

The quote from the *AISC Manual of Steel Construction* at the top of next page defines a limit state as a condition representing "structural usefulness." As mentioned previously, working stress design method suffered from the inability of the factor of safety to adequately address the variable nature of loading conditions. One of the advantages of the limit states approach is that it takes into account this variance by defining limit states which address *strength* and *serviceability*. The bridge designer can think of these terms in the following way:

❑ Strength is the limit state which defines the safe operation and adequacy of the structure. The criteria which are used to define this are yielding, ultimate strength, buckling, overturning, etc., under normal load conditions, or under extreme events.

❑ Serviceability is the limit state which defines the performance and behavior of the structure under nominal service loading. Some serviceability criteria are stress, fatigue, deflection, vibration, crack width, etc.

From the above, it is easy to see why limit states design codes, like those published by AISC and AASHTO, place a great deal of importance on the strength limit state, since this is the one that is concerned with "public safety for the life, limb and property of human beings" [Ref. 3.21]. This is why the strength limit state design is also often referred to as the *strength design*. Obviously, the limit states for strength will vary depending on the type of member being designed, its material properties, and the given loading condition.

Therefore, like working stress design, limit states design methods vary depending on the material being used and its related design specification. In general, though, we can define the limit states equation as

$$\text{Strength Provided} \geq \text{Strength Required} \qquad \text{(Eq. 3.18)}$$

The strength provided is defined by the specification applicable to the design of the member (e.g., ACI, AISC, AASHTO). The strength required is computed using applicable load combinations with appropriate load factors. This can be translated symbolically into an equation whose form is

$$\phi S_n \geq \Sigma \psi_i L_i \qquad \text{(Eq. 3.19)}$$

where ϕ = strength reduction factor pertaining to uncertainty of S_n
   S_n = nominal strength
   L_i = a service load acting on the member
   ψ_i = a load factor pertaining to uncertainty of L_i

Thus, the right half of Equation 3.19 represents the sum of individual loads, each multiplied by its specific load factor. See Table 3.4 and Table 3.5 for load combinations and the respective load factors for various type of loads used in the AASHTO LRFD Specifications.

3.6.3 Background and History

The development, application, and acceptance of a design methodology is not a trivial concern. Structural engineers spend four years at a university being educated in the general profession and specific disciplines. Another four

"A limit state is a condition which represents the limit of structural usefulness."

AISC LRFD CODE
[Ref. 3.21]

> Another question mark for the working stress approach is ... no matter how variable loads are, either in terms of frequency or magnitude, the factor of safety is always the same.

> One of the advantages of the limit states approach is that it takes into account this variance by defining limit states which address *strength* and *serviceability*.

> Perhaps the biggest factor which will spur the acceptance and use of a limit states approach, however, will be the instruction of it in civil engineering curriculums...

DID YOU KNOW

THAT in 1979 the Ontario Ministry of Transportation in Canada used the AASHTO specifications, but decided to develop their own code when vehicle loading was raised from 100,000 lb (445 kN) to 140,000 lb (623 kN)? After studying existing bridges within their province, ministry engineers determined that the structures had a significant reserve capacity. They also found that the bridges would fulfill limit states criteria. The new code was then developed around a limit states core [Ref. 3.22].

A ll of this educational effort is often built around a core design approach. One does not come by such an accumulation of expertise without a significant degree of plain, hard work.

U nlike concrete ... steel performs pretty much linearly right up to its yield point. This makes working stress better suited for steel than concrete.

T he important advantage ... with the limit states approach, ..., is the ability to "give proper weight to the degree of accuracy with which the various loads and resistances can be determined".

years are spent gaining experience and becoming licensed as a professional. Another decade or so could be invested afterward in the formulation of a specific expertise. All of this educational effort is often built around a core design approach. One does not come by such an accumulation of expertise without a significant degree of plain, hard work.

Then, all of a sudden, a designer can be faced with a radically new way of doing things. This was the case in 1971 for a great many structural engineers designing concrete structures. The working stress method was an accepted and proven way of building structures. No science, however, is static. Research and development initiated as early as the 1930's began investigating the ultimate strength of concrete beams. In 1963, the new release of the ACI Building Code (ACI 318-63) had a limit states approach published along with the traditional working stress approach [Ref. 3.5]. By 1971 the transformation was complete. Since then, for concrete structures, working stress design has been the *alternative* rather than the norm. The working stress design method was moved to an appendix in 1992. Since 2002, ACI Building Code (ACI318-02) has completely removed the working stress method from its publication.

Still, the progression toward a new approach is not an easy affair. Although concrete design has moved away from working stress, the design of steel structures still maintains a dual standards approach (see *Design Perspective*). The road that AISC took toward limit states, however, was somewhat different than that of ACI.

It would be easy, from a cursory review, to say that ACI was much more progressive than AISC in moving to limit states. As we discussed in Section 3.6.1, however, the elastic properties of steel are quite different from that of concrete. Unlike concrete, which reaches the proportional limit at only half its compressive strength, steel performs pretty much linearly right up to its yield point. This makes working stress better suited for steel than concrete. A comparison of Figures 3.17 and 3.18 illustrates why concrete professionals made a big push to refine the elastic design approach. Conversely, it also shows why steel professionals were in less of a hurry.

It should also be noted that, even though it was not until 1986 when AISC first issued its comprehensive limit states design specification, the working stress methodology was revised in 1978 to take into account the performance of steel at the limits states [Ref. 3.24]. The important advantage steel designers realize with the limit states approach, now codified in the AISC and AASHTO specifications, is the ability to "give proper weight to the degree of accuracy with which the various loads and resistances can be determined" [Ref. 3.21]. Although in theory AISC still has two sets of specifications, the working stress design specification has not been updated since 1986. It is being phased out when fewer and fewer structural engineers use the working stress design method.

Currently, there are two design specifications used in the United States. One is called AASHTO Standard Specifications, and the other is called AASHTO LRFD Specifications. In AASHTO Standard Specifications, both working stress design and load factor design (LFD) are used. LFD is also called strength design where service limit states are largely ignored.

Bridge engineers usually have less freedom to choose a design method than the building engineers. Each state requires bridges be designed with a specific design code and design method. Most bridges in the U.S. are currently designed using AASHTO LFD or LRFD methods. Although a few states are still using working stress design method, it will not be long before all bridges will be designed using LRFD method.

3.6.4 The Many Names of Working Stress and Limit States

At the top of Section 3.6, it was mentioned that the names by which working stress and limit states design were known varied "depending on the structural material being used, the design code being referenced, or even the era of publication." To someone new to the field, this statement may be a little confusing. As we will see, however, there exist about as many monikers for these two methods of design as there are organizations issuing design specifications. So far, throughout this section, the terms *working stress* and *limit states* have been intentionally used exclusive of any other labels. Where working stress and limit state describe the general (design method), the following terms reference the particular (design code).

Listed below are the principal names for working stress and limit states design the reader will come across in various bridge design–related specifications, publications, and literature.

1. **Allowable Stress Design.** For working stress design, AISC uses the designation "allowable stress design." The reader will also see this referred to by the acronym ASD. The design specifications for steel members are published in a separate, bound document which is titled *Manual for Steel Construction - Allowable Stress Design*. The ninth edition was published in 1986 and it is the last edition which will not be updated before it is phased out. The name is derived from the method's approach of designing for unit stresses which do not exceed an *allowable stress*.

> The name is derived from the method's approach of designing for unit stresses which do not exceed an *allowable stress*.

2. **Service Load Design.** AASHTO Standard Specifications calls working stress design the Service Load Design method in addition to referring to it as Allowable Stress Design. This reference is the same for both concrete and steel within that specifications. The reader will note, however, that the commentary also uses the term working stress. The name Service Load is taken from the unit stresses which are computed from the action of working or *service* loads which should not exceed the allowable stress.

3. **Load Factor Design.** In the standard Specifications, AASHTO uses the term in conjunction with the expression *strength design* (see below). It can be readily seen that the name comes from the factors applied to loads to compute the strength required of a member. AASHTO Standard Specifications currently provides both working stress and load factor methods. Typically the working stress code is presented first in a section. An entire topic is covered using working stress and then followed with a load factor design method, which is also known as LFD.

> AASHTO Standard Specifications currently provides both working stress and load factor methods.

4. **Strength Design.** ACI and AASHTO refer to load factor design method as *strength design*. Previous versions of the ACI code has used the

term *ultimate strength*. The vast majority of the ACI code is structured about this methodology. The name is derived from the general limit states equation which states that the *strength* provided must be greater than or equal to the *strength* required. The reader should note that the term strength design does not mean that a member actually yields or fails under loading conditions.

5. **Ultimate Strength.** Older versions of the ACI code referred to the limit states approach as the ultimate strength method. This was a reference to the strength provided as the ultimate strength. Since the term ultimate may denote a value which is impossible to reach, and was therefore somewhat misleading, ACI decided to remove the ultimate prefix.

6. **Load and Resistance Factor Design.** The designation for limit states design used by AISC and AASHTO is *load and resistance factor design*. This is often referred to by the acronym LRFD. In LRFD design specifications, structural members are designed to meet requirements of both strength and service limit states. The AASHTO LRFD design specification is published in separate documents to distinguish with the old specifications, and is becoming the mainstream design code.

> **A**ASHTO LRFD ... is becoming the mainstream design code.

3.7 INTERNAL FORCES

When a bridge is subjected to loads, as described in Section 3.5, its constituent elements develop internal forces which resist those loads. In general, the resisting forces take the form of

- ❏ Bending force
- ❏ Shear force

A SIMPLE SPAN, like the one shown in Figure 3.19, has longitudinal compression and tension as a result of bending. The stresses are greatest at the top and bottom *fibers*. The moments which create these types of stresses are called *positive moments*. For simple spans, the maximum moment is near the center of the span (depending on the type of loading). In continuous beam bridges, a condition arises in the girder where tension occurs at the top fiber and compression at the bottom fiber. When this happens, it is caused by *negative moment*.

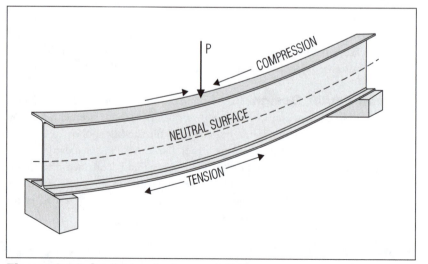

Figure 3.19 Bending in a simply supported beam.

❑   Torsional force
❑   Axial force

It is assumed that the reader has a basic understanding of statics and strength of materials so that the following discussion is intended to act simply as a refresher and offer an overview of how these internal forces affect bridge elements.

3.7.1   Bending Force

When a load is placed on a structural member as shown in Figure 3.19, the member will respond by bending. This bending is resisted by an internal rotational force or *moment*. These rotational forces are equal and opposite couples which act in a common plane. From basic statics, we know that a moment can be quantified as a force times a distance. Since the loads on bridges are relatively large, U.S. values are typically given as kip-ft where a kip is 1000 pounds force. The SI equivalent unit is kN-m. Stresses in a member that result from bending forces are referred to as bending stresses or sometimes as flexural (i.e., flexing) stresses.

In bridge design, primary members are the elements that are most affected by bending forces. Figure 3.19 shows a simply supported beam under bending. As the load acts downward, the girder resists by bending, the effects of which are compression (pushing in) at the top most part of the beam and tension (pulling out) at the bottom. It is at the top and bottom of the girder where stresses are the greatest. Stresses decrease to zero approaching the neutral surface of the girder.

3.7.2   Shear Force

A shear force will cause an internal force in a member which acts in the plane of the section. The shear stress will be referenced according to the particular plane in which it acts. In a wide flange girder, for example, vertical shear occurs in the beam cross section (i.e., the "I" shape) if the beam is loaded vertically. Horizontal shear acts along the length of a girder if the member is loaded longitudinally. One can visualize the effects of shear stress as one cross-sectional piece moving in one direction and another, adjacent cross-sectional piece moving in the opposite direction.

An internal shear force is induced by a load acting in the opposing direction. In a bridge, the greatest danger for shear occurs at supports where a load, combined with a beam reaction, can result in high shear stresses. From basic strength of materials, we know that average shearing stress is defined as the load divided by the resisting area. Taking a wide flange girder as an example, once again, vertical shear stress would be computed as the load divided by the beam web area.

3.7.3   Torsional Force

As discussed early in the sections covering steel and concrete box girders, torsion is a twisting about the longitudinal axis of a member. When

> **W**hen a load is placed on a structural member ... the member will respond by bending. This bending is resisted by an internal rotational force or *moment*.

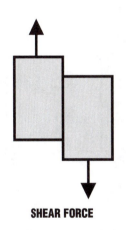

SHEAR FORCE

TYPICALLY, TORSION has an effect on beams which are weak on their minor axis. A torsional force, such as the one illustrated in Figure 3.20, can cause torsional buckling. Torsional buckling generally occurs at support points or concentrated load locations and is a function of both torsion and flexure. It is because of these torsional forces that secondary members such as channel diaphragms or cross frames are installed between girders in order to brace the primary members. Torsion can be introduced through wheel loads off the beam centerline or through wind loads.

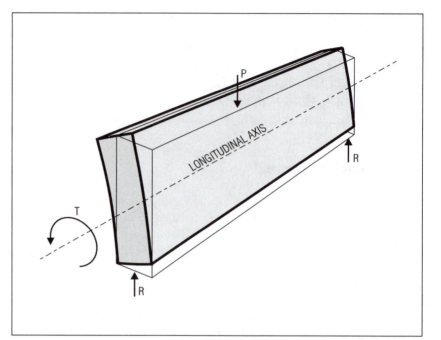

Figure 3.20 Torsion in a simply supported beam.

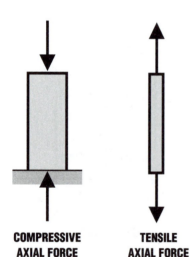

COMPRESSIVE AXIAL FORCE   **TENSILE AXIAL FORCE**

the effects of torsion are severe, box girder structures are used because of their ability to resist torsional forces. Torsional forces are caused by eccentric loads (i.e., loads which are not placed on the longitudinal neutral axis of the member).

In a highway bridge, torsional forces can result from wind forces, eccentric wheel loadings, or other overturning type loads. When a torsional force is applied to a member, the maximum stresses will occur at the outer face of the element.

3.7.4 Axial Force

An axial force is one which acts along the longitudinal axis of a member. Depending on the direction of the force, the axial force will induce either compression or tension. If the load is acting toward the member, it will be in compression, and if it acts away from the member, the member will be in tension. An example of an element under a compressive axial force would be a pier column. A tensile axial force would result in a cable, for example, of a suspension bridge.

3.8 LOAD DISTRIBUTION

So far, we have learned that bridge loads are transmitted from the deck to the superstructure and then to the supporting substructure elements. Exactly how are these loads transmitted though? If a truck is traveling over the top of a primary member, it is logical to say that this particular beam is resisting the truck load. This stringer, however, is connected to adjacent primary members through some form of secondary member (e.g., channel diaphragm, cross-frame). In addition to this, the bridge deck itself acts as a connection between longitudinal girders. This connectivity allows different members to work together in resisting loads.

Returning to the example of the truck traveling over the top of a specific primary member, it would be logical to assume that this specific girder is carrying most of the load. As a result of being connected with the girder in question, adjacent members assist in carrying *part* of the load. Exactly how much load they carry is a function of how the load is transmitted or *distributed* to them. Determining the fraction of load carried by a loaded member and the remainder distributed to other members is the focus of this discussion.

3.8.1 How Loads Are Distributed

The highway bridge, as mentioned previously, is not a collection of individual elements, each performing a specific function, but rather an integrated unit. The modeling of how a load is actually dispersed from the deck down through the substructure is not a trivial undertaking. A wide variety of parameters which range from the structure's geometry to element material properties influence exactly how loads are distributed.

Where defining a precise mathematical model of what happens to bridge loads in a structure is complicated, it is possible to examine the variables which influence the distribution. In essence, the influencing parameters are a function of the bridge superstructure cross-sectional properties. The following parameters determine how loads are distributed in a bridge superstructure. It should be kept in mind, however, that this is a general list and that other variables could potentially affect the distribution on loads. With this in mind, the influencing parameters are

- ❏ Type and depth of deck
- ❏ Span length
- ❏ Spacing between stringers
- ❏ Spacing of secondary members
- ❏ Stiffness of primary members
- ❏ Stiffness of secondary members
- ❏ Type of bracing employed (if any)
- ❏ Size and position of loads

As we have seen before with issues like the idealization of the dynamic effects of vehicle impact, in order to simplify the computation of load distribution, AASHTO Standard Specifications choose to utilize a distribution factor based on only two of the above referenced criteria: type of floor and stringer spacing. AASHTO LRFD Specifications, however, also considers the deck thickness, span length, and stringer stiffness. To account for the effects of load distribution, a load *distribution factor* (DF) is computed and applied to live load bending moments and shear forces.

Table 3.6 shows the AASHTO Standard Specifications wheel load distribution factors for various floor type and spacing configurations. Distribution will also vary depending on whether longitudinal or transverse

The modeling of how a load is actually dispersed from the deck down through the substructure is not a trivial undertaking. A wide variety of parameters ... influence exactly how loads are distributed.

...In order to simplify the computation of load distribution, AASHTO Standard Specifications chose to utilize a distribution factor based on only two ... criteria: type of floor and stringer spacing... AASHTO LRFD Specifications, however, also considers the deck thickness, span length, and stringer stiffness.

TYPE OF FLOOR	BRIDGE TRAFFIC LANES		NOTES
	ONE	TWO OR MORE	
TIMBER FLOOR			Dimensions are for nominal thickness.
Plank	$\dfrac{S}{4.0}$	$\dfrac{S}{3.75}$	Plank floors consist of lumber planks laid edge to edge with their wide face bearing on the supports.
Nail Laminated			Nail laminated floors consist of lumber pieces nailed together and laid face to face with their narrow edges bearing on the supports.
4" Thick or Multiple Layer Floors over 5" Thick	$\dfrac{S}{4.5}$	$\dfrac{S}{4.0}$	Multiple layer floors consist of two or more layers of lumber planks with each subsequent layer laid at an angle to the previous layer.
6" Thick or More	$\dfrac{S}{5.0}$ If **S** exceeds 5 ft, see note this row.	$\dfrac{S}{4.25}$ If **S** exceeds 6.5 ft, see note this row.	Assume the flooring between stringers acts as a simple beam with the load on each stringer being the wheel load reaction.
Glued Laminated Panels on Glued Laminated Stringers			Glued laminated floors consist of lumber pieces vertically glued laminated with their narrow edges bearing on the supports.
4" Thick	$\dfrac{S}{4.5}$	$\dfrac{S}{4.0}$	
6" Thick or More	$\dfrac{S}{6.0}$ If **S** exceeds 6 ft, see note this row.	$\dfrac{S}{5.0}$ If **S** exceeds 7.5 ft, see note this row.	Assume the flooring between stringers acts as a simple beam with the load on each stringer being the wheel load reaction.
On Steel Stringers			
4" Thick	$\dfrac{S}{4.5}$	$\dfrac{S}{4.0}$	
6" Thick or More	$\dfrac{S}{5.25}$ If **S** exceeds 5.5 ft, see note this row.	$\dfrac{S}{4.5}$ If **S** exceeds 7 ft, see note this row.	Assume the flooring between stringers acts as a simple beam with the load on each stringer being the wheel load reaction.
CONCRETE FLOOR			
On Steel I-Beam Stringers and Prestressed Concrete Girders	$\dfrac{S}{7.0}$ If **S** exceeds 10 ft, see note this row.	$\dfrac{S}{5.5}$ If **S** exceeds 14 ft, see note this row.	Assume the flooring between stringers acts as a simple beam with the load on each stringer being the wheel load reaction.
On Concrete T-Beams	$\dfrac{S}{6.5}$ If **S** exceeds 6 ft, see note this row.	$\dfrac{S}{6.0}$ If **S** exceeds 10 ft, see note this row.	Assume the flooring between stringers acts as a simple beam with the load on each stringer being the wheel load reaction.
On Timber Stringers	$\dfrac{S}{6.0}$ If **S** exceeds 6 ft, see note this row.	$\dfrac{S}{5.0}$ If **S** exceeds 10 ft, see note this row.	Assume the flooring between stringers acts as a simple beam with the load on each stringer being the wheel load reaction.
Concrete Box Girders	$\dfrac{S}{8.0}$ If **S** exceeds 12 ft, see note this row.	$\dfrac{S}{7.0}$ If **S** exceeds 16 ft, see note this row.	Assume the flooring between stringers acts as a simple beam ... as above. Omit sidewalk live load for interior and exterior girders designed with this criteria.
On Steel Box Girders	Find live load bending moment for each girder using: $$\text{FRACTION OF WHEEL LOAD} = 0.1 + 1.7R + 0.85/NW$$		$R = NW/\text{Number of Box Girders } (0.5 \le R \le 1.5)$ $NW = WC/12$ reduced to the nearest whole number $WC = $ Curb to curb or barrier to barrier width (feet)
On Prestressed Concrete Spread Box Beams	Find interior girder live load bending moment using: $$\text{FRACTION OF WHEEL LOAD} = (2NL/NB) + k(S/L)$$ For exterior girder assume flooring between stringers to act as a simple beam ... as above, but not less than $2NL/NB$.		$NL = $ Number of Design Traffic Lanes $NB = $ Number of Beams $(4 < NB < 10)$ $S = $ Beam Spacing $(6.57 < S < 11.00)$ (feet) $L = $ Span Length (feet); $W = $ Curb to Curb Width (feet) $k = 0.07W - NL(0.10NL - 0.26) - 0.20NB - 0.12$
STEEL GRID FLOOR			
Less than 4" Thick	$\dfrac{S}{4.5}$	$\dfrac{S}{4.0}$	
4" Thick or More	$\dfrac{S}{6.0}$ If **S** exceeds 6 ft, see note this row.	$\dfrac{S}{5.0}$ If **S** exceeds 10.5 ft, see note this row.	Assume the flooring between stringers acts as a simple beam with the load on each stringer being the wheel load reaction.
STEEL BRIDGE CORRUGATED PLANK FLOOR			
2" Minimum Depth	$\dfrac{S}{5.5}$	$\dfrac{S}{4.5}$	Factors based on a 6"x2" steel corrugated plank. Provides safer results if bending stiffness is greater than a 6"x2" steel corrugated plank.

Table 3.6 AASHTO Standard Specifications Wheel Load Distribution in Longitudinal Beams. (NOTE: Values are per wheel, multiply by $\frac{1}{2}$ if using axle value or lane load.). S = Average Stringer Spacing in Feet

members are being analyzed. It is important to note that these factors are applied to *wheel loads*. Figure 3.21 illustrates a typical scenario where an H20-44 truck is loading an interior stringer of a slab-on-stringer superstructure. When computing the bending moment due to live load, for example, a fraction of both the front and rear wheel loads is taken to act on a given interior stringer. Consulting Table 3.6, for a concrete deck (floor) with two or more lanes and a stringer spacing of less than 14 ft, the resultant distribution factor for an interior stringer will be

$$DF = \frac{S}{5.5} = \frac{7.0 \text{ ft}}{5.5} = 1.27$$

This value would be multiplied by half the weight of the design truck. The total weight of an H20-44 truck is 8,000 lb (front axle) + 32,000 lb (rear axle) or 40,000 lb. Therefore, one set of front and rear wheels would be half this

DESIGN PERSPECTIVE

AASHTO Load Distribution: Is it too Conservative?

*I*f someone wants to challenge the AASHTO Standard Specifications for being too conservative, one has to look no farther than the method employed for lateral load distribution. Within the past few years some designers have sought to address the conservatism of AASHTO's approach and offer alternative methods themselves.

Bogdan Kuzmanovic and Manuel Sanchez of Beiswenger, Hoch and Associates were faced with the need to economize the design of the Sunshine Skyway Bridge in Tampa, Florida. The AASHTO Standard Specifications method yielded a lane load fraction of 1.70 for a two-girder approach structure whose stringers were spaced at 23 ft (7 m). The designers felt this value to be high for a structure equipped with vertical cross bracing as well as lateral bracing located at the bottom flanges.

Realizing that the AASHTO Standard Specifications approach only takes into account stringer spacing and bridge floor configuration, Kuzmanovic and Sanchez investigated alternative methods that would take into account torsional properties of the structure in addition to the stiffness and spacing of secondary members. They also wanted a method that would facilitate the initial design process by not requiring definition of the entire bridge geometry (as is the case with a finite element model).

Four alternate methods were investigated, each of which took into account the enhanced torsional properties of the girder–cross-frame superstructure. The resulting lane load fractions ranged from 1.42 to 1.60 with an average of 1.493 (compared with the 1.70 AASHTO Standard Specifications value). The actual value used in the design was 1.53, resulting from one of the designer's alternates.

A subsequent finite element analysis performed by an AISC committee on the Sunshine Skyway Bridge computed a lane load fraction of 1.49 [Ref. 3.27].

Studies such as this have long since demonstrated that the AASHTO Standard Specifications approach represents a conservative simplification of the load distribution problem. It should not be forgotten, however, that what one designer calls conservative another may call safe. If nothing else, the AASHTO Standard Specifications have yielded designs which have been both safe and durable over the past several decades.

There is, though, always a call for improvement and refinement. As Kuzmanovic and Sanchez correctly point out in their analysis, the lateral distribution of loads on highway bridges is influenced by a host of factors which the AASHTO Standard Specifications simply does not account for at the present time.

AASHTO LRFD code takes the consideration of stringer spacing and stiffness, deck type and depth, bridge span length and stiffness of secondary members, thus improved the accuracy of predicting the load distribution factor.

DID YOU KNOW

THAT the Sunshine Skyway Bridge crossing Tampa Bay in Florida was constructed after a freighter struck a pier on the previous bridge, causing its collapse? The new structure has a main navigation span of 1200 ft (366 m) and a vertical clearance of 175 ft (53.4 m). The new structure is designed to withstand ship impacts of 6000 tons and hurricanes with winds up to 240 mph. For a discussion of how load distribution was refined for this structure's design, see the accompanying Design Perspective [Ref. 3.26].

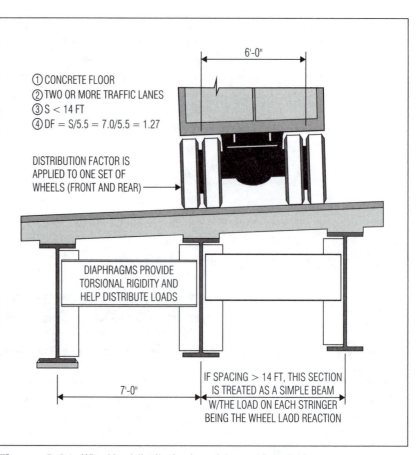

Figure 3.21 Wheel load distribution for a slab-on-stringer bridge.

amount or 20,000 lb or 20 kips. When computing bending moments, the distributed load used would be

$$\text{Distributed Load} = DF \times \text{One set of Wheels}$$
$$\text{Distributed Load} = 1.27 \times 20 \text{ kips} = 25.4 \text{ kips}$$

This means that 25.4 kips of the 40 kip H20-44 design truck acts on any given interior stringer and the remaining 14.6 kips are distributed amongst the other stringers. If the spacing between stringers had been greater than 14 ft, the concrete deck between the two adjacent interior stringers would be assumed to act as a simple beam. The wheel loads would then act on this simple beam and the resulting reactions taken as the load on any individual stringer. The reader should also note that if the bridge were carrying only one design traffic lane, the distribution factor would have been S/7.0 rather than S/5.5.

If the axle load is not at the support, the live load distribution factor for an interior stringer shear is the same as that for an interior stringer moment. If the axle load is at support, we should calculate the distribution factor for shear assuming the deck is simply supported by the stringers, similar to calculating live load distribution factor when stringer spacing is over 14 feet. This procedure is called "Level Rule". Note that when we calculate the maximum live load shear force at the support, "Level Rule" should only be applied to the axle load at the support. The normal live load distribution factor (as in Table 3.6) shall be applied to the rest axle loads.

AASHTO LRFD provides a more accurate and sophisticated formula to calculate the live load distribution factors. It is very important to remember that AASHTO LRFD uses axle load and lane load, instead of wheel load. In other words, the live load distribution factors in LRFD method is approximately half of these in the standard specifications, which uses wheel load or half of lane load. Therefore, we use 8 k, 32 k, and 32 k load for calculating HL-93 truck forces, but we use 4 k, 16 k, and 16 k for calculating HS-20 truck forces, although both trucks are identical.

The followings are equations of calculating live load distribution factors in AASHTO LRFD.

For concrete deck on stringer type bridges, the distribution factor for moment in interior stringers are:

One design lane loaded:

$$0.06+\left(\frac{S}{14}\right)^{0.4}\left(\frac{S}{L}\right)^{0.3}\left(\frac{K_g}{12.0Lt_s^3}\right)^{0.1} \qquad \text{(Eq. 3.20)}$$

Two or more design lanes loaded:

$$0.075+\left(\frac{S}{9.5}\right)^{0.6}\left(\frac{S}{L}\right)^{0.2}\left(\frac{K_g}{12.0Lt_s^3}\right)^{0.1} \qquad \text{(Eq. 3.21)}$$

The live load distribution factor for shear in interior stringers are:
One design lane loaded:

$$0.36+\frac{S}{25.0} \qquad \text{(Eq. 3.22)}$$

Two or more design lanes loaded:

$$0.2+\frac{S}{12}-\left(\frac{S}{35}\right)^{2.0} \qquad \text{(Eq. 3.23)}$$

To apply these equations, the bridge has to meet the following conditions:

$$3.5 \leq S \leq 16.0$$

$$4.5 \leq t_s \leq 12.0$$

$$20 \leq L \leq 240$$

$$10000 \leq K_g \leq 7000000$$

A ASHTO LRFD uses axle load and lane load, instead of wheel load. In other words, the live load distribution factors in LRFD method is approximately half of these in the standard specifications.

The minimum number of stringers is 4.

where S = spacing of stringers (ft)
L = span length (ft)
K_g = longitudinal stiffness parameter of the stringer (in^4)
t_s = depth of concrete slab (in)

$$K_g = n\left(I + Ae_g^2\right)$$

where n = ration of modulus of elasticity between stringer material and concrete deck
I = moment of inertia of the stringer (in^4)
A = section area of the stringer (in^2)
e_g = distance between the centers of gravity of the stringer and the deck (in)

For bridges that do not meet the above conditions, refined structural analysis such as finite element analysis may be used.

For other types of superstructure, the load distribution factors can be obtained in accordance with AASHTO LRFD Table 4.6.2.2b-1.

3.8.2 Different Types of Load Distribution

In addition to floor type and stringer spacing, the criteria governing load distribution vary depending on the orientation of the member being analyzed (longitudinal or transverse) and its position (interior or exterior). The following offers a general overview of some of the major types of floor systems and the related AASHTO requirements for distribution of loads.

1. **Interior Longitudinal Members.** As we have already discussed in the example in Section 3.8.1, the live load distribution factor of an interior stringer is determined from Table 3.6 (AASHTO 3.23.1), or AASHTO LRFD Table 4.6.2.2.2b-1. That accounts for lateral distribution of loads only. No longitudinal distribution of wheel loads is allowed. Live load bending moments are computed using one set of front and rear wheels (AASHTO Standard Specifications), or the whole truck (AASHTO LRFD), multiplied by the distribution factor.

2. **Exterior Longitudinal Members.** Depending on the girder arrangement, outside girders are often subjected to heavier loads than interior girders. Superimposed dead loads such as curbs, sidewalks, railings, barriers, etc., which are placed on an exterior girder *after the deck has cured*, can be distributed equally among all primary members (AASHTO 3.23.2.3.1.1). For a slab-on-stringer bridge *with four or more stringers,* the following distribution factors are used in AASHTO Standard Specifications:

$$DF = \frac{S}{5.5} \ (S \le 6 \text{ ft}) \quad \text{or} \quad DF = \frac{S}{4.0 + 0.25S} \ (6 < S \le 14 \text{ ft}) \qquad \textbf{(Eq. 3.24)}$$

where S = distance between exterior and adjacent interior stringer

From Equation 3.24 we see that the distribution factor will vary depending on the spacing of stringers. As is the case with many interior stringers, when the spacing between an exterior and adjacent interior stringer exceeds 14 ft, the flooring between the two stringers is taken to act as a simple beam with the load on each stringer being the resulting wheel load reaction.

In AASHTO LRFD Specifications, if only one lane is loaded, the load distribution factors for moment and shear can be obtained by positioning the truck wheel loads 2 feet from the parapet, and calculating the reaction from the exterior girder, assuming the deck is simply supported by the girders in the transverse direction. When two or more lanes are loaded, the live load distribution factor for moment can be obtained from Eq. 3.21, and modified by a factor:

$$0.77 + \frac{d_e}{9.1} \qquad \text{(Eq. 3.25)}$$

> When the spacing between an exterior and adjacent interior stringer exceeds 14 ft, the flooring between the two stringers is taken to act as a simple beam ... In no case should an exterior beam be designed smaller than interior girders.

When two or more lanes are loaded, the live load distribution factor for shear can be obtained from Eq. 3.23, and modified by a factor:

$$0.6 + \frac{d_e}{10} \qquad \text{(Eq. 3.26)}$$

where d_e = distance between the exterior web of exterior girder to the face of traffic barrier (ft.)   ($-1 \le d_e \le 5.5$)

If an exterior girder is under a sidewalk, the girder should be designed for truck load on the sidewalk.

It should be noted that in no case should an exterior girder be designed smaller than the interior girders, so that the bridge can be easily widened in the future.

> If an exterior stringer is under a sidewalk, the stringer should be designed for truck load on the sidewalk.

3. **Transverse Members.** The AASHTO specifications do not allow for any lateral distribution of loads for transverse members (e.g., floor beams). When there are no longitudinal members present and the deck is supported entirely by floor beams, the distribution factors, as outlined in AASHTO Table 3.23.3.1 or AASHTO LRFD Table 4.6.2.2.2f-1, may be used.

For concrete deck bridges, the distribution factors for both moment and shear is $S/6$. Where S is the spacing of the transverse beams. If S exceeds 6 feet (1.8 m), the distribution factor can be calculated by positioning the live load to obtain the maximum reaction at the floor beam, assuming the deck is simply supported by the floor beams. The distribution factors for both AASHTO Standard Specifications and AASHTO LRFD Specifications are similar.

3.23.4 STIFFNESS CONSTANT

The stiffness constant in Equation 3.27a is

$$K = \sqrt{\frac{I}{J}(1+\mu)}.$$

Listed below are values for various types of beams, which can be used by designers when performing a preliminary design (AASHTO 3.23.4.3).

Beam Type	K
Non-voided Rectangular	0.7
Rectangular w/Circular Voids	0.8
Box Section Beams	1.0
Channel Beams	2.2

3.23.4 TORSION CONSTANT

In lieu of more exact methods, the torsion constant J may be estimated using one of the following equations:

Nonvoided Rectangular Beams, Channels, and Tee Beams

$$J = \sum \left\{ \frac{1}{3} bt^3 \left(1 - 0.630 \frac{t}{b}\right) \right\}$$

where

b = length of each rectangular component within section

t = thickness of each rectangular component within section

Box-Section Beams

$$J = \frac{2 \cdot t \cdot t_f (b-t)^2 \cdot (d-t_f)^2}{b \cdot t + d \cdot t_f - t^2 - t_f^2}$$

where

b = overall width of box
d = overall depth of box
t = thickness of either web
t_f = thickness of either flange

4. Multibeam Concrete Decks (Concrete Panels). A multibeam concrete deck can be either conventionally reinforced or prestressed. Precast prestressed concrete panel decks were discussed in Section 3.2.3 briefly. These types of decks consist of concrete panels which run longitudinally and are placed next to one another. The panels are connected together with a shear key and lateral post-tensioning rods. A concrete overlay is usually applied to the top of concrete panels.

As with other longitudinal members, no longitudinal distribution of wheel loads is allowed. The AASHTO Standard Specifications takes into account the stiffness of the deck panels through use of a stiffness parameter C which is given as

$$C = \frac{W}{L}\sqrt{\frac{I}{J}(1+\mu)} = \frac{W}{L} \cdot K \qquad \text{for } W < L \qquad \text{(Eq. 3.27a)}$$

$$C = K \qquad \text{for } W \geq L \qquad \text{(Eq. 3.27b)}$$

where W = width of entire bridge perpendicular to beams, ft
$\quad\quad L$ = span length taken parallel to longitudinal girders, ft
$\quad\quad I$ = moment of inertia
$\quad\quad J$ = torsion constant (see sidebar)
$\quad\quad \mu$ = poisson's ratio for concrete, poisson's ratio can be assumed to be 0.2
$\quad\quad K$ = stiffness constant (see sidebar)

The boundary within which the stiffness parameter C falls and its value are used to define a parameter D, which is given by

$$D = (5.75 - 0.5N_L) + 0.7N_L(1 - 0.2C)^2 \qquad \text{(Eq. 3.27c)}$$

where N_L = number of traffic lanes

Therefore, like other members, the resultant distribution factor can be calculated as a function of the spacing between beams using the equation:

$$\text{Load Fraction} = \frac{S}{D} \qquad \text{(Eq. 3.27d)}$$

where S = width of a precast beam

If the value of $\sqrt{I/J}$ is greater than 5.0, or bridge skew angle exceeds 45 degrees, AASHTO Standard Specifications recommends that a "more precise method", such as grillage analysis, be used (AASHTO 3.23.4.3).

AASHTO LRFD uses slightly different equations to calculate load distribution factors for multibeam deck bridges. To calculate moment in interior and exterior beams, Tables 4.6.2.2.2b-1 and 4.6.2.2.2d-1 can be used. For shear in interior and exterior beams, Tables 4.6.2.2.3a-1 and 4.6.2.2.3b-1 can be used.

It can be seen that the value of the distribution factor is greatly dependent on the cross-sectional geometry of the precast panel. Both the moment of inertia and torsional constant are functions of the type of panel/beam used (e.g., voided section, solid beam, etc.). AASHTO provides a list of general constant values for use in the preliminary design of a multibeam bridge. The sidebar lists these preliminary values.

> **I**t can be seen that the value of the distribution factor is greatly dependent on the cross-sectional geometry and the span length of the precast panel.

3.8.3 Conclusions

As can be seen from the Design Perspective, in this section, the approach which AASHTO Standard Specifications takes for the distribution of loads has fostered some debate as to whether or not the method is too conservative. Regardless of the merits of such arguments, AASHTO LRFD has addressed the issue by certain extend. Both design methods will be further discussed in the design examples.

The AASHTO code places the distribution of loads for concrete slabs within the same section as that which describes the general design criteria for this element. With this in mind, the presentation of load distribution criteria for concrete slabs is offered in the following section. For load distribution criteria pertaining to other less common flooring, such as timber flooring, the reader is referred to the AASHTO specifications directly for information.

3.9 CONCRETE DECK SLABS

With this section, we begin the portion of the text which concerns the active design of structural elements in a highway bridge. Design examples will run parallel with text covering specifications and other related issues. These examples will always be positioned on the right-hand facing page. If there is insufficient room for the example to be completed on a single page, it will be continued on the subsequent right-hand facing page (the top of the design calculation page indicates the total number of pages in the example). For the most part, the associated text on the left-hand facing page and bottom of the right-hand page will be germane to the design example, although there is no guaranteed one-to-one correspondence.

Since both AASHTO standards and LRFD Specifications are currently used by bridge engineers in the United States, both will be presented in the design examples. In that way, this book can be used as a reference book no matter which method is required in your state. For students studying bridge engineering, it is to their benefit to learn both methods to broaden their knowledge, and to have a feeling of the advantages and disadvantages of each method.

We begin with the deck because the nature of the design process generally follows a top-down approach. While this is not to imply that, by any means, bridge design is a linear affair (it is not), it should serve to make the new designer aware that certain information must be available prior to an element's design. It is difficult to design the primary members if one does not know how much dead load the deck will contribute or to design the piers if the end reactions from the superstructure frame are unknown. Each element in a highway bridge plays off of the other. This means that there will be a certain degree of jumping back and forth between design examples before one can get a full appreciation of all the aspects that go into a bridge design.

As mentioned in Section 3.8.3, most of the design criteria governing the design of reinforced concrete deck slabs are derived from AASHTO 3.24, which covers both the design of slabs and distribution of wheel loads on the slab. A general note to the engineer new to bridge design: AASHTO utilizes the expression "continuous over more than two supports" when speaking of deck slabs. For the most part, this describes a slab continuous over multiple stringers. Therefore, if a concrete slab rests on seven wide flange stringers, this slab would be termed *continuous over more than two supports*. The reader should not be confused with a continuous span bridge which has been discussed previously. This implies a longitudinal continuity over a pier or other intermediate support.

> It is difficult to design the primary members if one does not know how much dead load the deck will contribute or to design the piers if the end reactions from the superstructure frame are unknown.

AASHTO STANDARD
3.24.2 PLACEMENT OF WHEEL LOADS FOR SLAB DESIGN

When designing a slab, the centerline of the wheel load is placed a distance of 1 ft (0.30 m) from the face of the curb. If there is no curb or sidewalk present, the loads are placed 1 ft from the face of the bridge railing.

When designing the sidewalk and associated slab, fascia stringer, etc., a wheel load *on the sidewalk* is placed 1 ft from the face of the bridge rail. If a barrier, rather than a railing, is present, this condition can be ignored. If a barrier is not present, though, the following allowances may be made:

LOAD FACTOR DESIGN

$\beta = 1.0$ rather than the 1.67 for slabs

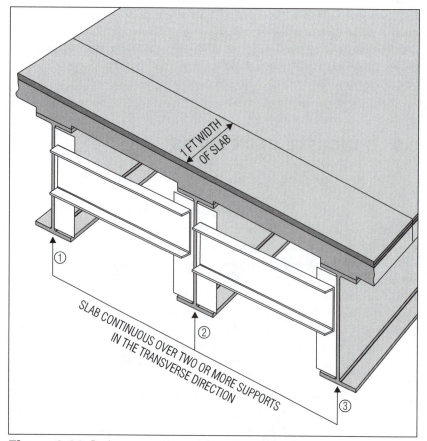

Figure 3.22 Design segment for a reinforced concrete deck slab.

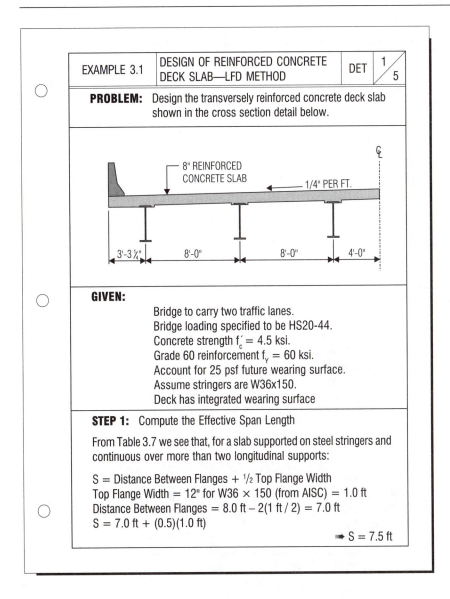

| EXAMPLE 3.1 | DESIGN OF REINFORCED CONCRETE DECK SLAB—LFD METHOD | DET | 1/5 |

PROBLEM: Design the transversely reinforced concrete deck slab shown in the cross section detail below.

8" REINFORCED CONCRETE SLAB

1/4" PER FT.

3'-3¼"   8'-0"   8'-0"   4'-0"

GIVEN:

Bridge to carry two traffic lanes.
Bridge loading specified to be HS20-44.
Concrete strength $f_c' = 4.5$ ksi.
Grade 60 reinforcement $f_y = 60$ ksi.
Account for 25 psf future wearing surface.
Assume stringers are W36x150.
Deck has integrated wearing surface

STEP 1: Compute the Effective Span Length

From Table 3.7 we see that, for a slab supported on steel stringers and continuous over more than two longitudinal supports:

S = Distance Between Flanges + ½ Top Flange Width
Top Flange Width = 12" for W36 × 150 (from AISC) = 1.0 ft
Distance Between Flanges = 8.0 ft – 2(1 ft / 2) = 7.0 ft
S = 7.0 ft + (0.5)(1.0 ft)

➡ S = 7.5 ft

DESIGN EXAMPLE 3.1

GIVEN PARAMETERS

The design of this slab will be performed using Load Factor Method (LFD) of AASHTO Standard Specifications.

The top flange width is found by consulting the AISC Manual of Steel Construction in the W Shapes Dimension section.

Although this bridge has a monolithic deck with integrated wearing surface, the design of the slab should account for a future wearing surface to be applied to the deck surface.

STEP 1: EFFECTIVE SPAN LENGTH

This step follows the verbiage of the AASHTO code explicitly. This makes the calculation of the effective span length somewhat involved. A more direct approach is to take

S = Center to Center Stringers - W/2

For slab on girder bridges with identical stringer properties, this is a more direct approach. For concrete girder bridges, however, the effective span length is the clear span length between the girder top flanges.

3.9.1 Effective Span Length

Figure 3.22 shows a typical design strip for a reinforced concrete deck slab. The deck is assumed to act like a beam which is continuous over its supports. In this case, the supports are the wide flange stringers used as primary members in the superstructure. A one-foot unit width is assumed for the *design beam*, with the beam running transversely (perpendicular to the primary members).

To simplify the design, a segment of the assumed slab-beam is taken and analyzed as a simple span. The length of this segment is called the *effective span length*. The size of the effective span length is dependent on

❑ Whether the slab is continuous over more than two supports
❑ The type of supports (e.g., steel or concrete stringers)
❑ How the slab is integrated with the supports

The deck is assumed to act like a beam which is continuous over its supports. In this case, the supports are the wide flange stringers used as primary members in the superstructure.

	SLAB CONFIGURATION	EFFECTIVE SPAN LENGTH	EXAMPLE
SIMPLE SPAN	Slab on two supports.	S = The distance center to center of supports S ≤ Clear Span + Slab Thickness	
CONTINUOUS OVER MORE THAN TWO SUPPORTS	Slab monolithic with beams. Slab monolithic with walls without haunches. Rigid top flange prestressed beams with top flange width to minimum thickness ratio less than 4.0.	S = Clear Span (Clear distance between faces of supports)	
	Slab supported on steel stringers. Slab supported on thin top flange prestressed beams with top flange width to minimum thickness ratio greater than or equal to 4.0.	S = Distance Between Edges of Top Flange + $\frac{1}{2}$ Top Flange Width	
	Slab supported on timber stringers.	S = Clear Span + $\frac{1}{2}$ Thickness of Stringer	

Table 3.7 AASHTO Effective Span Length Criteria for Concrete Slabs

Table 3.7 lists the AASHTO criteria governing the effective span length for reinforced concrete slabs (AASHTO 3.24.1). Also depicted in the table are representative types of structures that fall into the various groupings. Design Example 3.1 utilizes the third major grouping (a slab resting on more than two steel stringers), which is typical for the vast majority of slab-on-stringer bridges in use today. Load factor design (LFD) method per AASHTO Standard Specifications will be used for this example.

3.9.2 Calculation of Bending Moment

As mentioned in Section 3.9.1, the design of a concrete deck slab is performed on a per foot width of slab basis. AASHTO offers set criteria for specifying live load bending moment. The live load bending moment criteria

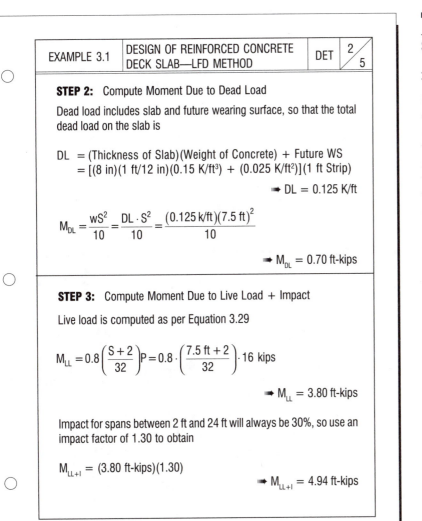

STEP 2: COMPUTE MOMENT DUE TO DEAD LOAD

The dead load is taken as a distributed load acting over the effective span length of the slab. The future wearing surface load was given as an area load which we take to act over the 1 ft wide unit strip of slab (see Figure 3.22). The moment due to dead load is computed in accordance with Equation 3.33. If the slab is continuous over more than two supports, as we have here, be careful not to use the standard $wL^2/8$ equation for a simple span under distributed load.

STEP 3: COMPUTE MOMENT DUE TO LIVE LOAD

Since the slab is continuous over more than two supports, we use Equation 3.29, which has the 0.8 multiplier. The value of P used is 16 kips since our live loading was specified to be HS20-44 (see the variable definitions for Equation 3.28). We computed the live load plus impact moment by multiplying the live load moment by 1.30. Another way of doing this is to compute an *impact only moment* by multiplying the live load moment by 0.30. Then the two moments are added together. This way saves a step.

If the designer so wishes, a more exact analysis can be performed using the AASHTO specified *tire contact area*. The contact area is based on a wheel of the standard H or HS design vehicles.

The placement of main reinforcement perpendicular to the direction of traffic typically occurs in structures where the concrete deck slab rests on a set of longitudinally oriented primary members.

vary depending on whether the main reinforcement is perpendicular or parallel to the direction of traffic. Additional criteria cover bending moments for cantilever slabs, slabs supported on four sides, and edge beams. The reader should keep in mind that the AASHTO bending moment equations *do not include impact*.

If the designer so wishes, a more exact analysis can be performed using the AASHTO specified *tire contact area*. For the standard HS-20 or Alternative Military Loadings, the contact area should have a length of 10 inches (in the traffic direction), and a width of 20 inches (AASHTO 3.30).

1. Main Reinforcement Perpendicular to Traffic. The placement of main reinforcement perpendicular to the direction of traffic typically occurs in structures where the concrete deck slab rests on a set of longitudinally oriented primary members. The most common example of

The placement of main reinforcement parallel to the direction of traffic occurs in structures where the slab resists major flexural forces or floor beams are present.

this is a slab-on-stringer bridge. The live load moment for slab spans simply supported in the transverse direction is calculated as follows:

$$M_{LL} = \left(\frac{S+2}{32} \right) P \qquad \text{(Eq. 3.28)}$$

where M_{LL} = live load moment per foot-width of slab, ft-lb
S = effective span length, ft
P = live load
= 16 kips for H20 and HS20 loading or
= 20 kips for H25 and HS25 loading

If the slab is continuous over more than two supports, AASHTO introduces a multiplier of 0.8 which is applied to both positive and negative moments. This modifies Equation 3.28 to become:

$$M_{LL} = 0.8 \left(\frac{S+2}{32} \right) P \qquad \text{(Eq. 3.29)}$$

The variable definitions are the same as for Equation 3.28. Both equations are applicable to effective spans which are between 2 ft and 24 ft inclusive (0.61 m to 7.31 m).

This range of lengths, therefore, means that the vehicle impact factor applied to live loads will always be 30 percent. Recall that

$$I = \frac{50}{L+125}$$

Therefore, for an extreme case of an effective span length of 24 ft, we would have $I = 0.33$ or 33 percent. Since I cannot be greater than 30 percent, we will always use an impact factor of 1.30 in calculating the effects of live load on a concrete slab.

2. Main Reinforcement Parallel to Traffic. The placement of main reinforcement parallel to the direction of traffic occurs in structures where the slab resists major flexural forces or floor beams are present. A truss bridge with floor beams but without stringers where concrete slab is supported by floor beams would be an example of this type of structure.

For these types of bridges, AASHTO specifies that the slab be analyzed as a beam having an effective width E, a length S, and a depth as described before, such that

$$E = 4 + 0.06S \qquad \text{(Eq. 3.30)}$$

where E = effective width of slab, ft
S = effective span length, ft

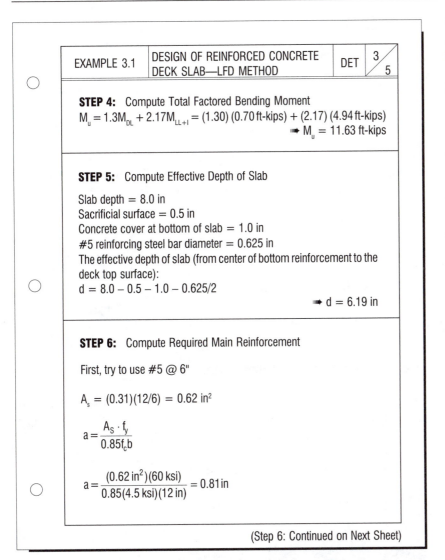

DESIGN EXAMPLE 3.1

STEP 4: COMPUTE TOTAL FACTORED MOMENT

The load factors are (see Table 3.2):
DL = 1.3
LL = 1.3 × 1.67 = 2.17

STEP 5: COMPUTE EFFECTIVE DEPTH OF SLAB

The effective depth of slab for bending moment capacity is the distance between the center of the main reinforcement and the top surface of the slab. Since this deck does not have a separate wearing surface, we assume 0.5 inch of the deck on top will be lost. We also assume a 1.0 inch concrete cover at bottom, and #5 bars will be used.

STEP 6: COMPUTE REQUIRED MAIN REINFORCEMENT

Next, we determine the actual bar spacing based on an assumed #5 bar. We first try to use #5 @ 6". Readers can refer to any reinforced concrete text books for calculating the bending moment capacity. AASHTO uses the same equations as ACI code.

The effective width cannot be greater than 7.0 ft (2.13 m). This value is given for truck wheel loading. If lane loading governs, though, a width of $2E$ is to be used. If the slab is simply supported, AASHTO specifies approximate maximum live load moments based on the loading conditions, where for HS20 loading

$$M_{LL} = 900S \quad \text{for} \ S \leq 50 \tag{Eq. 3.31a}$$

$$M_{LL} = 1000(1.30S - 20.0) \quad \text{for} \ 50 < S < 100 \tag{Eq. 3.31b}$$

where M_{LL} = live load moment, ft-lb
S = effective span length, ft

When the slab is continuous over two or more supports, truck or lane loads should be positioned so as to cause maximum positive and negative moment.

3. Dead Load Moments. For simple spans, the dead load moment can be taken as the maximum moment for a simply supported beam under a uniform distributed load. That is, for an effective span length of S

$$M_{DL} = \frac{wS^2}{8}$$ (Eq. 3.32)

For slabs continuous over more than two supports, however, an approximation must be made. Although AASHTO offers no specific dead load moment equation, the generally accepted expression is

$$M_{DL} = \frac{wS^2}{10}$$ (Eq. 3.33)

4. Total Factored Moment. For deck slab design, load group I (Table 3.2) should be used. The load factors for dead load and live load are 1.30 and 2.17 respectively.

3.9.3 Distribution Reinforcement

Whether or not the main reinforcement is parallel or perpendicular to the direction of traffic, *distribution reinforcement* will be required. Distribution reinforcement is used to account for the lateral distribution of live loads (AASHTO 3.24.10). By *lateral* we imply a direction transverse to the main reinforcement. Distribution reinforcement is located in the bottom of the deck slab. Culverts where the depth of fill over the slab exceeds 2 ft (0.61 m) are excluded from this requirement.

Distribution steel is used to account for the lateral distribution of live loads ... By *lateral* we imply a direction transverse to the main reinforcement.

THE INTRODUCTION of epoxy coated reinforcing steel used in bridge decks to protect against corrosion has significantly increased the bridge deck performance and their life expectancy. It has become the standard practice in regions where deicing salt is used in winters.

Figure 3.23 Reinforcing steel for a concrete deck slab about to be poured.

EXAMPLE 3.1	DESIGN OF REINFORCED CONCRETE DECK SLAB—LFD METHOD	DET	4/5

STEP 6: Compute Required Main Reinforcement (Continued)

$$\phi M_n = \phi A_s f_y \left(d - \frac{a}{2} \right)$$

$$\phi M_n = (0.9)(0.62)(60)\left(6.19 - \frac{0.81}{2} \right)\left(\frac{1}{12} \right)$$

$$\phi M_n = 16.14 \ K \cdot FT > M_u = 11.63 \ K \cdot FT$$

Since the reinforcement assumed is more than what is required, the designer can reduce the amount of reinforcing steel by increasing the rebar spacing to:

$$(6.0 \ in)\left(\frac{\phi \cdot M_n}{M_u} \right) = (6.0)\left(\frac{16.14}{11.63} \right) = 8.3 \ in$$

Now, use #5 @ 8" reinforcement

$$A_S = 0.31 \cdot \frac{12}{8} = 0.465 \ in^2$$

$$a = \frac{A_S \cdot f_y}{0.85 f_c b}$$

$$a = \frac{(0.465 \ in^2)(60 \ ksi)}{0.85(4.5 \ ksi)(12 \ in)} = 0.61 \ in$$

(Step 6: Continued on Next Sheet)

DESIGN EXAMPLE 3.1

STEP 6: COMPUTE REQUIRED MAIN REINFORCEMENT (CONTINUED)

The moment capacity in the first try is 39% more than the total factored moment. So we increase bar spacing by approximately 33%, using #5 @ 8". By recalculating the moment capacity, we know that the moment capacity is still more than what is required. Therefore, #5 @ 8" will be used for the design.

Like any reinforced concrete beams, the deck should also be checked for the minimum reinforcement requirement (AASHTO 8.17.1), and the maximum allowable reinforcement ratio (AASHTO 8.16.3.1).

To determine the amount of distribution steel required, the amount of main reinforcement needed is multiplied by a specified percentage. This percentage varies, depending on whether the main reinforcement is parallel or perpendicular to the direction of traffic.

For main reinforcement perpendicular to the direction of traffic the percentage is given as

$$\text{Percent of Main} = \frac{220}{\sqrt{S}} \leq 67 \text{ percent} \qquad \text{(Eq. 3.34)}$$

or, when the reinforcement is parallel to the direction of traffic, we use the expression

$$\text{Percent of Main} = \frac{100}{\sqrt{S}} \leq 50 \text{ percent} \qquad \text{(Eq. 3.35)}$$

where S = effective span length, ft

The limiting values of 67 percent and 50 percent specified in Equations 3.34 and 3.35, respectively, are maximum, not to exceed limits. The reason for locating the distribution steel at the bottom of the deck slab is that moments transverse to the main reinforcement cause tension which will be evidenced in the lower portion of the slab. If the main reinforcement is laid perpendicular to traffic, the distribution steel is to be placed on the middle half of the span, *between stringers*. Also, no less than 50 percent of the amount used in the middle is to be placed in the outer quarters of the span (AASHTO 3.24.10.3).

3.9.4 Minimum Slab Thickness

As mentioned in the last Did You Know? sidebar, the thickness of a concrete deck slab has a major impact on the overall longevity of the slab. The control of superstructure deflections is also affected by slab thickness. Toward this end, AASHTO has specified criteria which define the minimum thickness of reinforced concrete deck slabs for both simple spans and slabs continuous over more than two supports.

The minimum thickness in AASHTO Standard Specifications are defined for concrete flexural members so that they are provided with adequate stiffness to resist excessive deflections. For reinforced concrete slabs, this means a deck slab *whose main reinforcement is parallel to the direction of traffic*. For slabs which are simply supported, the minimum depth of slab (ft) is given as

$$t_{min} = \frac{1.2(S+10)}{30} \qquad \text{(Eq. 3.36)}$$

or, when the slab is continuous over more than two supports, the minimum slab thickness is defined as

$$t_{min} = \frac{(S+10)}{30} \geq 0.542 \qquad \text{(Eq. 3.37)}$$

where S = effective span length (feet).

AASHTO allows an adjustment to be made for variable depth members (e.g., a haunched slab) to account for changes in stiffness at positive and negative moment regions (AASHTO 8.9).

In AASHTO LRFD Specifications, the minimum depth of a concrete deck is 7.0 inch (178 mm), in addition to surface grooving and sacrificial surface.

3.9.5 Railing Loads

The portion of slab which resists loads induced by railing posts varies depending on whether a parapet is present or not (AASHTO 3.24.5.2). When

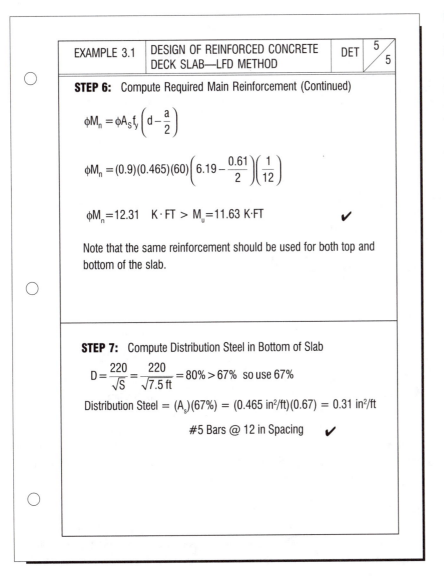

STEP 7: DISTRIBUTION STEEL IN BOTTOM OF SLAB

Distribution steel is computed in accordance with Equation 3.34. Since the value cannot be greater than 67 percent, we use this percentage to obtain the 0.31 in²/ft required distribution steel. #5 bars at a 12 in spacing gives 0.31 in²/ft.

In a real design, the maximum reinforcement and minimum reinforcement should also be check. See AASHTO 8.16.3.1 and 8.17.1 for details.

a parapet is not present, the effective length of slab resisting the post loads is given as

$$E = 0.8X + 3.75 \qquad \text{(Eq. 3.38)}$$

or, when a parapet is provided, the effective length of slab is defined by the following:

$$E = 0.8X + 5.0 \qquad \text{(Eq. 3.39)}$$

where E = effective length of slab resisting railing load, ft

X = distance from center of a post to point of analysis, ft

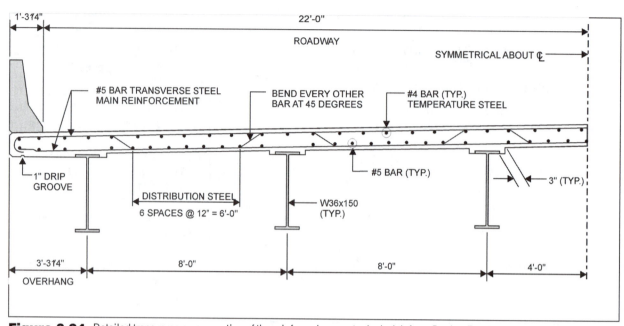

Figure 3.24 Detailed transverse cross-section of the reinforced concrete deck slab from Design Example 3.1.

Railing loads are not to be applied simultaneously with wheel loads. In AASHTO 2.7, guidelines are offered with regard to the application of railing loads. Designers should keep in mind, however, that the standards used by transportation departments for vehicular railings and barriers vary greatly from state to state. Many departments maintain their own design standards with regard to the application of railing loads which should be consulted prior to beginning the slab design.

3.9.6 AASHTO LRFD Method

So far we have only discussed concrete slab design, including Example 3.1, using AASHTO Standard specifications. AASHTO LRFD allows designers to use one of the following two approaches for the concrete deck slab design:

The first approach is the so called "Analytical Method". This method is almost identical to the method used in the Standard Specifications. The design truck wheel load P = 16 kips should be used in Equation 3.28 and Equation 3.29 to obtain live load bending moment.

The second approach is the so called "Empirical Design Method". To use this method, the minimum depth of the deck should not be less than 7.0 in (178 mm) excluding a sacrificial wearing surface where applicable, the effective span length of the deck should not exceed 13.5 ft (4.1 m), and the ratio of effective span length to deck depth is between 6.0 and 18.0. Some other conditions, as specified in AASHTO LRFD 9.7.2.4, should also be satisfied for Empirical Design Method to be used.

The Empirical Design Method specifies that the minimum amount of reinforcement for each bottom layer to be 0.27 in²/ft (572 mm²/m), and the minimum amount of reinforcement for each top layer to be 0.18 in²/ft (381 mm²/m). All reinforcement shall be straight bars except for hooks where required, and the maximum spacing is 18 in (457 mm).

> In addition to providing for sufficient reinforcement, the designer must also be concerned with appropriate detailing of the slab.

In Example 3.1, if we use the LRFD Empirical Design Method, we may use #5 @ 12" in both directions at the bottom slab (0.31 in²/ft, or 656 mm²/m), and use #5 @ 18" in both directions at the top slab (0.21 in²/ft, or 445 mm²/m). Note that the deck meets all conditions for the Empirical Design method. The reinforcement in the upper layer and the bottom layer shall be placed perpendicular to the slab supports such as stringers.

3.9.7 Slab Reinforcement Details

In addition to providing for sufficient reinforcement, the designer must also be concerned with appropriate detailing of the slab. Some of the major detailing concerns include, but are not limited to, the following:

- ❏ Minimum cover
- ❏ Length of bars
- ❏ Spacing between parallel bars
- ❏ Splicing of bars

Rules governing the above often vary depending on the owner's preferences and standards. Listed in the accompanying sidebar are some of the standards utilized by the New York State Department of Transportation in the design of concrete deck slabs.

3.9.8 Construction, Rehabilitation, and Maintenance

Too often, the subjects of rehabilitation and maintenance are divorced from the design process, and are treated either ancillary or unrelated to each other. Many a noble word has been spoken about the cause of an integrated design-maintain-rehab approach. The theory, however, rarely meets the practice. As we have discussed previously, concrete deck slabs continually sustain some of the harshest abuse of any bridge element. The increase in trucking loads, use of lighter, more flexible designs, and various environmental impacts all combine to make concrete decks highly susceptible to deterioration.

Related to rehabilitation and maintenance are issues concerning the construction details of a bridge. The design of a highway bridge should focus not only on the ability of the structure to resist design loads but also on its ability to function over a long period of time with minimal maintenance and repair operations.

There are a variety of construction, rehabilitation, and maintenance methods employed to increase the useful service lives of concrete bridge decks. Some methods can be employed at the initial construction of the deck while others represent remedial measures taken after deterioration has set in. The following details some of the more common methods of extending the service life of concrete bridge decks.

1. Increased Slab Thickness and Cover. A simple step in protecting bridge decks has already been touched on in one of this section's sidebars: increased slab thickness and cover for reinforcement. Especially when no wearing surface is present, sufficient cover is essential to protecting the deck from excessive wear. New York State requires 2.5 in (64 mm) of

---

SLAB DETAILING

The following are slab reinforcing steel detailing requirements used by the New York State DOT [Ref. 3.11].

MINIMUM COVER

The cover requirement for slabs with an integrated wearing surface is based on epoxy-coated bars being used in the top mat.

Top of Slab

w/Separate Wearing Surface	1¹⁄₂ in
w/Integrated Wearing Surface	2¹⁄₂ in

Bottom of Slab 1 in

BAR LENGTHS

The maximum length for reinforcing steel is 60 ft (18.29 m) since this is the longest length which most reinforcing steel plants in the United States produce bars.

SPLICING OF REBARS

Transverse bars under 60 ft long should be composed of a straight bar with a hook on each end (or as required) which is spliced halfway between the exterior and first interior stringer. If the length of a reinforcing bar exceeds 60 ft, then the requirement above is supplemented with an additional, staggered splice required in the straight bar halfway between interior stringers.

SPACING OF REBARS

The clear distance D between parallel bars is defined by the following criteria:

D < 24 in (0.61 m)
D > 1.5 × Nominal Diameter of Bars
D > 1.5 × Max Size of Coarse Aggregate
D > 1.5 in (38 mm)

Many a noble word has been spoken about the cause of an integrated design-maintain-rehab approach. The theory, however, rarely meets the practice.

cover on the top surface of slabs which have an integrated wearing surface. A minimum cover of 1.5 in (38 mm) is used when a wearing surface is present. The bottom of the slab is usually provided with 1 in (25 mm) of cover. Thicker slabs can also enhance the overall performance of bridges. Decks without a wearing surface are typically 8 to 8.5 in (203 to 216 mm) thick, while those with a wearing surface range upward from 7.5 in (190 mm). The more robust slab thickness is used to counteract the effects of cracking found in lighter bridge decks. As is the case with any concrete element, once cracks begin to propagate, the intrusion of moisture into the cracks results in corrosion of the reinforcement and all the deleterious effects that go along with it. These two basic steps, enacted by transportation departments in the 1970's, have gone a long way toward protecting deck slabs.

2. **Coated Reinforcement.** Since early 1980's, most reinforcing steel used in bridge deck has been coated with epoxy to inhibit corrosion by limiting the effects of moisture and chlorides. An epoxy-coated rebar is a standard, deformed bar which has been blast cleaned, heated, and then subjected to an electrostatic spray of dry powder. Initially, epoxy-coated bars are specified for the top mat of reinforcement in concrete bridge decks. A trend has been developed, however, to use epoxy-coated bars throughout the deck.

3. **Waterproofing Membrane.** Bridges with a bituminous wearing surface are sometimes equipped with a waterproofing membrane between the asphalt wearing course and concrete slab. A waterproofing membrane consists of a preformed layer of waterproofing material which, when combined with a primer coat, adheres to the concrete surface protecting it from corrosion caused by water and deicing chemicals. The primers are generally neoprene, resin, or solvent based and are applied to the deck with a spray or squeegee. Membrane sheets typically come in rubberized asphalt

> **A**n epoxy-coated rebar is a standard, deformed bar which has been blast cleaned, heated, and then subjected to an electrostatic spray of dry powder.

> **A** waterproofing membrane consists of a preformed layer of waterproofing material which, when combined with a primer coat, adheres to the concrete surface protecting it from corrosion.

THERE IS A LOT going on in Figure 3.25. First, one can see the reinforcing steel for a parapet which is integrated with the deck. Also visible are the bar supports or *bolsters* which are used to support the layers of reinforcement. Bolsters, like the ones shown in the photo, are typically preformed wire assemblies. They remain in place after the concrete has cured and are provided with at least some corrosion protection. The photo also shows the location at which the main transverse reinforcement is *lapped* to the end hooked bars. The 180 degree hook is also known as a candy cane for obvious reasons.

Figure 3.25 A bridge deck with a reinforcing layout similar to Design Example 3.1.

or modified bitumen sheets, which are placed like shingles (i.e., lapped) in the direction in which the water drains [Ref. 3.3]. After the waterproofing has been affixed to the top of the slab, the wearing course is placed on top of it. Earlier waterproofing membranes were composed of a bituminous material and a fiberglass cloth which acts as reinforcement. Other types included an epoxy resin system used in conjunction with a deck wearing course.

There are, however, some limitations and disadvantages to waterproofing membranes, which cause some agencies to shy away from them. Since slippage at the wearing surface–membrane-slab interface is a potential problem, waterproofing membranes cannot be installed on bridges with a vertical grade greater than 4 percent [Ref. 3.29]. From an inspection standpoint, waterproofing membranes, like stay-in-place forms underneath a slab, can hide deterioration to the slab taking place underneath the membrane layer (see Section 2.3.4, Part 1). Most agencies use waterproofing membrane in conjunction with epoxy coated reinforcement to provide better corrosion protection. This should illustrate to the reader, the extreme importance owners place on the integrity and quality of the structure's deck.

4. **Drainage.** Inadequate drainage facilities can severely limit the life span of a concrete deck. We touched on some of the major features of a deck drainage system in Section 2.3.5, Part 2. Some of the principal methods for draining runoff from the bridge deck are as follows:

- ❏ Deck swales
- ❏ Weep tubes
- ❏ Scuppers
- ❏ Catch basins
- ❏ Drop inlets

A deck swale is a V-shaped channel formed by opposing cross-slopes in the deck cross section; essentially acting as a large gutter. A weep tube is a piece of tubing, made out of PVC or some other material, which extends from the bottom of the wearing surface through the deck. Runoff is channeled toward the weep tube inlet and drained into the underpass. Scuppers are drain inlets, generally made of cast iron, which carry runoff from the bridge deck through the deck fascia. Figure 3.26 shows an open scupper drain. Catch basins and drop inlets are nodes in a stormwater collection facility which collect debris and lower the elevation of upstream and downstream pipes, respectively.

The adverse effects of inadequate deck drainage can range from traffic safety hazards to deterioration of the deck surface. First of all, excessive water collecting on the deck advances the risk of deterioration of the deck through the introduction of moisture into already cracked or spalled deck areas. Ponding on a bridge deck, while collecting water into a single, freestanding pool, can also accumulate deicing agents into the same concentrated location. From a traffic standpoint, excessive water on the bridge deck can lead to hydroplaning of vehicles in warm seasons and icy patches in cold ones.

> The adverse effects of inadequate deck drainage can range from traffic safety hazards to deterioration of the deck surface.

A PROBLEM ASSOCIATED with drains is the accumulation of debris. Outlets allowed to spill out onto the underpass can produce a great deal of refuse and garbage in addition to just runoff. If debris becomes excessive, it can accumulate and clog drains, such as the open drain scupper illustrated in Figure 3.26. When a drain becomes clogged with debris, it can cause a backup of water, which can lead to ponding and its associated adverse effects. A rigorous maintenance program should ensure that all existing drains are free of debris and functioning properly. This will require the periodic flushing out of drains and a consistent program of inspection.

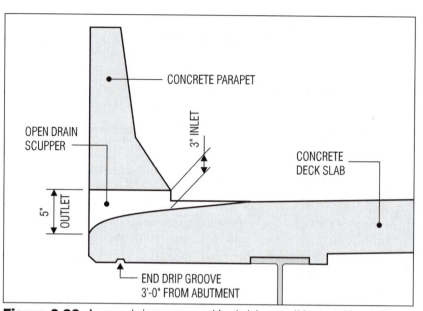

Figure 3.26 An open drain scupper used for draining runoff from a bridge deck.

When designing drainage facilities for a structure, two important criteria to keep in mind are that

❑ Drains should be constructed of corrosion resistant material.
❑ Drains should not discharge on other bridge elements or traffic passing underneath the structure (AASHTO 1.5).

From Figure 3.26 we see that the drip groove located on the bottom of the deck slab at the fascia girder is noted to stop 3 ft (0.91 m) from the face of the abutment. While this may seem to only make good common sense, the designer still must take care to ensure proper annotation on the contract documents so that these common sense details do not fall through the cracks.

In a rehabilitation design, the engineer cannot assume that the existing structure is provided with proper drainage facilities. A thorough drainage analysis should be conducted to ascertain if new, additional, or expanded facilities will be required. Particularly susceptible to drainage difficulties are bridges located on sag vertical curves or relatively flat grades.

The method of analysis most often used is the Rational Method (also known as the Lloyd-Davies Method in the United Kingdom). Most designers are quite familiar with the basic form of the rational method equation which relates runoff to rainfall intensity by the expression:

$$Q = kCiA$$

(Eq. 3.40)

where Q = peak runoff rate (ft³/s)
      C = runoff coefficient

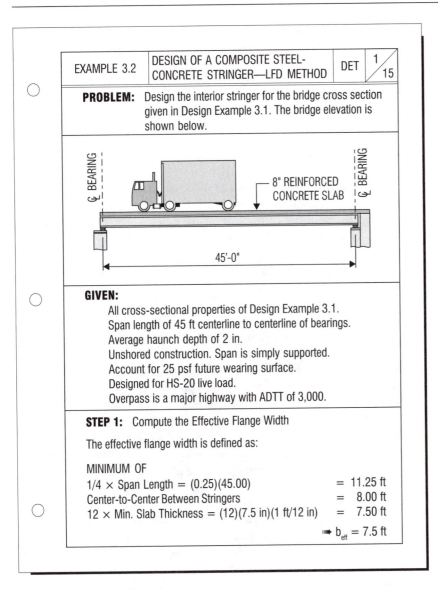

| EXAMPLE 3.2 | DESIGN OF A COMPOSITE STEEL-CONCRETE STRINGER—LFD METHOD | DET | 1 / 15 |

PROBLEM: Design the interior stringer for the bridge cross section given in Design Example 3.1. The bridge elevation is shown below.

8" REINFORCED CONCRETE SLAB

45'-0"

GIVEN:

All cross-sectional properties of Design Example 3.1.
Span length of 45 ft centerline to centerline of bearings.
Average haunch depth of 2 in.
Unshored construction. Span is simply supported.
Account for 25 psf future wearing surface.
Designed for HS-20 live load.
Overpass is a major highway with ADTT of 3,000.

STEP 1: Compute the Effective Flange Width

The effective flange width is defined as:

MINIMUM OF

1/4 × Span Length = (0.25)(45.00)	=	11.25 ft
Center-to-Center Between Stringers	=	8.00 ft
12 × Min. Slab Thickness = (12)(7.5 in)(1 ft/12 in)	=	7.50 ft

➡ b_{eff} = 7.5 ft

DESIGN EXAMPLE 3.2
GIVEN PARAMETERS

The design of the interior stringer will be performed using the Load Factor Design method of AASHTO Standard Specifications. This is a continuation of Design Example 3.1 so that the beam spacing of 8.0 ft and deck thickness of 8 in are used. A half inch wearing surface is assumed for the deck. An average haunch depth of 2 in is specified. The *haunch* is a small layer of concrete between the stringer and concrete slab. The span is simply supported (i.e., not continuous), so it may be analyzed as a simple beam. Unshored construction is specified so the beam must accommodate the dead load of the concrete slab.

STEP 1: EFFECTIVE FLANGE WIDTH

The criteria governing the effective flange width of a composite girder are defined by AASHTO 10.38.3.1. In this case, the last value (12 times the least thickness of slab) governs. We will use the effective flange width in Step 7 through Step 11 to compute the amount of concrete slab acting as a composite section with the steel stringer. Note that 8 in by 8.0 ft concrete deck is used to calculate the deck dead load.

i = average rainfall intensity (in/hr)
A = drainage area (acres)
k = 1.00083

The equation is called the rational method since it has a rational basis where Q is approximately equal to 1 if $C = 1$, $i = 1$, and $A = 1$ (i.e., 1 in of rainfall per hour equals 1 ft³/s per acre). The runoff coefficient is an approximation describing the permeability of the surface being analyzed. The sidebar gives values for various runoff coefficients [Ref. 3.30]. As can be seen from the table, the more permeable the surface (i.e., ability for water to infiltrate into the material) the lower the coefficient. Rainfall intensity, which varies from municipality to municipality, is determined from local records. This intensity will vary depending on the storm frequency and duration. For bridge design, a 10 year storm with a duration of 5 minutes is most often used.

RUNOFF COEFFICIENTS

The following are a listing of various runoff coefficients based on surface type. These values are applicable for storms with a 5 year to 10 year frequency [Ref. 3.30].

Surface	Runoff Coefficient
Pavement	
Asphalt	0.70 to 0.95
Concrete	0.70 to 0.95
Brick	0.70 to 0.85
Lawns (Sandy Soil)	
Flat (2%)	0.05 to 0.10
Average (2 to 7%)	0.10 to 0.15
Steep (7%)	0.15 to 0.20
Lawns (Heavy Soil)	
Flat (2%)	0.13 to 0.17
Average (2 to 7%)	0.18 to 0.22
Steep (7%)	0.25 to 0.35

When the elevation of adjacent spans is slightly off, the deck joint is extremely susceptible to being impacted by a snow plow's blade. This can cause damage not only to the bridge but the plow as well.

Once the quantity of runoff Q is determined, the bridge deck is analyzed for sheet flow. The width of deck carrying the runoff is sometimes defined as:

$$W = \text{Shoulder Width} + \frac{1}{3}(\text{Traffic Lane}) \qquad \text{(Eq. 3.41)}$$

where W = width of deck used in analysis

As mentioned earlier, a deck swale or gutter can be provided to drain water from the deck and/or roadway surface. The gutter should not be expected to handle all of the stormwater runoff. Therefore, some runoff can be anticipated to spill out into the travel lane [Ref. 3.31].

Depending on the circumstances, it may be desirous to tie into an existing drainage facility. Such a facility could range in size from earth swales and ditches to a major stormwater collection system composed of culverts, inlets, etc. If this is the case, it will be necessary to analyze the bridge as one component in the system in order to ascertain the magnitude of the impact which the additional runoff from the bridge site will have.

5. **Snow and Ice Removal.** In maintaining structures in cold climates, a thoughtful and efficient snow removal plan is an absolute necessity. Deck joints present a common problem point for snow plows during snow removal operations. When the elevation of adjacent spans is slightly off, the deck joint is extremely susceptible to being impacted by a snow plow's blade. This can cause damage not only to the bridge but the plow as well.

An added concern is when the skew angle of a bridge matches the plow blade angle. This problem can be addressed by using a plow with an adjustable blade angle or by raising the blade when approaching a bridge joint. Obviously, repeated impact to a deck joint can cause damage to both the joint and adjacent deck surfaces.

Snow removal crews should also be instructed to make sure snow is not left to accumulate along the curbs on a bridge. Especially when the bridge is oriented in a north-south direction, such an accumulation of snow can lead to the snow melting on the west side of the structure during daytime hours and then running off into the traffic lanes. As the day progresses and the sun begins to set in the west, this runoff will freeze causing icy, hazardous conditions.

Snow plows passing underneath the structure can sometimes cause problems when traveling with their blade raised through negligence or carelessness. If the vertical clearance is tight, the blade can impact primary members or, in concrete slab bridges, the deck itself.

Another problem in winter conditions is the formation of icicles on the deck fascias. These icicles can quite often become very large in size and pose a potential hazard to vehicles passing underneath the structure. During their removal, proper maintenance of traffic should be provided for underneath the structure.

6. **Patching.** When a deck has deteriorated to the point where its functionality comes into question, a decision by the owner must be made

EXAMPLE 3.2	DESIGN OF A COMPOSITE STEEL-CONCRETE STRINGER—LFD METHOD	DET	2/15

8'-0"

25 PSF FUTURE WEARING SURFACE

8"

2"

ASSUME 5% OF STRINGER WEIGHT FOR MISC. STEEL

ASSUME 100 LB/FT

12"

STEP 2: Compute the Dead Load on Stringer
The dead load is composed of the following items:

DL_{slab} = (b)(slab thickness)(w_{conc})
= (8.0 ft)(8.0 in)(1 ft / 12 in)(0.150 k/ft³) = 0.800 k/ft

DL_{haunch} = (haunch width)(haunch thickness)(w_{conc})
= (1.0 ft)(2.0 in)(1 ft / 12 in)(0.150 k/ft³) = 0.025 k/ft

DL_{steel} = (assumed stringer weight) + (misc. steel)
= (0.100 k/ft) + (5%)(0.100 k/ft) = 0.105 k/ft

➡ DL = 0.930 k/ft

STEP 3: Compute the Superimposed Dead Load on Stringer
Account for future wearing surface:

$$SDL_{ws} = \frac{(\text{width of roadway})(\text{future wearing surface})}{\text{number of stringers}}$$

$$= \frac{(44 \text{ ft})(0.025 \text{ k/ft}^2)}{6 \text{ Stringers}} = 0.183 \text{ k/ft}$$

(Step 3: Continued on Next Sheet)

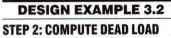

DESIGN EXAMPLE 3.2

STEP 2: COMPUTE DEAD LOAD

The dead load on the stringer is all weight placed *prior* to the concrete deck hardening and reaching full strength. In this case, the dead load on the stringer consists of the stringer itself, the slab and the haunch (the wearing course, parapet, etc., will be accounted for in Step 3). Since we do not yet know the exact size of the stringer, we will make an initial guess of 100 lb/ft for the stringer. We will assume 5 percent of the stringer weight to account for miscellaneous connection plates, diaphragms, etc. If stay-in-place deck form is used, it should also be included as a dead load in the design.

STEP 3: COMPUTE SUPERIMPOSED DEAD LOAD

Superimposed dead loads are those loads placed on the bridge after the deck has cured. These loads are resisted by the composite section. In this case, the superimposed dead load consists of the future wearing surface and parapet. From AASHTO 3.23.2.3.1.1 these loads are to be distributed equally among all stringers (see Section 3.5.2, Part 2).

whether to patch or replace the bridge deck. If the deterioration is localized enough and the integrity of the deck does not appear to be compromised, then patching can be an acceptable alternative to total deck replacement.

Prior to commencement of patching operations, an accurate field survey needs to be conducted indicating the location of the various distresses and whether the patches will constitute a shallow or deep repair, the former indicating removal of deficient concrete to a depth *above* the top mat of reinforcement and the latter removal *beneath* the first rebar layer. The goal, in either case, is to reach sound concrete. For this reason, it is not uncommon for full depth removal to be a blanket standard. Figure 3.27 shows a typical detail for partial depth removal of a deteriorated section of concrete deck.

Concrete is typically removed by jack hammering with saw cutting the concrete by 1/2" to 1" (12 mm to 25 mm), but the high pressure water jet is becoming popular in recent years. Care should be taken not to damage

> If the deterioration is localized enough and the integrity of the deck does not appear to be compromised, then patching can be an acceptable alternative to total deck replacement.

REMOVAL OF CONCRETE

can be accomplished by either jack hammering or using a high pressure water jet. The perimeter of the removal area shall be saw cut. When planning for the patching of a concrete deck, the estimators should account for future deterioration in the concrete deck by the time the project is let for construction. Depending on the rate of deterioration, quantities can increase anywhere from 10 to 25 percent of the initial condition of the deck. If new steel is needed to supplement the existing reinforcement, the ACI specification for required lap length of 30 times the bar diameter should be met. If a lap cannot be made, then drilling into the existing concrete will be required.

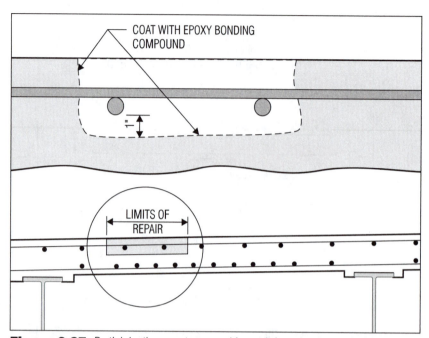

Figure 3.27 Partial depth concrete removal for a reinforced concrete deck slab.

> **I**n terms of rehabilitation, patching is generally considered to be a temporary, rather than permanent, measure ... delamination to the concrete deck slab often occurs right next to areas that have been previously patched.

> **I**f over 10% of the deck surface needs patching, but the deck is still generally solid, then patching in conjunction with a new deck overlay may be considered. Latex modified concrete is usually used as a deck overlay material.

existing reinforcing steel present. Once the concrete has been removed, the existing steel should be inspected to ascertain if any loss of section to the individual bars has taken place. If this is the case, additional bars should be installed. The existing steel and exposed concrete is then blast cleaned and the exposed concrete and reinforcement coated with an epoxy bonding compound. It is important that the surface be dry prior to placement of the epoxy bonding compound. The new concrete or repair compound is then placed into the void and allowed to cure. If the patch is especially thin and prone to quick drying, a piece of dampened burlap is typically placed over the patch to keep the concrete moist.

The new concrete placed should match the characteristics of the existing concrete as much as possible. Typically, portland cement is used in patching operations. Latex-modified concrete (see Section 3.3.2), as well as polymer-based and fast-setting concretes, are also used. These types of materials often require following a strict application sequence which varies somewhat from the process described above. To control the effects of shrinkage (see Section 3.5.4, Part 2) the contractor should use the minimum amount of water required for workability and strength.

In terms of rehabilitation, patching is generally considered to be a temporary, rather than permanent, measure. Studies have revealed that delamination to the concrete deck slab often occurs right next to areas that have been previously patched [Ref. 3.29]. This is not meant to imply that patching is a deficient solution; rather it denotes patching to be an interim solution to be applied until a larger scale rehabilitation is necessary (or possible). If over 10% of the deck surface needs patching, but the deck is still generally solid, then patching in conjunction with a new deck overlay may be considered. Latex modified concrete is usually used as a deck overlay material.

EXAMPLE 3.2	DESIGN OF A COMPOSITE STEEL-CONCRETE STRINGER—LFD METHOD	DET	3/15

STEP 3: Compute the Superimposed Dead Load (Continued):

Calculate weight of parapet by first computing the area of its cross section:

$$A_1 = (7 \text{ in})(21 \text{ in}) = 147.00 \text{ in}^2$$
$$A_2 = \tfrac{1}{2}(2.25 \text{ in})(21 \text{ in}) = 23.63 \text{ in}^2$$
$$A_3 = (9.25 \text{ in})(10 \text{ in}) = 92.50 \text{ in}^2$$
$$A_4 = \tfrac{1}{2}(6 \text{ in})(10 \text{ in}) = 30.00 \text{ in}^2$$
$$A_5 = (15.25 \text{ in})(3 \text{ in}) = \underline{45.75 \text{ in}^2}$$
$$A_P = 338.88 \text{ in}^2$$

$$w_P = (338.88 \text{ in}^2)(1 \text{ ft}^2/144 \text{ in}^2)(0.150 \text{ k/ft}^3)$$
$$= 0.353 \text{ k/ft}$$

There are two parapets on the bridge which are distributed over all six stringers:

$$SDL_P = 2 \text{ Parapets} \cdot \frac{w_P}{\text{No. Stringers}} = 2 \cdot \frac{0.353 \text{ k/ft}}{6 \text{ Stringers}} = 0.118 \text{ k/ft}$$

$$SDL = SDL_{ws} + SDL_P = 0.183 \text{ k/ft} + 0.118 \text{ k/ft}$$
$$\Rrightarrow SDL = 0.301 \text{ k/ft}$$

STEP 4: Compute Dead Load Moments and Shears

$$M_{DL} = \frac{wL^2}{8} = \frac{(0.930)(45.0^2)}{8} = 235.41 \text{ k} \cdot \text{ft}$$
$$\Rrightarrow M_{DL} = 235.41 \text{ k-ft}$$

$$V_{DL} = \frac{wL}{2} = \frac{(0.930)(45.0)}{2} = 20.93 \text{ k}$$
$$\Rrightarrow V_{DL} = 20.93 \text{ k}$$

(Step 4: Continued on Next Sheet)

DESIGN EXAMPLE 3.2

STEP 3: COMPUTE SUPERIMPOSED DEAD LOAD (CONTINUED)

The future wearing surface is applied over the width of roadway. From Figure 3.24 we see that the roadway width is 22 ft to the bridge centerline for a total width of 44 ft.

To compute the unit weight of the parapet, we break it down into rectangles and triangles, sum the areas, and then multiply it by the unit weight of concrete (150 lb/ft³). Like the wearing surface, this weight is distributed among all six stringers. The sum of the two values yields the total superimposed dead load on the stringer.

STEP 4: COMPUTE DEAD LOAD MOMENT AND SHEAR

The maximum moments and shear forces for dead load and superimposed dead load for a simple span are computed by Equation 3.49.

We separate superimposed dead loads from the rest of dead loads because when we calculate deflections, the composite section properties should be used for superimposed dead loads.

---

7. Sealing. The application of a protective, waterproofing sealer is another important measure used to extend the life of concrete elements, particularly concrete decks. The protective sealer is typically placed on the deck surface. In general, protective sealers are available in a variety of forms, some of the more popular types being

- ❑ Linseed oil
- ❑ Rubber and silicon resins
- ❑ Epoxy based sealants

Where most sealants coat the exterior face of the concrete, some, such as silicon resins, act as a *penetrating sealer*. This type of sealer actually penetrates the surface of the concrete element to provide a waterproofed surface. Linseed oil is usually mixed with another substance (such as kerosene) and applied to the concrete surface. In general, protective sealers are applied to new concrete elements and have limited success on a surface which already suffers from extensive deterioration.

8. Cathodic Protection. The adverse effects of chloride on concrete elements have already been discussed. Whether from deicing agents or seawater, chlorides cause some of the most severe deterioration that a concrete deck will see. To combat the corrosion induced by chlorides, an electrochemical system known as *cathodic protection* may be used to protect bridge decks (as well as other concrete elements).

> **W**hen chlorides are introduced to reinforced concrete, through cracks or other voids, an electrolyte and corresponding difference in electric potential is formed.

When chlorides are introduced to reinforced concrete, through cracks or other voids, an electrolyte and corresponding difference in electric potential is formed. The reinforcing steel acts as an anode and a cathode with ions being discharged and passed from one point on the steel to another, a process which causes corrosion of reinforcing steel and deterioration in concrete.

Cathodic protection introduces a separate metal to act as an anode so that the reinforcing steel becomes purely cathodic and causes the corrosion process to stop. There are two general cathodic protection systems in use today:

- ❑ Galvanic anode (sacrificial) system
- ❑ Impressed current system

The former uses anodes made of magnesium, zinc, or aluminum, which are sacrificed in order to protect the reinforcing steel. A difference in potential is created between the anode and the metal the anode is supposed to protect.

An impressed current system is more popular in bridge decks. A typical system is illustrated in Figure 3.28. The impressed current system

PLACEMENT OF ANODES in a conductive asphalt system varies depending on the geometry of the structure. Bridge decks that are less than 30 ft (10 m) wide are usually provided with one line of anodes placed along the deck centerline. Bridge decks 30 to 70 ft (21 m) wide use two rows of anodes, and bridges wider than 70 ft have three. The maximum spacing of anodes in a line should be less than every 25 ft (7.5 m) with the end anode not being more than 10 ft (3 m) from the end of the span. The anodes themselves are corrosion resistant and disc shaped with diameters up to 1 ft (300 mm) and a thickness of 1.5 in (37 mm) [Ref. 3.14].

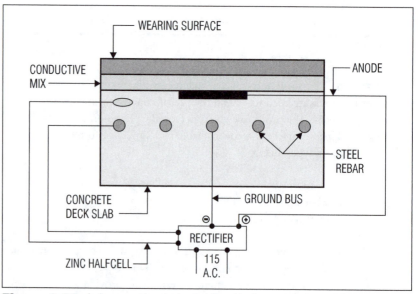

Figure 3.28 An impressed current cathodic protection system for a reinforced concrete deck. *(Adapted from Bridge Rehabilitation and Strengthening, Ref. 3.14.)*

EXAMPLE 3.2	DESIGN OF A COMPOSITE STEEL-CONCRETE STRINGER—LFD METHOD	DET	4 / 15

STEP 4: Compute Dead Load Moments and Shears (Continued):

$$M_{SDL} = \frac{wL^2}{8} = \frac{(0.301)(45.0)^2}{8} = 76.19 \text{ k·ft}$$

➟ $M_{SDL} = 76.19$ k-ft

$$V_{SDL} = \frac{wL}{2} = \frac{(0.301)(45.0)}{2} = 6.77 \text{ k}$$

➟ $V_{SDL} = 6.77$ k

STEP 5: Compute Live Load Moment and Shear:

We must first compute the wheel load distribution factor and impact factor. Referring to Table 3.6, for:

Concrete Floor
Two or More Traffic Lanes
On Steel I-Beam Stringers

The live load distribution factor for moment, and shear when axle load is not acting at support, can be calculated:

$$DF = \frac{S}{5.5} = \frac{8.0 \text{ ft}}{5.5} = 1.45$$

➟ $DF = 1.45$

For the rear axle at support, the live load distribution for shear when axle is acting at support can be calculated assuming deck is simply supported by the stringers (See the sketch on Sheet 5):

$$DF_R = \text{Left Support DF} + \text{Center Support DF} + \text{Right Support DF}$$

$$DF_R = \frac{4.0 \text{ ft}}{8.0 \text{ ft}} + 1 + \frac{2.0 \text{ ft}}{8.0 \text{ ft}}$$

➟ $DF_R = 1.75$

Impact is computed by Equation 3.15:

$$I = \frac{50}{L + 125} = \frac{50}{45 \text{ ft} + 125} = 0.29$$

➟ Use $I = 0.29$

(Step 5: Continued on Next Sheet)

DESIGN EXAMPLE 3.2

STEP 5: COMPUTE LIVE LOAD MOMENT AND SHEAR

Prior to computing the actual live load moment and shear, we need to calculate the wheel load distribution factor and impact factor to be applied to the moment and shear. The equation for the wheel load distribution factor is obtained from Table 3.6 (see also discussion in Section 3.8.1). In this example, we have a reinforced concrete slab (concrete floor) resting on wide flange stringers (steel I-beam stringers) with two traffic lanes. The load distribution factor is for *wheel loads,* so, when we compute the live load moment and shear, we will use half the axle loads indicated in Figure 3.12 (i.e., 4k, 16k, and 16k for an HS20-44 truck) or half of the lane load illustrated in Figure 3.13. The impact factor is a percentage which we add one to in order to create a straight multiplicative factor (see also, commentary on Step 3 for Design Example 3.1).

essentially reverses the current of the electrolyte solution through use of an applied direct current (DC) from a battery or rectifier. The metal anodes used vary somewhat depending on the type of impressed current system used.

A *conductive asphalt system* utilizes anodes which are disc shaped and made of graphite or high-silicon iron. The anodes are distributed throughout the deck (both longitudinally and transversely) and are charged by the DC current. When the current is applied, the potential of the reinforcing steel is lowered and the corrosion process is stopped [Ref. 3.14]. An *anode mesh* utilizes a similar approach, but rather than fixed, disc-shaped anodes, an anode mat made of either copper or titanium is placed on the deck and linked to adjoining mats in strips; covering the entire deck area. Other variations of these systems have been used, both in the construction of new bridge decks and the rehabilitation of existing ones.

From Figure 3.28 we can see that between the wearing surface and concrete deck is a layer of conductive mix, generally 2 to 3 in (51 to 76 mm) thick. Since concrete does not conduct electricity very well, the conductive mix provides for a uniform distribution of the electric current across the bridge deck. The conductive mix is generally a bituminous concrete-based mixture consisting of coke breeze, stone, sand, and asphalt cement. The coke breeze component acts as a course aggregate and provides for electric conductivity.

The DC rectifier uses AC line voltage which is regulated by a separate control panel located under the structure. The system must be monitored from time to time to ensure that the polarized charge is kept within a specified range. If the voltage falls too low, the system may not provide adequate protection to the deck, and if it rises too high, debonding of the overlay may occur.

Some of the drawbacks to cathodic protection are obvious. The need for a constant source of power and continued monitoring of the current adds to the maintenance operations required for a structure (although not as severe as having to patch or replace the deck). The problem of added dead load on the structure due to the need of a conductive layer is compounded by an increase in the depth of the structure, which may have an adverse effect on bridge-highway geometry constraints. Last, but never least, are the added costs associated with installing and maintaining the system.

Cathodic protection, however, is not a gimmick or experimental technology. In states such as California, the system has been implemented and has proved itself to be successful. It is entirely conceivable that, as the technology grows and develops, associated costs will be driven down and installation and maintenance simplified to the point where installing a cathodic protection system will be as standard as installing deck joints.

3.9.9 Conclusions

The design of the concrete deck slab, while perhaps not the most technically challenging activity, is critical to the overall performance of the structure. From a rehabilitation standpoint, owners will often decide whether to perform superficial maintenance or major rehabilitation based on the condition of the deck slab. In one way, the deck slab can be thought of as the barometer indicating bridge performance.

It is for these reasons that the detailing of the slab is so critical and we have spent so much time discussing the implementation of features which arrest the onset of deterioration. Whether it is incorporation of a drip groove at the deck fascia or use of epoxy-coated reinforcement, protection of the deck slab is an important issue which bridge engineers have been working on for the last half century. The items we have studied in Section 3.9.8 are the result of decades of research, implementation, and analyses. The waterproofing membrane has developed and grown over the years as the performance of early models was studied and the system refined. The same is now true for cathodic protection systems. Some engineers find it a bit disheartening when the profession seems to be less mathematical and more empirical. Half of the fun in civil engineering, however, is seeing how new ideas play out. An idea does not have to be born out of an equation so much as it does out of a

Cathodic protection, however, is not a gimmick or experimental technology. In states such as California, the system has been implemented and has proved itself to be successful.

Some engineers find it a bit disheartening when the profession seems to be less mathematical and more empirical. Half of the fun in civil engineering, however, is seeing how new ideas play out.

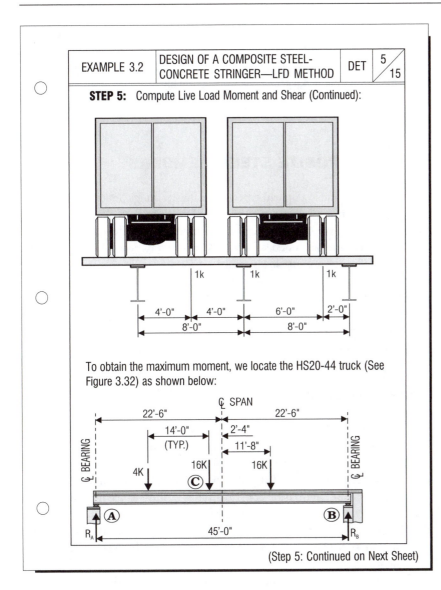

EXAMPLE 3.2	DESIGN OF A COMPOSITE STEEL-CONCRETE STRINGER—LFD METHOD	DET	5 / 15

STEP 5: Compute Live Load Moment and Shear (Continued):

1k   1k   1k

4'-0"   4'-0"   6'-0"   2'-0"

8'-0"   8'-0"

To obtain the maximum moment, we locate the HS20-44 truck (See Figure 3.32) as shown below:

℄ SPAN

22'-6"   22'-6"

14'-0" (TYP.)   2'-4"

11'-8"

℄ BEARING   ℄ BEARING

4K   16K   16K

Ⓒ

Ⓐ   Ⓑ

R_A 45'-0" R_B

(Step 5: Continued on Next Sheet)

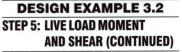

DESIGN EXAMPLE 3.2
STEP 5: LIVE LOAD MOMENT AND SHEAR (CONTINUED)

To calculate the live load distribution factor for shear when the axle load is at the support, we should locate trucks transversely to obtain the maximum reaction at the stringer, assuming the deck is simply supported by the stringers. This procedure is also called "Level Rule", which shall only be applied to the axle load at the support, not the rest of the axle loads.
To obtain the maximum live load moment for simply supported bridge due to HS-20 loading, the truck live load is placed as described in Figure 3.32.

knowledge of the way something should work. Often the more simple the solution, the more effective its implementation will be. While knowledge of mechanics and mathematics are important tools which the structural engineer uses in the design of a highway bridge, observation and analysis are equally important.

Coming back to the simple drip groove, it is easy for a designer to just copy the standard detail on to a set of plans without realizing that the specifications surrounding that detail are the result of a number of years of observation by maintenance personnel and designers. We have already mentioned that the groove must be terminated a given distance from the face of an adjacent element. This criterion comes about because inspectors in the field notice an accumulation of moisture on, for example, an abutment stem. They realize that, while the drip groove is draining away moisture from the deck fascia, it is dumping water someplace else where it should not.

Little by little, piece by piece, the overall performance of the deck slab is enhanced by the incorporation of the minutia that is detailing. It all begins and ends with rigorous observation and study. Consultants in private practice should spend time talking with their opposite numbers in public service, especially those in the maintenance department. It is only through this interaction and communication that the success of a design-maintain-rehab approach can be achieved.

3.10 COMPOSITE STEEL MEMBERS

One of the most popular types of highway bridge in use today is the composite steel beam bridge. In Section 3.2.1 we discussed the basic concepts behind composite construction and its inherit advantages. Reiterating from that section, a composite beam bridge utilizes a concrete slab deck which *works together* with steel girders in resisting loads placed on the bridge. In this section, we will discuss the fundamentals behind composite construction as well as present design examples which make use of both the LFD and LRFD specifications to designing composite steel-concrete girders. As with the previous section, we will also discuss construction, maintenance, and rehabilitation issues which concern composite slab-on-stringer bridges.

3.10.1 Composite Action

As discussed in the accompanying sidebar, the use of two dissimilar materials to form a single structural member is not a new technique. The advent of composite construction in bridge design, however, did not take effect until the mid to late 1940's. From a historical perspective, the time of the acceptance of composite construction is critical since it came almost concurrently with the nascent development of the U.S. Interstate. The new found economy of composite construction in the 1940's and 1950's led to the construction of thousands of composite steel beam bridges in the United States alone.

What is composite construction, though, and how does it offer such economy of materials? From basic strength of materials, the maximum stress in a beam subjected to pure bending is defined as

$$f = \frac{Mc}{I}$$

(Eq. 3.42)

where f = stress in beam
   M = bending moment
   c = distance from the neutral axis to extreme fiber
   I = moment of inertia of resisting cross section

This is often redefined using the *elastic section modulus* which is dependent only on the geometry of the resisting cross section and is simply given as

$$f = \frac{M}{S}$$

(Eq. 3.43)

where S = section modulus = $\dfrac{I}{c}$

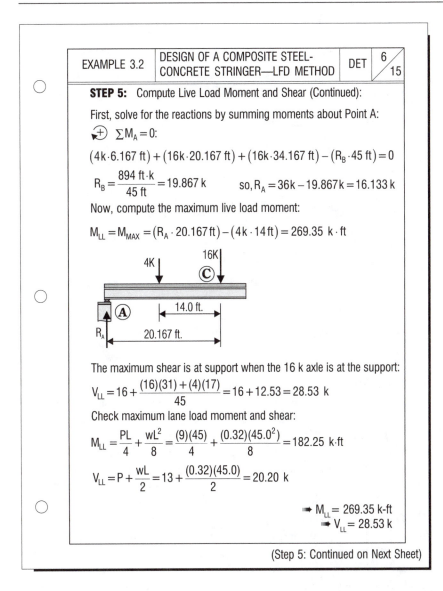

| EXAMPLE 3.2 | DESIGN OF A COMPOSITE STEEL-CONCRETE STRINGER—LFD METHOD | DET | 6/15 |

STEP 5: Compute Live Load Moment and Shear (Continued):

First, solve for the reactions by summing moments about Point A:

$\overset{+}{\curvearrowright} \ \Sigma M_A = 0:$

$(4k \cdot 6.167\,\text{ft}) + (16k \cdot 20.167\,\text{ft}) + (16k \cdot 34.167\,\text{ft}) - (R_B \cdot 45\,\text{ft}) = 0$

$R_B = \dfrac{894\,\text{ft} \cdot \text{k}}{45\,\text{ft}} = 19.867\,k \qquad \text{so, } R_A = 36k - 19.867k = 16.133\,k$

Now, compute the maximum live load moment:

$M_{LL} = M_{MAX} = (R_A \cdot 20.167\,\text{ft}) - (4k \cdot 14\,\text{ft}) = 269.35 \ \text{k} \cdot \text{ft}$

The maximum shear is at support when the 16 k axle is at the support:

$V_{LL} = 16 + \dfrac{(16)(31) + (4)(17)}{45} = 16 + 12.53 = 28.53 \ k$

Check maximum lane load moment and shear:

$M_{LL} = \dfrac{PL}{4} + \dfrac{wL^2}{8} = \dfrac{(9)(45)}{4} + \dfrac{(0.32)(45.0^2)}{8} = 182.25 \ \text{k} \cdot \text{ft}$

$V_{LL} = P + \dfrac{wL}{2} = 13 + \dfrac{(0.32)(45.0)}{2} = 20.20 \ k$

$\Rrightarrow M_{LL} = 269.35 \text{ k-ft}$
$\Rrightarrow V_{LL} = 28.53 \text{ k}$

(Step 5: Continued on Next Sheet)

First we calculate the reactions by summing moments about the left support (Point A). This yields the reaction at the right support. Both reactions combined must equal the total downward load of 36 k. Once we know the reactions, we can solve for the maximum live load moment which occurs at Point C (the center 16 k wheel load). We can solve for this moment by taking a section from the point in question to one support or the other, as shown in the free body diagram in the middle of the calculation sheet. The resulting live load moment is 269.35 k-ft. We should also calculate the lane load moment and shear and choose the most critical cases. If the reader refers to the Appendix of the AASHTO code to reference this value, they will notice that, for a 45 ft span under HS20-44 loading, an interpolated value will yield 538.7 k-ft or twice the 269.35 value computed. This is because the AASHTO table value is for *axle loads,* not the wheel loads we have been using. Designers should take note of this because it can lead to potential error when applying the wheel load distribution factor. If the AASHTO table is being used to obtain a moment (or axle loads are being used), the distribution factor or moment should be divided by 2.

By inspection, we see that the bigger the value of *S,* the smaller the resulting stress. Therefore, it is in the best interest of the designer to increase the section modulus as much as possible. This is where the principal advantage of composite action comes into play.

If a concrete slab simply rests on top of a steel beam, a phenomenon known as horizontal shear slippage occurs. As loads are placed on top of the slab, the top of both the slab and beam are in compression and the bottom of the slab and beam are in tension. In essence, both elements deflect like a beam, albeit independently. Since the bottom of the slab is in tension (i.e., pushing outward toward the ends of the beam) and the top of the beam is in compression (i.e., pushing inward toward the center of the beam), the resulting effect is one of the slab extending out over the ends of the beam (see Figure 3.29). In analyzing such a configuration, the slab and beam are treated independently, with the geometry of each element defining the neutral axis and moment of inertia of the slab and beam. Since the concrete slab alone has little strength

By inspection, we see that the bigger the value of *S,* the smaller the resulting stress. Therefore, it is in the best interest of the designer to increase the section modulus as much as possible.

SLIPPAGE OCCURS when there is no connection between a concrete slab and supporting beam. The natural bond between a slab and beam is not enough to resist the horizontal shear stress between the deck and the top flange of the beam. The strain diagrams in Figure 3.30 illustrate that, under non-composite action, the slab and beam act independently with two distinct neutral axes. The resulting slip can be defined as the tensile strain at the bottom of the slab and compressive strain at the top of beam. When shear connectors are introduced, they help resist the horizontal shear stress at the slab-beam interface to create a single *composite section* with its own unique neutral axis. Complete composite action is achieved when there is no horizontal shear slippage.

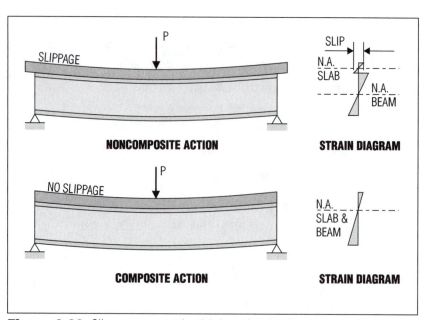

Figure 3.29 Slippage occurs at the slab-beam interface in noncomposite beams.

> I f the slab and beam ... were somehow integrated, they could resist loads as a single unit. In this arrangement, the neutral axis would be located somewhere in the middle of the section ...

compared with the stringers, the contribution of the strength from the deck is usually ignored for noncomposite superstructures.

If the slab and beam, however, were somehow integrated, they could resist loads as a single unit. In this arrangement, the neutral axis would be located somewhere in the middle of the section defined by the top of the slab and the bottom of the beam. With proper integration, the slab-beam would act as a unit with the top of the slab in compression and the bottom of the beam in tension and no slippage in between. This integration is accomplished through the incorporation of shear connectors between the slab and beam.

The shear connectors are generally metal element which extend vertically from the top flange of the supporting beam and are embedded into the slab. Several of these connectors are placed along the length of the beam to prevent slippage which is caused by horizontal shear stress at the slab-beam interface. Figure 3.30 shows a row of shear studs attached to a steel plate girder. Shear studs are the most common form of shear connector used today in composite concrete-steel beam bridges. The shear stud's installation is facilitated by the use of an automatic welding gun. This ease of installation and the relatively low cost of stud connectors has led to their popularity in composite construction.

For concrete girders, composite action is achieved by extending girder transverse stirrups into concrete deck to resist the horizontal shear stress between the deck and the girders.

With shear connectors in place, the slab and beam can now be analyzed as a single unit. Coming back to Equation 3.43, this increases the size of the section modulus which in turn allows the composite beam to resist heavier loads. In essence, the I-shaped beam is replaced by a T-shaped cross section composed of the slab and stringer, the advantages being

❏ A decrease in the size (and weight) of stringer required
❏ Longer possible span lengths

EXAMPLE 3.2	DESIGN OF A COMPOSITE STEEL-CONCRETE STRINGER—LFD METHOD	DET	7/15

STEP 5: Compute Live Load Moment and Shear (Continued):

The live load and impact forces acting on an interior stringer is:

$M_{LL+I} = M_{LL} \cdot DF \cdot (I+1) = (269.35)(1.45)(1+0.29)$

$V_{LL+I} = V_{LL} \cdot DF \cdot (I+1)$

$\qquad = (16.0)(1.75)(1+0.29) + (12.53)(1.45)(1+0.29)$

➡ $M_{LL+I} = 503.82$ k-ft

➡ $V_{LL+L} = 59.56$ k

STEP 6: Compute Factored Moment and Shear:

$M_u = 1.3[M_{DL} + M_{SDL} + 1.67(M_{LL} + I)]$

$\qquad = 1.3[(235.41 + 76.19 + (1.67)(503.82)]$

➡ $M_u = 1498.9$ k-ft

$V_u = 1.3[V_{DL} + V_{SDL} + 1.67(V_{LL} + I)]$

$\qquad = 1.3[(20.93 + 6.77 + (1.67)(59.56)]$

➡ $V_u = 165.3$ k

STEP 7: Choose a Preliminary Section:

We try section W24x76, using 50 ksi steel, and ignoring reinforcement in the deck.

First check the moment strength. The strength of concrete deck:

$0.85f'_c b_{eff} t_s = (0.85)(4.5)(90.0)(7.5) = 2581.9$ k

The strength of steel stringer:

$AF_y = (22.4)(50.0) = 1120.0$ k

$C = Min(2581.9, 1120.0)$

➡ $C = 1120.0$ k

(Step 7: Continued on Next Sheet)

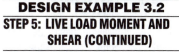

DESIGN EXAMPLE 3.2

STEP 5: LIVE LOAD MOMENT AND SHEAR (CONTINUED)

The maximum moment and shear in an interior stringer due to live load and impact are then calculated with appropriate load distribution factors.

STEP 6: CALCULATE FACTOR MOMENT AND SHEAR

By applying load factors from Table 3.2 (LFD Load Group I), we can obtain the total factored moment and shear for an interior stringer.

STEP 7: CHOOSE A PRELIMINARY SECTION

For a simply supported bridge, a range of 1/20 to 1/27 of the span length is normally used as the depth of the stringers. 50 ksi steel (painted or weathering steel) is commonly used for bridge construction. The concrete strength is 4.5 ksi.

We first try W24x76, which has a cross-section area of 22.4 in².

❑ A stiffer cross-section
❑ A reduction in live load stress and deflections
❑ An increase in load capacity
❑ Enhanced resistance to lateral loads

The way to calculate the bending capacity of composite concrete on steel stringers is similar to that of a reinforced concrete T section beam. Portion of the deck is in compression, and the steel stringer acts like reinforcing steel. See the Example 3.2 and Example 3.3 for the calculation details.

The economy of material realized by composite construction quickly led to its growth as a staple in highway bridge design. Standard rolled wide flange beams could now be used for much longer span lengths. The decrease in size of stringers also meant that beams could now be less deep than before.

THE SHEAR STUD has become the most popular form of shear connector. Early highway bridges made use of spiral shear connectors which consisted of a metal coil welded to the top flange of a steel beam. Installation of spiral connectors was an involved process generally not favored by contractors. The automatic welding gun welds a stud to the top flange through use of an electric arc, which melts a welding material at the bottom of the stud to the steel beam (the effects of which can be seen clearly in the center stud). The head of the shear stud is about 1/2 in larger in diameter than the shaft and is used to anchor the stud in the slab. Typically, the stud shaft has a diameter of 5/8, 3/4, or 7/8 in and a length of 3 to 5 in.

Figure 3.30 A shear stud installed at the top flange of a plate girder. Shear connectors are the key ingredient to preventing slippage and creating composite action.

Another added benefit is that the connection between slab and stringer acts like a diaphragm between adjacent stringers to resist lateral deformation.

The reader should be aware, however, that while we use the expression *composite beam* to imply a concrete slab resting on a steel girder, there are other forms of composite beams. In Section 3.1.2, Part 1, we discussed prestressed concrete girders, most of which are designed composite with concrete slab. For the purposes of the discussion in this section, though, we will use the expressions composite beam, composite action, and composite construction to describe a concrete slab-on-steel stringer type bridge.

> The reader should be aware, however, that while we use the expression *composite beam* to imply a concrete slab resting on a steel girder, there are other forms of composite beams.

3.10.2 Shored and Unshored Construction

The dead loads on a slab-on-stringer bridge consist principally of the slab and beam itself. Since concrete has to cure for 28 days before it reaches full strength, the slab and beam cannot be considered to work compositely in resisting dead loads. This means that, until the concrete has hardened to a sufficient point, the steel stringer itself must resist all dead loads.

Shored construction minimizes the amount of dead load the beam has to carry by providing support at intermediate locations along the length of the span. Once the concrete has reached sufficient strength, the shores are removed and the concrete dead load is carried by the composite section. Therefore, with shoring, smaller dead load deflection, and smaller dead load stress can be achieved. Conversely, unshored construction provides no support during casting concrete deck and expects the beam to resist all dead loads. For most spans, the costs associated with erecting shoring to support the beam are greater than the savings in steel realized. Therefore, shored construction is not a common practice.

> For most spans, the costs associated with erecting shoring to support the beam are greater than the savings in steel realized.

EXAMPLE 3.2	DESIGN OF A COMPOSITE STEEL-CONCRETE STRINGER—LFD METHOD	DET	8/15

STEP 7: Choose a Preliminary Section (Continued):
The compression block height at plastic moment:

$$a = \frac{C}{0.85f'_c b_{eff}} = \frac{1120.0}{(0.85)(4.5)(90.0)} = 3.3 \text{ in}$$

Since the compression block is within the concrete deck, it is considered as a compact section.

$$M_n = M_p = AF_y \left(d - \frac{a}{2} \right) = (1120.0)\left(\frac{23.92}{2} + 2 + 7.5 - \frac{3.3}{2} \right)\left(\frac{1}{12} \right)$$

$$\longrightarrow M_n = 1848.9 \text{ k-ft} > M_u = 1498.9 \text{ k-ft} \quad ✔$$

Then check the shear capacity.

$$\frac{D}{t_w} = \frac{23.92}{0.440} = 54.4$$

k = 5 for unstiffened stringer.

$$\frac{6000\sqrt{k}}{\sqrt{F_y}} = \frac{6000\sqrt{5}}{\sqrt{50000}} = 60.0 > \frac{D}{t_w}$$

so, C = 1.0

$$V_n = CV_p = C \cdot 0.58 F_y D t_w = (1.0)(0.58)(50.0)(23.92)(0.44)$$

$$\longrightarrow V_n = 305.2 \text{ k} > V_u = 165.3 \text{ k} \quad ✔$$

Therefore, the assumed section meets bending and shear strength requirements.

DESIGN EXAMPLE 3.2

STEP 7: CHOOSE A PRELIMINARY SECTION (CONTINUED)

The first step is to calculate the compression block height. If the compression block is within the concrete deck, then the section is considered compact, and the plastic moment is the composite section strength. If the plastic neutral axis is within the stringer web, then we will have to determine if the section is compact using Eq. 3.50 and Eq. 3.51. Eq. 3.55a or Eq. 3.55b can be used for compact sections. For non-compact sections, composite section elastic moment capacity shall be used.

Here "*a*" is the compression block height. It is obtained the same way as a regular reinforced concrete beam.

The plastic moment strength is also calculated the same way as a reinforced concrete beam if *a* < slab depth. The stringer is treated as reinforcement in the calculation.

The shear strength is the plastic capacity of the stringer's web, which is unstiffened.

Both moment and shear capacities exceed the factored forces, so the preliminary section meets the strength requirements.

3.10.3 Effective Flange Width

Even though the deck runs continuously across the supporting stringers, only a portion of the slab is taken to work in a composite fashion with the stringer. This portion of the slab acts as the top flange of a T-shaped girder (see Figure 3.31). This portion is termed the *effective flange width*. The definition of the effective flange width varies depending on whether the slab forms a T-shaped top flange (interior stringer) or is present on only one side of the stringer (exterior girder—see sidebar). For T-shaped cross sections, the effective flange width in AASHTO Standard Specifications is defined as the least of (AASHTO 10.38.3):

❏ One-fourth the span length of the stringer
❏ Center-to-center distance between stringers
❏ Twelve times the minimum thickness of the slab

> **E**ven though the deck runs continuously across the supporting stringers, only a portion of the slab is taken to work in a composite fashion with the stringer.

From inspection it can be seen that the first criterion will govern more often for short spans and the last for thin slabs. Otherwise, the stringer spacing will most likely hold true. For exterior stringer, the effective flange width should be taken as half of the effective width of the adjacent interior stringer, plus the least of:

❑ One-twelfth the span length
❑ Six times the slab thickness
❑ Deck overhang width

In the AASHTO LRFD Specifications, the contribution of the stringer web thickness and top flange width are also considered in determining the effective flange width of the concrete deck. For interior stringers, the effective flange width is defined (AASHTO LRFD 4.6.2.6) as the least of:

❑ One-fourth the span length of the stringer
❑ Center-to-center distance between stringers
❑ Twelve times the average thickness of the slab, plus the greater of stringer web thickness, or half the width of stringer top flange

For exterior stringers, AASHTO LRFD defines the effective flange width to be half of the effective width of the adjacent interior stringer, plus the least of:

❑ One-eighth the span length of the stringer
❑ The width of the overhang deck from exterior stringer
❑ Six times the average slab thickness, plus the greater of half of stringer web thickness, or 1/4 of the width of stringer top flange

THE EXTERIOR GIRDER shown in Figure 3.31 shows a conservative interpretation of the AASHTO effective flange width criteria. For overhangs where the deck is integrally reinforced *and monolithically poured* with the rest of the slab, the exterior slab-stringer configuration can be analyzed as a symmetrical T-beam section.

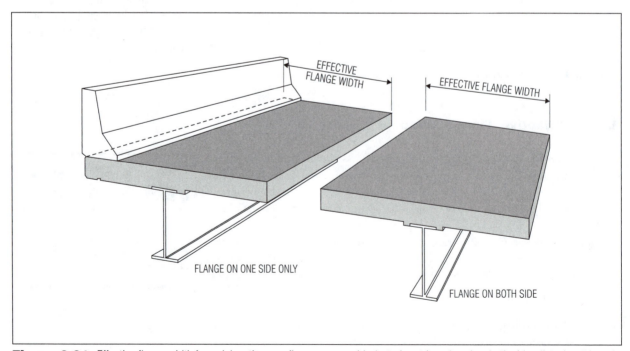

Figure 3.31   Effective flange width for a slab acting as a flange on one side (exterior stringer) and on both sides (interior stringer).

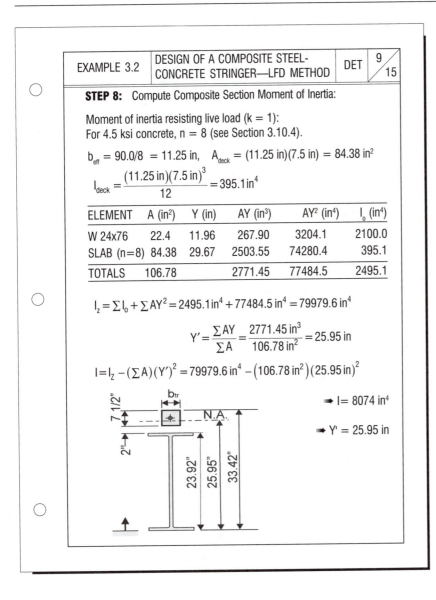

| EXAMPLE 3.2 | DESIGN OF A COMPOSITE STEEL-CONCRETE STRINGER—LFD METHOD | DET | 9/15 |

STEP 8: Compute Composite Section Moment of Inertia:

Moment of inertia resisting live load (k = 1):
For 4.5 ksi concrete, n = 8 (see Section 3.10.4).

$b_{eff} = 90.0/8 = 11.25$ in, $A_{deck} = (11.25\ \text{in})(7.5\ \text{in}) = 84.38\ \text{in}^2$

$I_{deck} = \dfrac{(11.25\ \text{in})(7.5\ \text{in})^3}{12} = 395.1\ \text{in}^4$

ELEMENT	A (in²)	Y (in)	AY (in³)	AY² (in⁴)	I_o (in⁴)
W 24x76	22.4	11.96	267.90	3204.1	2100.0
SLAB (n=8)	84.38	29.67	2503.55	74280.4	395.1
TOTALS	106.78		2771.45	77484.5	2495.1

$I_z = \sum I_o + \sum AY^2 = 2495.1\ \text{in}^4 + 77484.5\ \text{in}^4 = 79979.6\ \text{in}^4$

$$Y' = \frac{\sum AY}{\sum A} = \frac{2771.45\ \text{in}^3}{106.78\ \text{in}^2} = 25.95\ \text{in}$$

$I = I_z - (\sum A)(Y')^2 = 79979.6\ \text{in}^4 - (106.78\ \text{in}^2)(25.95\ \text{in})^2$

➡ I = 8074 in⁴

➡ Y' = 25.95 in

Before we design the shear studs, we have to calculate the composite section moment of inertia in order to calculate shear stresses due to live loads. For rolled section W24x76, we can refer to AISC for the section properties.

For composite section resisting live loads, we use the effective flange width calculated previously in Step 1. Using this transformed width of slab, the transformed area and moment of inertia of the slab are calculated. Note that k = 1 is used for calculating composite section for live loads.

A common datum located at the bottom of the bottom flange of the stringer is used. It is from this point that all references to the section neutral axis is given. The composite section moment of inertia is calculated following the steps indicated in Fig. 3.33.

The effective flange width is used to compute the section properties of the composite section and represents the portion of the deck which, together with the stringer, resists the applied loads.

3.10.4   The Transformed Section

When we calculate stresses or deflection of a structural under service loads, we usually assume the structure behaves elastically. To simplify the calculation of section properties of composite sections, we *transform* the section into a modified cross section where the concrete slab becomes an equivalent area of steel by the use of modular ratio. The modular ratio is defined as

$$n = \frac{E_s}{E_c}$$

(Eq. 3.44)

MOMENTS OF INERTIA ABOUT X-AXIS AT CG

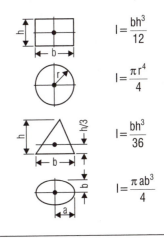

$I = \dfrac{bh^3}{12}$

$I = \dfrac{\pi r^4}{4}$

$I = \dfrac{bh^3}{36}$

$I = \dfrac{\pi ab^3}{4}$

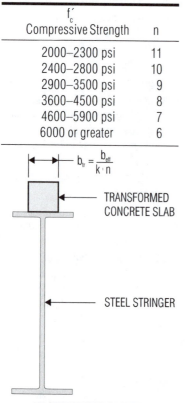

AASHTO STANDARD

10.38.1.3 MODULAR RATIO

AASHTO offers a table of modular ratio values to be used for various strengths of concrete in the design of composite members.

f_c' Compressive Strength	n
2000–2300 psi	11
2400–2800 psi	10
2900–3500 psi	9
3600–4500 psi	8
4600–5900 psi	7
6000 or greater	6

$b_{tr} = \dfrac{b_{eff}}{k \cdot n}$

TRANSFORMED CONCRETE SLAB

STEEL STRINGER

TRANSFORMED SECTION

where E_s = modulus of elasticity for steel
E_c = modulus of elasticity for concrete

The figure in the accompanying sidebar shows a visualization of what a transformed section could look like. The accepted value for the modulus of elasticity for steel is 29,000,000 psi (ACI 8.5.2, AASHTO 8.7.2 and 10.38.1.3). For normal weight concrete (approximately 145 lb/ft³), the modulus of elasticity is given as

$$E_c = 57,000\sqrt{f_c'} \qquad \text{(Eq. 3.45)}$$

where f_c' = compressive strength of concrete, lb/in²

If the actual unit weight of concrete used is known, the modulus of elasticity can be computed using

$$E_c = w^{1.5}33\sqrt{f_c'} \qquad \text{(Eq. 3.46)}$$

where w = unit weight of concrete, lb/ft³

For composite members, however, AASHTO offers a list of set modular ratio values which vary depending on the ultimate cylinder strength of the concrete used (AASHTO 10.38.1.3—see sidebar). Like Equation 3.45, these values are based on the use of normal weight concrete.

Once the modular ratio has been determined, the transformed width of the concrete slab can be calculated by simply dividing the effective width of the slab by the modular ratio:

$$b_{tr} = \frac{b_{eff}}{k \cdot n} \qquad \text{(Eq. 3.47)}$$

where b_{tr} = width of transformed concrete slab
k = multiplier accounting for creep (see Section 3.10.5)

This is the width used when computing the section properties of the composite section. The reader should keep in mind, however, that the center to center distance between stringers should be used when computing dead loads on the stringer.

3.10.5 Effects of Creep

In Section 3.5.4, Part 1, we defined creep as "the deformation of concrete caused by loads sustained over a period of time." When considering a composite member, this has an impact on superimposed dead loads such as wearing surface, curbs, railings, parapets, etc., which are placed after the deck

| EXAMPLE 3.2 | DESIGN OF A COMPOSITE STEEL-CONCRETE STRINGER—LFD METHOD | DET | 10/15 |

STEP 9: Compute Shear Range in the Stringer:

Ĉ SPAN

16K   16K   4K

$x_3 = 17'\text{-}0''$

$x_2 = 31'\text{-}0''$

$x_1 = 45'\text{-}0''$

Ĉ BEARING   Ĉ BEARING

x = 0

[x = 0] Positive Shear. From Step 5, we know that:

$+V_{x=0} = 59.56$ k

Note that live load distribution factors for shear, as well as live load impact are included.

[x = 0] Negative Shear

$-V_{x=0} = 0$

[x = 0] Total Shear Range

$V_{x=0} = +V_{x=0} - (-V_{x=0}) = 59.56$ k   ➠ $V_{x=0} = 59.56$ k

(Step 9: Continued on Next Sheet)

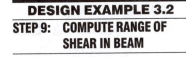

DESIGN EXAMPLE 3.2
STEP 9: COMPUTE RANGE OF SHEAR IN BEAM

We will compute the required number of shear connectors by examining the maximum positive and negative shear at various points along the length of the span. Naturally, we begin at the end of the span (x = 0).

Maximum shear is created by placing a design vehicle so that its rear axle is placed over the centerline of the bearings. As we stated in Step 5, the maximum positive shear at support due to live load and impact is 59.56 k for an interior stringer. At the end of the span, the negative shear is zero so it does not contribute to the total shear range. When calculating live load shear forces, in addition to the wheel load distribution factors, we must also apply an impact factor. In calculating the impact factor, for *truck load shear*, the loaded length of span is used for "L." This means we take the maximum of the "x" values shown in the figure, which in this case is 45 ft (the length of the span). This will vary for subsequent loading conditions (see Section 3.5.3, Part 7).

has cured and are sustained for the life of the structure (i.e., dead loads acting on the composite section).

To account for the effects of creep, AASHTO specifies a multiplier to be applied to the modular ratio when computing the width of the transformed slab (AASHTO 10.38.1.4). A multiplier of $k = 1$ is used for live load. For superimposed dead loads acting on the composite section, a multiplier of $k = 3$ is used.

Therefore, if a modular ratio of $n = 10$ were being used for the computation of stresses on the composite section due to live loads, a value of $3n = 30$ would be used for superimposed dead loads. This has the effect of reducing the width of the transformed slab and thereby reducing the size of the composite section modulus, which will increase the stress and deflection caused by the superimposed dead loads.

> To account for the effects of creep, AASHTO specifies a multiplier to be applied to the modular ratio when computing the width of the transformed slab.

AASHTO STANDARD

WHEN TRUCK LOADING GOVERNS

In Appendix A of the AASHTO Standard Specifications, the length of simple span where truck loading and lane loading govern are provided in tables listing the maximum vehicle loading moments, shears, and reactions. Truck loading governs for short spans and lane loading for long spans. The table below shows the range of simple span lengths where truck loading and lane loading govern.

BENDING MOMENT

Load	Span	Governs
H15	1 ft < L < 56 ft	Truck
H15	56 ft < L	Lane
HS15	1 ft < L < 140 ft	Truck
HS15	140 ft < L	Lane
H20	1 ft < L < 56 ft	Truck
H20	56 ft < L	Lane
HS20	1 ft < L < 140 ft	Truck
HS20	140 ft < L	Lane

END SHEAR & END REACTION

Load	Span	Governs
H15	1 ft < L < 32 ft	Truck
H15	32 ft < L	Lane
HS15	1 ft < L < 120 ft	Truck
HS15	120 ft < L	Lane
H20	1 ft < L < 33 ft	Truck
H20	33 ft < L	Lane
HS20	1 ft < L < 120 ft	Truck
HS20	120 ft < L	Lane

The method of selecting the stringer cross section will vary depending on whether a rolled section or plate girder is to be used.

3.10.6 Choosing a Rolled Section

The selection of the stringer cross-section geometry is accomplished through a trial and error process. The section is selected by performing five simple steps:

❑ First, assume a symmetrical steel section, based on the span length.
❑ Second, calculate the total factored bending moment and shear forces.
❑ Third, calculate the bending moment and shear capacities with the assumed section.
❑ Forth, revise, if necessary, the assumed steel section based on strength requirements.
❑ Fifth, check deflections and stringer working stresses (if required). Revise section if necessary.

There are a variety of methods which can be used to select steel stringers for composite beams. The method of selecting the stringer cross section will vary depending on whether a rolled section or plate girder is to be used. As an introduction, we will first discuss of designing rolled section stringers using LFD method. Design example using LRFD method is also introduced so readers can make comparison.

Bridge design is a trail and error process, so we first assume a reasonable stringer section based on the span length, and check if the section meets all AASHTO requirements. Revise the section if necessary until a satisfactory section is chosen.

1. Compute Design Moments and Shear Forces. The design moments and shear forces must be computed for:

❑ Dead load
❑ Superimposed dead load
❑ Live load plus impact

When computing the live load moments and shear forces, the designer must remember to take into account the wheel load distribution as outlined in Section 3.8, depending on which AASHTO specification is used. For longitudinally continuous stringers (i.e., stringers continuous over one or more piers) the computation of moments is significantly more complicated than for simple beams. Methods for computation of moments and shear in continuous beams will be discussed later in this section (see Section 3.12).

For simple spans, the dead load and superimposed dead load moments and shear forces at any point along the length of the span can be calculated from the standard equation for a beam under a uniform load:

$$M_x = \frac{wx}{2}(L-x)$$

(Eq. 3.48a)

EXAMPLE 3.2	DESIGN OF A COMPOSITE STEEL- CONCRETE STRINGER—LFD METHOD	DET	11 / 15

STEP 9: Compute the Shear Range in the Stringer (Continued):

16K   16K   4K

12'-6"

26'-6"

4'-6"   40'-6"

POSITIVE SHEAR

4K

NEGATIVE SHEAR

[x=4.5 ft] Positive Shear:

$$+V = DF\left(P_{16} \cdot \frac{x_1}{L} + P_{16} \cdot \frac{x_2}{L} + P_4 \frac{x_3}{L}\right)$$

$$= 1.45\left(16\,k \cdot \frac{40.5\,ft}{45.0\,ft} + 16\,k \cdot \frac{26.5\,ft}{45.0\,ft} + 4\,k \cdot \frac{12.5\,ft}{45.0\,ft}\right) = 36.15\,k$$

Impact: $\quad I = \dfrac{50}{125 + L_{max}} = \dfrac{50}{125 + 40.5\,ft} = 0.30$

So: $\quad +V_{x=4.5} = (I)(+V) = (1.30)(36.15\,k) = 47.00\,k$

[x = 4.5 ft] Negative Shear:

$$-V = DF\left(P_4 \cdot \frac{x}{L}\right) = 1.45\left(4\,k \cdot \frac{4.5\,ft}{45.0\,ft}\right) = -0.58\,k$$

Impact: $\quad I = \dfrac{50}{125 + 4.5\,ft} = 0.38 > 0.30 \quad$ So use $I = 0.30$

So: $\quad -V_{x=4.5} = (I)(-V) = (1.30)(-0.58\,k) = -0.75\,k$

[x = 4.5 ft] Total Shear Range

$V_{x=4.5} = +V_{x=4.5} - (-V_{x=4.5}) = 47.00\,k - (-0.75\,k)$

$\quad\quad\quad\quad\quad\quad\quad\quad\quad\quad\quad\quad \Rightarrow V_{x=4.5} = 47.75\,k$

(Step 9: Continued on Next Sheet)

DESIGN EXAMPLE 3.2

STEP 9: COMPUTE RANGE OF SHEAR IN BEAM (CONTINUED)

The process for calculating shear ranges continues. The beam is divided into tenth points proceeding toward the center of the span. There is no need to go any further because of symmetry. The first tenth point is 4.5 ft in from the left support.

The maximum positive shear is calculated by placing the rear axle of the HS20-44 design vehicle at the 4.5 ft point in question. Since we are no longer over the support (i.e., the center-line of bearings), we use the straight wheel load distribution factor of 1.45 for all axles. Remember that the impact factor is computed using the largest distance to the far support.

Maximum negative shear is computed with only the first 4k wheel load. This represents the maximum negative loading condition. Since the impact factor calculated using the 4.5 ft length is greater than the AASHTO specified maximum of 0.30, we use an impact factor of 1.30 applied to the calculated negative shear. The total shear is $+V-(-V)$ which yields 47.75 k.

$$V_x = w\left(\tfrac{L}{2} - x\right) \qquad \text{(Eq. 3.48b)}$$

where M_x = moment at a point x from an end support
$\quad\quad\; V_x$ = shear force at a point x from an end support
$\quad\quad\; w$ = uniformly distributed load in units of load per unit length
$\quad\quad\; x$ = distance from end support

The maximum moment for a simple span under a uniform distributed load occurs at the center of the span and is given by

$$M_{max} = \frac{wL^2}{8} \qquad \text{(Eq. 3.49a)}$$

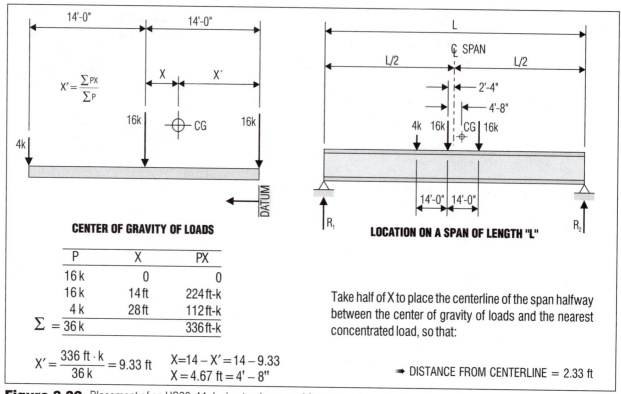

CENTER OF GRAVITY OF LOADS

P	X	PX
16 k	0	0
16 k	14 ft	224 ft-k
4 k	28 ft	112 ft-k
Σ = 36 k		336 ft-k

$$X' = \frac{336\ ft \cdot k}{36\ k} = 9.33\ ft \qquad \begin{array}{l} X = 14 - X' = 14 - 9.33 \\ X = 4.67\ ft = 4' - 8" \end{array}$$

Take half of X to place the centerline of the span halfway between the center of gravity of loads and the nearest concentrated load, so that:

➡ DISTANCE FROM CENTERLINE = 2.33 ft

Figure 3.32 Placement of an HS20-44 design truck on an arbitrary span in order to create maximum moment in the span.

The maximum shear force for a simple span under a uniform distributed load occurs at the support and is given by

$$V_x = \frac{wL}{2} \qquad \text{(Eq. 3.49b)}$$

where L = span length, centerline bearing to centerline bearing

It is important for the designer to calculate *two separate moments* for dead load and superimposed dead load since the computation of resulting stresses will vary because one is resisted by a noncomposite section and the other is resisted by a composite section. If LRFD is used, wearing surface load should also be calculated separately because it has a higher load factor than other dead loads.

The computation of the live load moment is slightly more involved. As we discussed in the section covering vehicle live loads (Section 3.5.3, Part 1), there are two types of vehicle live loading for AASHTO Standard Specifications: truck and lane loading. The rule of thumb followed by designers is that for short, simple spans, truck loading will generally govern. The definition of *short*, however, will vary depending on the type of loading being used. For bending moment induced by H20-44 loading, truck loading will govern for spans 56 ft (17 m) and less. However, for bending moment caused by HS20-44 loading, truck loading will govern for spans lengths

F or short, simple spans, truck loading will generally govern. The definition of *short* will vary depending on the type of loading used.

| EXAMPLE 3.2 | DESIGN OF A COMPOSITE STEEL-CONCRETE STRINGER—LFD METHOD | DET | 12/15 |

STEP 9: Compute the Shear Range in the Stringer (Continued):

[x = 9.0 ft] Positive Shear:

$$+V = DF\left(P_{16} \cdot \frac{x_1}{L} + P_{16} \cdot \frac{x_2}{L} + P_4 \cdot \frac{x_3}{L}\right)$$

$$= 1.45\left(16\,k \cdot \frac{36.0\,ft}{45.0\,ft} + 16\,k \cdot \frac{22.0\,ft}{45.0\,ft} + 4\,k \cdot \frac{8.0\,ft}{45.0\,ft}\right) = 30.93\,k$$

Impact: $I = \dfrac{50}{125 + 36.0\,ft} = 0.31 > 0.30$ So use $I = 0.30$

So: $+V_{x=9.0} = (I)(+V) = (1.30)(30.93\,k) = 40.21\,k$

[x = 9.0 ft] Negative Shear:

$$-V = DF\left(P_{16} \cdot \frac{x_1}{L} + P_4 \cdot \frac{x_2}{L}\right)$$

$$= 1.45\left(16\,k \cdot \frac{-9.0\,ft}{45.0\,ft} + 4\,k \cdot \frac{22.0\,ft}{45.0\,ft}\right) = -1.80\,k$$

So: $-V_{x=9.0} = (I)(-V) = (1.30)(-1.80\,k) = -2.34\,k$

[x = 9.0 ft] Total Shear Range

$V_{x=9.0} = +V_{x=9.0} - (-V_{x=9.0}) = 40.21\,k - (-2.34\,k) \Rightarrow V_{x=9.0} = 42.55\,k$

(Step 9: Continued on Next Sheet)

DESIGN EXAMPLE 3.2

STEP 9: COMPUTE RANGE OF SHEAR IN BEAM (CONTINUED)

The next tenth point is 9.0 ft from the left support. It should now be evident that as we move away from the support, the positive shear is decreasing and the negative shear increasing. The total shear range, however, is decreasing. This means that, when we compute the required shear connector spacing, the pitch at the end of the beam will be smaller than at the middle of the span (i.e., more studs at the end than at the center).

In this instance, with the point in question 9.0 ft from the support, the negative shear is computed with the front axle and center axle on the bridge. The center axle contributes the negative shear component. The distance to the near (left) support is taken for the 16 k load and the distance to the right support taken for the front wheel.

Again, the calculated live load impact value exceeds the 0.30 AASHTO specified maximum so we use an impact factor of 1.30.

140 ft (42.7 m) and less. When considering shear, span length ranges are different from those for moment depending on whether truck or lane loading governs. If the span length is greater than these lengths, then lane loading will govern. AASHTO provides a table of maximum moments and end shear reactions for various lengths of simply supported spans [Ref. 3.3]. The accompanying sidebar lists the span length ranges for which truck and lane loading govern for both bending moment and shear.

For the AASHTO LRFD Specifications, the design truck usually governs the design. But for short span bridges, design tandem may govern. Designers should calculate the force effects from both design truck and design tandem, and choose the most critical case to combine with the design lane load. Note that in LRFD, live load impact (dynamic load allowance) should only be applied to design truck or design tandem, not the design lane load.

The computation of the maximum live load moment induced by truck loading is made by moving a design truck along the length of the span so

> **F**or a moving load, the maximum moment occurs "when the center line of the span is midway between the center of gravity of loads and the nearest concentrated load."

as to induce maximum bending moment. For a moving load on simple span, the maximum moment occurs "when the center line of the span is midway between the center of gravity of loads and the nearest concentrated load" [Ref. 3.33].

Figure 3.32 shows that, for an HS20-44 truck (same as the design truck in LRFD Specifications), this value is 2'-4" or 2.33 ft (0.71 m). The center of gravity of the loads can be determined by referencing the distance of each load from a common datum. The sum of the product of each load times this distance is divided by the sum of all loads, yielding a distance from the center load of 4.67 ft (1.4 m). This is similar to the method for locating the center of gravity of a structural member. The right half of the figure shows an arbitrary span of length *L*. The group of loads is placed so that the centerline of the span falls between the center 16 k load and the center of gravity of the loads (2.33 ft from the centerline). This offset can now be used for any HS20-44 loading of a simple span.

After the loads have been placed on the span, the live load moment at a given location on a span is determined by analyzing the beam from one end of the beam to the point in question. For simple spans, the point at the 2'-4" offset (where the concentrated load is) represents the location of maximum moment.

The maximum live load shear force can be obtained by locating the 16 K wheel load near the support.

> **A**nother point of possible confusion is if axle loads, rather that wheel loads, are used. The distribution factor applies to *wheel loads* which are half the axle loads shown in Figure 3.12.

Once the maximum live load moment and shear forces are determined, the designer must also apply the required wheel load distribution factor which accounts for lateral distribution of the truck loads (see Section 3.8.1) and the dynamic effects of vehicle impact (see Section 3.5.3, Part 7). These multiplicative factors are applied directly to the live load moment and shear forces to yield a live load plus impact moment. The designer should keep in mind that the impact factor is a percentage, so that a value of $1 + I$ is applied to the live load forces. Another point of possible confusion is whether axle loads or wheel loads are used. In AASHTO Standard Specifications, the distribution factor applies to *wheel loads* which are half the axle loads shown in Figure 3.12. If the designer prefers to use axle loads in computations, then the distribution factors listed in Table 3.6 should be multiplied by $\frac{1}{2}$ to yield an axle load distribution factor (e.g., use a distribution factor of $S/11$ rather than $S/5.5$ in LFD method). In the AASHTO LRFD Specifications, axle loads and lane load are used instead of wheel loads.

> **I**f the designer prefers to use axle loads in computations, then the distribution factors listed in Tables 3.4 and 3.5 should be multiplied by $\frac{1}{2}$ to yield an axle load distribution factor.

2. **Total Factored Moment and Shear Forces.** The next step is to calculate the total factored forces. The designer should use the appropriate load factors depending on which AASHTO specification is used.

For AASHTO Standard Specifications, the load factor for dead load is 1.3, and load factor for live load is $1.3 \times 1.67 = 2.17$. See Table 3.2 for details.

For AASHTO LRFD Specifications, two load combinations are usually considered. For load combination Strength I, load factors for dead load, wearing surface and live load are 1.25, 1.50 and 1.75 respectively. For load combination Strength IV, the load factors for dead load and wearing

| EXAMPLE 3.2 | DESIGN OF A COMPOSITE STEEL-CONCRETE STRINGER—LFD METHOD | DET | 13/15 |

STEP 9: Compute the Shear Range in the Stringer (Continued):

[x = 22.5 ft] Positive Shear:

$$+V = DF\left(P_{16} \cdot \frac{x_1}{L} + P_{16} \cdot \frac{x_2}{L}\right)$$

$$= 1.45\left(16\,k \cdot \frac{22.5\,ft}{45.0\,ft} + 16\,k \cdot \frac{8.5\,ft}{45.0\,ft}\right) = 15.98\,k$$

Impact:

$$I = \frac{50}{125 + 36.0\,ft} = 0.31 > 0.30 \quad \text{So use } I = 0.30$$

So:

$$+V_{x=22.5} = (I)(+V) = (1.30)(15.98\,k) = 20.77\,k$$

[x = 22.5 ft] Negative Shear:

$$-V = DF\left(P_{16} \cdot \frac{x_1}{L} + P_{16} \cdot \frac{x_2}{L} + P_4 \cdot \frac{x_3}{L}\right)$$

$$= 1.45\left(16\,k \cdot \frac{-8.5\,ft}{45.0\,ft} + 16\,k \cdot \frac{-22.5\,ft}{45.0\,ft} + 4\,k \cdot \frac{8.5\,ft}{45.0\,ft}\right) = -14.89\,k$$

So:

$$-V_{x=22.5} = (I)(-V) = (1.30)(-14.89\,k) = -19.35\,k$$

[x = 22.5 ft] Total Shear Range:

$$V_{x=22.5} = +V_{x=22.5} - (-V_{x=22.5}) = 20.77\,k - (-19.35\,k) \Rightarrow V_{x=22.5} = 40.12\,k$$

DESIGN EXAMPLE 3.2

STEP 9: COMPUTE RANGE OF SHEAR IN BEAM (CONTINUED)

The last tenth point was at x = 9.0 ft. For the purposes of this example, we will skip the subsequent tenth point calculations as they follow pretty much the example set forth in the previous two calculation sheets. We will conclude the shear range calculations along the length of the span at the midspan location of the beam (x = 22.5 ft).

At this point, we place the rear axle at the midspan location. Because our span is only 45 ft long, the front 4 k wheel falls off of the span leaving us with the rear and center wheels only.

Maximum negative shear is created by placing the center wheel of the design vehicle at the midspan location. At the midspan location, negative shear is greatest and positive shear at its lowest value. The resulting 40.12 k shear range is not appreciably lower than the 42.55 k value calculated at the 9.0 ft offset. As can be seen from the past few sheets, calculating shear ranges is a somewhat tedious process that computer aided methods lend themselves well to handling.

---

surface are all 1.50, and no live load is considered. The larger moment and shear force from these two load combinations should be chosen for the design.

3. **Choosing a Section.** As we discussed earlier, choosing a steel stringer section that meets all design requirements is a trial and error process. Studies have shown that for a simple span bridge, the stringer depth should be in the range of 1/27 to 1/20 of the span length. Of course, the final section design will depend on the stringer spacing, steel strength, and the design live load.

AISC Steel Construction Manual (LRFD) offers a very useful tool for young engineers in choosing a preliminary section. Since we have already obtained the total factored bending moment, we can use the composite section bending moment capacity table to assist us in the stringer size selection. We should always keep in mind that no matter how we choose

We should always keep in mind that no matter how we choose the trial section, we should anticipate some revisions once detailed calculation is performed.

the trial section, we should anticipate some refinement once detailed calculation is performed.

4. **Composite Section Strength—LFD Method.** Once a preliminary section has been chosen based on the span length, factored moment and previous experiences, the selected section must be checked to determine the adequacy of the composite beam in resisting the factored bending moment and shear force.

For a composite section, the bending moment capacity depends on if the steel stringer is a *compact section*. A compact section is a symmetrical I-shaped beam with high resistance to local buckling and lateral or torsional buckling. Composite beams in positive moment regions shall qualify as compact sections if the neutral axis at the plastic moment is located above the web, or if the section satisfy the following requirements (AASHTO 10.50.1.1):

$$\frac{2D_{cp}}{t_w} \leq \frac{19,230}{\sqrt{F_y}} \qquad \text{(Eq. 3.50)}$$

$$\frac{D_p}{D'} \leq 5 \qquad \text{(Eq. 3.51)}$$

where D_{cp} = depth of the web in compression at the plastic moment assuming steel beam is fully yield
t_w = web thickness
F_y = steel yield stress (*psi*)
D_p = distance from the top of the slab to the neutral axis at plastic moment

$$D' = \beta \frac{(d + t_s + t_b)}{7.5}$$

where β = 0.9 for F_y = 36,000 psi
= 0.7 for F_y = 50,000 psi or 70,000 psi
d = depth of steel beam
t_s = thickness of the concrete slab
t_b = thickness of the concrete haunch above the beam top flange (to bottom of slab)

For compact section in positive bending regions, if the neutral axis of the plastic moment is above the web, or if $D_p < D'$, the maximum bending moment strength can be taken as the plastic bending strength.

To calculate the plastic moment strength, the composite section is treated as a conventional reinforced concrete beam. The steel beam acts like reinforcing steel, and concrete deck acts like concrete flange in a T beam. Compression reinforcing steel in the concrete deck is usually

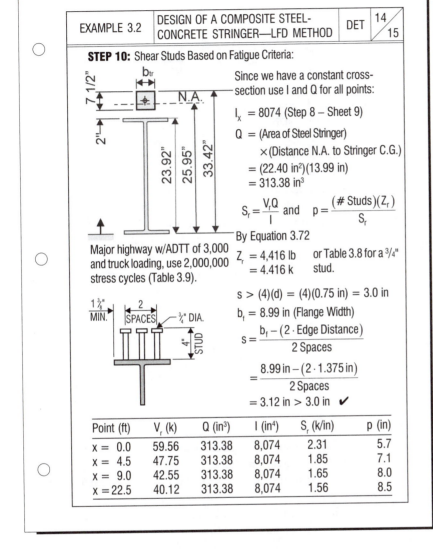

EXAMPLE 3.2	DESIGN OF A COMPOSITE STEEL-CONCRETE STRINGER—LFD METHOD	DET	14/15

STEP 10: Shear Studs Based on Fatigue Criteria:

Since we have a constant cross-section use I and Q for all points:

$I_x = 8074$ (Step 8 – Sheet 9)

Q = (Area of Steel Stringer)

$\times$ (Distance N.A. to Stringer C.G.)

$= (22.40 \text{ in}^2)(13.99 \text{ in})$

$= 313.38 \text{ in}^3$

$S_r = \dfrac{V_r Q}{I}$ and $p = \dfrac{(\text{\# Studs})(Z_r)}{S_r}$

By Equation 3.72

$Z_r = 4{,}416 \text{ lb}$ or Table 3.8 for a ¾"

$= 4.416 \text{ k}$ stud.

$s > (4)(d) = (4)(0.75 \text{ in}) = 3.0 \text{ in}$

$b_f = 8.99 \text{ in}$ (Flange Width)

$s = \dfrac{b_f - (2 \cdot \text{Edge Distance})}{2 \text{ Spaces}}$

$= \dfrac{8.99 \text{ in} - (2 \cdot 1.375 \text{ in})}{2 \text{ Spaces}}$

$= 3.12 \text{ in} > 3.0 \text{ in}$ ✔

Major highway w/ADTT of 3,000 and truck loading, use 2,000,000 stress cycles (Table 3.9).

Point (ft)	V_r (k)	Q (in³)	I (in⁴)	S_r (k/in)	p (in)
x = 0.0	59.56	313.38	8,074	2.31	5.7
x = 4.5	47.75	313.38	8,074	1.85	7.1
x = 9.0	42.55	313.38	8,074	1.65	8.0
x = 22.5	40.12	313.38	8,074	1.56	8.5

DESIGN EXAMPLE 3.2

STEP 10: COMPUTE REQUIRED PITCH FOR STUDS

The required pitch is a function of the range of horizontal shear at the slab-beam interface and the allowable stress for an individual stud. The former is computed using the live load plus impact shear ranges found in Step 9. The latter is taken from Table 3.8 and is based on the stud's diameter and the number of stress cycles. At the beginning of this Design Example we were given the type of overpass roadway and the estimated ADTT. This information is used to determine the number of stress cycles to design for (Table 3.9).

The designer must also make sure to check the geometric constraints detailed in Section 3.10.7, Part 2. In addition to the transverse spacing shown, the ratio of the stud length to diameter (L/d) must be greater than 4. Since the stud is 4 in long, this ratio is L/d = 4/0.75 = 5.33, which is greater than 4.

The table at left shows the resulting pitch values. These are the direct, calculated results which will be rounded *down* to present more reasonable field measurements (i.e., 5.5 in will be detailed instead as 5.7 in). See also Figure 3.35.

ignored. The compressive force in the concrete slab is equal to the smaller of:

$$C = 0.85 f_c' b t_s \qquad \text{(Eq. 3.52a)}$$

and

$$C = A F_y \qquad \text{(Eq. 3.52b)}$$

where b = effective width of the concrete slab

A = steel beam section area.

Like reinforced concrete beam, the depth of the concrete compression stress block in the concrete slab is:

$$a = \frac{C}{0.85 f_c' b} \qquad \text{(Eq. 3.53)}$$

When the compression stress block is within the concrete slab ($a < t_s$), the plastic moment can be calculated as:

$$M_p = C \cdot \left(d - \frac{a}{2} \right)$$

(Eq. 3.54)

where d = distance from the C.G. of stringer to the top of the concrete slab

If the compression stress block is beyond the deck thickness ($a > t$), then we will have to calculate the plastic neutral axis position, and calculate the plastic moment by adding all plastic forces times the moment arms for each component (i.e., slab, flanges, web). The plastic neutral axis is located where the compression force above it is equal to the tension force below it. All moment arms should be based on the neutral axis.

> The plastic neutral axis is located where the compression force above it is equal to the tension force below it.

Once we calculated the plastic moment capacity of the composite section, the maximum bending moment strength can be taken as:

For $\quad \dfrac{D_p}{D'} \le 1, \quad M_u = M_p ,$

(Eq. 3.55a)

For $\quad 1 < \dfrac{D_p}{D'} \le 5, \quad M_u = \dfrac{5M_p - 0.85M_y}{4} + \dfrac{0.85M_y - M_p}{4}\left(\dfrac{D_p}{D'} \right)$

(Eq. 3.55b)

Where M_y is the composite section elastic moment capacity which is equal to F_y times the section modulus with respect to the tension flange, using a transformed section and the modular ration n. In other words, M_y is the moment strength when bottom flange reaches the yield stress.

Please note that although most composite sections are compact, for a section that does not meet the compact requirements (Eq. 3.50 and Eq. 3.51), the maximum bending moment capacity shall be taken as M_y.

> Although most composite sections are compact, for a section that does not meet the compact requirements, the maximum bending moment capacity shall be taken as M_y.

Once we obtained the maximum bending strength of the composite section, we then compare it with the total factored moment. If the maximum bending strength is equal to or greater than the factored moment, the design is safe, otherwise the preliminary section size needs to be increased. Of course, if the section strength is far more than the factored moment, the preliminary section size should also be revised until a satisfactory size is finally chosen.

The next step is to check shear capacity. The shear strength of a composite section is the same as a noncomposite section because concrete deck is ignored in resisting shear. For a beam without stiffeners, the shear capacity

$$V_n = CV_p$$

(Eq. 3.56)

Where V_p is called plastic shear capacity and is determined as:

$$V_p = 0.58F_y D t_w$$

(Eq. 3.57)

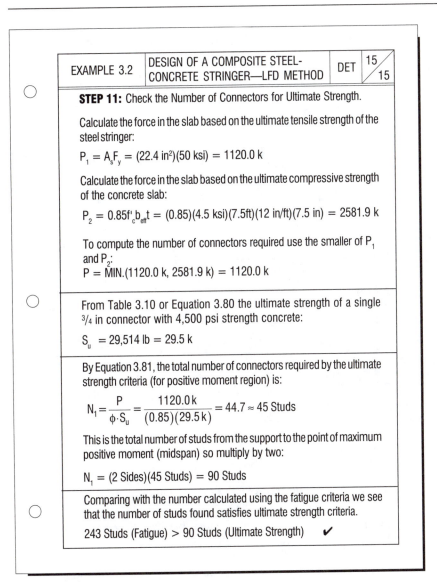

| EXAMPLE 3.2 | DESIGN OF A COMPOSITE STEEL-CONCRETE STRINGER—LFD METHOD | DET | 15/15 |

STEP 11: Check the Number of Connectors for Ultimate Strength.

Calculate the force in the slab based on the ultimate tensile strength of the steel stringer:

$P_1 = A_s F_y = (22.4 \text{ in}^2)(50 \text{ ksi}) = 1120.0 \text{ k}$

Calculate the force in the slab based on the ultimate compressive strength of the concrete slab:

$P_2 = 0.85 f'_c b_{eff} t = (0.85)(4.5 \text{ ksi})(7.5 \text{ft})(12 \text{ in/ft})(7.5 \text{ in}) = 2581.9 \text{ k}$

To compute the number of connectors required use the smaller of P_1 and P_2:
$P = \text{MIN.}(1120.0 \text{ k}, 2581.9 \text{ k}) = 1120.0 \text{ k}$

From Table 3.10 or Equation 3.80 the ultimate strength of a single $^3/_4$ in connector with 4,500 psi strength concrete:

$S_u = 29{,}514 \text{ lb} = 29.5 \text{ k}$

By Equation 3.81, the total number of connectors required by the ultimate strength criteria (for positive moment region) is:

$N_1 = \dfrac{P}{\phi \cdot S_u} = \dfrac{1120.0 \text{ k}}{(0.85)(29.5 \text{ k})} = 44.7 \approx 45 \text{ Studs}$

This is the total number of studs from the support to the point of maximum positive moment (midspan) so multiply by two:

$N_1 = (2 \text{ Sides})(45 \text{ Studs}) = 90 \text{ Studs}$

Comparing with the number calculated using the fatigue criteria we see that the number of studs found satisfies ultimate strength criteria.

243 Studs (Fatigue) > 90 Studs (Ultimate Strength) ✔

DESIGN EXAMPLE 3.2

STEP 11: CHECK STUDS FOR ULTIMATE STRENGTH

The first step in calculating the number of connectors required by the ultimate strength method is to compare the force in slab values. In this situation, the steel force is the smaller of the two values, so as per AASHTO 10.38.5.1.2, we use the steel value of 1120.0 k.

The ultimate strength of an individual connector is obtained from Table 3.10. The reader will recall that this value is a function of the diameter of the stud, the compressive strength of the concrete used in the slab and its associated modulus of elasticity. The values in Table 3.10 are calculated assuming normal weight concrete.

The number of studs required is computed by taking the ratio of these two forces and dividing by a 0.85 reduction factor. The designer should keep in mind that the number yielded by Equation 3.81 is for the connectors required "between the point of maximum positive moment and the adjacent support" (i.e., half the span length). So the resulting value is doubled and found to be less than that calculated for fatigue. See Fig. 3.35 for the final shear stud arrangement.

The constant C is equal to the buckling shear stress divided by the shear yield stress, and is determined as following:

for $\quad \dfrac{D}{t_w} < \dfrac{6{,}000\sqrt{k}}{\sqrt{F_y}} \qquad\qquad C = 1.0 \qquad\qquad$ (Eq. 3.58a)

for $\quad \dfrac{6{,}000\sqrt{k}}{\sqrt{F_y}} \le \dfrac{D}{t_w} \le \dfrac{7{,}500\sqrt{k}}{\sqrt{F_y}} \qquad C = \dfrac{6{,}000\sqrt{k}}{\left(\dfrac{D}{t_w}\right)\sqrt{F_y}} \qquad$ (Eq. 3.58b)

for $\quad \dfrac{D}{t_w} > \dfrac{7{,}500\sqrt{k}}{\sqrt{F_y}} \qquad\qquad C = \dfrac{4.5\times10^7 k}{\left(\dfrac{D}{t_w}\right)^2 F_y} \qquad$ (Eq. 3.58c)

SHEAR STUD GEOMETRIC CONSTRAINTS

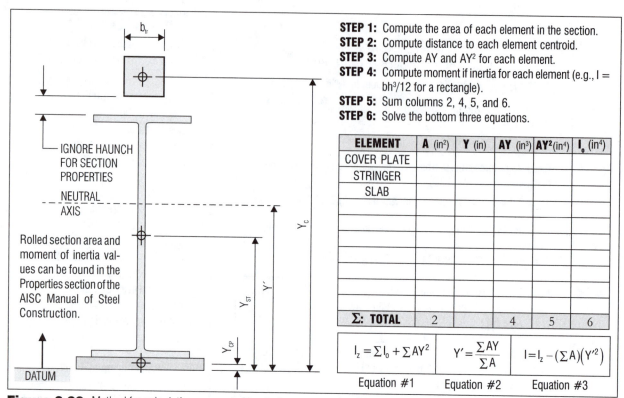

STEP 1: Compute the area of each element in the section.
STEP 2: Compute distance to each element centroid.
STEP 3: Compute AY and AY² for each element.
STEP 4: Compute moment if inertia for each element (e.g., I = bh³/12 for a rectangle).
STEP 5: Sum columns 2, 4, 5, and 6.
STEP 6: Solve the bottom three equations.

ELEMENT	A (in²)	Y (in)	AY (in³)	AY² (in⁴)	I_o (in⁴)
COVER PLATE					
STRINGER					
SLAB					
Σ: TOTAL	2		4	5	6

$$I_z = \Sigma I_o + \Sigma AY^2 \qquad Y' = \frac{\Sigma AY}{\Sigma A} \qquad I = I_z - (\Sigma A)(Y'^2)$$

Equation #1   Equation #2   Equation #3

Figure 3.33 Method for calculating moment of inertia for a composite section.

where $k = 5 + [5/(d_o/D)^2]$ is the bucking coefficient. ($k = 5$ for unstiffened beams).

D = clear, unsupported distance between flanges.

d_o = distance between transverse stiffeners.

When transverse stiffeners are provided ($d_o < 3D$), the shear capacity is increased to:

$$V_n = V_p\left(C + \frac{0.87(1-C)}{\sqrt{1+(d_o/D)^2}}\right) \qquad \text{(Eq. 3.59)}$$

If V_n is equal or larger than the factored shear force, the preliminary section is sufficient for shear forces. Otherwise, we may either increase the section size, or add transverse stiffeners to increase the shear capacity. Most rolled sections have sufficient shear strength compared with the bending strength, but if not, increasing section size (web thickness) is usually more economical than adding shear stiffeners. Shear stiffeners are usually used for plate girders (build-up sections) that have large D/t_w ratio.

> **M**ost rolled sections have sufficient shear strength compared with the bending strength, but if not, increasing section size (web thickness) is usually more economical than adding shear stiffeners.

5. Composite Section Strength—LRFD Method. The design approach for LRFD is very similar to that of LFD. A preliminary trial

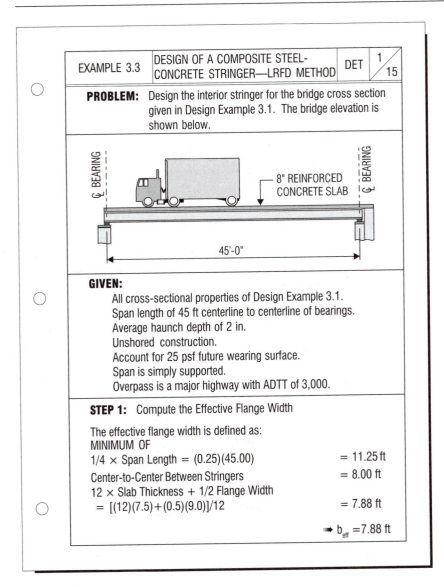

The design of the interior stringer will be performed using the AASHTO LRFD Specifications. This is the same structure as in Design Example 3.2 so that we can compare the two design methods. As in the previous example, the beam spacing of 8.0 ft and deck thickness of 8 in are used. A half inch wearing surface is assumed for the deck. An average haunch depth of 2 in is specified. The span is simply supported, and unshored construction is specified.

STEP 1: EFFECTIVE FLANGE WIDTH

The criteria governing the effective flange width of a composite girder are defined by AASHTO LRFD 4.6.2.6. In this case, the last value (12 times the average thickness of slab + 1/2 stringer flange width) governs. We will use the effective flange width in Step 8 through Step 13 to compute the amount of concrete slab acting as a composite section with the steel stringer. Note that 8 in by 8.0 ft concrete deck is used to calculate the deck dead load in Step 2.

section is chosen based on the span length, factored moment and previous experience. The selected section is then checked to determine the adequacy of the composite beam in resisting the factored bending moment and shear force.

For a composite section, the bending moment capacity depends on if the steel stringer is a *compact section*. The definition of a compact section in the LRFD specifications is slightly different from that of Standard Specifications. A composite section in positive bending region is considered compact if it meets the following requirements (AASHTO LRFD 6.10.6.2.2):

❏ the steel beam yield strength does not exceed 70 ksi,
❏ the web satisfies the requirement:

$$\frac{D}{t_w} \le 150 \qquad \text{(Eq. 3.60)}$$

❏ the section satisfies the web slenderness limit:

$$\frac{2D_{cp}}{t_w} \leq 3.76\sqrt{\frac{E}{F_{yc}}} \qquad \text{(Eq. 3.61)}$$

where D = depth of the web
D_{cp} = depth of the web in compression at the plastic moment assuming steel beam is fully yielded
t_w = web thickness
E = modulus of elasticity of the steel stringer
F_{yc} = compression flange steel yield stress

For compact sections in positive bending regions, if the neutral axis of the plastic moment is above 1/10 of the overall composite section depth ($D_p < 0.1D_t$), the maximum bending moment strength can be taken as the plastic bending strength:

$$M_n = M_p \qquad \text{(Eq. 3.62)}$$

Otherwise,

$$M_n = M_p\left(1.07 - 0.7\frac{D_p}{D_t}\right) \qquad \text{(Eq. 3.63)}$$

Like reinforced concrete beam, the depth of the concrete compression stress block in the concrete slab is:

$$a = \frac{AF_y}{0.85f_c'b} \qquad \text{(Eq. 3.64)}$$

When the compression stress block is within the concrete slab (a is less than the concrete deck thickness), the plastic moment can be calculated as:

$$M_p = AF_y\left(d - \frac{a}{2}\right) \qquad \text{(Eq. 3.65)}$$

where A = the area of the steel stringer
F_y = the yield strength of the steel stringer
d = the distance between the center of gravity of the steel stringer and the top of the concrete deck.

If the compression stress block is beyond the deck thickness, then we will have to calculate the plastic neutral axis position, and calculate the plastic moment by adding all plastic forces time the moment arms for each component (i.e., slab, flanges, web). The plastic neutral axis is located where

| EXAMPLE 3.3 | DESIGN OF A COMPOSITE STEEL-CONCRETE STRINGER—LRFD METHOD | DET | 2 / 15 |

8'-0"

25 PSF FUTURE WEARNIG SURFACE

8"

2"

ASSUME 5% OF STRINGER WEIGHT FOR MISC. STEEL

ASSUME 100 LB/FT

12"

STEP 2: Compute the Dead Load on Non-Composite Section
The dead load is composed of the following items:

DC_{slab} = (b)(slab thickness)(w_{conc})
= (8.0)(8.0/12)(0.150) = 0.800 k/ft

DC_{haunch} = (haunch width)(haunch thickness)(w_{conc})
= (1.0)(2.0/12)(0.150) = 0.025 k/ft

DC_{steel} = (assumed stringer weight) + (misc. steel)
= 0.100 + (5%)(0.100) = 0.105 k/ft

➡ DC_1 = 0.930 k/f

$M_{DC1} = \dfrac{wL^2}{8} = \dfrac{(0.930)(45.0^2)}{8} = 235.41 \text{k} \cdot \text{ft}$

➡ M_{DC1} = 235.41 k-ft

$V_{DC1} = \dfrac{wL}{2} = \dfrac{(0.930)(45.0)}{2} = 20.93 \text{ k}$

➡ V_{DC1} = 20.93 k

DESIGN EXAMPLE 3.3
STEP 2: COMPUTE DEAD LOAD ON NONCOMPOSITE SECTION

The dead load on the stringer is all weight placed *prior* to the concrete deck hardening and reaching full strength. In this case, the dead load on the stringer consists of the stringer itself, the slab and the haunch (the wearing course, parapet, etc., will be accounted for in Step 3 and Step 4). Since we do not yet know the exact size of the stringer, we will make an initial guess of 100 lb/ft for the stringer. We will assume 5 percent of the stringer weight to account for miscellaneous connection plates, diaphragms, etc. If stay-in-place deck form is used, it should also be included as a dead load in the design.

the compression force above it is equal to the tension force below it. All moment arms should be based on the plastic neutral axis.

Once we calculated the flexural strength, we can then check to see if the section meets the strength limit requirement:

$$M_u + \frac{1}{3} f_l S_{xt} \leq \phi_f M_n \qquad \text{(Eq. 3.66)}$$

where ϕ_t = the resistance factor for flexural (= 1.0, see AASHTO LRFD 6.5.4.2)

f_l = flange lateral bending stress in ksi. In most bridges, this item is zero.

M_n = nominal flexure resistance of the composite section in *k-in.*

M_u = factored bending moment about the major axis of the composite section in *k-in.*

S_{xt} = elastic section modulus about the major axis of the section to the tension flange as M_{yt}/F_{yt}.

M_{yt} = yield moment with respect to the tension flange in *k-in*.

Please note that although most composite sections are compact, for a section that does not meet the compact requirements (Eq. 3.60 and Eq. 3.61), the maximum bending moment capacity shall be taken as M_y.

The shear strength calculations in LRFD are almost identical to that of LFD specifications. For a beam without stiffeners, the nominal (without resistance factor) shear capacity is:

$$V_n = CV_p \qquad \text{(Eq. 3.67)}$$

Where V_p is called plastic shear capacity and is determined as:

$$V_p = 0.58F_y D t_w \qquad \text{(Eq. 3.68)}$$

The constant C is the ratio of the buckling shear resistance to the shear yield strength, and is determined as following:

if $\quad \dfrac{D}{t_w} \leq 1.12\sqrt{\dfrac{Ek}{F_y}} \qquad\qquad$ then: $C = 1.0 \qquad$ (Eq. 3.69a)

if $\quad 1.12\sqrt{\dfrac{Ek}{F_y}} < \dfrac{D}{t_w} \leq 1.40\sqrt{\dfrac{Ek}{F_y}} \qquad$ then: $C = \dfrac{1.12}{\left(\dfrac{D}{t_w}\right)}\sqrt{\dfrac{Ek}{F_y}} \qquad$ (Eq. 3.69b)

if $\quad \dfrac{D}{t_w} > 1.40\sqrt{\dfrac{Ek}{F_y}} \qquad\qquad$ then: $C = \dfrac{1.57}{\left(\dfrac{D}{t_w}\right)^2}\left(\dfrac{Ek}{F_y}\right) \qquad$ (Eq. 3.69c)

where $k = 5 + [5/(d_o/D)^2]$ is the shear bucking coefficient. ($k = 5$ for unstiffened beams).

D = clear distance between flanges.

d_o = distance between transverse stiffeners.

When transverse stiffeners are provided, the nominal shear capacity is taken as:

$$V_n = V_p\left(C + \dfrac{0.87(1-C)}{\sqrt{1+(d_o/D)^2}+d_o/D}\right) \qquad \text{(Eq. 3.70)}$$

The transverse stiffener spacing (if used) at end panel should not exceed $1.5D$.

The resistance factor ϕ_v for shear is 1.0 (AASHTO LRFD 6.5.4.2). If $\phi_v V_n$ is equal or larger than the factored shear force, the preliminary section is sufficient for shear forces. Otherwise, we may either increase the web thickness, or add transverse stiffeners to increase the shear capacity.

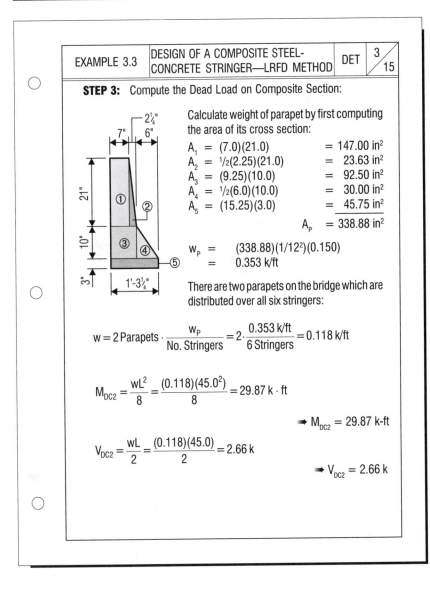

EXAMPLE 3.3	DESIGN OF A COMPOSITE STEEL-CONCRETE STRINGER—LRFD METHOD	DET	3/15

STEP 3: Compute the Dead Load on Composite Section:

Calculate weight of parapet by first computing the area of its cross section:

$$A_1 = (7.0)(21.0) = 147.00 \text{ in}^2$$
$$A_2 = \tfrac{1}{2}(2.25)(21.0) = 23.63 \text{ in}^2$$
$$A_3 = (9.25)(10.0) = 92.50 \text{ in}^2$$
$$A_4 = \tfrac{1}{2}(6.0)(10.0) = 30.00 \text{ in}^2$$
$$A_5 = (15.25)(3.0) = 45.75 \text{ in}^2$$
$$A_p = 338.88 \text{ in}^2$$

$$w_P = (338.88)(1/12^2)(0.150)$$
$$= 0.353 \text{ k/ft}$$

There are two parapets on the bridge which are distributed over all six stringers:

$$w = 2 \text{ Parapets} \cdot \frac{w_P}{\text{No. Stringers}} = 2 \cdot \frac{0.353 \text{ k/ft}}{6 \text{ Stringers}} = 0.118 \text{ k/ft}$$

$$M_{DC2} = \frac{wL^2}{8} = \frac{(0.118)(45.0^2)}{8} = 29.87 \text{ k} \cdot \text{ft}$$

➡ $M_{DC2} = 29.87$ k-ft

$$V_{DC2} = \frac{wL}{2} = \frac{(0.118)(45.0)}{2} = 2.66 \text{ k}$$

➡ $V_{DC2} = 2.66$ k

DESIGN EXAMPLE 3.3

STEP 3: COMPUTE DEAD LOAD ON COMPOSITE SECTION

Superimposed dead loads are those loads placed on the bridge after the deck has cured. These loads are resisted by the composite section. In AASHTO LRFD Specifications, wearing surface and utilities have a larger load factor than the rest of the dead loads. Therefore, we must separate wearing surface and utility (if applicable) when we calculate the superimposed dead loads. In this example, the superimposed dead load consists of the future wearing surface and parapet. Here only concrete parapets are calculated in this step. The future wearing surface will be calculated in Step 4.

All superimposed dead loads are to be distributed equally among all stringers.

To prevent permanent deformation, the maximum stress in the bottom flange, under Service II load combination, should not exceed 95 percent of the steel yield stress (AASHTO LRFD 6.10.4.2).

6. **Conclusions.** If the computed moment and shear capacities for the composite section exceed the total factored forces, then the preliminary section can be accepted as final. Should the factored forces be higher than the section capacity, a refinement of the section must be performed. For a rolled section, the designer can either

❏ Choose a larger rolled section
❏ Add a cover plate to the bottom of the section

Obviously it is a goal of the design to choose a section which minimizes the size of the girder while still maintaining a safe design. Larger sections

Shear Connector Design

10.38.5 FATIGUE CONSTANT FOR STUD CONNECTORS

Fatigue is induced by repetitive loading and unloading of a structure. AASHTO accounts for this by incorporation of a multiplicative factor based on the number of live loading cycles. AASHTO 10.38.5.1.1 gives the following factors:

Cycles	α
100,000	13,000
500,000	10,600
2,000,000	7,850
Over 2,000,000	5,500

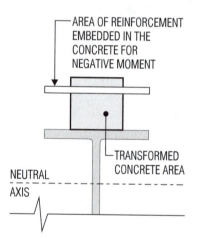

Q IS THE STATICAL MOMENT OF THE TRANSFORMED CONCRETE AREA ABOUT THE NEUTRAL AXIS OF THE COMPOSITE SECTION OR THE AREA OF REINFORCEMENT EMBEDDED IN THE CONCRETE FOR NEGATIVE MOMENT (AASHTO 10.38.5.1)

STATICAL MOMENT - Q

In a rehabilitation design, it is often desirable to remove the existing spiral connectors and replace them with shear studs when deck replacement is performed.

have the potential of impacting vertical clearance constraints (through an increase in beam depth), total weight of the structure, and associated costs. If a suitable rolled section or rolled section cover plate configuration cannot be found, a plate girder approach can be investigated.

3.10.7 Shear Connector Design

We have already discussed that composite action is enabled by the incorporation of shear connectors at the top flange of a steel stringer. In designing shear connectors, it is important to keep in mind the principal function of the connectors, which is to transfer horizontal shear to prevent movement between the slab and stringer, so that the steel stringer and the concrete deck will act as a single composite section.

Our discussion in this section will focus on the design of stud type connectors. As mentioned earlier, many older bridges are equipped with spiral shear connectors. In a rehabilitation design, it is often desirable to remove the existing spiral connectors and replace them with shear studs when deck replacement is performed. It is difficult to keep spiral connectors during the deck removal operation.

AASHTO requires that shear connectors be designed to account for fatigue and checked for ultimate strength. Discussed below are the parameters governing fatigue and ultimate strength criteria as well as various geometric constraints for placement of shear stud connectors.

1. **Fatigue.** In the early days of composite construction, shear connectors were designed under a strict elastic approach. As horizontal shear varied along the stringer, shear connectors were spaced accordingly. The composite steel-concrete beam was taken to act as a unit up to its ultimate strength with the overall goal being the elimination of slip at the slab-beam interface [Ref. 3.35]. This approach led to an overly conservative number of shear connectors being specified.

   Current practice bases the design of shear connectors on the ultimate flexural strength of a composite beam. Under such an approach, fatigue can become the governing criteria. Fatigue is caused by the repetitive loading and unloading of a structural member. Under an elastic approach for analyzing the effects of fatigue, it is the range of shear acting upon a connector rather than its magnitude of total shear which is considered [Ref. 3.36]. By a range of shear forces, we imply the difference between the maximum and minimum shear forces. The design approach and equations for both AASHTO Standard Specifications and LRFD Specifications are almost identical, except that in the Standard Specifications, service load is used for fatigue, while in LRFD specifications, only one truck with a load factor of 0.75 is used for fatigue design.

   The range of shear stress in the interface between stringer and the concrete deck is:

   $$S_r = \frac{V_r Q}{I} \qquad \text{(Eq. 3.71)}$$

   where S_r = range of horizontal shear at slab-beam interface, k/in
   V_r = range of shear due to live load plus impact, k

EXAMPLE 3.3	DESIGN OF A COMPOSITE STEEL-CONCRETE STRINGER—LRFD METHOD	DET	4 / 15

STEP 4: Compute Wearing Surface on Composite Section:

$$DW = \frac{(\text{width of roadway})(\text{future wearing surface})}{\text{number of stringers}}$$

$$= \frac{(44 \text{ ft})(0.025 \text{ k/ft}^2)}{6 \text{ Stringers}} \qquad = 0.183 \text{ k/ft}$$

$$M_{DW} = \frac{wL^2}{8} = \frac{(0.183)(45.0)^2}{8} = 46.32 \text{ k} \cdot \text{ft} \qquad \Rightarrow M_{DW} = 46.32 \text{ k}$$

$$V_{DW} = \frac{wL}{2} = \frac{(0.183)(45.0)}{2} = 4.12 \text{ k} \qquad \Rightarrow V_{DW} = 4.12 \text{ k}$$

STEP 5: Compute Live Load Distribution Factor:

We first assume the stringer size W24x76:

$$A = 22.4 \text{ in}^2, \qquad I = 2100 \text{ in}^4, \qquad d = 23.92 \text{ in}^2$$

The distance between the C.G. of the stringer and the C.G. of the deck:

$$e_g = \frac{7.5}{2} + 2.0 + \frac{23.92}{2} = 17.71 \text{ in}$$

For 4.5 ksi concrete, n = 8.

$$K_g = n\left(I + Ae_g^2\right) = (8)[2100 + (22.4)(17.71)^2] = 73,005 \text{ in}^4$$

Live load distribution factor for moment—Strength Limit State

$$DF_m = 0.075 + \left(\frac{S}{9.5}\right)^{0.6} \left(\frac{S}{L}\right)^{0.2} \left(\frac{K_g}{12.0 L t_s^3}\right)^{0.1}$$

$$= 0.075 + \left(\frac{8.0}{9.5}\right)^{0.6} \left(\frac{8.0}{45.0}\right)^{0.6} \left(\frac{73,005}{12.0 \cdot 45.0 \cdot 7.5^3}\right)^{0.1}$$

$$\Rightarrow DF_m = 0.645$$

(Step 5: Continued on Next Sheet)

DESIGN EXAMPLE 3.3

STEP 4: COMPUTE WEARING SURFACE ON COMPOSITE SECTION

The future wearing surface is equally distributed among all 6 stringers. Since wearing surface has different load factor, we separate it from the rest of superimposed dead loads.

STEP 5: COMPUTE LIVE LOAD DISTRIBUTION FACTORS

Prior to computing the actual live load moment and shear, we need to calculate the live load distribution factor for the moment and shear. For the two-lane bridge, the live load distribution factor for moment is given by Eq. 3.21, and the live load distribution factor for shear is given by Eq. 3.23. (Both are for Strength Limit States). Also see discussion in Section 3.8.1 for the other equations. Note that the live load distribution in LRFD is for *axle loads*.

Since live load distribution factor is a function of the section properties of the stringer, we have to assume a section based on experience to begin the design process.

Q = statical moment about neutral axis (see sidebar), in^3

I = moment of inertia of composite beam, in^4

For shear stud type connectors, this range of shear stress must be less than or equal to a corresponding allowable range of horizontal shear. This allowable range is given by

$$Z_r = \alpha \cdot d^2 \qquad\qquad (\text{Eq. 3.72})$$

where Z_r = allowable range of horizontal shear on one stud, k

α = constant based on number of stress cycles (see sidebar)

d = diameter of stud, in

STUD SIZE	100,000 CYCLES	500,000 CYCLES	2,000,000 CYCLES	2,000,000+ CYCLES
5/8 in	5,078	4,141	3,066	2,148
3/4 in	7,312	5,962	4,416	3,094
7/8 in	9,953	8,116	6,010	4,211

Table 3.8 Allowable Range of Horizontal Shear Z_r in Pounds for One Stud

AASHTO STANDARD DIVISION II
11.3.3 STUD SHEAR CONNECTORS

AASHTO specifies the tensile properties of welded shear stud connectors to be based on the following minimum requirements:

Tensile Strength 60,000 psi
Yield Strength 50,000 psi
Elongation 20% in 2 in
Reduction of Area 50%

The yield strength is determined using a 0.2% offset method (AASHTO, II, 11.3.3.1)

In AASHTO LRFD, an equation is given for α:

$$\alpha = 34.5 - 4.28 \log N \quad (\alpha \geq 2.75) \quad \text{(Eq. 3.73)}$$

where N = number of truck loading cycles (assuming 75 years) which can be calculated by (AASHTO LRFD 6.6.1.2.5):

$$N = (365)(75)n \cdot p(ADTT) \quad \text{(Eq. 3.74)}$$

where n = cycle per truck passage. For simple span or continuous span not near interior support, $n = 2$ if span is no more than 40 feet, *and* $n = 1$ if span is greater than 40 feet. For continuous span near interior support, $n = 2$ if span is no more than 40 feet, otherwise $n = 1.5$.

p = fraction of truck traffic in a single lane, which is equal to 1.0, 0.85 or 0.80 for one lane, two lanes, and three or more lanes (in one direction) respectively.

$ADTT$ = average number of trucks per day in one direction.

In AASHTO Standard Specifications, N is estimated as shown in Table 3.9.

So, the design of the composite beam's shear stud connectors should be such that

$$S_r \leq Z_r \quad \text{(Eq. 3.75)}$$

As we discussed in Section 3.10.1, there are three standard size shear stud connectors most commonly used in bridge construction: 5/8, 3/4 and 7/8 in. These dimensions represent the diameter of the stud shaft (i.e., not the head). Using these values, we can substitute into Equation 3.72 to define the allowable range of horizontal shear per stud for common size connectors. The results are displayed in Table 3.8.

The number of cycles used to define the allowable range of stress varies depending on the type of road the bridge is carrying. The number of cycles is mainly impacted by the amount of truck traffic traveling over the structure. Table 3.9 lists the number of cycles to be used for various types of overpass roadways. The ADTT columns represents the average daily truck traffic traveling in *one direction* over the bridge.

Shear stud type connectors are placed next to each other transversely along the top flange of a steel stringer to form a single row (see Figure 3.29).

...**t**here are three standard size shear stud connectors most commonly used in bridge construction: 5/8, 3/4, and 7/8 in.

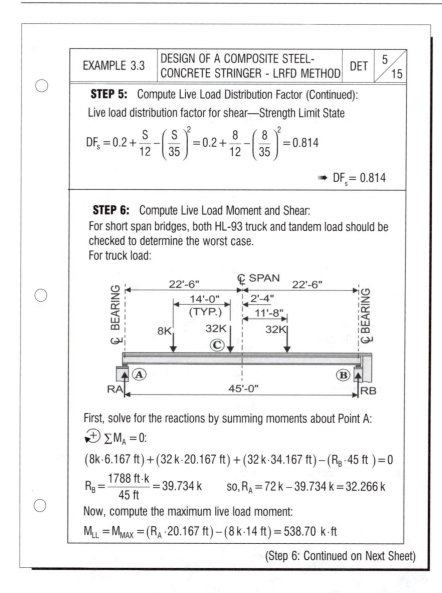

STEP 5: Compute Live Load Distribution Factor (Continued):

Live load distribution factor for shear—Strength Limit State

$$DF_s = 0.2 + \frac{S}{12} - \left(\frac{S}{35}\right)^2 = 0.2 + \frac{8}{12} - \left(\frac{8}{35}\right)^2 = 0.814$$

➠ $DF_s = 0.814$

STEP 6: Compute Live Load Moment and Shear:

For short span bridges, both HL-93 truck and tandem load should be checked to determine the worst case.
For truck load:

First, solve for the reactions by summing moments about Point A:

$\circlearrowleft^{+} \ \Sigma M_A = 0$:

$$(8k \cdot 6.167\ ft) + (32\ k \cdot 20.167\ ft) + (32\ k \cdot 34.167\ ft) - (R_B \cdot 45\ ft) = 0$$

$$R_B = \frac{1788\ ft \cdot k}{45\ ft} = 39.734\ k \qquad so, R_A = 72\ k - 39.734\ k = 32.266\ k$$

Now, compute the maximum live load moment:

$$M_{LL} = M_{MAX} = (R_A \cdot 20.167\ ft) - (8\ k \cdot 14\ ft) = 538.70\ k \cdot ft$$

(Step 6: Continued on Next Sheet)

DESIGN EXAMPLE 3.3

STEP 5: COMPUTE LIVE LOAD DISTRIBUTION FACTORS (CONTINUED)

Note that live load distribution factor for shear is different from that of moment. Also, distribution factors for exterior girders are different from interior stringers. See AASHTO LRFD 4.6.2.2.2.

STEP 6: COMPUTE LIVE LOAD MOMENT AND SHEAR

The live load for LRFD Specifications is composed of a truck or a tandem, combined with a 0.64 k/ft lane load. Both truck and tandem loads should be analyzed to obtain the worst effect.

First we calculate the maximum live load moment due to the design truck. The design truck is identical to the HS-20 load in Example 3.2. We use the same approach to obtain the maximum moment. Note that axle loads are used for the calculation.

Rows of connectors are then placed one after the other, longitudinally along the length of the stringer. The distance between rows of shear studs is known as the *pitch*. The limiting criteria defined in Equation 3.75 is used to determine the required pitch of the shear connectors.

To calculate the required pitch of shear connectors, we take the ratio of

$$p = \frac{n \cdot Z_r}{S_r} \qquad \text{(Eq. 3.76)}$$

where p = pitch (spacing) of shear connectors, in

n = number of shear connectors in a transverse row

Z_r = allowable range of horizontal shear (Tables 3.8 and 3.9)

S_r = range of horizontal shear at the point in question

With regard to the pitch of shear stud type connectors, the general rule of thumb is: the larger the diameter of the shear stud, the greater the spacing.

Rows of connectors are then placed one after the another ... along the length of the stringer. The distance between rows of shear studs is known as the *pitch*.

With regard to the pitch of shear stud type connectors, the general rule of thumb is: the larger the diameter of the shear stud, the greater the spacing.

TYPE OF ROAD	CASE	ADTT	TRUCK LOADING	LANE LOADING
Freeways, Expressways, Major Highways, and Streets	I	2,500 or more	2,000,000	500,000
Freeways, Expressways, Major Highways, and Streets	II	less than 2,500	500,000	100,000
Other Highways and Streets not included in Case I or II	III		100,000	100,000

Table 3.9 Number of Stress Cycles for Longitudinal Load Bearing Members

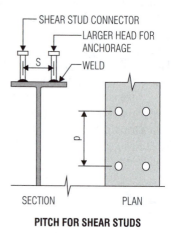

PITCH FOR SHEAR STUDS

In general, AASHTO limits the maximum spacing of shear connectors to 24 in (0.61 m), the exception to this rule being at the interior supports of longitudinally continuous stringers. For such structures it may be desirable to space the connectors at wider intervals in order to avoid areas of high tension in the top flange of the stringer. This situation occurs at locations of negative moment. For negative moment regions such as this, AASHTO does not require any shear connectors, provided that the reinforcing steel in the concrete slab is *not* taken to be part of the overall composite section (AASHTO 10.52.1). If reinforcing steel in the negative moment region is considered as part of the composite section, shear connectors should be provided.

Shear studs can be spaced equally throughout the length of the stringer based on the shear range at support. Greater economy, however, can be realized by using variable spacing based on the horizontal shear along the length of the stringer. For a simple span bridge, this means that there will

THE STEEL DECK FORMS in Figure 3.34 are waiting for installation at a bridge project staging area. Previously, steel deck forms were used predominately in building structures. Their use in bridge projects, however, has been gaining acceptance over the past several years. These forms are permanent, which also leads to them being referred to as "stay-in-place forms" (see also Figure 2.8). When the forms shown in Figure 3.34 are eventually installed in the bridge, they will be placed perpendicular to the primary members. During installation, they are fastened to supporting members and to adjacent form sections which are lapped to provide a tight joint and avoid potential mortar loss during placement of the concrete.

Figure 3.34 Steel deck forms, like those above, can affect composite construction.

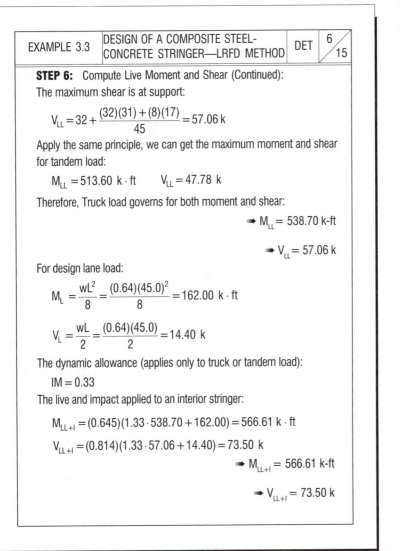

To obtain the maximum shear force at the support, we place the 32 k axle at the support, and the another 32 k axle and the 8 k axle on the span. That yields the maximum shear force of 57.06 k.

Following the same procedure, we can obtain the maximum moment and shear for the design tandem load, which is composed of a pair of 25 k axle loads, spaced at 4 feet. For maximum moment, one axle load should be placed 1 ft from the span center, and the other be placed 3 ft from the center. (See Figure 3.32 for details). For maximum shear force at support, one axle load should be placed at the support, and the other be placed 4 feet from the support.

The more critical forces from design truck and design tandem (in this case, the design truck for both moment and shear) should then be added to the design lane load (0.64 k/ft). The dynamic load allowance of 0.33 should not apply to the lane load.

be a greater number of shear studs at the ends of the beam (i.e., a closer spacing between rows of shear studs) than at the center of the span.

2. **Additional Geometric Constraints.** In addition to the longitudinal spacing of shear connectors, there are other geometric parameters which affect the size and placement of shear stud connectors. In a transverse direction, shear studs in a row should not be less than an inch from the edge of the stringer flange to the edge of the shear connector. The minimum spacing between shear studs (dimension s in the accompanying sidebar figure) is defined as (AASHTO 10.38.2.4)

$$s \geq 4 \cdot d \qquad \text{(Eq. 3.77)}$$

where s = spacing center to center between connectors in a row
  d = diameter of stud

Whatever size shear stud connector is selected, the same size should be used throughout the entire bridge structure.

AASHTO SPECIFICATION

10.2.2 MINIMUM YIELD POINT FOR STRUCTURAL STEEL

AASHTO provides a table (AASHTO Table 10.2A) which details the various minimum yield point or minimum yield strength (F_y) values for various types of structural steel. The modulus of elasticity of all steel is taken as 29,000,000 psi.

Type of Steel	Grade	F_y
Structural Carbon Steel	36	36 ksi plates up to 4" thick incl.
High Strength	50	50 ksi plates up to 4" thick incl.
Low Alloy Steel High Strength Low Alloy Steel	50W	50 ksi plates up to 4" thick incl.
Quenched and Tempered Low Alloy Steel	70W	70 ksi plates up to 4" thick incl.
High Yield Strength Quenched and Tempered Alloy Steel	100 & 100W	100 ksi plates up to 2½" thick incl.
High Yield Strength Quenched and Tempered Alloy Steel	100 & 100W	90 ksi plates over 2½" thick to 4" incl.

In the late 1960's and early 1970's, the advent of ultimate strength theory led to the incorporation of an ultimate strength approach in shear connector design.

There should also be at least 2 in (50 mm) of concrete cover over the top of the shear connector. The shear stud should also extend at least 2 in (50 mm) above the bottom of the concrete deck slab (AASHTO 10.38.2.3). Another geometric constraint is that the ratio of the length of the connector to its diameter should not be less than 4.

When a haunch is being used over the top flange of a stringer, this will obviously have an impact on the length of the stud used. In New York State, the Department of Transportation recommends using 4 in (100 mm) long studs for haunches which are 2 in (50 mm) and under. For haunches 2 in to 4 in deep, 6 in (150 mm) studs are to be used [Ref. 3.11]. Whatever size shear stud connector is selected, the same size should be used throughout the entire bridge structure. Haunches larger than 4 in deep are usually reinforced so that 4 or 5 in long studs can be used.

3. Effect of Stay-in-Place Forms. Another factor which can affect the placement of shear studs is the presence of steel deck forms (also see Section 2.3.4, Part 1). These forms, which remain in place after the concrete has cured (stay-in-place forms), behave differently depending on the way they are oriented on the bridge. If the ribs of the forms, like those shown in Figure 3.34, are placed parallel to the primary members, the deck essentially behaves like a haunched slab. If the ribs are placed orthogonally to the stringers, however, a potential shear failure due to insufficient shear stud penetration may occur.

To counteract these effects, shear studs should extend at least 1.5 inches (38 mm) above the steel deck form rib. Steel deck form rib sizes up to 1.5 in generally have no effect on the stiffness or other section properties of the composite beam. Forms with ribs in excess of 1.5 inches in depth, while not impacting the section modulus of the beam at the bottom flange, have an adverse (i.e., decreasing) effect on the section modulus of the slab [Ref. 3.37].

4. Ultimate Strength. Once the connectors have been designed for fatigue, they must be checked for ultimate strength. At the top of this discussion, we stated that the early design of shear connectors (circa 1957) was concerned with the limitation of shear stresses at the slab-beam interface. This limiting criterion, however, proved to be irrelevant since studies showed that a composite beam develops its full flexural capacity as long as the aggregate of the ultimate strength of each connector is at least equal to the total horizontal shear (from the point of zero to maximum moment) [Ref. 3.37].

In the late 1960's and early 1970's, the advent of ultimate strength theory led to the incorporation of an ultimate strength approach in shear connector design. Using an ultimate strength method, it became possible to determine the minimum number of shear connectors required to develop full flexural strength of the composite section.

In later editions of the bridge design code, AASHTO specified that the ultimate strength of all shear connectors must be greater than or equal to the ultimate strength of the concrete slab in compression or the steel

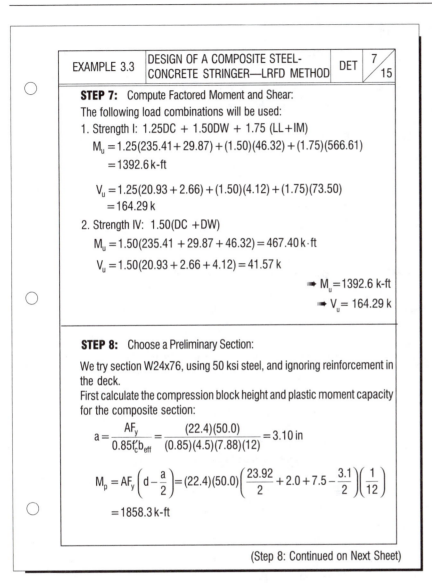

STEP 7: CALCULATE FACTOR MOMENT AND SHEAR

By applying load factors from Table 3.4 AND Table 3.5, we can obtain the total factored moment and shear for an interior stringer.

Note that both Strength I and Strength IV load combinations are calculated to obtain the worst situation for the stringer design. In most cases, Strength I will govern the design.

STEP 8: CHOOSE A PRELIMINARY SECTION

For a simply supported bridge, a range of 1/20 to 1/27 of the span length is normally used as the depth of the stringers. 50 ksi steel (painted or weathering steel) is commonly used for bridge construction.

The first step is to calculate the plastic compression block height, and the plastic moment strength. If the compression block is within the concrete slab, then the plastic moment strength can be calculated as if it were a reinforced concrete beam. (The steel stringer is treated as reinforcement in the concrete beam.)

stringer in tension. The smaller of the two values is taken. AASHTO differentiates between sections of a span where there is

- ❏ Maximum positive moment
- ❏ Maximum negative moment
- ❏ Points of contraflexure

The first condition occurs in simply supported spans and the last two criteria are found in longitudinally continuous bridges. With regard to points of maximum positive moment, the ultimate tensile strength of the steel stringer is given as

$$P_1 = A_s F_y \qquad \text{(Eq. 3.78)}$$

where P_1 = tension force in the stringer

A_s = total area of steel stringer including cover plates

F_y = minimum yield point of steel used

DID YOU KNOW

THAT a great deal of the research on the ultimate strength of shear connectors was conducted at Lehigh University in Bethlehem, Pennsylvania? In 1971 Jorgen Ollgaard, Roger Slutter, and John Fisher published a paper defining the ultimate strength of a single shear stud as

$$Q_u = 0.5 A_s \sqrt{f'_c \cdot E_c}$$

which, for all intents and purposes, is the one used today in the both AASHTO codes [Ref. 3.38].

STUD SIZE	f'_c 3,000 psi	f'_c 3,500 psi	f'_c 4,000 psi	f'_c 4,500 psi
5/8 in	15,122	16,975	18,763	20,496
3/4 in	21,775	24,444	27,019	29,514
7/8 in	29,638	33,271	36,775	40,172

Table 3.10 Nominal Strength S_n in Pounds for One Stud and Normal Weight Concrete

Likewise, the ultimate compressive strength of the concrete slab is given by the expression

$$P_2 = 0.85 f'_c \cdot b_{eff} \cdot t \qquad \text{(Eq. 3.79)}$$

where P_2 = compression force in the slab
f'_c = 28 day compressive strength of concrete used
b_{eff} = effective flange width (See Section 3.10.3)
t = thickness of concrete slab

For shear stud type connectors, the ultimate strength of the connector itself is

$$S_n = 0.5 A \sqrt{f'_c E_c} \leq A F_u \qquad \text{(Eq. 3.80)}$$

where S_n = nominal strength of a single shear connector, kips
A = cross-section area of stud, in^2
f'_c = 28 day compressive strength of concrete used, ksi
E_c = modulus of elasticity of concrete, ksi
F_u = specified tensile strength of shear stud, ksi

As mentioned at the end of Part 2 above, the ratio of the length of the stud to its diameter should be greater than 4. This criteria must be met in order for Equation 3.80 to hold. The modulus of elasticity of concrete is defined as outlined in Section 3.10.4.

Once all three ultimate strengths have been computed, it is possible to compute the minimum number of shear connectors required. It is important to note that the number of shear connectors calculated using the ultimate strength approach is used *as a check* of the number determined using the fatigue approach. The number of shear connectors specified for the final design must satisfy both of these criteria (i.e., the ultimate strength method is not an alternative approach, but a required check). With this in mind, the minimum number of shear connectors is given as

It is important to note that the number of shear connectors calculated using the ultimate strength approach is used *as a check* of the number determined using the fatigue approach.

$$N_1 = \frac{P}{\phi \cdot S_n} \qquad \text{(Eq. 3.81)}$$

where N_1 = number of shear connectors (see below)
P = minimum of P_1 and P_2
ϕ = resistance factor = 0.85
S_n = nominal strength of a shear connector (Equation 3.80)

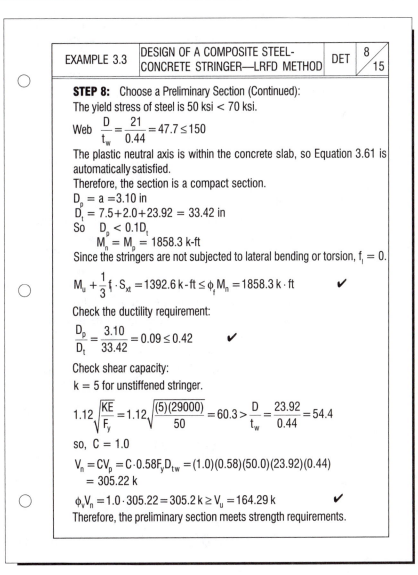

EXAMPLE 3.3	DESIGN OF A COMPOSITE STEEL-CONCRETE STRINGER—LRFD METHOD	DET	8 / 15

STEP 8: Choose a Preliminary Section (Continued):

The yield stress of steel is 50 ksi < 70 ksi.

Web $\dfrac{D}{t_w} = \dfrac{21}{0.44} = 47.7 \leq 150$

The plastic neutral axis is within the concrete slab, so Equation 3.61 is automatically satisfied.

Therefore, the section is a compact section.

$D_p = a = 3.10$ in

$D_t = 7.5 + 2.0 + 23.92 = 33.42$ in

So $D_p < 0.1 D_t$

$M_n = M_p = 1858.3$ k-ft

Since the stringers are not subjected to lateral bending or torsion, $f_l = 0$.

$M_u + \dfrac{1}{3} f_l \cdot S_{xt} = 1392.6 \text{ k-ft} \leq \phi_f M_n = 1858.3 \text{ k} \cdot \text{ft}$ ✔

Check the ductility requirement:

$\dfrac{D_p}{D_t} = \dfrac{3.10}{33.42} = 0.09 \leq 0.42$ ✔

Check shear capacity:

$k = 5$ for unstiffened stringer.

$1.12 \sqrt{\dfrac{KE}{F_y}} = 1.12 \sqrt{\dfrac{(5)(29000)}{50}} = 60.3 > \dfrac{D}{t_w} = \dfrac{23.92}{0.44} = 54.4$

so, $C = 1.0$

$V_n = C \cdot V_p = C \cdot 0.58 F_y D_{tw} = (1.0)(0.58)(50.0)(23.92)(0.44)$
$\qquad = 305.22$ k

$\phi_v V_n = 1.0 \cdot 305.22 = 305.2 \text{ k} \geq V_u = 164.29 \text{ k}$ ✔

Therefore, the preliminary section meets strength requirements.

DESIGN EXAMPLE 3.3
STEP 8: CHOOSE A PRELIMINARY SECTION (CONTINUED)

In LRFD, if a composite section with steel stringer yield stress not exceeding 70 ksi, and the web meets the requirements of Eq. 3.60, and the depth of steel web in compression (if any) meets the requirements of Eq. 3.61, then the section is considered compact. In this example, we have a compact section. For compact section in positive bending regions, if the plastic neutral axis is above 1/10 of the overall compact section depth, the moment capacity equals to the plastic bending strength. See Part 5 of Section 3.10.6 for details.

Once moment strength is calculated, we first use Eq. 3.66 to check strength requirement, and then check ductility requirement.

The shear strength is the plastic capacity of the stringer's web, which is unstiffened.

Both moment and shear capacities exceed the factored forces, so the preliminary section meets the strength requirements.

The number of shear connectors defined by Equation 3.81 is the minimum number of connectors required between points of maximum positive moment and the adjacent end supports. The value of *P* used is the smaller of the ultimate concrete compressive and ultimate steel tensile strengths found by Equations 3.78 and 3.79.

Table 3.10 presents the various values of shear stud nominal strengths for different strengths of concrete. These values are based on Equation 3.80 as well as Equation 3.45 for the modulus of elasticity of normal weight concrete. The designer should keep in mind that these values must be multiplied by the 0.85 resistance factor.

Another potential source for error is if the designer uses the transformed effective flange width in Equation 3.79. The *full effective flange width* of the slab should be used in computing the ultimate compressive strength of the concrete slab.

> **T**he value of *P* used is the smaller of the ultimate concrete compressive and ultimate steel tensile strengths ...

> **T**he *full effective flange width* of the slab should be used in computing the ultimate compressive strength of the concrete slab.

So far, we have discussed the parameters involved in determining the number of shear connectors required for points located within regions of positive moment only. In areas between maximum positive moment and adjacent maximum negative moment the minimum number of shear connectors required is given as

$$N_2 = \frac{P + P_3}{\phi \cdot S_n}$$
(Eq. 3.82)

where N_2 = number of shear connectors
P = minimum of P_1 and P_2
P_3 = force in slab at points of maximum negative moment
ϕ = resistance factor = 0.85
S_n = nominal strength of a shear connector (Equation 3.80)

The force in the slab at points of maximum negative moment is taken as zero when reinforcement located at the top surface of the concrete slab is not used in calculating the properties of the composite section resisting negative moments. Otherwise, this force is computed by the following:

For Load Factor Design (AASHTO Standard Specifications):

$$P_3 = A_s^r \cdot F_y^r$$
(Eq. 3.83)

For the LRFD method, P_3 is taken as the lesser of:

$$P_3 = A_s F_y$$
(Eq. 3.84a)

$$P_3 = 0.45 f_c' \cdot b_{eff} \cdot t$$
(Eq. 3.84b)

where P_3 = force in slab at points of maximum negative moment
A_s^r = total area of reinforcement within the effective flange width at the interior support
F_y^r = minimum yield stress of reinforcing steel
b_{eff} = effective flange width (see section 3.10.3)
t = thickness of concrete slab
A_s = total cross-section area of the stringer
F_y = yield stress of the stringer

Note that AASHTO LRFD Specifications takes a more conservative approach in dealing with concrete slab in tension than AASHTO Standard Specifications. The 45% of the deck compressive strength represents the combined contribution of deck reinforcement and the tensile strength of the concrete. In the AASHTO Standard Specifications, only reinforcement in the deck is considered in resisting tension, therefore requiring less shear studs to resist the horizontal shear at negative moment region.

| EXAMPLE 3.3 | DESIGN OF A COMPOSITE STEEL-CONCRETE STRINGER—LRFD METHOD | DET | 9 / 15 |

STEP 9: Compute Composite Section Moment of Inertia:

For superimposed dead loads, use 3n (= 24):

$$b_f = \frac{b_{eff}}{3n} = \frac{7.88 \cdot 12}{3 \cdot 8} = 3.94 \text{ in} \qquad I_{deck} = \frac{(3.94 \text{ in})(7.5 \text{ in})^3}{12} = 138.5 \text{ in}^4$$

ELEMENT	A (in²)	Y (in)	AY (in³)	AY² (in⁴)	I₀ (in⁴)
W 24x76	22.4	11.96	267.90	3204.1	2100.0
SLAB (3n)	29.55	29.67	876.75	26013.1	138.5
TOTALS	51.95		1144.65	29217.2	2238.5

$$I_z = \Sigma I_0 + \Sigma AY^2 = 2238.5 \text{ in}^4 + 29217.2 \text{ in}^4 = 31{,}456 \text{ in}^4$$

$$Y' = \frac{\Sigma AY}{\Sigma A} = \frac{1144.65 \text{ in}^3}{51.95 \text{ in}^2} = 22.03 \text{ in}$$

$$I = I_z - (\Sigma A)(Y')^2 = 31{,}456 \text{ in}^4 - (51.95 \text{ in}^2)(22.03 \text{ in})^2$$

$$= 6243.3 \text{ in}^4$$

$$S = \frac{I}{y'} = \frac{6243.3 \text{ in}^4}{22.03 \text{ in}} = 283.40 \text{ in}^3$$

For live loads, use n (=8):

$$b_f = \frac{b_{eff}}{n} = \frac{7.88 \cdot 12}{8} = 11.82 \text{ in} \qquad I_{deck} = \frac{(11.82 \text{ in})(7.5 \text{ in})^3}{12} = 415.5 \text{ in}^4$$

ELEMENT	A (in²)	Y (in)	AY (in³)	AY² (in⁴)	I₀ (in⁴)
W 24x76	22.4	11.96	267.90	3204.1	2100.0
SLAB (n=8)	88.65	29.67	2630.25	78039.4	415.5
TOTALS	111.05		2898.15	81243.5	2515.5

(Step 9: Continued on Next Sheet)

DESIGN EXAMPLE 3.3
STEP 9: COMPUTE COMPOSITE SECTION MOMENT OF INERTIA

Before we check service limit state, and design the shear studs, we have to calculate the composite section moment of inertia in order to calculate stresses due to live loads and superimposed dead loads. For rolled section W24x76, we can refer to AISC for the section properties.

For composite section, we use the effective flange width calculated previously in Step 1. Using this transformed width of slab, the transformed area and moment of inertia of the slab are calculated. Note that k = 1 is used for calculating the composite section for live loads, and k = 3 for calculating the composite section for superimposed dead loads.

A common datum located at the bottom of the bottom flange of the stringer is used. It is from this point that all references to the section neutral axis is given. The composite section moment of inertia is calculated following the steps indicated in Fig. 3.33.

In positive moment regions, this longitudinal reinforcing steel is typically ignored since its impact is negligible. As was illustrated in Figure 3.30, in positive moment regions, compression is taken up by the slab and tension by the steel stringer.

Whether or not the reinforcing steel is taken as part of the composite section, however, is an option which is left up to the designer. As mentioned above, if the longitudinal reinforcing steel is not taken as part of the composite section, the value of P_3 goes to zero. If this is the case, then additional shear connectors must be provided at points of contraflexure.

The number of additional shear connectors required at points of contraflexure for each beam is given as

$$N_c = \frac{A_r^r \cdot f_r}{Z_r} \qquad \text{(Eq. 3.85)}$$

[3.10.7, Part 4]

A WAY TO LAY OUT shear connectors is presented in Figure 3.35. The calculated spacing at the various beam locations is plotted as a curve passed through the points. Obviously, the more points taken the more accurate the plot. In Design Example 3.2, four such points were taken. Since, for a simple span, shear is greatest at the supports, the greatest variation is seen here. When selecting the break point, the designer must take care that the specified spacing falls *below* the plotted curve. This will ensure the most conservative result. Our breakpoint is at x = 9.2 ft from the support. While, at this point, an 8 in spacing fall below the curve, so we are O.K. at this point. The total number of studs is

$3 \times (21\,\text{Studs} + 39\,\text{Studs} + 21\,\text{Studs})$

since we have three studs per row, for a total of 243 studs.

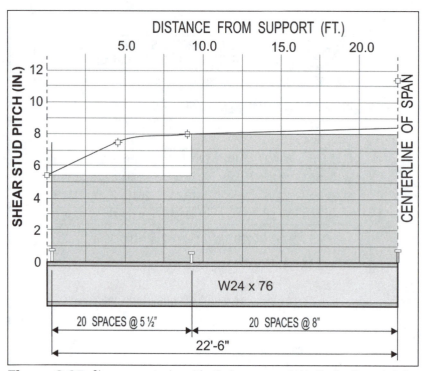

Figure 3.35 Shear connector layout for the beam presented in Design Example 3.2.

where N_c = number of additional connectors required
 A_r^s = total area of longitudinal slab reinforcement for each beam over interior support
 f_r = range of stress due to live load plus impact in the slab reinforcement over the support
 Z_r = allowable range of horizontal shear (Table 3.8 and Equation 3.72)

If an accurate calculation of f_r is not available, an assumed value of 10,000 psi may be used instead. These additional connectors are placed next to the point of dead load contraflexure within a distance which is defined as

$$d = \frac{b_{\text{eff}}}{3}$$ (Eq. 3.86)

where b_{eff} = effective flange width

Any field splices should be located so as not to interfere with the shear connectors (AASHTO 10.38.5.1.3).

3.10.8 Cover Plates

A cover plate is a separate steel plate welded to the bottom flange of a rolled section stringer. We have already mentioned that when a rolled section does not satisfy the design requirements of the beam, welding of a cover plate may be a way of *beefing up* the section properties of a composite beam. Discussed below

> **W**hen a rolled section ... does not satisfy the design requirements of the beam, welding of a cover plate may be a desirable way of *beefing up* the section properties ...

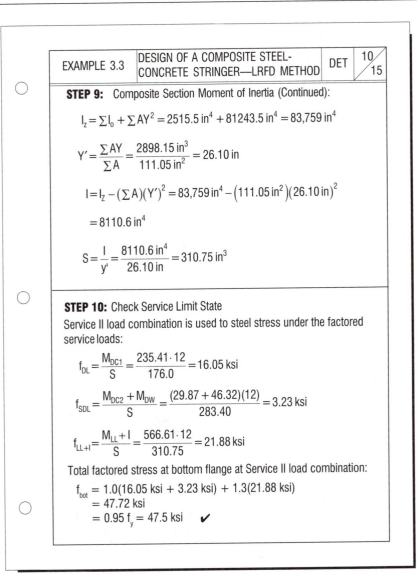

Steel stringers are checked for maximum tensile stress under Service II load combinations. So the elastic composite section modulus of bottom extreme fiber is calculated here.

STEP 10: CHECK SERVICE LIMIT STATE

The total stress is composed of dead load stress, superimposed dead load stress, and live load (including dynamic allowance, or impact) stress.

Net steel section is used to calculate dead load stress. Composite section with k = 3 is used to calculate superimposed dead load stress, and composite section with k = 1 is used to calculate live load stress.

The load factors used in Service II load combination can be obtained from Table 3.4. (1.0 for dead load and superimposed dead loads, and 1.3 for live load).

The maximum factored stress in steel should not exceed 95 percent of the steel yield stress (AASHTO LRFD 6.10.4.2).

are some of the major benefits gained by using cover plates as well as some of the associated principal design and performance issues.

1. **Advantages of a Cover Plate.** The principal advantages of a cover plate can be summarized as

   ❏ An increase in the section modulus of the composite section
   ❏ A moving downward of the center of gravity of the stringer
   ❏ Potential cost savings

The first item has already been discussed in detail. The second advantage is particularly useful when the plastic neutral axis falls within the concrete slab. From Equation 3.54 we can see that the addition of a cover plate will not only increase the steel beam area, it will also increase the moment arm d, and thus significantly increase the moment strength.

DID YOU KNOW

THAT conventional rolled beam girders can be used for spans up to 70 ft in length? The addition of a cover plate, however, allows rolled beams to be used for spans up to 90 ft. Composite beams with spans greater than 90 ft. use a plate girder as the steel stringer. A plate girder is formed by different steel plate elements which are welded, bolted, or riveted together, forming an I-beam cross section [Ref. 3.39].

A general rule of thumb is that when the economy realized by incorporation of a cover plate is less than 7 lb/ft, their use should be avoided.

This cutoff point can be defined as the point where the moment diagram for the beam without a cover plate intersects the moment diagram for the beam with a cover plate.

With regard to the last advantage for adding a cover plate, there is some reasoning which must accompany such a rationale. AISC does not include cover plates in their composite beam selection tables because they find that the fabrication costs are too great to warrant their incorporation (although they do not prohibit the use of cover plates in general). If this is so, when does use of a cover plate become a cost effective alternative to simply selecting a larger rolled section?

A general rule of thumb is that, when the economy realized by incorporation of a cover plate is less than 7 lb/ft, their use should be avoided. However, should the cover plate offer a savings of more than 12 lb/ft, their use can be justified based on economic considerations [Ref. 3.32].

2. Cover Plate Area. From a design standpoint there are two major considerations which the designer must address when adding a cover plate to a rolled beam:

❑ The area of the plate in section
❑ The length of the plate in elevation

With regard to the area of the plate in section, this is a function of the maximum factored moment of the stringer. AASHTO specifies that the thickness of a cover plate welded to a rolled beam should not be greater than two times the thickness of the flange (AASHTO 10.13.3). The width of the cover plate, however, can be larger or smaller than that of the bottom flange. The plate width, however, should confirm to AASHTO welding criteria (see Part 6 below).

The designer must first assume a preliminary rolled beam section to be used. If the composite section moment strength is less than the total factored moment, a cover plate may be added to the bottom flange. The section area of the cover plate may be chosen as the area of the preliminary stringer times the percentage of the moment strength deficiency.

Once the cover plate is chosen, the composite section strength needs to be recalculated to confirm that the moment strength is sufficient to resist the factored moment.

3. Cover Plate Length. The length of the cover plate is generally determined by the bending moment along the length of the stringer. Cover plates can be classified as either *full length*, meaning that they run the entire length of the stringer, or *partial length*, meaning they are located about the center of the beam at offsets from each support.

The location where a partial cover plate ends is known as the *cutoff point*. This cutoff point can be defined as the point where the moment diagram for the beam without a cover plate intersects the moment diagram for the beam with a cover plate [Ref. 3.32]. Figure 3.36 shows a partial length cover plate along with the graphical depiction of the location of the cutoff points.

It is also possible to determine the approximate length of cover plate required through use of a mathematical expression based on the parabolic

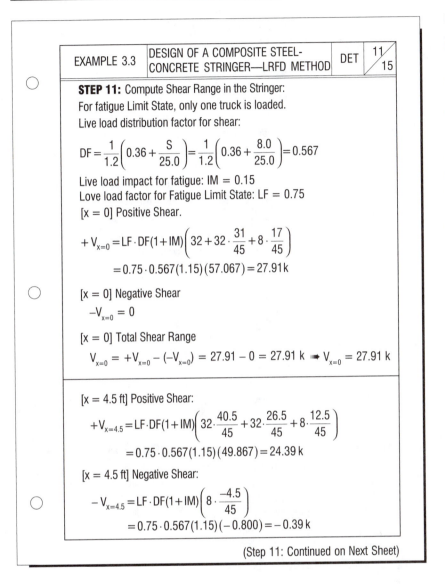

| EXAMPLE 3.3 | DESIGN OF A COMPOSITE STEEL-CONCRETE STRINGER—LRFD METHOD | DET | 11/15 |

STEP 11: Compute Shear Range in the Stringer:

For fatigue Limit State, only one truck is loaded.

Live load distribution factor for shear:

$$DF = \frac{1}{1.2}\left(0.36 + \frac{S}{25.0}\right) = \frac{1}{1.2}\left(0.36 + \frac{8.0}{25.0}\right) = 0.567$$

Live load impact for fatigue: IM = 0.15

Love load factor for Fatigue Limit State: LF = 0.75

[x = 0] Positive Shear.

$$+V_{x=0} = LF \cdot DF(1+IM)\left(32 + 32 \cdot \frac{31}{45} + 8 \cdot \frac{17}{45}\right)$$
$$= 0.75 \cdot 0.567(1.15)(57.067) = 27.91k$$

[x = 0] Negative Shear

$$-V_{x=0} = 0$$

[x = 0] Total Shear Range

$$V_{x=0} = +V_{x=0} - (-V_{x=0}) = 27.91 - 0 = 27.91\ k \implies V_{x=0} = 27.91\ k$$

[x = 4.5 ft] Positive Shear:

$$+V_{x=4.5} = LF \cdot DF(1+IM)\left(32 \cdot \frac{40.5}{45} + 32 \cdot \frac{26.5}{45} + 8 \cdot \frac{12.5}{45}\right)$$
$$= 0.75 \cdot 0.567(1.15)(49.867) = 24.39\ k$$

[x = 4.5 ft] Negative Shear:

$$-V_{x=4.5} = LF \cdot DF(1+IM)\left(8 \cdot \frac{-4.5}{45}\right)$$
$$= 0.75 \cdot 0.567(1.15)(-0.800) = -0.39\ k$$

(Step 11: Continued on Next Sheet)

(Step 11: Continued on Next Sheet)

DESIGN EXAMPLE 3.3
STEP 11: COMPUTE RANGE OF SHEAR IN BEAM

We will compute the required number of shear connectors by examining the maximum positive and negative shear at various points along the length of the span. Naturally, we begin at the end of the span (x = 0).

For Fatigue Limit State, only one design truck is loaded on the bridge. Therefore, we should use Eq. 3.22, divided by 1.2, for distribution factor for the live load shear (AASHTO LRFD 3.6.1.1.2). The load factor for Fatigue Limit State is 0.75 (see Table 3.4).

The dynamic allowance (impact) for live load is 0.15 (not 0.33 used for strength limit states). For fatigue limit state, average truck weight (75% of the maximum) is used, while in strength limit states, the maximum values are used.

Maximum shear at support is created by placing a design vehicle so that its rear axle is placed over the centerline of the bearings, as is shown in Step 9 of Example 3.2, except that axle loads of 32k, 32k and 8k should be used to represent an HL-93 truck.

The negative shear at support for a simply supported beam is zero. So the maximum shear range at support is equal to the maximum positive shear.

geometry of the bending moment diagram. The point of cutoff, illustrated in Figure 3.36 as the dimension x, can be calculated using the ratio

$$\frac{x^2}{(L/2)^2} = \frac{b}{y} \qquad \text{(Eq. 3.87)}$$

where x = half the theoretical length of cover plate
L = length of span
b = difference between resisting moment of beam with a cover plate and without a cover plate
y = resisting moment of beam with cover plate

The resisting moments are computed using Equation 3.54 for the beam with and without the cover plate attached to the rolled beam, provided the section is a compact section.

Furthermore, the end of a partial length cover plate should extend "beyond the theoretical end by the terminal distance ...

Due to the fact that cover plates are most often welded to the bottom flange of a rolled beam, they are extremely susceptible to the adverse effects of fatigue ...

THE CUTOFF POINT is determined by first calculating the *theoretical* termination point and then adding a specified length on top of this theoretical length. The theoretical length of a partial length cover plate is that length where the total factored moment at the end of the plate is at or near the moment capacity. Equation 3.87 can be used to get an approximate length. The designer should keep in mind, however, that the end of the cover plate has to be checked for fatigue. For simple spans the stress range at the end of the plate is the stress due to live load plus impact.

AASHTO specifies the minimum length of a cover plate added to a rolled beam as (AASHTO 10.13.1)

$$L_p > 2d + 3 \qquad \text{(Eq. 3.88)}$$

where L_p = length of cover plate, ft
d = depth of beam, ft

Furthermore, the end of a partial length cover plate should extend "beyond the theoretical end by the terminal distance, **and** it shall extend to a section where the stress range in the beam flange is equal to the allowable fatigue stress range for base metal adjacent to or connected by fillet welds" (AASHTO 10.13.4). That is, once the theoretical length is computed, a terminal distance is added to each end, which is

❏ 2 times the nominal cover plate width for cover plates *not* welded across their ends
❏ 1½ times the nominal cover plate width for cover plates which are welded across their ends

Another geometric constraint, which the designer must observe, is that the width at the end of a tapered cover plate cannot be less than 3 in (76 mm) (AASHTO 10.13.4).

4. Fatigue—AASHTO Standard Specifications. An important issue facing the designer in the use of cover plates is the problem of fatigue. Due to the fact that cover plates are most often welded to the bottom flange of a rolled beam, they are extremely susceptible to the adverse

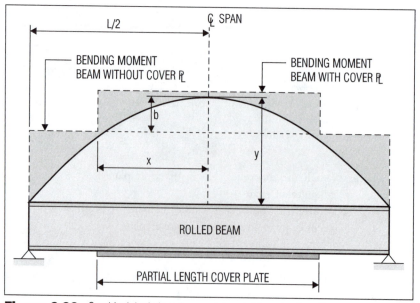

Figure 3.36 Graphical depiction of cover plate cutoff based on bending moment capacity.

| EXAMPLE 3.3 | DESIGN OF A COMPOSITE STEEL- CONCRETE STRINGER—LRFD METHOD | DET | 12/15 |

STEP 11: Compute Shear Range in the Stringer (Continued):

[x = 4.5] Total Shear Range

$V_{x=4.5} = +V_{x=4.5} - (-V_{x=4.5}) = 24.39 - (-0.39) = 24.78 \text{ k}$

$$\Rightarrow V_{x=4.5} = 24.78 \text{ k}$$

[x = 9.0] Positive Shear.

$+V_{x=9.0} = LF \cdot DF(1+IM)\left(32 \cdot \frac{36}{45} + 32 \cdot \frac{22}{45} + 8 \cdot \frac{8}{45}\right)$

$= 0.75 \cdot 0.567(1.15)(42.667) = 20.87 \text{ k}$

$-V_{x=9.0} = LF \cdot DF(1+IM)\left(32 \cdot \frac{-9}{45} + 8 \cdot \frac{22}{45}\right)$

$= 0.75 \cdot 0.567(1.15)(-2.489) = -1.22 \text{ k}$

[x = 9.0] Total Shear Range

$V_{x=9.0} = +V_{x=9.0} - (-V_{x=9.0}) = 20.87 - (-1.22) = 22.09 \text{ k}$

$$\Rightarrow V_{x=9.0} = 22.09 \text{ k}$$

[x = 22.5 ft] Positive Shear:

$+V_{x=22.5} = LF \cdot DF(1+IM)\left(32 \cdot \frac{22.5}{45} + 32 \cdot \frac{8.5}{45}\right)$

$= 0.75 \cdot 0.567(1.15)(22.044) = 10.78 \text{ k}$

[x = 22.5 ft] Negative Shear:

$-V_{x=22.5} = LF \cdot DF(1+IM)\left(32 \cdot \frac{-8.5}{45} + 32 \cdot \frac{-22.5}{45} + 8 \cdot \frac{8.5}{45}\right)$

$= 0.75 \cdot 0.567(1.15)(-20.533) = -10.04 \text{ k}$

(Step 11: Continued on Next Sheet)

DESIGN EXAMPLE 3.3
STEP 11: COMPUTE RANGE OF SHEAR IN BEAM (CONTINUED)

The process for calculating shear ranges continues. The beam is divided into tenth points proceeding toward the center of the span. There is no need to go any further because of symmetry. The first tenth point is 4.5 ft in from the left support.

The maximum positive shear is calculated by placing the rear axle of the design truck at the 4.5 ft point in question. Maximum negative shear is computed with only the first 8k wheel load, which represents the maximum negative loading condition. The total shear is +V −(−V) which yields 24.78 k.

The next tenth point is 9.0 ft from the left support. It should now be evident that as we move away from the support, the positive shear is decreasing and the negative shear increasing. The total shear range, however, is decreasing. In this instance, with the point in question 9.0 ft from the support, the negative shear is computed with the front axle and center axle on the bridge. The center axle contributes the negative shear component. The distance to the near (left) support is taken for the 32k load and the distance to the right support taken for the front wheel.

---

effects of fatigue which result from the repetitive loading and unloading of a structure. As bridges began to evidence fatigue in the late 1960's and early 1970's, AASHTO moved to introduce fatigue criteria which would address this situation. The first fatigue criteria appeared in the 1965 specifications. Subsequently in 1971 and 1974, revisions and enhancements based on experimental data were issued [Ref. 3.40]. While the issue of fatigue is very broad and pertains to a wide variety of elements (as we have just seen with shear connectors), the following discussion focuses on its effects concerning cover plates only.

With regard to fatigue, the major point of concern is at the ends of the cover plate. The AASHTO criteria vary depending on the type of connection and the number of stress cycles the structure is subjected to. Cover plates fall into categories E and E' (AASHTO 10.3.1). These categories are applicable to partial length cover plates that fulfill the criteria given in Table 3.11.

The E and E' categories are two of the most severe of all the AASHTO stress categories (with E' being the more extreme of the two). The severity

Flange Thickness	Plate Width	Weld Across End	Stress Category
≤ 0.8 in	Narrower than Flange	with or without	E
≤ 0.8 in	Wider than Flange	with	E
≤ 0.8 in	Wider than Flange	without	E'
> 0.8 in	Narrower than Flange	with or without	E'
> 0.8 in	Wider than Flange	with	E'
> 0.8 in	Wider than Flange	without	E'

Table 3.11 Stress Categories for Different Types of Partial Length Cover Plates

Indeed, AASHTO takes the issue of fatigue so seriously that allowable stresses are broken down according to structures with and without redundant load paths.

is such that, if the structure has a non-redundant load path (i.e., failure of a member causes failure of the entire structure), a partial length cover plate cannot be welded to a flange greater than 0.8 in (20 mm) in thickness (AASHTO 10.13.2). Indeed, AASHTO takes the issue of fatigue so seriously that allowable stresses are broken down according to structures with and without redundant load paths.

An example of an element which has no redundant load path would be a two girder bridge. These members are also referred as *fractual critical members*. Multibeam bridges such as the one in Design Examples 3.1

AASHTO STANDARD

10.3.1 ALLOWABLE FATIGUE STRESS RANGES

Table 3.12 shows the allowable fatigue stress ranges for various types of stress categories. There are, however, certain caveats pertaining to stress categories A, C, and E which are detailed below:

STRESS CATEGORY A

The second row of allowable stress ranges pertain to unpainted weathering steel, A709 (all grades).

STRESS CATEGORY C

The second row of allowable stress ranges pertain to transverse stiffener welds on girder webs or flanges.

STRESS CATEGORY E

For nonredundant load path structures, a partial length cover plate is not to be used on flanges with a thickness in excess of 0.8 in.

STRESS CATEGORY	100,000 CYCLES	500,000 CYCLES	2,000,000 CYCLES	2,000,000+ CYCLES
\multicolumn{5}{c}{Redundant Load Path Structures}				
A (see sidebar)	63.0 ksi	37.0 ksi	24.0 ksi	24.0 ksi
	49.0	29.0	18.0	16.0
B	49.0	29.0	18.0	16.0
B'	39.0	23.0	14.5	12.0
C (see sidebar)	35.5	21.0	13.0	10.0
				12.0
D	28.0	16.0	10.0	7.0
E	22.0	13.0	8.0	4.5
E'	16.0	9.2	5.8	2.6
F	15.0	12.0	9.0	8.0
\multicolumn{5}{c}{Nonredundant Load Path Structures}				
A (see sidebar)	50.0 ksi	29.0 ksi	24.0 ksi	24.0 ksi
	39.0	23.0	16.0	16.0
B	39.0	23.0	16.0	16.0
B'	31.0	18.0	11.0	11.0
C (see sidebar)	28.0	16.0	10.0	9.0
			12.0	11.0
D	22.0	13.0	8.0	5.0
E	17.0	10.0	6.0	2.3
E'	12.0	7.0	4.0	1.3
F	12.0	9.0	7.0	6.0

Table 3.12 Allowable Fatigue Stress Ranges

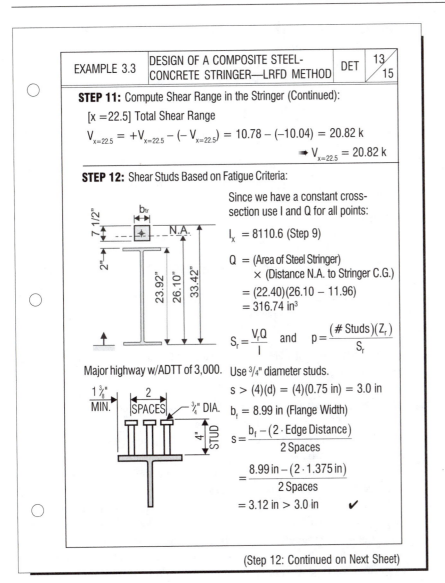

| EXAMPLE 3.3 | DESIGN OF A COMPOSITE STEEL-CONCRETE STRINGER—LRFD METHOD | DET | 13/15 |

STEP 11: Compute Shear Range in the Stringer (Continued):

[x = 22.5] Total Shear Range

$$V_{x=22.5} = +V_{x=22.5} - (-V_{x=22.5}) = 10.78 - (-10.04) = 20.82 \text{ k}$$

$$\Rightarrow V_{x=22.5} = 20.82 \text{ k}$$

STEP 12: Shear Studs Based on Fatigue Criteria:

Since we have a constant cross-section use I and Q for all points:

$$I_x = 8110.6 \text{ (Step 9)}$$

$$\begin{aligned} Q &= \text{(Area of Steel Stringer)} \\ &\quad \times \text{(Distance N.A. to Stringer C.G.)} \\ &= (22.40)(26.10 - 11.96) \\ &= 316.74 \text{ in}^3 \end{aligned}$$

$$S_r = \frac{V_r Q}{I} \quad \text{and} \quad p = \frac{(\# \text{Studs})(Z_r)}{S_r}$$

Major highway w/ADTT of 3,000.   Use 3/4" diameter studs.

$$s > (4)(d) = (4)(0.75 \text{ in}) = 3.0 \text{ in}$$

$$b_f = 8.99 \text{ in (Flange Width)}$$

$$s = \frac{b_f - (2 \cdot \text{Edge Distance})}{2 \text{ Spaces}}$$

$$= \frac{8.99 \text{ in} - (2 \cdot 1.375 \text{ in})}{2 \text{ Spaces}}$$

$$= 3.12 \text{ in} > 3.0 \text{ in} \quad ✔$$

(Step 12: Continued on Next Sheet)

For the purposes of this example, we will skip some tenth point calculations as they follow pretty much the example set forth in the previous two calculation sheets. We will conclude the shear range calculations along the length of the span at the midspan location of the beam (x = 22.5 ft).

At this point, we place the rear axle at the midspan location. Because our span is only 45 ft long, the front 8 k wheel falls off of the span leaving us with the rear and center wheels only.

Maximum negative shear is created by placing the center wheel of the design truck at the midspan location. At the midspan location, negative shear is greatest and positive shear at its lowest value. The resulting 20.82 k shear range is not appreciably lower than the 22.09 k calculated at the 9.0 ft offset.

STEP 12: SHEAR STUDS BASED ON FATIGUE CRITERIA

Shear stud design is usually controlled by fatigue limit state. Composite section for live load (as calculated in Step 9) is used for live load shear forces in the studs.

and 3.2 are considered to have redundant load paths. We should avoid designing new bridges that have fracture critical members.

As was illustrated previously for shear connectors, the number of stress cycles for longitudinal load bearing members is mainly based on the Average Daily Truck Traffic (ADTT). The number of cycles can be determined from Table 3.9. Table 3.12 shows the allowable fatigue stress ranges for the entire group of stress categories and their associated stress cycles. The range of stress is defined as the algebraic difference between the maximum and minimum stresses. Tension and compression are expected to have opposite signs (i.e., negative or positive).

Cover plates are designed for fatigue in a fashion very similar to that performed for shear connectors. For a cover plate, the critical point is at the ends of the plate. The shear stress is computed at the end of the plate (due to live load plus impact only) and compared to the appropriate allowable stress given in Table 3.12. If the computed shear stress is less than the allowable, then the design can stand.

C over plates are designed for fatigue in a fashion very similar to that which is performed for shear connectors.

5. Fatigue—AASHTO LRFD Specifications. In the AASHTO Standard Specifications, we use service load (unfactored) to calculate fatigue stress, but in the LRFD Specifications, Fatigue Limit State (live load factor of 0.75) is used to calculate fatigue stresses (Table 3.4) and only one truck is considered in the calculation.

When using Equation 3.20 or 3.22 for line load distribution factors, the multiple presence factor of 1.2 should be deducted from these equations (AASHTO LRFD 3.6.1.1.2).

Structures are designed for a 75 year life, so the allowable fatigue stress depends on the fatigue detail category, and the average daily truck traffic, which can be expressed as:

$$(\Delta F)_n = \left(\frac{A}{N}\right)^{\frac{1}{3}} \geq \frac{1}{2}(\Delta F)_{TH} \qquad \text{(Eq. 3.89)}$$

where N = number of cycles the structure is subjected to the truck load (Eq. 3.74, Part 1 of Section 3.10.7)

A = detail category constant in ksi^3 (see Table 2.13)

$(DF)_{TH}$ = constant-amplitude fatigue thresholds in ksi (also see Table 3.13). Table 3.13).

The stresses calculated using Fatigue Limit State load combination should not exceed the allowable fatigue stress expressed in Eq. 3.89.

6. Welds. The most common type of weld used at the end of a cover plate is a fillet weld. The ultimate strength of the weld metal should be equal or greater than that of the base metal (AASHTO 10.56.1.2). The welds at the ends of the cover plate must be checked for longitudinal shear force and fatigue stress.

The longitudinal force in the cover plate due to the factored loads at the theoretical end is resisted by welds placed between the theoretical and actual ends. Plastic base metal shear strength should be used. This will determine how long the cover plate should be extended beyond the theoretical end point.

The stress range at the actual end should satisfy the fatigue requirements, as discussed in Part 4 or 5 above. Allowable fatigue for Stress Category E or E' should be used depending on the bottom flange thickness.

Detail Category	Detail Category Constant A ($\times 10^8$ ksi^3)	Constant-Amplitude Fatigue Thresholds (ksi)
A	250.0	24.0
B	120.0	16.0
B'	61.0	12.0
C	44.0	10.0
C'	44.0	12.0
D	22.0	7.0
E	11.0	4.5
E'	3.9	2.6
A 325 Bolts	17.1	31.0
A 490 Bolts	31.5	38.0

Table 3.13 AASHTO LRFD Fatigue Category Constant and Thresholds

EXAMPLE 3.3	DESIGN OF A COMPOSITE STEEL-CONCRETE STRINGER—LRFD METHOD	DET	14/15

STEP 12: Shear Stud Based on Fatigue Criteria (Continued):

$$N = 365 \cdot 75 \cdot n \cdot p \cdot (ADTT) = 365 \cdot 75 \cdot 1 \cdot 1.0 \cdot 3000$$

$$= 82.1 \cdot 10^6 \text{ (assuming two-way traffic)}$$

$$\alpha = 34.5 - 4.28 \log N = 34.5 - 4.28 \log (82.1 \cdot 10^6) = 0.627$$

$$Z_r = \alpha \cdot d^2 \geq \frac{5.5d^2}{2}$$

so: $Z_r = \dfrac{(5.5)(0.75)^2}{2} = 1.55 \, k$ $p = \dfrac{3 \cdot Z_r}{S_r}$

Point (ft)	V_r (k)	Q (in^3)	I (in^4)	S_r (k/in)	p (in)
x = 0.0	27.91	316.74	8,111	1.090	4.3
x = 4.5	24.78	316.74	8,111	0.968	4.8
x = 9.0	22.09	316.74	8,111	0.863	5.4
x = 22.5	20.82	316.74	8,111	0.813	5.7

W24 x 76

25 SPACES @ 4"   34 SPACES @ 5"

CENTERLINE OF SPAN

22'-6"

Shear Stud Spacing

DESIGN EXAMPLE 3.3

STEP 12: SHEAR STUDS BASED ON FATIGUE CRITERIA (CONTINUED)

The required pitch is a function of the range of horizontal shear at the slab-beam interface and the allowable stress for an individual stud. The former is computed using the live load plus impact shear ranges found in Step 11. The latter is calculated with Eq. 3.72 and is based on the stud's diameter and the number of stress cycles, which is a function of the estimated ADTT. See Eq. 3.73 in Part 1 of Section 3.10.7.

The designer must also make sure to check the geometric constraints detailed in Section 3.10.7, Part 2. In addition to the transverse spacing shown, the ratio of the stud length to diameter (L/d) must be greater than 4. Since the stud is 4 in long, this ratio is L/d = 4/0.75 = 5.33, which is greater than 4.

The table at left shows the resulting pitch values. These are the direct, calculated results which will be rounded *down* to present more reasonable field measurements. Note that the most popular shear studs are of 7/8" diameter. To use 3 rows of such studs, we may want to choose stringers with little bid wider flanges.

The thickness of a fillet weld used is dependent on the thickness of the cover plate and the flange it is connected to. The governing material being the thicker of the two. If the thicker of the two is less than or equal to $\frac{3}{4}$ in (19 mm) then a $\frac{1}{4}$ in (6 mm) minimum fillet weld is to be used. If the plate or flange is greater than $\frac{3}{4}$ in then a $\frac{5}{16}$ in (8 mm) minimum fillet weld should be used (AASHTO 10.23.2.2).

Fillet welds at cover plates are also to be checked for fatigue in addition to the longitudinal shear force. This type of weld falls into stress category B. As was the case with shear connectors, the range of shear is calculated at the end of the cover plate using the general form of Equation 3.71 (S = VQ/I). It has been mentioned previously that the welds located at the ends of cover plates are extremely susceptible to the adverse effects of fatigue. This should serve as notice to the designer to ensure that a thorough investigation is performed.

The thickness of a fillet weld used is dependent on the thickness of the cover plate and the flange it is connected to.

AASHTO STANDARD

10.2.2 MINIMUM TENSILE STRENGTH FOR STEEL (F_u)

AASHTO provides a table (AASHTO Table 10.2A) which details the various minimum tensile strengths (F_u) for various types of structural steel. The modulus of elasticity of all steel is taken as 29,000,000 psi.

Type of Steel	Grade	F_u
Structural Carbon Steel	36	58 ksi plates up to 4" thick incl.
High Strength	50	65 ksi plates up to 4" thick incl.
Low Alloy Steel High Strength Low Alloy Steel	50W	70 ksi plates up to 4" thick incl.
Quenched and Tempered Low Alloy Steel	70W	90 ksi plates up to 4" thick incl.
High Yield Strength Quenched and Tempered Alloy Steel	100 & 100W	110 ksi plates up to $2^{1}/_{2}$" thick incl.
High Yield Strength Quenched and Tempered Alloy Steel	100 & 100W	100 ksi plates over $2^{1}/_{2}$" thick to 4" incl.

THE MINIMUM DISTANCE from the end of a rolled beam to the point where a cover plate is terminated varies depending on the preferences of the owner. In Figure 3.37, the cover plate is terminated 1 ft (0.3 m) from the edge of the bearing sole plate. Some states have a maximum end distance of 1 ft from the edge of the beam itself. Still others have distances upwards of 5 ft (1.5 m) from the end of beam. The distance specified is usually a result of a particular agency's experience and based on the data provided by inspections taken over several years.

7. Problems with Cover Plates. A fundamental problem with cover plates is the introduction of a *stress concentration* at the ends of the plate. A stress concentration can be caused by a sudden change in cross-section of a structural member. The change in cross-section of a cover plated beam, from rolled section only to a rolled section with a larger bottom flange creates such a situation. The resulting stress concentration causes high, localized stresses which occur at the point of discontinuity.

These stress concentrations can cause cracks to form at the toe of the cover plate welds. Extreme conditions can lead to cracks propagating right through the bottom flange of the beam. Severe cracks can even lead to the total failure of the beam. The adverse effects of stress concentrations in

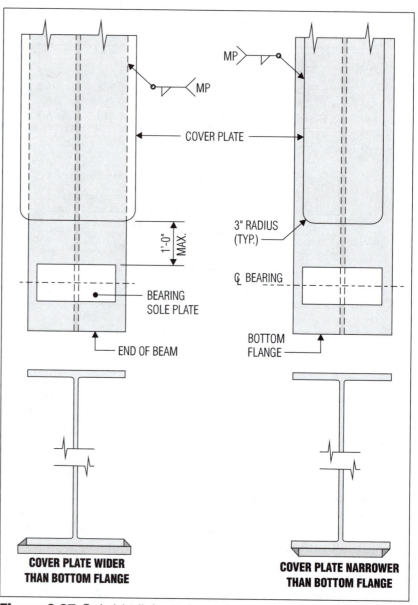

Figure 3.37 Typical details for attachment of a cover plate to a rolled beam.

EXAMPLE 3.3	DESIGN OF A COMPOSITE STEEL-CONCRETE STRINGER—LRFD METHOD	DET	15/15

STEP 13: Check Shear Studs Based on Strength Limit State:

$$P_1 = A_s F_y = 22.4 \cdot 50.0 = 1120 \text{ k}$$

$$P_2 = 0.85 f_c' \cdot b_{eff} \cdot t = 0.85 \cdot 4.5 \cdot (7.88 \cdot 12) \cdot 7.5 = 2713 \text{ k}$$

$$P = \text{MIN}(P_1, P_2) = 1120 \text{ k}$$

$$Q_n = 0.5 A_{sc} \sqrt{f_c' \cdot E_c} \le A_{sc} \cdot F_u$$

$$A_{sc} = \frac{\pi \cdot (0.75)^2}{4} = 0.442 \text{ in}^2$$

$$E_c = 1820 \sqrt{f_c'} = 1820 \sqrt{4.5} = 3860 \text{ ksi} \qquad \text{(AASHTO LRFD 5.4.2.4)}$$

$$0.5 A_{sc} \sqrt{f_c' \cdot E_c} = 0.5 \cdot 0.442 \sqrt{4.5 \cdot 3860} = 29.13 \text{ k}$$

$$A_{sc} \cdot F_u = 0.442 \cdot 60.0 = 26.52 \text{ k}$$

Therefore, $Q_n = 26.52 \text{ k}$

$$\text{Number of studs required} = \frac{P}{\phi Q_n} = \frac{1120}{0.85 \cdot 26.52} = 50$$

Number of studs provided $= 3 \cdot (25 + 34) = 177$ ✔

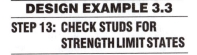
The first step in calculating the number of connectors required by the strength limit states is to compare the force in slab and the stringer. In this situation, the steel force is the smaller of the two values, so we use the value of 1120.0 k from steel stringer.

The ultimate strength of an individual connector is obtained from Eq. 3.80. The ultimate strength of a shear stud is a function of the diameter, the compressive strength of the concrete used in the slab and its associated modulus of elasticity.

The number of studs required is computed by taking the ratio of these two forces and dividing by a 0.85 performance factor. The designer should keep in mind that the number yielded by Equation 3.81 is for the connectors required "between the point of maximum positive moment and the adjacent support" (i.e., half the span length). So the resulting value is doubled and found to be less than that calculated for fatigue.

cover plated beams led to the introduction of specifications which call for partial length cover plates to extend beyond the theoretical cutoff points (see Part 3 above). Some state transportation departments even go so far as to prohibit the use of partial length cover plates all together. Others specify a maximum distance from the end of the stringer where a cover plate should terminate [e.g., within 5 ft (1.5 m) from the end of the stringer]. The designer should make sure to check all owner specific standards regarding the use and application of cover plates with rolled beam stringers.

> **E**xtreme conditions can lead to cracks propagating right through the bottom flange of the beam. Severe cracks can even lead to the total failure of the beam.

3.10.9 Bearing Stiffeners with Rolled Beams

Rolled beams generally do not require intermediate or longitudinal stiffeners. In general, stiffeners are used in conjunction with plate girders. In

A BEARING STIFFENER is used to resist the reactions which occur at the end of a beam. The bearing stiffener is designed to act as a column which helps carry the entire reaction, transmitting the force to the bearing below. Although not visible in Figure 3.38, it is often desirable to place stiffeners on both sides of the web. If the stiffener extends all the way to the bottom flange, then the stiffener must be checked for bearing stress. In Figure 3.38, the stiffener has a bevel cut near the web to facilitate placement of a fillet weld. Stiffeners connected in such a fashion are designed so that only the area of the plate bearing on the flange is taken as resisting the reaction. For rolled beams, stiffeners are used when the unit shear in the web at the bearing exceeds 75 percent of the allowable shear for the girder web.

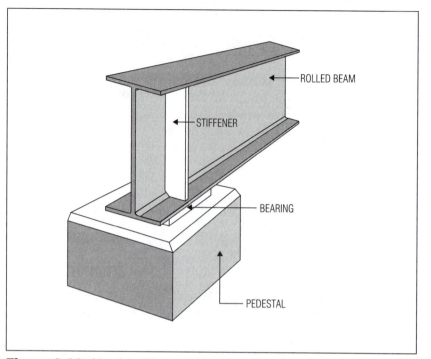

Figure 3.38 A bearing stiffener used in conjunction with a rolled beam.

> **B**earing stiffeners are required when the unit shear in the web at the bearing location is greater than 75 percent of the allowable shear for girder webs.

most cases, however, bearing stiffeners are used in conjunction with rolled beams at supports to resist concentrated reaction forces. A typical bearing stiffener is illustrated in Figure 3.38. Bearing stiffeners are also required when the unit shear in the web at the bearing location is greater than 75 percent of the shear capacity for girder webs (AASHTO 10.33.2). For more on stiffeners in general, and bearing stiffeners in particular, see the section on plate girders below (Section 3.11.2, Part 7).

3.10.10 Deflections

Designers must also check the deflection caused by live load plus impact on a stringer to ensure that it falls below a certain maximum value. AASHTO Standard Specifications specifies the maximum allowable deflection for a conventional highway bridge to be (AASHTO 10.6.2):

$$\Delta_{LL+I} \leq \frac{1}{800} \cdot L \qquad \text{(Eq. 3.90a)}$$

where Δ_{LL+I} = deflection due to live load plus impact
L = span length

If the structure, however, is located in an urban area where it is used by pedestrians, the limiting value is taken as (to increase pedestrian' comfort level):

$$\Delta_{LL+I} \leq \frac{1}{1000} \cdot L \qquad \text{(Eq. 3.90b)}$$

In the AASHTO LRFD Specifications, a live load deflection check is optional.

Exact computation of live load deflections can be somewhat complicated if the beam is non-prismatic (i.e., the beam does not possess a constant cross section throughout its length). The most general example of a non-prismatic beam is a rolled beam with a cover plate. As a simplification, deflections are computed based on the moment of inertia of the beam at the point of maximum positive moment, so that, in essence, the variations in sectional geometry are ignored. Although a certain degree of error is introduced as a result of this assumption, for most conditions the deviation is negligible (on the order of less than 3 percent).

To compute the live load deflection, conventional methods of structural mechanics can be employed (e.g., conjugate beam method). Actual deflections, however, are typically 15 to 20 percent higher than calculated values [Ref. 3.32]. This increase is due to a variety of factors, the foremost of which is the increased stiffness of the composite section. This enhanced stiffness can potentially lead to an increase in the percentage of deflections due to shear.

The designer should investigate the deflection for all three loading conditions: dead load, superimposed dead load, and live load plus impact. The maximum dead load deflections are computed using

$$\Delta_{DL/SDL} = \frac{5wL^4}{384EI}$$ (Eq. 3.91)

where $\Delta_{DL/SDL}$ = deflection due to dead or superimposed dead load
w = distributed load in units of load per unit length
L = length of span
E = modulus of elasticity of steel used for beam
I = moment of inertia of resisting section

The same conventions apply as before with regard to the moment of inertia. That is, the steel section is taken only for dead load and a composite section with $k = 3$ for superimposed dead load.

In addition to knowing the maximum dead load deflection, it is also necessary to compute the dead load deflections along the length of the span. At any point along the beam, the deflection due to a uniformly distributed dead or superimposed dead load is given by

$$\Delta_x = \frac{wx}{24EI}\left(L^3 - 2Lx^2 + x^3\right)$$ (Eq. 3.92)

where Δ_x = deflection at a point x on the beam
x = distance from support

> **A**s a simplification, deflections are computed based on the moment of inertia of the beam at the point of maximum positive moment.

> **I**n addition to knowing the maximum dead load deflection, it is also necessary to compute the dead load deflections along the length of the span.

LIVE LOAD DEFLECTION

When computing live load deflection, the distribution factor is not always the same as that applied to moments. For live load deflection, it is assumed that all stringers act together and have an equal deflection.

Deflections along the length of the span due to dead loads need to be calculated for a variety of reasons. Some of the principal uses of these deflections being

❑ Calculation of final overpass roadway elevations
❑ Calculation of the varying depth of deck slab haunches
❑ Calculation of beam camber

For the most accurate calculation of live load deflections, a truck should be placed to create maximum moment (as illustrated in Figure 3.32). An approximation, however, can be made where a single, concentrated load is placed at midspan and the maximum deflection calculated by the following expression:

$$\Delta_{LL+I} = \frac{PL^3}{48EI}$$

(Eq. 3.93)

where Δ_{LL+I} = deflection due to live load plus impact
  P = concentrated load

The concentrated load P can be taken as:

$$P = \text{Wheel Load} \cdot DF \cdot (1+I)$$

(Eq. 3.94)

where DF = wheel load distribution factor (see sidebar)
  I = impact factor (Equation 3.15)

Alternately, the designer can choose to employ more rigorous methods in calculating deflections ... either in the form of traditional hand calculation methods or, if available, computer-aided means.

Alternately, the designer can choose to employ more rigorous methods in calculating deflections due to live load, either in the form of traditional hand calculation methods or, if available, computer-aided means. Obviously, long span, continuous beam bridges will require a closer investigation than short span, simply supported structures we have discussed thus far.

It is important to reiterate that any dead loads placed on a composite beam before the slab has reached at least 75 percent of its full strength will be carried by the *steel section only* (unless temporary shoring is provided). Therefore, any corresponding dead load deflections will impact this resisting section without the benefits of composite action.

The reasons behind the limitations on deflections are to minimize excessive vibrations to the structure and reduce the risk of potential impact to primary members by underpass traffic.

The reasons behind the limitations on deflections are to minimize excessive vibrations to the structure and reduce the risk of potential impact to primary members by underpass traffic. It is recommended that the designer new to bridges take a walk over a structure with heavy traffic so they can experience the former first hand.

3.10.11 Camber

We have just discussed how dead loads on a structure can cause the primary members to deflect downward under their weight. This downward deflection, if severe, can cause excessive sagging in the beam. In addition to this, beams which drop below their horizontal plane too much can cause extreme fluctuations in the haunch depth (i.e., the layer of concrete between the slab and steel beam).

To minimize or eliminate this problem, steel beams are often *cambered* to offset the effects of dead load deflections, vertical curve requirements, and/or other factors which affect the profile of a steel stringer. By *camber*, we imply a deflection of the beam. Negative camber is the downward sagging of a girder and positive camber, the upward curving. In general, however, when one uses the expression *camber* they usually imply a slight bending upward of the beam in an effort to offset the anticipated downward deflection.

Figure 3.39 illustrates the difference between negative and positive camber. A working line is established at the top of the web at each end of the stringer. If any portion of the final structure falls beneath this working line than the girder is said to have negative camber [Ref. 3.11]. Obviously, this is not a desirable condition. Cambering of a girder requires the beam to be literally curved upward.

The question then arises: When is cambering of a beam necessary? Generally, when the anticipated downward deflection of the stringer is greater than 0.75 in (19 mm) cambering of the stringer will be required. Both rolled beams and plate girders can be cambered, although by slightly different methods.

Rolled beams are cambered through the local application of heat to the girder [Ref. 3.33]. Any variations in the profile of the girder are taken up by the deck haunch. It is important to note here that the haunch between the girder and slab *varies along the length of the span.* Later we will see how this variable depth is computed. Plate girders are typically cambered by cutting the web plate elements to the camber specified.

Some designers will camber the primary members so that there is a slight upward deflection resulting after the dead loads are placed on the structure. The reason for this is that bridges which are truly level give the illusion of actually sagging. A slight upward deflection is incorporated into the beam in order to compensate for this [Ref. 3.32]. A table based on the dead load deflections and other controlling criteria is incorporated into the final contract documents for fabrication of the beams.

A table based on the dead load deflections and other controlling criteria is incorporated into the final contract documents for fabrication of the beams.

ONE OF THE BIGGEST problems with negative camber is of an aesthetic rather than structural nature. Put simply, bridges which have negative camber (or sag) look like they are going to fall down to someone driving underneath them. The only instance where some negative camber is typically allowed is when the feature crossed by the structure is a body of water. In addition to the term "negative camber" which is used in the text and Figure 3.39, the reader will sometimes notice the term *sag camber* which refers to the same thing. In addition to deflections caused by dead load and superimposed dead load, the geometry of the vertical curve (e.g., a sag vertical curve) can adversely affect camber.

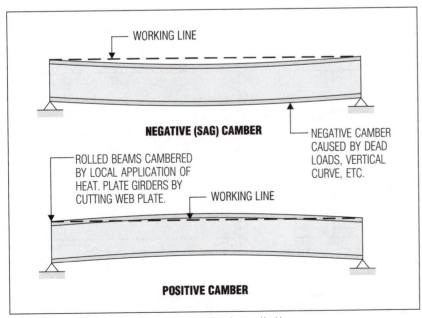

Figure 3.39 Positive and negative camber for a rolled beam.

3.11 PLATE GIRDERS

We have already seen how predefined rolled beams can be used in composite construction. Once the design moments and shears are calculated, an appropriate beam can be selected from a variety of sizes set forth in the AISC specifications. For long span bridges in general, and longitudinally continuous bridges in particular, a greater economy can be realized by using plate girders in lieu of the predefined rolled beam shapes.

A *plate girder* is a beam with an "I" cross section composed of steel plate elements which are connected together by welds, bolts, or rivets. As the Did You Know? sidebar points out, early plate girder elements utilized rivets which were eventually replaced by high strength bolts which in turn gave way to the welded plate girder. The "I" cross section itself is comprised of two flange plates (one on top and the other on the bottom) and a web plate as illustrated in Figure 3.40.

Rolled beam bridges have the advantage of quick erection, straight forward fabrication, and an overall simplicity of design. Plate girder structures, however, benefit from the ability to customize the fabrication of primary members to the specific moments and shears dictated by the design. This customization of the girder cross-section leads to an overall economy of materials in the superstructure. When span lengths reach upwards of 60 ft (18 m) the designer should begin investigating the use of plate girders (although they are more economically feasible at 90 ft).

To be sure, the design of welded plate girders is closely associated with the design of longitudinally continuous bridges (Section 3.12). However, we will first discuss some of the important issues concerning the specific design

A VARIATION IN PLATE sizes may represent a girder with the least weight; however, this may not be the most economical girder. In the specification of plate girder elements, the designer must always be aware of the increase in fabrication costs which are associated with excessive variations in plate sizes. There are a variety of factors which the designer must play off of each other in order to realize the greatest economy of materials. Should a thicker web be used or a thinner one with some stiffeners? Should the flange thickness be varied or kept constant? Should the girder be haunched or have a uniform cross-section? These are all questions which the designer must answer before a specific design can be chosen.

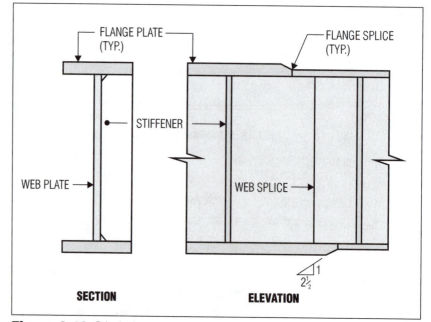

Figure 3.40 Principal components of a welded plate girder.

of plate girders before moving into the more general arena of continuous bridges.

3.11.1 Hybrid Girders

A *hybrid girder* is a plate girder with load-bearing plates of varying steel types. An example of this would be a plate girder with high strength steel used for the top and bottom flanges and a lower strength steel for the web. A plate girder which utilizes the same strength steel throughout its cross-section is said to be a *homogeneous girder*. The reader should take care not to confuse hybrid girders with built-up members. A *built-up member* utilizes various AISC rolled shapes which are combined in order to enhance section properties.

In a typical hybrid girder design, the webs are designed using steel with a yield strength of 36 ksi or 50 ksi (248 or 345 MPa) and the flanges with steel having a higher yield strength (50 ksi or 70 ksi). The principal advantage of the hybrid design is the reduction in size of the flange plate elements. The decision on whether or not to use a hybrid design is generally based on the economic advantages of such an approach. Studies have shown that the advantages of hybrid girder design is generally small. Compared to a homogeneous girder, using 50 ksi or 70 ksi steel throughout, the savings offered by a hybrid girder are usually on the order of 1 to 2 percent. It should also be noted that these estimates are based on steel which will eventually be painted. As we will see later on, the use of unpainted weathering steel will have an impact on some of these and other design considerations.

Note that the yield stress of web should not be less than 70 percent of the yield stress of the flanges.

3.11.2 Elements of a Plate Girder

In Figure 3.40, the constituent elements of a welded plate girder are depicted. In this section we will use the term plate girder to imply a *welded* plate girder. The discussion of riveted or bolted girders is beyond the scope of this text and the reader is referred to the appropriate design specifications (i.e., AASHTO, AISC) for more information on this type of plate girder. The specific plate girder elements along with the general criteria governing their design are presented below.

1. **Flange Plate Thickness.** The flange of a welded plate girder is actually a series of plates which are married to each other, end to end, using full penetration butt welds. A full penetration butt weld implies a weld where the flange plates come together at a *butt joint* (i.e., where two pieces of steel lie approximately in the same horizontal plane). The weld, also known as a *complete penetration groove weld*, which extends completely through the flanges to be joined, is designed to transmit the total load, and has higher strength than that of the flange plates. This type of weld is much more difficult to produce than the fillet welds discussed earlier in the section on cover plate design (Section 3.10.8, Part 6). Compared to a fillet weld, though, the groove weld provides for a stronger connection.

In a typical hybrid girder design, the webs are designed using steel with a yield strength of 36 ksi or 50 ksi and the flanges with steel having a higher yield strength (50 or 70 ksi).

The yield stress of web should not be less than 70 percent of the yield stress of the flanges.

AASHTO STANDARD

10.48.1 WELDED PLATE GIRDER FLANGE PLATES

To meet compact section requirements, the compression flange width to its thickness ratio (b_f/t) and web depth to its thickness ratio (D/t_w) shall not to exceed the following:

Yield Strength	b_f/t	D/t_w
36 ksi	21.7	101
50 ksi	18.4	86
70 ksi	15.5	72

AASHTO SPECIFICATIONS
WEB PLATE DEPTH TO THICKNESS RATIO (D/t_w)

The minimum thickness of web plates shall meet the following requirements:

WITHOUT LONGITUDINAL STIFFENER		
Yield Strength	Standard	LRFD
36 ksi	192	150
50 ksi	163	150
70 ksi	138	150

WITH LONGITUDINAL STIFFENER		
Yield Strength	Standard	LRFD
36 ksi	385	300
50 ksi	326	300
70 ksi	276	300

> **S**tudies by the Bethlehem Steel Corporation showed that the total number of flange plates should *not* exceed three for field sections up to 130 ft.

THE BUTT JOINT shown below depicts two plates of the same thickness being joined together. When two plates *of different thickness* are spliced together, AASHTO specifies a taper based on a uniform slope of not more than 1 in 2¹/₂ with respect to the surface of either plate to be used (AASHTO 10.18.5.5). This type of bevel is illustrated in Figure 3.40.

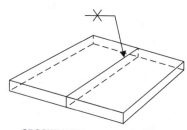

GROOVE WELD AT A BUTT JOINT

The ratio of the projecting compression flange plate width to its thickness should be designed so that no local buckling will occur. AASHTO Standard Specifications specify that the compression flange should meet the following requirements:

❑ To meet compact section requirements (AASHTO 10.48.1.1):

$$\frac{b_f}{t} \leq \frac{4,110}{\sqrt{F_y}}$$

(Eq. 3.95)

❑ For noncompact section (braced) (AASHTO 10.48.2.1):

$$\frac{b_f}{t} \leq 24$$

(Eq. 3.96)

AASHTO LRFD Specifications have the following requirements for both compression and tension flanges (AASHTO LRFD 6.10.2.2):

$$\frac{b_f}{2t} \leq 12.0$$

(Eq. 3.97)

$$b_f \geq \frac{D}{6}$$

(Eq. 3.98)

$$t \geq 1.1 t_w$$

(Eq. 3.99)

where b_f = flange width
   t = thickness of flange plate
   t_w = thickness of web plate
   F_y = steel yield stress (psi)
   D = depth of web plate

In addition, the moment of inertia of the compression flange (about vertical axis in the plane of web) should not be 10 times greater or 10 times smaller than that of the tension flange.

2. Flange Plate Economy. A design based solely on the minimum weight of steel would produce a flange with multiple variations in thickness. Such an approach, however, would also increase the number of splices required in the flange plate and thus raise fabrication costs. Studies by the Bethlehem Steel Corporation showed that the total number of flange plates should *not* exceed three for field sections up to 130 ft (40 m) (i.e., no more than two shop splices). A rule of thumb is that the average savings in steel realized by varying the flange plate thickness is approximately 700 lb (318 kg) [Ref. 3.1]. The practice of varying the width of the flange is generally discouraged because of the excessive fabrication costs.

3. Web Thickness. A web plate can either be of constant or varying depth. A plate girder whose web varies in depth is known as a *haunched girder*. In the sidebar accompanying Figure 3.1, we discussed how high fabrication costs have made haunched girders increasingly unattractive for spans less than 400 ft (122 m) in length [Ref. 3.1]. The focus of our discussion in this section will be on girders with webs of constant depth.

In designing the web of a plate girder, one must specify the depth of the plate (which is dependent on the maximum moment) and its thickness (which is dependent on the maximum shear). The minimum web thickness is to prevent it from local buckling under the design loads. The thickness limits in AASHTO Standard Specifications and LRFD Specifications are slightly different. The following are the summary of these limitations (AASHTO 10.48 and AASHTO LRFD 6.10.2.1):

❑ To meet compact section requirements:

$$\frac{D}{t_w} \le \frac{19,230}{\sqrt{F_y}} \quad \text{(AASHTO Standard)} \qquad \text{(Eq. 3.100a)}$$

$$\frac{D}{t_w} \le 150 \quad \text{(AASHTO LRFD)} \qquad \text{(Eq. 3.100b)}$$

❑ For transversely stiffened girders:

$$\frac{D}{t_w} \le \frac{36,500}{\sqrt{F_y}} \quad \text{(AASHTO Standard)} \qquad \text{(Eq. 3.101a)}$$

$$\frac{D}{t_w} \le 150 \quad \text{(AASHTO LRFD)} \qquad \text{(Eq. 3.101b)}$$

❑ For longitudinally stiffened girders:

$$\frac{D}{t_w} \le \frac{73,000}{\sqrt{F_y}} \quad \text{(AASHTO Standard)} \qquad \text{(Eq. 3.102a)}$$

$$\frac{D}{t_w} \le 300 \quad \text{(AASHTO LRFD)} \qquad \text{(Eq. 3.102b)}$$

where t_w = thickness of web
D = depth of web
F_y = yield stress of web steel (psi)

The minimum web thickness for typical steel is listed in the sidebar. Since web stiffeners can prevent web plates from local buckling, the web thickness can be reduced by introducing transverse and/or longitudinal stiffeners. These stiffeners will be discussed in details in Part 5 and Part 8 of this section.

4. Web Plate Economy. When defining the thickness of the web plate, the general rule of thumb is that as the depth of the web increases, so does its thickness. The area of the flange, however, will decrease as the depth of the web increases. This implies that a certain degree of comparison will be required in order to accurately determine the most cost effective solution.

> Since web stiffeners can prevent web plates from local buckling, the web thickness can be reduced by introducing transverse and/or longitudinal stiffeners.

The Bethlehem Steel studies found that for span lengths of 200 ft (61 m) and less, longitudinally stiffened girders were *not* cost effective.

In Part 3 above, it was demonstrated that when a beam is longitudinally stiffened, the thickness of the web may be decreased. As we saw with the varying of flange plate thickness, however, this reduction in web thickness does not always translate into a more economical solution. The Bethlehem Steel studies found that for span lengths of 200 ft (61 m) and less, longitudinally stiffened girders were *not* cost effective. While the reduction in web thickness results in weight savings of anywhere from 1 to 12 percent, the associated fabrication costs resulted in designs will be 1 to 3 percent higher than if the beam were not longitudinally stiffened. For hybrid girders, the costs were 4 to 7 percent higher. Based on these results, longitudinal stiffeners are not recommended unless the span length exceeds 300 ft (91.5 m) [Ref. 3.1].

5. **Transverse Intermediate Stiffeners.** In order for the web thickness criteria defined in Part 3 above to hold true, the web must be able to resist the applied shear forces, and it is adequately provided with stiffeners. There are two general types of transverse stiffeners:

- Bearing stiffeners, located at the supports of a span and
- Intermediate stiffeners, located over the length of the span.

A bearing stiffener attached to a rolled beam stringer was depicted in Figure 3.38. Intermediate stiffeners are located at points in between the supports. Another type of stiffener, known as a longitudinal stiffener, will be discussed in more detail later. The following discussion details the various aspects concerning the design and use of transverse intermediate stiffeners with plate girders.

Intermediate stiffeners are provided in order to prevent the web of a girder from buckling. Thin, deep webs are especially prone to web buckling.

■ **When Stiffeners Are Required.** There are several boundary conditions which determine whether or not intermediate stiffeners will be required. It is helpful, however, to explain why intermediate stiffeners are used in the first place. Intermediate stiffeners are provided in order to prevent the web of a girder from buckling. Thin, deep webs are especially prone to web buckling. To determine whether intermediate stiffeners are required at a specific point along the span, the designer must determine the total factored shear force of the web at the point in question. An intermediate stiffener is *not* required if the web shear capacity without web stiffeners exceeds the factored shear force. The shear capacity is calculated with Equation 3.56 or Equation 3.67, depending on if LFD or LRFD method is used in the design.

If the web shear capacity is less than the factored shear force, one can either increase the web thickness, increase the web depth (provided the minimum web thickness requirements are still met), or add transverse shear stiffeners.

■ **Spacing of Stiffeners.** If it is determined that intermediate stiffeners are indeed required, then the spacing of the stiffeners must be calculated. The spacing specified is required to satisfy conditions which affect the first and subsequent intermediate stiffeners. The first step in determining the spacing of the stiffeners is to calculate the web buckling coefficient, C. This value is dependent on a buckling constant, k, which is given as:

$$k = 5 + \frac{5}{(d_o/D)^2}$$ (Eq. 3.103)

where d_o = spacing of intermediate stiffener, in
D = unsupported depth of web between flanges, in

Next, an upper and lower limit describing the web slenderness must be computed. These limits are based on the constant k defined in Equation 3.103 above and the yield strength of the steel used in the web plate. The lower limit is given as:

$$C_{lower} = \frac{6000\sqrt{k}}{\sqrt{F_y}}$$ (Eq. 3.104)

and the upper limit as:

$$C_{upper} = \frac{7500\sqrt{k}}{\sqrt{F_y}}$$ (Eq. 3.105)

Once these two limits are determined, the value of the web buckling coefficient, C, can be determined using Table 3.14 below. As can be seen from the table, the value of C varies depending on where the slenderness ratio D/t_w falls.

The spacing of intermediate stiffeners specified must be such so that the factored shear force is less than the shear capacity as outlined in Equation 3.106 (LFD) or Equation 3.108 (LRFD).

$$V_n = V_p\left(C + \frac{0.87(1-C)}{\sqrt{1+(d_o/D)^2}}\right)$$ (Eq. 3.106)

and

$$V_p = 0.58F_y D t_w$$ (Eq. 3.107)

where V_p = plastic shear capacity of the web.

Note that in AASHTO LRFD Specifications, shear capacity is slightly different:

$$V_n = V_n\left(C + \frac{0.87(1-C)}{\sqrt{1+(d_o/D)^2} + d_o/D}\right)$$ (Eq. 3.108)

> The spacing of intermediate stiffeners specified must be such so that the factored shear force is less than the shear capacity ...

The designer should also take care that the maximum spacing specified for the first intermediate stiffener is such that:

$$d_o < 1.5 \cdot D \qquad \text{(Eq. 3.109)}$$

and for other intermediate transverse stiffeners:

$$d_o < 3.0 \cdot D \qquad \text{(Eq. 3.110)}$$

In computing the factored shear force, the designer should place the live load in such a way so as to create the maximum shear at the point in question. This can be accomplished in a fashion similar to that demonstrated earlier for determining maximum shear range for shear stud design (see Design Example 3.2, Step 9).

For AASHTO LRFD design, the web should also be checked for special fatigue requirement if intermediate transverse stiffeners are used. For webs with or without longitudinal stiffeners, the shear force in the web should not be larger than the shear-buckling resistance (AASHTO LRFD 6.10.5.3):

$$V_u \leq V_{cr} \qquad \text{(Eq. 3.111)}$$

and
$$V_{cr} = V_n = C \cdot V_p = C \cdot 0.58 F_y D t_w \qquad \text{(Eq. 3.112)}$$

where V_u = shear in the web at the section under consideration due to unfactored permanent load plus twice the load factored for fatigue live load. The load factor of 1.5 represents the heaviest truck to cross the bridge in 75 years. The dynamic allowance should be 0.15.

V_{cr} = shear buckling resistance.

V_n = web nominal shear strength.

and C should be taken from Table 3.14.

> In computing the factored shear force, the designer should place the live load in such a way so as to create the maximum shear at the point in question.

CONDITION	C
$D/t_w < C_{lower}$	1.0
$C_{lower} < D/t_w < C_{upper}$	$\dfrac{6000\sqrt{k}}{\left(D/t_w\right)\sqrt{F_y}}$
$D/t_w > C_{upper}$	$\dfrac{4.5 \times 10^7 \cdot k}{\left(D/t_w\right)^2 F_y}$

Table 3.14 Web Buckling Coefficient Values

This special fatigue provision should not be applied to unstiffened webs or the end panels (between the bearing stiffeners and the nearest intermediate transverse stiffeners) of stiffened webs.

■ **Single and Dual Stiffeners.** AASHTO allows intermediate stiffeners to be connected on either one or both sides of the plate girder web. In both cases, the stiffener consists of a plate which is welded to the girder web (typically with a fillet weld on both sides of the stiffener plate). If stiffeners are placed on both sides of the web, then the plate needs to be tightly fitted to the compression flange plate. Stiffener plates placed on one side only have to bear on the compression flange, but need not be attached to it. Transverse stiffeners need not be in bearing with the tension flange. An exception to this provision would be if the stiffener plates are connected to the secondary members (e.g., channel diaphragm, cross-frame, etc.) in which case the transverse stiffener should be rigidly connected to both top and bottom flanges (AASHTO 10.48.5.3, LRFD 6.10.11.1). When transverse stiffeners are welded to the tension flange, a fatigue check should be performed. See Step 10 of Design Example 3.5 for more details.

> **...I**f the stiffener plates are connected to the secondary members (e.g., channel diaphragm, cross-frame, etc.) in which case the transverse stiffener should be rigidly connected to both top and bottom flanges.

■ **Geometric Requirements.** For transverse stiffeners to be effective, the designer must ensure that the stiffeners meet the geometric constraints, principal of which is the minimum required area of the stiffeners (AASHTO 10.48.5.3 and LRFD 6.10.11.1.4). The minimum gross cross-section area of intermediate transverse stiffeners is:

$$A = Y \cdot \left(0.15 \cdot B \cdot D \cdot t_w \left(1 - C \right) \left(\frac{V_u}{V_n} \right) - 18 \cdot t_w^2 \right)$$ (Eq. 3.113)

Where Y is the ratio of web yield stress to stiffener plate yield stress; $B = 1.0$ for stiffener pairs, 1.8 for single angle, and 2.4 for single plate, C can be obtained from Table 3.14; V_u is the factored shear force, and V_n is the plastic or buckling shear force calculated by Equation 3.112.

In addition to the area requirements described above, AASHTO also specifies certain dimensional criteria which must be followed in detailing the stiffener and its connection to the plate girder (AASHTO 10.34.4.10 and LRFD 6.10.11.1.2). With regard to the former, the width of the intermediate stiffener plate, b_p should be specified such that:

$$b_t \geq 2 + \frac{d}{30} \quad \text{and} \quad \geq \frac{b_f}{4}$$ (Eq. 3.114)

where d = depth of girder
b_f = full width of girder flange

DID YOU KNOW

THAT proponents of the use of steel in highway bridges sight steel's recyclable nature as one of its principal advantages? The raw material used in fabricating rolled beams and plate girders utilizes scrap steel as a principal component. In 1990, when Comiskey Park, in Chicago, was razed to make way for a new stadium, all of the old structure's steel was melted in roughly a day and a half and used to make new beams [Ref. 3.44].

As is the case with any design requirement, however, a consistency in satisfying design criteria does not imply the right to forego the process of checking.

AASHTO SPECIFICATION
REQUIRED AREA OF STIFFENERS

If the limiting value for the gross cross-sectional area of intermediate stiffeners computed by Equation 3.113 is found to be approaching zero or negative, then the stiffeners are only required to meet the moment of inertia requirements detailed by Equations 3.116 and 3.117 and the plate dimension criteria defined earlier.

Also, the thickness of the intermediate stiffener plate, t_p, should be specified such that:

$$t_p \geq \frac{b_t}{16}$$ (Eq. 3.115)

■ **Stiffener Moment of Inertia.** In addition to satisfying the geometric requirements the designer must also ensure that the moment of inertia of a stiffener is greater than a specified limit. The moment of inertia for a stiffener *on one side of the web only* is taken about the face which is in contact with the web. If stiffeners are present *on both sides of the web*, then the moment of inertia is taken about the centerline of the web plate (AASHTO 10.48.5.3 and LRFD 6.10.11.1.3).

Once the moment of inertia of a given stiffener, I, is known, it must be checked to see that:

$$I > d_o \cdot t_w^3 \cdot J$$ (Eq. 3.116)

where d_o = transverse spacing between stiffeners, in
t_w = thickness of web, in
J = required ratio of rigidity of one stiffener to the web

AASHTO defined the required ratio of rigidity for a single stiffener to that of the web plate as:

$$J = 2.5 \cdot \left(\frac{D}{d_o}\right)^2 - 2 \text{ but not less than } 0.5$$ (Eq. 3.117)

where D = unsupported depth of web plate between flange components for transversely stiffened girders, or maximum subpanel depth for longitudinally stiffened girders.

Generally speaking, most stiffeners will consistently meet the moment of inertia requirement. As is the case with any design requirement, however, a consistency in satisfying design criteria does not imply the right to forego the process of checking.

■ **Welding Transverse Intermediate Stiffeners.** With respect to the connection of the stiffener plate to the plate girder, an intermediate stiffener is not required to be in bearing with the tension flange of the plate girder unless it is used to connect diaphragms. One of the reasons for this is that when a stiffener is welded to the tension flange of a plate girder, the tension flange will be subject to fatigue [Ref. 3.43].

Therefore, it is permissible to stop the stiffener short of the tension flange plate. The distance between the end of the stiffener weld and the fillet weld at the closest edge of the web-flange interface, d_{weld}, should be such that:

$$4t_w \leq d_{weld} \leq 6t_w$$ (Eq. 3.118)

where t_w = thickness of web plate

Figure 3.41 illustrates a typical stiffener connection detail at the web plate and compression flange plate. The constraints defined by Equation 3.118 are denoted at the bottom (tension) flange of the plate girder.

As we discussed earlier, when a stiffener is welded to the tension flange of a plate girder, effects similar to those discussed before at the end of a cover plate can occur (e.g., fatigue, brittle fracture).

6. Transverse Intermediate Stiffener Economy. From an economy standpoint, transverse stiffeners should be placed on one side of the plate girder web only, whenever possible [Ref. 3.1]. Exceptions to this general rule would be at diaphragm connections for interior stringers or other points intended to support concentrated loads.

7. Bearing Stiffeners. In Section 3.10.9 we briefly discussed the use of bearing stiffeners in conjunction with rolled beams. An illustration of a bearing stiffener was also presented in Figure 3.38. Welded plate girders are required to have bearing stiffeners at the end bearing locations and intermediate bearings of longitudinally continuous structures. At these locations, the bearing stiffener is designed to resist the total end reactions. As shown in Figure 3.38, bearing stiffeners should extend to the outer edges of the top and bottom flange plates as much as possible (AASHTO 10.34.6.1).

AASHTO recommends that a pair of stiffeners be used (i.e., a stiffener plate on either side of the web). It is even possible that when a girder is excessively deep, the web is designed to be equipped with two pairs of plates. If this is the case, the plates should be offset sufficiently to permit proper welding.

> **W**hen a stiffener is welded to the tension flange of a plate girder, effects similar to those discussed before at the end of a cover plate can occur (e.g., fatigue, brittle fracture).

> **F**rom an economy standpoint, transverse stiffeners should be placed on one side of the plate girder web only, whenever possible.

WHEN A STIFFENER is attached to only one side of a web plate, AASHTO requires that the stiffener must be in bearing against, but need not be attached to, the compression flange in order to be effective (AASHTO 10.48.5.3). An exception to this rule would be if the stiffener plate were also acting as a connection plate for a secondary member (see Section 3.11.2, Part 5, *Single and Dual Stiffeners*). In Figure 3.41, stiffeners are provided on both sides of the web plate and are connected to the compression flange with a fillet weld to both sides of the plate. The main functions of the stiffeners are to resist compression forces which are transmitted directly from the web and stiffen the web during buckling. Figure adapted from Ref. 3.43.

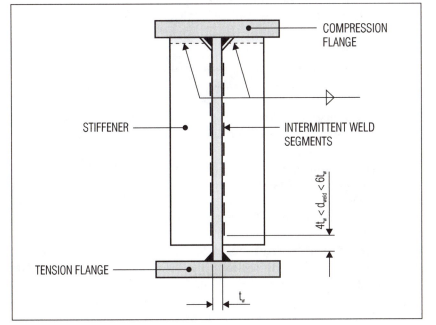

COMPRESSION FLANGE

STIFFENER

INTERMITTENT WELD SEGMENTS

$4t_w < d_{weld} < 6t_w$

TENSION FLANGE

t_w

Figure 3.41 Connection of an intermediate stiffener to a plate girder.

[3.11.2, Part 7]

> I t is even possible that, when a girder is excessively deep, the web is designed to be equipped with two pairs of plates ... the plates should be offset sufficiently to permit proper welding.

As mentioned in the sidebar accompanying Figure 3.38, bearing stiffeners are designed as columns, resisting the end reactions of the span. The width of each projecting bearing stiffener should satisfy (AASHTO LRFD 6.10.11.2.2):

$$b_f \leq 0.48 t_p \sqrt{\frac{E}{F_y}} \qquad \text{(Eq. 3.119)}$$

where b_f = width of stiffener, in
F_y = yield strength of steel used for stiffener, ksi
t_p = thickness of projecting stiffener element, in

If two plates on either side of the web plate are used, the width of the section *acting as the resisting column* is taken as the width of the two plates themselves plus the web thickness located in between them. The web plate width is limited to 9 times its thickness on each side of the stiffeners. If more than one pair of bearing stiffeners are used, the resisting column section is composed of all stiffeners plus the girder web extending no more than 9 times the web thickness on each side of the outer stiffeners.

Bearing stiffeners should also be designed to resist the factored bearing forces. The factored bearing resistance can be calculated (AASHTO LRFD 6.10.11.2.2):

$$(R_{sb})_r = \phi_b (R_{sb})_n \qquad \text{(Eq. 3.120)}$$

where $(R_{sb})_r$ = factored bearing resistance
ϕ_b = resistance factor of bearing (= 1.0, AASHTO LRFD 6.5.4.2)
$(R_{sb})_n = 1.4 \, A_{pn} F_y$ = nominal bearing resistance
A_{pn} = area of bearing stiffeners directly bearing against webs.

The area clipped to clear the web-to-flange fillet weld, and the area beyond the edge of flange, if any, should not be included in calculating the bearing resistance.

In detailing the interface of the stiffener and flanges, the designer has two options; either the stiffener can be:

❑ Milled to bear against the flange through which they receive the total end reaction

❑ Connected to the flange using full penetration groove welds

8. **Longitudinal Stiffeners.** A longitudinal stiffener, like transverse intermediate stiffeners, is welded to the web plate of a plate girder. The longitudinal stiffener, as its name would imply, runs along the length of the stringer. We have already demonstrated in Part 3 above that incorporation of a longitudinal stiffener reduces the required thickness of the web plate by one half.

Longitudinal stiffeners are typically provided on only one side of the web. In addition to allowing for an overall reduction in web thickness, a longitudinal stiffener also serves to:

❑ Increase the shear and bending strength of the girder
❑ Increase lateral stiffness

While these advantages would seem to lead toward a consistent use of longitudinal stiffeners in the design of plate girders, increased fabrication costs and other issues also play a factor in deciding whether or not they are implemented (see Part 9 below).

■ **Longitudinal Stiffener Moment of Inertia.** Like an intermediate transverse stiffener, the designer must ensure that the moment of inertia of a longitudinal stiffener is greater than a specified limit. Once the moment of inertia for a given longitudinal stiffener is known, it must be checked to ensure that it is greater than a prescribed minimum (AASHTO 10.48.6.3):

$$I \geq D \cdot t_w^3 \left(2.4 \frac{d_o^2}{D^2} - 0.13 \right)$$

(Eq. 3.121)

where I = minimum required moment of inertia, in⁴
    D = unsupported distance between flange plates, in
    t_w = thickness of web, in
    d_o = spacing between transverse stiffeners, in

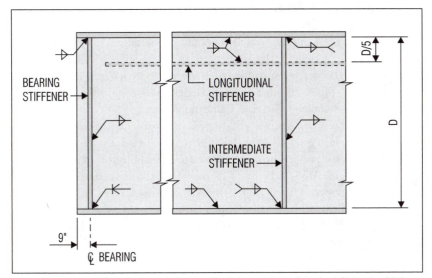

A LONGITUDINAL stiffener's centerline is located a distance of D/5 from the inside surface of the compression flange (AASHTO 10.48.6.1). In this particular detail, the longitudinal stiffeners are to be stopped 2½ in (63.5 mm) short from the point where they intersect connection plates and web splice plates. Longitudinal stiffeners are not required to be continuous and may be cut at intersections with transverse intermediate stiffeners. In AASHTO LRFD (6.10.11.3), the designer should determine the stiffener location so that both service limit state and strength limit state requirements are satisfied.

Figure 3.42 Typical plate girder detail. *(Adapted from Standard Plans for Highway Bridges, Volume II, Structural Steel Superstructures, FHWA, Ref. 3.9.)*

This moment of inertia is taken about the edge in contact between the longitudinal stiffener and the web plate.

This moment of inertia is taken about the edge in contact between the longitudinal stiffener and the web plate.

The radius of gyration of the stiffener should also satisfy:

$$r \geq \frac{d_o \sqrt{F_y}}{23,000} \quad \text{(AASHTO Standard)} \quad \text{(Eq. 3.122a)}$$

$$r \geq 0.253 d_o \sqrt{\frac{F_y}{E}} \quad \text{(AASHTO LRFD)} \quad \text{(Eq. 3.122b)}$$

In calculating the radius of gyration, a centrally located web strip equal to $18 t_w$ in width should be considered as a part of the longitudinal stiffener. For hybrid girders, some modification to Equation 3.122b is required by AASHTO LRFD (6.10.11.3.3).

■ **Geometric Requirements.** While AASHTO does not specify a minimum required area for longitudinal stiffeners, a minimum thickness is defined. The width of longitudinal stiffener should not be wider than (AASHTO LRFD 6.10.11.3.2):

$$b_l \leq 0.48 t_s \sqrt{\frac{E}{F_y}} \quad \text{(Eq. 3.123)}$$

where b_l = width of stiffener
t_s = thickness of the stiffener

This requirement is intended to prevent local buckling of the longitudinal stiffener.

9. **Longitudinal Stiffener Economy.** We mentioned earlier that longitudinal stiffeners are typically placed on one side of the web plate only. A way of improving the overall economy of the fabricated plate girder is to place the longitudinal stiffener on the side opposite from the one containing the transverse stiffeners. Such an approach will minimize the number of times a longitudinal stiffener intersects with a transverse stiffener and thereby decrease fabrication costs.

The economy studies conducted by Bethlehem Steel, discussed previously in Parts 2, 4, and 7 above, indicated that longitudinally stiffened plate girders are not economically feasible for spans less than 200 ft (61 m) [Ref. 3.1]. Indeed, the studies demonstrated that plate girders equipped with both longitudinal and transverse stiffeners were not competitive with those equipped with only transverse stiffeners until the span lengths exceeded 300 ft (91.5 m). For more on this issue, see Part 4 above.

Studies demonstrated that plate girders equipped with both longitudinal and transverse stiffeners were not competitive with these quipped with only transverse stiffeners until the span lengths exceeded 300 ft.

10. **Miscellaneous Economy Issues.** The Bethlehem Steel studies bore out some other results, with regard to plate girder economy, which are

worth mentioning here. So far we have discussed the economy with respect to the geometry of an individual girder. The reduction of the number of girders throughout the cross section of the superstructure can also play a role in reducing the overall cost of the structure.

While fewer girders will result in deeper beams and a thicker deck slab, there are also associated reductions in the number of bearings, secondary members, connection plates, etc., which can provide substantial savings. The studies recommended a 10 ft (3.05 m) minimum spacing between girders [Ref. 3.1].

Related to the reduction of the number of girders in cross section is the use of precast, prestressed concrete decks in conjunction with plate girders (see also Section 3.2.3). The use of precast deck panels can result in larger girder spacings and therefore fewer girders. These types of deck panels, however, have been predominately used in rehabilitation projects so that associated savings in steel costs could be potentially offset by increased deck construction costs.

All of this should serve as notice to the engineer that design of a plate girder is an iterative (and at times subjective) process which calls on the designer to play various options off of each other in an effort to determine the optimum design.

Although reducing the number of girders can usually reduce the costs, we should not design a bridge with fewer than four girders. Otherwise it will be very difficult in the future to replace the deck in stages (to maintain traffic in half of the deck while replacing the other half). Designers should always keep the future maintenance and rehabilitation in mind when designing new bridges.

> The reduction of the number of girders throughout the cross section of the superstructure can also play a role in reducing the overall cost of the structure.

> Although reducing the number of girders can usually reduce the costs, we should not design a bridge with fewer than four girders.

3.11.3 Lateral Bracing for Plate Girders

Lateral bracing was discussed earlier in the section on secondary members (Section 3.1.4, Part 2). In summary, lateral bracing is a system of cross frames located in the horizontal plane and installed at a beam's flange in order to resist lateral deformation. Lateral deformation is induced by loads which act normal to the centerline of primary members. Wind loads are the major contributing loading condition which determine whether or not lateral bracing will be required.

Since plate girders can become exceedingly deep (in comparison to their rolled beam cousins) the need for lateral bracing is of greater concern. This increase in girder depth creates a larger surface area over which wind loads can act. The following is a discussion of the general parameters which define the specification of lateral bracing for plate girders.

> Since plate girders can become exceedingly deep (in comparison to their rolled beam cousins) the need for lateral bracing is of greater concern.

1. Where Bracing Is Located. The need for lateral bracing should be investigated not only for the final stage, but also for construction stages. Lateral bracing at final stage is *not* required at a flange which is attached to a concrete deck or a deck of similar rigidity. Put simply, lateral bracing for highway bridges is typically located at the bottom flange only. Exceptions to this rule would be precast, prestressed concrete deck panels or timber planks which do not have a secure attachment to primary members. In such a situation, the need for lateral bracing at the top flange should be investigated. Lateral bracing designed for construction stages may be removed for the final condition.

2. Bracing as a Function of Span Length. Previous editions of the AASHTO specifications required lateral bracing for all spans greater than 125 ft (38.1 m). More recent editions, however, do not rely on span length as a steadfast rule for incorporating lateral bracing. Rather, the stress induced by wind loads is used to determine the need for a bracing system at the bottom flange. Lateral bracing is usually designed in conjunction with cross-frames or diaphragms to resist lateral loads.

3. Placement and Types of Lateral Bracing. Should lateral bracing be required, it is placed in the exterior bays (i.e., between the fascia stringer and first interior stringer) between the secondary members. The bracing is to be placed in the horizontal plane of the flange being braced.

Typically, lateral bracing is composed of steel angles or tees. The minimum size of angle allowed is 3 in × 2¹/₂ in (76.2 mm × 63.5 mm). A minimum of two welds or fasteners are required at the end of each connection (AASHTO 10.21.6).

Figure 3.43 shows a typical lateral bracing layout for a plate girder superstructure. The bracing, located in the exterior bay, is composed of WT rolled T sections (see the figure in the accompanying sidebar). The bracing is bolted to T-gusset plates which are in turn bolted to the plate

> **S**hould lateral bracing be required, it is placed in the exterior bays (i.e., between the fascia stringer and first interior stringer) between the secondary members.

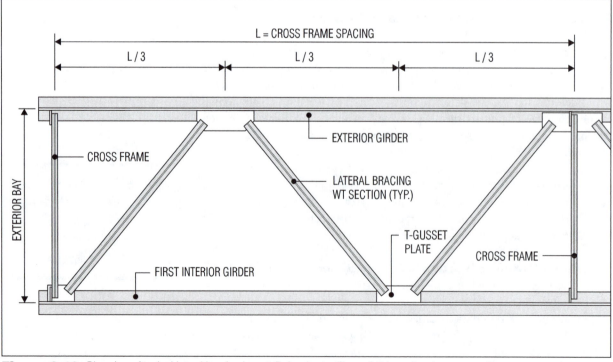

Figure 3.43 Plan view of typical lateral bracing layout. Refer also to Figure 3.5 for a view in cross section.

girder's web plate. Each lateral bracing element is located at third points between cross frame type secondary members. In lieu of the triangular pattern with single diagonal members illustrated in the figure, it is also possible to use a crossing (X) configuration with dual diagonals.

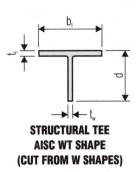

**STRUCTURAL TEE
AISC WT SHAPE
(CUT FROM W SHAPES)**

4. Eliminating Lateral Bracing. Some transportation departments wish to eliminate the use of lateral bracing. In certain instances, there may be no way to avoid the incorporation of some form of lateral bracing system. There are, however, some design approaches which may eliminate the need for lateral bracing.

One such approach is to reduce the spacing between cross frames (the *L* dimension in Figure 3.43). Another method is to increase the thickness of the flange plate. Wind forces are generally going to be most severe at cutoff points in the bottom flange (i.e., those locations where that flange thickness changes). As we saw earlier with cover plates, locations with such a discontinuity are prone to stress concentrations and should be looked at closely when attempting to eliminate the need for a lateral bracing system.

The designer and owner should note, however, that lateral bracing systems may be desirous from an ease of construction standpoint (if not a design one). As was mentioned in Section 3.1.4, Part 2, lateral bracing also provides added stability to the superstructure frame during and even after construction.

5. Economy of Lateral Bracing. We have already demonstrated that, for the plate girder itself, there are a variety of factors which determine what type of final geometry presents the most economical solution. The same rationale holds true with regard to the implementation of lateral bracing systems.

Increasing the flange thickness or reducing the spacing between cross frames does indeed work toward eliminating the need for lateral bracing. The designer must keep in mind, however, that taking these steps can potentially increase the overall cost of the plate girder. A thicker flange will result in increased material costs. A reduced cross frame spacing means more cross frames with the associated increase in cost as a result of more materials and additional fabrication. These factors, combined with the benefits lateral bracing has in the field (with regard to erection) should play in the final decision as to implement lateral bracing or not.

> **A** reduced cross frame spacing means more cross frames with the associated increase in cost as a result of more materials and additional fabrication.

3.11.4 Cross-Frames for Plate Girders

As discussed in Part 1 of Section 3.1.4, a cross-frame is typically composed of steel angles in cross (X) or vee (V) configurations. The primary functions of a cross-frame are:

- ❏ Transforming lateral force from bottom flange to top flange and concrete deck
- ❏ Providing stability for compression flanges
- ❏ Distributing vertical loads among girders

Cross-frames are typically placed at bearing lines, and at intermediate locations as required. The need for intermediate cross-frames should be evaluated with the lateral wind load, the flange stiffness, and the use of lateral bracing. If the bridge is skewed more than 20°, intermediate cross-frames should be placed perpendicular to the girders (AASHTO LRFD 6.7.4.2).

The spacing of the cross-frames should be chosen to balance the cost of the cross-bracing, and the cost of increasing the bottom flange size due to bending from the lateral wind. The cross-frames should be designed to resist wind load acting on the bottom half of the exterior girder. The force should be transmitted to the top flange that is connected to the concrete deck.

3.12 CONTINUOUS BEAMS

Up to this point, we have dealt exclusively with simply supported highway bridge structures. With our knowledge of both composite construction (Section 3.10) and plate girder design (Section 3.11), we are now ready to discuss the benefits and design of continuous beam bridges. While this section will concern itself with steel plate girder type structures, the reader should be aware that prestressed concrete can also be used in the construction of continuous beam bridges. Issues concerning the design of prestressed structures will be presented later in Section 3.15. When the term *continuous beam* is used in this section, it implies a longitudinally continuous span with primary members extending across a pier (support) uninterrupted.

3.12.1 Advantages of Continuous Beams

There are many benefits to be realized by the use of continuous beams in highway bridge construction. Compared to a simply supported structure, continuous bridges offer the advantages of:

- ❑ Reducing the number of deck joints
- ❑ Reducing the number of bearings
- ❑ Increasing span lengths
- ❑ Reducing the amount of material required

Probably the most significant item listed above is the first: elimination of deck joints. The reader who has careful studied Section 2 will recall the often mentioned problems associated with leakage at deck joints. From a long term cost standpoint, the detrimental effects of joint leakage have a severe impact on the overall cost of a structure throughout its life. Damage from this type of deterioration can affect not only the superstructure but the substructure as well. By removing the need for joints at piers, a continuous span greatly reduces the life cycle cost of the bridge and helps minimize the amount of maintenance required by the owner.

For simple spans, since they begin and end at a support point (pier) a bearing is required at the end of the first span and beginning of the subsequent span. Continuous spans, however, which run uninterrupted over the pier will require only one bearing, thereby reducing the number of bearings by half at any given pier. This is beneficial, not only from the initial cost savings, but also with regard to having to maintain fewer bearings over the life of the bridge (see Figure 3.44). Having one line of bearings also reduces the width of the pier bent.

By removing the need for joints at piers, a continuous span greatly reduces the life cycle cost of the bridge and helps minimize the amount of maintenance required by the owner.

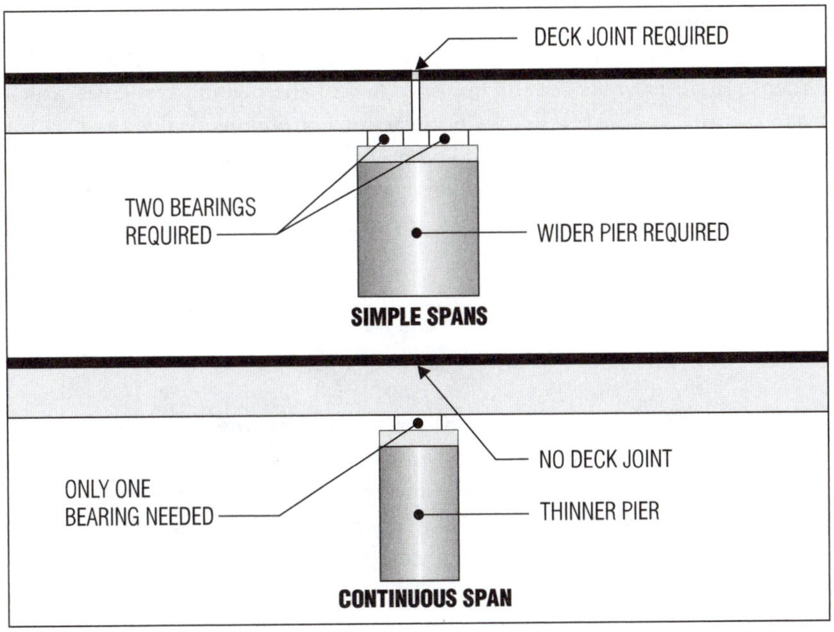

Figure 3.44 Simple spans require two bearings at a support; continuous only one.

COMPOSITE BRIDGES with continuous spans present a different situation for the designer. In regions of negative moment the deck is considered to be cracked due to the tensile forces at the top of the section. We saw in the design of shear connectors for composite bridges with continuous spans (Section 3.10.7, Part 4), however, that the reinforcing steel in the concrete slab can actually be taken as part of the composite section. This means that the tensile properties of the reinforcing steel can assist in resisting the tension which exists in the top flange of the composite section. This is just one example of the challenges continuous bridges presents to the designer.

Continuous bridges, however, incur greater fabrication costs than their simply supported counterparts. Where a simply supported span can be designed and erected relatively quickly, the design of continuous spans is more involved and their construction impacted by the need for customized plate girders, splices, etc. Continuous span bridges are also more susceptible to settlement problems than simply supported bridges. All things being equal, simple spans are generally best suited for short crossings and where speed of construction is an issue. Continuous bridges are typically favored when a sound foundation is available and span lengths are greater.

3.12.2 Rolled Sections as Continuous Beams

While this section will concern itself primarily with the design of plate girder type continuous beams, for short spans rolled beam primary members can also be used. These rolled beams, however, in many cases may require cover plates in regions of maximum *negative moment*. Figure 3.19 showed a simple span with positive moment only. So far we have only studied beams in this state; where the top flange is in compression and the bottom flange is in tension. With continuous beams, though, the beam will also have regions of negative moment where the top flange is in tension and the bottom flange is in compression. As we will see later, this presents certain design conditions affecting both the superstructure and the substructure which the engineer must account for.

Regardless of whether a rolled beam, plate girder, or even prestressed concrete beam is used, because of the nature of the structural response, the section properties of a continuous beam will be nonprismatic (i.e., not of a constant section geometry).

> **R**egardless of whether a rolled beam, plate girder or even prestressed concrete beam is used, because of the nature of the structural response, the section properties of a continuous beam will be nonprismatic.

Like simply supported spans, continuous beams benefit from the use of composite construction (see Section 3.10.1). A decrease in the depth of girder and stiffer cross section are only two of the major advantages which make composite construction as popular for continuous bridges as it is for simple spans. As the sidebar to Figure 3.44 indicates, however, continuous spans present some technical challenges not found in simply supported structures. The presence of tension at the top flange requires the designer to either:

❏ Ignore composite action at regions of negative moment
❏ Take into account the effects of reinforcing steel in the slab

In regions of positive moment, however, the behavior of the slab and beam is the same as that discussed previously for simple spans. The controlling design criteria for continuous spans will be the regions of negative moment which occur at the supports. Forces in these areas are generally greater than the points of maximum positive moment found near the center of a span.

3.12.3 Moment Distribution

The 1960's and 1970's ...**t** saw a veritable burgeoning of continuous beam analysis software ... many engineers rely on such software to perform the design of continuous beam bridges.

The analysis of continuous beam bridges is somewhat complicated because of the physical continuity over a support and the variable nature of the beam's cross section. Because of this complexity, the 1960's and 1970's saw a veritable burgeoning of continuous beam analysis software. Today, many engineers rely on such software to perform the design of continuous beam bridges. While use of continuous beam programs is more the norm than the exception today, it is also important for the bridge engineer to be able to perform the necessary analysis by hand. Where hand calculation methods are concerned, the moment distribution method, developed by Professor Hardy Cross, remains the standard for analysis of continuous beam bridges (see Did You Know? sidebar). Provided below is an overview of the basic principles behind moment distribution for continuous beams.

1. **Overview.** Moment distribution is essentially an iterative approach for solving beam problems of a variety of complexities. Moment distribution is generally favored as a hand calculation method because it:

   ❏ Converges to a solution quickly
   ❏ Provides for the direct calculation of moments, shears, and reactions
   ❏ Is easy to learn

   Another advantage of this approach is that it is not bounded by the loading conditions. General relationships are first developed and then applied to determine resulting moments, shears, etc. A general limitation on the use of moment distribution is that joints are not allowed to translate laterally (i.e., sway). Also, moment distribution does not take into account the effects of settlement at support points. This may be accounted for in a separate calculation.

The approach utilized in this section for moment distribution is slightly different from the conventional method detailed in many structural analysis texts. This approach utilizes modified stiffness factors (see Part 5 below) and carry over factors (Part 7), which allows for a quicker convergence to a solution than the conventional approach. The moment distribution method detailed below results in distribution factors (Part 5) which are different from the standard method. The final fixed end moments, however, will be the same, regardless of the approach taken [Ref. 3.48]. The reader should be aware that there are a variety of moment distribution methodologies which can be used in a similar fashion.

2. Fixed End Moments. A concept which is central to moment distribution is that of the fixed end moment. A *fixed end moment* (FEM) is a couple located at the ends of a beam, induced by loads on the beam when the ends are fixed against rotation. This moment is developed in order to keep the ends of the beam horizontal.

A calculation begins with the entire structure restrained or *locked* and the fixed end moments determined. Then each joint is *unlocked* (i.e., allowed to rotate) one at a time while the others are still restrained. The joint is then *balanced* by redistributing moments and shears to the members adjacent to that node. Once the equilibrium position of the unlocked joint is known, it is locked in this position and then the next joint is calculated, and so on. As each joint is balanced in this fashion, the analysis moves toward an equilibrium condition for the entire structure at which time the calculation is completed [Ref. 3.47].

The sign convention used to describe fixed end moments is a source of potential confusion in moment distribution. Positive and negative fixed end moments do not correspond to the way we have used positive and negative moment thus far in the text. As mentioned above, a fixed end moment is that moment which is applied to keep a member's end fixed against rotation, so that if the restraining moment is clockwise the sign is positive and if the restraining moment is counterclockwise, the sign is negative. The figure in the accompanying sidebar illustrates this convention for a beam subjected to a concentrated load. In this example, at the right end, to resist the upward reaction and keep the end horizontal, a clockwise moment is needed, the sign of which is positive.

3. Relative Beam Stiffness. Each member in the structure is said to possess a *relative stiffness*. This stiffness is defined by the type of material in the member, its cross-sectional properties, and the length. The general equation which quantifies the relative stiffness, R, is :

$$R = \frac{E \cdot I}{L} \qquad \text{(Eq. 3.124)}$$

where E = modulus of elasticity of material in member
  I = moment of inertia for member
  L = length of member

The *EI* component of Equation 3.124 is known as the *stiffness* of the beam.

> The sign convention used to describe fixed end moments is a source of potential confusion in moment distribution.

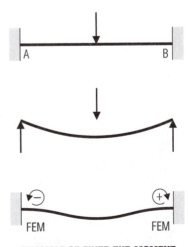

EXAMPLE OF FIXED END MOMENT SIGN CONVENTION

FIXED END MOMENTS are provided with a dual subscript. The first subscript indicates the joint at which the moment takes place. The first and second subscript together indicate the span which is being loaded. So that, for example, the moment M_{BC} denotes a moment at joint B for span BC. This convention applies to other variables in the moment distribution process such as stiffness, distribution and carry over factors.

DESIGNATION OF FIXED END MOMENT

The moment which is transmitted to the fixed end is known as the *carry over moment*. The portion of the moment which is transmitted is quantified by a *carry over factor*.

4. **Fixity Factor.** Each joint in the structure is assigned a fixity factor which varies depending on whether the joint is a pin or built-in (fixed). The fixity factor, F, is either:

- ❏ $F = 0$ if joint is a pin
- ❏ $F = 1$ if joint is built-in.

The reader should keep in mind that this is fixity against *rotation only* (i.e., not against translation).

5. **Stiffness Factor.** The stiffness factor, also known as the angular spring constant, is defined by the relative stiffness calculated as shown in Part 3 above and the fixity of the joint *opposite from the joint in question*. The stiffness factor, K, is given as:

$$K = \left(3 + F_{opposite}\right)R \qquad \text{(Eq. 3.125)}$$

where $F_{opposite}$ = fixity factor for opposite joint (see Part 4)
R = relative stiffness (see Part 3)

The standard approach would be to always use a stiffness factor of $K = 4R$.

6. **Distribution Factor.** At any given joint, the moment at that joint is going to be distributed to all adjacent members. The amount that goes to each member is a function of the stiffness of the joint in question and all members tributary to that joint. So that, the distribution factor, D, is given as:

$$D = \frac{K_n}{\sum K} \qquad \text{(Eq. 3.126)}$$

where K = stiffness factor for joint in question

ΣK = sum of stiffness factors for all tributary members

Two exceptions to Equation 3.126 occur at end points which are defined as either:

- ❏ $D = 0$ at a built-in end
- ❏ $D = 1$ at a simply supported end

7. **Carry Over Factor.** As mentioned above, a moment at a simply supported end is partially transmitted to an adjacent fixed end. The moment which is transmitted to the fixed end is known as the *carry over moment*. The portion of the moment which is transmitted is quantified by a *carry over factor*. Like the stiffness factor, the carry over factor is dependent

on the fixity of the joint *opposite from the joint in question*. The carry over factor, C, is given as:

$$C = \frac{2F_{opposite}}{3 + F_{opposite}}$$ (Eq. 3.127)

where $F_{opposite}$ = fixity factor for opposite joint (see Part 4)

8. **Method Synopsis.** Tables 3.15A and 3.15B provide a step by step synopsis of the moment distribution method (adapted from Ref. 3.48). Parts 2 through 7 above represent the constituent components required to complete a moment distribution calculation. The table explains how to use these values in a complete example. This explanation is combined with a worked example of a two span continuous beam. For fixed moment calculations, Tables 3.16A and 3.16B contain standard fixed end moments for a variety of beam loading configurations.

3.12.4 Influence Lines

Further complicating the analysis of continuous beam bridges is the presence of moving loads on the structure. Influence lines are useful tools which allow the designer to determine the maximum loading conditions for shear and moment based on a set of moving loads. Influence lines are plotted in a coordinate system where the x-axis represents the length of the structure and the y-axis the magnitude of the shear or moment *at the point in question*.

We highlight, "at the point in question" because it is easy for the novice designer to confuse an influence line with a shear or moment diagram. Figure 3.45 shows a typical influence line diagram for a three span structure. The plotted curve is for a load placed at the third panel point. The curve shows what the bending moment will be *at point 3* if the load is placed at a given panel point along the length of the structure, so that based on the influence diagram shown in Figure 3.45, the maximum moment occurs when the load is placed at point 3 itself.

> Influence lines are plotted in a coordinate system where the x-axis represents the length of the structure and the y-axis the magnitude of the shear or moment *at the point in question*.

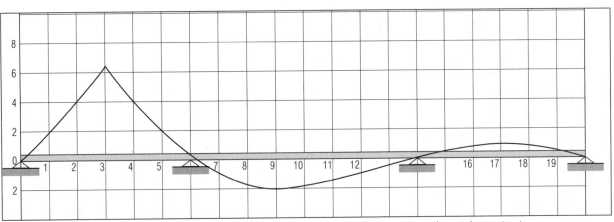

Figure 3.45 Sample bending moment influence line at panel point 3 for a three span, continuous beam structure.

STEP	DESCRIPTION	WORKED EXAMPLE
0	Given the beam shown at right, determine the resultant moments at Points A, B, and C. Assume that the beam from point A to C is composed of the same material. The cross-sectional properties, however, vary between spans AB and BC as indicated by the moment of inertia values shown.	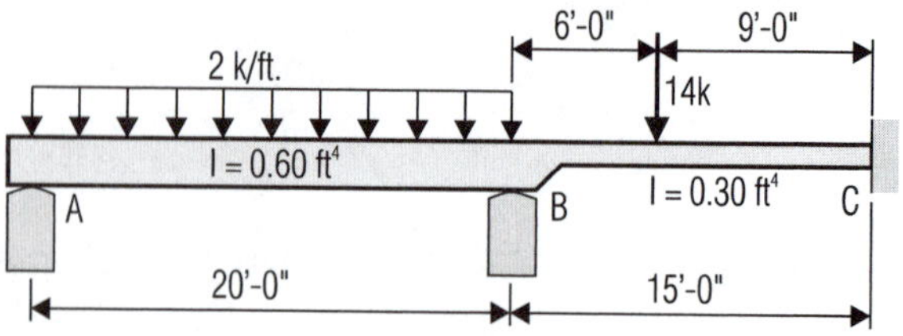
1	Divide the beam into independent spans. Assume all ends to be built-in.	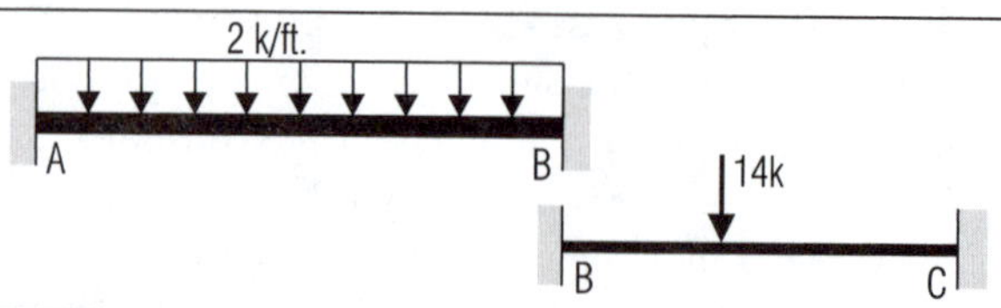
2	Calculate the relative stiffness of each span identified in Step 1. If either the modulus of elasticity, E, or the moment of inertia, I, is constant along the entire length of the structure they may be set equal to 1.	$R_{AB} = \dfrac{E \cdot I}{L} = \dfrac{1 \cdot 0.60 \text{ ft}^4}{20 \text{ ft}} = 0.03$ $R_{BC} = \dfrac{E \cdot I}{L} = \dfrac{1 \cdot 0.30 \text{ ft}^4}{15 \text{ ft}} = 0.02$
3	Calculate the fixity factors for each joint going in each direction. If the joint is capable of rotating, F = 0. If the joint is built in or is a continuous support, F = 1.	$F_{AB} = 0$ (End is free to rotate) $F_{BA} = 1$ (Continuous support) $F_{BC} = 1$ (Continuous support) $F_{CB} = 1$ (Built in)
4	Calculate the stiffness factors for each joint going in each direction. Remember that the fixity factor, F, used is from the opposite joint, not the joint in question.	$K_{AB} = (3 + F_{opposite})R = (3 + 1)(0.03) = 0.12$ $K_{BA} = (3 + F_{opposite})R = (3 + 0)(0.03) = 0.09$ $K_{BC} = (3 + F_{opposite})R = (3 + 1)(0.02) = 0.08$ $K_{CB} = (3 + F_{opposite})R = (3 + 1)(0.02) = 0.08$
5	Calculate the distribution factors based on the stiffness factors calculated in Step 4 above. The denominator (ΣK) is the aggregate of all tributary spans to the joint in question. At built-in ends use D = 0 and at simply supported ends D = 1.	$D_{AB} = 1$ (Simply supported end) $D_{BA} = \dfrac{K_n}{\Sigma K} = \dfrac{K_{BA}}{K_{BA} + K_{BC}} = \dfrac{0.09}{0.09 + 0.08} = 0.53$ $D_{BC} = \dfrac{K_n}{\Sigma K} = \dfrac{K_{BC}}{K_{BA} + K_{BC}} = \dfrac{0.08}{0.09 + 0.08} = 0.47$ $D_{CB} = 0$ (Built in end)
6	Calculate the carry over factors for each joint going in each direction. Remember that the fixity factor, F, used is from the opposite joint, not the joint in question. (Continued in Table 3.15B)	$C_{AB} = \dfrac{2 \cdot F_{opposite}}{3 + F_{opposite}} = \dfrac{2 \cdot F_{BA}}{3 + F_{BA}} = \dfrac{2 \cdot 1}{3 + 1} = 0.50$ $C_{BA} = \dfrac{2 \cdot F_{opposite}}{3 + F_{opposite}} = \dfrac{2 \cdot F_{AB}}{3 + F_{AB}} = \dfrac{2 \cdot 0}{3 + 0} = 0$ $C_{BC} = \dfrac{2 \cdot F_{opposite}}{3 + F_{opposite}} = \dfrac{2 \cdot F_{CB}}{3 + F_{CB}} = \dfrac{2 \cdot 1}{3 + 1} = 0.50$ $C_{CB} = \dfrac{2 \cdot F_{opposite}}{3 + F_{opposite}} = \dfrac{2 \cdot F_{BC}}{3 + F_{BC}} = \dfrac{2 \cdot 1}{3 + 1} = 0.50$

Table 3.15A Synopsis and Example of Moment Distribution Method

STEP	DESCRIPTION	WORKED EXAMPLE
7	Calculate the fixed end moments for each joint going in each direction using Tables 3.16A and 3.16B. Make sure to use the proper sign convention (i.e., clockwise positive and counter-clockwise negative) and be consistent throughout. The appropriate loading condition is based on the independent spans established in Step 1. At the onset, all ends are taken to be built in.	(diagram: $w = 2$ k/ft on span AB, $L = 20'\text{-}0"$; span BC with $a = 6'\text{-}0"$, $b = 9'\text{-}0"$, 14k load, $L = 15'\text{-}0"$) $M_{AB} = -\dfrac{wL^2}{12} = -\dfrac{(2\text{k/ft})(20\text{ ft})^2}{12} = -66.67 \text{ ft} \cdot \text{k}$ $M_{BA} = +\dfrac{wL^2}{12} = \dfrac{(2\text{k/ft})(20\text{ ft})^2}{12} = 66.67 \text{ ft} \cdot \text{k}$ $M_{BC} = -\dfrac{Pb^2a}{L^2} = -\dfrac{(14\text{k})(9\text{ ft})^2(6\text{ ft})}{(15\text{ ft})^2} = -30.24 \text{ ft} \cdot \text{k}$ $M_{CB} = +\dfrac{Pa^2b}{L^2} = -\dfrac{(14\text{k})(6\text{ ft})^2(9\text{ ft})}{(15\text{ ft})^2} = 20.16 \text{ ft} \cdot \text{k}$

Step 8

Balance any unbalanced moments by using a counter moment which is calculated using the appropriate joint distribution factor. The counter moments used for balancing are:
- Built-in End: 0
- Interior Joint: - (unbalance)
- Pinned End: - (unbalance)
- Semi Restrained End: - (1-F)(unbalance)

At an interior support the *unbalance* is the amount which has to be added to each joint in order to balance them. At joint B we use:

$$\text{unbalance} = -(M_{BA} + M_{BC})$$

Don't forget to take *the negative value* of the unbalance and multiply it by the distribution factor of the joint in question.

At an exterior, pinned joint the moment must equal zero, so the FEM is immediately balanced by either adding or subtracting the amount (depending on the sign of the FEM).

MOMENT DISTRIBUTION TABLE

LENGTH	20.0		15.0	
EI	0.60		0.30	
R	0.03		0.02	
JOINT	AB	BA	BC	CB
F	0.00	1.00	1.00	1.00
K	0.12	0.09	0.08	0.08
D	1.00	0.53	0.47	0.00
C	0.50	0.00	0.50	0.50
FEM	−66.67	+66.67	−30.24	+20.16
BALANCE	+66.67	+19.31	−17.12	0.00
CARRY OVER	0.00	+33.33	0.00	−8.56
BALANCE	0.00	−17.66	−15.66	0.00
CARRY OVER	0.00	0.00	0.00	−7.83
TOTAL	0.00	+63.03	−63.02	+3.77

Step 9

Carry over the distributed balanced moments to the opposite end of the span; *the same sign is used*. So that, for a span AB, the carry over moment in the AB column would be M_{BA} times C_{BA} and the carry over moment in the BA column would be M_{AB} times C_{AB}.

As an example, the first set of calculations are given:
1st Balance:
AB = +66.67 to set pinned end = 0
BA = $-(M_{BA} + M_{BC})D_{BA} = -(66.67 - 30.24)0.53 = -19.31$
BC = $-(M_{BA} + M_{BC})D_{BC} = -(66.67 - 30.24)0.47 = -17.12$
CB = 0 (Fixed End)

Step 10

Repeat Steps 8 and 9 until the appropriate joints are zeroed out (fixed ends do not need to be zeroed). Total all the rows of all the columns to obtain the final moments.

1st Carry Over:
AB = $(M_{BA})(C_{BA}) = (-19.31)(0) = 0$
BA = $(M_{AB})(C_{AB}) = (+66.67)(0.50) = +33.33$
BC = $(M_{CB})(C_{CB}) = (0.00)(0.50) = 0.00$
CB = $(M_{BC})(C_{BC}) = (-17.12)(0.50) = -8.56$

Table 3.15B Synopsis and Example of Moment Distribution Method (Continued)

[3.12.4]

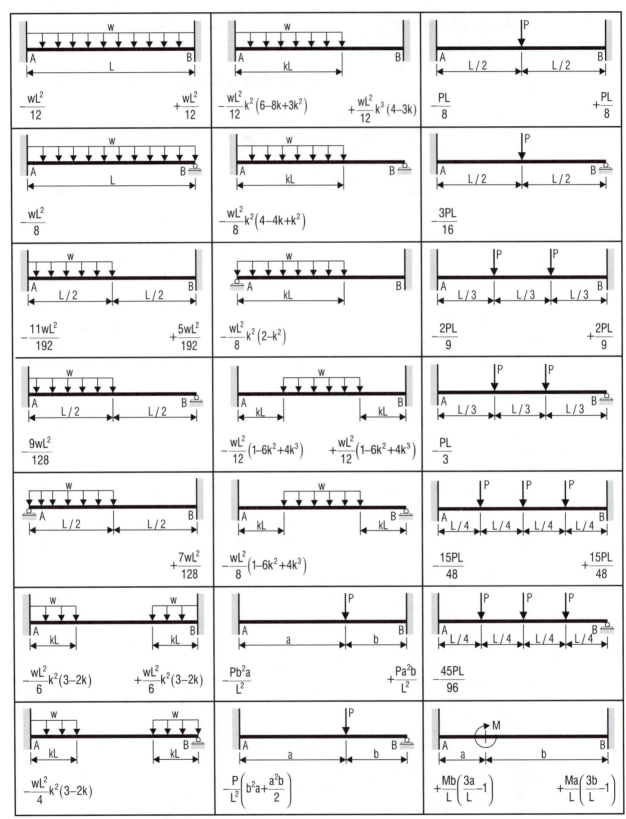

Table 3.16A Fixed End Moments for Common Beam Loadings (Adapted from Ref. 3.45 and 3.48)

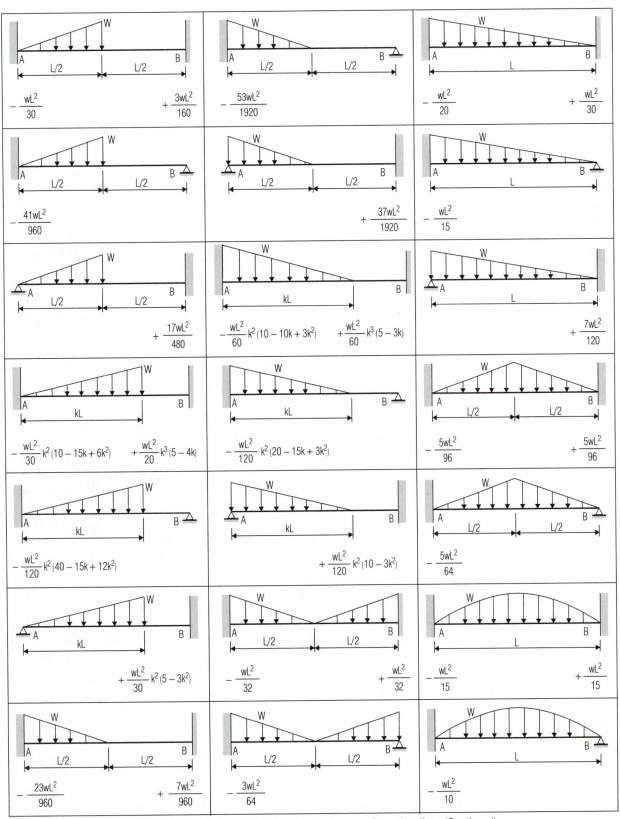

Table 3.16B Fixed End Moments for Common Beam Loadings (Continued)

Determining the actual moment or shear from an influence diagram varies depending on the type of load present. If the load is a concentrated load, the ordinate value can be used directly. If the load is a uniform distributed load, the area under the curve is used.

Influence diagrams can be developed using a variety of methods. The influence lines can be developed using graphical methods, using the method of virtual displacement, or even moment distribution. The most tedious aspect of this process is that influence lines have to be developed at individual points along each span.

> **T**he most tedious aspect of this process is that influence lines have to be developed at individual points along each span.

Probably the most common way of obtaining an influence line is through the use of predefined tables. These tables offer influence line coordinate data for a variety of multispan continuous beam structures. The tables are broken down by varying ratios of span lengths. An example of this would be a three span structure where the end spans are taken as length L and the center span with a length of $2L$. These tables eliminate a great deal of tedious hand calculations, provided the span ratios match up with those provided in the tables. Generally the ordinates are provided at tenth point increments along the length of each span.

For the purposes of this discussion, we will describe the procedure for developing influence lines for bending moment using the moment distribution method. This method is essentially a three step process. The following, along with Design Example 3.4, illustrate this approach which can be applied to any continuous beam.

1. **General Moment Support Equation.** The first step is to develop a general equation which describes the internal moments at support points based on a load at any point on the structure. This equation is developed using the moment distribution approach described in Section 3.12.3.

   An assumed fixed end moment is placed at the left side of the first interior support (i.e., $M_{BA} = 100$ ft-k). All other joints are set free to rotate (i.e., $M_{mn} = 0$ where mn denotes a support location). The moment distribution method of balancing and carrying over is conducted until the system reaches equilibrium. At this time all supports are totaled to yield the first set of moments which will be used as coefficients in the resultant moment support equation.

   This process is repeated with a unit moment placed on the other side of the first interior support (i.e., $M_{BC} = 100$ ft-k) and all other supports set to zero. Upon completing this step, all information necessary for the first support is available. Moments at subsequent supports are calculated in a similar fashion.

> **I**f there is symmetry present (i.e., two equal end spans, four equal spans, etc.) only the supports before the line of symmetry need to be calculated.

   If there is symmetry present (i.e., two equal end spans, four equal spans, etc.), only the supports before the line of symmetry need to be calculated. In Design Example 3.4, for a three span structure comprising three equal spans, only the two sides of the first interior support are required to be solved because of symmetry (i.e., the equations at the second support are the mirror image of the first support).

The general form of the moment support equation for a unit load placed in the first span (AB) is presented below as:

$$M_{BA} = \left(M_{AB}^{unit} \cdot M_{AB}^{FEM} \right) + \left(M_{BA}^{unit} \cdot M_{BA}^{FEM} \right) \qquad \text{(Eq. 3.128)}$$

where M_{BA} = internal support moment at left side of first support

M_{BA}^{FEM} = moment due to unit moment found using moment distribution

M_{BA}^{FEM} = fixed end moment calculated by placing a unit load $P = 1$ at a point on a span

A similar equation is prepared for the right side of the first interior support, and both sides of all subsequent supports. The unit moments used in Equation 3.128 are those found by placing the 100 ft-k unit on the left side of the first interior support. In the equation for the internal moment at the right side of the first support (M_{BC}) the unit moments used would be those resulting from the 100 ft-k moment placed on the right side of the support (and all other supports set equal to zero). This convention is repeated for all subsequent supports.

2. **Unit Loads.** Once the support moment equations have been established, the next step is to develop the influence ordinates at all of the support points. This is done by placing a unit load at tenth points along each span. The resulting fixed end moments are then computed, as before, using Table 3.16A (for a concentrated load). Each fixed end moment is multiplied by the appropriate unit moment as described in Equation 3.128.

In building a table of influence ordinates, this will result in a column of ordinates for each support. Table 3.17A illustrates what the influence ordinates table will look like at this stage. For a load placed at any tenth point, we now have influence data at all support points. As can be seen from the table, however, the ordinates at points within each span for a given unit load still need to be calculated.

3. **Influence Data at Intermediate Points.** In order to complete the influence data at intermediate points, the designer must:

❏ Take each span as a simple beam and determine the bending moment at tenth points and then

❏ Proportion the negative moment (determined in Part 2 above) throughout the span and combine with the simple beam bending moment.

We will take the three span continuous beam described in Design Example 3.4 and Table 3.17A as an example. A unit load of 1 is placed

> Once the support moment equations have been established, the next step is to develop the influence ordinates at all the support points.

Unit Load at		SPAN 1											SPAN 2									
		A	.1	.2	.3	.4	.5	.6	.7	.8	.9	B	.1	.2	.3	.4	.5	.6	.7	.8	.9	C
SPAN 1	A	0										0										0
	.1	0										-.026										.007
	.2	0										-.051										.013
	.3	0										-.073										.018
	.4	0										-.090										.022
	.5	0										-.100										.025
	.6	0										-.102										.026
	.7	0										-.095										.024
	.8	0										-.077										.019
	.9	0										-.046										.011
SPAN 2	B	0										0										0
	.1	0										-.039										-.015
	.2	0										-.064										-.032
	.3	0										-.077										-.049
	.4	0										-.080										-.064
	.5	0										-.075										-.075
	.6	0										-.064										-.080
	.7	0										-.049										-.077
	.8	0										-.032										-.064
	.9	0										-.015										-.039
SPAN 3	C	0										0										0
	.1	0										.011										-.046
	.2	0										.019										-.077
	.3	0										.024										-.095
	.4	0										.026										-.102
	.5	0										.025										-.100
	.6	0										.022										-.090
	.7	0										.018										-.073
	.8	0										.013										-.051
	.9	0										.007										-.026
	D	0										0										0

Table 3.17A Moment Influence Ordinates for Three Equal Spans After Solving the Moment Support Equations (through 3.12.4, Part 2)

A unit load of 1 is placed at the first tenth point in Span 1. Taking the span to act as a simply supported beam, the bending moment is calculated at each tenth point along its length.

at the first tenth point in Span 1. Taking the span to act as a simply supported beam, the bending moment is calculated at each tenth point along its length.

The negative moment at joint B of Span AB must now be proportioned throughout the span. In Table 3.17A this value is -0.026. To proportion this amount we take a tenth of this amount (i.e., -0.0026) and add a proportional amount to each tenth point. At each tenth point the proportioned amount would be:

- ❏ 0.1L = 1 times -0.0026
- ❏ 0.2L = 2 times -0.0026
- ❏ 0.3L = 3 times -0.0026
- ❏ and so on

EXAMPLE 3.4	INFLUENCE LINES FOR A THREE SPAN CONTINUOUS BEAM STRUCTURE	DET	1 / 6

PROBLEM: Develop a table of influence ordinates for bending moment for a three span continuous beam structure. All three spans are equal.

GIVEN: The structure as depicted below.

STEP 1: Divide the beam into independent spans and apply a unit moment of 100 at the end of Span AB.

STEP 2: Calculate the Relative Stiffness for Each Span.

$$R_{AB} = \frac{E \cdot I}{L} = \frac{(1)(1)}{L} = \frac{1}{L} = R_{BA} = R_{BC} = R_{CB} = R_{CD} = R_{DC} = R$$

STEP 3: Calculate the Fixity Factors for Each Span.

$F_{AB} = 0$	$F_{BA} = 1$	$F_{BC} = 1$	$F_{CB} = 1$	$F_{CD} = 1$	$F_{DC} = 0$
Free to Rotate	Contin. Support	Contin. Support	Contin. Support	Contin. Support	Free to Rotate

STEP 4: Calculate the Stiffness Factors for Each Span.

$$K_{AB} = (3 + F_{opposite})R = (3 + 1)R \qquad K_{AB} = 4R$$
$$K_{BA} = (3 + F_{opposite})R = (3 + 0)R \qquad K_{BA} = 3R$$
$$K_{BC} = (3 + F_{opposite})R = (3 + 1)R \qquad K_{BC} = 4R$$
$$K_{CB} = (3 + F_{opposite})R = (3 + 1)R \qquad K_{CB} = 4R$$
$$K_{CD} = (3 + F_{opposite})R = (3 + 0)R \qquad K_{CD} = 3R$$
$$K_{DC} = (3 + F_{opposite})R = (3 + 1)R \qquad K_{DC} = 4R$$

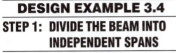

DESIGN EXAMPLE 3.4

STEP 1: DIVIDE THE BEAM INTO INDEPENDENT SPANS

The three span structure is divided into three independent spans, AB, BC, and CD. A unit moment of 100 is applied to the B end of Span AB. All other supports are set free to rotate so their fixed end moments will be zero. Recall our sign convention of a clockwise moment being positive.

STEP 2: CALCULATE RELATIVE STIFFNESS FACTORS

For the development of the influence ordinate data, we will assume a prismatic beam (i.e., of uniform cross section) and constant material properties. Therefore, both the modulus of elasticity E and moment of inertia, I, can be set to unity (1). Since we have three equal spans, all relative stiffness values will be equal. We will call this value R (Equation 3.124).

STEP 3: CALCULATE FIXITY FIXITY FACTORS

All continuous supports, as a rule, are set equal to one. Since the ends are free to rotate, they are set equal to zero.

STEP 4: CALCULATE STIFFNESS FACTORS

Remember to use the fixity factor of the joint which is *opposite* from the current joint in question (Equation 3.125).

The proportioned amount at each tenth point is then applied to each tenth point value of the bending moment calculated taking the beam to be simply supported. These values can now be incorporated into the first row of blank intermediate span ordinates for Span 1 for a unit load at the first tenth point.

4. Predefined Tables. From the above, it is obvious that creating all of the influence data for a continuous beam bridge is a rather tedious affair. As mentioned previously, there exists a variety of sources from which the designer can access predefined tables of influence data. AISC provides such a reference with their *Moments, Shears and Reactions for Continuous Highway Bridges*. First published in 1959 and later revised in 1983, this document offers the designer with a set of common continuous bridge configurations [Ref. 3.49].

In addition to presenting influence lines for general continuous beam configurations, the AISC publication provides tables which give the

> From the above, it is obvious that creating all of the influence data for a continuous beam bridge is a rather tedious affair.

Unit Load at		A	.1	.2	.3	.4	.5	.6	.7	.8	.9	B	.1	.2	.3	.4	.5	.6	.7	.8	.9	C
						SPAN 1										SPAN 2						
SPAN 1	A	0	0	0	0	0	0	0	0	0	0	0	0	0	0	0	0	0	0	0	0	0
	.1	0	.087	.075	.062	.049	.037	.024	.012	-.001	-.014	-.026	-.023	-.020	-.017	-.013	-.010	-.007	-.003	.000	.003	.007
	.2	0	.075	.150	.125	.100	.074	.049	.024	-.001	-.026	-.051	-.045	-.038	-.032	-.026	-.019	-.013	-.006	.000	.006	.013
	.3	0	.063	.125	.188	.151	.114	.076	.039	.002	-.036	-.073	-.064	-.055	-.046	-.036	-.027	-.018	-.009	.000	.009	.018
	.4	0	.051	.102	.153	.204	.155	.106	.057	.008	-.041	-.090	-.078	-.067	-.056	-.045	-.034	-.022	-.011	.000	.011	.022
	.5	0	.040	.080	.120	.160	.200	.140	.080	.020	-.040	-.100	-.088	-.075	-.063	-.050	-.038	-.025	-.013	.000	.013	.025
	.6	0	.030	.060	.089	.119	.149	.179	.108	.038	-.032	-.102	-.090	-.077	-.064	-.051	-.038	-.026	-.013	.000	.013	.026
	.7	0	.021	.041	.061	.082	.102	.123	.143	.064	-.016	-.095	-.083	-.071	-.060	-.048	-.036	-.024	-.012	.000	.012	.024
	.8	0	.012	.025	.037	.049	.062	.074	.086	.099	.011	-.077	-.067	-.058	-.048	-.038	-.029	-.019	-.010	.000	.010	.019
	.9	0	.003	.006	.009	.022	.027	.033	.038	.044	.049	-.046	-.040	-.034	-.029	-.023	-.017	-.011	-.006	.000	.006	.011
SPAN 2	B	0	0	0	0	0	0	0	0	0	0	0	0	0	0	0	0	0	0	0	0	0
	.1	0	-.004	-.008	-.012	-.016	-.020	-.023	-.027	-.031	-.035	-.039	.053	.046	.038	.031	.023	.015	.007	.000	-.007	-.015
	.2	0	-.006	-.013	-.019	-.026	-.032	-.038	-.045	-.051	-.058	-.064	.019	.102	.086	.069	.052	.035	.018	.002	-.015	-.032
	.3	0	-.008	-.015	-.023	-.031	-.039	-.046	-.054	-.062	-.064	-.077	-.004	.069	.141	.114	.087	.060	.033	.005	-.022	-.049
	.4	0	-.008	-.016	-.024	-.032	-.040	-.048	-.056	-.064	-.072	-.080	-.018	.043	.105	.166	.128	.090	.051	.013	-.026	-.064
	.5	0	-.008	-.015	-.023	-.030	-.038	-.045	-.053	-.060	-.068	-.075	-.025	.025	.075	.125	.175	.125	.075	.025	-.025	-.075
	.6	0	-.006	-.013	-.019	-.026	-.032	-.038	-.045	-.051	-.058	-.064	-.026	.013	.051	.090	.128	.166	.105	.043	-.018	-.080
	.7	0	-.005	-.010	-.015	-.020	-.025	-.029	-.034	-.039	-.044	-.049	-.022	.005	.033	.060	.087	.114	.141	.069	-.004	-.077
	.8	0	-.003	-.006	-.010	-.013	-.016	-.019	-.022	-.026	-.029	-.032	-.015	.002	.018	.035	.052	.069	.086	.102	.019	-.064
	.9	0	-.002	-.003	-.005	-.006	-.008	-.009	-.011	-.012	-.014	-.015	-.007	.000	.008	.015	.023	.031	.038	.046	.053	-.039
SPAN 3	C	0	0	0	0	0	0	0	0	0	0	0	0	0	0	0	0	0	0	0	0	0
	.1	0	.001	.002	.003	.005	.006	.007	.008	.009	.010	.011	.006	.000	-.006	-.011	-.017	-.023	-.029	-.034	-.040	-.046
	.2	0	.002	.004	.006	.008	.010	.012	.013	.015	.017	.019	.010	.000	-.010	-.019	-.029	-.038	-.048	-.058	-.067	-.077
	.3	0	.002	.005	.007	.010	.012	.014	.017	.019	.021	.024	.012	.000	-.012	-.024	-.036	-.048	-.060	-.071	-.083	-.095
	.4	0	.003	.005	.008	.010	.013	.015	.018	.021	.023	.026	.013	.000	-.013	-.026	-.038	-.051	-.064	-.077	-.090	-.102
	.5	0	.003	.005	.008	.010	.013	.015	.018	.020	.023	.025	.013	.000	-.013	-.025	-.038	-.050	-.063	-.075	-.088	-.100
	.6	0	.002	.005	.007	.009	.011	.013	.016	.018	.020	.022	.011	.000	-.011	-.022	-.034	-.045	-.056	-.067	-.078	-.090
	.7	0	.002	.004	.006	.007	.009	.011	.013	.015	.016	.018	.009	.000	-.010	-.018	-.027	-.036	-.046	-.055	-.064	-.073
	.8	0	.001	.003	.004	.005	.006	.008	.009	.010	.012	.013	.006	.000	-.006	-.013	-.019	-.026	-.032	-.038	-.045	-.051
	.9	0	.001	.001	.002	.003	.003	.004	.005	.005	.006	.007	.003	.000	-.003	-.007	-.010	-.013	-.017	-.020	-.023	-.026
	D	0	0	0	0	0	0	0	0	0	0	0	0	0	0	0	0	0	0	0	0	0

Table 3.17B Moment Influence Ordinates for Three Equal Spans After Solving Intermediate Points (through Step 3)

designer the maximum reactions, shears, and moments based on the standard AASHTO HS20-44 loading. This loading is applied to a variety of continuous beam geometries and saves the designer the step of having to apply the AASHTO loading to general purpose influence lines for shear and moment.

When using the AISC or similar tables, the designer should note whether *axle* or *wheel* loads are being used. As mentioned before in Section 3.10.6, Part 1, this can be a source of potential confusion and error in using these types of predefined tables. The AISC tables, for example, utilize axle loads rather than wheel loads, so that when a wheel load distribution is applied using AASHTO Standard Specifications (e.g., S/5.5), one half of the table value should be used.

It would be impossible for any reference to cover all possible span configurations. Therefore, it may still be incumbent upon the designer to

> **W**hen using the AISC or similar tables, the designer should note whether *axle* or *wheel* loads are being used ... this can be a source of potential confusion ...

EXAMPLE 3.4	INFLUENCE LINES FOR A THREE SPAN CONTINUOUS BEAM STRUCTURE	DET	2/6

STEP 5: Calculate the Distribution Factors for Each Span.

$D_{AB} = 1$ (Simply Supported End)

$$D_{BA} = \frac{K_n}{\sum K} = \frac{K_{BA}}{K_{BA} + K_{BC}} = \frac{3R}{3R + 4R} = \frac{3}{7} = 0.43$$

$$D_{BC} = \frac{K_n}{\sum K} = \frac{K_{BC}}{K_{BA} + K_{BC}} = \frac{4R}{3R + 4R} = \frac{4}{7} = 0.57$$

$$D_{CB} = \frac{K_n}{\sum K} = \frac{K_{CB}}{K_{CB} + K_{CD}} = \frac{4R}{4R + 3R} = \frac{4}{7} = 0.57$$

$$D_{CD} = \frac{K_n}{\sum K} = \frac{K_{CD}}{K_{CB} + K_{CD}} = \frac{3R}{4R + 3R} = \frac{3}{7} = 0.43$$

$D_{DC} = 1$ (Simply Supported End)

STEP 6: Calculate the Carry Over Factors for Each Span.

$$C_{AB} = \frac{2 \cdot F_{opposite}}{3 + F_{opposite}} = \frac{2 \cdot F_{BA}}{3 + F_{BA}} = \frac{(2)(1)}{3 + 1} = \frac{2}{4} = 0.50$$

$$C_{BA} = \frac{2 \cdot F_{opposite}}{3 + F_{opposite}} = \frac{2 \cdot F_{AB}}{3 + F_{AB}} = \frac{(2)(0)}{3 + 0} = \frac{0}{3} = 0$$

$$C_{BC} = \frac{2 \cdot F_{opposite}}{3 + F_{opposite}} = \frac{2 \cdot F_{CB}}{3 + F_{CB}} = \frac{(2)(1)}{3 + 1} = \frac{2}{4} = 0.50$$

$$C_{CB} = \frac{2 \cdot F_{opposite}}{3 + F_{opposite}} = \frac{2 \cdot F_{BC}}{3 + F_{BC}} = \frac{(2)(1)}{3 + 1} = \frac{2}{4} = 0.50$$

$$C_{CD} = \frac{2 \cdot F_{opposite}}{3 + F_{opposite}} = \frac{2 \cdot F_{DC}}{3 + F_{DC}} = \frac{(2)(0)}{3 + 0} = \frac{0}{3} = 0$$

$$C_{DC} = \frac{2 \cdot F_{opposite}}{3 + F_{opposite}} = \frac{2 \cdot F_{CD}}{3 + F_{CD}} = \frac{(2)(1)}{3 + 1} = \frac{2}{4} = 0.50$$

DESIGN EXAMPLE 3.4

STEP 5: CALCULATE THE DISTRIBUTION FACTORS

The distribution factors are calculated using the stiffness factors determined earlier in Step 4. The denominator is the sum of the stiffness factors of all tributary spans to the joint in question. As a rule, simply supported ends are given a distribution factor of one. If either end were built-in, they would have been given a distribution factor of zero (Equation 3.126).

STEP 6: CALCULATE CARRY OVER FACTORS

The carry over factors are calculated using the fixity factors determined earlier in Step 3. Note that the fixity factor *opposite* the joint in question is used. Since the ends are free to rotate, their fixity factors are zero, which means that the first interior support of exterior spans will have a carry over factor of zero. All other carry over factors are 0.50 (Equation 3.127).

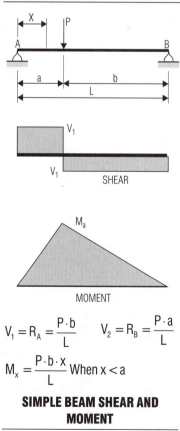

$$V_1 = R_A = \frac{P \cdot b}{L} \qquad V_2 = R_B = \frac{P \cdot a}{L}$$

$$M_x = \frac{P \cdot b \cdot x}{L} \text{ When } x < a$$

SIMPLE BEAM SHEAR AND MOMENT

generate the influence data by hand. Naturally this exercise is not necessary if computer software is available. The designer should keep these tables on hand, though, to utilize in a checking capacity. As we have consistently stated throughout this text, the designer should corroborate all computer solutions with a hand check. Predefined tables offer a quick and handy method of checking computer output.

5. Using Influence Lines. The novice designer must be aware that the influence line *does not represent a shear or moment diagram* itself. The influence data are simple ordinates, off of which shear and moment diagrams can be created. Using the influence line for moment given in Table 3.17B as an example, each row of data represents the ordinates to the bending moment diagram for a load placed at the specified load point, so that the first row of data are the ordinates for the bending moment diagram with a unit load placed a distance of one tenth the length of the first span from support A. Because of symmetry, the vertical columns for the third span of the structure are not provided in the table.

The shaded diagonal represents the maximum ordinates possible for any given unit load. If, for example, a unit load were placed at 0.3 of the first span, the maximum ordinate would be 0.188. These shaded values are ordinates to the maximum positive moment envelope induced by a single, moving concentrated load.

The way a shear or moment diagram is developed from an influence line varies depending on whether the beam is loaded with a concentrated load or a uniform distributed load. To determine the actual shear and moment values from an influence line, the following rules must be observed [Ref. 3.49]:

■ **Reactions and Shears Due to Concentrated Load.** To find the actual reaction or shear value due to a concentrated load, the ordinate is multiplied by the value of the concentrated load.

■ **Reactions and Shears Due to Uniform Load.** To find the actual reaction or shear value due to a uniformly distributed load, the area under the influence line is multiplied by the product of the distributed load (in units of weight per unit length) and the length of the *shorter* span.

■ **Moments Due to Concentrated Load.** To find the actual bending moment value due to a concentrated load, the ordinate is multiplied by the product of the weight of the concentrated load and the length of the *shorter* span.

■ **Moments Due to Uniform Load.** To find the actual bending moment value due to a uniformly distributed load, the area under the influence line is multiplied by the product of the distributed load (in units of weight per unit length) and the *square* of the length of the *shorter* span.

The area taken, for a specific panel point, is defined by a *column* of influence ordinates. In Table 3.17B, for example, the area would be computed for the curve defined by the first column of ordinates (i.e., 0, .087, .075, .063 ... .002, .001, .001, 0). Many predefined tables include the area under this curve for computing moments due to a uniform load.

There are a variety of methods for calculating the area under a curve defined by set of points. The most basic approach would be to plot the curve and break it down into triangles and rectangles and then sum the areas of each part. Obviously, such an approach would prove tedious for all but the most basic two span continuous structures. Another approach would be to use a spreadsheet program or mathematics software package after entering the influence ordinates in table form. Some handheld calculators even provide predefined programs for computing the area under a curve defined by a set of points. If such computer methods are unavailable, however, the following section offers a hand calculation method which is relatively straightforward and provides results quickly.

> The way a shear or moment diagram is developed from an influence line varies depending on whether the beam is loaded with a concentrated load or a uniform ... load.

> Some handheld calculators even provide predefined programs for computing the area under a curve defined by a set of points.

EXAMPLE 3.4	INFLUENCE LINES FOR A THREE SPAN CONTINUOUS BEAM STRUCTURE		DET	3/6

STEP 7: Use Moment Distribution to get the Support Equation Coefficients.

MOMENT DISTRIBUTION – UNIT MOMENT OF 100 @ BA

LENGTH EI R	L 1 R		L 1 R		L 1 R	
JOINT	AB	BA	BC	CB	CD	DC
F **K** **D** **C**	0.00 4R 1.00 0.50	1.00 3R 0.43 0.00	1.00 4R 0.57 0.50	1.00 4R 0.57 0.50	1.00 3R 0.43 0.00	0.00 4R 1.00 0.50
FEM	0.00	100.00	0.00	0.00	0.00	0.00
BALANCE **CARRY OVER**	0.00 0.00	-43.00 0.00	-57.00 0.00	0.00 -28.50	0.00 0.00	0.00 0.00
BALANCE **CARRY OVER**	0.00 0.00	0.00 0.00	0.00 8.12	16.24 0.00	12.25 0.00	0.00 0.00
BALANCE **CARRY OVER**	0.00 0.00	-3.49 0.00	-4.63 0.00	0.00 -2.31	0.00 0.00	0.00 0.00
BALANCE **CARRY OVER**	0.00 0.00	0.00 0.00	0.00 0.66	1.32 0.00	0.99 0.00	0.00 0.00
BALANCE **CARRY OVER**	0.00 0.00	-0.28 0.00	-0.38 0.00	0.00 -0.19	0.00 0.00	0.00 0.00
BALANCE **CARRY OVER**	0.00 0.00	0.00 0.00	0.00 0.05	0.11 0.00	0.08 0.00	0.00 0.00
BALANCE **CARRY OVER**	0.00 0.00	-0.02 0.00	-0.03 0.00	0.00 -0.01	0.00 0.00	0.00 0.00
TOTAL	0.00	+53.21	-53.21	-13.34	+13.32	0.00

DESIGN EXAMPLE 3.4
STEP 7: GET MOMENT SUPPORT EQUATION COEFFICIENTS

A unit moment of 100 is placed at the B end of span AB (the next step will place this same unit moment on the other side of this joint). All other joints are set free to rotate with FEMs of zero.

Recall that, in moment distribution, balancing is conducted at the ends of the beam and at joints between common spans (e.g., BA-BC and CB-CD). The carry over process is done within an individual span (e.g., BA carried over to AB and AB carried over to BA). The horizontal arrows indicate a balancing operation and the crossing arrows a carry over. The factors EI, R, F, K, D, and C are taken from Steps 2 through 6. For more on moment distribution, see Section 3.12.3 and Tables 3.15A and 3.15B.

The moment distribution converges after seven balancing and carry over operations. We will round the resulting values for use in subsequent calculations to 53.2 and 13.3. As would be expected, the two ends of the structure, AB and DC, are equal to zero since the moments at the ends of the continuous beam are zero.

6. Area Under an Influence Line. The *method of coordinates* offers a quick and efficient way to calculate the area under a given influence line. This is a general purpose method which can be used in diverse applications such as the computation of the area enclosed by a traverse. As the name implies, the area under the influence line will be computed by taking each ordinate as part of an *x-y* coordinate pair.

A coordinate pair is taken such that the *x*-coordinate is the length along the span (e.g., 0.1, 0.2, 0.3, etc.) and the *y*-coordinate is the actual influence ordinate at that point [Ref. 3.48]. The general form of the equation used is given as:

$$A = \left| \frac{1}{2} \left(\sum_{i=1}^{n} y_i \left(x_{i-1} - x_{i+1} \right) \right) \right|$$

(Eq. 3.129)

However, it is easier to compute the area by arranging the coordinate pairs in the following fashion:

$$\frac{x_1}{y_1} \diagdown \frac{x_2}{y_2} \diagdown \frac{x_3}{y_3} \diagdown \frac{x_4}{y_4} \diagdown \frac{x_1}{y_1}$$

where the above example would be used for a curve defined by four separate points. The actual area is determined using the following expression:

$$A = \left| \frac{1}{2} \left(\sum \text{Full Line Products} - \sum \text{Dotted Line Products} \right) \right| \quad \textbf{(Eq. 3.130)}$$

Taking the four point example given in Equation 3.130, this would translate into the absolute value of:

$$0.50 \left| (x_1 y_2 + x_2 y_3 + x_3 y_4 + x_4 y_1) - (x_2 y_1 + x_3 y_2 + x_4 y_3 + x_1 y_4) \right|$$

The method of coordinates, described above, offers a relatively simple approach to finding the area under an influence line. A recommended method of attack would be to take all of the positive moment regions and compute their area and then take all of the negative moment regions and compute their area. The total area under the curve would be the combination of the positive and negative regions.

The reader should note that the total area is not taken as the absolute value. This means that the negative moment area is subtracted from the positive moment area. Therefore, it is possible that the total area under an influence line is a negative value if the area under the negative portion of the influence curve is greater than that under the positive portion.

As mentioned earlier, there are a variety of other analytical methods which can be employed to achieve the same result. For curves with relatively linear segments, the trapezoidal rule can be used. Simpson's rule is a method which is more popular when the boundary is curved or parabolic. The reader is referred to general civil engineering reference texts such as Ref. 3.48 for more information on these approaches.

7. **Conclusions.** In this section, the word tedious has been used repeatedly in reference to influence lines. If the designer's organization has access to a continuous beam software package, the point is moot (many such systems can even output influence line data in addition to the complete analysis of a structure). For the student in a classroom environment, or engineer without such software, the ability to create a set of influence lines as painlessly as possible is paramount if one hopes to conduct the design of a continuous beam bridge in a reasonable time frame.

It has been said that "a good carpenter uses the tools at his disposal." The same can be said of the design engineer. In today's work environment, the number of engineers who have no access whatsoever to even a personal

---

> The method of coordinates, described above, offers a relatively simple approach to finding the area under an influence line.

> It has been said that "a good carpenter uses the tools at his disposal." The same can be said of the design engineer.

EXAMPLE 3.4	INFLUENCE LINES FOR A THREE SPAN CONTINUOUS BEAM STRUCTURE	DET	4/6

STEP 8: Use Moment Distribution to get the Support Equation Coefficients.

MOMENT DISTRIBUTION – UNIT MOMENT OF 100 @ BC

LENGTH EI R	L 1 R		L 1 R		L 1 R	
JOINT	AB	BA	BC	CB	CD	DC
F	0.00	1.00	1.00	1.00	1.00	0.00
K	4R	3R	4R	4R	3R	4R
D	1.00	0.43	0.57	0.57	0.43	1.00
C	0.50	0.00	0.50	0.50	0.00	0.50
FEM	0.00	0.00	-100.00	0.00	0.00	0.00
BALANCE	0.00	43.00	57.00	0.00	0.00	0.00
CARRY OVER	0.00	0.00	0.00	28.50	0.00	0.00
BALANCE	0.00	0.00	0.00	-16.24	-12.25	0.00
CARRY OVER	0.00	0.00	-8.12	0.00	0.00	0.00
BALANCE	0.00	3.49	4.63	0.00	0.00	0.00
CARRY OVER	0.00	0.00	0.00	2.31	0.00	0.00
BALANCE	0.00	0.00	0.00	-1.32	-0.99	0.00
CARRY OVER	0.00	0.00	-0.66	0.00	0.00	0.00
BALANCE	0.00	0.28	0.38	0.00	0.00	0.00
CARRY OVER	0.00	0.00	0.00	0.19	0.00	0.00
BALANCE	0.00	0.00	0.00	-0.11	-0.08	0.00
CARRY OVER	0.00	0.00	-0.05	0.00	0.00	0.00
BALANCE	0.00	0.02	0.03	0.00	0.00	0.00
CARRY OVER	0.00	0.00	0.00	0.01	0.00	0.00
TOTAL	0.00	+46.79	-46.79	+13.34	-13.32	0.00

DESIGN EXAMPLE 3.4
STEP 8: GET MOMENT SUPPORT EQUATION COEFFICIENTS

The process illustrated previously in Step 7 is repeated here. This time, however, the unit moment of 100 is placed on the other side of joint B. Also note the sign change of the unit moment based on our previously established convention.

The magnitude of the values in each column is identical to those found in Step 7. The only difference is in the sign associated with each value.

The resulting totals show a change in magnitude at joints BA and BC while CB and CD remain the same except for the change in sign. As before, we will round these values for use later on, the rounded values being 46.8 and 13.3.

Because of the symmetry of the structure, it is not necessary to perform a moment distribution calculation at joints CB and CD. The resulting coefficients used will be a mirror image of those established for joints BA and BC in Steps 7 and 8. The next step will be to define the general moment support equations.

utilize computer facilities even if fully featured bridge specific software is not available.

A quick review of Table 3.18 illustrates that creation of influence data can, at the very least, be facilitated with the use of a simple spreadsheet program. Indeed, even the tabular nature of moment distribution lends itself well toward automation with a spreadsheet. While to some this may seem like an obvious point, it is not at all uncommon to see the design calculations from large engineering firms done entirely by hand. It is easy for an engineer to lament the absence of bridge specific design software and utilize the tried and true hand calculation methods they have always employed. The good carpenter, however, should make use of even the most basic tools. A spreadsheet program falls into this category. Particularly in today's computing environment, where interactive, Windows-based spreadsheet software provides the designer with a robust suite of graphing functions, every automation tool must be exploited to its fullest potential.

	Point	a	b	EQUATION 1	EQUATION 2	FEM 1	FEM 2	COEFF 1	COEFF 2	M
SPAN 1	A	1.0	0.0	0	0	0	0	0	0	0
	1	0.9	0.1	0	$b^2a + 0.50a^2b$	0	0.0495	0	-0.532	-0.0263
	2	0.8	0.2	0	$b^2a + 0.50a^2b$	0	0.0960	0	-0.532	-0.0511
	3	0.7	0.3	0	$b^2a + 0.50a^2b$	0	0.1365	0	-0.532	-0.0726
	4	0.6	0.4	0	$b^2a + 0.50a^2b$	0	0.1680	0	-0.532	-0.0894
	5	0.5	0.5	0	$b^2a + 0.50a^2b$	0	0.1875	0	-0.532	-0.0998
	6	0.4	0.6	0	$b^2a + 0.50a^2b$	0	0.1920	0	-0.532	-0.1021
	7	0.3	0.7	0	$b^2a + 0.50a^2b$	0	0.1785	0	-0.532	-0.0950
	8	0.2	0.8	0	$b^2a + 0.50a^2b$	0	0.1440	0	-0.532	-0.0766
	9	0.1	0.9	0	$b^2a + 0.50a^2b$	0	0.0855	0	-0.532	-0.0455
SPAN 2	B	0.0	1.0	0	0	0	0	0	0	0
	11	0.1	0.9	$-b^2a$	$+a^2b$	-0.0810	0.0090	0.468	-0.133	-0.0391
	12	0.2	0.8	$-b^2a$	$+a^2b$	-0.1280	0.0320	0.468	-0.133	-0.0642
	13	0.3	0.7	$-b^2a$	$+a^2b$	-0.1470	0.0630	0.468	-0.133	-0.0772
	14	0.4	0.6	$-b^2a$	$+a^2b$	-0.1440	0.0960	0.468	-0.133	-0.0802
	15	0.5	0.5	$-b^2a$	$+a^2b$	-0.1250	0.1250	0.468	-0.133	-0.0751
	16	0.6	0.4	$-b^2a$	$+a^2b$	-0.0960	0.1440	0.468	-0.133	-0.0641
	17	0.7	0.3	$-b^2a$	$+a^2b$	-0.0630	0.1470	0.468	-0.133	-0.0490
	18	0.8	0.2	$-b^2a$	$+a^2b$	-0.0320	0.1280	0.468	-0.133	-0.0320
	19	0.9	0.1	$-b^2a$	$+a^2b$	-0.0090	0.0810	0.468	-0.133	-0.0150
SPAN 3	C	0.0	1.0	0	0	0	0	0	0	0
	21	0.1	0.9	$-(b^2a + 0.50a^2b)$	0	-0.0855	0	-0.133	0	0.0114
	22	0.2	0.8	$-(b^2a + 0.50a^2b)$	0	-0.1440	0	-0.133	0	0.0192
	23	0.3	0.7	$-(b^2a + 0.50a^2b)$	0	-0.1785	0	-0.133	0	0.0237
	24	0.4	0.6	$-(b^2a + 0.50a^2b)$	0	-0.1920	0	-0.133	0	0.0255
	25	0.5	0.5	$-(b^2a + 0.50a^2b)$	0	-0.1875	0	-0.133	0	0.0249
	26	0.6	0.4	$-(b^2a + 0.50a^2b)$	0	-0.1680	0	-0.133	0	0.0223
	27	0.7	0.3	$-(b^2a + 0.50a^2b)$	0	-0.1365	0	-0.133	0	0.0182
	28	0.8	0.2	$-(b^2a + 0.50a^2b)$	0	-0.0960	0	-0.133	0	0.0128
	29	0.9	0.1	$-(b^2a + 0.50a^2b)$	0	-0.0495	0	-0.133	0	0.0066
	D	0.0	1.0	0	0	0	0	0	0	0

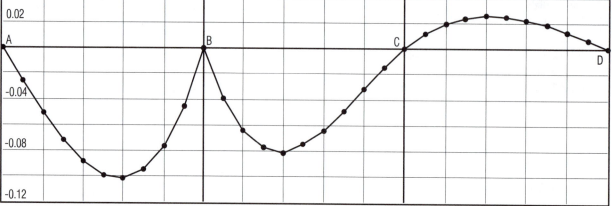

Table 3.18 & Figure 3.46 Spreadsheet format and plot of influence ordinates at Support B for Design Example 3.4.

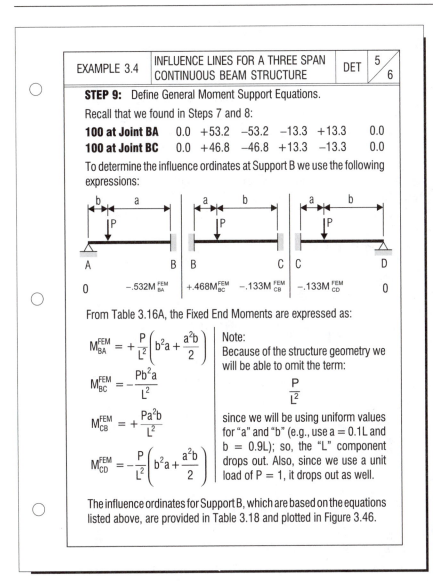

| EXAMPLE 3.4 | INFLUENCE LINES FOR A THREE SPAN CONTINUOUS BEAM STRUCTURE | DET | 5 / 6 |

STEP 9: Define General Moment Support Equations.

Recall that we found in Steps 7 and 8:

100 at Joint BA 0.0 +53.2 −53.2 −13.3 +13.3 0.0

100 at Joint BC 0.0 +46.8 −46.8 +13.3 −13.3 0.0

To determine the influence ordinates at Support B we use the following expressions:

0   −.532M$_{BA}^{FEM}$ +.468M$_{BC}^{FEM}$ −.133M$_{CB}^{FEM}$ −.133M$_{CD}^{FEM}$ 0

From Table 3.16A, the Fixed End Moments are expressed as:

$$M_{BA}^{FEM} = +\frac{P}{L^2}\left(b^2a + \frac{a^2b}{2}\right)$$

$$M_{BC}^{FEM} = -\frac{Pb^2a}{L^2}$$

$$M_{CB}^{FEM} = +\frac{Pa^2b}{L^2}$$

$$M_{CD}^{FEM} = -\frac{P}{L^2}\left(b^2a + \frac{a^2b}{2}\right)$$

Note:
Because of the structure geometry we will be able to omit the term:

$$\frac{P}{L^2}$$

since we will be using uniform values for "a" and "b" (e.g., use a = 0.1L and b = 0.9L); so, the "L" component drops out. Also, since we use a unit load of P = 1, it drops out as well.

The influence ordinates for Support B, which are based on the equations listed above, are provided in Table 3.18 and plotted in Figure 3.46.

To develop the general moment support equations, we utilize the resulting moments from the moment distribution conducted using a unit moment of 100. In the support equations, these values are factored back down by 100 (i.e., yielding a unit moment of 1). The value of 100 is used for convenience in dealing with significant figures. If so desired, a unit moment of 1 could have been applied at the onset. The resulting values are depicted in Table 3.18 and plotted in Figure 3.46. The table is built by moving a concentrated unit load of P = 1 across the entire structure at uniform intervals. The resulting moments are determined by computing the fixed end moments as depicted at left. These moments are then multiplied by the appropriate coefficients determined by placing the unit moment on either side of joint B. Note that when the load is on the middle span, the total moment is the sum of both fixed end moments multiplied by their respective coefficients. Because of symmetry, the values at joint C will be the mirror image (from top to bottom) of those at B. See also Tables 3.17A and 3.17B.

Just like any other software solution, however, spreadsheet utilities should have an independent check to ensure their accuracy.

3.12.5 Alternate Method for Analysis of Continuous Beams

We have already discussed how continuous beams can be analyzed using moment distribution and influence lines to determine the shear and moments which result from various loading conditions. In addition to performing this hand calculation, computer solutions which implement the influence line method, matrix displacement, or some form of finite element analysis may also be employed to provide similar results for continuous beam type bridges.

Another approach for analyzing continuous beams has been presented by Zuraski [Ref. 3.50]. The Zuraski methodology provides for the calculation of end moments for interior spans of a continuous beam structure through general

Just like any other software solution, however, spreadsheet utilities should have an independent check to ensure their accuracy.

The Zuraski methodology provides for the calculation of end moments in spans of a continuous beam structure through general, closed-form expressions.

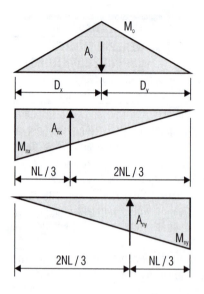

closed-form expressions. This general purpose approach allows for the calculation of the end moments on either side of any interior joint, provided the following criteria are met:

❑   The beams must be of constant flexural stiffness (*EI*)
❑   The exterior spans must be of equal length
❑   All interior spans must be of equal length

The concise and well defined nature of the Zuraski approach lends itself well toward incorporation into computer solutions. The reader is referred to Ref. 3.50 for a detailed discussion of the derivation of the following expressions.

The general expression for the moment on the left side of an interior support can be defined as:

$$M_x = \frac{6kM_oF_x}{\left(q_x c_{nx} + c_{nx-1}\right) + c_{ny}\left(\dfrac{c_x^*}{c_y^*}\right)} \qquad \text{(Eq. 3.131)}$$

and on the right side as:

$$M_y = \frac{6kM_oF_y}{\left(q_y c_{ny} + c_{ny-1}\right) + c_{nx}\left(\dfrac{c_y^*}{c_x^*}\right)} \qquad \text{(Eq. 3.132)}$$

The variables which comprise Equations 3.131 and 3.132 are either geometry dependent or a function of the conjugate beam moments of the loaded and adjacent spans. The sidebar figure illustrates conjugate beam loads

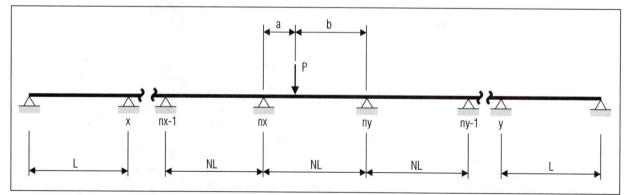

Figure 3.47 Notation for a typical continuous beam bridge with an interior span loaded.

EXAMPLE 3.4	INFLUENCE LINES FOR A THREE SPAN CONTINUOUS BEAM STRUCTURE	DET	6 / 6

STEP 10: Calculate the Intermediate Influence Ordinates at 0.1L

At load at 0.1L compute the moment for the span as a simple beam:

$M_{x=0} = 0$

$M_{MAX} = \dfrac{Pab}{L} = \dfrac{(1)(0.1L)(0.9L)}{L} = 0.09L$

$M_{x=L} = 0$

$M_{MAX} = 0.09L$, $P = 1$, $x = 0.1L$, A, B

x	0.0	0.1	0.2	0.3	0.4	0.5	0.6	0.7	0.8	0.9	1.0	x
M_x	0.0	0.09	0.08	0.07	0.06	0.05	0.04	0.03	0.02	0.01	0.0	M_x

From Step 9 and Table 3.18, at a = 0.1L of the continuous beam, the influence ordinate for the moment at the support B is –0.0263. This is proportioned across the entire span as follows:

$$p = \dfrac{-0.0263}{10 \text{ points}} = -0.00263$$

$M_x = M_{simple} + np$ where: n = Point in span for n = 1 to 9

$M_{x=0.0} = 0.00 + (0)(-0.00263) = 0.0000$
$M_{x=0.1} = 0.09 + (1)(-0.00263) = 0.0874$
$M_{x=0.2} = 0.08 + (2)(-0.00263) = 0.0747$
$M_{x=0.3} = 0.07 + (3)(-0.00263) = 0.0621$
$M_{x=0.4} = 0.06 + (4)(-0.00263) = 0.0494$
$M_{x=0.5} = 0.05 + (5)(-0.00263) = 0.0368$
$M_{x=0.6} = 0.04 + (6)(-0.00263) = 0.0242$
$M_{x=0.7} = 0.03 + (7)(-0.00263) = 0.0116$
$M_{x=0.8} = 0.02 + (8)(-0.00263) = -0.0010$
$M_{x=0.9} = 0.01 + (9)(-0.00263) = -0.0137$
$M_{x=1.0} = 0.09 + (10)(-0.00263) = -0.0263$

DESIGN EXAMPLE 3.4
STEP 10: INTERMEDIATE INFLUENCE ORDINATES

For the sake of brevity, we will only show the calculation for intermediate points at one location. We will take the case where a unit load is placed one tenth the length of the first span in from the first support.

The first step is to take the span to act as a simple beam and compute the bending moment at tenth points along the span. From Step 9 and Table 3.18, we see that, under this loading condition, the influence ordinate at Support B is –0.0263. This amount is proportioned along the length of the first span and combined with the simple beam moment to yield the intermediate influence ordinates.

The proportioning takes one tenth of the negative moment at support B and distributes it amongst each panel point, with the full amount being proportioned at support B and none at support A. These resulting values can be seen in the first row of Table 3.17B.

A similar approach is taken for the remaining spans and loading conditions present.

for the loaded span depicted in Figure 3.47. With regard to these figures, we take the variable *k* to be the following:

$$k = \dfrac{\text{Area of Moment Diagram}}{(\text{Span Length})(M_o)} \qquad \text{(Eq. 3.133)}$$

where M_o = maximum ordinate to simple beam moment diagram

Typical values for *k* would be $\frac{1}{2}$ for a triangular simple beam moment diagram and $\frac{2}{3}$ for a uniform load parabola. In essence, the *k* value accounts for the shape of the simple beam moment diagram.

DID YOU KNOW

THAT one of the main advantages of the conjugate beam method is its ability to handle beams of varying cross section and material? A drawback, however, is its difficulty in dealing with beams in which both ends are built-in [Ref. 3.48]. Although the methodology described in Section 3.12.5 utilizes conjugate beam relationships, it is applicable only for beams which have a constant flexural stiffness.

Unit Load at		REACTIONS				SHEARS					
		R_A	R_B	R_C	R_D	V_{AB}	V_{BA}	V_{BC}	V_{CB}	V_{CD}	V_{DC}
SPAN 1	A	1.0	0	0	0	1.0	0	0	0	0	0
	.1	.8736	.1594	-.0396	.0066	.8736	-.1264	.0330	.0330	-.0066	-.0066
	.2	.7488	.3152	-.0768	.0128	.7488	-.2512	.0640	.0640	-.0128	-.0128
	.3	.6272	.4638	-.1092	.0182	.6272	-.3728	.0910	.0910	-.0182	-.0182
	.4	.5104	.6016	-.1344	.0224	.5104	-.4896	.1120	.1120	-.0224	-.0224
	.5	.4000	.7250	-.1500	.0250	.4000	-.6000	.1250	.1250	-.0250	-.0250
	.6	.2976	.8304	-.1536	.0256	.2976	-.7024	.1280	.1280	-.0256	-.0256
	.7	.2048	.9142	-.1428	.0238	.2048	-.7952	.1190	.1190	-.0238	-.0238
	.8	.1232	.9728	-.1152	.0192	.1232	-.8768	.0960	.0960	-.0192	-.0192
	.9	.0544	1.0026	-.0684	.0114	.0544	-.9456	.0570	.0570	-.0114	-.0114
	B	0	1.0	0	0	0	-1.0/0	0/1.0	0	0	0
SPAN 2	.1	-.0390	.9630	.0910	-.0150	-.0390	-.0390	.9240	-.0760	.0150	.0150
	.2	-.0640	.8960	.2000	-.0320	-.0640	-.0640	.8320	-.1680	.0320	.0320
	.3	-.0770	.8050	.3210	-.0490	-.0770	-.0770	.7280	-.2720	.0490	.0490
	.4	-.0800	.6960	.4480	-.0640	-.0800	-.0800	.6160	-.3840	.0640	.0640
	.5	-.0750	.5750	.5750	-.0750	-.0750	-.0750	.5000	-.5000	.0750	.0750
	.6	-.0640	.4480	.6960	-.0800	-.0640	-.0640	.3840	-.6160	.0800	.0800
	.7	-.0490	.3210	.8050	-.0770	-.0490	-.0490	.2720	-.7280	.0770	.0770
	.8	-.0320	.2000	.8960	-.0640	-.0320	-.0320	.1680	-.8320	.0640	.0640
	.9	-.0150	.0910	.9630	-.0390	-.0150	-.0150	.0760	-.9240	.0390	.0390
	C	0	0	1.0	0	0	0	0	-1.0/0	0/1.0	0
SPAN 3	.1	.0114	-.0684	1.0026	.0544	.0114	.0114	-.0570	-.0570	.9456	-.0544
	.2	.0192	-.1152	.9728	.1232	.0192	.0192	-.0960	-.0960	.8763	-.1232
	.3	.0238	-.1428	.9142	.2048	.0238	.0238	-.1190	-.1190	.7952	-.2048
	.4	.0256	-.1536	.8304	.2976	.0256	.0256	-.1280	-.1280	.7024	-.2976
	.5	.0250	-.1500	.7250	.4000	.0250	.0250	-.1250	-.1250	.6000	-.4000
	.6	.0224	-.1344	.6016	.5104	.0224	.0224	-.1120	-.1120	.4896	-.5104
	.7	.0182	-.1092	.4638	.6272	.0182	.0182	-.0910	-.0910	.3728	-.6272
	.8	.0128	-.0768	.3152	.7488	.0126	.0128	-.0640	-.0640	.2512	-.7488
	.9	.0066	-.0396	.1594	.8736	.0066	.0066	-.0330	-.0330	.1264	-.8736
	D	0	0	0	1.0	0	0	0	0	0	-1.0

Table 3.19A Reaction and Shear Influence Ordinates for Three Equal Spans

For a span subjected to a concentrated load, the maximum ordinate referenced in Equation 3.133 is defined as:

$$M_o = \frac{Pab}{NL}$$

(Eq. 3.134)

where P = concentrated load

a = distance from left support to concentrated load

b = distance from right support to concentrated load

NL = interior span length

In the term NL the variable N is used to define the ratio of the interior span length to the exterior span length (e.g., if the interior span were 100 ft long and the exterior span 80 ft, the ratio N would be 1.25).

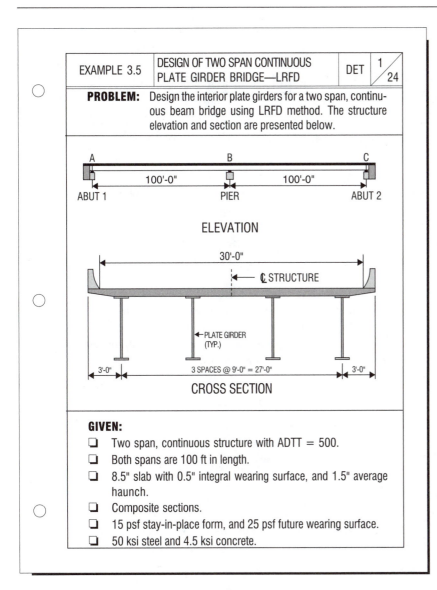

| EXAMPLE 3.5 | DESIGN OF TWO SPAN CONTINUOUS PLATE GIRDER BRIDGE—LRFD | DET | 1/24 |

PROBLEM: Design the interior plate girders for a two span, continuous beam bridge using LRFD method. The structure elevation and section are presented below.

ELEVATION

CROSS SECTION

GIVEN:
- ❏ Two span, continuous structure with ADTT = 500.
- ❏ Both spans are 100 ft in length.
- ❏ 8.5" slab with 0.5" integral wearing surface, and 1.5" average haunch.
- ❏ Composite sections.
- ❏ 15 psf stay-in-place form, and 25 psf future wearing surface.
- ❏ 50 ksi steel and 4.5 ksi concrete.

DESIGN EXAMPLE 3.5
GIVEN PARAMETERS

In this example, we will combine the principles outlined in Section 3.11 and 3.12 to provide for the design of a continuous plate girder bridge. The design will be facilitated by the AISC's table of moments, shears, and reactions. (Ref. 3.49).

The bridge will be designed using AASHTO LRFD specifications. Only an interior girder will be designed. The design of an exterior girder is similar, but the dead load and live load distribution factors are different.

To simplify the calculations, all live load and dead load moments, shears and reactions are given for this example to save paper space. In read design, these forces are obtained by using structural analysis software, or by using reference book such as the tables in Reference 3.49. If the designer has no access to computer software or reference tables, he or she can develop influence lines (similar to Design Example 3.4), and obtain the member forces and reactions by hand calculations.

> ❝ Figuring moment distributions of bridge loads at supports for continuous spans was extremely laborious ... until the last 30 years or so, most designers chose to take the path of least resistance—several simple spans. ❞
>
> EDWARD WASSERMAN
> [Ref. 3.51]

In the first moment diagram, shown in the previous sidebar, the distances from the left and right supports to the centroid of the moment diagram are defined as:

$$D_x = \frac{NL + a}{3} \quad \text{and} \quad D_y = \frac{NL + b}{3} \qquad \text{(Eqs. 3.135 and 3.136)}$$

where NL = interior span length

These distances are used to compute the amount of moment diagram area which is transmitted to each support:

$$F_x = \frac{D_y}{NL} \quad \text{and} \quad F_y = \frac{D_x}{NL} \qquad \text{(Eqs. 3.137 and 3.138)}$$

In Equations 3.131 and 3.132, a coefficient q is used in the denominator of each expression. This variable is a function of the ratio of the adjacent

Area		SPAN 1										SPAN 2									
	A	.1	.2	.3	.4	.5	.6	.7	.8	.9	B	.1	.2	.3	.4	.5	.6	.7	.8	.9	C
+ Area	0	.040	.070	.090	.100	.100	.090	.070	.040	.020	.017	.015	.030	.055	.070	.075	.070	.055	.030	.015	.017
- Area	0	-.005	-.010	-.015	-.020	-.025	-.030	-.035	-.040	-.065	-.117	-.070	-.050	-.050	-.050	-.050	-.050	-.050	-.050	-.070	-.117
Total	0	.035	.060	.075	.080	.075	.060	.035	.000	-.045	-.100	-.055	-.020	.005	.020	.025	.020	.005	-.020	-.055	-.100

Table 3.19B Moment Influence Areas for Three Equal Spans (see also Table 3.17B)

span length to the loaded span length on either side and is defined by the equation:

$$q = 2 \cdot \left(\frac{\text{Adjacent Span Length}}{\text{Loaded Span Length}} + 1 \right) \quad \text{(Eq. 3.139)}$$

> To complete the calculation of the end moments, we need to determine the ratios of interior joint moments near the loaded span to that at the first interior support ...

To complete the calculation of the end moments, we need to determine the ratios of interior joint moments near the loaded span to that at the first interior support, c_i. Values for these ratios are presented in Table 3.20. Similar coefficients which define a cross-span compatibility, and are used in Equations 3.131 and 3.132 are given as:

$$c_x^* = \left(\frac{q_x c_{nx} + c_{nx-1}}{F_x} - \frac{c_{nx}}{F_y} \right) \quad \text{(Eq. 3.140)}$$

and

$$c_y^* = \left(\frac{q_y c_{ny} + c_{ny-1}}{F_y} - \frac{c_{ny}}{F_x} \right) \quad \text{(Eq. 3.141)}$$

The components of Equations 3.140 and 3.141 have been previously defined by Equations 3.133 through 3.139 and Table 3.20.

INTERIOR END MOMENT	Moment at Joint in Question / Moment at First Interior Joint
1st	1
2nd	$-\dfrac{2N+2}{N}$
3rd	$\dfrac{7N+8}{N}$
4th	$-\dfrac{26N+30}{N}$
5th	$\dfrac{97N+112}{N}$
6th	$-\dfrac{362N+418}{N}$

Table 3.20 Ratio of a Given Joint Moment to First Interior Moment

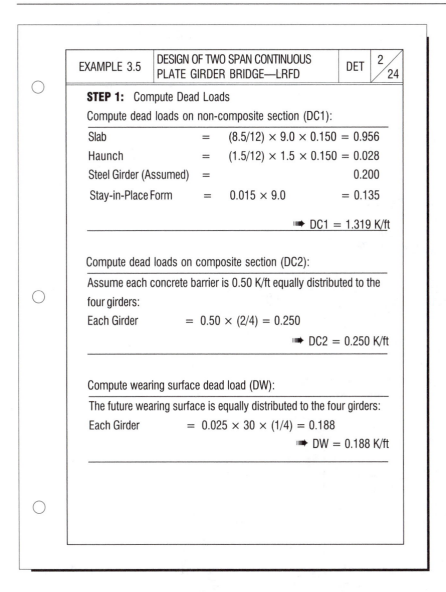

STEP 1: COMPUTE DEAD LOADS

As the design of any bridges, the first step is always to compute the dead loads.

In AASHTO LRFD specifications, dead loads are classified into three categories (based on if they act on composite section, and their load factors). They are:

DC1 - Dead loads act on noncomposite section. They include concrete slab and haunch weight, steel girder and miscellaneous steel members, and stay-in-place steel forms. Since we do not know the girder size yet, we make an initial guess of 200 lb/ft, including miscellaneous connection plates and diaphragms, etc.

DC2 - Dead loads act on composite section, excluding dead loads listed in DW below. They include concrete barriers and sidewalks (if any).

DW - Wearing surface and utilities (if any). They also act on composite section, but have higher load factors than these in DC2 due to greater uncertainty of the magnitude of these loads.

The value of N used in Table 3.20 to define the various c ratios is given by the following expression:

$$N = \frac{\text{Interior Span Length}}{\text{Exterior Span Length}} \qquad \text{(Eq. 3.142)}$$

In the equations defined above, the subscript notation of x is used to denote the first interior joint to the left of the joint in question. Conversely, the

Area	REACTIONS				SHEARS					
	R_A	R_B	R_C	R_D	V_{AB}	V_{BA}	V_{BC}	V_{CB}	V_{CD}	V_{DC}
+ Area	.4500	1.2000	1.2000	.4500	.4500	.0167	.5833	.0833	.6167	.0500
- Area	-.0500	-.1000	-.1000	-.0500	-.0500	-.6167	-.0833	-.5833	-.0167	-.4500
Total	.4000	1.1000	1.1000	.4000	.4000	-.6000	.5000	-.5000	.6000	-.4000

Table 3.21 Reaction and Shear Areas for Three Equal Spans (see also Table 3.19A)

STEP	DESCRIPTION	WORKED EXAMPLE
0	Given the beam shown at right, determine the resultant moments at supports B and C when the center span is subjected to an 18 k load 12 ft from support B. Assume that the beam from point A to D is composed of the same material and has a constant moment of inertia.	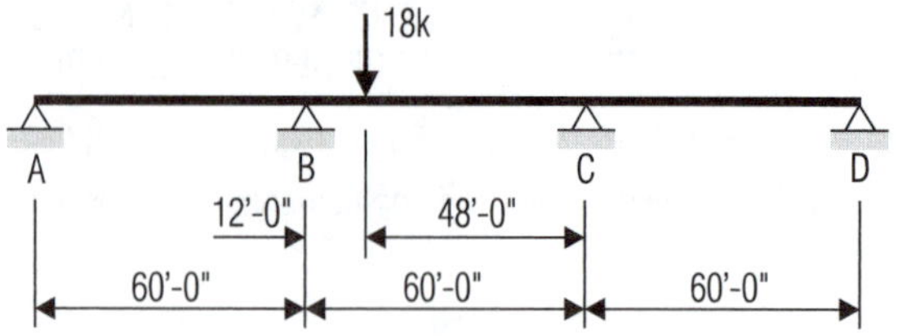
1	Determine the following geometric variables: a = Distance from load to left support b = Distance from load to right support nx = Number of interior joints to left side ny = Number of interior joints to right side NL = Interior Span Length $N = \dfrac{\text{Interior Span Length}}{\text{Exterior Span Length}}$	$a = 12\,\text{ft}$ $b = 48\,\text{ft}$ $nx = 1; \quad nx - 1 = 0$ $ny = 1; \quad ny - 1 = 0$ $NL = 60\,\text{ft}$ $N = \dfrac{60\,\text{ft}}{60\,\text{ft}} = 1$
2	Determine the ratios of given joint moment to first interior moment. Enter Table 3.20 with the interior end moment desired (either nx, ny, nx–1, or ny–1) and the value of N computed in Step 1. If the example had five spans and the load was in the second span, then we would have nx = 1 (use the row labeled 1st), and so on.	$c_{nx} = c_1 = 1$ $c_{nx-1} = c_0 = 0$ $c_{ny} = c_1 = 1$ $c_{ny-1} = c_0 = 0$
3	Compute the amount of the moment diagram area which is transmitted to each support. Equations 3.135 through 3.138 can be combined as shown at right.	$F_x = \dfrac{D_y}{NL} = \dfrac{NL+b}{3NL} = \dfrac{60\,\text{ft} + 48\,\text{ft}}{(3)(60\,\text{ft})} = 0.60$ $F_y = \dfrac{D_x}{NL} = \dfrac{NL+a}{3NL} = \dfrac{60\,\text{ft} + 12\,\text{ft}}{(3)(60\,\text{ft})} = 0.40$
4	Compute the ratio of the adjacent span length to the load span length variable as defined by Equation 3.139. Since this example has equal spans, the value for both the left side (x) and the right side (y) are equal to 4.	$q_x = 2 \cdot \left(\dfrac{\text{Adjacent Span Length}}{\text{Loaded Span Length}} + 1 \right) = 2 \cdot \left(\dfrac{60\,\text{ft}}{60\,\text{ft}} + 1 \right) = 4$ $q_y = 2 \cdot \left(\dfrac{\text{Adjacent Span Length}}{\text{Loaded Span Length}} + 1 \right) = 2 \cdot \left(\dfrac{60\,\text{ft}}{60\,\text{ft}} + 1 \right) = 4$
5	Calculate the maximum ordinate of the moment diagram based on the magnitude of the concentrated load and its position (Equation 3.134).	$M_o = \dfrac{P_{ab}}{NL}$ $M_o = \dfrac{(18\,\text{k})(12\,\text{ft})(48\,\text{ft})}{60\,\text{ft}} = 172.8\,\text{ft}\cdot\text{k}$

Table 3.22A Synopsis and Example of Zuraski Method for Calculating Support Moments in Continuous Beams

STEP	DESCRIPTION	WORKED EXAMPLE
6	Calculate the coefficients which define the cross-span compatibility relationship for the left side of the first interior support as given in Equation 3.140.	$$c_x^* = \left(\frac{q_x c_{nx} + c_{nx-1}}{F_x} - \frac{c_{nx}}{F_y} \right)$$ $$c_x^* = \left(\frac{(4)(1)+0}{0.6} - \frac{1}{0.4} \right) = 4.167$$
7	Calculate the coefficients which define the cross-span compatibility relationship for the right side of the first interior support as given in Equation 3.141.	$$c_y^* = \left(\frac{q_y c_{ny} + c_{ny-1}}{F_y} - \frac{c_{ny}}{F_x} \right)$$ $$c_y^* = \left(\frac{(4)(1)+0}{0.4} - \frac{1}{0.6} \right) = 8.333$$
8	Define the ratio of the area of the moment diagram to the product of the span length and the maximum simple beam moment ordinate (Equation 3.133). This value is taken as 1/2 for a triangular-shaped simple beam moment diagram.	$k = 1/2$
9	Calculate the resulting moment for the continuous beam at Support B using Equation 3.131.	$$M_B = M_x = \frac{6kM_oF_x}{(q_x c_{nx} + c_{nx-1}) + c_{ny}\left(\dfrac{c_x^*}{c_y^*}\right)}$$ $$M_B = M_x = \frac{(6)(1/2)(172.8)(0.6)}{(4)(1)+(1)\left(\dfrac{4.167}{8.333}\right)} \quad \Rrightarrow M_B = 69.12 \text{ ft-k}$$
10	Calculate the resulting moment for the continuous beam at Support C using Equation 3.132.	$$M_C = M_y = \frac{6kM_oF_y}{(q_y c_{ny} + c_{ny-1}) + c_{nx}\left(\dfrac{c_y^*}{c_x^*}\right)}$$ $$M_C = M_y = \frac{(6)(1/2)(172.8)(0.4)}{(4)(1)+(1)\left(\dfrac{8.333}{4.167}\right)} \quad \Rrightarrow M_C = 34.56 \text{ ft-k}$$
NOTES	Using this method the following sign convention applies: ❑ A positive moment indicates a moment whose curvature is concave down. ❑ A negative moment indicates a moment whose curvature is concave up. This method requires both exterior spans to be of equal length and all interior spans to be of equal length. This method requires beams to have a constant flexural stiffness (EI). For this example, using influence lines for a three span continuous beam yields identical results (see text).	

Table 3.22B Synopsis and Example of Zuraski Method for Calculating Support Moments in Continuous Beams (Continued)

When using the Zuraski method in solving for support moments ... the sign convention used is opposite from that which we have established previously.

subscript notation *y* is used to describe the first interior joint to the right of the joint in question. The subscript *nx* refers to the number of *interior* joints to the left of the loaded span and *ny* refers to the number of *interior* joints to the right of the loaded span.

When using the Zuraski method in solving for support moments, it is important for the designer to note that the sign convention used is opposite from that which we have established previously. In using this approach a positive moment indicates a moment whose curvature is concave down and a negative moment, one which is concave up.

Table 3.22 shows a worked example using the Zuraski method. For the sake of comparison to the influence line approach, a structure with three equal spans of 60 ft is chosen. The interior span is loaded with a single concentrated 18k load placed a distance of 12 ft from support B (i.e., at panel point 0.2L).

Using the influence data developed earlier and detailed in Table 3.17B, one would reference the row of data for a unit load in Span 2 at 0.2L (i.e., the 13th row of influence data). The moment at support B would be computed as follows:

$$M_B = (18 \text{ k})(60 \text{ ft})(-0.064) = -69.12 \text{ k}$$

and the moment at Support C would be calculated by:

$$M_C = (18 \text{ k})(60 \text{ ft})(-0.032) = -34.56 \text{ k}$$

Comparing the results above to the values determined in the worked example of Tables 3.22A and 3.22B, we see there is an exact match. The reader should keep in mind the difference in the sign convention noted above. For beams with a constant flexural stiffness, the Zuraski methodology offers a straightforward and well-defined approach for calculating support moments. Indeed, the flexible nature of the equations used (with regard to being able to handle various numbers of spans) make it ideal for implementation in computer analysis packages.

3.12.6 Live Load on Continuous Beam Structures

In AASHTO Standard Specifications, a bridge should be designed with either truck loading or lane loading, whichever produce the larger forces. It has been previously mentioned that, for longer spans, lane loading is more likely to govern than truck loading. Since continuous beam bridges allow for the creation of long span lengths, the issue of lane loading becomes more important. The point where truck loading or lane loading governs is a function of the geometry of the structure and can either be determined by trial and error or through general rules of thumb. In general, for spans of equal length, greater than 41 ft (12.5 m) in length, lane loading governs for maximum negative moment at an interior support [Ref. 3.12].

When using lane loading, the designer must take care to adhere to the specifications as defined in AASHTO Standard Specifications 3.11.3. In Section 3.5.3, Part 1, we touched on this code requirement which calls for an additional 18 k load to be placed in an adjacent span in order to induce maximum negative moment. Both of these loads are used in conjunction with a uniform distributed load of 0.640 k/ft. As with the concentrated load, the

EXAMPLE 3.5	DESIGN OF TWO SPAN CONTINUOUS PLATE GIRDER BRIDGE—LRFD	DET	$\frac{3}{24}$

STEP 2: Live Load Distribution Factor

Only interior girders are designed in this example. (Exterior girders have different live load distribution factors, but the design procedure is the same). To obtain the load distribution factor, the following section is assumed.

Section 1: Maximum Moment (Positive Flexure) @ 0.4L

Assume top flange 1"×12", web 1/2"×40", and bottom flange 1"×16". Steel net section is used to compute moment of inertia:

ELEMENT	A (in²)	Y (in)	AY (in³)	AY² (in⁴)	I_o (in⁴)
Top Flange	12.00	41.5	498.0	20667	1
Web	20.00	21.0	420.0	8820	2667
Bottom Flange	16.00	0.5	8.0	4	1
TOTALS	48.00		926.0	29491	2669

$$I_z = \sum I_o + \sum AY^2 = 2669\,in^4 + 29491\,in^4 = 32160\,in^4$$

$$Y' = \frac{\sum AY}{\sum A} = \frac{926.0\,in^3}{48.00\,in^2} = 19.29\,in$$

$$I = I_z - (\sum A)(Y')^2 = 32160\,in^4 - (48.00\,in^2)(19.29\,in)^2$$

$$I = 14,299\,in^4$$

$$e_g = \frac{8.0}{2} + 1.5 + (42 - 19.29) = 28.21\,in$$

$$n = 8 \text{ (for 4.5 ksi concrete)}$$

$$k_g = n(I + Ae_g^2) = 8[14299 + 48.00(28.21)^2]$$

$$= 419,981\,in^4$$

(Step 2: Continued on Next Sheet)

DESIGN EXAMPLE 3.5
STEP 2: LIVE LOAD DISTRIBUTION FACTOR

Recall that in Section 3.8.1, we discussed how live loads are distributed among girders. In AASHTO LRFD specifications, live load distribution is a function of girder spacing, bridge span length, the deck slab thickness, and the steel girder section properties.

In order to calculate live load distribution factors, the designer will have to first guess a girder section. These requires extensive knowledge and experience, but for a starter, one can use 1/30 to 1/25 of span length (for continuous spans) as the girder depth. In this example, we assume 1"×12" as top flange, 1/2"×40" as web, and 1"×16" as bottom flange at positive bending region.

Steel net section properties are calculated for determining the live load distribution factors.

As having been mentioned many times, the bridge design is a trial and error process. It may involve several cycles before member sizes are refined, and a final design computation is produced.

uniform load is placed in certain spans so as to create maximum moment. When computing positive moment, only one concentrated load is used.

Note that it is possible that truck loading controls some part of the design, while lane loading controls other parts for the same bridge.

In AASHTO LRFD, designers do not have to determine whether lane loading or truck loading should be used, because both load effects must be combined for the design. However, designers still need to separate the forces caused from the design truck and lane load because the dynamic load allowance (impact) only applies to the truck loading, not the lane load portion of the live load.

The following discussion pertains to some of the key issues and techniques involved in the application of live loads on continuous beam bridge structures.

1. Negative Moment Using Influence Lines.

There is probably no other phrase which is more aggravating to both the novice and

There is probably no other phrase which is more aggravating to both the novice and experienced bridge designer than "place loads to create maximum moment."

experienced bridge designer than "place loads to create maximum moment." A great deal of this frustration comes from this one little phrase causing so much work on the part of the designer. Fortunately, the techniques we have learned thus far, such as the creation and use of influence lines, greatly simplify the task of identifying the points of maximum moment.

For example, if we want to determine the maximum negative moment at a support for the lane load (AASHTO Standard Specifications) using influence lines in Table 3.17B, we can reference the influence data and proceed down the Support B column of the table. The maximum negative influence ordinates are found to be located at 0.6L of Span 1 and 0.4L of Span 2. An 18k load is placed at each of these panel points. Figure 3.46, which shows a plot of this influence data, also shows that the curve is completely in the negative region for the first two spans and positive for the third. Therefore, the uniform distributed load of 0.640 k-ft is applied *only in these two spans.*

We saw earlier that the moment due to a distributed load is computed by determining the area under the influence line and multiplying it by the distributed load and the square of the shorter span. If we were to load all three spans, the resulting negative moment would be less than if only the first two are loaded. To arrive at the maximum moment, we take the area under the curve as it proceeds from Support A to Support C. This value is given in Table 3.19B. The final, maximum negative moment at Support B is calculated by summing the three constituent moments.

As we have seen before, however, the designer needs to take care when applying live load distribution factors to the resulting moments. In AASHTO Standard Specifications, the distribution factors apply to *wheel loads* rather than axle loads. When the 18 k concentrated load and 0.640 k/ft uniform distributed load are applied to the structure, they simulate the presence of the design vehicle axle. Therefore, prior to applying the wheel distribution and impact factors, the resulting moment should be halved. But in AASHTO LRFD Specifications, axle loads and lane load are used, so no modification is necessary.

This should serve as notice to the designer that when dealing with design loads, the engineer must be consistently aware of exactly what the load is intended to represent. The lane load should be thought of as the train of vehicle it is intended to represent; not just an abstract distributed load. Such an approach helps ensure a more accurate analysis and design of the structure.

2. **Special Load Points.** The reader, at this point, may be thinking, "boy, it sure is convenient that the maximum influence ordinates fall at tenth points along each span." In truth, the actual maximum ordinates often fall at points in between the tenth point intervals established for calculating the influence ordinates. These points can be identified based on the type of lane loading being applied and the geometry of the structure (i.e., for maximum positive or negative moment, for short spans or long spans, etc.).

AISC presents some of these special load points in their collection of predefined tables [Ref. 3.49]. Tables are also provided which identify not only the location of the maximum ordinates but their value as well. An

> T his should serve as notice to the designer that ... the engineer must be consistently aware of exactly what the load is intended to represent.

> T he reader, at this point, may be thinking, "boy, it sure is convenient that the maximum influence ordinates fall at tenth points along each span."

EXAMPLE 3.5	DESIGN OF TWO SPAN CONTINUOUS PLATE GIRDER BRIDGE—LRFD	DET	4 / 24

STEP 2: Live Load Distribution Factor (Continued)

Live Load Distribution Factor for Positive Bending
When two lanes loaded:

$$DF = 0.075 + \left(\frac{S}{9.5}\right)^{0.6}\left(\frac{S}{L}\right)^{0.2}\left(\frac{K_g}{12.0 \cdot t_s^3}\right)^{0.1}$$

$$DF = 0.075 + \left(\frac{9.0}{9.5}\right)^{0.6}\left(\frac{9.0}{100.0}\right)^{0.2}\left(\frac{419,981}{12.0 \times 100.0 \times 8.0^3}\right)^{0.1}$$

⇒ DF = 0.651

When one lane loaded:

$$DF = 0.06 + \left(\frac{S}{14}\right)^{0.4}\left(\frac{S}{L}\right)^{0.3}\left(\frac{K_g}{12.0 \cdot t_s^3}\right)^{0.1}$$

$$DF = 0.06 + \left(\frac{9.0}{14}\right)^{0.4}\left(\frac{9.0}{100.0}\right)^{0.3}\left(\frac{419,981}{12.0 \times 100.0 \times 8.0^3}\right)^{0.1}$$

⇒ DF = 0.452

Live Load Distribution Factor for Shear
When two lanes loaded:

$$DF = 0.2 + \frac{S}{12} - \left(\frac{S}{35}\right)^2 = 0.2 + \frac{9}{12} - \left(\frac{9}{35}\right)^2$$

⇒ DF = 0.884

(Step 2: Continued on Next Sheet)

DESIGN EXAMPLE 3.5
STEP 2: LIVE LOAD DISTRIBUTION FACTOR (CONTINUED)

Recall that, in Section 3.8.1, we discussed how to calculate live load distribution factors for moments and shears. In AASHTO LRFD, live load distribution factors for interior girders and exterior girders are different. Also, live loads distribution factors for one lane structures are different from these of multiple lane bridges.

Although this is a two-lane bridge, we need to calculate live load distribution factors for both two lane loaded and one lane loaded. For Strength Limit States and Service Limit States, the girder should be designed assuming both lanes are loaded. But for Fatigue Limit State, only one lane should be loaded.

Equation 3.20 and Equation 3.21 should be used to calculate live load distribution factors for bending in an interior girder. Equation 3.22 and Equation 3.23 should be used to calculate live load distribution factors for shear forces in an interior girder.

Note that the live load distribution factors at positive and negative bending regions are different because the girder section properties are different.

---

example of such a special load point is at 0.5774L from the exterior support of the shorter span. A load placed at this special load point creates the maximum negative moment at the first interior support due to the load placed in the shorter span [Ref. 3.49].

In this example, the maximum ordinate for the first span is not actually −0.102 but −0.1026 and the maximum value in the second span is not −0.080 but −0.0801. In this case, the resulting differential is negligible. Using the tenth point values we find a negative moment of −466.13 ft-k as opposed to a value of −466.2 ft-k.

Naturally, the use of computer-aided methods allows for precise analysis and pinpointing of key points along spans. Should such facilities not be available, however, tables such as those provided by AISC eliminate a great deal of the grunt work involved in computing maximum positive and negative moments due to live load.

3. Maximum Shear. In continuous beams, shear is computed along the spans using influence lines in a fashion similar to that discussed previously for moment. A difference, however, is that in AASHTO Standard specifications, truck loading generally governs for shear except for very long spans. That is, where lane loading may govern for moment, it is quite possible that truck loading governs for shear. Should lane loading govern, however, the designer should note that the concentrated load used is 26 k rather than the 18 k load used for moment (AASHTO 3.7.1.2).

There exist, approximate span length limits where truck loading will govern for shear. If a span length falls below the limit listed below, truck loading will generally govern [Ref. 3.12]. Larger values usually indicate a geometry where lane loading controls. These limits are defined as:

- ❏ Shear and Reaction at the End Support: Up To 140 ft
- ❏ Shear at Left of First Interior Support: Up To 110 ft
- ❏ Shear at Right of First Interior Support: Up To 110 ft
- ❏ Reaction at First Interior Point: Up To 58 ft

These numbers are just guidelines. Designers should calculate both lane loading and truck loading, and design each component based on the most critical loading. Of course, if AASHTO LRFD is used, we have to add lane loading to truck or tandem loading to get the design forces.

For exterior spans, it is usually sufficient to calculate shear at certain key points such as the end supports, the point 0.4L from the closest end support, and in the negative shear region just to the left of the first interior support. These points can then be connected by straight line segments to develop the final shear diagram.

4. Impact for Continuous Beams. In AASHTO Standard Specifications, Equation 3.15 in Section 3.5.3, Part 7, defined the application of live load impact. However, when computing the live load impact factor for a continuous beam the question arises as to what the value of L (the length of the loaded span) is for a continuous beam.

The value used for L will vary depending on whether the beam is being analyzed for positive or negative moment, as outlined below (AASHTO 3.8.2.2):

- ❏ Positive Moment: Length of Span in Question
- ❏ Negative Moment: Average of Two Adjacent Loaded Spans

When spans of varying length are used, the designer should take care to note the variable nature of the impact factor for continuous beams.

> When spans of varying length are used, the designer should take care to note the variable nature of the impact factor for continuous beams.

In AASHTO LRFD Specifications, live load impact is not affected by the configuration of the structure. The impact of 33% should be used except for fatigue, and for fracture limit states, 15% should be used. For deck joints, a 75% impact for all limit states must be used. Note that no impact should be applied to the lane loading in any case.

| EXAMPLE 3.5 | DESIGN OF TWO SPAN CONTINUOUS PLATE GIRDER BRIDGE—LRFD | DET | 5/24 |

STEP 2: Live Load Distribution Factor (Continued)

When one lane loaded:

$$DF = 0.36 + \frac{S}{25.0} = 0.36 + \frac{9}{25.0}$$

⟹ DF = 0.720

Section 2:   Maximum Negative Moment @ Pier

Assume top flange 1"×18", web 1/2"×40", and bottom flange 1.5"×18". Steel net section is used to compute moment of inertia:

ELEMENT	A (in^2)	Y (in)	AY (in^3)	AY^2 (in^4)	I$_0$ (in^4)
Top Flange	18.00	42.0	756.0	31752	2
Web	20.00	21.5	430.0	9245	2667
Bottom Flange	27.00	0.75	20.25	15	5
TOTALS	65.00		1206.25	41012	2674

$$I_z = \sum I_0 + \sum AY^2 = 2674 \text{ in}^4 + 41012 \text{ in}^4 = 43686 \text{ in}^4$$

$$Y' = \frac{\sum AY}{\sum A} = \frac{1206.25 \text{ in}^3}{65.00 \text{ in}^2} = 18.56 \text{ in}$$

$$I = I_z - (\sum A)(Y')^2 = 43686 \text{ in}^4 - (65.00 \text{ in}^2)(18.56 \text{ in})^2$$

$$I = 21,295 \text{ in}^4$$

$$e_g = \frac{8.0}{2} + 1.5 + (42.5 - 18.56) = 29.44 \text{ in}$$

n = 8 (for 4.5 ksi concrete)

(Step 2: Continued on Next Sheet)

(Step 2: Continued on Next Sheet)

DESIGN EXAMPLE 3.5
STEP 2: LIVE LOAD DISTRIBUTION FACTOR (CONTINUED)

With the live load distribution factors for positive bending region already computed, we now need to compute the live load distribution factors for negative bending region.

Similar to the way we calculated live load distribution factors for positive bending region, we first have to assume a steel girder section. Typically, the girder section over piers are larger than the sections at the positive mending region. Here we assume the top flange as 1"×18", the web as 1/2"×40", and the bottom flange as 1.5"×18". The net section properties are used in calculating live load distribution factors.

Note that if the assumed section needs to be changed either because it is too small or because it is too large, we will have to go back to recalculate live load distribution factors. For that reason, hand calculation such as this example is primarily used for design check. Most designs are now performed by computer software. But as a designer, it is absolutely essential that he or she be able to design or check a design by hand.

3.12.7 Composite Section in Negative Bending

For composite sections in negative bending region, the concrete deck is in tension, so concrete should be ignored in calculating the section modulus or flexural strength. Whether or not the longitudinal reinforcement in the deck is considered as part of the structural section depends on if the section is designed as a composite section by providing sufficient shear studs in the negative bending region. (Refer to Section 3.10.7, Part 4.)

The design of composite sections in negative bending is similar to the design of non-composite sections, except that the tension reinforcement in the deck is considered part of the composite section with the steel girder.

1. AASHTO Standard Specifications. In AASHTO Standard Specifications, if the steel girder is a compact section, then the strength can be calculated as the plastic moment:

$$M_n = F_y Z \qquad \text{(Eq. 3.143)}$$

> For composite sections in negative bending region, the concrete deck is in tension, so concrete should be ignored in calculating the section modulus or flexural strength.

Otherwise, the elastic strength should be used:

$$M_n = F_y S \qquad \text{(Eq. 3.144)}$$

Where F_y = yield stress of the steel
Z = plastic section modulus
S = elastic section modulus

To be designated as a compact section, the girder needs to meet several conditions to prevent buckling (Eqs. 3.95 and 3.100a). For new design, it is always a good idea to choose sections to meet these conditions so that plastic section modulus can be used to maximize the strength for the negative bending.

2. AASHTO LRFD Specifications. AASHTO LRFD takes a more conservative approach in designing composite sections in negative bending. It treats compression flanges as compression members under axial and bending forces, or under axial and torsional forces. So the scope of the design is to prevent the compression flange from buckling under various strength limit load combinations. To achieve that objective, it specifies the maximum flange design stress under the strength limit states. The maximum design stress is a function of the girder section properties, and the spacing of the lateral bracing for the compression flange.

> The maximum design stress is a function of the girder section properties, and the spacing of the lateral bracing for the compression flange.

For discretely braced compression flange, the maximum design stress under strength limit states should be taken as:

$$F_{nc} = R_b F_y \qquad \text{(Eq. 3.145)}$$

where F_y = yield stress of the flange steel
R_b = web load-shedding factor (AASHTO LRFD 6.10.1.10.2)

If longitudinal stiffeners are provided, and

$$\frac{D}{t_w} \le 0.95 \sqrt{\frac{Ek}{F_y}} \qquad \text{(Eq. 3.146a)}$$

or

$$\frac{2D_c}{t_w} \le \lambda_{rw} \qquad \text{(Eq. 3.146b)}$$

then $R_b = 1.0$. Otherwise,

$$R_b = 1 - \left(\frac{a_{wc}}{1200 + 300a_{wc}} \right) \left(\frac{2D_c}{t_w} - \lambda_{rw} \right) \le 1.0 \qquad \text{(Eq. 3.147)}$$

EXAMPLE 3.5	DESIGN OF TWO SPAN CONTINUOUS PLATE GIRDER BRIDGE—LRFD	DET	6/24

STEP 2: Live Load Distribution Factor (Continued)

$$k_g = n(I + Ae_g^2) = 8[21,295 + 65.0(29.44)^2]$$
$$= 621,051 \, in^4$$

Live Load Distribution Factor for Negative Bending
When two lanes loaded:

$$DF = 0.075 + \left(\frac{S}{9.5}\right)^{0.6}\left(\frac{S}{L}\right)^{0.2}\left(\frac{K_g}{12.0 \cdot t_s^3}\right)^{0.1}$$

$$DF = 0.075 + \left(\frac{9.0}{9.5}\right)^{0.6}\left(\frac{9.0}{100.0}\right)^{0.2}\left(\frac{621,051}{12.0 \times 100.0 \times 8.0^3}\right)^{0.1}$$

➠ DF = 0.674

When one lane loaded:

$$DF = 0.06 + \left(\frac{S}{14}\right)^{0.4}\left(\frac{S}{L}\right)^{0.3}\left(\frac{K_g}{12.0 \cdot t_s^3}\right)^{0.1}$$

$$DF = 0.06 + \left(\frac{9.0}{14}\right)^{0.4}\left(\frac{9.0}{100.0}\right)^{0.3}\left(\frac{621,051}{12.0 \times 100.0 \times 8.0^3}\right)^{0.1}$$

➠ DF = 0.467

Live load distribution factors for shear at both abutment and pier locations are the same.

(Step 2: Continued on Next Sheet)

DESIGN EXAMPLE 3.5
STEP 2: LIVE LOAD DISTRIBUTION FACTOR (CONTINUED)

In Section 3.8.1, we discussed how to calculate live load distribution factors for moments and shears. In AASHTO LRFD, live load distribution factors for interior girders and exterior girders are different. Also, live loads distribution factors for one lane structures are different from these of multiple lane bridges.

For Strength Limit States and Service Limit States, live load distribution factors should be calculated assuming both lanes are loaded. But for Fatigue Limit State, only one lane should be loaded when calculating live load distribution factors.

Equation 3.20 and Equation 3.21 should be used to calculate live load distribution factors for bending in an interior girder. Equation 3.22 and Equation 3.23 should be used to calculate live load distribution factors for shear forces in an interior girder.

Again we must remember that the live load distribution factors at positive and negative bending regions are different because the girder section properties are different.

In which
$$\lambda_{rw} = 5.7\sqrt{\frac{E}{F_y}} \qquad\qquad (Eq. 3.148)$$

$$a_{wc} = \frac{2D_c t_w}{b_{fc} t_{fc}} \qquad\qquad (Eq. 3.149)$$

where D_c = depth of the web in compression in the elastic range
t_w = web thickness
k = bend-buckling coefficient (See Eq. 3.69)
b_{fc} = compression flange width
t_{fc} = compression flange thickness

If the compression flange is noncompact, i.e.:

$$\frac{b_{fc}}{2t_{fc}} > 0.38\sqrt{\frac{E}{F_y}}$$

(Eq. 3.150)

then the compression flange is subjected to local buckling. A reduction factor should be calculated and applied to Equation 3.145 to obtain the maximum design stress in the compression flange to prevent compression flange from local buckling (AASHTO LRFD 6.10.8.2.2).

The compression flange should also be checked for lateral-torsional buckling. If the compression flange unbraced length:

$$L_b \leq L_p = 1.0 r_t \sqrt{\frac{E}{F_y}}$$

(Eq. 3.151)

In which:

$$r_t = \frac{b_{fc}}{\sqrt{12\left(1 + \frac{1}{3}\frac{D_c t_w}{b_{fc} t_{fc}}\right)}}$$

(Eq. 3.152)

Then the compression flange is not subjected to lateral torsional buckling, and Equation 3.145 need not be modified.

If

$$L_p < L_b \leq L_r$$

then

$$F_{nc} = C_b \left(1 - 0.3\frac{L_b - L_p}{L_r - L_p}\right) R_b F_y \leq R_b F_y$$

(Eq. 3.153)

If

$$L_b > L_r = \pi \cdot r_t \sqrt{\frac{E}{F_y}}$$

(Eq. 3.154)

then

$$F_{nc} = F_{cr} \leq R_b F_y$$

(Eq. 3.155)

Where C_b is the moment gradient modifier.

If $f_{mid} > f_2$, or $f_2 = 0$

$$C_b = 1.0$$

(Eq. 3.156a)

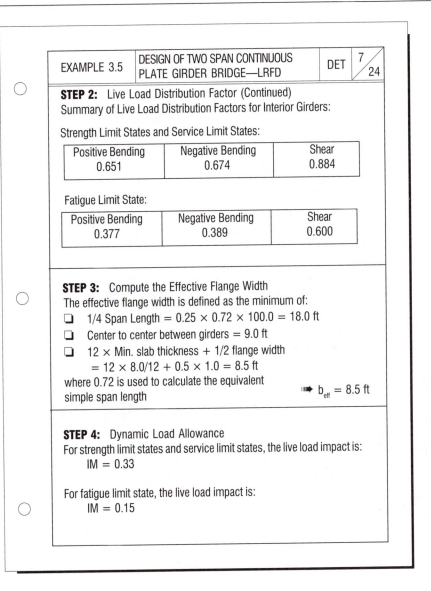

| EXAMPLE 3.5 | DESIGN OF TWO SPAN CONTINUOUS PLATE GIRDER BRIDGE—LRFD | DET | 7/24 |

STEP 2: Live Load Distribution Factor (Continued)
Summary of Live Load Distribution Factors for Interior Girders:

Strength Limit States and Service Limit States:

Positive Bending	Negative Bending	Shear
0.651	0.674	0.884

Fatigue Limit State:

Positive Bending	Negative Bending	Shear
0.377	0.389	0.600

STEP 3: Compute the Effective Flange Width
The effective flange width is defined as the minimum of:
- ❏ 1/4 Span Length = 0.25 × 0.72 × 100.0 = 18.0 ft
- ❏ Center to center between girders = 9.0 ft
- ❏ 12 × Min. slab thickness + 1/2 flange width
  = 12 × 8.0/12 + 0.5 × 1.0 = 8.5 ft
where 0.72 is used to calculate the equivalent
simple span length   ➠ b_{eff} = 8.5 ft

STEP 4: Dynamic Load Allowance
For strength limit states and service limit states, the live load impact is:
    IM = 0.33

For fatigue limit state, the live load impact is:
    IM = 0.15

DESIGN EXAMPLE 3.5
STEP 2: LIVE LOAD DISTRIBUTION FACTOR (CONTINUED)

Having calculated the live load distribution factors for both positive bending and negative bending regions, we can summerize these factors here.

For Fatigue Limit State the Multiple Presence Factor of 1.2 should be deducted from Eqs. 3.20 and 3.22 (AASHTO LRFD 3.6.1.1.2).

STEP 3: COMPUTE EFFECTIVE FLANGE WIDTH

The effective flange width of the composite section is calculated per Section 3.10.3. Note that 8" is used for deck thickness (the 1/2" on top is consider non-structural, but should be considered as part of the dead loads).

STEP 3: DYNAMIC LOAD ALLOWANCE

In AASHTO LRFD specifications, an impact factor of 0.33 is used for Strength Limit States and Service Limit States, while 0.15 is used for Fatigue Limit State. These factors should be *added* onto the truck live loads (i.e., a total factor of 1.33 or 1.15 should be used for truck live load). They should not be applied to lane load portion of the live load.

Otherwise: $C_b = 1.75 - 1.05\left(\dfrac{f_1}{f_2}\right) + 0.3\left(\dfrac{f_1}{f_2}\right)^2 \leq 2.3$ (Eq. 3.156b)

$$F_{cr} = \frac{C_b R_b \pi^2 E}{\left(\dfrac{L_b}{r_t}\right)^2}$$ (Eq. 3.157)

where f_{mid} = factored maximum stress at the middle of the unbraced
        compression flange (compression as positive)
    f_2 = factored maximum stress at either end of the unbraced
        compression flange (compression as positive). If it is in
        tension, $f_2 = 0$.

$f_0 =$ factored maximum stress at the brace point opposite to the one corresponding to f_2 (compression as positive)

$$f_1 = 2f_{mid} - f_2 \geq f_0 \qquad \text{(Eq. 3.158)}$$

Note that when calculating the stresses f_{mid}, f_2 and f_0, strength limit load combinations should be used. The stress from lateral bending, if any, should not be included (AASHTO LRFD 6.10.8.2.3).

The maximum design stress for tension flanges is the yield stress of the tension flange steel (AASHTO LRFD 6.10.8.3). The tension stress under the strength limit states can be calculated using elastic section modulus, ignoring concrete in the deck. Whether or not the reinforcing steel in the deck should be used depends on if the bridge is designed as a composite section in the negative flexural regions.

If there is an out-of-plane bending (in the weak axis of the girder), both compression and tension flanges should be designed for the combined stresses. In that case, Equation 3.66 should be used for the strength limit states.

> **F**or continuous span bridges, the negative bending regions can either be designed as a composite section by providing sufficient shear studs, or be designed as non-composite sections, ...

3. Conclusions. For continuous span bridges, the negative bending regions can either be designed as a composite section by providing sufficient shear studs, or be designed as non-composite sections, even though the bridges are designed as composite in the positive bending regions. When a continuous span bridge is designed using a composite section over piers, the designer should be aware that the yield stress of reinforcing steel is normally different from that of structural steel when calculating plastic section modulus and bending moment strength. If AASHTO LRFD is used, we only use elastic section modulus; in that case, we can use the same modulus of elasticity for both reinforcing steel and structural steel. See Example 3.5 for details.

No matter whether or not the negative flexural regions are designed as composite sections, we should always provide sufficient longitudinal reinforcement in these regions to control cracks where concrete deck is in tension.

3.12.8 Beam Splices

While splices can be utilized for any type of beam, they are most prevalent in continuous beam type structures. There are a variety of reasons why a beam splice may be required in a continuous beam bridge. Some of the major conditions which can lead to the incorporation of some type of beam splice are:

❑ The required length of beam is not available from the fabricator
❑ A splice is more economical than a single, large beam
❑ A splice aids in cambering of the beam
❑ A splice may be required to facilitate a change in section
❑ A splice is required for transportation or erection

The type of splice used will vary depending on whether the splice is to be installed in the shop or in the field [Ref. 3.43]. When a splice is installed in the

EXAMPLE 3.5	DESIGN OF TWO SPAN CONTINUOUS PLATE GIRDER BRIDGE—LRFD	DET	8/24

STEP 5: Unfactored Moments and Shears

For simplicity, only maximum positive and maximum negative bending moments are designed here. For shear forces, these at supports (abutment and pier) are calculated.

Since we have a symmetrical structure (both spans are of equal length), we only need to design one span.

The following forces are obtained from AISC's Manual (Ref. 3.49):

For DC1 = 1.319 K/ft

The Maximum Positive Moment = 927.3 k-ft
The Maximum Negative Moment = 1648.8 k-ft
The Maximum Shear at Abutment = 49.46 k
The Maximum Shear at Pier = 82.44 k
The Maximum Reaction at Abutment = 49.46 k
The Maximum Reaction at Pier = 164.88 k

For DC2 = 0.250 K/ft

The Maximum Positive Moment = 175.8 k-ft
The Maximum Negative Moment = 312.5 k-ft
The Maximum Shear at Abutment = 9.38 k
The Maximum Shear at Pier = 15.63 k
The Maximum Reaction at Abutment = 9.38 k
The Maximum Reaction at Pier = 31.25 k

(Step 5: Continued on Next Sheet)

DESIGN EXAMPLE 3.5

STEP 5: UNFACTORED MOMENTS AND SHEARS

As discussed earlier, most structure member design forces are obtained by using computer design software. For hand calculations, most engineers use AISC's "Moments, Shears and Reactions Tables for Continues Highway Bridges" (Ref. 3.49). Of course, should such design tools be unavailable, engineers cab always develop the influence lines for continuous spans (See Design Example 3.4).

The shortcoming of these design tables is that one can only obtain the maximum or minimum forces at certain locations (typically at supports, midspan and over piers). If the designer wishes to obtain the moment or shear diagram or envelope, he or she will have to reply on computer software, or using influence lines.

The dead loads for a noncomposite section (DC1) and a composite section (DC2) were calculated in Step 1. For each load class, we obtained the maximum positive and negative moments, maximum shears at the abutment and the pier, and reactions at the abutment and the pier. Table 2.0 of Ref. 3.49 was used.

---

field, a bolted connection is typically used in lieu of a welded one due to the difficult nature of field-welding large girder elements. Weld splices are typically used for shop splices for economics and simplicity.

The following discussion covers both types of connections and presents some of the principal issues concerning their incorporation into continuous beam elements.

1. Required Strength. A splice, quite naturally, is designed for the moment and shear which occurs at the location of the splice. Elements of a typical splice configuration are illustrated in Figure 3.48. In essence, a splice is designed to allow the two separate beams function as an integrated unit (i.e., in the same way they would if no splice were required).

Traditionally, the splice was designed "for not less than the average of the required strength at the point of the connection and the strength of the member at the same point but, in any event, not less than 75 percent of

---

When a splice is installed in the field, a bolted connection is typically used in lieu of a welded one due to the difficult nature of field-welding large girder elements.

the strength of the member" (AASHTO 10.19.1.1). If two different size sections are to be connected, the smaller section is used for determining the required splice characteristics. But in AASHTO LRFD Specifications, some minor modifications have been introduced so that it does not have to be designed too conservatively. See Parts 4 and 5 of this section for details.

The designer should use caution with the term "point of the connection." Splices, like the one illustrated in Figure 3.48, do not occur at a specific point but rather cover a length of beam which can range from 1 to 2 ft. Along this length, both moments and shears will vary. This variation must be accounted for by the designer. As with any bolted connection, the loads on the splice should be taken to act on the center of gravity of the bolt group [Ref. 3.43].

Splices are typically located at points of low shear and moment (see sidebar accompanying Figure 3.48). In some instances where the splices are constructed in the shop, the decision as to where splices should be located is left to the fabricator.

2. **Welded Splices.** As mentioned above, welded splices are most often installed in the shop rather than the field. Such connections are made using full penetration butt welds without the use of splice plates (AASHTO 10.18.5.1). Welded field splices should be avoided due to quality control and potential fatigue problems associated with field welding.

A typical welded splice for a continuous plate girder will be located in the flange plate to accommodate a change in thickness. This type of connection was discussed in Section 3.11.2, Parts 1 and 2.

Full penetration butt welds, irrespective of the difficulties listed above, can offer a sound connection which is as strong as the base material it joins. As long as the welds are closely inspected during the fabrication process, they may prove to be an attractive alternative to bolted connections.

The designer should use caution with the term "point of the connection." Splices ... do not occur at a specific point but rather cover a length of beam which can range from 1 to 2 ft.

Full penetration butt welds, irrespective of the difficulties listed above, can offer a sound connection which is as strong as the base material it joins.

WHEN DESIGNING a splice such as the one depicted in Figure 3.48, the engineer should keep in mind that the splice itself may be 1 to 2 ft in length. Along this length both the moment and shear will vary. The location of the splice along the length of the span, therefore, is important. Some state transportation agencies identify specific locations where splices are to be placed. In continuous beams, a desirable location for splices is at the point of dead load contraflexure. The general rule of thumb, as one would expect, is to locate splices in regions where both the shear and moment are low.

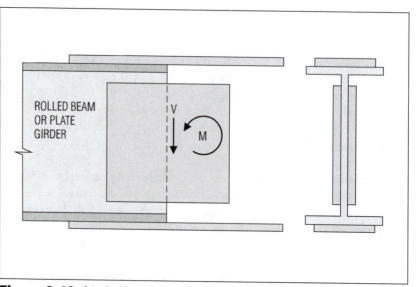

Figure 3.48 A typical four plate beam splice. *(Adapted from Ref. 3.43.)*

| EXAMPLE 3.5 | DESIGN OF TWO SPAN CONTINUOUS PLATE GIRDER BRIDGE—LRFD | DET | 9/24 |

STEP 5: Unfactored Moments and Shears (Continued)

For DW = 0.188 K/ft
The Maximum Positive Moment = 132.2 k-ft
The Maximum Negative Moment = 235.0 k-ft
The Maximum Shear at Abutment = 7.05 k
The Maximum Shear at Pier = 11.75 k
The Maximum Reaction at Abutment = 7.05 k
The Maximum Reaction at Pier = 23.50 k

HL-93 live load is composed of Track or Tandem load (whichever governs) plus a 0.64 k/ft U.D.L. The following forces caused by live loads were obtained from a structural analysis software:

For Design Truck:
The Maximum Positive Moment = 1233.9 k-ft
The Maximum Negative Moment = 663.4 k-ft
The Maximum Shear at Abutment = 63.7 k
The Maximum Shear at Pier = 67.8 k
The Maximum Reaction at Abutment = 63.7 k
The Maximum Reaction at Pier = 71.1 k

For Design Tandem:
The Maximum Positive Moment = 989.5 k-ft
The Maximum Negative Moment = 479.8 k-ft
The Maximum Shear at Abutment = 48.9 k
The Maximum Shear at Pier = 49.5 k
The Maximum Reaction at Abutment = 48.9 k
The Maximum Reaction at Pier = 50.0 k

(Step 5: Continued on Next Sheet)

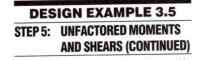

DESIGN EXAMPLE 3.5
STEP 5: UNFACTORED MOMENTS AND SHEARS (CONTINUED)

In a process similar to that performed in the previous sheet, we compute the maximum positive and negative moments, the maximum shears and reactions at both the abutment and the pier for the wearing surface dead load (DW). For two-span continues span, the maximum positive moment is at near 4/10 span from the abutment.

In AASHTO LRFD specifications, the live load is composed of a design truck or a design tandem (whichever governs), plus a design lane load. The designer will have to obtain the maximum forces for both loading, and choose the larger ones to be added to the design lane load as the final design forces. Bear in mind that dynamic load allowance (Obtained in Step 4) needs to be applied only to the truck or tandem loads, not the lane load.

The maximum live load forces for the design truck and tandem can be obtained either from design reference books, computer software, or influence lines. Note that for every force category, the design truck controls the design. That is usually the case for long and median span bridges.

3. **Bolted Splices.** When a splice must be installed in the field, a bolted connection is, in many instances, the only option for contractors. Connections at webs and flanges are made with the use of splice plates which are placed symmetrically about each side of the joint which are joined to the girders with high strength bolts.

In continuous spans, splices should be made at or near point of dead load contraflexure where the bending moment is the smallest.

If the member joined by the splice is in compression, the strength of the members connected by the high strength bolts is based on the gross section. If the member joined is primarily in bending, then the gross section is used unless more than 15 percent of each flange area is removed. The tensile stress on the net section is not to exceed $1.0F_u$. The amount in excess of the 15 percent value should be subtracted from the gross area (AASHTO 10.18.1.1).

> In continuous spans, splices should be made at or near point of dead load contraflexure where the bending moment is the smallest.

AASHTO LRFD SPEC
VALUES FOR K_h

For standard holes	1.00
For oversize and short-slotted holes	0.85
For long-slotted holes with the slot perpendicular to the direction of the force	0.70
For long-slotted holes with the slot parallel to the direction of the force	0.60

VALUES FOR K_s

for Class A surface conditions	0.33
for Class B surface conditions	0.33
for Class C surface conditions	0.33

Class A Surface: unpainted clean mill scale, and blast-cleaned surfaces with Class A coatings.

Class B Surface: unpainted blast-cleaned surfaces and blast-cleaned surfaces with Class B coatings.

Class C Surface: hot-dip galvanized surfaces roughened by brushing after galvanizing.

The standard bolt hole diameters should be 1/16 in larger than the bolt diameters (AASHTO LRFD 6.13.2.4.2). The minimum spacing between centers of bolts should not be less than three times the diameter of the bolts (AASHTO LRFD 6.13.2.6.1).

In designing web splices, the plate and connections are to be specified such that they resist not only the design moment acting on the web but also the moment induced by shear at the splice combined with eccentricity introduced by the splice connection. That is, the presence of shear at bolts offset from the joint will induce an eccentric moment which should be accounted for (AASHTO 10.18.2.3).

With regard to the geometry of the web splice, AASHTO requires that splice plates designed for shear extend the full length of the girder between the flanges. A minimum of two rows of bolts on each side of the joint is also required.

Flange splice plates are designed to accommodate only that part of the design moment which is not resisted by the web. If an angle is to be used as a flange splice, two angles are to be used, with one installed on each side of the stringer.

High-strength bolt splices may be designed as either slip-critical or bearing-type connections. Bearing-type connections are primarily for compression members. For girder splices, slip-critical connections should be designed to resist service loads (AASHTO LRFD 6.13.2.1.1).

The shear resistance at slip-critical connection at service limit state may be calculated as:

$$R_r = R_n = K_h K_s N_s P_t \qquad \text{(Eq. 3.159)}$$

where K_h = hole size factor (see sidebar)
K_s = surface condition factor (also see sidebar)
N_s = number of slip planes per bolt
P_t = minimum required bolt tension (kip)

For ASTM A325 bolts, the required tension in bolts are 28 kips, 39 kips, and 51 kips for 3/4", 7/8", and 1" bolts respectively.

From Equation 3.159 we can calculate that for a 7/8" diameter A325 bolt with standard bolt hole, and is used in class A surface condition, the single surface shear capacity at Service Limit II is 12.87 kips.

The factored shear resistance of a bolt connection at the Strength Limit State should be taken as (AASHTO LRFD 6.13.2.7):

$$R_r = \varphi_s R_n \qquad \text{(Eq. 3.160)}$$

If thread are excluded from the shear plane, then:

$$R_n = 0.48 A_b F_{ub} N_s \qquad \text{(Eq. 3.161a)}$$

If thread are included from the shear plane, then:

$$R_n = 0.38 A_b F_{ub} N_s \qquad \text{(Eq. 3.161b)}$$

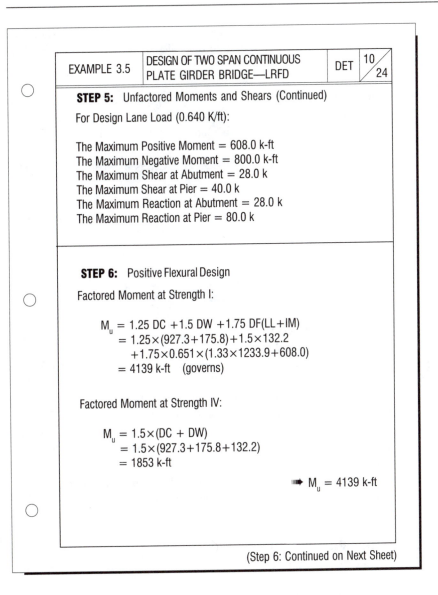

EXAMPLE 3.5	DESIGN OF TWO SPAN CONTINUOUS PLATE GIRDER BRIDGE—LRFD	DET	10/24

STEP 5: Unfactored Moments and Shears (Continued)

For Design Lane Load (0.640 K/ft):

The Maximum Positive Moment = 608.0 k-ft
The Maximum Negative Moment = 800.0 k-ft
The Maximum Shear at Abutment = 28.0 k
The Maximum Shear at Pier = 40.0 k
The Maximum Reaction at Abutment = 28.0 k
The Maximum Reaction at Pier = 80.0 k

STEP 6: Positive Flexural Design

Factored Moment at Strength I:

$$M_u = 1.25 \, DC + 1.5 \, DW + 1.75 \, DF(LL+IM)$$
$$= 1.25 \times (927.3 + 175.8) + 1.5 \times 132.2$$
$$+ 1.75 \times 0.651 \times (1.33 \times 1233.9 + 608.0)$$
$$= 4139 \text{ k-ft} \quad \text{(governs)}$$

Factored Moment at Strength IV:

$$M_u = 1.5 \times (DC + DW)$$
$$= 1.5 \times (927.3 + 175.8 + 132.2)$$
$$= 1853 \text{ k-ft}$$

➠ $M_u = 4139$ k-ft

(Step 6: Continued on Next Sheet)

For live load, only one span should be loaded to obtain the maximum positive moment and shear at abutment. Table A2.0 of Ref. 3.49 may be used for hand calculation.

Most bridge design software automatically obtain the most critical forces caused by the design live load (HL-93). But for hand calculations, we have to obtain forces caused by the design truck, the design tandem, and the design lane load separately, so that we can choose the worst case between the truck load and tandem load, and to avoid adding live load impact to the design lane load.

STEP 6: POSITIVE FLEXURAL DESIGN

The assumed sections needs to be checked for Strength Limit States, Service Limit States, and Fatigue Limit State.

For positive bending at Strength Limit States, both Strength I and Strength IV load combinations should be checked to obtain the worst case. The load factors should be obtained from Table 3.4 and Table 3.5.

where φ_s = resistance factor for bolts in shear (= 0.80)
A_b = cross-section area of the bolt
F_{ub} = specified minimum tensile strength of the bolt (ksi). For A325 bolts with diameters 0.5 through 1.0 in, F_{ub} = 120 ksi (AASHTO LRFD 6.4.3.1).
N_s = number of slip planes per bolt

Therefore, for a 7/8" diameter A325 bolt (threads are excluded from the shear plane), the factored shear capacity at the strength limit state for a single slip plane is 27.7 kips.

Note that when the bolted connections are longer than 50 inches, a modification factor of 0.8 should be applied to equations 3.161a and 3.161b. This modification is to account for uneven distribution of shear forces among the large number of bolts. In bolted splice design, this 50 inch is measured for one side of the splice bolts from the center of the splice.

4. Bolted Web Splices. Web splice plates and their connections should be designed for shear, the moment due to eccentricity of the shear force at the splice, and the portion of bending moment resisted by the web at the splice location.

The design shear force V_{uw} should be taken as the following (AASHTO LRFD 6.13.6.1.4b).

> Web splice plates and their connections should be designed for shear, the moment due to eccentricity of the shear force at the splice, and the portion of bending moment resisted by the web at the splice location.

If $\qquad V_u < 0.5\varphi_v V_n \quad$ then $\quad V_{uw} = 1.5V_u \qquad$ (Eq. 3.162a)

otherwise $$V_{uw} = \frac{V_u + \varphi_v V_n}{2}$$ (Eq. 3.162b)

where φ_v = resistance factor for shear (= 1.0)
V_u = factored shear at the point of splice
V_n = nominal shear resistance of the web at the splice location.

In earlier editions of AASHTO, the splice shear was designed for the factored shear at the splice, or 75% of the web shear strength, whichever is more critical. The old approach tends to provide an over-conservative design when the factored shear force is relatively small at the splice locations.

The eccentricity of the design shear should be taken as the distance from the point of the splice to the centroid of the bolt group under consideration.

5. Bolted Flange Splices. The flange splice plates and their connections should be designed for the force $F_{cf}A_e$ at the strength limit state (AASHTO LRFD 6.13.6.1.4c). Where A_e is the effective flange area of the smaller flange connected by the splice plate. For compression flanges, it should be taken as the gross area of the flanges. For tension flanges, it should be taken as:

$$A_e = \frac{\varphi_u F_u}{\varphi_y F_y} A_n \le A_g$$ (Eq. 3.163)

F_{cf} is the design stress, and should be taken as:

$$F_{cf} = \frac{|f_{cf}| + \varphi_f F_y}{2} \ge 0.75\varphi_f F_y$$ (Eq. 3.164)

For splice plates in tension, the factored strength should be taken as the lesser of:

$$P_r = \varphi_y F_y A_g$$ (Eq. 3.165a)

| EXAMPLE 3.5 | DESIGN OF TWO SPAN CONTINUOUS PLATE GIRDER BRIDGE—LRFD | DET | 11/24 |

STEP 6: Positive Flexural Design (Continued)

For composite section (ignore reinforcing steel in the concrete deck), the compression block height:

$$a = \frac{AF_y}{0.85f_c'b_{eff}}$$

$$a = \frac{48.00 \times 50.0}{0.85 \times 4.5 \times (8.5 \times 12)} = 6.15 \text{ in}$$

$$d = 8.0 + 1.5 + 42.0 - 19.29 = 32.21 \text{ in}$$

$$M_p = A_s F_y \cdot \left(d - \frac{a}{2}\right)$$

$$M_p = 48.0 \times 50.0 \times \left(32.21 - \frac{6.15}{2}\right) \times \frac{1}{12} = 5827 \text{ k} \cdot \text{ft}$$

Since $D_p = a = 6.15 \text{ in} > 1/10 \, D_t = 1/10 \times (8+1.5+42) = 5.15 \text{ in}$

$$M_n = M_p \cdot \left(1.07 - 0.7\frac{D_p}{D_t}\right)$$

$$M_n = 5827 \cdot \left(1.07 - 0.7\frac{6.15}{51.5}\right) = 5748 \text{ k} \cdot \text{ft}$$

Since the plastic neutral axis is within the concrete slab, it is considered as a compact section for positive bending.

(Step 6: Continued on Next Sheet)

DESIGN EXAMPLE 3.5
STEP 6: POSITIVE FLEXURAL DESIGN (CONTINUED)

The way in calculating the plastic bending strength of a composite section is similar to that of a rectangular or T section reinforced concrete beam. Here instead of having tension reinforcement, we have the steel girder in tension.

First we assume the plastic neutral axis is within the concrete slab. Since $a = 6.15''$, which is less than the deck thickness of 8'' (excluding the 1/2'' wearing surface), we know that the assumption is correct. (Should a be greater that 8'', we would have to recalculate the plastic neutral axis location, and would have to use complicated equations to calculate the plastic moment strength — See AASHTO LRFD Table D6.1-1 for details).

The d in the calculation sheet is the center of gravity of the steel girder to the top of the concrete deck. Note that the number 19.29 (in) is the distance from the bottom of the steel girder to the c.g. of the girder, which was calculated in Step 2 of this design example.

Since the plastic neutral axis is more than 1/10 of the overall section depth, we use Equation 3.63 to obtain the nominal flexural strength.

$$P_r = \varphi_u F_u A_n \qquad \text{(Eq. 3.165b)}$$

For splice plates in compression, the factored strength should be taken as:

$$R_r = \varphi_c F_y A_s \qquad \text{(Eq. 3.166)}$$

where φ_u = resistance factor for fracture of tension member (=0.80)
  φ_y = resistance factor for yielding of tension member (=0.95)
  F_u = minimum tension strength (AASHTO LRFD Table 6.4.1-1)
  F_y = specified yield strength
  A_n = net area of flange
  A_g = gross area of flange

f_{cf} = maximum flexural stress at the center of the controlling flange at the point of the splice, under the factored loads

φ_f = resistance factor for flexure $(= 1.0)$

φ_c = resistance factor for compression $(= 0.90)$

A_s = gross area of the splice plate

Like the bolted connections in the web plates, the connections in flanges should be checked for slip under Service II load combinations.

3.12.9 Hanger Assemblies

For long, continuous bridges, it is possible to use intermediate, suspended spans. The intermediate span is actually supported by two cantilevered or anchor spans on either side. The joint at which the suspended span meets the cantilevered span acts as a hinge and must allow for movement at this location. Typically, this joint is located at the expansion ends of the suspended span.

For short spans, the use of a pedestal built into the supporting beam can be used since there will be minimal movement. Longer spans, however, demand a more robust connection to account for the necessary translation and rotation at the joint. One such connection which allows for this movement in long span, continuous beam bridges is the expansion hanger or pin and hanger assembly (see Figure 3.49).

In essence, a hanger assembly performs much in the same way as a bearing in that it is designed to accommodate both translation and rotation and transmit vertical and horizontal loads. Also, like a bearing, a hanger assembly can be thought of as a mechanical system with all of the associated maintenance concerns.

Translation is facilitated through the ability of both the top and bottom pins to rotate. As shown in Figure 3.49, the web of the cantilever span extends over the web of the suspended span. These two webs are in turn joined together by the top and bottom pins and a steel hanger plate. At the opposite end of the girder, a traditional fixed bearing is provided which allows for rotation only.

> **L**ike the bolted connections in the web plates, the connections in flanges should be checked for slip under Service II load combinations.

> **I**n essence, a hanger assembly performs much in the same way as a bearing in that it is designed to accommodate both translation and rotation and transmit vertical and horizontal loads.

LIKE A BEARING a pin and hanger assembly functions much in the same fashion, in that it allows for both translation and rotation at the joint. The primary difference, however, is that, where a bearing is located over a substructure component and transmits its loads to the substructure pedestal, the pin and hanger assembly is located in between substructure support points. Like a bearing, however, the pin and hanger assembly must undergo rigorous inspection to ensure that the assembly components are free to move as they were designed and that excessive corrosion has not inhibited its ability to function.

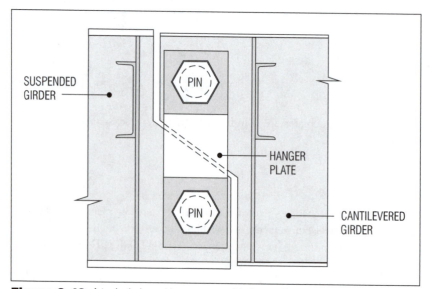

Figure 3.49 A typical pin and hanger assembly for a welded plate girder.

EXAMPLE 3.5	DESIGN OF TWO SPAN CONTINUOUS PLATE GIRDER BRIDGE—LRFD	DET	12/24

STEP 6: Positive Flexural Design (Continued)

$\phi_f \cdot M_n = 1.0 \times 5748 = 5827 \, k \cdot ft > M_u = 4139 \, k \cdot ft$

The section satisfies the strength limit state requirements. ✔

Check for ductility requirement:

$\dfrac{D_p}{D_t} = \dfrac{6.15}{51.5} = 0.12 < 0.42$ ✔

Check for Service Limit State:
Service II load combination is used to control steel from yielding under normal service conditions.
The composite section for live load (n = 8)

$b_f = \dfrac{b_{eff}}{n} = \dfrac{102}{8} = 12.75 \, in$ $I_{deck} = \dfrac{12.75 \times 8.0^3}{12} = 544 \, in^4$

ELEMENT	A (in²)	Y (in)	AY (in³)	AY² (in⁴)	I₀ (in⁴)
Steel Section	48.00	19.29	926	17861	14299
Concrete Slab	102.0	47.5	4845	230138	544
TOTALS	150.0		5771	247,999	14,843

$I_z = \sum I_o + \sum AY^2 = 14843 \, in^4 + 247999 \, in^4 = 262,842 \, in^4$

$Y' = \dfrac{\sum AY}{\sum A} = \dfrac{5771 \, in^3}{150.0 \, in^2} = 38.47 \, in$

$I = I_z - (\sum A)(Y')^2 = 262842 \, in^4 - (150.0 \, in^2)(38.47 \, in)^2$

$I = 40,851 \, in^4$ $S_b = \dfrac{I}{y'} = \dfrac{40,851}{38.47} = 1062 \, in^3$

(Step 6: Continued on Next Sheet)

DESIGN EXAMPLE 3.5
STEP 6: POSITIVE FLEXURAL DESIGN (CONTINUED)

The factored positive flexural strength is greater than the factored positive moment, so the section meets the strength requirement.

The ductility requirement is to ensure that the steel girder is not too large so that the concrete might crush in compression prior to when the steel girder is fully yielded.

The steel girder should also be checked for Service Limit States so that it will not yield under normal service loads. Service II load combination should be used for steel members.

To calculate the service load stress, we have to first calculate the composite and non-composite section properties. To calculate live load stress, the composite section with n = 8 (elastic modulus ration between steel and concrete) is used. For superimposed dead load stresses, 3n = 24 is used for calculating composite section properties. For dead load stress, a net steel section is used.

Steel girder section properties calculated in Step 2 are used here to obtain the composite section.

As mentioned above, the maintenance of pin and hanger assemblies is a critical operation which no transportation department treats lightly. Probably the most infamous pin and hanger assemblies are those that were provided on the Silver and Mianus River Bridges. The former pin and hanger assembly failed in 1967 and the latter in 1983. Both failures were catastrophic and led to a heightened awareness with the maintenance difficulties associated with this type of mechanical system.

To accommodate the movements, deck expansion joints must be provided at the hanger assemblies, which create additional challenges for the maintenance of the bridge. For these reasons, hanger assemblies are no longer used for new bridges.

Like the inspection of bearings discussed earlier, hanger assemblies should be inspected to ensure that they are free to move. Movement can be inhibited by corrosion of any of the assembly components or a misalignment of the

Probably the most infamous pin and hanger assemblies are those that were provided on the Silver and Mianus River Bridges. The former ... failed in 1967 and the latter in 1983.

Whether it is the use of paint systems or weath-ering steel ... engineers are becoming increasingly aware of the importance of ensuring the longevity of the structure they design.

girders. Impact from underpass traffic is another concern for the inspector. Like cover plates, hanger assemblies can also suffer from the adverse effects of fatigue, which are the major causes for the two bridge failures.

3.13 PROTECTING STEEL SUPERSTRUCTURES

So far we have discussed the design of steel highway bridges with a focus on the analytical aspects of the design process. Of equal importance, however, is the specification of systems designed to protect the steel superstructure after its construction. Whether it is the use of paint systems or weathering steel, in today's design environment engineers are becoming increasingly aware of the importance of ensuring the longevity of the structure they design.

To many designers, the application of a protective coating to a steel superstructure may almost be an afterthought. There is an obvious need to protect an exposed steel superstructure against the corrosive effects of natural and man-made elements. In the minds of many engineers (both old and young) the specification of a paint system would seem to be a simple, boiler plate operation. As we will see, however, the advanced state of deterioration of many steel structures combined with a heightened awareness of the environmental impact of many protective systems has led to the protection of steel superstructures becoming a prime issue for many transportation agencies.

The following discussion will focus on the two major ways of protecting steel superstructures:

- ❏ Protective coating systems
- ❏ Weathering steel

We will also look at the important issue of paint removal and the impact it has on the rehabilitation of existing structures.

3.13.1 Protective Coating Systems

One of the main arguments proponents of concrete bridges use in lobbying against steel structures is the susceptibility of steel to corrosion from the elements. The incorporation of a high quality protective coating system, however, can go a long way toward extending the life span of a steel structure and reducing maintenance costs in the future. Obviously, the paint coatings used by transportation agencies did not evolve overnight, but rather have become refined and modified as a result of their use and performance. Prior to discussing the main coating systems in use today, an investigation into the origins of these systems is beneficial.

1. Background and History. The origin of the modern protective coating system can be traced back to the middle 19th century [Ref. 3.53]. A prime example of how protective coating systems have developed can be found in the Firth of Forth Bridge in Scotland. The Forth Bridge was first opened to traffic in 1889 [Ref. 3.54]. For a bridge constructed more than one hundred years ago, the paint system applied to the structure bears a striking similarity to those present in many bridge still in use today.

EXAMPLE 3.5	DESIGN OF TWO SPAN CONTINUOUS PLATE GIRDER BRIDGE—LRFD	DET	$\frac{13}{24}$

STEP 6: Positive Flexural Design (Continued)

Composite Section for Superimposed Dead Loads, Use 3n = 24:

$$b_f = \frac{b_{eff}}{3n} = \frac{102}{24} = 4.25 \text{ in} \qquad I_{deck} = \frac{4.25 \times 8.0^3}{12} = 181.3 \text{ in}^4$$

ELEMENT	A (in²)	Y (in)	AY (in³)	AY² (in⁴)	I_o (in⁴)
Steel Section	48.00	19.29	926	17861	14299
Concrete Slab	34.00	47.5	1615	76713	181.3
TOTALS	82.00		2541	94,574	14,480

$$I_z = \sum I_o + \sum AY^2 = 14480 \text{ in}^4 + 94574 \text{ in}^4 = 109,054 \text{ in}^4$$

$$Y' = \frac{\sum AY}{\sum A} = \frac{2541 \text{ in}^3}{82.0 \text{ in}^2} = 30.99 \text{ in}$$

$$I = I_z - (\sum A)(Y')^2 = 109,054 \text{ in}^4 - (82.0 \text{ in}^2)(30.99 \text{ in})^2$$

$$I = 30,303 \text{ in}^4 \qquad S_b = \frac{I}{y'} = \frac{30,303}{30.99} = 977.8 \text{ in}^3$$

For non-composite section (see Step 2):

$$I = 14,299 \text{ in}^4$$

$$y' = 19.29 \text{ in}^4$$

$$S_b = \frac{I}{y'} = \frac{14,299}{19.29} = 741.3 \text{ in}^3$$

Dead load stress:

$$f_{DL} = \frac{M_{DL1}}{S} = \frac{927.3 \times 12}{741.3} = 15.01 \text{ ksi}$$

(Step 6: Continued on Next Sheet)

DESIGN EXAMPLE 3.5
STEP 6: POSITIVE FLEXURAL DESIGN (CONTINUED)

For Service Limit States, elastic section properties should be used for all composite and noncomposite sections. For steel bridges, the objective of the Service Limit States is to avoid the steel from yielding under normal load conditions, therefore to avoid permanent plastic deflections.

The elastic composite section properties are calculated using the steps stipulated in Figure 3.33. Once the composite section moment of inertia "I" is calculated, the elastic section modulus of bottom flange can be calculated by dividing "I" by the distance between the bottom of girder and the c.g. of the composite section.

The total steel bottom flange stress under the Service II load combination is calculated by adding the dead load stress, the superimposed dead load stress, and the live load stress. Note that the load factor for both dead load and superimposed dead load is 1.0. The load factor for live load is 1.3. See Table 3.4 for details.

To protect the structure, a red lead/linseed oil primer was applied in the shop with a second coating provided once the members were in the field. The steel was provided with an additional coat of red oxide intermediate along with one coat of red oxide finish. Tube areas were re-coated with two coats of white lead and oil [Ref. 3.53].

The red lead/linseed oil primers, red lead/iron oxide intermediate coats, and white lead and oil finish coats, as stated above, are very similar to those used in the United States in the first half of the twentieth century. The red lead/linseed oil primer could be applied to surfaces with almost no surface preparation, making it an attractive coating solution. The introduction of chromium green oxide pigments for finished coats is one variation that most readers will notice as the familiar color of many steel highway bridges.

The red lead/white lead systems eventually gave way to the so-called *Basic Lead Silico Chromate* (BLSC) system. This system offered more stability in the color which, although orange by nature, could be modified into a

> The red lead/linseed oil primer could be applied to surfaces with almost no surface preparation, making it an attractive coating solution.

> "Engineers who must prevent bridges and other steel structures from corroding have found there's a revolution brewing in their paint buckets."

RITA ROBISON
[Ref. 3.52]

---

variety of other colors. The BLSC system, over the course of several years and associated modifications, eventually evolved into the AASHTO M 229 standard in 1950's.

In terms of service life, the BLSC systems applied to bridges in the 1950's and 1960's showed life spans in the range of five to ten years and sometimes even twelve years. Enhancements and modifications (particularly in the area of polymer chemistry) raised the bar, so to speak, for protective coating systems into the realm of fifteen to thirty years of useful performance.

By the 1980's high ratio zinc silicates were being offered by a variety of vendors as *high performance* primers (see Did You Know? sidebar). Complicating the issue further is the use of micaceous iron oxide (MIO) coatings. MIO coatings, long used in Europe, are attempting to gain a foothold in the lucrative United States bridge maintenance marketplace. Although more expensive than traditional coating systems, the MIO coating system has been given high marks for longevity and overall performance (see below). With so many choices and, as we will see, strict environmental regulations, the application of protective coating systems to steel superstructures is indeed becoming an involved issue.

2. **The Nature of Steel Corrosion.** Like the corrosion of reinforced concrete (discussed earlier in the section on cathodic protection, Section 3.9.8, Part 8), corrosion of steel is an electrochemical process. When two different metals are placed in an electrolyte, and electrical current is created between the two metals. An example of an electrolyte would be salt water. In essence, one metal acts as the anode and the other as the cathode with deterioration being the end result. This process of deterioration is known as *galvanic corrosion.*

Whether or not a particular steel structure is more susceptible to corrosion than another is dependent on many factors. The presence of an electrolyte like salt water, be it through deicing agents or a marine environment, can greatly accelerate the deterioration of steel structures. Other factors which can accelerate corrosion are the presence of carbon dioxide and hydrogen sulfide as well as extremely high temperatures.

In general, there are some basic measures which can be taken to limit corrosion of steel. One approach would be to reduce the contact between dissimilar metals. Another would be to galvanize the surface of the metal. Lastly, the surfaces can be separated by a different material such as rubber or paint.

From the latter item, we see what is naturally intuitive: a layer of paint shields and protects the underlying steel from the elements. Of course, the actual system which protects the steel is significantly more complicated than a simple coat of paint; but the concept is essentially the same. Where steel bridges begin to suffer, however, is when the protective coating begins to break down and exposes the underlying material to the adverse effects of the surrounding environment. Because of the complete exposure of a steel superstructure to the elements, this deterioration can cause significant loss of section to structural members and impact the integrity of the bridge as a whole.

Where steel bridges begin to suffer, however, is when the protective coating begins to break down and expose the underlying material ...

EXAMPLE 3.5	DESIGN OF TWO SPAN CONTINUOUS PLATE GIRDER BRIDGE—LRFD	DET	14/24

STEP 6: Positive Flexural Design (Continued)

Superimposed dead load stress:

$$f_{SDL} = \frac{M_{DL2} + M_{DW}}{S} = \frac{(175.8 + 132.2) \times 12}{977.8} = 3.78 \text{ ksi}$$

Live load stress:
Live load factor for Service Limit State II is 1.3.

$$M_{LL} = 1.3 \times 0.651 \times (1.33 \times 1233.9 + 608.0) = 1903 \text{ k} \cdot \text{ft}$$

$$f_{LL} = \frac{M_{LL}}{S} = \frac{1903 \times 12}{1062} = 21.51 \text{ ksi}$$

The total factored stress at bottom flange at Service Limit State II is:

$$f_{bot} = 15.01 + 3.78 + 21.51 = 40.30 \text{ ksi} < 0.95\, f_y = 47.5 \text{ ksi} \ ✔$$

STEP 7: Negative Flexural Design

Factored Moment at Strength Limit State I:
$$M_u = 1.25\, DC + 1.5\, DW + 1.75\, DF\, (LL + IM)$$
$$= 1.25 \times (1648.8 + 312.5) + 1.5 \times 235.0$$
$$+ 1.75 \times 0.674 \times (663.4 \times 1.33 + 800.0)$$
$$= 4788 \text{ k-ft}$$

Factored Moment at Strength Limit State IV:
$$M_u = 1.5\, (DC + DW)$$
$$= 1.5 \times (1648.8 + 312.5 + 235.0)$$
$$= 3294 \text{ k-ft}$$

➠ $M_u = 4788$ k-ft

(Step 7: Continued on Next Sheet)

DESIGN EXAMPLE 3.5
STEP 6: POSITIVE FLEXURAL DESIGN (CONTINUED)

The reader should note that, although both live load and superimposed dead loads act on composite sections, the section modulus used in calculating stresses are different. Live load is a short-term load, so the creep of concrete will not affect the steel stress. The superimposed dead loads are long-term loads, so we have to consider the effect of concrete creep. Therefore we use *3n* to transform the concrete slab into equivalent steel for superimposed dead load, while using *n* for live load.

The total stress under the factored loads (Service II load combination) is equal to 40.30 ksi, which is less than the allowable stress (95% of the yield stress of the girder) which is 47.5 ksi. Therefore, the assumed section meets the Service Limit States requirements.

STEP 7: NEGATIVE FLEXURAL DESIGN

As in positive flexural design, we first determine the factored bending moments using load combination Strength I and Strength IV, and choose the more critical one as the design moment.

When using a protective coating system, corrosion of steel members is controlled through the use of one of the following mechanisms [Ref 3.53]:

❑ Inhibitive primers
❑ Sacrificial primers
❑ Barrier coatings

The coatings used can come in a variety of forms. The major types of coatings being metallic, organic, and inorganic in composition. Further complicating the issue is the application of such systems to existing steel structures. In this instance, the designer must not only be concerned with the protective system to be applied, but must also deal with removal or encapsulation of an existing protective coating which may have been in place for several decades. All of these factors make the decision as to what system to use, an important one.

> **t**he designer must not only be concerned with the protective system to be applied, but must also deal with removal or encapsulation of an existing protective coating ...

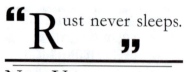

"Rust never sleeps. **"**

NEIL YOUNG

There is ... a general concern over the toxic nature of both of these types of primers. The intensity of this concern has grown rapidly since the 1980's.

---

3. Inhibitive Primers. A primer is the initial coat of paint which is applied to the virgin surface of a steel member. The quality of a primer is indicated by its ability to adhere to the surface of the steel. An inhibitive primer functions through use of an organic coating which stops corrosion through a process of chemical or mechanical inhibition. This *inhibition* is designed to prevent deterioration caused by moisture and oxygen.

The pigments of inhibitive primers give the coating their inhibitive characteristics. A pigment, by definition, is a fine, insoluble powder which is dispersed into the liquid portion of the paint. The pigment gives the paint its color, hardness, and corrosion resisting properties and can be either organic or inorganic. The two basic types of pigments used in inhibitive primers are:

- ❏ Partially soluble hexavalent chromium salt
- ❏ Basic lead compounds

The two most predominate forms of inhibitive primers are red lead and BLSC. While the former has 100 percent toxic agent in its weight, the latter has only 25 percent. Also, where red lead paint can only be used as a primer, the BLSC system can also function as a second coat and even a top coat.

There is, however, a general concern over the toxic nature of both of these types of primers. The intensity of this concern has grown rapidly since the 1980's. New regulations in the United States enacted by the Occupational Safety and Health Administration (OSHA) and the Environmental Protection Agency (EPA) have significantly impacted the cost of using lead based primers. Some estimates show that the cost of repainting a structure has risen from $2 per square foot to the range of $5-$10 per square foot or even $30 per square foot [Ref. 3.52]. The focus of these regulations is to minimize the amount of lead which is released into the surrounding atmosphere. Lead can be released into the air at any time the structural steel is either painted or blast cleaned in the field. For these reasons, lead based paint has been totally eliminated in the United States by late 1980's.

Research and development has been conducted which has produced a variety of less toxic pigments but the general consensus has been that the inhibitive characteristics of these new products still do not perform as well as these of chromate and lead based pigments. While this does not mean that nontoxic inhibitive primers are unacceptable, their widespread use in the mainstream transportation arena, however, has yet to develop to its full potential [Ref. 3.53].

4. Sacrificial Primers. Like an anode in a cathodic protection system (see Section 3.9.8, Part 8), a sacrificial or galvanic primer protects the underlying steel surface by creating a surface which is electrochemically negative in relation to the steel. This results in the steel becoming completely cathodic and eliminating potential deterioration. Zinc is the most common material used to make the primer act as an anode. The zinc is dispersed through the paint film as a pigment and applied directly to the steel surface [Ref. 3.53].

EXAMPLE 3.5	DESIGN OF TWO SPAN CONTINUOUS PLATE GIRDER BRIDGE—LRFD	DET	15/24

STEP 7: Negative Flexural Design (Continued)
Elastic Composite Section Property:

The total reinforcing steel $A_s = 10.37$ in^2. (5.93 in from top of steel girder). Only reinforcement inside the effective flange width should be used.

ELEMENT	A (in^2)	Y (in)	AY (in^3)	AY^2 (in^4)	I_o (in^4)
Steel Girder	65.00	18.56	1206.4	22391	21295
Reinf. Steel	10.37	48.43	502.2	24322	0
TOTALS	75.37		1708.6	46713	21295

$$I_z = \sum I_o + \sum AY^2 = 21295\,in^4 + 46713\,in^4 = 68008\,in^4$$

$$Y' = \frac{\sum AY}{\sum A} = \frac{1708.6\,in^3}{75.37\,in^2} = 22.67\,in$$

$$I = I_z - (\sum A)(Y')^2 = 68008\,in^4 - (75.37\,in^2)(22.67\,in)^2$$

$$I = 29,275\,in^4$$

$$S_{bot} = \frac{I}{y'} = \frac{29275}{22.67} = 1291\,in^3$$

$$S_{top} = \frac{I}{y'} = \frac{29275}{42.5 - 22.67} = 1476\,in^3$$

Stress in Compression Flange:

$$\lambda_{rw} = 5.7\sqrt{\frac{E}{F_y}} = 5.7\sqrt{\frac{29000}{50}} = 137.3 \quad (Eq.\ 3.148)$$

(Step 7: Continued on Next Sheet)

DESIGN EXAMPLE 3.5
STEP 7: NEGATIVE FLEXURAL DESIGN (CONTINUED)

For continuous span bridges, the negative bending regions can either be designed as a composite section, or a noncomposite section. The concrete deck is in tension, so it will be ignored. The reinforcing steel in the deck is also ignored if a noncomposite section is assumed in the design. If the section is assumed as a composite section, then the reinforcing steel in the deck can be considered as part of the composite section.

As we discussed in the Section 3.10.7, Part 4 that in order to take advantage of using composite section at negative bending region, sufficient shear studs should be provided in that region.

In this design example, a composite section is assumed in the negative bending region. A total reinforcement of 10.37 in^2 is assumed to be placed within the effective width of the concrete slab. Longitudinal reinforcement in both top and bottom layers may be considered. In this example, the center of gravity of the longitudinal reinforcement is 5.93" above the top of the steel girder.

An advantage that zinc based sacrificial primers has is that, compared to chromate or lead based inhibitive primers, the zinc is relatively nontoxic. The zinc can either be mixed with an inorganic substance such as a silicate or phosphate just prior to application or an organic vehicle (i.e., the liquid part of the paint) such as rubber, epoxies, or vinyls. A limitation of inorganic, sacrificial primers is that the surface must receive a *near white blast cleaning* prior to application (see below).

One difficulty found in the application of zinc based sacrificial primers is the difficulty in determining which areas are the base metal and which areas have been newly primed. Research is being conducted in which zinc is replaced with another form of conductive pigment. The advantage of these new pigments is that they will allow for an easier determination as to which areas have been primed and which areas have not. However, the jury is still out as to their performance in relationship to the more traditional zinc based systems.

One difficulty found in the application of zinc based sacrificial primers is the difficulty in determining which areas are the base metal and which areas have been newly primed.

[3.13.1, Part 5]

5. Barrier Coatings. A barrier system is designed to prevent water, oxygen, and ionic material from coming in contact with the underlying steel surface. A barrier system is typically composed of multiple layers of essentially the same substance [Ref. 3.53]. Types of barrier system coatings are:

- ❏ Coal-tar enamels
- ❏ Low-build vinyl lacquers
- ❏ Epoxy and aliphatic urethanes
- ❏ Coal-tar epoxies

While the thickness of coats used in barrier systems is often insufficient in preventing moisture and oxygen from precipitating the cathodic reaction which causes deterioration, the system has proven reliable in protecting steel superstructures. The reason for this is the ionic impermeability of the barrier systems. Even though moisture gets through the barrier, it is usually of such high electrical resistance that the cathodic reaction, from cathode to anode, is minimal.

In order to take advantage of this property, it is important that the vehicle selected be low in moisture and oxygen transmission rates so as to complement the characteristics of the barrier system. Examples of vehicles which offer these characteristics are vinyls, chlorinated rubbers, and coal-tar.

6. Surface Preparation. It was mentioned earlier that the principal function of a primer is to adhere to the underlying steel surface; creating a bond which is both sound and secure. This bond should at best eliminate and at worst minimize the intrusion of water and oxygen to the steel below. Damage to the base metal from corrosion arises when this bond is compromised and the cathodic reaction of corrosion, discussed in Part 2

Cleaning Methodology	Normalization of Substrate	Removal of Interference Material	Increase in Surface Area	Removal of Soluble Salts
Hand-Tool Cleaning	Poor	Poor-Fair	Poor-Fair	Poor
Power-Tool Cleaning	Fair	Fair	Fair	Poor-Fair
Brush-Blast Cleaning	Fair	Fair	Good	Poor-Fair
Commercial Blast Cleaning	Good	Good	Excellent	Good
Near-White Blast Cleaning	Very Good	Very Good	Excellent	Very Good
White-Blast Cleaning	Excellent	Excellent	Excellent	Very Good
Water Blasting	Good	Good	Poor	Fair
High-Pressure Water Blast	Very Good	Good-Very Good	Poor	Good
Wet Abrasive Blasting	Very Good-Excellent	Very Good-Excellent	Excellent	Excellent

Table 3.23 Effectiveness of Various Methods of Surface Preparation. *(Adapted from Ref. 3.53.)*

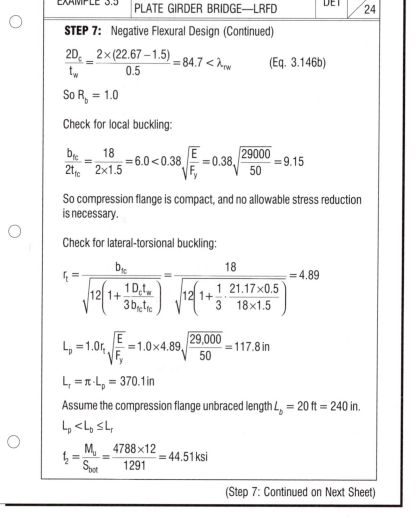

In AASHTO LRFD specifications, the maximum compression stress under the factored strength limit state load combinations is calculated and compared with the allowable compression stress. The allowable stress is generally the steel yield stress, and modified by reduction factors due to potential compression flange local buckling and the potential lateral-torsional buckling of the steel girder. See Section 3.12.7, Part 2 for details.

In according to Equation 3.150, the compression flange of the assumed section is a compact, so it will not be subjected to local buckling.

The lateral-torsional buckling (or global buckling) force is a function of the unbraced length of the compression flange. In this example, the unbraced length is 20 feet. Equation 3.153 should be used to determine the allowable compression stress due to the potential global buckling.

To apply to Equation 3.153, the maximum stresses at the pier, at the other brace point (20 ft from the pier), and at the mid point between (10 ft from the pier) need to be calculated.

A first step toward ensuring that the protective coating system performs its intended function is to properly prepare the surface for application of the primer and subsequent coats.

above, is initiated. A first step toward ensuring that the protective coating system performs its intended function is to properly prepare the surface for application of the primer and subsequent coats.

The method of preparing the steel surface varies depending on the type of protective coating used. Lead based, inhibitive primers generally require less surface preparation than sacrificial and barrier systems. It is no wonder, then, that the development of these new protective coatings has also led to the development of enhanced surface preparation techniques.

Since the lead based inhibitive primers, favored in the first half of the twentieth century required less surface preparation, hand cleaning with various power tools was commonly used to prepare the steel surface. The more sensitive, nontoxic systems, however, demanded more robust methods. These systems led directly to the use of abrasive blasting in order to gain an underlying steel surface which was as clean and pure as possible.

> **N**ot only does proper sur-face preparation increase the bonding action between primer and base metal, it also creates a uniform surface upon which to place the coating system ...

It should be kept in mind that, although the paint itself is an expense, the surface preparation and eventual application of the protective coating is often several times the cost of that for the basic materials.

The importance of a sound surface preparation program, however, cannot be understated. Not only does proper surface preparation increase the bonding action between primer and base metal, it also creates a uniform surface upon which to place the coating system and thereby minimize the amount of foreign particles which could potentially accelerate the cathodic reaction. These particles could take the form of chloride or sulfate ions on the steel surface. The principal methods presently utilized for surface preparation of steel are:

❑ Hand cleaning
❑ Solvent cleaning
❑ Blast cleaning
❑ Power cleaning

Each of the methods listed above offers various levels of quality and is appropriate for use with certain types of protective coating systems. Surface preparation also varies depending on whether new steel is being used or an existing structure is being repainted. When considering the quality and thoroughness of the surface preparation of steel, there are two fundamental properties which must be taken into account:

❑ The physical appearance of the steel
❑ The chemical cleanliness of the substrate

> **B**y "chemically clean" we mean a surface which is free from iogenic material which can initiate the cathodic reaction (e.g., chlorides and sulfates).

By "chemically clean" we mean a surface which is free from iogenic material which can initiate the cathodic reaction (e.g., chlorides and sulfates). Table 3.23 lists several methods of surface preparation and rates their ability to satisfy the following requirements:

❑ Normalization of the surface
❑ Exposing of reactive steel
❑ Increasing the real surface area of the steel
❑ Removing all iogenic materials

In Europe, the removal of chemical impurities has been given a higher level of importance than it has in the United States [Ref. 3.53]. As Table 3.23 demonstrates, however, there is no method of surface preparation which can be deemed *excellent* across the board.

Regardless of the method used, whether it be as primitive as the use of hand tools or as sophisticated as wet abrasive blasting, the control of toxic materials when cleaning steel in the field has become one of the principal concerns when preparing steel for painting in the field. Since field preparation of steel is mainly carried out on older structures, this concern is exacerbated by the predominate use of lead based primers in bridge structures of this vintage.

The following discussion pertains to some of the more basic methods of surface preparation and their associated benefits and deficiencies.

EXAMPLE 3.5	DESIGN OF TWO SPAN CONTINUOUS PLATE GIRDER BRIDGE—LRFD	DET	17/24

STEP 7: Negative Flexural Design (Continued)

At middle of the braced point (10 ft from the pier):

$$M_{DC1} = 890.3 \text{ k-ft}$$
$$M_{DC2} = 168.8 \text{ k-ft}$$
$$M_{DW} = 126.9 \text{ k-ft}$$
$$M_{truck} = 597.1 \text{ k-ft}$$
$$M_{lane} = 432.0 \text{ k-ft}$$

$$M_u = 1.25DC + 1.5DW + 1.75DF(LL + IM)$$
$$M_u = 1.25 \times (890.3 + 168.8) + 1.5 \times 126.9$$
$$\quad + 1.75 \times 0.674 \times (1.33 \times 597.1 + 432.0)$$
$$M_u = 2960 \text{ k-ft}$$

Assume at 0.9L, the section is the same as that over pier.

$$f_{mid} = \frac{2960 \times 12}{1291} = 27.51 \text{ ksi}$$

At the brace point (20 ft from the pier):

$$M_{DC1} = 263.8 \text{ k-ft}$$
$$M_{DC2} = 50.0 \text{ k-ft}$$
$$M_{DW} = 37.6 \text{ k-ft}$$
$$M_{truck} = 530.8 \text{ k-ft}$$
$$M_{lane} = 192.0 \text{ k-ft}$$

$$M_u = 1.25DC + 1.5DW + 1.75DF(LL + IM)$$
$$M_u = 1.25 \times (263.8 + 50.0) + 1.5 \times 37.6$$
$$\quad + 1.75 \times 0.674 \times (1.33 \times 530.8 + 192.0)$$
$$M_u = 1508 \text{ k-ft}$$

(Step 7: Continued on Next Sheet)

DESIGN EXAMPLE 3.5
STEP 7: NEGATIVE FLEXURAL DESIGN (CONTINUED)

To calculate the maximum stresses at the middle of the braced points, we have to first obtain the maximum bending moment at that point. The moments due to dead loads and live loads may be calculated from influence lines, or can be obtained from running bridge design computer software. In this design example, these moments are given to simplify the calculation.

In a similar fashion, the bending moments due to dead loads and live loads at the brace point (20 feet from the pier) are also given in this design example.

The load combination for Strength I is used to obtain the factored moments at these points. The factored maximum compression stresses at these points are then calculated by dividing these moments by the respective section modulus.

■ **Hand and Power Tool Cleaning.** As a method of surface preparation, the use of power or hand tools by themselves is generally insufficient and does not satisfy any of the major requirements of surface preparation listed above. The use of hand and power tools is typically confined to the removal of heavy rust scale, loose paint, etc., after which a more robust method of surface preparation is used. Hand and power tools should be used to remove surface rust and paint and should not be expected to reach the bare steel below.

An adverse effect of power and hand tools is their tendency to force corrodent back into the steel surface itself. Therefore, any use of this method should be undertaken with care taken that the surface of the steel is not damaged.

■ **Dry Abrasive Blasting.** Dry abrasive blasting (i.e., without water) cleans the steel surface by blasting small, abrasive particles at the steel

> The use of hand and power tools is typically confined to the removal of heavy rust scale ... after which a more robust method of surface preparation is used.

surface which strips off the layers of paint, rust, etc. above the bare steel. Dry abrasive blasting can be performed using one of two different approaches:

- ❏ Centrifugal blasting
- ❏ Air blasting

The former utilizes multiple, rotating blades which launch the abrasives at the steel surface at extremely high speed. An advantage of the centrifugal blasting approach is that the abrasives are generally reusable and thus offers a cost savings over multiple cleanings. If and when abrasives are reused, however, they should be cleaned to ensure that they are free of oils and other contaminants which could adversely affect future cleanings. Air blasting works under a similar premise, except in lieu of the rotating blades, a stream of compressed air is used to propel abrasives such as silica, sand, or crushed flint at the surface of the steel.

It is even possible to use grits that are zinc based which, as we saw earlier, has the advantage of arresting the cathodic reaction. Conversely, abrasives which contain copper should be avoided because they are prone to accelerating cathodic reaction. Also, as shown in Table 3.23, a drawback to dry blasting in general is its weak performance in eliminating chemical contaminants on the steel surface. This deficiency is more pronounced when the dry blasting is being conducted in the field rather than the shop.

■ Water Blasting. Water or hydroblasting, as the name would imply, uses a stream of water at very high pressures to remove any paint and rust from the surface of a steel member. These high pressures (as high as 20,000 psi but usually 5,000 psi for highway bridges) can lead to potential hazards for the operator. One of the main advantages of the water blasting approach is that it is good at removing chloride contaminants from the steel surface. Another benefit is that the water does not scarify (i.e., scratch) the surface of the steel as mechanical methods are prone to do.

■ Water Abrasive Blasting. Wet abrasive blasting is essentially a synthesis of the two previous methods described above. Water and abrasives are air-blasted toward the steel surface, removing rust, paint, and ionic materials from the steel surface. While the results, as shown in the ratings in Table 3.23, may appear to indicate that wet abrasive blasting is the optimum solution for steel surface preparation, there are, however, certain drawbacks.

One such drawback is the sludge by-products created as a result of the process (a problem which has particularly adverse results when traffic is passing underneath the structure). Another problem associated with this method is the potential of the steel to begin to corrode in between cleaning and application of the primer.

Similar to the use of zinc abrasives described above, wet abrasive blasting has been augmented to utilize inhibitive solutions which are introduced through the water used in blasting. Inhibitors, such as chromates and phosphates, can be applied in an effort to minimize the potential for rusting in between cleaning and application of the primer coat.

> An advantage of the centrifugal blasting approach is that the abrasives are generally reusable and thus offers a cost savings over multiple cleanings.

| EXAMPLE 3.5 | DESIGN OF TWO SPAN CONTINUOUS PLATE GIRDER BRIDGE—LRFD | DET | 18/24 |

STEP 7: Negative Flexural Design (Continued)

Assume as 0.8L, the section is the same as that over pier.

$$f_0 = \frac{1508 \times 12}{1291} = 14.02 \, \text{ksi}$$

$$f_1 = 2f_{mid} - f_2 > f_0 \qquad \text{(Eq. 3.158)}$$

$$2f_{mid} - f_2 = 2 \times 27.51 - 44.51 = 10.51 \, \text{ksi} < f_0$$

Therefore: $f_1 = f_0 = 14.02 \, \text{ksi}$

$$C_b = 1.75 - 1.05\left(\frac{f_1}{f_2}\right) + 0.3\left(\frac{f_1}{f_2}\right)^2 \leq 2.3 \qquad \text{(Eq. 3.156b)}$$

$$C_b = 1.75 - 1.05\left(\frac{14.02}{44.51}\right) + 0.3\left(\frac{14.02}{44.51}\right)^2$$

$$C_b = 1.449 < 2.3$$

$$F_{nc} = C_b\left(1 - 0.3\frac{L_b - L_p}{L_r - L_p}\right)R_b F_y \leq R_b F_y$$

$$F_{nc} = 1.449\left(1 - 0.3\frac{240 - 117.8}{370.1 - 117.8}\right) \times 1.0 \times 50 \qquad \text{(Eq. 3.153)}$$

$$F_{nc} = 61.92 \, \text{ksi} > R_b F_y = 50 \, \text{ksi}$$

Therefore, $F_{nc} = 50 \, \text{ksi}$

(Step 7: Continued on Next Sheet)

DESIGN EXAMPLE 3.5
STEP 7: NEGATIVE FLEXURAL DESIGN (CONTINUED)

Once the factored maximum stresses at the both brace points, and the middle point are calculated, the moment gradient modifier C_b can be obtained using Equation 3.156b. By substitute C_b into Equation 3.153, we can obtain the allowable compression stress for the girder due to the lateral-torsional buckling.

In this design example, the final allowable compressive stress is 50 ksi that is the yield stress of the steel, which means that the girder is neither subjected to the local buckling, nor is subjected to the global buckling.

The reader should keep in mind that it may be more economical to increase the spacing of the lateral supports to reduce the costs of diaphragms. In doing so, the allowable compressive stress may also be reduced. For straight bridges, most engineers use diaphragm spacing of 20 to 30 feet. For curved bridges, smaller spacing may be used to reduce the torsion in girders.

Should the steel indeed corrode after cleaning, another blasting will be required to clean off this layer of rust. Obviously such an occurrence will increase the cost of the blasting process. One method of minimizing the risk of corrosion after blasting is to dry the steel. This drying can be accomplished either via dry blasting or blowing the steel dry after the wet abrasive blasting has been performed.

Despite these deficiencies, however, wet abrasive blasting offers a method for satisfying most of the primary requirements for surface preparation detailed in Table 3.23 with very little associated air pollution.

■ **Spot Cleaning.** In the laboratory, or with field experimentation, it is relatively easy to quantify which method offers the cleaner surface, the better bond between steel and primer, etc. In the real world, however, the limitation of available funds, for all practical purposes, can make any study irrelevant. While limited funds may reduce the amount of work a

O ne method of minimizing the risk of corrosion after blasting is to dry the steel ... either via dry blasting or blowing the steel dry ...

I n the real world, however, the limitation of available funds, for all practical purposes, can make any study irrelevant.

transportation agency can perform in maintaining the surface of a steel superstructure, it does not eliminate the need for protecting the steel as much as possible given the funds available.

Because of the conflict between limited funds and the need for steel maintenance, spot cleaning has become a common practice in cleaning paint surfaces on existing steel bridges. Spot cleaning generally entails cleaning and priming only the deteriorated regions of a steel member and then applying full coats of conventional intermediate and/or finish coats. These full coats are placed over the isolated areas which have been cleaned as well as the areas of the steel where the paint is still in good condition.

The new coats are typically oil/alkyd based. When painting over existing film the same rules, with regard to chemical cleanliness, apply to this surface as would the bare steel. Since this film is now essentially the substrate to which the new coating system while adhere to, it must be free of chlorides, dirt, and other debris that would adversely impact the bond between the new coat and the old.

7. **Overcoating.** A method of applying a protective coating to existing steel bridges, which is based on the spot cleaning approach, is known as *overcoating* [Ref. 3.55]. Under the overcoating approach, corroded areas are cleaned using hand and/or power tools to remove broken down paint, loose rust, and old coatings. The entire steel, regardless of condition, receives a thorough cleaning through the use of a power water wash which removes dirt and a certain percentage of chlorides which are embedded in the surface of the steel.

Once the steel surface is prepared as described above, a three step painting process is conducted where:

> ❏ Any exposed steel areas are spot primed with a surface tolerant one-component moisture cure polyurethane aluminum primer
> ❏ A polyurethane intermediate coat is applied to the entire bridge surface
> ❏ A light-stable polyurethane top coat is applied to the structure

In addition to the obvious cost savings, when compared to complete surface cleaning, overcoating also offers the benefit of greatly limiting the amount of hazardous waste associated with more extensive surface preparation methods. The main danger for the emission of toxic material when overcoating occurs is the use of hand and power tools. Any debris generated by this spot cleaning must be contained and disposed of.

However, when the entire surface of a steel superstructure, coated with a lead based protective coating system, is cleaned, there is an extremely high cost associated with containing and collecting the existing paint. In addition to this expense, all of the contaminated abrasive and other materials must also be disposed of. With the fiscal constraints imposed on many transportation departments, such an approach is becoming increasingly unacceptable as costs associated with this type of operation continue to rise.

Under the overcoating approach, corroded areas are cleaned using hand and/or power tools to remove broken down paint, loose rust, and old coatings.

EXAMPLE 3.5	DESIGN OF TWO SPAN CONTINUOUS PLATE GIRDER BRIDGE—LRFD	DET	19/24

STEP 7: Negative Flexural Design (Continued)

The maximum stress in compression flange:

$$f_c = \frac{M_u}{S_{bot}} = \frac{4788 \times 12}{1291} = 44.51 \, \text{ksi} < F_{nc} = 50 \, \text{ksi} \qquad ✔$$

Check allowable stress in tension flange:

The allowable tension stress is $F_{nt} = F_y = 50$ ksi.

$$f_t = \frac{M_u}{S_{top}} = \frac{4788 \times 12}{1476} = 38.93 \, \text{ksi} < F_{nt} = 50 \, \text{ksi} \qquad ✔$$

STEP 8: Shear at Abutment

Factored shear at Strength I:
$V_u = 1.25 \, DC + 1.5 \, DW + 1.75 \, DF \, (LL + IM)$
$V_u = 1.25 \times (49.46 + 9.38) + 1.5 \times 7.05$
$\qquad + 1.75 \times 0.884 \times (1.33 \times 63.7 + 28.0)$
$V_u = 258.5 \, k$

Factored shear at Strength IV:
$V_u = 1.5 \, (DC + DW)$
$V_u = 1.5 \times (49.46 + 9.38 + 7.05)$
$V_u = 98.8 \, k$

⬛▶ $V_u = 258.5 \, k$

$$\frac{D}{t_w} = \frac{40}{0.5} = 80.0$$

Assume $k = 5$ (no transverse stiffeners)

(Step 8: Continued on Next Sheet)

DESIGN EXAMPLE 3.5

STEP 7: NEGATIVE FLEXURAL DESIGN (CONTINUED)

Having determined the allowable compressive stress, we must now calculate the maximum compressive stress due to the factored loads. Since the maximum compressive stress is less than the allowable stress, the assumed girder section meets the strength requirements for compression.

Next we have to determine the maximum tensile stress. The allowable tensile stress is the yield stress of the steel, which is greater than the maximum tensile stress under the factored loads. Therefore, the assumed girder section also meets the strength requirements for tension.

STEP 8: SHEAR AT ABUTMENT

Having determined that the assumed sections meet flexural strength and service limit requirements, we now have to determine if the design meets the shear strength requirements.

At abutment, the factored shear at both Strength I and Strength IV load combinations are calculated, and the more critical shear is used for the design.

Not all structures, however, are candidates for overcoating. Some key factors which could affect the decision to overcoat are:

❑ The amount of rusted areas on the steel
❑ The severity of the corrosion
❑ Adhesion of the existing coating
❑ Type of paint presently used

If the corrosion is extensive or if the existing coating is such that adhesion of the new coats will be impaired (e.g., as with leafing or non-leafing aluminum pigments) then overcoating may not be possible.

8. Micaceous Iron Oxide (MIO) Coatings. MIO coatings have been called "Europe's best kept secret" [Ref. 3.56]. The success of MIO coatings on such prominent European structures as the Eiffel Tower (see Did You Know? sidebar) and the Royal Albert Bridge as well as the Sydney Harbor

Bridge in Australia have led to MIO becoming a de facto standard for bridges overseas. In the United States, however, only the Virginia Department of Transportation has used MIO coatings extensively [Ref. 3.56].

What is it then that makes MIO such a good coating system and why has it yet to catch on in the United States? With regard to the first part of the question, it is the structure of the MIO coating which makes it so successful. MIO coatings form a protective layer over steel members using opaque flakes which align themselves in a fashion similar to shingles on a roof. This arrangement provides a barrier to moisture attempting to penetrate the coating while at the same time allowing moisture trapped beneath the surface to *escape*, thus preventing potential blistering and delamination failures [Ref. 3.52]. The structure of MIO coatings can be thought of as a "release-valve" which allows trapped moisture to escape but still reduces moisture permeability [Ref. 3.56].

MIO coatings have proved themselves to be corrosion resistant, even in saltwater environments. MIO primers can also be applied over a wet, or sometimes even oily, surface. Another advantage is that MIO coatings have excellent adhesion properties, meaning that subsequent coats can be readily placed over existing ones. With all of these advantages, the question raised at the top of the section persists: why have MIO protective coating systems failed to catch on in the United States?

Proponents of MIO coatings would argue that one of the disadvantages that the system has in becoming marketable in the U.S. is that Australia is the primary source of the proven pigment [Ref. 3.56]. Since this requires importing the pigment, potential marketers and users of MIO coatings are discouraged by the price. The natural color of MIO coatings is a dark grey, which many transportation departments in the United States are hesitant to use. The color, however, can be modified with other pigments.

MIO coatings also call on maintenance personnel to change their concept of protective coating systems. Most people tend to think of paint as a barrier that keeps

> **M** IO coatings form a protective layer over steel members using opaque flakes which align themselves in a fashion similar to shingles on a roof.

DESIGN PERSPECTIVE

Is Lead Bridge Paint Hazardous?

W hen someone first thinks of lead paint it is almost reflexive to assume that it presents an environmental and health risk. But is lead *bridge* paint dangerous to the environment? A report issued by the National Cooperative Highway Research Program (NCHRP) says maybe not.

The Environmental Protection Agency defines "hazardous" based on the paint's exposure in a municipal landfill environment. In such a setting the lead paint would be exposed to acetic acid, a by-product of municipal waste. When lead is combined with acetic acid to form the extremely soluble compound lead acetate, the likelihood of lead residues exceeding the EPA limit of 5 ppm is relatively high.

However, it is not common construction practice to dump lead paint residues in a municipal landfill. Typically all abrasive paint residue is placed with other construction waste. In this environment, rather than forming lead acetate, less soluble com-

pounds such as lead oxide and lead chromate are formed. These compounds are virtually insoluble in rainwater, groundwater, or even in freshwater lakes and streams.

Based on the latter scenario detailed above, the NCHRP report suggested that lead buried in such a fashion posed little threat of leaching into the groundwater.

The other side of the safety coin involves worker safety in removing lead based paints. In this respect, lead is extremely dangerous. Lead can contaminate a worker through a variety of methods which range from simply breathing-in the lead or eating or drinking from material contaminated with lead particles.

To minimize the adverse effects of lead to workers, a variety of safety and protective equipment from helmets to respirators are required for even the most basic operations. Research is being conducted by OSHA and other organizations to develop better equipment and removal techniques in an effort to reduce the health risk faced by crews in the field [Ref. 3.57].

EXAMPLE 3.5	DESIGN OF TWO SPAN CONTINUOUS PLATE GIRDER BRIDGE—LRFD	DET	20/24

STEP 8:   Shear at Abutment (Continued)

$$1.4\sqrt{\frac{Ek}{F_y}} = 1.4\sqrt{\frac{29{,}000 \cdot 5}{50}} = 75.4$$

Since $\dfrac{D}{t_w} > 1.4\sqrt{\dfrac{E \cdot k}{F_y}}$

$$C = \frac{1.57}{\left(\dfrac{D}{t_w}\right)^2}\left(\frac{E \cdot k}{F_y}\right) \qquad \text{(Eq. 3.69c)}$$

$$C = \frac{1.57}{(80.0)^2}\left(\frac{29{,}000 \cdot 5}{50}\right) = 0.711$$

$$V_n = CV_p = C(0.58 F_y D t_w) \qquad \text{(Eq. 3.67 \& Eq. 3.68)}$$

$$V_n = 0.711 \times 0.58 \times 50 \times 40 \times 0.5$$

$$V_n = 412.4\ k$$

$$\varphi_v V_n = 1.0 \times 412.4 = 412.4\ k > V_u = 258.5\ k \qquad ✔$$

Therefore, no shear stiffeners are required at abutment when using the assumed sections.

DESIGN EXAMPLE 3.5
STEP 8: SHEAR AT ABUTMENT (CONTINUED)

We now calculate the shear strength of the assumed girder. For plate girders, only the web plate is considered to resist shear. The top and bottom flanges are completely ignored.

Most bridges do not use longitudinal stiffeners due to the high fabrication costs. Whether or not transverse stiffeners are provided depends on the shear strength requirement.

In this example, we first try to determine if transverse shear stiffeners are required by assuming $k = 5$ (no transverse shear stiffener). By using Equations 3.67 to 3.69, we calculated the factored shear strength without shear stiffeners. Since it is greater than the factored shear force at the abutment, so the assumed web plate meets the shear strength requirements, and no shear stiffeners are required at abutment.

Readers should note that although no shear stiffeners are required at the abutment, we should provide bearing stiffeners over the bearing. See Section 3.11.2, Part 7 and Figure 3.42 for details.

---

moisture out. MIO coatings, however, have a "designed permeability" which allows moisture to penetrate. This moisture, though, is stripped of its contaminants as its enters the MIO "shingle" structure and is then released [Ref. 3.56].

The reader should not get the impression, however, that MIO coatings are completely absent from the bridge scene in the United States. Slowly, MIO is gaining acceptance through its use in such structures as the Astoria Bridge crossing the Columbia River in Oregon, where a coating system containing MIO was used [Ref. 3.52].

9. Conclusions. By now the reader should have a feeling as to the basic types of protective coating systems in use and the various methods of preparing the steel components on which they are applied. The issue becomes even more complicated by certain types of coatings being combined with others to form a composite system.

> **W**ith all of these advantages, the question raised at the top of the section persists: why has MIO protective coating systems failed to catch on in the United States?

DID YOU KNOW

THAT one of the more famous structures to be protected using an MIO coating system is the Eiffel Tower? First applied in 1919, the coating system utilized red lead linseed oil which was topcoated with MIO linseed oil [Ref. 3.56].

It has often been said that familiarity breeds contempt, but in the world of bridge projects it could be said that familiarity breeds another contract.

It is relatively easy for one to rush to conclusions as to which method is better than another based on the findings of one study versus another. The factors which go into formulating a final decision, however, are quite often not cut and dry. Everything from the weather conditions at the bridge site to available funds to experience and familiarity with one system goes into the process of selecting one system over another. If anything proves this point, it is the fact that, based on performance alone, lead based systems are proven winners when it comes to protecting steel superstructures. The liability of lead based systems with regard to environmental concerns, however, has doomed them to obsolescence.

It is also easy, as we see from above, to attempt to draw comparisons from Europe to the United States; but the vast geography of the United States combined with its disproportionately larger number of highway bridge structures begs for a closer analysis. What may work for a transportation department whose bridge structures cross the dry sands of Arizona may not necessarily be applicable to the pile bent supported simple span bridges crossing the brackish waters of Florida.

There is also something to be said for experience with a given system and the level of comfort associated with this experience. It has often been said that familiarity breeds contempt, but in the world of bridge projects it could be said that familiarity breeds another contract. Writing a specification for a certain type of protective coating system is no small feat and, to be sure, those involved in writing one are probably not that terribly eager to begin changing the structure of the specification all around.

If the evidence is there, however, that a new system will provide the savings its developers promise, then transportation department personnel will gravitate toward the better solution. The difficulty many protective coating systems have, with this respect, is proving something will last 15 years on an owner's bridges when a single coat of their product has yet to be applied to a single stringer. With the advent of the strong environmental regulations, though, the eyes and ears of many bridge maintenance groups have turned to this important area and they are more willing now to see and listen than any time before.

3.13.2 Containment and Disposal of Paint Waste

At the top of this discussion, we mentioned the severe impact new regulations concerning the removal, containment, and disposal of the toxic by-products has on the application of protective coating systems. So far we have touched on (to a limited degree) the process of removing paint and debris from the surface of steel members. Two questions arise, however, after the issue of removing the paint has been resolved:

❑ How do you collect the waste? (containment)
❑ Where does the waste go after its collected? (disposal)

These are very large issues which have caused the price tag associated with protecting steel superstructures to skyrocket. To put things in perspective, today transportation agencies actually examine the alternative of putting new steel in rather than just painting it.

To put things in perspective, today transportation agencies actually examine the alternative of putting new steel in rather than just painting it.

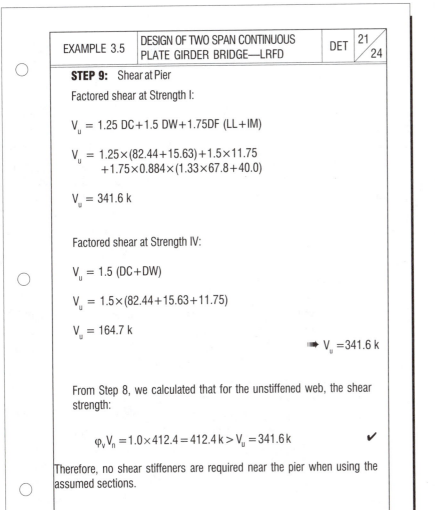

| EXAMPLE 3.5 | DESIGN OF TWO SPAN CONTINUOUS PLATE GIRDER BRIDGE—LRFD | DET | 21/24 |

STEP 9: Shear at Pier

Factored shear at Strength I:

$$V_u = 1.25\,DC + 1.5\,DW + 1.75\,DF\,(LL+IM)$$

$$V_u = 1.25 \times (82.44 + 15.63) + 1.5 \times 11.75 + 1.75 \times 0.884 \times (1.33 \times 67.8 + 40.0)$$

$$V_u = 341.6\,k$$

Factored shear at Strength IV:

$$V_u = 1.5\,(DC + DW)$$

$$V_u = 1.5 \times (82.44 + 15.63 + 11.75)$$

$$V_u = 164.7\,k$$

$$\Rightarrow V_u = 341.6\,k$$

From Step 8, we calculated that for the unstiffened web, the shear strength:

$$\varphi_v V_n = 1.0 \times 412.4 = 412.4\,k > V_u = 341.6\,k \qquad ✔$$

Therefore, no shear stiffeners are required near the pier when using the assumed sections.

DESIGN EXAMPLE 3.5
STEP 9:   SHEAR AT PIER

The web plate used over the pier is identical to that used at the abutment, so they should have the same shear strength if no shear stiffeners are used.

At the pier, the factored shear force under both Strength I and Strength IV load combinations are calculated, and the more critical shear is used for the design. In most cases, Strength I controls the design, unless the bridge has very high dead load to live load ratio.

As with live load moments, the live load shear is composed with design truck load and design lane load. The live load impact should only be applied to the truck load, not the lane load portion of the live load. Live load distribution factor (obtained in Step 2) should also be applied to the live load.

Since the factored shear force is less than the factored shear strength of the web, the assumed section meets the shear strength requirements at the pier, and no intermediate (shear) stiffeners are required.

The following discussion provides a background on how these regulations originated and the ramifications they have on the safety of the public: both in terms of the hazardous waste and the protection of bridge superstructures.

1. **Background and History.** When the postwar boom gave birth to the U.S. Interstate, environmental concerns were, to say the least, not on the forefront of conversations taking place in transportation departments across the United States. As we discussed back in Section 1.2, thousands of miles of highway and thousands of highway bridges began to spring up on drafting tables and into the field almost overnight. While it may be presumptuous to say that the designers of that era gave little or no attention to the removal and disposal of the lead based coating systems that were being applied to these new structures; it is probably pretty much true. Engineers in those days had a great deal of latitude as to the decisions that they made. Even if someone did question their

While it may be presumptuous to say that the designers of that era gave little or no attention to the removal and disposal of the lead based coating systems ... it is probably pretty much true.

authority (and that was rarely done) the professional integrity of the engineer was usually enough to sway opinion.

All of that changed substantially by the mid 1960's and the early 1970's. During these years the environmental movement gained momentum and suddenly engineers found themselves adapting to a very new world. This is not to say that transportation departments themselves did not take the initiative in formulating programs to deal with environmental concerns. As early as the 1960's, states like Louisiana and California had begun to formulate programs which addressed the problems associated with lead and chromate based paints. As the hazards of lead paint became more fully understood, state agencies sought to tackle the most glaring problem areas. Specifically, the states sought to address the entry of lead particles into:

❏ Streams
❏ Adjacent lands
❏ Groundwater supplies

This concern led to some of the initial methods of containment (i.e., preventing toxic by-products from leaving the project site). Many of these early efforts met with limited success. It was soon found, however, that containment was only one part of the puzzle. For even if all of the contaminated debris was collected (and it wasn't) the question of what to do with it posed almost as much difficulty.

Even with new regulations being put into place, by the early 1980's, only a few transportation agencies were aggressively pursuing the issue of containment and disposal [Ref. 3.57]. By the mid-1980's, however, with enforcement of these regulations becoming more severe, transportation departments began to actively study the problem in an effort to develop techniques and guidelines that would help them conform with the new laws while at the same time perform their function of ensuring that the highway bridges they managed were adequately protected.

With regard to the last statement, it is easy for one to empathize with the position many transportation department engineers found themselves in. The new regulations, while designed to protect the public, were enacted without any real concern with how the maintenance departments would protect their structures. Engineers in state transportation departments throughout the United States were forced to develop the methods of removal, containment, and disposal on-the-fly so to speak.

Some states, such as Pennsylvania, went so far as to hire an independent research contractor to investigate the problem in an effort simply to develop guidelines with which to perform the work within the framework of the environmental regulations [Ref. 3.57]. By the late 1980's manufacturers were also investing research and development dollars into the development of new systems to aid in the containment, recycling, disposal, and processing of the waste.

The new regulations, while designed to protect the public, were enacted without any real concern with how the maintenance departments would protect their structures.

2. Containment Devices. A containment device is required during paint removal operations to confine and collect waste and debris caused by surface preparations. The containment device itself is either an

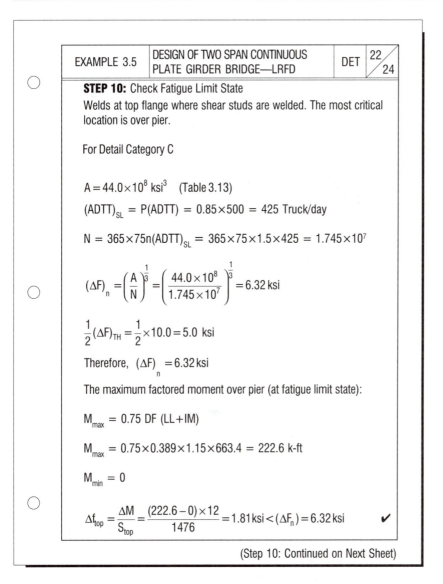

| EXAMPLE 3.5 | DESIGN OF TWO SPAN CONTINUOUS PLATE GIRDER BRIDGE—LRFD | DET | $\frac{22}{24}$ |

STEP 10: Check Fatigue Limit State

Welds at top flange where shear studs are welded. The most critical location is over pier.

For Detail Category C

$A = 44.0 \times 10^8 \text{ ksi}^3$ (Table 3.13)

$(ADTT)_{SL} = P(ADTT) = 0.85 \times 500 = 425 \text{ Truck/day}$

$N = 365 \times 75n(ADTT)_{SL} = 365 \times 75 \times 1.5 \times 425 = 1.745 \times 10^7$

$$(\Delta F)_n = \left(\frac{A}{N}\right)^{\frac{1}{3}} = \left(\frac{44.0 \times 10^8}{1.745 \times 10^7}\right)^{\frac{1}{3}} = 6.32 \text{ ksi}$$

$$\frac{1}{2}(\Delta F)_{TH} = \frac{1}{2} \times 10.0 = 5.0 \text{ ksi}$$

Therefore, $(\Delta F)_n = 6.32 \text{ ksi}$

The maximum factored moment over pier (at fatigue limit state):

$M_{max} = 0.75 \text{ DF (LL+IM)}$

$M_{max} = 0.75 \times 0.389 \times 1.15 \times 663.4 = 222.6 \text{ k-ft}$

$M_{min} = 0$

$$\Delta f_{top} = \frac{\Delta M}{S_{top}} = \frac{(222.6 - 0) \times 12}{1476} = 1.81 \text{ ksi} < (\Delta F_n) = 6.32 \text{ ksi} \quad ✔$$

(Step 10: Continued on Next Sheet)

DESIGN EXAMPLE 3.5
STEP 10: CHECK FATIGUE LIMIT STATE

Now that the design moments and shears have been computed, we are ready to check if the design meets Fatigue Limit State requirement. Since we do not use cover plates, we only need to check the welds at shear studs and welds at intermediate stiffeners (used for diaphragms).

We first check the weld at shear studs over the pier where the tensile stress in the top flange is the maximum. The connection detail is classified as category C. From Table 3.13, we can obtain the Detail Category Constant A, and the Constant-Amplitude Fatigue Thresholds. The number of cycles the structure is subjected to the truck load (N) is obtained from Equation 3.74. Using Equation 3.89, we can determine the allowable fatigue stress, which is 6.32 ksi.

Next we must determine the stress range of the top flange over the pier. Note that for Fatigue Limit State, the live load factor is 0.75, the live load impact is 0.15, and a single lane should be used to calculate live load distribution factor. (See Step 2). Since the stress range is less than the allowable fatigue stress, the shear stud welds will not cause fatigue problem.

enclosure or barrier which is placed under or attached onto the bridge structure proper. The type of containment device will vary depending on a variety of factors which could include:

❏ Method of surface preparation
❏ Extent of assembly required
❏ Cost

While there are no steadfast rules or specifications governing the type of containment device to be used in all instances, the following discussion outlines some of the more basic methods of containing paint waste and debris [Ref. 3.57].

■ **Free-Hanging Enclosures.** A free-hanging enclosure is typically a tarp or plastic sheet supported on only two corners. An example of such

> The containment device itself is either an enclosure or barrier which is placed under or attached onto the bridge structure proper.

a containment device would be a tarp pinned at the top to the concrete fascia of a bridge deck and left to hang down to the underpass roadway surface.

An obvious difficulty with such an approach is the "sailing" of the tarp, which can be caused by high winds. If the blowing is severe enough, it is possible that the enclosure will be pulled from its supports and fall to the underpass below. This sail effect can present a danger, not only to the crews working on the bridge, but also to underpass traffic underneath or adjacent to the structure. Because of this danger, free-hanging enclosures on particularly high bridges is not recommended.

One solution to the wind problems associated with hanging tarps is to use a sheet which allows a certain amount of air to pass through the sheet. This screen, however, must still be of sufficient strength to perform its function.

Naturally, tarps and plastic sheets are attractive choices to contractors because they are relatively inexpensive. A deficiency with this type of containment device is that they merely deflect abrasive debris rather than collect and support the load itself. Typically the debris which is deflected off of the tarps falls to collection points at the base of the structure.

> **T**his sail effect can present a danger, not only to the crews working on the bridge, but also to underpass traffic underneath or adjacent to the structure.

■ **Complete Structure Enclosures.** A more extreme alternative to the free-hanging enclosure is to completely enclose the structure. Such an enclosure can be fashioned with a steel or wood framework, cable structures, or prefabricated panels. While such a method definitely produces a secure environment within which debris can be contained and eventually disposed; it is not without potential difficulties.

One difficulty is visibility within the enclosures. The bridge is surrounded by a solid structure while at the same time blasting or cleaning operations will be generating large quantities of dust and debris. Proper lighting and protective equipment for the crews is an absolute necessity when a complete structure enclosure is used. Circulation of air within the enclosure must also be maintained. Otherwise dust could leak from the enclosure.

From a safety standpoint, the enclosure itself is a structure which must be properly designed to withstand a variety of loads ranging from the workers within the enclosure to wind loads on the outside of it.

> **W**hile such a method definitely produces a secure environment ... it is not without potential difficulties.

Inside the structure there must be appropriate facilities to allow workers to get at the bridge itself. In many instances these platforms will need to be elevated to reach superstructure elements so that appropriate safety concerns must also be addressed here.

One advantage of using a complete structure enclosure is the potential for reusing the enclosure components on subsequent bridge maintenance projects. This is especially beneficial on large structures where the enclosure unit can be broken down after completion of work at one point on the bridge and reassembled at the next point of work.

An obvious drawback to complete structure enclosures are the associated costs incurred in acquiring the materials as well as designing and then assembling the enclosure.

■ **Negative Pressure Containment.** As mentioned above, a danger with enclosing a structure is the potential risk of dust particles escaping the

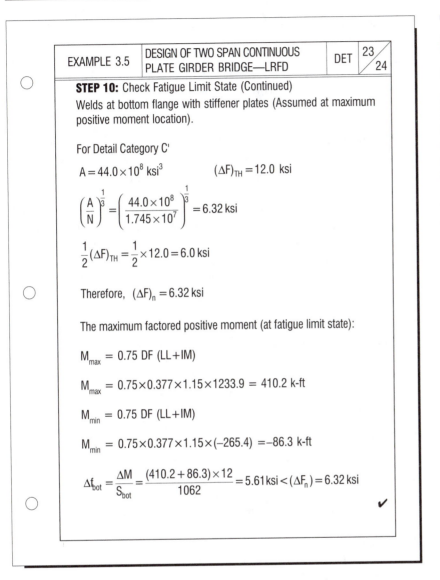

| EXAMPLE 3.5 | DESIGN OF TWO SPAN CONTINUOUS PLATE GIRDER BRIDGE—LRFD | DET | 23/24 |

STEP 10: Check Fatigue Limit State (Continued)

Welds at bottom flange with stiffener plates (Assumed at maximum positive moment location).

For Detail Category C'

$$A = 44.0 \times 10^8 \text{ ksi}^3 \qquad (\Delta F)_{TH} = 12.0 \text{ ksi}$$

$$\left(\frac{A}{N}\right)^{\frac{1}{3}} = \left(\frac{44.0 \times 10^8}{1.745 \times 10^7}\right)^{\frac{1}{3}} = 6.32 \text{ ksi}$$

$$\frac{1}{2}(\Delta F)_{TH} = \frac{1}{2} \times 12.0 = 6.0 \text{ ksi}$$

Therefore, $(\Delta F)_n = 6.32$ ksi

The maximum factored positive moment (at fatigue limit state):

$$M_{max} = 0.75 \text{ DF (LL+IM)}$$

$$M_{max} = 0.75 \times 0.377 \times 1.15 \times 1233.9 = 410.2 \text{ k-ft}$$

$$M_{min} = 0.75 \text{ DF (LL+IM)}$$

$$M_{min} = 0.75 \times 0.377 \times 1.15 \times (-265.4) = -86.3 \text{ k-ft}$$

$$\Delta f_{bot} = \frac{\Delta M}{S_{bot}} = \frac{(410.2 + 86.3) \times 12}{1062} = 5.61 \text{ ksi} < (\Delta F_n) = 6.32 \text{ ksi}$$

✔

DESIGN EXAMPLE 3.5

STEP 10: CHECK FATIGUE LIMIT STATE (CONTINUED)

The next step is to check the fatigue requirement for the welds between the bottom flange and the intermediate web stiffeners. In this design example, we do not need and transverse shear stiffeners, but we must provide stiffeners for the diaphragms.

To simplify the calculation, we assume the diaphragm connection plates are located at the maximum positive bending location (0.4 L from the abutment). Of course, in the real design, we should try to avoid placing transverse stiffeners at the maximum bending location.

The connection detail is classified as category C'. From Table 3.13, we can obtain the Detail Category Constant A, and the Constant-Amplitude Fatigue Thresholds. The number of truck loading cycles is calculated in the previous sheet. Using Equation 3.89, we can determine the allowable fatigue stress, which is 6.32 ksi.

Next we must determine the maximum stress range of the bottom flange. The minimum bending moment at 0.4L is given here. It can be obtained from bridge design software, or from influence lines. Since the maximum stress range is less than the allowable fatigue stress, the weld connection will not cause fatigue problem within the design life of 75 years.

---

enclosure. One method of preventing this is to create negative pressure by drawing air from outside the enclosure into the enclosure. The air is passed along the surface being worked on and then passed out of the enclosure through a filter.

Since techniques such as blasting are used, the pressure used to move the air through the enclosure must be capable of overcoming that of the surface preparation method. In essence this approach controls the passage of particles into a known path.

Negative pressure containment demands specialized equipment to blow air into the enclosure, filter the debris, and vacuum the air out of the enclosure. The enclosure also needs to be designed to accommodate air intakes and escape ducts. While theoretically the system should eliminate particles from escaping the enclosure, the reality shows that maintaining constant negative pressure is difficult to achieve. Even with negative

Negative pressure containment demands specialized equipment to blow air into the enclosure, filter the debris, and vacuum the air out of the enclosure.

pressure systems in place, workers both inside and outside of enclosures are exposed to extreme health risks from inhaling contaminated air. Negative pressure systems hold a great deal of promise in containing lead debris and is becoming the standard practice in lead paint removal operation. However, work still needs to be done in perfecting their operation.

■ **Power Tool Debris Containment.** While the debris generated by power tools is more easily contained (when compared to blasting methods, for example), the waste still has the same volume of lead paint as that generated by other methods. Indeed, the lead is more concentrated when power tools are used and should thus be carefully controlled to avoid entry into environmentally sensitive areas. Vacuums provide an efficient way of containing debris generated by power tool cleaning methods.

As mentioned in Section 3.13.1, Part 6, power tools should not be expected to remove material down to the bare steel surface. They are, however, capable of removing the layer of paint which contains the lead contaminants. Therefore, one method that has been employed is the use of power tools in conjunction with blasting. This so called *two-step cleaning* process takes advantage of the localized containment possible with hand tools while at the same time providing a thorough surface preparation. Power tools are used in conjunction with attached vacuums to contain all of the hazardous lead waste. Then, an open abrasive method employs partial containment, essentially to control the escape of dust.

■ **Collecting Fallen Abrasives and Debris.** Even with attached vacuum devices, like those described above, debris will invariably fall to the ground. When blasting methods are utilized, abrasives will be distributed in the work site and need to be channeled and eventually collected. Methods ranging from the primitive (sweeping and shoveling) to the more sophisticated (vacuuming and mechanical conveyors) can be used to contain and collect this waste.

Particularly when dealing with abrasives, a regular collection plan (preferably once per day) should be employed to remove abrasives and wastes. When using suspended tarps or screens to collect abrasives, it is important that the abrasives not be allowed to accumulate in excessive amounts, which could lead to the containment system failing. Once collected, the waste is stored in drums or dumpsters. A hazardous waste should be appropriately identified on the container.

Another method of containing debris is to channel it through a tube like conduit and directly into disposal containers located below. The California Department of Transportation encloses the scaffolding, where workers blast a steel superstructure, with burlap funnels which channel debris to a cylindrical snorkel-like containment which is suspended from the enclosure to the ground [Ref. 3.57].

Containing fallen abrasives and debris for structures which cross bodies of water is even more complicated. One solution often employed is to collect debris on barges located under the structure which can then be used to haul the debris away.

> This so-called *two-step cleaning* process takes advantage of the localized containment possible with hand tools while at the same time providing a thorough surface preparation.

EXAMPLE 3.5	DESIGN OF TWO SPAN CONTINUOUS PLATE GIRDER BRIDGE—LRFD	DET	24/24

STEP 11: Shear Connectors

Follow Design Example 3.3 for shear connector design. Since we have provided detailed calculations in Example 3.3, we will not repeat it here. Note that shear studs in negative bending region should be designed separately.

Once we finish the design of an interior girder, the next step is to design an exterior girder.

As we stated earlier, the dead loads and live load distribution factors between interior girders and exterior girders are different. We should never design an exterior girder that is weaker than an interior girder. The reason is that in the future, the bridge might be widened. So it should be at least as strong as interior girders.

If filed splices are provided, they should be designed as well. Please refer to Section 3.12.8 for details.

Substructure is usually designed after the superstructure design is completed (or at least a preliminary design is completed).

DESIGN EXAMPLE 3.5

STEP 11: SHEAR CONNECTORS

We must now compute the number of shear studs for the composite sections. Since we have provided detailed calculations in Design Example 3.3, we will not repeat it here.

Since the assumed girder sections have been checked for Strength Limit States, Service Limit States, and Fatigue Limit State, we now can conclude that the girder meets all AASHTO LRFD requirements. Of course, if it were a real design, we may want to refine the sections and to produce a more economical design. As I mentioned earlier, bridge design is a trial and error process, with an objective of producing a safe, economical, and durable structure.

3. **Recycling Abrasives.** One ecologically sound method of minimizing the waste resulting from surface preparation operations is to recycle abrasives used in blasting methods. Recycling abrasives is accomplished through a two step process where the abrasives are:

❏ Collected and then
❏ Reclaimed to separate out the reusable abrasive

The collection of abrasives for recycling is somewhat more complicated than for simple disposal since the abrasive must be separated from dirt and debris. The abrasive can either be collected at the nozzle or after blasting.

Once collected, the abrasives are placed into a reclaimer where the reusable abrasive is separated out. Also separated out is any dust, paint, or other debris which may have made its way into the collected abrasives.

> **O**ne ecologically sound method of minimizing the waste resulting from surface preparation operations is to recycle abrasives used in blasting methods.

There are three principal methods used for separating out the reusable abrasives from the associated paint, dust, and debris. The main systems currently being used are:

- Air-wash separators
- Cyclone separators
- Rotary vibratory separators

These systems, while providing adequate results, by no means produce a completely pure abrasive upon separation. The recycled abrasive can often suffer from being too "dusty" with the same dust being recycled through the system on several occasions [Ref. 3.57]. This dust can lead to various visibility and health problems for the cleaning work crews.

4. Disposal Methods. Disposal of paint and abrasive debris from a project site used to be a relatively easy affair. Spent abrasive was either hauled away to landfills or deposited in rivers [Ref. 3.57]. Obviously, given the current tight environmental regulation and our present knowledge concerning the adverse effects of lead based coating systems, such an approach is no longer feasible.

Disposal of paint wastes can be thought of as the third leg of a cost triangle associated with maintaining steel superstructures. One leg of the triangle is the cost of surface preparation, the other containment and collection of wastes at the project. The third and final link is disposal of the waste. When the waste to be disposed of is designated as hazardous, the cost will dramatically increase.

In 1990, the United States EPA enacted regulations which forbade the land disposal of hazardous waste. This means that all hazardous wastes must be first treated or detoxified. Once treated properly, the waste is no longer considered hazardous and may then be disposed of. This regulation is also known as the *Land Ban*.

The process of treating the hazardous waste can be conducted on one of two levels. The hazardous waste can either be:

- Separated out from the nonhazardous waste or
- Converted to a nonhazardous form

The process of disposing of hazardous waste is further complicated (and made more expensive) by regulations which concern the handling, packaging, storing, transporting, and testing of the waste. Treatment of the waste can be conducted on or off site by physical or chemical methods; with each having its particular impacts on the overall cost of the process.

The following discussion concerns the various methods for both physically and chemically treating wastes. In performing this treatment, the general goal is to get the leachable lead content below the EPA maximum allowable of 5 ppm. For more on the EPA requirements and the hazards associated with lead bridge paint, the reader is referred to the accompanying *Design Perspective*.

> In 1990, the United States EPA enacted regulations which forbade the land disposal of hazardous waste. This means that all hazardous wastes must be first treated or detoxified.

■ **Physical Methods.** As the name implies, physical methods entail physically separating out the hazardous component of the generated waste. The principal methods for separating out the hazardous components are:

❑ Screening
❑ Crushing or grinding
❑ Air wash
❑ Flotation
❑ Magnetism

The specific physical method used for separating out hazardous components is generally dependent on the nature of the abrasive used during surface preparation. Metallic abrasives lend themselves well to air-wash filtration while nonmetallic abrasives may not react well to this process [Ref. 3.57].

> The specific physical method used for separating out hazardous components is generally dependent on the nature of the abrasive used during surface preparation.

■ **Chemical Methods.** Chemical processing of the debris is designed to eliminate the hazardous risk of paint wastes through one of two principal methods which are to either:

❑ Vaporize the lead in the debris
❑ Make the lead particles insoluble

The former could involve the use of high-temperature incineration while the latter the addition of portland cement to the debris. In some instances, the waste is even treated on site (although such an alternative is subject to strict requirements by EPA).

5. **Conclusions.** In the last two sections, we have seen the magnitude of the problems facing the application and subsequent maintenance of protective coating systems in highway bridges. The apparent simplicity of simply "slapping a couple coats of paint" on a steel superstructure certainly belies the impact removing, containing, and disposing lead based systems has had on today's transportation agencies.

Both the alacrity and severity with which new regulations have hit maintenance departments has created a situation where environmental concerns have come face to face with other safety issues. To the layperson, an environmental regulation usually implies that the public is, by default, being protected. It is difficult, however, to draw a straight analogy between protecting wetlands and painting bridges.

Maintenance engineers are faced with sets of regulations which are often contradictory in the goals they seek to achieve. EPA wants all lead by-products to be contained so that they do not contaminate the environment by, for example, seeping into groundwater. However, in so containing lead dust and other such hazardous waste, workers are more at risk because they are exposed to the lead-laden dust within the confines of an enclosure structure; a situation which OSHA is acutely aware of.

> Maintenance engineers are faced with sets of regulations which are often contradictory in the goals they seek to achieve.

If this were not enough to contend with, there are the associated costs which come with attempting to meet all of these regulations. Transportation departments are already limited in the amount of funds

> Like any answer to a complex problem, however, a successful solution will be achieved through a combination of experience and perseverance.

they can spend. If the monetary resources are not available then, by default, certain bridges will go unpainted. If the steel is allowed to deteriorate to the point where significant loss of section occurs, then the traveling public is put at risk.

In summary, engineers in maintenance departments are put in the middle of three conflicting needs in that they are required by law to satisfy:

- ❏ Environmental safety
- ❏ Worker safety
- ❏ The safety of traffic over a structure

DESIGN PERSPECTIVE

Weathering Steel Environments: This One's Just Right.

If Goldilocks were employed by a transportation department, she might find herself having to decide if weathering steel should be used at a particular site.

"This one's too dry," she may say. If their are insufficient wet-dry cycles, weathering steel may not adequately create the protective oxide coating. Another danger is if the steel will be continually exposed to spray from contaminants such as industrial fumes or deicing agents [Ref. 3.58].

Moving on to the next site Goldilocks may be overheard muttering, "... and this one's too wet." Excessive moisture on the surface of weathering steel can cause extreme corrosion. When moisture clings to the weathering steel surface for extended periods of time, the steel will also not properly develop the protective oxide coating (see Section 3.13.3, Part 2).

Finally, Goldilocks comes upon the ideal site for weathering steel, "This one's just right!" she exclaims. Climates which have regular wet/dry cycles and are not prone to the harsh effects of marine environments can prove adequate in allowing the weathering steel to develop its protective coating.

Topography at the bridge site is another factor which can impact how weathering steel performs. If one side of the bridge is shaded and the other exposed to sunlight, then the protective coating may not develop uniformly. Even the presence of weeds can impede air circulation and hinder the performance of the steel [Ref. 3.58].

Another obvious impact on the performance of weathering steel is the presence of deck joints and their associated leaking if not properly sealed. Opponents of weathering steel would note this and other concerns as reasons not to use the material, while proponents would counter that problems like deicing agents and joint leakage have an adverse impact on any material.

Like any material, however, weathering steel is a viable alternative provided it is implemented with care and not thought of as a panacea to the protective coating issue.

Trying to meet these goals is a problem as difficult as any continuous beam analysis or foundation design, and the resources being applied prove it.

In the preceding text we have touched on some of the major methods used to remove, contain, and dispose of lead waste. These are by no means the only solutions and methods available. Due to the severity of the problem, a great deal of research and development has been, and is being, conducted to help on issues as diverse as ventilating enclosure structures to chemically treating waste.

While both public and private institutions are at work on these problems, the principal responsibility (at least in the United States) rests with the owner of the structures involved. The so-called cradle-to-grave policy mandates that it is the transportation department which is ultimately responsible for proper disposal of all waste associated with the painting of a structure [Ref. 3.57]. While the burden may be on the agency, the problem is too big for any one organization to solve. Like any answer to a complex problem, however, a successful solution will be achieved through a combination of experience and perseverance.

3.13.3 Weathering Steel

Having just discussed the plethora of problems associated with protective coating systems, we now turn our attention to a steel designated as ASTM A588 and A709: weathering steel. On the surface, weathering steel would appear to be the answer to the many problems and the costs associated with conventional protective coating systems. The reality, which we will see, is not as good as it may first seem but not as bad as some would paint it. The following is a discussion of the basic properties of weathering steel, its benefits, and associated difficulties.

1. **Background and History.** Weathering steel possesses the unique material property of providing a protective coating to the steel by rusting. As weathering steel oxidizes, it forms a protective coating which actually inhibits continuous rusting. The benefits of such a material in bridge design are obvious. Weathering steel would not have to be painted and thereby would require little or no maintenance to its steel components. The nascent use of weathering steel in bridge design was extremely positive. As experience with the material grew, however, problems were soon discovered.

   Weathering steel was originally developed for use in the fabrication of unpainted coal cars [Ref. 3.58]. Its introduction into the world of highway bridges did not occur until the 1960's. The promise which weathering steel held and the initial positive feedback led to its quick incorporation into the standards of many highway transportation departments.

   One such example is the Michigan Department of Transportation. The state's first weathering steel bridge was built in Detroit in 1963. The initial positive feedback on the steel's performance led to weathering steel being adopted throughout the state in 1969. By the 1970's over 600 highway bridges were constructed using weathering steel in the state of Michigan [Ref. 3.59]. A 1987 survey indicated that there were approximately 2,300 weathering steel structures in use on state highway systems alone. Such positive reaction seemed to indicate that weathering steel was the wave of the future. Investigations into the performance of these structures, however, began to raise a cloud over the use of this promising material.

2. **Material Properties of Weathering Steel.** Weathering steel is a carbon steel base alloyed with roughly 2 percent of copper, nickel, chromium, and silicon coming in yield strength of 50 to 100 ksi. Highway bridge structure typically makes use of ASTM A588 and A709. A new quenched and tempered weathering steel known as ASTM A852 is also available and has a yield strength of 70 ksi [Ref. 3.60]. For the purposes of this discussion we will refer to weathering steel as ASTM A588.

   Weathering steel requires moisture and airborne contaminants to develop the hard coating which protects the steel. Rainwater washes over the structure in several wet/dry cycles allowing the protective coating to develop over the steel [Ref. 3.58]. While moisture is essential to form the protective coating, continuous moisture can adversely affect the

> Like any answer to a complex problem, however, a successful solution will be achieved through a combination of experience and perseverance.

> Weathering steel was originally developed for use in the fabrication of unpainted coal cars.

performance of weathering steel. Some sources of continuous moisture include:

- ❏ Nightly condensation
- ❏ Cooling from the deck causing moisture to run down web
- ❏ Capillary moisture
- ❏ Absorption by corrosion products
- ❏ Leaking joints
- ❏ Spray from traffic

A high relative humidity, nightly fog, and moisture which evaporates from nearby bodies of water will also spur the development of moisture over the surface [Ref. 3.60]. As we will see, these environmental conditions play an important role concerning how weathering steel will perform.

> As we will see, these environmental conditions play an important role concerning how weathering steel will perform.

3. **Environmental Considerations.** From the above, it becomes readily visible that the environment in which weathering steel is placed plays an important role in how the material will perform (see also the accompanying *Design Perspective*). Environments which are too dry do not have the necessary wet/dry cycles required to create the protective oxide coating or *patina*. Likewise, environments which are too wet or susceptible to continuous moisture (e.g., through excessive humidity) will also serve to hinder the development of a sound patina.

What does all of this mean? First and foremost, it means that weathering steel must be used in an environment which is conducive to its inherit material properties and their benefits. An example where this has been done successfully is in the state of Maine. Engineers at the state transportation department have undertaken an aggressive implementation of weathering steel structures. This use of weathering steel, however, is not made without a certain measure of prudence. Outlying coastal areas, which are susceptible to saltwater spray, are intentionally avoided, while inland lakes, streams, and waterways are targeted sites [Ref. 3.61].

On the other side of the coin, the state of Michigan has seen some of the worst deterioration associated with weathering steel. A combination of constant contamination from deicing salts and extended exposure to moisture has led to numerous structures undergoing excessive corrosion [Ref. 3.58]. The problems were so severe that in 1979 a partial moratorium was issued which was then followed by a complete ban on the use of weathering steel in 1980 [Ref. 3.59].

4. **Maintenance of Weathering Steel.** With two extremes, such as those detailed above, the question arises "Is weathering steel a viable alternative to protective coatings or not?" The qualified answer is yes, provided that the environmental situation is conducive and the steel is *properly maintained*.

The latter item may come as a surprise to the novice bridge designer. After all, the main advantage of weathering steel would appear to be its ability to be "left alone" without having to be repeatedly painted. No engineering structure, be it a highway bridge or sewer system, is maintenance free. Many of the problems associated with weathering steel stem from its implementation in areas where it simply cannot perform well. When weathering steel is placed in the right environmental setting, it will perform well but will still require limited maintenance.

In reference to the state of Maine example detailed above, the state has a maintenance program where each weathering steel structure receives an annual washing to remove salt-laden sand from the decks. This washing also serves to flush out curbs, gutters, and drains. The underside of the structure also receives a high pressure wash using a water sprayer which cleans the bearings and interior girders. In the process of washing a bridge, maintenance personnel "kill two birds with one stone" by performing a cursory inspection of the structure to detect any possible cracking which could allow salts to penetrate into the weathering steel [Ref. 3.61].

Anyone who has seen a weathering steel structure will no doubt notice the rather unattractive streaks of rust which often stain the light grey surface of the concrete substructure. These rust blemishes often spoil the look of what are otherwise striking bridge structures. Staining of the substructure, however, can be prevented by temporarily wrapping piers and abutments throughout construction with heavy gauge polyethylene sheeting [Refs. 3.60 and 3.58]. In addition to this protective measure, liquid silicone or epoxy based coatings can be applied to the substructure in order to protect them.

If joints are present, however, they will eventually leak and this will create the telltale streaking blemishes at the support locations. Another potential source of these rust streaks is dripping from girders which is somehow channeled to the piers and abutments. In such situations, the only recourse a maintenance department will have will be to either leave the streaks or attempt to clean the substructure elements with blast cleaning or chemical stain removers [Ref. 3.60].

5. **Inspection of Weathering Steel.** When a steel bridge which has been painted undergoes inspection, the assigned personnel look for rusting to detect whether or not the protective coating system has failed. How does someone inspect a structure, however, which, by design, is covered with rust to protect itself? The answer is: very closely.

Close inspection is required in order to detect whether the protective oxide coating has fully developed over the steel surface. During regular biennial inspections, the weathering steel is inspected to check the color and texture of the oxide film. This inspection is undertaken using a hammer and wire brush to ascertain whether the rust on the surface of the steel adheres to the underlying steel or has become *debonded*. Debonding is evidenced by flaking of the rust or peeling off in laminar sheets when either banged with a hammer or wire brushed [Ref. 3.60].

If the protective oxide coating has ceased to function properly, then the size and depths of any pitting must be logged in an effort to determine the severity of the deterioration as well as possible causes for the steel corrosion.

With regard to the latter item, it is also important for the inspectors to note any and all drainage problems and other site conditions which could be potential causes for corrosion of the steel. Malfunctioning of joints, vegetation growth around end supports, and the presence of excessive dust or other materials on the surface of the steel are just a few of the conditions which can propagate deterioration in weathering steel.

Many of the problems associated with weathering steel stem from its implementation in areas where it simply cannot perform well.

Anyone who has seen a weathering steel structure will no doubt notice the rather unattractive streaks of rust which often stain the light grey surface of the concrete substructure.

How does someone inspect a structure ... which, by design, is covered with rust to protect itself? The answer is: very closely.

Another difficulty associated with the inspection of weathering steel structures is in the detection of fatigue cracks. When a structure is painted, the rust emitted from a crack is readily visible by contrast to the painted background. In a bridge constructed with weathering steel, however, the crack not only blends in with the rust colored background, but is also filled with newly formed rust. Due to this difficulty in visually detecting cracks, fatigue cracks in weathering steel structures are not usually detected until the member has fractured [Ref. 3.60]. Therefore, fatigue crack detection tools are usually used for inspections. Dye penetrant is normally used for visual inspections. Magnetic field, ultrasonic test, or X-ray may be used to detect cracks.

6. Rehabilitation of Weathering Steel. When a weathering steel structure begins to shows signs of wear, like those detailed in Part 5 above, then some form of rehabilitation must be undertaken to preserve the integrity of the steel superstructure. The most basic method which can be employed is to paint the steel. This involves many of the headaches discussed in Section 3.13.2 as well as some additional concerns. The surface of weathering steel is, by nature, extremely rough. Therefore, the protective coating system to be used must be able to withstand excessive dry film thickness variations. Another adverse effect of weathering steel's rough surface is the collection of debris and contaminants within the pitted surface itself.

This can lead to difficulties when paint crews attempt to meet transportation department specifications calling for near white blast cleaned surface quality [Ref. 3.60]. Because it is difficult, if not impossible, to achieve such a condition, it may be desirable to have any pertinent specifications revised when the underlying steel is A588 or comparable.

A form of preventive maintenance is to paint the ends of girders 5 to 10 ft (1.5 to 3.0 m) from each side of a joint [Ref. 3.58]. An inorganic zinc coating can be used with a pigment that matches the color of the weathering steel. If a persistent drainage problem causes water to be deposited on the steel, the incorporation of details to carry water away from the steel should be investigated.

7. Conclusions. Whenever a material (or any other product for that matter) holds out the promise of being a cure all solution, it is liable to undergo harsh criticism if it does not perform as expected. Weathering steel can definitely fall into this category. The examples detailed above concerning the states of Maine and Michigan serve to bear this out. The experiences of these two transportation departments with weathering steel also serve to illustrate the long-term nature of the problems associated with bridge engineering in general.

The initial feedback which the Michigan DOT had on the performance of weathering steel was generally positive; leading to its widespread use in that state. It was not until several years later that the problems mentioned earlier began to surface. Because bridge engineers are designing structures intended to last decades in a harsh environment, no amount of

> **D**ue to this difficulty in visually detecting cracks, fatigue cracks in weathering steel structures are not usually detected until the member has fractured.

laboratory investigation or analysis can adequately predict how a certain material, or even design, will stand up to any *given bridge site.*

There is an expression which says "the scout catches all the arrows," and in this instance, by being on the cutting edge of a new technology, Michigan was catching its share of arrows. Once the idea of a panacea is stripped away from weathering steel, however, it can be viewed as just another material which, when properly implemented, can be quite useful in the building of bridges. The experience of Maine would seem to bear this out and it is not the only example. The New York State Thruway Authority opted for using weathering steel for the structure replacing the collapsed Schoharie Creek Bridge. The New Jersey Turnpike is also undergoing an aggressive implementation of weathering steel structures [Ref. 3.58]. The percentage of weathering steel used in the United States increased significantly since early 1990's. By early 2000's, more than half of the steel bridges built in the United States have used weathering steel.

Given the success of many weathering steel structures, it would be wrong to dismiss the material as unusable. On the other hand it must still be recognized that weathering steel structures will still require their own unique type of maintenance to ensure their longevity (see Part 4 above). Like so many other details on a bridge structure, weathering steel will benefit from the experience gained by those in the field and their efforts to improve upon what is already in use. Research and development into specialized coating systems for weathering steel is just one area where, over time, the benefits of weathering steel can be further enhanced and thus make it more accepted in the industry.

3.13.4 Galvanizing

Another method of protecting steel superstructures is by galvanizing the steel components. While galvanizing is a popular method for protecting metal in many diverse applications, its use in highway bridges and other civil engineering projects has been somewhat limited. Probably the most well known application of galvanizing in bridge design is the suspension cables of the Brooklyn Bridge (see accompanying Did You Know? sidebar [Ref. 3.62]). To be sure, the Brooklyn Bridge is a notable example, but in today's design environment, galvanizing can be more readily discovered in bridge railings than in primary members.

Like any protective method galvanizing is not without its shortcomings. Recently, the impact of new environmental regulations has caused some engineers to revisit this method of protecting steel elements. The following discussion presents an overview of the basic principles behind galvanizing, its benefits, and inherit limitations.

1. Overview. Galvanizing steel is a process whereby a protective coating is applied by immersing the steel member in a bath of molten zinc [Ref. 3.62]. This process is also known as hot dipping. The coating provides a barrier against oxygen, inhibiting its contact with the base metal, while at the same time offering cathodic protection against corrosion. For the most

DID YOU KNOW

THAT the Brooklyn Bridge, completed in the spring of 1883 has a central span of 1,595.5 ft (486.3 m), side spans which are each 930 ft (283.5 m) long, and a total length, including approaches, of 5,989 ft (1,825.4 m)? The width of the bridge is 85 ft (25.9 m). The four cables each contain 5,434 parallel, galvanized steel, oil-coated wires which are wrapped into a cylinder 15.75 in (40 cm) in diameter [Ref. 3.54].

There is an expression which says "the scout catches all the arrows," and in this instance, by being on the cutting edge of a new technology, Michigan was catching its share of arrows.

While galvanizing is a popular method for protecting metal in many diverse applications, its use in highway bridges and other civil engineering projects has been somewhat limited.

part, galvanizing is an option for new steel components only. Most steels can be readily galvanized. Weathering steel, however, with a silicon content of 0.15 percent to 0.75 percent cannot be galvanized.

2. Benefits and Drawbacks.

Similar to weathering steel, the principal benefit of galvanized steel is its ability to withstand corrosion. The performance of galvanized steel is such that little or no maintenance or painting is required. There are, however, two major drawbacks to galvanizing steel.

First, galvanizing is an expensive process with the cost of hot dipping steel generally more expensive than conventional painting. Second, and probably more serious, is the limited size of the baths within which the steel members are immersed. While galvanizing bath sizes vary, most can only handle beams up to 75 ft (22.9 m) in length. This imposes a severe limitation on many continuous bridges with large span lengths.

Due to the limited use of galvanizing in highway bridges, there are relatively few galvanizers in business with facilities that can accommodate the large sizes found in highway bridges; this has the effect of driving up the cost of galvanizing. Proponents would argue that the initial cost is offset by the savings in maintenance down the road. While such an argument makes sense, it is often a tough sell.

With regard to the problem of galvanizing large elements, one potential solution is to hot dip the ends of a beam and then metallize the center portion of the beam [Ref. 3.62]. Where galvanizing immerses the metal into a bath, metallizing applies the protective coating with a flame spray. Metallizing, however, requires a near white blast cleaning which brings with it some of the same difficulties found in protective coatings discussed earlier.

There are numerous examples of galvanized bridges in the United States which have performed well over a number of years. While most of these structures are small to medium in size, this does not diminish the performance of their coating system. It may be true that only smaller steel members can be hot dipped, it is also true that there are a lot of small to medium size bridges being built. Even though a long 500 ft (152.4 m) structure cannot be galvanized easily, this should not preclude investigating the advantages of galvanizing small bridges or even culverts.

In the United States, most of the impact of galvanizing steel can be found in the Midwest due to a larger presence of galvanizing facilities in the so-called Rust Belt [Ref. 3.62]. As mentioned above and throughout this section, tough, new environmental regulations are forcing engineers to investigate options for protecting steel that, otherwise, may have been overlooked.

> **e**ven though a long 500 ft structure cannot be galvanized easily, this should not preclude investigating the advantages of galvanizing small bridges or even culverts.

3.13.5 Conclusions

To the reader it may seem that the preceding discussion has been rather exhaustive. At the onset of the section, it was mentioned that many engineers may tend to trivialize the issue of protecting steel superstructures. If nothing else, this section should serve as an indicator of how serious and real the problems are confronting a vast majority of the bridges in the United States and throughout the world.

There is, however, no single solution to the problem. Not MIO. Not weathering steel. Not galvanizing. None of these coatings or materials can, by itself, solve the dilemma of how to protect steel superstructures. When maintaining a highway bridge structure, solutions are not discovered, they evolve. In a quote from Arthur Elliot, mentioned earlier, it was said that "it is probably safe to say that a completely satisfactory deck joint has not yet been designed" [Ref. 3.12]. One could substitute "protective coating" for "deck joint" and the quote would be just as valid.

3.14 LOAD RATING

We have already discussed how important sound inspection data is to a transportation maintenance department. One of the main functions of this data is to provide an agency with feedback as to exactly how their bridges are performing in the field. In addition to sound inspection data, however, a maintenance department requires more quantitative information regarding how an individual bridge can withstand loads. This quantitative benchmark of bridge performance is known as the load rating.

While the load rating is based upon the precepts set forth in the general AASHTO Specifications, the guidelines for developing a highway bridge load rating value are set forth in the AASHTO publication *Manual for Condition Evaluation of Bridges* [Ref. 3.63]. It is important for the reader to recognize that the calculated load rating value of a bridge is not a magical number. The load rating, like inspection data, is only a gauge of bridge performance and one component in the overall profile of a structure.

The use of load rating values varies depending on the specific bridge in question. At one end of the spectrum a load rating may be used to determine the type and scope of rehabilitation a structure receives in order to bring the bridge up to current standards. Another use of load rating values would be in the posting of a bridge, limiting the type and/or weight of vehicles passing over the structure.

The following discussion is meant only to offer the novice designer an overview of the general concepts behind the load rating of a highway bridge. For more information on the technical aspects of load rating, the reader is referred to Ref. 3.63.

3.14.1 Inventory and Operating Ratings

AASHTO differentiates between lower and upper ranges of bridge performance. The lower range of performance implies safe use of a highway bridge on a day to day basis. Naturally, since this day to day use of a bridge will imply the largest amount of traffic passing over a structure, the factor of safety built into the rating will be relatively large. This lower rating is called the *inventory rating*. This rating represents "a load level which can safely utilize an existing structure for an indefinite period of time" [Ref. 3.63].

There are instances, however, when vehicles (generally trucks) have to carry abnormally large loads over a structure. While a structure can withstand

"Highway bridges have historically had very high reliability levels even when compared to other mass produced structural systems..."

MICHEL GHOSN AND FRED MOSES
[Ref. 3.64]

When maintaining a highway bridge structure, solutions are not discovered, they evolve.

It is important for the reader to recognize that the calculated load rating value of a bridge is not a magical number.

these loads on special occasions, it is not desirable to have them repeatedly pass over a structure. This upper range of bridge load capacity uses a smaller factor of safety to maximize the capabilities of the bridge to withstand loads and is known as the *operating rating*. This rating represents "the maximum permissible live load to which the structure may be subjected" [Ref. 3.63].

Unlike the bridge inspector's rating assigned to a bridge (see Section 2.3.2) the inventory and operating ratings are calculated using analytical rather than subjective methods. The live loadings used are the standard AASHTO H and HS trucks depicted earlier in Figure 3.12. The final load rating values can be developed using either the working stress or load factor methods with the former approach generally yielding more conservative results.

When an existing structure is being load rated, the presence of as-built plans (see Section 2.7) greatly aids in calculation of a load rating value. Should as-built plans be unavailable, then a thorough site inspection must be conducted to obtain detailed field measurements to fill in the missing gaps.

3.14.2 Field Measurements and Inspection

In Section 2 and above we have touched upon the importance of field measurements. Regardless of whether detailed as-built plans are available or not, field measurements which describe the present day condition of a structure are absolutely essential. With regard to steel superstructures, measurements of primary members (e.g., flange and web thickness) aid in creating an accurate picture of what loads a bridge can withstand.

If a bridge has lost 20 percent of its cross-sectional properties, this can result in a greatly reduced load rating (depending on the location of the deterioration). This same principle applies to concrete and timber superstructures as well. In addition to loss of section any other defects such as misalignment, bends, eccentricities, or kinks in compression members should also be noted [Ref. 3.63]. In general, the inspecting engineer should be on the lookout for any physical conditions which he or she feels can impact the load carrying capacity of the structure.

3.14.3 Loading the Structure

The load rating of a bridge is based on the structure's ability to withstand both dead loads and live loads. Dead loads are computed using the unit weights of materials and is a relatively straightforward affair [Ref. 3.63]. Live loads are usually calculated using the standard AASHTO H and HS trucks. Special truck loading configurations, however, are used by different agencies. The *Manual for Condition Evaluation of Bridges* itself has its own set of design vehicles (see page 74, Ref. 3.63). Designers should check with the owner prior to beginning a load rating calculation to ascertain the loading configuration desired by the agency.

Placement of loads on a bridge are made in accordance with the AASHTO specifications (see Sections 3.5 and 3.8). The AASHTO *Manual for Condition Evaluation of Bridges*, however, adds the following requirements [Ref. 3.63]:

❑ Roadways whose widths are 18 to 20 ft (5.5 to 6.1 m) are given two design lanes equal to half the roadway width each. Live loads are centered in the design lanes.

Regardless of whether detailed as-built plans are available or not, field measurements which describe the present day condition of a structure are absolutely essential.

In general, the inspecting engineer should be on the look out for any physical conditions which he or she feels can impact the load carrying capacity of the structure.

❏ Roadways whose widths are less than 18 ft are given only one traffic lane.

AASHTO permits a reduction in traffic lanes if the designer believes that the present volume of traffic and movement over the structure so warrants such a reduction.

As would be expected, impact is also applied to all live loads. Again, AASHTO allows a reduction in impact should alignment conditions, enforced speed limit postings, etc., warrant such a reduction. Such conditions, if utilized in reducing the impact factor, should be deemed to significantly reduce the speed of vehicles passing over the structure.

Distribution of loads across the superstructure is also performed in accordance with the general AASHTO specifications. If special loading conditions are being utilized, then the applicable distribution factors should be applied.

As mentioned above, either the working stress method, load factor method or LRFD method can be used in calculating the load rating of a structure. The following discussion, however, will focus on the working stress and load factor approaches for calculating a highway bridge's load rating.

3.14.4 Working Stress Method

As we have already seen, the working stress method is built around the concept of the stress in members falling under a specified *allowable stress*. This also leads to the method being known as the allowable stress method. The AASHTO *Manual for Condition Evaluation of Bridges* provides guidelines for applying the working stress (and load factor) method in computing the load rating for structures constructed out of a variety of materials such as:

> **A**s we have already seen, the working stress method is built around the concept of the stress in members falling under a specified *allowable stress.*

❏ Steel and wrought iron
❏ Conventionally reinforced and prestressed concrete
❏ Timber

The general equation for load rating is:

$$RF = \frac{C - D}{L(I + 1)}$$
(Eq. 3.167)

where RF = rating factor
C = the allowable stress
D = the stress due to dead loads
$L(I + 1)$ = the stress due to live load and impact.

The allowable stress C depends on whether the bridge is rated for inventory level or operating level. For inventory level rating, the allowable stress for any material is the same as that used in new bridge design using allowable stress method. For operating level rating, a higher allowable stress is allowed. See Part 1 of this section for more details.

From Equation 3.167 we can see that load rating is to calculate how much live load a particular structural member can resist. If the rating factor is greater than one, it means that member can carry more than the rated live load. Each superstructure member should be rated for various forces (i.e., moment, shear, etc.). The smallest rating factor from every member will be the rating factor for the whole structure.

For example, if a bridge under HS-20 loading has a rating factor of 0.90 for inventory level, and 1.15 for operating level, it means that it can carry 90% of HS-20 loading (or HS-18) at inventory level, and it can resist 115% of HS-20 loading (or HS-23) at operating level.

If there is no visible overstress, the substructure is usually not required to be rated.

The following provides an overview of the basic criteria governing these various materials.

1. Steel and Wrought Iron.
In rating an existing steel structure, these allowable stresses will vary depending on the following:

❏ Whether an inventory or operating rating is calculated
❏ The type of steel present

With regard to the latter item, it is quite possible that, for older structures, the type of steel used is unknown. Such a situation can arise from the absence of as-built plans. However, even if as-built or other plans are available, it is quite possible that the type of steel used was not labeled on the plans in the first place.

For this reason, AASHTO provides minimum tensile strength and yield strength values for steel constructed during various years (see also Section 2.3.4, Part 2). These values are based on the probable type of steel used in construction during certain eras (e.g., A7 steel was quite popular during the 1950's).

In addition to this, AASHTO also provides various allowable stresses based on the loading condition the member is subjected to. Some examples of these loading conditions are:

❏ Axial tension
❏ Compression in extreme fiber of beams
❏ Compression in concentrically loaded columns
❏ Shear in girder webs

For steel structures, the principal difference between inventory and operating ratings is the reduction factor applied to the minimum yield strength. For *inventory ratings* the following allowable stresses are used:

$0.55F_y$ for tension or compression
$0.33F_y$ for web shear

> **I**t is quite possible that, for older structures, the type of steel used is unknown. Such a situation can arise from the absence of as-built plans.

and for *operating ratings* the allowable stresses are:

$0.75F_y$ for tension or compression
$0.45F_y$ for web shear

There are, however, exceptions to these criteria depending on the loading and physical conditions (e.g., bearing on milled stiffeners). When a girder with transverse intermediate stiffeners is being investigated, the spacing of the stiffeners does not require checking unless the web has severely deteriorated and/or the spacing of the stiffeners exceeds the depth of the web.

For wrought iron structures, the maximum unit stress for tension and bending is defined as:

Inventory = 14,600 psi
Operating = 20,000 psi

2. Conventionally Reinforced and Prestressed Concrete.

For conventionally reinforced concrete, AASHTO Standard Specifications can be used for various modular ratios for different strengths of concrete. Allowable stresses for various grades of reinforcing steel in tension are also presented. Inventory and operating allowable stresses are given for structures constructed prior to 1954 (18 ksi and 25 ksi), Grade 40 billet (20 ksi and 28 ksi), Grade 50 rail (20 ksi and 32.5 ksi), and Grade 60 (24 ksi and 36 ksi). These values are used without reduction.

Allowable stresses for concrete in compression are:

Inventory = $0.4f_c'$
Operating = $0.6f_c'$

> **A**llowable stresses for various grades of reinforcing steel in tension are also presented.

Prestressed concrete structures should be rated for both allowable stress and the strength. At inventory level, the allowable concrete strength is $6\sqrt{f_c'}$ in tension, and $0.6f_c'$ in compression (where stresses are in psi). At operating level, only strengths (moment, shear, etc.) are rated. See Section 3.14.5 for load factor method for strength evaluation details.

3. Timber.

In load rating timber structures, AASHTO relies heavily on the judgment of the investigating engineer [Ref. 3.63]. The general criterion governing the load rating of timber structures, however, is that the maximum allowable operating unit stress should not exceed 1.33 times the allowable stresses for stress-grade lumber as set forth in the standard AASHTO specifications. Criteria governing the rating of timber columns are also provided.

3.14.5 Load Factor Method

So far we have covered some of the basic guidelines for rating a bridge as set forth in the AASHTO *Manual for Condition Evaluation of Bridges* using allowable stress method. Some states are still using allowable stress method to

> **S**ome states are still using allowable stress method to rate old bridges that were designed using the same method. But most bridge are being rated using load factor method.

> **W**hen rating any structure, the basic requirement an engineer seeks to check is whether the capacity of the structure is greater than the loads it is subjected to.

rate old bridges that were designed using the same method. But most bridge are being rated using load factor method. This method is based on a strength evaluation and is also detailed in Ref. 3.63.

Compared with allowable stress method, load factor method for rating bridges has improved the load rating results (increased the consistency of structural safety) and has addressed the following concerns:

❑ Reduce the amount variation in ratings between structures as mentioned above
❑ Provide more realistic ratings through use of a load factor methodology (similar to AASHTO load factor design)

A belief that is fairly widespread in the transportation community is that the working stress approach in general, and the working stress method load rating methodology in particular, is overly conservative in the analysis of bridges. A major focus of the strength evaluation criteria is to offer a more realistic image of a structure's actual capacity. The load factor (or strength) evaluation methodology is based upon the design practice of using AASHTO load factor design, which was the main stream design practice in the United States in the past 20 years.

When rating any structure, the basic requirement an engineer seeks to check is whether the capacity of the structure is greater than the loads it is subjected to. The rating equation is expressed as:

$$RF = \frac{C - A_1 D}{A_2 L(I+1)}$$

(Eq. 3.168)

where RF = rating factor
$\qquad C$ = capacity of the member (moment, shear, torsion, etc.)
$\qquad D$ = dead load affects
$\qquad L(I+1)$ = live load and impact effects
$\qquad A_1$ = load factor for dead loads
$\qquad A_2$ = load factor for live load

The dead load factor (A_1) is equal to 1.3. The live load factor (A_2) depends on whether the structure is rated for inventory level or operating level. For inventory rating, a live load factor of 2.16 (similar to the AASHTO LFD design) is used. For operating level, a reduced live load factor of 1.3 is used. As we discussed earlier, inventory level represents the strength requirements for the new design, while operating level represents the minimum level of safety the bridge is expected to carry the specified live load.

The capacity (C) can be obtained using AASHTO Standard Specification's load factor method. Like any other load rating calculations, each structure member should be rated for various load conditions (i.e., moment, shear, etc.), and the lowest rating factor from all members should be taken as the overall rating for the structure.

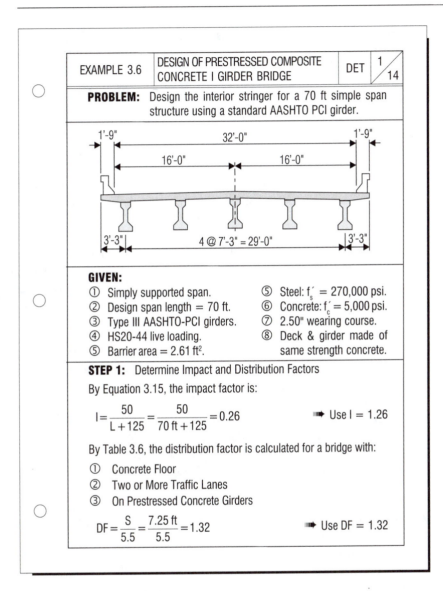

| EXAMPLE 3.6 | DESIGN OF PRESTRESSED COMPOSITE CONCRETE I GIRDER BRIDGE | DET | 1 / 14 |

PROBLEM: Design the interior stringer for a 70 ft simple span structure using a standard AASHTO PCI girder.

1'-9"   32'-0"   1'-9"

16'-0"   16'-0"

3'-3"   4 @ 7'-3" = 29'-0"   3'-3"

GIVEN:
① Simply supported span.
② Design span length = 70 ft.
③ Type III AASHTO-PCI girders.
④ HS20-44 live loading.
⑤ Barrier area = 2.61 ft².

⑤ Steel: $f_s' = 270,000$ psi.
⑥ Concrete: $f_c' = 5,000$ psi.
⑦ 2.50" wearing course.
⑧ Deck & girder made of same strength concrete.

STEP 1: Determine Impact and Distribution Factors

By Equation 3.15, the impact factor is:

$$I = \frac{50}{L + 125} = \frac{50}{70\,\text{ft} + 125} = 0.26 \qquad \Rrightarrow \text{Use } I = 1.26$$

By Table 3.6, the distribution factor is calculated for a bridge with:

① Concrete Floor
② Two or More Traffic Lanes
③ On Prestressed Concrete Girders

$$DF = \frac{S}{5.5} = \frac{7.25\,\text{ft}}{5.5} = 1.32 \qquad \Rrightarrow \text{Use } DF = 1.32$$

DESIGN EXAMPLE 3.6
GIVEN PARAMETERS

In this example we will design the interior girder of a prestressed concrete structure. AASHTO Standard Specifications will be used. The 70 ft design span is to be simply supported and subjected to HS20-44 live loading. The superstructure cross section consists of five equally spaced girders with concrete barriers over each fascia girder. Two traffic lanes are carried by the bridge.

STEP 1: DETERMINE IMPACT AND DISTRIBUTION FACTORS

As we have seen with steel superstructures, we need to compute the live load impact and distribution factors. The impact factor is computed using Equation 3.15 and a value of one added to the percentage to create a straight multiplicative factor.

The distribution factor equation used is obtained from Table 3.6. Since we are using prestressed girders, the equation used is identical to that seen previously in Design Example 3.2 for steel I-beam stringers. Note that if we were using a concrete box girder, for example, this would not be the case.

It is worth noticing that when load factor method is used for load rating, the engineer only needs to calculate the inventory level rating. The rating factor for operating level is always proportional to that of inventory level with a factor of 2.17/1.3 = 1.67. Therefore, if the rating factor of a bridge is 1.10 for HS-20 loading at inventory level, the rating factor at operating level should be 1.84.

3.14.6 LRFD Method

In working stress method or load factor method, the bridge structural conditions or the traffic conditions are not considered in the load rating calculations. To address these concerns, a method based on limit states approach has been introduced by AASHTO in the *Guide Specifications for Strength Evaluation of Existing Steel and Concrete Bridges* [Ref. 3.65].

Although load rating using LRFD method is not widely used in the United States yet mainly because the vast majority of the existing bridges were designed either using allowable stress method, or using load factor method (LFD), as we discussed earlier, AASHTO load factor design will be completely replaced by AASHTO LRFD after 2007. Therefore, readers should be prepared to take the challenges of using LRFD as a primary method in the near future.

It is beyond the scope of this book to offer a thorough examination of the load and resistance factor method for rating bridge structures. However, the following is an overview of the basic concepts behind the method and some of the major points of concern designers will have in utilizing this approach.

1. **Overview.** Where the allowable stress method compensates for uncertainty with a factor of safety, the limit states method (LRFD, and to some extend, load factor method as well) takes a "probabilistic approach" to safety through the use of load and resistance factors [Ref. 3.65]. The resulting load rating is developed by comparing *factored loads* with the *factored resistance* of key sections.

The AASHTO Guide Specification believes that the LRFD rating is more realistic and more advantageous than the allowable stress or load factor methods because it provides for:

❑ A more uniform and consistent evaluation of bridges
❑ Flexibility in making evaluations
❑ Uniform levels of reliability based on performance histories
❑ An incorporation of traffic and response data
❑ The use of site specific data in the evaluation

2. **The Concept of Safe Evaluation.** The load and resistance factor method is based on the concept of *safe evaluation*. By safe evaluation, we imply an approach which takes into account the function and site specifics of a structure in order to render a rating. This is made in contrast to the methodology previously discussed, which is, for all intents and purposes, a straight analytical approach (although it may be argued that a similar safe evaluation has been built into the allowable stresses through their refinement over the years).

At first blush, the reader may get the impression that the limit states evaluation approach will consistently produce ratings which are higher than the traditional, working stress or load and resistance factor approaches. This, however, is not always the case. A bridge which possesses a redundant load path, is well maintained, and has well enforced traffic regulations will most likely produce an operating rating larger than was previously computed. A structure, however, which has significant deterioration, non-redundant components, and heavy truck traffic may produce an inventory rating which is below its previous rating.

Like any limit states method, the strength evaluation approach for rating bridges lives and dies by the quality of the load and resistance factors used. If one were to draw the analogy between load factors and pasta sauce it would be prudent for an engineer to be able to say "It's in there." What

Like any limit states method, the strength evaluation approach for rating bridges lives and dies by the quality of the load and resistance factors used.

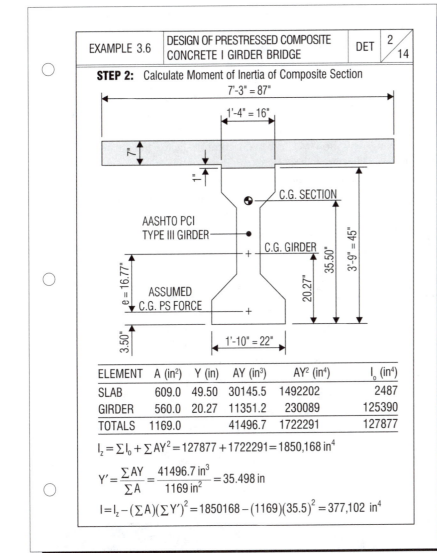

| EXAMPLE 3.6 | DESIGN OF PRESTRESSED COMPOSITE CONCRETE I GIRDER BRIDGE | DET | 2/14 |

STEP 2: Calculate Moment of Inertia of Composite Section

ELEMENT	A (in²)	Y (in)	AY (in³)	AY² (in⁴)	I_0 (in⁴)
SLAB	609.0	49.50	30145.5	1492202	2487
GIRDER	560.0	20.27	11351.2	230089	125390
TOTALS	1169.0		41496.7	1722291	127877

$$I_z = \sum I_0 + \sum AY^2 = 127877 + 1722291 = 1850{,}168 \text{ in}^4$$

$$Y' = \frac{\sum AY}{\sum A} = \frac{41496.7 \text{ in}^3}{1169 \text{ in}^2} = 35.498 \text{ in}$$

$$I = I_z - (\sum A)(\sum Y')^2 = 1850168 - (1169)(35.5)^2 = 377{,}102 \text{ in}^4$$

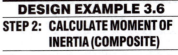

DESIGN EXAMPLE 3.6
STEP 2: CALCULATE MOMENT OF INERTIA (COMPOSITE)

When solving for the effective width for an interior girder (see Section 3.15.2, Part 2), the latter of the three criteria (overhang not to exceed one-half clear distance) governs. In this example we will assume the concrete used is the same for the slab and the girder so that we do not have to worry about a modular ratio.

One of the given parameters was an AASHTO PCI Type III girder. This girder is fully dimensioned in Figure 3.2. The values of:

$$I = 125{,}390 \text{ in}^4 \quad \text{and} \quad Y' = 20.27 \text{ in}$$

are obtained from predefined tables and handbooks similar to the AISC Manual of Steel Construction. See Table 3.24 for an overview of prestressed girder properties.

We will assume that the center of gravity of the prestressing force is located a distance of 3.50 in from the bottom of the girder. This yields an eccentricity of 16.77 in to the center of gravity of the girder only. These distances are annotated on the figure in the accompanying calculation sheet.

about a heavy volume of traffic?" A skeptic may ask; "It's in there." "What about vigorous maintenance work?", again "It's in there." "Dead loads, live loads, rough approaches, heavy deterioration." The response again would be "Yes, it's in there."

A sound limit states approach, however, is more than the simple presence of these load factors. Their magnitude must also be accurate and reflect the practices and desires of the owner. This accuracy must be both in terms of structural and economic performance. Quite naturally, it would take any design engineer or transportation department a period of time before confidence in both the method and the ratings it produces is achieved.

3. Conclusions. From the above, it is obvious that the limit states evaluation approach to rating bridges places a great deal of responsibility, not only on the engineer as an individual, but the transportation department as a whole. It is one thing to say, "gee this road doesn't have that much truck

> **I**t is obvious that the limit states evaluation approach to rating bridges places a great deal of responsibility ... on the engineer ...

[3.14.6, Part 3]

DID YOU KNOW

$\overline{\text{THAT}}$ the basic concepts behind
prestressed concrete were first
formulated in the period 1885–
1890 in Germany and the
U.S. by C. F. W. Doehring and
P. H. Jackson, respectively? It
was not until 1955, however,
when the first design criteria
for the design of prestressed
bridges was published by the
Bureau of Public Roads.
[Refs. 3.66 and 3.67].

traffic" and quite another to incorporate that into a final rating. It is quite accurate to say that a limit states approach offers flexibility, but with flexibility comes responsibility.

This subjectivity could also lead to some conflict between those who design and those who maintain. No engineer can say that he or she has never encountered disagreement with fellow engineers examining the same situation. For example, it is not uncommon to have two separate traffic analyses performed with each producing a different conclusion. Like anything new, however, a certain comfort factor has to be built into the process. The more limit states approaches, like the one described above, are used, the more engineers will begin to trust both the method and their own judgment. Now, we are approaching the point that the limit states approaches are accepted by most bridge engineers and have become the standard practice.

3.15 PRESTRESSED CONCRETE

So far we have discussed the use of steel primary members in bridge design. In this section we will examine the use of prestressed concrete in bridge superstructures. The use of prestressed concrete in bridge construction is a relatively new phenomenon (1950's and onward). One of the major contributing factors to the acceptance and use of prestressed concrete was the reduced availability of steel following the Second World War.

In Section 3.1.2, Part 1 we discussed the basic principles behind prestressed concrete. In this section we will expand on these fundamental concepts and discuss some of the major design and maintenance issues concerning the use

OUTSIDE OF THE U.S. the use of prestressed concrete in highway bridges developed in a somewhat different fashion. In the U.S. after World War II, there existed a relatively high labor to material cost. This led to the development of standardized, precast components which lent themselves well to mass production. Outside of the U.S., the opposite was true, with a high ratio of material to labor costs prevailing. This led to the development of long-span bridges and comparatively complicated structures. Today, bridges within the U.S. and overseas, such as the one shown in Figure 3.50, possess many similarities, with each design community learning from the other [Ref. 3.5].

Figure 3.50 A prestressed concrete bridge carries dual roadways over a busy underpass in Singapore.

EXAMPLE 3.6	DESIGN OF PRESTRESSED COMPOSITE CONCRETE I GIRDER BRIDGE	DET	3 / 14

STEP 3: Calculate Dead Load on Prestressed Girder

The dead load is composed of the following items:

DL_{slab} = (b_{eff})(slab thickness)(w_{conc})
= (7.25 ft)(7 in)(1 ft/12 in)(0.150 k/ft³)   = 0.634 k/ft

DL_{haunch} = (haunch width)(haunch thickness)(w_{conc})
= (1.33 ft)(1 in)(1 ft/12 in)(0.150 k/ft³)   = 0.017 k/ft

DL_{girder} = (girder area)(w_{conc})
= (560 in²)(1 ft²/144 in²)(0.150 k/ft³)   = 0.583 k/ft

$DL_{barrier}$ = (2 barriers)(barrier area)(w_{conc})/5 Girders
= (2)(2.61 ft²)(0.150 k/ft³)/5 Girders   = 0.157 k/ft

$DL_{wearing}$ = (w.c. thick.)(pave. width)(w_{pave})/5 Girders
= (2.5 in)(1/12)(32 ft)(0.150 k/ft³)/5   = 0.200 k/ft

➠ DL = 1.591 k/ft

STEP 4: Compute Dead Load Moments

Dead Load Moments by Equation 3.49:

$$M_{slab} = \frac{wL^2}{8} = \frac{(0.634 + 0.017)(70\text{ ft})^2}{8}$$ ➠ M_{slab} = 399 ft-k

$$M_{girder} = \frac{wL^2}{8} = \frac{(0.583\text{ k/ft})(70\text{ ft})^2}{8}$$ ➠ M_{girder} = 357 ft-k

$$M_{barrier} = \frac{wL^2}{8} = \frac{(0.157\text{ k/ft})(70\text{ ft})^2}{8}$$ ➠ $M_{barrier}$ = 96 ft-k

$$M_{wearing} = \frac{wL^2}{8} = \frac{(0.200\text{ k/ft})(70\text{ ft})^2}{8}$$ ➠ $M_{wearing}$ = 123 ft-k

➠ M_{DL} = 975 k/ft

DESIGN EXAMPLE 3.6
STEP 3: CALCULATE DEAD LOAD ON PRESTRESSED GIRDER

The dead loads for the various elements are calculated for the 7'-3" effective flange width. The area of the barrier is taken from a California Standard [Ref. 3.15] and, along with the wearing course thickness, was given at the beginning of the calculation. Both the barrier and the wearing course are distributed over the five girders. The wearing course is placed over the 32 ft width between the faces of each traffic barrier.

STEP 4: COMPUTE DEAD LOAD MOMENTS

As we saw earlier in Step 4 of Design Example 3.2, the dead load moments are calculated using the standard equation for a uniform distributed load (Equation 3.49).

The next step will be to calculate the maximum live load plus impact moment. Since we have a simple span, this will be created by placing a design truck with the center of gravity of loads offset a given distance from the centerline of the span.

Note that the slab and girder dead loads act on the non-composite section, while barrier and wearing surface act on the composite section.

---

of prestressed concrete in highway bridge superstructures. Also presented in the section is a design example of a small bridge constructed with prestressed concrete girders.

3.15.1 Overview of Prestressed Concrete

Recapping from Section 3.1.2, prestressed concrete utilizes an applied force which increases internal compression in the concrete beam thereby reducing or eliminating stresses due to tension once the beam is loaded. There are a variety of methods for applying a prestressing force to a concrete member. A primitive example is illustrated in Figure 3.51 where a rectangular beam is subjected to a uniform distributed live load. The beam is concentrically prestressed with the resulting stress distribution depicted below the beam.

To apply the prestressing force, such as the one depicted in Figure 3.51, jacks can be placed at either end of the beam and made a permanent part of

STRESSES AT THE bottom fiber of the beam in Figure 3.51 which are caused by dead and live loads can only be eliminated if the compressive stress induced by the prestressing force, P, is equal to the magnitude of the tensile stresses induced by the applied loads.

Like conventional reinforced concrete, prestressed concrete must also account for the effects of shrinkage and creep. If the beam is to eliminate all tensile stresses, then the prestressing force applied must be greater than the tensile stresses alone in order to account for the additional deformational loads (see Section 3.5.4, Parts 1 and 2).

One drawback to this process is that the top fiber of the beam must resist both the compressive forces from the applied loads and the prestressing force [Ref. 3.67].

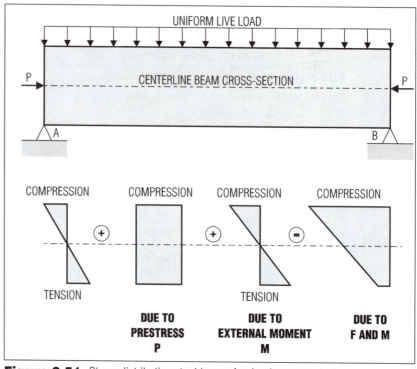

Figure 3.51 Stress distribution at midspan of a simple rectangular beam prestressed concentrically.

the structure. Such a configuration, however, would be extremely susceptible to movement at the supports which could lead to a reduction in the prestress force.

A more popular solution is to utilize a steel cable or *tendon* which is embedded within the concrete beam and anchored at the ends of the member. When the prestressing force is applied to the tendon prior to the concrete being poured, the beam is said to be pretensioned. When the force is applied after the concrete has hardened the beam is called posttensioned. The following explains some of the basic properties, advantages, and disadvantages of each method.

1. Pretensioned Beams. In a pretensioned beam, prior to the placement of concrete steel, tendons are stressed by application of a tensile force (usually with hydraulic jacks). The magnitude of the prestressing force varies depending on the beam itself and the loads to be applied (see Figure 3.51 sidebar). Once the concrete has hardened around the tendons, they are released. The tendons immediately seek to restore themselves to their original length. It is this response that introduces the compressive forces which in turn eliminate tension at the bottom fiber of the beam under service loads.

Pretensioned beams are sometimes fabricated in casting yards where the tendons are anchored between large abutments known as *pretensioning beds,* which can be as much as 500 ft (152.4 m) apart [Ref. 3.67]. An alternative method to this approach is to embed the anchors within the beam itself.

| EXAMPLE 3.6 | DESIGN OF PRESTRESSED COMPOSITE CONCRETE I GIRDER BRIDGE | DET | 4/14 |

STEP 5: Calculate Live Load Plus Impact Moment

From Figure 3.32, we locate the HS20-44 truck as shown below:

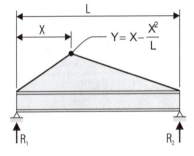

First, solve for the reactions by summing moments about Point A:

$\curvearrowright$ $\Sigma M_A = 0$:

$$(4k \cdot 18.67\,ft) + (16k \cdot 32.67\,ft) + (16k \cdot 46.67\,ft) - (R_B \cdot 70\,ft) = 0$$

$$R_B = \frac{1344\,ft\cdot k}{70\,ft} = 19.20\,k \qquad \text{so, } R_A = 36\,k - 19.20\,k = 16.80k$$

Now, compute the maximum live load moment:

$$M_{LL} = M_{MAX} = (R_A \cdot 32.67\,ft) - (4k \cdot 14\,ft) = 492.80\,ft \cdot k$$

Apply the impact and wheel load distribution factors:

$$M_{LL+I} = M_{LL} \cdot DF \cdot I$$

$$M_{LL+I} = (492.80\,ft\text{-}k)(1.32)(1.26)$$

➠ $M_{LL+I} = 819.62\,ft\text{-}k$

Earlier in Step 5 of Design Example 3.2 and Figure 3.32 we described the placement of an HS20-44 truck to induce maximum moment on a simply supported span. Note that in AASHTO Standard Specifications, only wheel load (not a whole truck) is used.

Recapping, the truck is placed so that the centerline of the span is halfway between the center of gravity of loads and the nearest concentrated load. The maximum moment occurs at the middle concentrated load (16k).

Another way of solving this problem is to use an influence line as shown below:

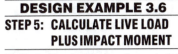

After the live load moment is computed, the impact and distribution factors, which were calculated earlier in Step 1, are applied.

One major advantage of the pretensioning approach is that it lends itself well to the mass production of beams. As prestressed bridges became more popular, and standard beam sizes accepted, fabricators found themselves producing prestressed pretensioned concrete beams much in the same fashion steel fabricators had been churning out wide flange beams.

One method of enhancing the performance of pretensioned beams is to deflect the prestressing tendons upward and downward along the length of the beam. This process is known as *draping* or *harping*. Draping tendons upward near supports can reduce the tension stress at the top fiber near supports. It can also increase shear capacity due to the inclied prestressing steel.

2. Posttensioned Beams. In a posttensioned beam, the steel tendons are stressed after the concrete has had time to harden. The tendons are

> One major advantage of the pretensioning approach is that it lends itself well to the mass production of beams.

LINEAR PRESTRESSING SYSTEMS

There are a wide variety of patented systems for both pretensioning and posttensioning. The United States, Germany, France, and Russia are some countries where these technologies have been developed. Listed below are some of the more popular methods for stressing and anchoring tendons [Ref. 3.68].

PRETENSIONING

STRESSING METHODS

- Against buttresses or stressing beds
- Against central steel tube
- Continuous stressing against molds
- Electric current to heat steel

ANCHORING METHODS

- During prestressing:
  Wires and Strands
- For transfer of prestress:
  Bond (for strands and small wires)
  Corrugated clips (for big wires)

POSTTENSIONING

STRESSING METHODS

- Steel against concrete
- Concrete against concrete
- Expanding cement
- Electric prestressing
- Bending steel beams

ANCHORING METHODS

- Wires, by frictional grips
- Wires, by bearing
- Wires, by loops and other methods
- Bars, by bearing and by grips
- Strands, by bearing
- Strands, by friction grips

> **A** major problem encountered by the early fabricators of prestressed concrete beams was a low prestress which led to an eventual loss of prestress due to creep and shrinkage.

incorporated into the concrete beam in either one of the following two fashions:

- ❑ Bonded
- ❑ Unbonded

Bonded tendons are placed within preformed voids in the concrete member. These voids could be formed by metal ducts or plastic tubes. Plastic tubes may crack and cause potential corrosion of prestressing steel, so most bridges use metal ducts. After the concrete has hardened and the posttensioning stress is applied, the space between the hole and the tendon is filled with grout so that the tendon/tube assembly becomes *bonded* to the surrounding concrete beam.

Unbonded tendons are simply greased and wrapped in paper. After the posttensioning force is applied, they are left as is or *unbonded* to the surrounding concrete beam. To protect the tendons a waterproofing paper is sometimes used to guard against potential corrosion. The grease used may also be provided with an anticorrosion component [Ref. 3.67]. With respect to bridge design, bonded tendons are more the norm with unbonded tendons primarily used in building construction. Both of these methods require the incorporation of an anchorage at the ends of the posttensioned member.

Where pretensioning has the advantage of being well suited to mass production, posttensioning is advantageous when very large elements are being fabricated which cannot be transported to the project site. The ability to posttension precast or cast-in-place members is another advantage which provides the designer with added flexibility. Where pretensioned beams are typically produced in standard sizes and geometries, posttensioned girders can be customized to fit site-specific conditions. Also, pretensionning steel can either be straight or draped. Posttensioning steel can, however, be of any shape, so it is usually designed to follow the moment diagram of the girder.

3. **Application of Pre- and Posttensioned Concrete.** The general rule of thumb is that pretensioned beams are utilized for short spans and posttensioned beams for longer, more complicated spans. For short spans with simple alignment and clearance constraints, the pretensioned beam offers a straightforward, economical solution.

Larger spans, however, which can be cast-in-place at or near the project site, are better suited to posttensioning. Another advantage of posttensioned construction is that the tendons can be placed on nonlinear paths (something that is very difficult to do when the beam is pretensioned). Thus, when complicated overpass alignment geometries are present, posttensioning is the preferred approach.

4. **Prestressing Steels.** A major problem encountered by the early fabricators of prestressed concrete beams was a low prestress, which led to an eventual loss of prestress due to creep and shrinkage [Ref. 3.5]. This was a direct result of the use of conventional structural steel. To compensate for the effects of creep and shrinkage, high strength steel is needed which can allow for the application of a high initial stress.

EXAMPLE 3.6	DESIGN OF PRESTRESSED COMPOSITE CONCRETE I GIRDER BRIDGE	DET	5/14

STEP 6: Calculate Stresses at Top Fiber of Girder

Recapping from Step 2, the centroid distances and moments of inertia for the composite and noncomposite sections are:

NONCOMPOSITE Type III Girder	COMPOSITE 7" Slab & Type III Girder
I = 125,390 in^4	I = 377,102 in^4
y_t = (45–20.27) in = 24.73 in	y_t = (45–35.50) in = 9.50 in
y_b = 20.27 in	y_b = 35.50 in

The stresses at the top fiber of the girder is calculated using the standard expression defined by Equation 3.42 ($f = Mc / I$):

	Element	Equation	Top Fiber
Noncomposite	Slab	$\dfrac{(399\ \text{ft·k})(12\ \text{in/ft})(24.73\ \text{in})}{125,390\ \text{in}^4}$	= 0.944 ksi
Noncomposite	Type III Girder	$\dfrac{(357\ \text{ft·k})(12\ \text{in/ft})(24.73\ \text{in})}{125,390\ \text{in}^4}$	= 0.845 ksi
Composite	LL+I	$\dfrac{(820\ \text{ft·k})(12\ \text{in/ft})(9.50\ \text{in})}{377,102\ \text{in}^4}$	= 0.248 ksi
Composite	Barrier	$\dfrac{(96\ \text{ft·k})(12\ \text{in/ft})(9.50\ \text{in})}{377,102\ \text{in}^4}$	= 0.029 ksi
Composite	Wear. Course	$\dfrac{(123\ \text{ft·k})(12\ \text{in/ft})(9.50\ \text{in})}{377,102\ \text{in}^4}$	= 0.037 ksi
	TOTAL	f_{top}	= 2.103 ksi

DESIGN EXAMPLE 3.6
STEP 6: CALCULATE STRESSES AT TOP FIBER OF GIRDER

Now that we know the section properties of both the composite and non-composite sections and the design service moments, we can calculate the stresses at the top and bottom fiber of the prestressed girder.

For the top fiber, we need to compute the distance from the centroid to the top fiber *of the girder*. The distance to the centroid for the composite section was determined earlier in Step 2. The distance to the centroid for the girder proper can be found in Table 3.24. Both of these values are referenced from the *bottom* of the girder.

The stresses for the slab and girder are computed based on the noncomposite section properties, while those for live load plus impact, the barrier, and wearing course are determined using the composite section properties calculated in Step 2. The expression used to compute the stresses is defined by Equation 3.42. The individual stresses are then totaled to yield an overall stress at the extreme top fiber of the Type III prestressed girder.

For example, the typical loss in prestress (regardless of the type of steel used) is in the range of 15 ksi to 50 ksi. If a steel tendon were used with a yield point of 40 ksi with an initial stress of 30 ksi applied, the entire prestress could potentially be lost to the normal behavior of the surrounding concrete [Ref. 3.67]. This phenomenon led to the incorporation of high-strength steel tendons for prestressed concrete.

There are three basic groupings of prestressing steels. Specifically, these types of steel are:

❏ Uncoated stress-relieved wires
❏ Uncoated stress-relived strand
❏ Uncoated high strength steel bars

The properties of these various types of prestressing steel are covered by ASTM specifications (A 421, A 416, and A 722 respectively). The reader is referred to these specifications and Ref. 3.67 for more information on these steels and their properties.

5. Concrete for Prestressing. We saw earlier that for conventionally reinforced concrete, concrete with compressive strengths in the range of 3000 to 4000 psi are typically used. For elements like concrete deck slabs, use of any higher strength concrete would present minimal advantages.

For prestressed concrete, however, high strength concrete with compressive strengths in the range of 5000 to 6000 psi is the norm. The principal reasons for this are that:

❑ A reduction in weight and therefore cost can be achieved
❑ High strength concrete undergoes smaller volume changes

With regard to the latter item, it is important that the concrete utilized has a composition which limits the effects of creep and shrinkage (see Section 3.5.4, Parts 1 and 2). As we have already discussed, significant volume changes in the concrete can lead to a potential loss of prestress.

The effects of shrinkage on prestressed concrete, however, are quite different from these on conventionally reinforced concrete. In regular reinforced concrete, the compressive forces due to shrinkage are taken up by the reinforcing steel. In prestressed concrete, however, the steel is completely in tension so that the compressive forces act on the concrete only. This has the effect of increasing the deformation due to shrinkage. In addition to the volumetric changes caused by shrinkage and creep, the designer must also account for the effects of deformations caused by temperature variations.

3.15.2 Composite Beams

For medium size highway bridges, composite prestressed concrete structures which utilize precast beams and a cast-in-place deck are a viable and popular solution. There are many similarities to be drawn between this type of structure and the steel-concrete composite structures presented earlier in Section 3.10. Discussed below are some of the major issues concerning the design of composite prestressed beams:

1. Advantages. One of the main advantages of using a composite beam when dealing with prestressed concrete is that it allows for fabrication of the girders at a location off-site where conditions are generally more favorable. Like steel wide flange beams which are typically designed as unshored, precast prestressed girders are sized and designed to accommodate both the dead loads and future live loads so that falsework is typically not needed. This feature, combined with the ready availability of primary members, allows for relatively quick erection and construction.

One of the main advantages of using a composite beam when dealing with prestressed concrete is that it allows for fabrication of the girders at a location off-site ...

EXAMPLE 3.6	DESIGN OF PRESTRESSED COMPOSITE CONCRETE I GIRDER BRIDGE	DET	6 / 14

STEP 7: Calculate Stresses at Bottom Fiber of Girder

Recapping from Step 2, the centroid distances and moments of inertia for the composite and noncomposite sections are:

NONCOMPOSITE Type III Girder	COMPOSITE 7" Slab & Type III Girder
$I = 125,390 \text{ in}^4$	$I = 377,102 \text{ in}^4$
$y_t = (45 - 20.27) \text{ in} = 24.73 \text{ in}$	$y_t = (45 - 35.50)\text{in} = 9.50 \text{ in}$
$y_b = 20.27 \text{ in}$	$y_b = 35.50 \text{ in}$

The stresses at the bottom fiber of the girder is calculated using the standard expression defined by Equation 3.42 ($f = Mc / I$):

	Element	Equation	Bot. Fiber
Noncomposite	Slab	$\dfrac{(399 \text{ ft·k})(12 \text{ in/ft})(20.27 \text{ in})}{125,390 \text{ in}^4}$	$= 0.774 \text{ ksi}$
	Type III Girder	$\dfrac{(357 \text{ ft·k})(12 \text{ in/ft})(20.27 \text{ in})}{125,390 \text{ in}^4}$	$= 0.692 \text{ ksi}$
Composite	LL + I	$\dfrac{(820 \text{ ft·k})(12 \text{ in/ft})(35.50 \text{ in})}{377,102 \text{ in}^4}$	$= 0.926 \text{ ksi}$
	Barrier	$\dfrac{(96 \text{ ft·k})(12 \text{ in/ft})(35.50 \text{ in})}{377,102 \text{ in}^4}$	$= 0.108 \text{ ksi}$
	Wear. Course	$\dfrac{(123 \text{ ft·k})(12 \text{ in/ft})(35.50 \text{ in})}{377,102 \text{ in}^4}$	$= 0.139 \text{ ksi}$
	TOTAL	f_{bot}	$= 2.639 \text{ ksi}$

DESIGN EXAMPLE 3.6
STEP 7: CALCULATE STRESSES AT BOTTOM FIBER

Having already computed the top fiber stresses, stresses at the bottom fiber of the prestressed girder are calculated in a similar fashion. The text below parallels that for the top fiber stress computation.

For the bottom fiber, we need to compute the distance from the centroid to the bottom fiber *of the girder*. The distance to the centroid for the composite section was determined earlier in Step 2. The distance to the centroid for the girder proper can be found in Table 3.24. Both of these values are referenced from the *bottom* of the girder.

The stresses for the slab and girder are computed based on the noncomposite section properties, while those for live load plus impact, the barrier, and wearing course are determined using the composite section properties calculated in Step 2. The expression used to compute the stresses is defined by Equation 3.42. The individual stresses are then totaled to yield an overall stress at the extreme bottom fiber of the Type III prestressed girder.

Section Type	Section Area (in²)	Moment of Inertia (in⁴)	Y′ (in)	Span Range (ft)
I	276	22,750	12.59	30–45
II	369	50,980	15.83	40–60
III	560	125,390	20.27	55–80
IV	789	260,730	24.73	70–100
V	1013	521,180	31.96	90–120
VI	1085	733,320	36.38	110–140

Table 3.24 Properties of Various AASHTO PCI Beam Sections

In Figure 3.52 a typical composite slab-prestressed girder configuration is illustrated. Like their steel-concrete cousins, prestressed composite beams require a means of transferring horizontal shear between the two components. For small shears, the bond between the girder and slab may be enough to accomplish this. When larger shears are present, however, a reinforcing rod which ties the two elements together is required (see Figure 3.52). Unlike other concrete components, a shear key is generally not used to achieve this functionality. Like concrete-steel composite beams which utilize welded shear stud connectors, the steel tie utilized in concrete-concrete composite construction allows both components to act as one unit in resisting loads and increases the flexural strength of the superstructure.

2. Effective Flange Width. Like steel-concrete beams, prestressed composite beams utilize a girder which is integrated with a slab to form a T-girder configuration. The portion of the slab which acts as the top flange of the T-girder cross section is known as the effective flange width (see Section 3.10.3). The criteria governing the size of the effective flange width are very similar to that for steel-concrete composite beams. For concrete-concrete composite beams, AASHTO defines the effective flange width for an interior girder as (AASHTO 8.10.1.1):

- ❏ Total width not to exceed one-fourth the span length
- ❏ Overhang on each side of web not to exceed six times the thickness of the slab
- ❏ Overhang on each side of web not to exceed one-half clear distance to adjacent web

The first and last criteria are very similar to that seen earlier, with the wording slightly different. As we saw before, there are separate

> **T**he criteria governing the size of the effective flange width is very similar to that for steel-concrete composite beams.

THE BENEFITS OF composite construction that are realized by steel-concrete beams are much the same for composite prestressed beams. The composite slab-girder section offers greater flexural strength than if the two members were to act independently. Composite action is gained through the incorporation of a steel tie which binds the deck to the girder, serving the same function as shear stud connectors. The design of composite prestressed beams also has similarities with a section moment of inertia and neutral axis being calculated just as for steel-concrete beams. Although an I girder shape is shown in Figure 3.52, other beams, such as the Bulb-T girders illustrated earlier in Figure 3.3 can also be used.

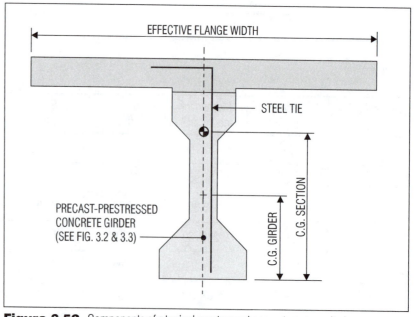

Figure 3.52 Components of a typical prestressed concrete composite beam.

EXAMPLE 3.6	DESIGN OF PRESTRESSED COMPOSITE CONCRETE I GIRDER BRIDGE	DET	7/14

STEP 8: Calculate Initial Prestressing Force

In Step 2, we assumed an eccentricity of: $e = 16.77$ in.

The square of the radius of gyration is calculated as:

$$r^2 = \frac{I}{A} = \frac{125{,}390 \text{ in}^4}{560 \text{ in}^2} = 223.91 \text{ in}^2$$

Calculate effective prestressing force:

$$C = P_f = \frac{f_{bot} \cdot A}{1 + \frac{e \cdot y_b}{r^2}} = \frac{(2.639 \text{ ksi})(560 \text{ in}^2)}{1 + \frac{(16.77 \text{ in})(20.27 \text{ in})}{223.91 \text{ in}^2}} = 586.9 \text{ k}$$

Calculate effective stress:

f_e = Allowable Initial Stress – Assumed Losses

By AASHTO 9.15.1 for low relaxation strands:
Allowable Initial Stress = $0.75 f'_s = (0.75)(270 \text{ ksi}) = 202.50$ ksi

By Table 3.25 for pretensioned strands:
Assumed Losses = 35 ksi

$f_e = 202.50 \text{ ksi} - 35.0 \text{ ksi} = 167.50$ ksi

Calculate area of steel:

$$A_s^* = \frac{P_f}{f_e} = \frac{586.9 \text{ k}}{167.5 \text{ ksi}} = 3.50 \text{ in}^2$$

Assume losses due to elastic shortening. So:
Losses After Transfer = 35 ksi – 13 ksi = 22 ksi

The initial prestressing force is:

$P_i = P_f + (\text{Losses After Transfer})(A_s^*) = 586.9 \text{ k} + (22 \text{ ksi})(3.50 \text{ in}^2)$

➠ $P_i = 663.9$ k

DESIGN EXAMPLE 3.6
STEP 8: CALCULATE INITIAL PRESTRESSING FORCE

Recall that in Step 2 we assumed an eccentricity based on a 3.50 in offset to the center of gravity of the prestressing force. We also need to determine the radius of gyration of the section which is defined by the ratio of the section's inertia to its area.

The effective prestressing force is determined by solving Equation 3.175 for C. We use the stress at the bottom fiber of the section determined earlier in Step 7.

We now need to account for the effect of prestress loss. The effective stress is defined as the allowable stress less prestress losses. For the sake of brevity, rather than calculating losses due to creep, shrinkage, etc., we will use the assumed value from Table 3.25. The area of steel is therefore the ratio of the effective prestressing force and the effective area.

Some of these losses, however, will have already taken place when the girder is stressed (i.e., elastic shortening— see Section 3.15.4, Part 1). We assume 13 ksi and then determine our initial prestressing force.

Description of Loss	Pretensioning (psi)	Posttensioning (psi)
Elastic Shortening of Concrete	12,000	N/A
Sequence Stressing	N/A	5,000
Creep of Concrete	11,000	11,000
Shrinkage of Concrete	6,000	4,000
Creep of Steel	6,000	5,000
TOTAL	35,000	25,000

Table 3.25 Classic Estimate of Prestress Losses

Type of Prestressing Steel	Total Loss	
	$f'_c = 4,000$ psi	$f'_c = 5,000$ psi
Pretensioning Strand	N/A	45,000 psi
Posttensioning Wire or Strand	32,000 psi	33,000 psi
Posttensioning Bars	22,000 psi	23,000 psi

Table 3.26 AASHTO Estimate of Prestress Losses (AASHTO 9.16.2.2)

criteria for girders which have a slab on only one side of their web. In such instances, the effective flange width is defined as not to exceed (AASHTO 8.10.1.2):

❏ One-twelfth the span length
❏ Six times the slab thickness
❏ One-half the clear distance to the next web

As with steel-concrete beams, the effective flange width is used to determine section properties of the T-girder cross section. The actual flange width should be used to calculate the dead load acting on the beam.

> As with steel-concrete beams, the effective flange width is used to determine section properties of the T-girder cross section.

3. Horizontal Shear. We have touched upon the need to develop a shear connection between the prestressed girder and the concrete deck. The design of this shear connection is based on the general expression (AASHTO 9.20.4.3, also see ACI 17.5):

$$V_u \le \phi \cdot V_{nh} \qquad \text{(Eq. 3.169)}$$

where V_u = factored shear force at section considered
ϕ = strength reduction factor (0.85 for shear)
V_{nh} = nominal horizontal shear strength

The nominal horizontal shear strength, V_{nh}, is the strength of the joint between the two surfaces (i.e., the top of the girder flange and bottom of the slab), and can be calculated from (AASHTO 9.20.4.3):

❏ $80b_v d$ (lb) when ties *are not* provided and the contact surface is clean, free of laitance, and intentionally roughened. With regard to roughness, AASHTO and ACI specify the full amplitude as approximately 0.25 in (6.35 mm).

❏ $80b_v d$ (lb) when minimum ties *are* provided (see Eq. 3.170) and the contact surface is clean and free of laitance, but *not* intentionally roughened.

❏ $350b_v d$ (lb) when both conditions above are met.

❏ For each percent of tie reinforcement in excess of the required minimum (Eq. 3.170), shear strength may be increased by $(160f_y/40,000)b_v d$ (lb).

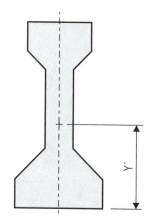

**LOCATION OF GIRDER
CENTER OF GRAVITY**

EXAMPLE 3.6	DESIGN OF PRESTRESSED COMPOSITE CONCRETE I GIRDER BRIDGE	DET	8/14

STEP 9: Calculate Fiber Stresses in Beam

Compute stresses at top and bottom using Eqs 3.174 and 3.175:

TOP FIBER	BOTTOM FIBER
$1 + \dfrac{e \cdot y_t}{r^2}$	$1 + \dfrac{e \cdot y_b}{r^2}$
$1 + \dfrac{(16.77\text{ in})(-24.73\text{ in})}{223.91\text{ in}^2} = -0.85$	$1 + \dfrac{(16.77\text{ in})(20.27\text{ in})}{223.91\text{ in}^2} = 2.52$
$f_{top} = -0.85\dfrac{P}{A} \pm f_{time}$	$f_{bot} = 2.52\dfrac{P}{A} \pm f_{time}$

	Time of Stress	Equation	Stress
Top Fiber	At time of prestressing	$-0.85 \cdot \dfrac{-663.9\text{ k}}{560\text{ in}^2} - 0.845\text{ ksi}$	$= 0.163$ ksi T
	At time slab is placed	$-0.85 \cdot \dfrac{-586.9\text{ k}}{560\text{ in}^2} - 1.789\text{ ksi}$	$= -0.898$ ksi C
	At design load	$-0.85 \cdot \dfrac{-586.9\text{ k}}{560\text{ in}^2} - 2.103\text{ ksi}$	$= -1.212$ ksi C
Bottom Fiber	At time of prestressing	$2.52 \cdot \dfrac{-663.9\text{ k}}{560\text{ in}^2} + 0.692\text{ ksi}$	$= -2.295$ ksi C
	At time slab is placed	$2.52 \cdot \dfrac{-586.9\text{ k}}{560\text{ in}^2} + 1.466\text{ ksi}$	$= -1.175$ ksi C
	At design load	$2.52 \cdot \dfrac{-586.9\text{ k}}{560\text{ in}^2} + 2.639\text{ ksi}$	$= -0.002$ ksi C

DESIGN EXAMPLE 3.6
STEP 9: CALCULATE FIBER STRESSES IN BEAM

First we will calculate the geometric parameters of Equations 3.174 and 3.175 for the top and bottom fibers of the girder. Keep in mind our sign convention outlined in Section 3.15.3 where distances below the centroid are positive and above are negative.

We will calculate the stresses at three different times. When the beam is prestressed, when the slab is placed, and under design loading conditions.

At the time of prestressing only the girder dead load is considered, so that the time dependent stress is the "Type III Girder" stress calculated in Step 6 for the top and Step 7 for the bottom. At the time the slab is placed, the time dependent stress is the sum of the "Slab + Type III Girder" values in Steps 6 and 7. The design load time dependent stresses are the total values at the bottom of Steps 6 and 7.

Note that, with the sign convention used, compression is negative and tension positive. We see that, under design loads, the stress in the bottom fiber of the prestressed girder is essentially zero.

The reinforcement used to ensure a sound shear connection usually takes the form of ties. This reinforcement extends from the girder into the cast-in-place deck slab. If the designer so desires, AASHTO allows shear reinforcement already present in the girder to be extended into the slab to satisfy the minimum tie reinforcement requirement.

This minimum tie reinforcement requirement is defined by the following (AASHTO 9.20.4.5):

$$\frac{50 \cdot b_v \cdot s}{f_y} \qquad \text{(Eq. 3.170)}$$

where b_v = width of cross section at contact surface
  s = tie spacing which cannot exceed four times the least web width of support element nor 24 in
  f_y = specified yield strength of reinforcement

> **T**he reinforcement used to ensure a sound shear connection usually takes the form of ties or extended stirrups.

If ties are used, they may be made up of single bars or wire, multiple leg stirrups, or vertical legs of welded wire fabric (AASHTO 9.20.4.5). Regardless of the type of tie used, it should be securely anchored to the connected elements, either by embedment or hooks.

If dissimilar concretes are used for the deck slab and the girder, a modular ratio must be computed just as before for steel-concrete composite girders. Quite naturally, this modular ratio will be much smaller than that computed for steel-concrete structures since the materials used will be closer in strength than steel and concrete are. For example, if the beam is fabricated with concrete having a compressive strength of 4,500 psi and the slab with 3,500 psi concrete, the modular ratio would be 1.13 (as compared to values for steel-concrete composite beams which range from 6 to 11).

When such a modular ratio is required, the slab is transformed to the girder in a fashion similar to that illustrated in Design Example 3.2, Step 8. For more on steel-concrete composite beams, the reader is referred to Section 3.10.

3.15.3 Required Prestress Force

The design stresses are computed at the top and bottom fiber of the resisting section using the section properties of the beam, or if composite, beam and slab. Once these design stresses are known, it is possible to determine the required prestress force.

For the rectangular beam loaded concentrically in Figure 3.51, the general equation for combined stresses is given as:

> **I**f dissimilar concretes are used for the deck slab and the girder, a modular ratio must be computed just as before for steel-concrete composite girders.

WHEN COMPUTING the stress acting on an eccentrically loaded beam, three geometric variables are important to know. The first is the eccentricity, e, itself. This is the distance from the center of gravity of the prestressing force to the centroid of the cross section. The distance y is that from the fiber is question (i.e., either top or bottom fiber) and the centroid of the cross section. The third variable is the radius of gyration of the section. From basic mechanics, recall that the square of the radius of gyration r^2 is defined as the ratio of the moment of inertia of the cross section to the area of the cross section. When compared to concentrically prestressing a beam, eccentrically loading will lead to an improved economy.

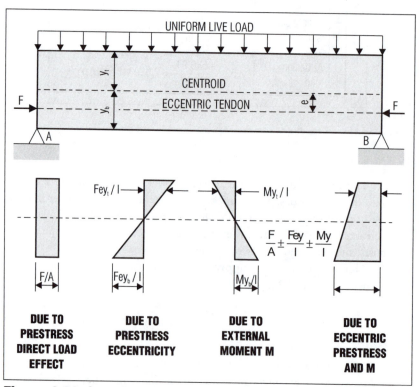

Figure 3.53 Stress distribution at midspan of a simple rectangular beam prestressed eccentrically.

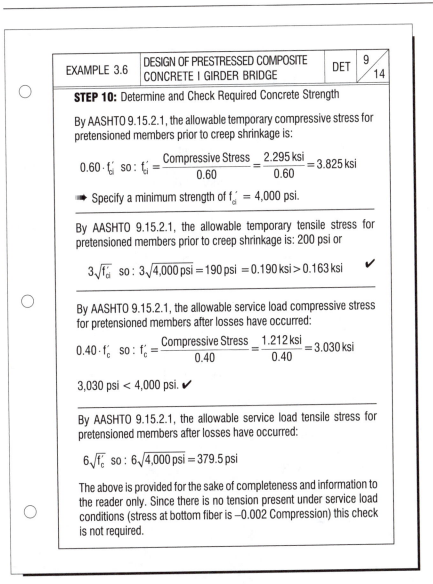

| EXAMPLE 3.6 | DESIGN OF PRESTRESSED COMPOSITE CONCRETE I GIRDER BRIDGE | DET | 9/14 |

STEP 10: Determine and Check Required Concrete Strength

By AASHTO 9.15.2.1, the allowable temporary compressive stress for pretensioned members prior to creep shrinkage is:

$$0.60 \cdot f_{ci}' \quad \text{so}: f_{ci}' = \frac{\text{Compressive Stress}}{0.60} = \frac{2.295\,\text{ksi}}{0.60} = 3.825\,\text{ksi}$$

➡ Specify a minimum strength of $f_{ci}' = 4{,}000$ psi.

By AASHTO 9.15.2.1, the allowable temporary tensile stress for pretensioned members prior to creep shrinkage is: 200 psi or

$$3\sqrt{f_{ci}'} \quad \text{so}: 3\sqrt{4{,}000\,\text{psi}} = 190\,\text{psi} = 0.190\,\text{ksi} > 0.163\,\text{ksi} \quad ✔$$

By AASHTO 9.15.2.1, the allowable service load compressive stress for pretensioned members after losses have occurred:

$$0.40 \cdot f_c' \quad \text{so}: f_c' = \frac{\text{Compressive Stress}}{0.40} = \frac{1.212\,\text{ksi}}{0.40} = 3.030\,\text{ksi}$$

3,030 psi < 4,000 psi. ✔

By AASHTO 9.15.2.1, the allowable service load tensile stress for pretensioned members after losses have occurred:

$$6\sqrt{f_c'} \quad \text{so}: 6\sqrt{4{,}000\,\text{psi}} = 379.5\,\text{psi}$$

The above is provided for the sake of completeness and information to the reader only. Since there is no tension present under service load conditions (stress at bottom fiber is −0.002 Compression) this check is not required.

DESIGN EXAMPLE 3.6
STEP 10: DETERMINE REQUIRED CONCRETE STRENGTH

Based on the stresses calculated in Step 9, we must determine and check the required concrete strength. This is done in accordance with AASHTO 9.15.2.1.

The strength is checked for adequacy in resisting compressive and tensile stresses prior to creep and shrinkage taking effect and after the losses have occurred.

Under compressive stress conditions, prior to creep and shrinkage we find that a 4,000 psi strength concrete will meet this requirement. This strength concrete also fulfills the requirements of all other conditions. In real design, a minimum of 5,000 psi concrete should be used for prestressed concrete members.

With regard to tension under service load conditions, since there is no tension present in this condition, a check is not needed. However, if this condition did exist, the allowable stress value is provided in the accompanying calculation sheet.

$$f = \frac{F}{A} \pm \frac{M \cdot y}{I} \qquad \text{(Eq. 3.171)}$$

where f = fiber stress

F = prestressing force

A = area of cross section

I = moment of inertia of cross section

When a beam is prestressed concentrically as shown in Figure 3.51, however, the top fiber must resist compressive stresses due to both prestressing *and* dead and live loads acting on the beam. Because of this phenomenon, tendons are typically placed a given distance from the centroid of the beam cross section. This distance is known as the eccentricity and is denoted by the variable *e*. Figure 3.53 shows a beam, similar to the one illustrated in Figure 3.51, with an eccentrically prestressed concrete beam.

In this instance, the beam which is eccentrically prestressed requires roughly half the prestress needed if the beam were prestressed concentrically.

> **W**hen a beam is prestressed concentrically … the top fiber must resist compressive stresses due to both prestressing *and* dead and live loads acting on the beam.

Another benefit is that the top fiber is not called upon to resist any compressive stress as a result of the eccentric prestressing [Ref. 3.67]. Therefore, the obvious benefit of eccentrically prestressing a beam is an enhanced economy. To further better the economy of the section, it is sometimes permissible to allow some nominal tensile stresses, resulting from service loads, to act on the section.

The moment due to prestressing is the product of the prestressing force and the eccentricity, *e*. In the sidebar accompanying Figure 3.53, we note that the radius of gyration of the section is also needed. Recall from basic mechanics that the square of the radius of gyration is defined as:

$$r^2 = \frac{I}{A}$$

(Eq. 3.172)

where I = moment of inertia of cross section
A = area of cross section

so that the expression defined in Equation 3.171 can be rewritten in the following way:

$$f = \frac{F}{A}\left(1 \pm \frac{e \cdot y}{r^2}\right)$$

(Eq. 3.173)

where f = fiber stress
F = prestressing force
A = area of cross section
M = moment acting on cross section
e = eccentricity

STEEL VS. CONCRETE. The perpetual nature of the debate concerning which material is better for highway bridges seems to be as much a part of bridge engineering as truck loading. The general perception among designers is that one type of structure must be chosen over the other. As Figure 3.54 illustrates, however, steel and concrete often coexist in the same environment. Indeed, sometimes prestressed girders are used in conjunction with steel girders *on the same structure*. Whether one material is better than the other is, of course, open to debate. As with any design issue, however, there should always be room for open-minded discussion. Such an approach only serves to make each type of bridge better in the long run.

Figure 3.54 A steel plate girder structure passes over a prestressed concrete bridge in Florida. Steel and prestressed concrete often coexist in the same environment.

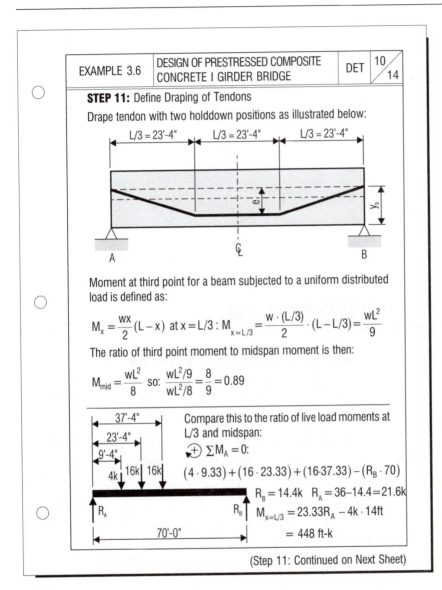

| EXAMPLE 3.6 | DESIGN OF PRESTRESSED COMPOSITE CONCRETE I GIRDER BRIDGE | DET | 10/14 |

STEP 11: Define Draping of Tendons

Drape tendon with two holddown positions as illustrated below:

$L/3 = 23'-4"$ $L/3 = 23'-4"$ $L/3 = 23'-4"$

Moment at third point for a beam subjected to a uniform distributed load is defined as:

$$M_x = \frac{wx}{2}(L-x) \text{ at } x = L/3 : M_{x=L/3} = \frac{w \cdot (L/3)}{2} \cdot (L - L/3) = \frac{wL^2}{9}$$

The ratio of third point moment to midspan moment is then:

$$M_{mid} = \frac{wL^2}{8} \text{ so: } \frac{wL^2/9}{wL^2/8} = \frac{8}{9} = 0.89$$

Compare this to the ratio of live load moments at L/3 and midspan:

$\circlearrowleft \Sigma M_A = 0$:

$$(4 \cdot 9.33) + (16 \cdot 23.33) + (16 \cdot 37.33) - (R_B \cdot 70)$$

$$R_B = 14.4k \quad R_A = 36 - 14.4 = 21.6k$$

$$M_{x=L/3} = 23.33 R_A - 4k \cdot 14ft$$

$$= 448 \text{ ft-k}$$

(Step 11: Continued on Next Sheet)

We will drape the tendon using two holddown points. Draping is also sometimes known as harping. To check the adequacy of this approach, we must determine the stresses resulting from the draped geometry of the tendon.

We will use the stresses computed earlier and apply a multiplier to get the values at the third points along the beam. This multiplier will be the ratio of the third point moment to the midspan moment. To compute this ratio we will take the general moment expressions for dead load and live load.

Calculating dead load moments is relatively straightforward since we have a uniform distributed load. Calculating the moment at the third point with the standard midpoint (maximum) moment results in a ratio of 0.89.

Live load, however, is a little more complicated. For maximum moment at the third point we position a truck with its center wheel over the beam's third point. Summing moments about support B we take a section just past the third point and solve for the moment.

y = distance from fiber to centroid of cross section

r = radius of gyration (Equation 3.172)

This general expression can be used to define separate fiber stresses at the top and bottom fiber of the beam cross section. In order to create uniform expressions, it is important to maintain a uniform sign convention. In this text we will use the convention put forth by James Libby in Ref. 3.67. Using this convention the following items are considered to be positive:

❏ Tensile stresses
❏ Forces in tension
❏ Strains and elongations
❏ Moments causing tensile stresses in the bottom fiber
❏ Increases in stress, strains, etc.
❏ Slopes of stress diagrams for positive bending
❏ Downward offsets from the centroidal axis (e.g., y and e)

In order to create uniform expressions, it is important to maintain a uniform sign convention.

" It's hard to get
people to change
details and designs.
Once an agency locks
into a standard they just
go on and on with it. **"**

BRUCE NOEL

[Ref. 3.58]

Conversely, concrete shrinkage is considered to be negative. As is the case with any sign convention, consistency is the rule and as long as the designer adheres to whatever standard he or she establishes, the results should be the same.

When such a consistent sign convention, as the one described above, is employed, the expression defined by Equation 3.173 can be defined for both the top and bottom fibers of the prestressed girder as:

$$f_{top} = \frac{C}{A}\left(1 + \frac{e \cdot y_t}{r^2}\right)$$ (Eq. 3.174)

and

$$f_{bot} = \frac{C}{A}\left(1 + \frac{e \cdot y_b}{r^2}\right)$$ (Eq. 3.175)

where C = resultant compressive force acting on section
y_t = distance from centroid to top of section (negative)

DESIGN PERSPECTIVE

Steel vs. Concrete: Which One Is Better for Bridges?

*A*t the onset of Section 3, regarding superstructure element selection, it was mentioned that "no other component elicits so much discussion, and even downright controversy, as to the type of elements to be utilized in construction." In essence, this boils down to steel vs. concrete.

While it would be foolish for anyone to answer "Which one is better?" one can examine the trends and discuss the advantages and disadvantages of each.

First concrete. A 1990 FHWA study indicated that, out of 723 new bridges slated for construction, 414 were to be constructed out of prestressed concrete: just over 57 percent.

Proponents of concrete site the fact that concrete structures do not require painting and therefore have a lower life-cycle cost when compared to steel (see Section 3.13). They would also note such design advantages as speed of construction as well as enhanced de-

flection control and overload capacity when compared to steel. Perhaps most damaging, however, is the claim that prestressed concrete structures are significantly more durable than their steel counterparts [Ref. 3.69].

Quite naturally, advocates of the use of steel would beg to differ on many, if not all of these points. With regard to maintenance, steel proponents would argue that, while steel shows corrosion more readily than concrete, it is more easily maintained because the deterioration is visible. Concrete, they argue, hides deterioration until spalling has occurred. If a prestressing tendon fails, then replacement rather than maintenance is required.

With regard to overload capacity, steel proponents counter that prestressed girders are designed to accommodate certain loads just as steel bridges are.

Indeed, sometimes each pro and con becomes indistinguishable from the other. Concrete advo-

cates claim their material is quicker to erect; so do those who promote steel [Ref. 3.44].

One thing few designers will admit, however, is that they are driven by what they know best and if that is steel, then they will gravitate toward these types of structures. If the engineer is more familiar with concrete, then a prestressed concrete structure will more than likely win out. The accompanying quote by Bruce Noel bears this out. Although in this particular instance, the engineer was referring to protective coating systems, the same is true for any design detail.

There is nothing inherently bad about this. In fact, it is only human nature. Both steel and concrete offer quality products. There are too many functional structures out there for it to be otherwise. As professionals, we must work toward making proper use of each material and applying it in as unbiased a fashion as possible.

| EXAMPLE 3.6 | DESIGN OF PRESTRESSED COMPOSITE CONCRETE I GIRDER BRIDGE | DET | 11/14 |

STEP 11: Define Draping of Tendons (Continued)

The maximum moment (near midspan) calculated earlier in Step 5 was found earlier to be: M_{max} = 492.80 ft-k

The ratio of third point to midpoint moments can be taken as:

$\dfrac{448 \text{ ft·k}}{492.8 \text{ ft·k}} = 0.91$ Since this is relatively close to 0.89 we will use 0.89 as our multiplier.

STEP 12: Fiber Stresses at Third Points of Beam

The multiplier is applied to the "time dependent" stresses calculated in Steps 6 and 7.

	Time of Stress	Equation	Stress
Top Fiber	At time of prestressing	$-.85 \cdot \dfrac{-663.9k}{560 \text{ in}^2} - (.845)(.89)$	= 0.257 ksi T
	At time slab is placed	$-.85 \cdot \dfrac{-586.9k}{560 \text{ in}^2} - (1.789)(.89)$	= −0.701 ksi C
	At design load	$-.85 \cdot \dfrac{-586.9k}{560 \text{ in}^2} - (2.103)(.89)$	= −0.981 ksi C
Bottom Fiber	At time of prestressing	$2.52 \cdot \dfrac{-663.9k}{560 \text{ in}^2} + (0.692)(.89)$	= −2.372 ksi C
	At time slab is placed	$2.52 \cdot \dfrac{-586.9k}{560 \text{ in}^2} + (1.466)(.89)$	= −1.336 ksi C
	At design load	$2.52 \cdot \dfrac{-586.9k}{560 \text{ in}^2} + (2.639)(.89)$	= −0.292 ksi C

DESIGN EXAMPLE 3.6
STEP 11: DEFINE DRAPING OF TENDONS (CONTINUED)

To compute the live load ratio we also need the midspan moment. The maximum moment was calculated earlier in Step 5 at a point close to midspan. The actual midspan moment is 490 ft-k so the difference is negligible. The live load ratio is therefore 0.91. Since this is relatively close to 0.89 we will use 0.89 as our multiplier.

STEP 12: FIBER STRESSES AT THIRD POINTS

Taking our expressions from Step 9, the dead and live load stresses are multiplied with the third point ratio. This produces resulting stresses where the tension at the time of prestressing is greater than that found at midspan.

We will now need to check the concrete strength requirements to see if the 4,000 psi strength concrete specified earlier will satisfy the AASHTO requirements of 9.15.2.1.

For more information on the expressions used in the accompanying table, refer to Step 9 as well as Section 3.15.3.

> As is the case with any sign convention, consistency is the rule and as long as the designer adheres to whatever standard he or she establishes, the results should be the same.

> A factor which can significantly impact the design of prestressed concrete members is the presence of conventional reinforcement in the beam.

y_b = distance from centroid to bottom of section (positive)
e = eccentricity. Distance from centroid to center of gravity of prestressing force (positive if below centroid)

so that when the designer computes the required prestressing force he or she solves for C, substituting in the design stress at the bottom fiber of the section and the miscellaneous geometric parameters.

A factor which can significantly impact the design of prestressed concrete members is the presence of conventional reinforcement in the beam. Such reinforcement may be present to facilitate construction or meet strength and serviceability requirements [Ref. 3.67]. When such reinforcement is present in the beam, it will also become prestressed and thus impact the design of the section. Most people will simply ignore non-prestressing reinforcing steel when calculating section properties. If you choose to consider it, you must transform reinforcing steel area into an equivalent concrete area by multiplying modulus ration *n*. A detailed discussion of these effects is beyond the scope of this text, and the reader is referred to Ref. 3.67 for more information on the subject.

3.15.4 Loss of Prestress

> Eventually, there will be a loss of prestress in the tendons which ... can be initiated by several contributing factors.

Eventually, there will be a loss of prestress in the tendons which must be accounted for by the designer. This loss of prestress can be initiated by several contributing factors. Some of the principal phenomena which can cause a loss of prestress are [Ref. 3.68]:

❑ Immediate elastic shortening of concrete under compression
❑ Shrinkage of concrete during drying
❑ Creep under sustained compression
❑ Frictional force between tendons and concrete during tensioning
❑ Relaxation in steel under tension
❑ Slippage and slackening of tendons during anchoring

Discussed below is an overview of some of the above referenced contributing factors which lead to a loss of prestress.

1. Elastic Shortening of Concrete. When the prestressing force is applied to the beam the surrounding concrete will undergo a deformation. This deformation typically results in the concrete around the tendons compressing causing the beam to shorten slightly. This small shortening, which takes place over a short period of time, is called elastic shortening. One potential side effect of this phenomenon is a loss of prestress.

The loss of prestress due to pretensioning a member can be defined by the following expression (AASHTO 9.16.2.1.2):

$$ES = \Delta f_s = n \cdot f_{cir} \qquad \text{(Eq. 3.176)}$$

where Δf_s = loss of prestress in steel
n = modular ratio (see Equations 3.177 and 3.178 below)
f_{cir} = concrete stress at the center of gravity of the prestressing steel due to prestressing force F and dead load of beam immediately after transfer

In the above expression, the modular ratio is defined by the following expression:

$$n = \frac{E_s}{E_{ci}} \qquad \text{(Eq. 3.177)}$$

where
$$E_{ci} = 33w^{3/2}\sqrt{f_{ci}'} \qquad \text{(Eq. 3.178)}$$

and E_s = modulus of elasticity of prestressing steel, psi (typically assumed as 28×10^6 psi)
E_{ci} = modulus of elasticity of concrete at stress transfer, psi (defined by Equation 3.178)
w = concrete unit weight, lb/ft^3
f_{ci}' = concrete compressive strength at time of initial prestress, psi

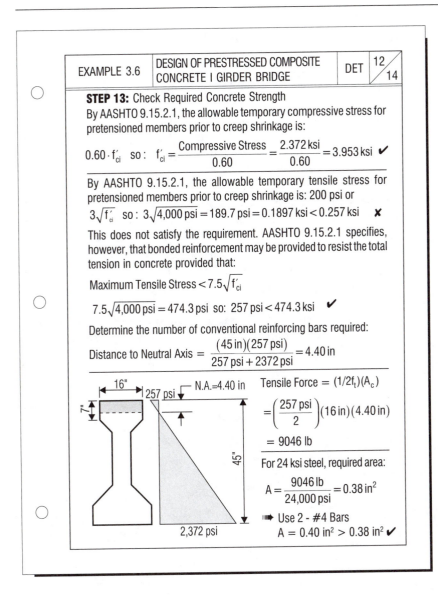

As before, we check for temporary compressive stress and find that the 4,000 psi strength concrete specified earlier is adequate.

We now check for temporary tensile stress and find that our computed stress is greater than the allowable. This does not mean, however, that we have to use a higher strength concrete. AASHTO allows us to supplement the cross section with bonded reinforcement provided that the overstress does not exceed a specified limit. Checking this upper limit, we see that we can use the supplemental reinforcement.

To calculate the amount of additional steel which will be required, we first locate the neutral axis based on the maximum tensile and compressive stresses and the depth of girder.

Once the neutral axis is located we can compute the tensile force and associated area of reinforcing steel required. We will use allowable stress of 24 ksi. To satisfy the calculated 0.38 in² area we choose two #4 bars which have an area of 0.40 in².

> If a beam is posttensioned, ... tendons are generally stressed individually ... the change in stress is averaged and taken to act on all of the tendons equally.

> When every posttensioned tendon is stressed above the initial prestressing force by the anticipated loss, then no losses resulting from elastic shortening need to be accounted for.

When a beam is pretensioned, all tendons are stressed simultaneously, meaning that a single stress change occurs all at once. If a beam is posttensioned, however, tendons are generally stressed individually. In the latter case, the change in stress is averaged and taken to act on all of the tendons equally.

This is done by calculating the loss in the first tendon and then using half of that amount as the average loss in all tendons. When every posttensioned tendon is stressed above the initial prestressing force by the anticipated loss, then no losses resulting from elastic shortening need to be accounted for [Ref. 3.68].

AASHTO defines elastic shortening for posttensioned beams similar to that for pretensioned. In this instance, however, we use the expression (AASHTO 9.16.2.1.2):

$$ES = \Delta f_s = 0.5 \cdot n \cdot f_{cir} \qquad \text{(Eq. 3.179)}$$

where Δf_s = loss of prestress in steel

    n = modular ratio (see Equations 3.177 and 3.178 above)

    f_{cir} = concrete stress at the center of gravity of the prestressing steel due to F and DL of beam immediately after transfer

AASHTO, though, stipulates that certain types of tensioning may alter the losses due to elastic shortening. Essentially, however, the differences between pretensioning and posttensioning are taken up by the 0.5 multiplier.

2. Shrinkage of Concrete. In Section 3.5.4, Part 2, we discussed the effects of shrinkage on conventional concrete. In prestressed concrete, we again see the impact of moisture loss on the performance of the member. Unlike elastic shortening, shrinkage takes place over a long period of time. While it may take several years before the member reaches 100 percent of its losses due to shrinkage roughly 80 percent will take place in the first year [Ref. 3.68].

AASHTO accounts for losses due to shrinkage based on the mean annual relative humidity of the region where the bridge is being

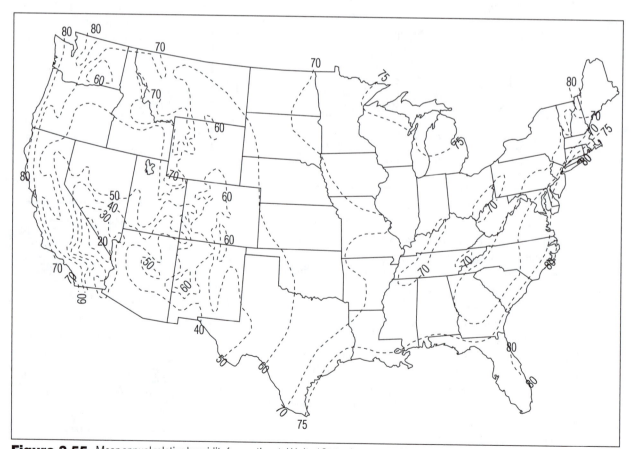

Figure 3.55 Mean annual relative humidity for continental United States in percent. *(Adapted from Standard Specifications for Highway Bridges, 17th Edition, Ref. 3.3.)* Consult map in the AASHTO specifications for more detail.

| EXAMPLE 3.6 | DESIGN OF PRESTRESSED COMPOSITE CONCRETE I GIRDER BRIDGE | DET | 13/14 |

STEP 14: Check Flexural Strength

Compute prestressing steel ratio defined as:

$$p^* = \frac{A_s^*}{b \cdot d} \quad \left| \begin{array}{l} A_s^* = 3.50 \text{ in}^2 \text{ (Step 8)} \\ b = \text{Effective Flange Width} = 7' - 3'' = 7.25 \text{ ft} = 87 \text{ in} \\ d = \text{Girder-Slab Depth above PS} = 53 \text{ in} - 3.5 \text{ in} = 49.5 \text{ in} \end{array} \right.$$

$$p^* = \frac{3.50 \text{ in}^2}{(87 \text{ in})(49.5 \text{ in})} = 8.13 \times 10^{-4}$$

Using Equation 3.187 to compute average stress in prestressing steel at ultimate load for bonded members:

$$f_{su}^* = f_s' \left[1 - \left(\frac{\gamma^*}{\beta_1} \right) \left(\frac{p^* \cdot f_s'}{f_c'} \right) \right] \quad \left| \begin{array}{l} p^* = 8.13 \times 10^{-4} \text{ (Above)} \\ f_s' = 270 \text{ ksi (Given)} \\ f_c' = 4,000 \text{ psi} = 4 \text{ ksi} \end{array} \right.$$

$$= 270 \text{ ksi} \cdot \left[1 - \left(\frac{0.28}{0.85} \right) \left(\frac{8.13 \times 10^{-4} \times 270 \text{ ksi}}{4 \text{ ksi}} \right) \right] = 265 \text{ ksi}$$

where : $\gamma^* = 0.28$ (Given), $\beta_1 = 0.85$ (for 4 ksi concrete)

$$a = \frac{A_s^* \cdot f_{su}^*}{0.85 f_b' b} = \frac{3.50 \times 265}{0.85 \times 4 \times 87} = 3.14 \text{ in}$$

Thickness of Slab = 7 in > a = 3.14 in:

Neutral axis is located in the flange meaning that we design for a rectangular section

(Step 14: Continued on Next Sheet)

We must first compute a ratio of prestressing steel. Recall that in Step 8 we determined the area of prestressing steel required. This area is divided by the area bounded by the effective flange width and the depth of the section above the center of gravity of prestressing steel.

We use this value to compute the average stress in the prestressing steel at ultimate load. Since we assumed that the deck and girder would be made out of the same concrete, we use the concrete strength of 4,000 psi determined earlier. Otherwise we would use the strength of the deck here which is typically lower than that for the prestressed girder.

We use $\gamma^* = 0.28$ for low relaxation prestressing steel, which is typical, for this bridge.

We next need to determine the location of the neutral axis for ultimate load to see if it is located in the web or the flange. This will tell us whether we treat the section as a flanged or rectangular section. If the neutral axis falls in the flange area, we treat it as a rectangular section. Since the resulting value is less than the 7 in slab thickness, we treat the section as a rectangular one.

---

constructed. For pretensioned bridge structures, the expression which defines the loss of prestress due to shrinkage is given by (AASHTO 9.16.2.1.1):

$$SH = 17,000 - 150 \cdot RH \qquad \text{(Eq. 3.180)}$$

and for posttensioned structures

$$SH = 0.80 \cdot (17,000 - 150 \cdot RH) \qquad \text{(Eq. 3.181)}$$

where RH = mean annual ambient relative humidity in percent

AASHTO provides a map of the United States with relative humidity values plotted as contours. Figure 3.55 shows these relative humidity

> **A**ASHTO provides a map of the United States with relative humidity values plotted as contours ... if necessary, however, more refined methods can be used.

contours for the continental United States only. If necessary, however, more refined methods can be used.

3. **Creep of Concrete.** In Section 3.5.4, Part 1, we discussed the effects of creep on conventional concrete. Like shrinkage, creep is time dependent and acts on the member over a given period of time when the beam is subjected to sustained loads. The onset of creep is assumed to occur after the prestressing force has been applied and the superimposed dead loads are placed on the member.

> The onset of creep is assumed to occur after the prestressing force has been applied and the superimposed dead loads are placed on the member.

To compute losses due to creep, the concrete stress at the center of gravity of the prestressing steel is reduced by the tensile strain which occurs as a result of the placement of superimposed dead loads. Specifically, AASHTO defines the loss due to creep of concrete with the following expression (AASHTO 9.16.2.1.3):

$$CR_c = 12 \cdot f_{cir} - 7 \cdot f_{cds} \qquad \text{(Eq. 3.182)}$$

where f_{cir} = concrete stress at the center of gravity of the prestressing steel due to F and DL of beam immediately after transfer
f_{cds} = concrete stress at the center of gravity of the prestressing steel due to all DL except DL present at time F is applied

This expression is used to define losses due to creep of concrete for both pretensioned and posttensioned members.

4. **Friction.** In general, the stress in a tendon at a point away from the tensioning end is lower due to the friction which occurs between the tendon and surrounding concrete or sheathing [Ref. 3.68]. One factor which influences the loss due to friction is known as the length effect. This length or wobbling effect is the amount of friction which would occur if the tendon were perfectly straight. Since this is not the case, a certain amount of friction results between the prestressing steel and surrounding material.

Obviously, many factors impact the amount of friction which results from this phenomenon, some of which are:

❏ Length of the tendon
❏ Stress in the tendons
❏ Friction coefficient
❏ Type of duct used

Another component of friction loss is known as the curvature effect. This loss results from the curve the prestressing tendon is intended to follow. The two basic contributing factors impacting the curvature effect are:

❏ Pressure on surrounding concrete caused by the tendon
❏ Friction coefficient

EXAMPLE 3.6	DESIGN OF PRESTRESSED COMPOSITE CONCRETE I GIRDER BRIDGE	DET	14 / 14

STEP 14: Check Flexural Strength (Continued)

For a rectangular section, we must check that ...

$$\frac{p^* \cdot f_{su}^*}{f_c'} = \frac{(8.13 \times 10^{-4})(265 \text{ ksi})}{(4 \text{ ksi})} = 0.05$$

... does not exceed the following limit (AASHTO 9.18.1):

$$0.36 \cdot \beta_1 = (0.36)(0.85) = 0.31 \text{ so} : 0.05 < 0.31 \ ✔$$

By Equation 3.189, the flexural strength of a rectangular section is taken as:

$$\phi \cdot M_n = \phi \cdot \left[A_s^* \cdot f_{su}^* \cdot \left(d - \frac{a}{2} \right) \right]$$

$$\phi \cdot M_n = \frac{1.0 \cdot \left[(3.50 \text{ in}^2) \cdot (265 \text{ ksi}) \cdot (49.5 - 0.5 \times 3.14) \right]}{12 \text{ in/ft}}$$

$$\phi \cdot M_n = 3705 \text{ ft} \cdot k$$

Taking the moment defined by the load factored group loading (see Table 3.2):

$$M = \gamma \cdot \left[\beta_{DL} \cdot M_{DL} + \beta_{LL+I} \cdot M_{LL+I} \right]$$

Using the dead load moment determined in Step 4 and the live load plus impact moment found in Step 5:

$$M = 1.3 \cdot \left[(1.0)(975 \text{ ft} \cdot k) + (1.67)(819.62 \text{ ft} \cdot k) \right] = 3047 \text{ ft} \cdot k$$

So, we are O.K. since we have:

3047 ft-k < 3705 ft-k ✔

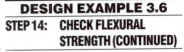

DESIGN EXAMPLE 3.6
STEP 14: CHECK FLEXURAL STRENGTH (CONTINUED)

The prestressing steel is checked to ensure that the steel is yielding as ultimate capacity is approached (AASHTO 9.18.1). The beta factor used is 0.85 for concrete with strengths up to and including 4,000 psi (AASHTO 8.16.2.7). For concrete strengths over 4,000 psi, the 0.85 beta value is reduced by 0.05 for each 1000 psi of strength over 4,000 psi. The beta value, however, cannot be less than 0.65.

We next check the design flexural strength of the section. By Equation 3.189, for factory produced, precast prestressed concrete girders the strength reduction factor (ϕ) is taken to be 1.0.

Substituting in we calculate the flexural strength of the section. Using the load factor method and associated load factors from Table 3.2 (AASHTO 3.22), the design moment is computed. The dead load moment was tabulated in Step 4 and the live load plus impact moment in Step 5. Solving, we see that the capacity of the selected section is adequate.

In real design, the minimum reinforcement should also be checked (AASHTO 9.18.2).

The variable nature of friction loss is further complicated by the type of lubricants used and the types of surfaces in contact with each other; each influencing the magnitude of the friction coefficient. As we have consistently seen, however, the complex and variable physical conditions which lead to friction loss are defined using an idealized model. This idealization is made using coefficients known as the *friction wobble coefficient* and the *friction curvature coefficient*. Table 3.27 presents AASHTO recommended values, for each coefficient, which can be used when experimental data for the materials used is unavailable (AASHTO 9.16.1).

The friction losses at any point along the tendon is defined by AASHTO 9.16.1 as:

As we have consistently seen, however, the complex and variable physical conditions which lead to friction loss are defined using an idealized model.

$$T_o = T_x \cdot e^{(KL + \mu\alpha)}$$

(Eq. 3.183)

Type of Steel	Type of Duct	K = Wobble/ft	μ = Curvature
Wire or ungalvanized strand	Bright metal sheathing	0.0020	0.30
	Galvanized metal sheathing	0.0015	0.25
	Greased or asphalt-coated and wrapped	0.0020	0.30
	Galvanized rigid	0.0002	0.25
High-strength bars	Bright metal sheathing	0.0003	0.20
	Galvanized metal sheathing	0.0002	0.15

Table 3.27 AASHTO Wobble and Curvature Coefficients for Various Types of Prestressing Steels and Ducts

where T_o = steel stress at the jacking end

T_x = steel stress at point along tendon in question

e = base of naperian logarithms

K = wobble coefficient per foot of tendon (see Table 3.27)

L = length of tendon from jack to point in question

μ = curvature coefficient (see Table 3.27)

α = total angular change of tendon in radians from jacking end to point in question

Friction losses will be minimized if tendons are greased properly and wrapped in plastic tubes [Ref. 3.68]. When bonded tendons are used, another method of reducing the impact of friction losses is to lubricate the tendon during tensioning operations and then flush it clean with water. Tendon overtensioning and jacking from each end of the tendon are two additional methods which are used to compensate for predicted friction losses.

In Equation 3.183, an approximation is allowed when the $(KL + \mu\alpha)$ term is found to be less than 0.30. When such a condition occurs, the friction loss can be approximated by:

> When bonded tendons are used, another method of reducing the impact of friction losses is to lubricate the tendon during tensioning operations and then flush it clean with water.

$$T_o = T_x \cdot (1 + KL + \mu\alpha) \qquad \text{(Eq. 3.184)}$$

Although friction losses take place before anchoring, they should be "estimated for design and checked during stressing operations" by the contractor [Ref. 3.3]. Typically, friction loss data (e.g., friction coefficients, minimum jacking forces, etc.) are annotated on the contract documents to facilitate this checking process.

> Although friction losses take place before anchoring, they should be "estimated for design and checked during stressing operations" by the contractor.

Rigid ducts are to be sufficiently strong so that they hold the designed alignment without visible wobble during the placement of concrete. These ducts can be fabricated using welds or interlocking seams. AASHTO does not require galvanizing of welded seams (AASHTO 9.16.1).

5. Relaxation of Prestressing Steel. Where creep is the change in strain which results from a member under constant stress, relaxation is the loss of stress for a member under stress and at constant strain [Ref. 3.67]. The higher the stress the tendon is subjected to, the more the loss due to relaxation will be. Relaxation in steel is affected primarily by the type of prestressing steel used and the method of prestressing.

For both pretensioning and posttensioning, the loss due to relaxation is determined using previously calculated values for losses resulting from elastic shortening, shrinkage, and creep of concrete. When the beam is posttensioned, friction losses are also considered in determining the losses due to relaxation.

For *pretensioned members* the loss to relaxation of prestressing steel are given by the following expressions (AASHTO 9.16.2.1.4):

for   250 ksi to 270 ksi Stress Relieved Strand

$$CR_s = 20,000 - 0.40ES - 0.20 \cdot (SH + CR_c) \qquad \text{(Eq. 3.185a)}$$

for   250 ksi to 270 ksi Low Relaxation Strand

$$CR_s = 5,000 - 0.10ES - 0.05 \cdot (SH + CR_c) \qquad \text{(Eq. 3.185b)}$$

For *posttensioned members* the loss to relaxation of prestressing steel are given by the following expressions (AASHTO 9.16.2.1.4):

for   250 ksi to 270 ksi Stress Relieved Strand

$$CR_s = 20,000 - 0.30FR - 0.40ES - 0.20 \cdot (SH + CR_c) \qquad \text{(Eq. 3.185c)}$$

for   250 ksi to 270 ksi Low Relaxation Strand

$$CR_s = 5,000 - 0.07FR - 0.10ES - 0.05 \cdot (SH + CR_c) \qquad \text{(Eq. 3.185d)}$$

for   240 ksi Wire

$$CR_s = 18,000 - 0.30FR - 0.40ES - 0.20 \cdot (SH + CR_c) \qquad \text{(Eq. 3.185e)}$$

for   145 ksi to 160 ksi Bars

$$CR_s = 3,000 \qquad \text{(Eq. 3.185f)}$$

> Where creep is the change in strain which results from a member under constant stress, relaxation is the loss of stress for a member under stress and at constant strain.

AASHTO SPECIFICATION
9.15 VARIABLES USED FOR
PRESTRESSED CONCRETE

f_c' = Concrete Compressive Strength at 28 days

f_{ci}' = Concrete Compressive Strength at time of initial prestress

f_s' = Prestressing Steel Ultimate Strength

f_y^* = Prestressing Steel Yield Point

These expressions for relaxation in steel result from prestressed beams possessing a level of steel strain which is always changing. This change takes place concurrently with creep.

A more expedient method of accounting for the losses in prestress is to use predefined tables which contain estimated losses.

The friction loss *FR* used is in units of pounds per square inch and is taken as the stress reduction below a level of *0.70f′ₛ* at the point in question along the tendon.

These expressions for relaxation in steel result from prestressed beams possessing a level of steel strain which is always changing. This change takes place concurrently with creep. The actual loss caused by relaxation is therefore calculated as a function of the immediate losses caused by elastic shortening and the long term losses resulting from shrinkage and creep in the concrete. AASHTO also notes that the "relaxation losses are based on an initial stress equal to the stress at [the] anchorages" [Ref. 3.3].

6. **Total Loss.** It is therefore intuitively obvious that the total loss of prestress is defined as:

$$\Delta f_s = SH + ES + CR_c + CR_s \qquad \text{(Eq. 3.186)}$$

where Δf_s = total loss excluding friction, psi
   SH = loss due to concrete shrinkage, psi
   ES = loss due to elastic shortening, psi
   CR_c = loss due to creep of concrete, psi
   CR_s = loss due to relaxation of prestressing steel, psi

7. **Estimated Losses.** A more expedient method of accounting for the losses in prestress is to use predefined tables which contain estimated losses. Two such tables are presented in Tables 3.25 and 3.26. Typically these values (such as the current AASHTO estimates in Table 3.26) are based on the use of:

- ❏ Normal weight concrete
- ❏ Normal prestress levels
- ❏ Average exposure conditions

For small structures these tables may prove adequate. Larger, more complex structures, however, require more precise methods such as the one outlined above. Depending on the magnitude of the project, it may even be desirous to use a more exact methodology based on exact prestress loss data.

3.15.5 Allowable Stresses

It has been mentioned earlier that prestressed concrete structures generally use higher strength concrete when compared to conventionally reinforced structures. For prestressed concrete bridges, concrete with a compressive strength of 5,000 psi or 6,000 psi (35 MPa or 40 MPa) is generally used. Higher strength concrete may result in an economy of materials, provided that it is readily accessible to the contractor.

Based on this type of concrete, AASHTO presents allowable stresses for both concrete and prestressing steel (although the allowable stress values are applicable to prestressed concrete which is composed of lower concrete strengths). The allowable stresses are presented in Table 3.28 in

	Method	Description	Allowable Stress
PRESTRESSING STEEL	Pretensioned	Stress at anchorages after seating for stress relieved strands	$0.70 \cdot f'_s$
	Pretensioned	Stress at anchorages after seating for low relaxation strands	$0.75 \cdot f'_s$
		Slight overstressing up to $0.80f'_s$ for short periods of time permitted	
	Posttensioned	Stress at anchorages after seating	
		Slight overstressing up to $0.90f^*_y$ for short periods of time permitted	$0.70 \cdot f'_s$
	Both	Stress at service load after losses (does not include overload)	$0.80 \cdot f^*_y$
CONCRETE	Pretensioned	Compression: Temporary stresses	$0.60 \cdot f'_{ci}$
	Posttensioned	Compression: Temporary stresses	$0.55 \cdot f'_{ci}$
	Both	Tension: Temporary stresses: Precompressed tensile zone	None specified
	Both	Tension: Temporary stresses: Areas with no bonded reinforcement	200 psi or $3\sqrt{f'_{ci}}$
	Both	Compression: Stresses at service load after losses	$0.40 \cdot f'_c$
	Both	Tension: Stresses at service load after losses	
		Precompressed tensile zone, members with bonded reinforcement	$6\sqrt{f'_c}$
		Precompressed tensile zone, severe corrosive exposure conditions	$3\sqrt{f'_c}$
		Precompressed tensile zone, members with no bonded reinforcement	0
	Both	Cracking stress: Normal weight concrete	$7.5\sqrt{f'_c}$
		Cracking stress: Sand-lightweight concrete	$6.3\sqrt{f'_c}$
		Cracking stress: All other lightweight concrete	$5.5\sqrt{f'_c}$
	Posttensioned	Anchorage bearing stress: Posttensioned anchorage at service load Not to exceed $0.90f'_{ci}$	3,000 psi

Table 3.28 Allowable Stresses for Prestressing Steel and Concrete (AASHTO 9.15)

synopsis format. The stresses typically vary depending on the duration (temporary vs. long term) and the nature of the loading condition (compression vs. tension).

3.15.6 Flexual Strength

In addition to the service load stress requirements stipulated in Table 3.28, prestressed concrete members must also meet the strength requirements.

In addition to the service load stress requirements..., prestressed concrete members must also meet the strength requirements.

When calculating flexural strength, most designers ignore non-prestressing reinforcing steel. The equations used to calculate prestressed concrete beam are similar to these used in conventional reinforced concrete beams, except that the allowable stress for prestressing steel should be calculated as:

$$f_{su}^* = f_s' \left[1 - \left(\frac{\gamma^*}{\beta_1} \right) \left(\frac{\rho^* f_s'}{f_c'} \right) \right]$$

(Eq. 3.187)

where f_{su}^* = allowable stress for prestressing steel
f_s' = ultimate stress for prestressing steel
γ^* = factor for type of prestressing steel (= 0.28 for low-relaxation steel)
β_1 = factor for concrete strength (= 0.85 for 4 ksi concrete, and 0.80 for 5 ksi concrete)
ρ^* = ration of prestressing steel (= A_s^*/bd)
f_c' = concrete strength

The concrete compression block height:

$$a = \frac{A_s^* \cdot f_{su}^*}{0.85 f_c' b}$$

(Eq. 3.188)

where A_s^* = area of prestressing steel
b = effective flange width

If the compression stress block height a is less than the concrete deck thickness, the flexural strength can be calculated as:

$$\phi \cdot M_n = \phi \cdot A_s^* \cdot f_{su}^* \left(d - \frac{a}{2} \right)$$

(Eq. 3.189)

where d is the distance between the centroid of prestressing steel and the top of concrete slab.

If a is greater than the concrete slab thickness, or if non-prestressing steel is considered in flexural strength calculation, detailed calculations may be performed. See AASHTO 9.17 for complete equations.

The section should also be checked for maximum and minimum reinforcement requirements (ductility requirements). See AASHTO 9.18 or Step 14 of Example 3.6 for details.

3.16 PRESTRESSED CONCRETE MAINTENANCE

The number of prestressed concrete highway bridge structures in use and being constructed has increased dramatically. In 2003, 47% of highway bridges in the United States made use of prestressed concrete elements. As we have already discussed, however, the widespread use of prestressed concrete (particularly in the United States) is a relatively new phenomenon, especially when compared to steel structures (see Did You Know That?). While it may be somewhat inaccurate to say that maintenance and rehabilitation methods for prestressed concrete highway bridges are embryonic, the techniques are at best in their early stages of development.

To be sure, prestressed concrete offers many advantages as a material for bridge construction (see *Design Perspective: Steel vs. Concrete*). Like steel, or any other material for that matter, prestressed concrete requires a thorough and attentive maintenance program to ensure that the structure serves its function at a high level of performance.

The following discussion presents an overview of some of the major issues which can impact the performance of prestressed concrete bridges and influence an owner's inspection and maintenance program.

3.16.1 Overview

Any bridge structure will eventually deteriorate. In prestressed concrete structures the deterioration process is accelerated if the designer did not adequately account for design conditions (e.g., loss of prestress, overload conditions, etc.) or the contractor employed improper techniques during

Figure 3.56 A prestressed concrete box structure under construction.

THIS CONCRETE BOX structure under construction will eventually require rehabilitation, but when? The general rule of thumb is that concrete structures, like this one, need retrofitting after approximately 6,000 days. This translates into roughly 15 years of service. The time dependent effects of creep and shrinkage play an important role in the performance of prestressed concrete structures. Another factor which can influence the level of deterioration in prestressed concrete structures is the environment within which it is located. Prestressed concrete structures in a marine environment often fair worse than structures in less severe surroundings.

> It is important for the reader to appreciate that prestressed concrete is not so much a material but rather a method of construction.

> The impact which pre-stressing steel has on the performance of a structure is great, particularly in light of the resulting adverse effects which can occur should the tendons fail.

construction. With regard to the maintenance and rehabilitation of pre-stressed concrete bridges, it is important for the reader to appreciate that prestressed concrete is not so much a material but rather a method of construction [Ref. 3.70]. Maintenance and rehabilitation of prestressed concrete differs from that of conventionally reinforced structures in two basic ways. These differences being that prestressed concrete makes use of higher strength concrete and prestressing tendons are used to develop its strength.

Since higher strength concrete is generally the rule of thumb, the concrete component of a prestressed element will, on the whole, perform better than that of a conventionally reinforced element. Because of this, much attention is focused on the performance of the prestressing steel.

The impact which prestressing steel has on the performance of a structure is great, particularly in light of the resulting adverse effects which can occur should the tendons fail. What makes maintenance of prestressed structures different from steel bridges is the difficulty in inspecting the hidden elements (i.e., prestressing steel) of a prestressed component.

This difficulty also leads to associated problems with rehabilitation. Since a prestressed girder is essentially a self-contained, enclosed assembly, it is difficult to rehabilitate portions of a span as can be done with a steel girder. In many instances replacement rather than rehabilitation is the only solution available to an owner.

Prestressed concrete bridges are not without their share of failures either. Failures of prestressed concrete structures have occurred both within the United States and overseas. In spite of these difficulties, however, prestressed concrete structures have gained popularity because of their durability. As the first generation of prestressed concrete bridges has grown older, new methods for their maintenance have also developed.

3.16.2 Deterioration of Prestressed Concrete

Prestressed concrete suffers from some of the same types of deterioration as conventionally reinforced elements (e.g., cracking and scaling). The presence of prestressing steel, however, leads to some subtle and not so subtle differences.

In general, corrosion of prestressed concrete takes place as a result of several mechanisms [Ref. 3.70]. Some of the major contributing factors which initiate and propagate corrosion are:

- ❏ Pitting corrosion
- ❏ Stress corrosion
- ❏ Hydrogen embrittlement

The most severe consequence which can result from corrosion to a prestressed concrete member is a total loss of prestress in the steel tendons which can ultimately lead to failure of the structure. The seriousness of this necessitates the development of a sound and thorough maintenance program which can detect deterioration in its early stages and thus identify potential problem areas in advance. While there are a variety of advanced tools available to facilitate the inspection process (e.g., radiography, exposure of prestressing steel, etc.), the basis of any maintenance operations will be the visual inspection. For this reason, we need to discuss the principal forms of deterioration which an inspector will be faced with in inspecting prestressed concrete elements.

Provided below is an outline of some of the major forms of deterioration prestressed concrete members are subjected to.

1. **Cracking.** Like conventionally reinforced concrete, prestressed concrete is susceptible to cracking. Map cracking and other types of cracks can result from many of the same conditions as discussed previously for conventional concrete. Chief among the causes of such cracking are the intrusion of chlorides and other harmful agents which are typical of marine and cold weather environments. Such cracking can initiate abnormal expansion and lead to a loss of strength of the member [Ref. 3.70].

Other forms of cracking include plastic shrinkage cracks and drying shrinkage cracks, which can result from improper drying of the concrete. Settlement cracks may also occur as a result of either poor workmanship during construction or settlement of the structure's foundation.

Principal causes for structural cracks can be detailed by the following [Ref. 3.70]:

- ❏ Inadequate moment and shear capacity
- ❏ Incorrect allowance for thermal forces
- ❏ Incorrect allowance for stresses from tendon curvature
- ❏ Poor construction techniques
- ❏ Poor tolerances requirements for locating strands
- ❏ Use of under strength materials

The impact which such cracking will have on a structure will vary. Some cracks will naturally be more severe than others. Because of the naturally occurring phenomena of shrinkage and creep, it is impossible to completely eliminate all cracking. Cracking, however, can be limited by avoiding some of the design and fabrication pitfalls detailed above. Flexural cracks, for example, indicate an improper or inadequate accounting for stresses due to tension at the extreme fiber of the resisting beam cross section. Indeed, although creep and shrinkage are unavoidable, as we saw in Section 3.15, they can and should be accounted for during the design process.

The same is true for cracks caused by thermal forces which, in some structures, can cause stresses even greater than live loading conditions. Thermal cracks are evidenced by vertical cracks located close to intermediate supports. Another key point is at tendon anchorage locations where cracks may develop as a result of improper design and/or construction.

Similar to plate girders, shear cracks will predominately affect girder webs where they are inclined at approximate 45 degree angles. Shear cracks are generally located in the area between the span support and inflection point [Ref. 3.70].

While there are a variety of advanced tools available to facilitate the inspection process ... the basis of any maintenance operations will be the visual inspection.

Chief among the causes of such cracking are the intrusion of chlorides and other harmful agents which are typical of marine and cold weather environments.

Because of the naturally occurring phenomena of shrinkage and creep, it is impossible to completely eliminate all cracking.

2. Other Forms of Concrete Corrosion. In addition to cracking, other forms of concrete corrosion which can affect the performance of a structure are:

- ❏ Scaling
- ❏ Honeycombing
- ❏ Air pockets
- ❏ Popouts resulting from internal pressure
- ❏ Surface deposits (e.g., efflorescence)
- ❏ Wear from traffic
- ❏ Erosion
- ❏ Chemical attacks

Scaling, honeycombing, and air pockets typically result from poor construction methods. Chemical attacks, as mentioned earlier, result from environmental factors. Prestressed concrete will also suffer from the cathodic action discussed earlier in Section 3.9.8, Part 8. This can lead to damage to both the prestressing steel (see Part 3 below) and surrounding concrete.

3. Deterioration of Prestressing Steel. As mentioned above, prestressing steel is subjected to the same cathodic action that conventional reinforcing steel is. The principal physical difference between deterioration of conventional reinforcing bars and prestressing steel is that the latter is subjected to higher stresses and is therefore more susceptible to corrosion than the comparatively lightly stressed reinforcing steel. For the most part, however, this differential is negligible. The more extreme difference between the reinforcing bars and prestressing steel is that the consequences of an excessively deteriorated prestressing tendon is much greater than for a conventional reinforcing bar.

Corrosion to steel components of a prestressed girder can be accelerated through the existence of cracks as described above. The presence of such cracks provides an excellent vehicle for water, chlorides, and other harmful agents to penetrate the surface of the concrete and reach the underlying steel.

Another source of deterioration is the often mentioned deck joint leakage. This is of particular concern in prestressed concrete girders as the end anchorages can potentially be affected. When water penetrates to the end anchorage location it will generally travel down the entire length of the tendon damaging both the prestressing steel and the surrounding concrete. This will in turn lead to unbonding, which will greatly accelerate the deterioration process.

> **t**he consequences of an excessively deteriorated prestressing tendon is much greater than for a conventional reinforcing bar.

3.16.3 Inspection of Prestressed Concrete

In Section 2 we discussed the general procedures associated with a detailed site inspection. With regard to prestressed concrete structures, there are certain key issues which need to be addressed. In this section we have already touched on the importance of a thorough visual inspection in order to formulate an accurate and coherent maintenance plan. Likewise, it can be said that the condition of the bridge will predicate the level of detail awarded to the inspection process.

The list of key items indicating deterioration is not at all surprising and could just as well apply to a conventionally reinforced structure [Ref. 3.70]. Basic features or conditions which should be identified by the inspector can be defined as:

❑ Cracking
❑ Wet spots
❑ Spalling
❑ Excessive deflection/deformation of members
❑ Presence of efflorescence
❑ Scaling
❑ Settlement or uplift of the structure

Of particular concern, however, is the condition of the prestressing tendons. One of the drawbacks to prestressed structures is that it is difficult if not impossible to adequately inspect the prestressing steel located within a girder using visual methods alone. If corrosion of the tendons is suspected, however, there are methods available to more closely ascertain the condition of the prestressing steel.

One method is to drill holes in the member and visibly inspect the steel. The location of the holes is based on tell tale signs of deterioration underneath such as:

❑ Rust stains
❑ Wet spots
❑ Test results indicating high chloride content

> **T**he list of key items indicating deterioration is not at all surprising and could just as well apply to a conventionally reinforced structure.

> **O**ne of the drawbacks to prestressed structures is that it is difficult if not impossible to adequately inspect the prestressing steel located within a girder using visual methods alone.

BUCKET SNOOPERS like the one shown in Figure 3.57 offer inspection personnel access to the underside of a structure. This is particularly advantageous when the bridge crosses a body of water or has an extremely large underpass clearance making inspection from a cherry picker beneath the bridge impossible. Many transportation departments maintain their own standards for inspection. One rule that transcends all organizations, however, is safety first. This means hard hats for all inspection personnel, reflective vests, and proper maintenance of traffic when required. In Figure 3.57, a truck equipped with a flashing arrow board can be seen in the background providing protection to the crews inspecting the bridge.

Figure 3.57 A bucket snooper is used to inspect the underside of bridge over water.

The obvious danger associated with such an approach is that the inspection itself could damage the girder and accelerate deterioration. Because of this risk, it is important that the utmost care be taken in the drilling process. To remove the concrete and expose the underlying strands, an electric chipping hammer can be used [Ref. 3.70].

In posttensioned structures coring to a given depth is acceptable, provided that it stops short of the tendon duct. The remaining concrete is removed with a chipping hammer and the tendon inspected. A method developed in Germany utilizes a drill equipped with a magnetic sensor which stops the drill just short of the underlying steel.

In addition to these basic methods, advanced methods which are based on ultrasonic, electrical, and radiographic techniques can be used to indicate possible delaminations in the concrete or corrosion to the prestressing steel. Some of these approaches were covered previously in Section 2.

In general, the inspection of a prestressed concrete structure should focus on the most sensitive areas of the bridge. An obvious candidate for consistent inspection is at anchorage zones and beam ends. As mentioned earlier, these areas are particularly susceptible to joint leakage and the intrusion of water at the anchorage will carry moisture along the tendon through capillary action, accelerating deterioration. In addition to the presence of moisture, anchorage zones are also susceptible to cracking due to high stresses at this location.

Like steel girders, prestressed girders are also prone to vehicle impact when located over underpasses with a tight vertical clearance. Such impact can lead to a chipping away of concrete, exposure of prestressing strands, or even damage to the strands themselves.

3.16.4 Rehabilitation of Prestressed Concrete

If an inspection indicates that remedial measures need to be taken, there are several basic steps an owner can take to both protect and repair a prestressed concrete structure. One basic step is to ensure proper drainage of the bridge deck and to repair or replace any deficient joints. Indeed, such measures should be undertaken consistently by a maintenance department as a form of preventive maintenance.

It is inevitable, however, that individual structures will, at one time or another, require rehabilitation. This rehabilitation could be necessitated by factors which can be grouped as:

❑ Deterioration related
❑ Accidental damage related

Accidental damage, such as impact from overheight trucks, is typically localized and can be repaired in a discrete fashion.

Methods for rehabilitating prestressed concrete structures will vary depending on which of the two groups the problem lies in. Accidental damage, such as impact from overheight trucks, is typically localized and can be repaired in a discrete fashion. Deterioration related repairs, however, must deal with the possibility that the problem will not be contained by the remedial measure. For example, the intrusion of chlorides can spread throughout a girder over a period of time. The risk is always present that the measure employed will slow but not arrest deterioration.

Discussed below are some of the basic methods employed to repair damage to prestressed concrete elements. As mentioned above, however, the applicability of the methods will vary depending on the origin of the deficiency.

1. Patching. For small, localized areas of deterioration, patching offers a quick low cost remedial measure which maintenance departments often rely on. In comparing the patching of a prestressed concrete element to a conventionally reinforced element, it is important to note that the size of the patch for prestressed elements is of great importance in that extensive patching could adversely influence the strength of the member. Therefore, any patching of a significant nature should also be accompanied by a structural analysis to determine the impact the repair work will have on the performance of the element.

This becomes of particular concern when the patch is located in an area that is normally in compression. If such a situation occurs, the member should be preloaded to simulate the effects of live load on the structure [Ref. 3.70]. These loads should be maintained until the patch has attained its specified strength. If this is not done, cracks will develop, generally at the bond line or in the existing concrete next to the patch because the patch material is generally of a higher strength than the existing base concrete.

A deficiency with patching is that when the deteriorated area has suffered from corrosion damage due to chloride intrusion, the patching may actually *accelerate* deterioration. In Section 3.9.8, Part 8 we described the process of cathodic action which causes deterioration. By patching a chloride-contaminated area with patch material of a different chloride-oxygen content, the effect will be to cause the formation of stronger corrosion cells. One solution to this problem is to use a dielectric material for patching (e.g., a polymer mortar), although even this is not foolproof since corrosion cells can still develop if the repair work is not impervious [Ref. 3.70].

> A deficiency with patching is that when the deteriorated area has suffered from corrosion damage due to chloride intrusion, the patching may actually *accelerate* deterioration.

In Section 3.9.8, Part 6 we discussed the process of patching concrete deck elements. The process, as it is applied to the patching of prestressed concrete elements, is remarkably similar. The principal difference, however, is that in the patching of concrete bridge decks, it is feasible (and often an economic necessity) to leave in place adjacent sections of concrete which, while contaminated, are still relatively sound. This same philosophy cannot be uniformly applied to prestressed concrete elements.

The main reason for this is that it is difficult to ascertain the future performance of a prestressed concrete element once the patching has been performed. In the most extreme and dire scenario, extensive corrosion can seriously impact the structural adequacy of the structure. Conversely, however, there are very few alternative methods presently available to repair the type of surface damage usually addressed with patching. It is therefore recommended that patches, when they are made, be consistently monitored to gauge the level of performance of the repair. Such inspection can be performed either visually or through the use of sounding.

2. Permanent Formwork. When prestressed concrete girders have been subjected to accidental damage which causes the exposure of prestressing steel, a form of permanent formwork or enclosure of the damaged area is often used. Figure 3.58 illustrates a metal sleeve splice which is used to repair such damage. As an alternate method, jacketing of the damaged area with new concrete is sometimes used. When such an approach is taken, the formwork is generally left in place to provide added protection to the repaired segment. In essence, both of these repairs are similar to a patch and therefore come with the caveats associated with such repairs detailed above.

3. **Crack Injection.** When a girder is subjected to an overload condition which induces cracking, the injection of epoxy resin is often a suitable repair method. Since overloading is, for the most part, a one-time occurrence, the likelihood that the crack will reappear is minimal. Conversely, if the crack is subjected to constant reopening through general levels of live load or

> **W**hen a girder is subjected to an overload condition which induces cracking, the injection of epoxy resin is often a suitable repair method.

PREFABRICATED METAL sleeves, like the one illustrated in Figure 3.58, can be used to repair prestressed concrete girders which have sustained damage due to vehicle impact or some other accidental damage.

The metal sleeve is usually fabricated from A36 steel with a thickness no less than $5/16$ in. Although the sleeve can be fabricated in either the field or the shop, a minimum of one field weld will be required to assemble the sleeve. While the sleeve does not restore prestress, it is designed to possess at least as much strength as the severed strands.

To bond the sleeve to the girder, epoxy resin is applied using pressure injection. The epoxy is injected into a $1/16$ in gap which is formed through the use of metal spacers attached to the inside surfaces of the splice plates. Each end of the girder is then sealed with epoxy mortar. This same principle has been applied to other structural elements such as columns, cap beams, and marine pilings.

An alternate to the metal sleeve would be to jacket the entire girder with new concrete and leave the formwork in place. Although the formwork itself does not provide added strength, it does offer additional protection to the underlying girder. [Ref. 3.70]

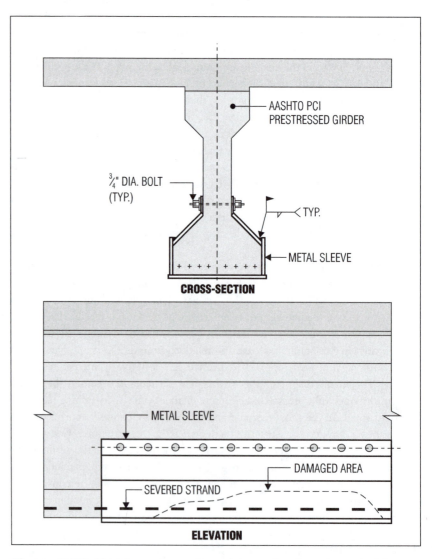

Figure 3.58 Metal sleeve splice used to repair damaged prestressed concrete girders. *(Adapted from: NCHRP Synthesis of Highway Practice 140, Ref. 3.70.)*

other deformational loads (e.g., thermal loads), then crack injection is not recommended since the crack will simply reform again. In that case, the structure should be strengthened prior to crack injection. As mentioned above for patching, it may be necessary to preload the member with simulated live load until the injection material has reached sufficient strength.

4. **Sealers.** As discussed earlier in Section 3.9.8, Part 7, concrete sealers are designed to prevent the intrusion of moisture to the underlying concrete. In this sense, sealers are most suitable as methods of preventive maintenance, rather than outright repair. Sometimes, however, sealers are applied to already corroded areas in an attempt to slow deterioration.

5. **Strengthening.** At times it may be necessary to improve the strength of a prestressed concrete member. Strengthening of a prestressed girder can be accomplished using a variety of methods, some of which include the use of:

   ❑ Bonded external reinforcement
   ❑ Tendon replacement
   ❑ External posttensioning

   Bonded external reinforcement makes use of steel plates or fiber reinforced polymer material which are bonded with epoxy to the soffits of beams which show signs of cracking [Ref. 3.70]. The second method, tendon replacement, is not very popular for highway bridges because bonded construction is the norm and access to tendon anchorages is limited. An example of the last method, external posttensioning, is illustrated in Figure 3.59.

   In this approach, symmetrical jacking corbels are placed on either side of the girder web at the lower sloping face of the girder's bottom flange. The corbels are attached to the girder with expansion bolts or similar devices. A prestressing force is then applied to strands or high strength rods located in the corbels providing the additional strength required by the girder.

   External posttensioning is also used for concrete box-girder bridges. External posttensioning strands can be installed inside the box girder to provide additional strength.

6. **Conclusions.** From the above, it is clear that prestressed concrete possesses its own unique maintenance and rehabilitation requirements. This should serve as a warning to new designers that any material, regardless of what their specific proponents may say, will require attentive maintenance and care in order to ensure that the structure performs at the level of service it was designed for.

   With regard to prestressed concrete, it is helpful to revisit the statement made earlier that prestressed concrete is not so much a material as it is a *method* of construction. As this *method* has developed over the years, the design and construction of prestressed concrete structures has benefited from the knowledge gained through maintenance and

...any material, regardless of what their specific proponents may say, will require attentive maintenance and care in order to ensure that the structure performs at the level of service it was designed for.

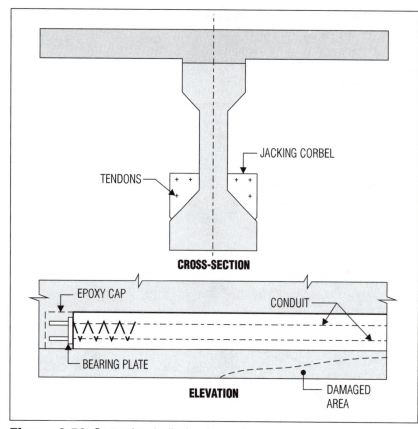

JACKING CORBEL

TENDONS

CROSS-SECTION

EPOXY CAP

CONDUIT

BEARING PLATE

ELEVATION

DAMAGED AREA

Figure 3.59 Posttensioned splice for a damaged prestressed concrete girder. *(Adapted from NCHRP Synthesis of Highway Practice 140, Ref. 3.70.)*

TO INCREASE THE strength of a prestressed concrete girder, external posttensioning is often used. Using this method, jacking corbels are attached to the prestressed girder, which is then posttensioned using high strength rods or prestressing strands.

As illustrated in Figure 3.59, the corbels are attached to the sloping face of the girder's lower flange and the lower portion of the girder's web, generally using expansion bolts or reinforcement inserted into specially drilled holes. When connecting the corbels to the prestressed girder, it is important that the connection devices do not interfere with the girder's existing prestressing steel. Also, to enhance the contact between the corbel and the girder, the surface in contact is roughened. Although the repair must be designed using prestress which provides adequate strength, it is important not to overstress girder sections which are already precompressed [Ref. 3.70]

rehabilitation efforts. Once again we see the benefits of an integrated design-maintain-rehabilitate approach which was touched upon earlier in Section 3.9.9. It is only through a tight integration of all three facets that engineers can improve the performance of highway bridges. The difficulty encountered by designers in achieving this integration is that the development takes place at a very slow and often imperceptible rate. At the onset of this section we stated that repair typically is warranted at about twenty years into the life of a prestressed concrete structure. In terms of both design and maintenance, a lot can change in twenty years. With patience and fortitude, however, engineers stand a real chance at extending the life of the structures they design.

REFERENCES

3.1 Knight, Richard P., "Economical Steel Plate Girder Bridges," *Engineering Journal/AISC,* Second Quarter, 1984.

3.2 *Market Research—The Bridge Market 2003.* Portland Cement Association, October 2004.

3.3 *Standard Specifications for Highway Bridges,* 17th ed., American Association of State Highway and Transportation Officials, Washington, D.C., 2002.

3.4 *Standard Plans for Highway Bridges,* vol. I, *Concrete Superstructures,* U.S. Department of Transportation, Federal Highway Administration, Washington, D.C., 1990.

3.5 Winter, George and Nilson, Arthur H., *Design of Concrete Structures,* 9th ed., McGraw-Hill, New York, 1979.

3.6 Gutkowski, Richard M. and Williamson, Thomas G., "Timber Bridges: State-of-the-Art," *Journal of Structural Engineering,* American Society of Civil Engineers, pp. 2175–2191, vol. 109, No. 9, September, 1983.

3.7 Scofield, W. Fleming and O'Brien, W.H., *Modern Timber Engineering,* 4th ed., p. 144, Southern Pine Association, New Orleans, 1954.

3.8 *Timber Construction Manual,* 3rd ed., American Institute of Timber Construction, pp. 5-360 to 5-363, John Wiley & Sons, New York, 1985.

3.9 *Standard Plans for Highway Bridges,* vol. II, *Structural Steel Superstructures,* U.S. Department of Transportation, Federal Highway Administration, Washington, D.C., 1982.

3.10 "Rehabilitation and Replacement of Bridges on Secondary Highways and Local Roads," NCHRP Report 243, Transportation Research Board, pp. 10–12, Washington, D.C., December, 1981.

3.11 *Standard Details for Highway Bridges,* New York State Department of Transportation, Albany, 1989.

3.12 Elliot, Arthur L., "Steel and Concrete Bridges," *Structural Engineering Handbook,* Edited by Gaylord, Edwin H., Jr., and Gaylord, Charles N., McGraw-Hill, New York, 1990.

3.13 *AASHTO Manual for Bridge Maintenance,* American Association of State Highway and Transportation Officials, pp. 77–104, Washington, D.C., 1987.

3.14 *Bridge Rehabilitation and Strengthening,* Organisation for Economic Co-Operation and Development, Paris, 1983.

3.15 *AASHTO LRFD Bridge Design Specifications,* American Association of State Highway and Transportation Officials, Washington, D.C., 2004.

3.16 *Bridge Design Practice Manual,* California Department of Transportation, p. 1-11, Sacramento, 1993.

3.17 Page, Robert A. et al., *Goals, Opportunities, and Priorities for the USGS Earthquake Hazards Reduction Program,* U.S. Geological Survey, p. 3, Washington, D.C., 1992.

3.18 Walley, W.J., and Purkiss, J.A., "Bridge Abutments and Piers," pp. 836–837, *The Design and Construction of Engineering Foundations,* Edited by Henry, F.D.C., Chapman and Hall, New York, 1986.

3.19 *Building Code Requirements for Reinforced Concrete and Commentary,* American Concrete Institute, Detroit, 2002.

3.20 Peck, Ralph B., Hanson, Walter E., Thornburn, and Thomas H., *Foundation Engineering,* p. 59, John Wiley & Sons, New York, 1974.

3.21 *Load and Resistance Factor Design Manual of Steel Construction,* 2nd ed., American Institute of Steel Construction, Chicago, 1998.

3.22 Green, Peter, "Bridge Code Updated," *Engineering News Record,* vol. 227, pp. 33–34, 15 July 1991.

3.23 Brazil, Aine, et al., "LRFD: Still Waiting," *Civil Engineering,* American Society of Civil Engineers, vol. 61, pp. 47–48, June 1991.

3.24 Salmon, Charles G. and Johnson, John E., *Steel Structures: Design and Behavior,* 2nd ed., Harper & Row, New York, 1980.

3.25 *Building Code Requirements for Reinforced Concrete (ACI 318–89)* (Revised 1992) and *Commentary-ACI 318R-89* (Revised 1992), American Concrete Institute, Detroit, 1992.

3.26 Troitsky, M. S., *Cable-Stayed Bridges,* pp. 135–137, Van Nostrand Reinhold, New York, 1988.

3.27 Kuzmanovic, Bogdan O., and Sanchez, Manuel R., "Lateral Distribution of Live Loads on Highway Bridge," *Journal of Structural Engineering,* American Society of Civil Engineers, vol. 112, no. 8, pp. 1847–1862, August 1986.

3.28 Banks, Ralph K., "Bridge Decks: Their Problems and Solutions," *Public Works,* vol. 117, pp. 26–28, December, 1986.

3.29 "Rehabilitation and Replacement of Bridges on Secondary Highways and Local Roads," NCHRP Report 243, Transportation Research Board, pp. 2–7, Washington, D.C., December, 1981.

3.30 *Design and Construction of Sanitary and Storm Sewers,* American Society of Civil Engineers and the Water Pollution Control Federation, pp. 42–57, 1969.

3.31 *A Policy on Geometric Design of Highways and Streets,* 4th ed., American Association of State Highway and Transportation Officials, Washington, D.C., 2001.

3.32 Cook, John P., *Composite Construction Methods,* Robert E. Krieger Publishing Co., Malabar, Florida, 1985.

3.33 *Allowable Stress Design Manual of Steel Construction,* 9th ed., American Institute of Steel Construction, Chicago, 1989.

3.34 *Manual of Steel Construction, LRFD,* 3rd ed., American Institute of Steel Construction, Chicago, 2003.

3.35 Slutter, Roger G. and Driscoll, George C., "Flexural Strength of Steel-Concrete Composite Beams," *Journal of Structural Engineering,* American Society of Civil Engineers, vol. 91, no. ST2, pp. 71–99, April, 1965.

3.36 Slutter, Roger G. and Fisher, John W., "Fatigue Strength of Shear Connectors," *Highway Research Record,* no 147, Highway Research Board, Washington, D.C., 1966.

3.37 Viest, Ivan M., Chairman, Task Committee on Composite Construction, "Composite Steel Construction," *Journal of Structural Engineering,* American Society of Civil Engineers, vol. 100, no. ST5, pp. 1085–1139, May, 1974.

3.38 Ollgaard, Jorgen G., Slutter, Roger G., and Fisher, John W., "Shear Strength of Stud Connectors in Lightweight and Normal-Weight Concrete," *Engineering Journal/AISC,* pp. 55–64, April, 1971.

3.39 Hooper, Ira, Grubb, Michael A., and Viest, Ivan M. "Design of Composite Members," pg. 14–22, *Structural Engineering Handbook,* Edited by Gaylord, Edwin H., Jr., and Gaylord, Charles N., McGraw-Hill, New York, 1990.

3.40 "Rehabilitation and Replacement of Bridges on Secondary Highways and Local Roads," NCHRP Report 243, Transportation Research Board, pp. 17–22, Washington, December, 1981.

3.41 *Bridge Code,* 3rd ed., Ontario Ministry of Transportation, p. 294, Toronto, 1992.

3.42 *Latex-Modified Concretes and Mortars,* NCHRP Synthesis of Highway Practice 179, Transportation Research Board, Washington, D.C., August, 1992.

3.43 Salmon, Charles G. and Johnson, John E., *Steel Structures: Design and Behavior,* 3rd ed., Harper Collins, New York, 1990.

3.44 Johnson, Andy, "Steel Weighs In," *Civil Engineering,* American Society of Civil Engineers, vol. 62, pp. 69–71, July, 1992.

3.45 *Bridge Design Practice Manual,* 3rd ed., California Department of Transportation, Sacramento, 1971.

3.46 Large, George E., *Basic Reinforced Concrete Design: Elastic and Creep,* 2nd ed., p. 126, The Ronald Press Company, New York, 1957.

3.47 Pecknold, David A., "Structural Analysis," pp. 1-39 to 1-41, *Structural Engineering Handbook,* Edited by Gaylord, Edwin H., Jr., and Gaylord, Charles N., McGraw-Hill, New York, 1990.

3.48 Lindeburg, Michael R., *Civil Engineering Reference Manual*, 5th ed., Professional Publications, Belmont, California, 1989.

3.49 *Moments, Shears and Reactions for Continuous Highway Bridges*, American Institute of Steel Construction, Chicago, 1986.

3.50 Zuraski, Patrick D., "Continuous-Beam Analysis for Highway Bridges," *Journal of Structural Engineering*, American Society of Civil Engineers, vol. 117, no. 1, pp. 80–99, January, 1991.

3.51 Wasserman, Edward P., "Jointless Bridge Decks," *Engineering Journal/ AISC*, pp. 93-100, Third Quarter, 1987.

3.52 Robison, Rita, "Safeguarding Steel," *Civil Engineering*, American Society of Civil Engineers, vol. 62, pp. 50-53, April, 1992.

3.53 Hare, Clive H., "Protective Coatings for Bridge Steel," NCHRP Synthesis of Highway Practice 136, Transportation Research Board, pp. 1-107, Washington, D.C., December, 1987.

3.54 Steinman, D. B., and Watson, S. R., *Bridges and Their Builders*, 2nd ed., Dover Publications Inc., New York, 1957.

3.55 Angeloff, Carl, "Overcoating Bridges Containing Lead-Based Paints: An Economical Alternative," *Public Works*, vol. 124, pp. 56-57, January, 1993.

3.56 "Europe's Best Kept Secret: MIO Bridge Coatings," *Public Works*, vol. 123, pp. 39–40, January, 1992.

3.57 Appleman, Bernard R., "Bridge Paint: Removal, Containment, and Disposal," NCHRP Synthesis of Highway Practice 176, Transportation Research Board, pp. 1–37, Washington, D.C., February, 1992.

3.58 Robison, Rita, "Weathering Steel: Industry's Stepchild," *Civil Engineering*, American Society of Civil Engineers, vol. 58, pp. 42–45, October, 1988.

3.59 Culp, James D., Reincke, Jon W., and Tinklenberg, Gary L., "Total Shop Painting of Steel Bridges," *Public Works*, vol. 119, pp. 48–50, November, 1988.

3.60 "Weathering Steel: Can Rust Be a Friend?" *Public Works*, vol. 121, pp. 168–182, September, 1990.

3.61 "Maine Benefits from Weathering Steel Bridges," *Public Works*, vol. 122, pg. 74, January, 1991.

3.62 Robison, Rita, "A New Look at Galvanized Bridges," *Civil Engineering*, American Society of Civil Engineers, vol. 61, pp. 52–55, July, 1991.

3.63 *Manual for Condition Evaluation of Bridges*, American Association of State Highway and Transportation Officials, Washington, D.C., 2003.

3.64 Ghosn, Michel and Moses, Fred, "Reliability Calibration of Bridge Design Code," *Journal of Structural Engineering*, American Society of Civil Engineers, vol. 112, no. 4, pg. 745, April, 1986.

3.65 *Guide Specifications for Strength Evaluation of Existing Steel and Concrete Bridges,* American Association of State Highway and Transportation Officials, Washington, D.C., 1989.

3.66 Wang, Chu-Kia and Salmon, Charles G., *Reinforced Concrete Design,* 4th ed., Harper & Row Publishers, New York, 1985.

3.67 Libby, James R., *Modern Prestressed Concrete,* 4th ed., Van Nostrand Reinhold, New York, 1990.

3.68 Lin, T.Y. and Zia, Paul, "Design of Prestressed-Concrete Structural Members," p. 13-7, *Structural Engineering Handbook,* Edited by Gaylord, Edwin H., Jr., and Gaylord, Charles N., McGraw-Hill, New York, 1990.

3.69 Freyermuth, Clifford L., "Sizing up Segmentals," *Civil Engineering,* American Society of Civil Engineers, vol. 62, pp. 66–69, July, 1992.

3.70 Manning, David G., "Durability of Prestressed Concrete Highway Structures," NCHRP Synthesis of Highway Practice 140, Transportation Research Board, pp. 1–65, Washington, D.C., November, 1988.

3.71 Gaylord, Edwin H., and Gaylord, Charles N., *Design of Steel Structures,* McGraw-Hill, New York, 1972.

4

Design of Substructure Elements

Of all the elements which make up a highway bridge, substructure elements present some of the most visibly striking features. A towering column or hammerhead pier can provide a certain sense of majesty which leaves a lasting image upon the traveler passing under a bridge. To be sure, for larger bridges, the superstructure elicits much, if not more, of the same feeling. For the majority of highway bridges, however, the only striking aspect of the design is found in the substructure. Even a row of reinforced earth modular units, snaking out along an abutment side slope, can be quite aesthetically pleasing.

If it can be said that the design of superstructure components varies greatly depending on geographic location and transportation department preferences, the same would be equally true for substructure components. In this section, we will cover the basic principles behind the design, rehabilitation, and maintenance of substructure components. Specifically the three major components which will be discussed are: abutments, piers, and bearings.

As with the presentation of superstructures provided in Section 3, the focus of the discussion will be on general concepts rather than specific forms of elements which vary greatly from region to region.

Figure 4.1 A highway bridge superstructure is supported by bearings, piers and abutments.

4.1 ABUTMENTS

An abutment is a structure located at the end of a bridge which provides the basic functions of:

❑ Supporting the end of the first or last span
❑ Retaining earth underneath and adjacent to the approach roadway, and, if necessary
❑ Supporting part of the approach roadway or approach slab

To provide this functionality, a variety of abutment forms are used. The style of abutment chosen for a given bridge varies depending on the geometry of the site, size of the structure, and preferences of the owner. A simplification would be to think of an abutment as a retaining wall equipped with a bridge seat. The following discussion describes some of the most popular types of abutments in use, presents a design example for a typical abutment, and covers some of the general maintenance and rehabilitation issues.

4.1.1 Types of Abutments

As mentioned above, most abutment types are variations on retaining wall configurations. With the exception of a crib wall, most any retaining wall system, when equipped with a bridge seat and designed to withstand the severe live loading conditions present in highway bridge structures, can be used as an abutment. Another difference between a conventional retaining wall system and a bridge abutment is that the latter is typically equipped with adjoining, flared walls known as *wingwalls*.

Figure 4.2 A reinforced earth abutment is used to support this composite steel bridge.

Figure 4.3 A single span bridge under construction crossing a stream.

WINGWALLS, like the ones shown in Figure 4.3, are provided to assist an abutment in confining the earth behind an abutment. In this instance, the abutments are an integral component of the entire structure, which is not uncommon for structures possessing a relatively short underpass crossing. When a backwall, wingwall, and footing form a single structural system, the analysis becomes very complicated. In such a case the designer has two options available: either rely on a set of conservative assumptions and approximations or utilize computer aided solutions such as finite element analysis. The latter is generally performed by most bridge engineers.

Wingwalls are designed to assist the principal retaining wall component of an abutment in confining the earth behind the abutment. Examples of wingwalls are given in Figures 1.6, 1.8, and 4.3. The principal retaining wall component mentioned above is usually called the *backwall* or *stem* of the abutment. The *bridge seat*, upon which the superstructure actually rests, is typically composed of either freestanding pedestals or a continuous breastwall. The pedestals or breastwall is designed to support bearings which in turn support individual primary member and transfer girder reactions to the foundation. They are located just in front of the backwall and sit on top of the abutment footing. In general, the major types of abutments presently in use are given by the following ten types.

> **W**ingwalls are designed to assist the principal retaining wall component of an abutment in confining the earth behind the abutment.

1. **Gravity Abutment.** A gravity abutment resists horizontal earth pressure with its own dead weight. By nature, this leads to abutments which are rather heavy. Gravity abutments are most often constructed using concrete; however, stone masonry is also sometimes used. As described above, a gravity abutment is composed of a backwall and flared wingwalls which rest on top of a footing (see also Figure 1.2).

2. **U Abutment.** When the wingwalls of a gravity abutment are placed at right angles to the backwall, the abutment is known as a U abutment. The name "U abutment" comes from the shape the abutment has when viewed in plan. The wingwalls are typically cast monolithically with the abutment backwall and cantilevered vertically from the footing. Some wingwalls may have portion cantilevered horizontally as well. Because there is a tendency for the wingwalls to overturn, their footings are cast monolithically with the abutment footing.

3. **Cantilever Abutment.** A cantilever abutment is virtually identical to a cantilever retaining wall (i.e., a wall or stem extending up from a footing) except that a cantilever abutment is designed to accommodate larger vertical loads and is equipped with a bridge seat.

> **A** cantilever abutment is virtually identical to a cantilever retaining wall ... except that a cantilever abutment is designed to accommodate larger vertical loads and is equipped with a bridge seat.

WHEN AN ABUTMENT has a large breastwall or backwall tied together with adjacent wingwalls, the structure is known as a U abutment. This name is derived from the "U" shape the abutment makes when viewed in plan. The abutment under construction in Figure 4.4 still has its *formwork* in place. Formwork is the entire system of forms, supports, and related elements which together act as a mold for a concrete element until the element has the required strength to support itself. Sometimes, prefabricated reusable forms are used; these type of forms are known as *ganged forms*.

Figure 4.4 A typical gravity abutment with wingwalls under construction.

The stem of a cantilever abutment, along with its breastwall or pedestals, is rigidly attached to the footing and acts as a cantilever beam, from which the name is derived. The stem transmits horizontal earth pressures to the footing with stability being maintained through the abutment's own dead weight and the soil mass resting on the rear part of the footing. The front face of an abutment footing is known as the *toe* and the rear face as the *heel*. At times it may be desirable to vary the thickness of the stem to achieve an economy of materials. Cantilever abutments are feasible for heights up to approximately 21 ft (6.5 m). If the required height exceeds this value, an alternative, such as a counterfort abutment (see Part 7 below) should be investigated.

4. **Full Height Abutment.** A full height abutment is a cantilever abutment which extends from the underpass grade line (either roadway or water body) to the grade line of the overpass roadway above.

5. **Stub Abutment.** Stub abutments are relatively short abutments which are placed at the top of an embankment or slope. Unless sufficient rock exists at the site, stub abutments generally are supported on piles which extend through the embankment.

6. **Semi-Stub Abutment.** As its name would imply, a semi-stub abutment is in between the size of a full height and stub abutment. A semi-stub abutment is founded at an intermediate location along the embankment. This type of abutments are also called semi-cantilever abutments.

7. **Counterfort Abutment.** A counterfort abutment, similar to a counterfort retaining wall, utilizes a stem and footing which is braced with thin vertical slabs, known as counterforts, which are spaced at intervals

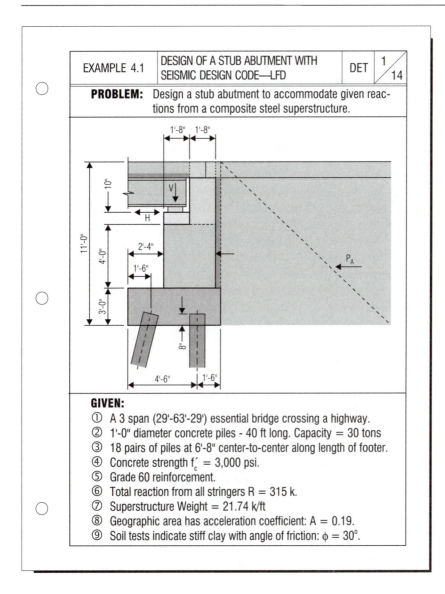

| EXAMPLE 4.1 | DESIGN OF A STUB ABUTMENT WITH SEISMIC DESIGN CODE—LFD | DET | 1 / 14 |

PROBLEM: Design a stub abutment to accommodate given reactions from a composite steel superstructure.

GIVEN:
① A 3 span (29'-63'-29') essential bridge crossing a highway.
② 1'-0" diameter concrete piles - 40 ft long. Capacity = 30 tons
③ 18 pairs of piles at 6'-8" center-to-center along length of footer.
④ Concrete strength f'_c = 3,000 psi.
⑤ Grade 60 reinforcement.
⑥ Total reaction from all stringers R = 315 k.
⑦ Superstructure Weight = 21.74 k/ft
⑧ Geographic area has acceleration coefficient: A = 0.19.
⑨ Soil tests indicate stiff clay with angle of friction: $\phi = 30°$.

In this example we will design a stub abutment using LFD to accommodate seismic loads. The abutment geometry in cross section is illustrated in the accompanying calculation sheet. In plan, the abutment is equipped with 18 pairs of 1 ft diameter, 40 ft long concrete piles spaced at a distance of 6'-8" center to center. The face of the stem is assumed to be smooth.

It can be assumed that the abutment can be displaced horizontally without significant restraint. Given this condition, we will utilize the pseudo-static Mononobe-Okabe method for computing lateral active soil pressures under seismic loading. All references to the AASHTO seismic code contained in Division I-A of that specification will be followed by the "I-A" identifier (e.g., AASHTO 3.3 I-A).

The loads from 16 stringers which are transmitted to the abutment are given as 315 k. The bridge is located in a geographic area which, when referenced to Figure 3.15, provides an acceleration coefficient of 0.19. Assume earth with a unit weight of 120 pounds per cubic foot and concrete with a unit weight of 150 pounds per cubic foot.

along the length of the footing (see Figure 4.5). These thin slabs join with the stem and footing at right angles. The counterforts allow the abutment breastwall to be designed as a horizontal beam between the counterforts rather than as a cantilevered stem. Generally, counterfort abutments are used when very high walls are required.

8. Spill-through Abutment. A spill-through abutment utilizes two or more vertical columns or buttresses which have a cap beam on top of them. The cap beam is in turn used to support the bridge seat upon which the superstructure rests. The fill extends from the bottom of the cap beam and is allowed to *spill through* the open spaces between the vertical columns so that only a portion of the embankment is retained by the abutment.

9. Pile Bent Abutment. Similar in nature to a spill-through abutment, a pile bent abutment consists of a single cap beam, acting as a bridge seat,

> **T**he counterforts allow the abutment breastwall to be designed as a horizontal beam between the counterforts rather than as a cantilevered stem.

supported by one or two rows of piles. Batter piles are used to prevent sliding.

10. MSE Systems. In the Did You Know? sidebar at the top of this section, it was mentioned that the name "reinforced earth" is a trademarked name for specific types of retaining wall systems. Reinforced earth systems are produced by The Reinforced Earth Company. MSE systems utilize modular facing units, generally made of unreinforced concrete, with metal or polymeric reinforcement (either in the form of strips or mesh) attached to the back. The facing units are cast in the form of a geometric shape which lends itself to being assembled into a uniform wall (e.g., hexagon, diamond). The reinforcement strips or mesh are thereby layered in the retained fill which is compacted. These strips act as "reinforcement," transforming the granular soil into a coherent material which can support both its own weight and that of applied vertical loading [Ref. 4.1].

The name "reinforced earth" is derived from this effect. A more generic name that is normally used by engineers is that of a *Mechanically Stabilized Earth (MSE) system*. The reader should keep in mind that "reinforced earth" is a proprietary designation.

Two obvious concerns with these systems are their longevity and future maintenance requirements. The metal used to reinforce the earth

> **A** more generic name that is normally used by engineers is that of *mechanically stabilized earth system.*

A COUNTERFORT retaining wall, like the one illustrated in Figure 4.5, is generally not economically feasible unless the height from the bottom of the footing to the top of the stem is greater than 20 to 25 ft (6.1 to 7.6 m). The economy of a counterfort retaining wall is typically a function of the relative cost of forms, concrete, reinforcing, and labor. The spacing between counterforts is determined by a trial and error approach with an obvious limiting constraint being cost. Generally, a spacing of approximately one third to one half of the height is most economical [Ref. 4.2]. This space in between counterforts is backfilled with soil.

From a structural standpoint, the earth is retained by the stem which acts as a continuous beam spanning in between counterforts. The counterforts, in turn, act as cantilevers. The intensity of loading on the stem increases with depth, which can be accommodated by increasing the thickness of the stem (as shown in the figure) or the amount of reinforcement [Ref. 4.1].

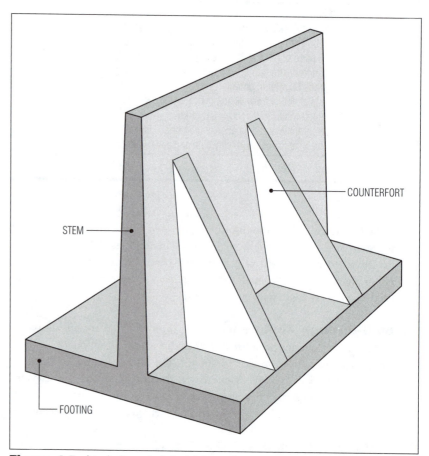

Figure 4.5 A typical counterfort retaining wall.

| EXAMPLE 4.1 | DESIGN OF A STUB ABUTMENT WITH SEISMIC DESIGN CODE—LFD | DET | 2/14 |

STEP 1: Determine Type of Seismic Analysis and Other Criteria

For an "essential bridge" by AASHTO 3.3 I-A we have:

IC = Importance Classification = I

With an importance classification of "I" by AASHTO 3.4 I-A for:

$0.09 < A < 0.19$ and IC = I

SPC = Seismic Performance Category = B

The bridge has an unchanging cross section, with similar supports, and a uniform mass and stiffness, so it is considered to be:

Regular (By AASHTO 4.2 I-A)

For a Regular Bridge, SPC = B, and 2 to 6 spans, we choose to use: Method 2 = Single-Mode Spectral Analysis (By AASHTO 4.2 I-A)

For stiff clay, by AASHTO 3.5 I-A:

Soil Profile Type II: S = Site Coefficient = 1.2

Response Modification Factor (AASHTO 3.7 I-A)

Abutment Stem: R = 2 (Treat as a wall-type pier)

Abutment Footing: R = One-Half R for Abutment Stem
                    $= R/2 = 2/2 = 1$ (AASHTO 6.2.2 I-A)

Combination of Seismic Forces (AASHTO 3.9 I-A):

Case I: |100% Longitudinal Motion| + |30% Transverse Motion|

Case II: |30% Longitudinal Motion| + |100% Transverse Motion|

Load Grouping (AASHTO 6.2.1 I-A):

1.0(DL + Buoyancy + Stream Flow + Earth Pressure + Earthquake)
          (N/A)   (N/A)

DESIGN EXAMPLE 4.1
STEP 1: DETERMINE SEISMIC ANALYSIS AND CRITERIA

In Section 3.5.3, Part 2 we discussed the nature of temporary loads in general, and seismic loads in particular. Prior to beginning design, we need to determine the seismic criteria which will determine which type of analysis will be required: either the more straightforward single-mode spectral analysis or the more complex multimode spectral analysis.

The type of analysis used is dependent on the geometry of the structure (i.e., is the cross section uniform or not) and the location of the bridge in the transportation network (i.e., acceleration coefficient). Based on our given parameters for the structure, we determine that the single-mode spectral analysis method will be sufficient.

Other seismic criteria which need to be calculated are the response modification factors which will be used to determine seismic design forces for individual members by dividing elastic forces by the R factors. Finally, the load combinations and groupings are defined. Note that AASHTO I-A modifies the load factors in Table 3.2 so that γ and β are equal to 1.0.

---

is typically protected through use of a galvanized coating. Since the use of MSE systems is still, in the terms of bridge life, relatively young, "the jury is still out" so to speak as to whether or not MSE abutments compare favorably to traditional, reinforced concrete implementations. Many transportation departments, however, have begun utilizing MSE as an abutment material because of the obvious economic and even aesthetic reasons. Exactly how these abutments will be performing over a 75-year life cycle, though, remains to be seen.

4.1.2 Coulomb Earth Pressure Theory

An abutment, like a retaining wall, must be designed to satisfy two basic design requirements. These requirements are, safety against possible failure by:

❏ Overturning and excessive settlement
❏ Sliding

> **E**xactly how these abutments will be performing over a thirty or forty year life cycle, though, remains to be seen.

DID YOU KNOW

THAT the basic principles describing
the effects of earth pressure against a retaining wall were developed by a French army engineer, Charles Augustin Coulomb (1736–1806)? His earth pressure theory was first published in 1773. Later in his career he made fundamental contributions to the fields of friction, electricity, and magnetism [Ref. 4.3].

For an abutment, the structure must be designed to resist both earth pressures and applied loads from the superstructure. Many factors influence the design process, including the type of soil present, drainage, and seismic loading. With regard to the latter, more detail will be provided in Section 4.1.7. Prior to the discussion of the seismic design of an abutment, however, it is necessary to review the basic principles behind Coulomb earth pressure theory. The seismic analysis utilized is an extension of the basic principles described in this section.

Figure 4.6 illustrates the basic forces acting on an abutment (also included in the diagram are seismic forces which will be discussed later). The principal force acting on an abutment is the active earth pressure, designated by the variable P_{AE} in Figure 4.6. The triangular area defined by the sloping line proceeding from the heel of the footing/stem to the top of backfill is known as the failure wedge. Coulomb theory is based on the following assumptions [Ref. 4.2]:

❑ The soil is isotropic and homogeneous
❑ The soil possesses both internal friction and cohesion
❑ The rupture surface is a plane surface
❑ The friction forces are distributed uniformly along the plane rupture surface
❑ The failure wedge is a rigid body

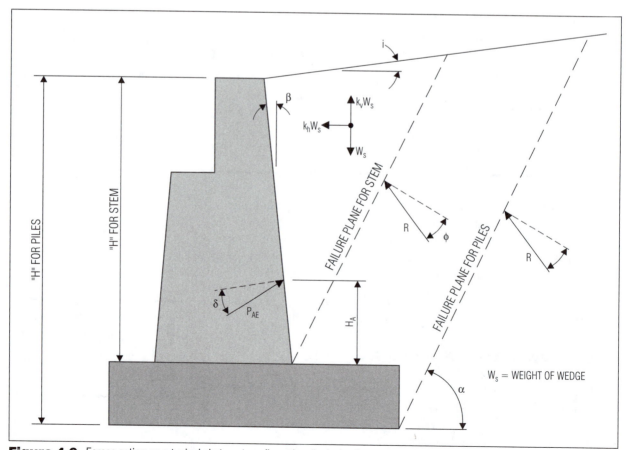

Figure 4.6 Forces acting on a typical abutment configuration (includes forces due to seismic loading (k_h and k_v).

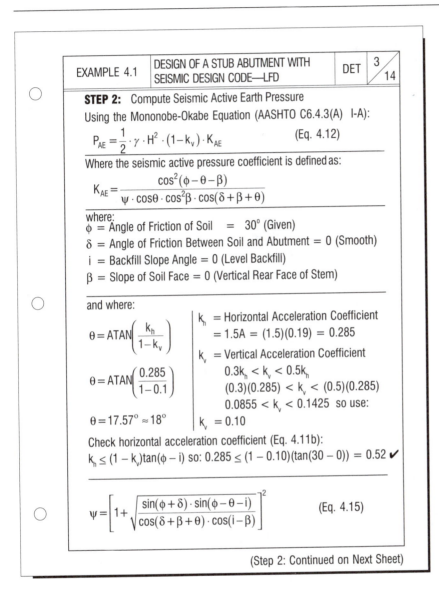

EXAMPLE 4.1	DESIGN OF A STUB ABUTMENT WITH SEISMIC DESIGN CODE—LFD	DET	3 / 14

STEP 2: Compute Seismic Active Earth Pressure

Using the Mononobe-Okabe Equation (AASHTO C6.4.3(A) I-A):

$$P_{AE} = \frac{1}{2} \cdot \gamma \cdot H^2 \cdot (1 - k_v) \cdot K_{AE} \qquad \text{(Eq. 4.12)}$$

Where the seismic active pressure coefficient is defined as:

$$K_{AE} = \frac{\cos^2(\phi - \theta - \beta)}{\psi \cdot \cos\theta \cdot \cos^2\beta \cdot \cos(\delta + \beta + \theta)}$$

where:
ϕ = Angle of Friction of Soil = 30° (Given)
δ = Angle of Friction Between Soil and Abutment = 0 (Smooth)
i = Backfill Slope Angle = 0 (Level Backfill)
β = Slope of Soil Face = 0 (Vertical Rear Face of Stem)

and where:

$$\theta = \text{ATAN}\left(\frac{k_h}{1 - k_v}\right)$$

$$\theta = \text{ATAN}\left(\frac{0.285}{1 - 0.1}\right)$$

$$\theta = 17.57° \approx 18°$$

k_h = Horizontal Acceleration Coefficient
= 1.5A = (1.5)(0.19) = 0.285

k_v = Vertical Acceleration Coefficient
$0.3 k_h < k_v < 0.5 k_h$
$(0.3)(0.285) < k_v < (0.5)(0.285)$
$0.0855 < k_v < 0.1425$ so use:
$k_v = 0.10$

Check horizontal acceleration coefficient (Eq. 4.11b):
$k_h \leq (1 - k_v)\tan(\phi - i)$ so: $0.285 \leq (1 - 0.10)(\tan(30 - 0)) = 0.52$ ✔

$$\psi = \left[1 + \sqrt{\frac{\sin(\phi + \delta) \cdot \sin(\phi - \theta - i)}{\cos(\delta + \beta + \theta) \cdot \cos(i - \beta)}}\right]^2 \qquad \text{(Eq. 4.15)}$$

(Step 2: Continued on Next Sheet)

(Step 2: Continued on Next Sheet)

DESIGN EXAMPLE 4.1
STEP 2: COMPUTE SEISMIC ACTIVE EARTH PRESSURE

The AASHTO seismic code specifies that, for abutments, the pseudo-static Mononobe-Okabe analysis method is to be used (AASHTO 1998 Commentary C6.4.3(A)). This method utilizes a modified Coulomb equation to compute the active earth pressure acting on the abutment.

This method makes use of the acceleration coefficient (based on the geographic location of the bridge), which is decomposed into horizontal and vertical components. For free standing abutments, the horizontal acceleration coefficient k_h is taken as half of the acceleration coefficient A (i.e., A / 2). However, if batter piles are present as exist in our case, then the value for k_h is taken as 1.5A (AASHTO 6.4.3 I-A). The range for the vertical acceleration coefficient given is a generally accepted limit.

To compute the active earth pressure we also need to identify certain physical parameters concerning the soil present and the abutment physical characteristics. The horizontal acceleration coefficient is checked to ensure that it falls under the AASHTO specified limit.

❏ As the failure wedge moves along the wall friction forces are developed
❏ A unit length of wall is considered over an infinitely long body

One of the main deficiencies with the Coulomb earth pressure theory is that it assumes an ideal soil and that the rupture surface is defined by a plane. In reality, however, the failure surface is more accurately defined by a surface possessing a slight curvature. Coulomb himself recognized that the rupture surface was curved, but decided to replace the curve with a plane as an approximation.

Given the variable definition presented in Figure 4.6, the general expression defining the active earth pressure acting on the abutment is defined as:

$$P_A = \frac{1}{2} \cdot \gamma \cdot H^2 \cdot K_A \qquad \text{(Eq. 4.1)}$$

One of the main deficiencies with the Coulomb earth pressure theory is that it assumes an ideal soil and that the rupture surface is defined by a plane.

Coulomb, himself, recognized that the rupture surface was curved, but decided to replace the curve with a plane as an approximation.

where γ = unit weight of soil
H = height of soil face
K_A = active pressure coefficient

The active pressure coefficient is in turn defined by the following expression:

$$K_A = \frac{\cos^2(\phi - \beta)}{\psi \cdot \cos^2\beta \cdot \cos(\delta + \beta)} \qquad \text{(Eq. 4.2)}$$

where ϕ = angle of friction of soil
δ = angle of friction between soil and abutment
β = slope of soil face

and

$$\psi = \left[1 + \sqrt{\frac{\sin(\phi + \delta) \cdot \sin(\phi - i)}{\cos(\delta + \beta) \cdot \cos(i - \beta)}}\right]^2 \qquad \text{(Eq. 4.3)}$$

where i = backfill slope angle

Similarly, *passive earth pressure* is pressure in which the abutment is being pushed *into the backfill*. This is calculated in a very similar fashion with the expression:

$$P_P = \frac{1}{2} \cdot \gamma \cdot H^2 \cdot K_P \qquad \text{(Eq. 4.4)}$$

where γ = unit weight of soil
H = height of soil face
K_P = passive pressure coefficient

The passive pressure coefficient is in turn defined by the following expression:

$$K_P = \frac{\cos^2(\phi - \beta)}{\Gamma \cdot \cos^2\beta \cdot \cos(\delta - \beta)} \qquad \text{(Eq. 4.5)}$$

where in this case we use a denominator multiplier defined by the following:

$$\Gamma = \left[1 + \sqrt{\frac{\sin(\phi + \delta) \cdot \sin(\phi - i)}{\cos(\delta - \beta) \cdot \cos(i - \beta)}}\right]^2 \qquad \text{(Eq. 4.6)}$$

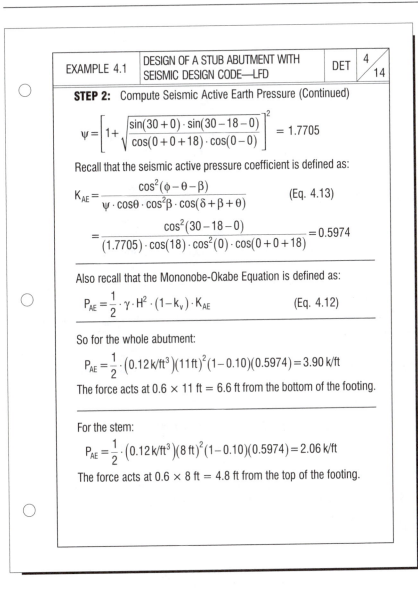

| EXAMPLE 4.1 | DESIGN OF A STUB ABUTMENT WITH SEISMIC DESIGN CODE—LFD | DET | 4 / 14 |

STEP 2: Compute Seismic Active Earth Pressure (Continued)

$$\psi = \left[1 + \sqrt{\frac{\sin(30+0) \cdot \sin(30-18-0)}{\cos(0+0+18) \cdot \cos(0-0)}} \right]^2 = 1.7705$$

Recall that the seismic active pressure coefficient is defined as:

$$K_{AE} = \frac{\cos^2(\phi - \theta - \beta)}{\psi \cdot \cos\theta \cdot \cos^2\beta \cdot \cos(\delta + \beta + \theta)} \qquad \text{(Eq. 4.13)}$$

$$= \frac{\cos^2(30 - 18 - 0)}{(1.7705) \cdot \cos(18) \cdot \cos^2(0) \cdot \cos(0 + 0 + 18)} = 0.5974$$

Also recall that the Mononobe-Okabe Equation is defined as:

$$P_{AE} = \frac{1}{2} \cdot \gamma \cdot H^2 \cdot (1 - k_v) \cdot K_{AE} \qquad \text{(Eq. 4.12)}$$

So for the whole abutment:

$$P_{AE} = \frac{1}{2} \cdot \left(0.12 \, k/ft^3\right)\left(11 \, ft\right)^2 \left(1 - 0.10\right)\left(0.5974\right) = 3.90 \, k/ft$$

The force acts at 0.6×11 ft = 6.6 ft from the bottom of the footing.

For the stem:

$$P_{AE} = \frac{1}{2} \cdot \left(0.12 \, k/ft^3\right)\left(8 \, ft\right)^2 \left(1 - 0.10\right)\left(0.5974\right) = 2.06 \, k/ft$$

The force acts at 0.6×8 ft = 4.8 ft from the top of the footing.

DESIGN EXAMPLE 4.1
STEP 2: SEISMIC ACTIVE EARTH PRESSURE (CONTINUED)

The seismic active earth pressure requires the computation of one more constant, after which the active earth pressure coefficient K_{AE} and the resultant P_{AE} value can be computed.

We will need to calculate two values, one for the stem and the other for the whole abutment. These pressures will be used to describe the *dynamic pressure* acting on the abutment. The *static pressure* acting on the abutment will be computed in the next step using the traditional Coulomb expression (i.e., $\theta = k_v = 0$).

Note that the forces are calculated based on a one-foot vertical strip.

For abutment stem design, the dynamic pressure will be taken to act at a distance of 0.6H above the top of footing. The static pressure acts at a distance of H/3 above the top of footing. For that reason, these two forces have to be calculated separately.

For pile design, the 0.6H and H/3 should be measured from the bottom of footing.

For the era in which it was developed, and the stage of his career, Coulomb's approach is remarkably analytical. The active and passive earth pressures represent maxima and minima values which can be used to determine the size of a retaining wall or abutment based on a trial and error approach.

As we will see shortly, the seismic analysis method utilizes much of the same methodology with the only difference being the incorporation of horizontal and vertical acceleration coefficients to account for the effects of earthquake motion.

The active earth pressure represents the minimum lateral earth pressure. Most abutments are very rigid and are not free to move or rotate, therefore, the actual earth pressure are higher than the active earth pressure. To account for that, AASHTO recommends to use the so called "at-rest" lateral earth

> For the era in which it was developed, and the stage of his career, Coulomb's approach is remarkably analytical.

pressure, which is calculated by the following equation (AASHTO 5.5.2 or AASHTO LRFD 3.11.5.2):

$$K_o = 1 - \sin \phi \qquad \text{(Eq. 4.7)}$$

where ϕ is the effective angle of internal friction.

If no approach slab is used behind the abutment backwall, an equivalent of 2 feet soil surcharge load should be applied to the abutment to account for lateral earth pressure caused by live loads.

4.1.3 Abutment Stability—Service Load Design Method

Traditionally, all bridge foundations were designed using service load method in the USA. Although most states have adopted LFD or LRFD for superstructure design, many of them still use ASD for foundation design. Therefore, it is important for young engineers to understand the service load design method.

When service load design method is used, no load factors or performance factors are applied. Instead, a minimum Factor of Safety (F.S.) is required. It was mentioned earlier that an abutment must be designed to provide safety against failure due to overturning or sliding. With regard to the former, the factor of safety against overturning can be defined by the following expression:

$$F.S._{overturn} = \frac{\sum \text{Moments to Resist Overturning}}{\sum \text{Overturning Moments}} \qquad \text{(Eq. 4.8a)}$$

A generally accepted safety factor for overturning is 2.0. If the footing is supported on rock, a value of 1.5 is acceptable (AASHTO 5.5.5 and 7.5.2.1).

With regard to sliding, the safety factor against sliding is given by the following expression:

$$F.S._{slide} = \frac{\sum \text{Resisting Forces}}{\sum \text{Driving Forces}} \qquad \text{(Eq. 4.8b)}$$

For cohesionless backfill, the resulting safety factor should be at least 1.5. If cohesive backfill is present, the suggested safety factor is approximately 2.0 [Ref. 4.2]. Since granular materials are used for almost all abutment backfill, AASHTO recommends 1.5 as the minimum factor of safety against sliding.

Even if overall stability is provided, however, special investigations may be required if the abutment is constructed on top of soft subsoils. These investigations could consist if:

- ❏ Special explorations
- ❏ Testing
- ❏ Other analyses

to determine if any potentially unacceptable long term settlements or horizontal movements will occur.

> When services load design method is used, no load factors or performance factors are applied. Instead, a minimum Factor of Safety (F.S.) is required.

INCREASING SLIDING RESISTANCE

METHOD I
INCLINE UNDERSIDE OF FOOTING

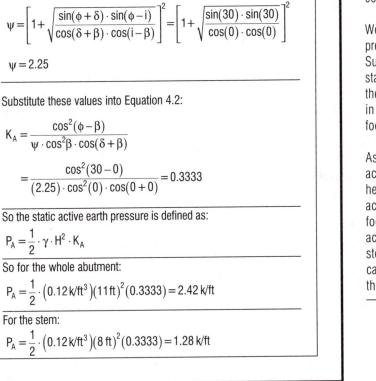

| EXAMPLE 4.1 | DESIGN OF A STUB ABUTMENT WITH SEISMIC DESIGN CODE—LFD | DET | 5/14 |

STEP 3: Compute Static Active Earth Pressure

The static active earth pressure coefficient is defined as:

$$K_A = \frac{\cos^2(\phi - \beta)}{\psi \cdot \cos^2\beta \cdot \cos(\delta + \beta)} \qquad \text{(Eq. 4.2)}$$

where:

$$\psi = \left[1 + \sqrt{\frac{\sin(\phi + \delta) \cdot \sin(\phi - i)}{\cos(\delta + \beta) \cdot \cos(i - \beta)}}\right]^2 = \left[1 + \sqrt{\frac{\sin(30) \cdot \sin(30)}{\cos(0) \cdot \cos(0)}}\right]^2$$

$$\psi = 2.25$$

Substitute these values into Equation 4.2:

$$K_A = \frac{\cos^2(\phi - \beta)}{\psi \cdot \cos^2\beta \cdot \cos(\delta + \beta)}$$

$$= \frac{\cos^2(30 - 0)}{(2.25) \cdot \cos^2(0) \cdot \cos(0 + 0)} = 0.3333$$

So the static active earth pressure is defined as:

$$P_A = \frac{1}{2} \cdot \gamma \cdot H^2 \cdot K_A$$

So for the whole abutment:

$$P_A = \frac{1}{2} \cdot (0.12 \, k/ft^3)(11 \, ft)^2 (0.3333) = 2.42 \, k/ft$$

For the stem:

$$P_A = \frac{1}{2} \cdot (0.12 \, k/ft^3)(8 \, ft)^2 (0.3333) = 1.28 \, k/ft$$

DESIGN EXAMPLE 4.1
STEP 3: STATIC ACTIVE EARTH PRESSURE

As Stated in Step 2, for the static active earth pressure, θ and $k_v = 0$. So we need to recompute the active earth pressure coefficient for the static condition (designated by K_A). First we must recompute the value of ψ for the static condition.

We now compute the static active earth pressure coefficient using θ and $k_v = 0$. Substituting in, we determine the final static active earth pressure acting over the whole wall. The reader should keep in mind that these values are per unit foot of wall length.

As we mentioned earlier, the static active earth pressure acts at 1/3 of the height. So for the whole abutment, it acts at 3.67 ft from the bottom of the footing. For the stem only, the force acts at 2.67 ft from the bottom of the stem. These arm lengths will be used to calculate bending moments caused by the static earth pressure.

Obviously, when computing the factor of safety for both overturning and sliding, a great deal of importance should be placed on what constitutes the numerator and denominator in Equations 4.8a and 4.8b.

Normally, the passive earth pressure at footing toe side is ignored. We should not rely on the passive earth pressure to resist overturning or sliding, because that soil may be lost due to erosion or regrading in the future.

There are a variety of methods which can be employed to increase sliding resistance of an abutment or retaining wall. One method is to incline the bottom surface of the footing, sloping it back toward the backfill. If the base is founded on soils, this angle of inclination should not exceed 10 degrees. If the footing is founded on rock, however, the angle selected can be such that all forces are normal to it [Ref. 4.1]. Another method is to include a rib or extrusion from the base of the footing, also to enhance resistance. This rib can be placed at either the toe or heel of the footing, or under the stem. The resistance developed, however, will vary depending on the location of the rib selected.

INCREASING SLIDING RESISTANCE

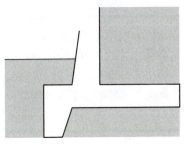

METHOD II
INCLUDE RIB IN FOOTING BASE

4.1.4 Load Factor Design Method

In AASHTO Standard Specifications, load factor design for foundations is treated as an alternative design method. As we mentioned in Section 4.1.3, most engineers in the USA are used to the service load design method for bridge foundations.

The LFD approach for substructure is the same as for superstructure discussed in Section 3. Load factors for load combinations I or VII (where earthquake is considered) are usually used. The resistance factors for strength limit states are summarized in Tables 4.10.6-1 to 4.10.6-3 of the AASHTO Standard Specifications [Ref. 4.4].

Note that when LFD is used, we still need to check the serviceability of the foundation such as excessive movements of the foundation, or excessive vibrations caused by dynamic loadings (AASHTO 5.13.1). Service load (unfactored) should be used for these serviceability check.

4.1.5 Load and Resistance Factor Design Method

In AASHTO LRFD [Ref. 4.5], foundations are designed for strength limit states and service limit states. Extreme event limit states such as seismic loading, scour, vessel or vehicular collision, should also be considered if applicable.

The strength limit states mainly deal with structural safety issues, which include:

- ❑ Bearing resistance (except presumptive capacity is used in design)
- ❑ Sliding at the base of footing
- ❑ Excessive loss of contact (scour)
- ❑ Loss of lateral support
- ❑ Structural Capacity

Similar to LFD approach, the resistance factors for various types of foundations are specified in Table 1 through Table 3 in AASHTO LRFD 10.5.5. Load factors for strength limit states as specified in Table 3.4 should be used.

Since traditionally foundations are designed using the service load method, and many geotechnical engineers still give soil bearing capacity based on the service load method, AASHTO LRFD allows engineers to use the Service I load combination to check bearing capacity if the presumptive resistance value is used.

For earthquake load, load combination for Extreme Event I should be used. Unlike AASHTO Standard Specifications, a certain percentage of live load should be considered when combined with earthquake load. AASHTO LRFD does not give a specific value for live load factor, but it indicates that 0.50 can be used for normal average daily truck traffic.

Foundations should also be designed for service limit states. They should include (AASHTO LRFD 10.5.2):

- ❑ Settlement and lateral displacement
- ❑ Overall stability (slope stability)
- ❑ Bearing resistance if presumptive bearing capacity is used

AASHTO LRFD allows engineers to use Service I load combination to check bearing capacity if presumptive resistance value is used.

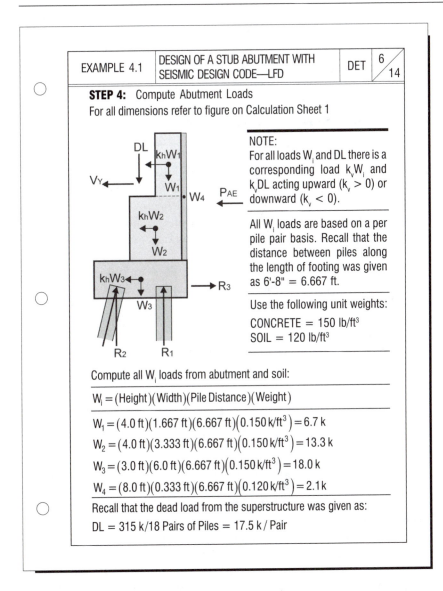

| EXAMPLE 4.1 | DESIGN OF A STUB ABUTMENT WITH SEISMIC DESIGN CODE—LFD | DET | 6 / 14 |

STEP 4: Compute Abutment Loads
For all dimensions refer to figure on Calculation Sheet 1

NOTE:
For all loads W_i and DL there is a corresponding load $k_v W_i$ and k_vDL acting upward ($k_v > 0$) or downward ($k_v < 0$).

All W_i loads are based on a per pile pair basis. Recall that the distance between piles along the length of footing was given as 6'-8" = 6.667 ft.

Use the following unit weights:
CONCRETE = 150 lb/ft³
SOIL = 120 lb/ft³

Compute all W_i loads from abutment and soil:

$$W_i = (\text{Height})(\text{Width})(\text{Pile Distance})(\text{Weight})$$

$$W_1 = (4.0\,\text{ft})(1.667\,\text{ft})(6.667\,\text{ft})(0.150\,\text{k/ft}^3) = 6.7\,\text{k}$$

$$W_2 = (4.0\,\text{ft})(3.333\,\text{ft})(6.667\,\text{ft})(0.150\,\text{k/ft}^3) = 13.3\,\text{k}$$

$$W_3 = (3.0\,\text{ft})(6.0\,\text{ft})(6.667\,\text{ft})(0.150\,\text{k/ft}^3) = 18.0\,\text{k}$$

$$W_4 = (8.0\,\text{ft})(0.333\,\text{ft})(6.667\,\text{ft})(0.120\,\text{k/ft}^3) = 2.1\,\text{k}$$

Recall that the dead load from the superstructure was given as:
DL = 315 k/18 Pairs of Piles = 17.5 k / Pair

DESIGN EXAMPLE 4.1
STEP 4: COMPUTE ABUTMENT LOADS

We must now compute the loads due to the abutment and soil at the rear face over the footing along with the superstructure dead loads acting on the abutment. As usual, we will assume the effects of passive pressure to be negligible.

The loading diagram shows the loads induced by the weight of each section of the abutment (W_i) as well as the horizontal component of the seismic loads (k_h). The reader should keep in mind, however, that a vertical component of seismic loads, k_v, is also present but not illustrated in the diagram. These loads will either act upward or downward, depending on the sign of k_v.

The loads are computed based on a *per pile pair* basis. We were given a distance of 6'-8" between piles at the beginning of this example. Also given were the unit weights of concrete and soil to be used.

The last load to be computed in this step is that of the superstructure dead loads, which are distributed over the 18 pairs of piles.

Load factors for Service Limit State I should be used. Resistance factors for the service limit state should be taken as 1.0.

Note that no matter which design method is used, the nominal earth pressure as discussed in Section 4.1.2 and Section 4.1.7 should be the same. The difference is that they use different load factors and resistance factors. In the case of service load design method, no load factor or resistance factor is used, but rather a factor of safety is used.

4.1.6 Other Related Foundation Topics

The preceding text offers only the most cursory discussion of the fundamental principles governing the design of retaining walls and abutments. It is intended only to give the reader the simplest of introductions to the subject matter and provide a common basis for discussion within this section. For further discussion on the subjects already covered, such as Coulomb earth pressure theory and abutment stability, as well as topics such as Rankine earth pressures, the design of piles, and other related topics which were not covered, the reader is referred to References 4.1 through 4.3, all of which offer thorough and complete discussions on these and related topics.

4.1.7 Mononobe-Okabe Analysis

A topic which is becoming of particular concern in the bridge design profession is that of seismic design. Particularly in light of recent earthquakes, such as the Loma Prieta earthquake of 1989 and the earthquake which struck Southern California in 1994, the conventional design of substructure components is no longer acceptable. Indeed, one of the most frequently asked questions of a bridge engineer is, "Are highway bridges safe enough to handle an earthquake?"

Transportation departments in states such as New York, where seismic activity does not garner the same headlines as that on the west coast, have undertaken rigid new guidelines concerning the seismic design of highway bridges. It is because of this heightened awareness in seismic design that the design example in this section has been structured to take into account the effects of seismic loading.

There are two fundamental issues which face bridge engineers with regard to seismic loading:

❏ Seismic retrofitting of existing structures
❏ Design of new structures to accommodate seismic loads

Where the seismic design of bridges definitely requires new details for the design of various components, it also requires a different type of analysis. In Section 3.5.3, Part 2 we discussed the unique loading conditions imposed by the application of seismic forces on a bridge structure. With regard to bridge abutments, one such analysis method used to account for seismic loading is the so-called Mononobe-Okabe analysis method.

For a freestanding abutment or retaining wall which can displace horizontally without "significant restraint," AASHTO recommends that the pseudo-static Mononobe-Okabe method of analysis be used to determine the effects of lateral active soil pressures during seismic loading (AASHTO Division I-A, 6.4.3(A)). An example of "significant restraint" would be tiebacks or battered piles which prevent abutment stem from horizontal or rotational movement.

The following discussion provides a background and overview of the basic concepts behind the Mononobe-Okabe analysis method. The nomenclature and variable designation used in this section is consistent with that presented in Figure 4.6 and Section 4.1.2.

1. Background. The Mononobe-Okabe method was developed in the 1920's and is frequently used for the calculation of the effects of seismic soil forces acting on a bridge abutment [Ref. 4.4]. This method is essentially an extension of the Coulomb sliding wedge theory (see Section 4.1.2), which takes into account horizontal and vertical inertia forces acting on the soil. These are illustrated, in part, in Figure 4.6, by the forces designated

Indeed, one of the most frequently asked questions a bridge engineer hears is, "Are highway bridges safe enough to handle an earthquake?"

The Mononobe-Okabe method was developed in the 1920's and is frequently used for the calculation of the effects of seismic soil forces acting on a bridge abutment.

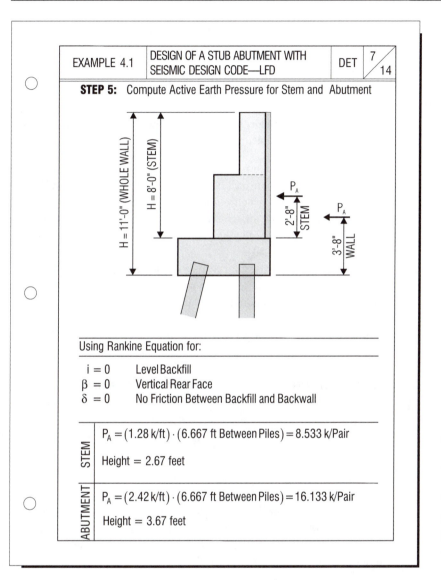

| EXAMPLE 4.1 | DESIGN OF A STUB ABUTMENT WITH SEISMIC DESIGN CODE—LFD | DET | 7/14 |

STEP 5: Compute Active Earth Pressure for Stem and Abutment

Using Rankine Equation for:

$i = 0$ Level Backfill
$\beta = 0$ Vertical Rear Face
$\delta = 0$ No Friction Between Backfill and Backwall

STEM

$P_A = (1.28 \text{ k/ft}) \cdot (6.667 \text{ ft Between Piles}) = 8.533 \text{ k/Pair}$

Height = 2.67 feet

ABUTMENT

$P_A = (2.42 \text{ k/ft}) \cdot (6.667 \text{ ft Between Piles}) = 16.133 \text{ k/Pair}$

Height = 3.67 feet

DESIGN EXAMPLE 4.1
STEP 5: COMPUTE ACTIVE EARTH PRESSURES STEM/WALL

We will compute two separate active earth pressures, one acting on the stem alone and the other acting on the entire abutment. The resultant forces will act at a distance of one-third the height of the member under consideration (see accompanying figure).

To compute the active earth pressures, we will utilize the Rankine equation, which reduces to the expression shown in the calculation sheet because of the geometry of the abutment and relationship between the stem and backfill with regard to friction.

The active earth pressures were computed earlier in Step 3. The pressures for both the stem and entire abutment were computed over a unit width. The forces in this sheet are based on per pair of piles. The forces for the entire abutment are used for pile design (which is not part of the example), while the forces for the stem are used to design the stem.

The distance between the pair of piles are 6'-8", which was given at the beginning of this example.

as $k_h W_s$ and $k_v W_s$ (where W_s is the weight of the soil located within the wedge) located in the active wedge force diagram.

The design of the abutment should take into account "forces which arise from seismically induced lateral earth pressures, additional forces arising from wall inertia effects and the transfer of seismic forces from the bridge deck through the bearing supports which do not slide freely." An example of "bearing supports which do not slide freely" would be fixed bearings.

The inertia forces due to the mess of the abutment itself is normally ignored in current seismic design procedures. That is not a conservative assumption, and many engineers believe that the force should be included in the design (See Part 6 of this section).

The failure of a highway bridge in general due to the failure or displacement of an abutment during an earthquake is well documented.

Causes of damage can be associated with any one of the following factors:

❏ Fill settlement or slumping
❏ Displacement caused by high lateral earth pressures resulting from seismic activity
❏ The transfer of high longitudinal or transverse inertia forces from the bridge superstructure

Potential adverse by-products of the above listed factors include settlement of the abutment backfill, damage to the abutment and damage to the bridge deck, all of which can lead to the possibility of a bridge being closed to access. Because of this condition, seismic design of abutments plays a critical part in the ability of the structure as a whole to resist seismic forces during an earthquake.

Difficulties in designing abutments to withstand seismic loading lie not only in the complex nature of earthquake motion but also in the great variety of abutment configurations in use. In Section 4.1.1 we listed ten basic forms of abutments alone and this does not even include all of the permutations of these basic forms. To model the effects of an earthquake on an abutment requires "many simplifying assumptions" [Ref. 4.4].

> To model the effects of an earthquake on an abutment requires "many simplifying assumptions."

2. Horizontal and Vertical Seismic Coefficients. The Mononobe-Okabe method utilizes horizontal and vertical seismic coefficients. The horizontal seismic coefficient is equal to:

$$k_h = \frac{A}{2} \qquad \text{(Eq. 4.9)}$$

where A = acceleration coefficient

The acceleration coefficient A is determined by referencing the bridge site location with a map which depicts accelerations in terms of contours. Such a map, for the continental United States is presented in Figure 3.15. A more detailed version is presented in the AASHTO specifications for the entire United States including the states of Hawaii and Alaska.

As mentioned in Section 3.5.3, Part 2, the acceleration coefficient is a dimensionless constant which is used to describe ground motion. If the acceleration coefficient exceeds 0.19, the bridge is said to be in an area of high seismic activity. As a frame of reference, Southern California has acceleration coefficient values in the range of 0.60 and higher and New York values are in the realm of 0.10.

Equation 4.9 applies to freestanding abutments or retaining walls which can be displaced horizontally without significant restraint. However, if a freestanding abutment, which is restricted from horizontal displacement through the implementation of anchors or batter piles, is present, AASHTO recommends a first approximation of:

$$k_h = 1.5 \cdot A \qquad \text{(Eq. 4.10)}$$

be used instead of Equation 4.9 for the calculation of maximum lateral earth pressure.

With regard to the vertical seismic coefficient, k_v, AASHTO

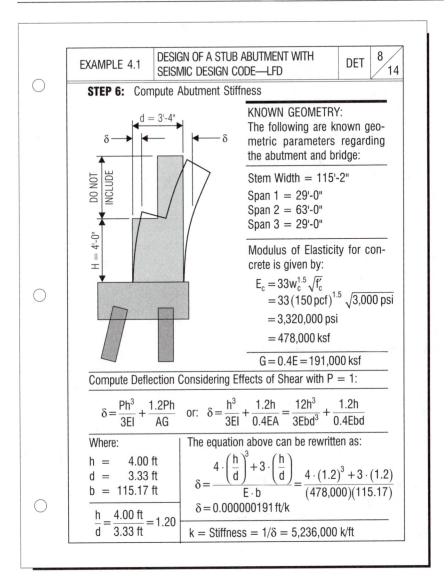

| EXAMPLE 4.1 | DESIGN OF A STUB ABUTMENT WITH SEISMIC DESIGN CODE—LFD | DET | 8 / 14 |

STEP 6: Compute Abutment Stiffness

KNOWN GEOMETRY:
The following are known geometric parameters regarding the abutment and bridge:

Stem Width = 115'-2"

Span 1 = 29'-0"
Span 2 = 63'-0"
Span 3 = 29'-0"

Modulus of Elasticity for concrete is given by:

$$E_c = 33 w_c^{1.5} \sqrt{f_c'}$$
$$= 33 (150\,\text{pcf})^{1.5} \sqrt{3{,}000\,\text{psi}}$$
$$= 3{,}320{,}000\,\text{psi}$$
$$= 478{,}000\,\text{ksf}$$

$$G = 0.4E = 191{,}000\,\text{ksf}$$

Compute Deflection Considering Effects of Shear with P = 1:

$$\delta = \frac{Ph^3}{3EI} + \frac{1.2Ph}{AG} \quad \text{or:} \quad \delta = \frac{h^3}{3EI} + \frac{1.2h}{0.4EA} = \frac{12h^3}{3Ebd^3} + \frac{1.2h}{0.4Ebd}$$

Where:

h = 4.00 ft
d = 3.33 ft
b = 115.17 ft

$$\frac{h}{d} = \frac{4.00\,\text{ft}}{3.33\,\text{ft}} = 1.20$$

The equation above can be rewritten as:

$$\delta = \frac{4 \cdot \left(\dfrac{h}{d}\right)^3 + 3 \cdot \left(\dfrac{h}{d}\right)}{E \cdot b} = \frac{4 \cdot (1.2)^3 + 3 \cdot (1.2)}{(478{,}000)(115.17)}$$

$$\delta = 0.000000191\ \text{ft/k}$$

$$k = \text{Stiffness} = 1/\delta = 5{,}236{,}000\ \text{k/ft}$$

(Diagram labels: d = 3'-4", δ, δ, DO NOT INCLUDE, H = 4'-0")

DESIGN EXAMPLE 4.1
STEP 6: COMPUTE ABUTMENT STIFFNESS

In order to compute the effects of longitudinal earthquake motion on the abutment, we first need to determine the stiffness of the abutment. To calculate the stiffness we will apply a unit load of P = 1 on the abutment assuming it acts as a cantilevered beam fixed at the footing. We will compute the deflection due to this unit load and, by definition, the stiffness will be the inverse of this value.

We are given a total width of stem of 115'-2" and an end span length of 29'-0" (which will be used later). Because the height to depth ratio is not great, we need to take into account the effects of shear when computing the deflection. To simplify the calculation, the general deflection equation is rewritten using a parameter of h/d.

The value of "h" is taken as 4.00 ft and the top portion of the abutment (backwall) ignored because the superstructure is supported by the bearings. Therefore the backwall height is not included when computing the stiffness for the abutment in longitudinal earthquake motion.

specifies that the effects of vertical acceleration may be omitted. If the designer deems it necessary, however, to incorporate the effects of vertical acceleration into the design, a general accepted range for this coefficient is:

$$0.30 k_h < k_v < 0.50 k_h \qquad \text{(Eq. 4.11a)}$$

and

$$k_h \le (1 - k_v)\tan(\phi - i) \qquad \text{(Eq. 4.11b)}$$

where ϕ and i are the same as used in Equation 4.3.

The vertical seismic coefficient is used to determine the upward and downward motion of the structure during seismic loading.

3. Basic Assumption. The Mononobe-Okabe method makes certain basic assumptions. These are identified in AASHTO 1998 Commentary, C6.4.3(A) as:

❑ The abutment is free to yield enough to allow full soil strength or active pressure conditions to be mobilized,
❑ The backfill is cohesionless, and
❑ The backfill is unsaturated so that liquefaction problems will not arise.

With the assumptions described above, equilibrium considerations of the soil wedge behind the abutment are used to determine the active earth pressure acting on the soil mass by the abutment and vice versa [Ref. 4.4].

If the abutment is rigid and unable to move, the seismic earth pressure will be much higher than the Mononobe-Okabe method predicts.

4. Active Earth Pressure. The seismically induced active earth pressure looks very similar to the one defined early using conventional Coulomb earth pressure theory (Equations 4.1 through 4.3). In this case, the active earth pressure is given as:

$$P_{AE} = \frac{1}{2} \cdot \gamma \cdot H^2 \cdot (1 - k_v) \cdot K_{AE}$$ (Eq. 4.12)

where γ = unit weight of soil
H = height of soil face
K_{AE} = active pressure coefficient

$$K_{AE} = \frac{\cos^2(\phi - \theta - \beta)}{\psi \cdot \cos\theta \cdot \cos^2\beta \cdot \cos(\delta + \beta + \theta)}$$ (Eq. 4.13)

where ϕ = angle of friction of soil
δ = angle of friction between soil and abutment
β = slope of soil face
θ = seismic internal angle

The seismic internal angle, θ, is the parameter which differentiates the seismic active earth pressure coefficient from its static version presented earlier in Equation 4.2. This angle is defined as:

$$\theta = \arctan\left(\frac{k_b}{1 - k_v}\right)$$ (Eq. 4.14)

| EXAMPLE 4.1 | DESIGN OF A STUB ABUTMENT WITH SEISMIC DESIGN CODE—LFD | DET | 9 / 14 |

STEP 7: Compute Earthquake Load on Abutment

29'-0"   63'-0"   29'-0"

w = Weight of Deck
= 21.74 k/ft

2" (TYP)

P_0 P_0 P_0

V_s

Compute static displacement v_s with $P_o = 1$:

$$v_S = \frac{P_o \cdot L}{k} = \frac{(1)(29.0 \text{ ft})}{5,236,000 \text{ k/ft}} = 5.54 \times 10^{-6} \text{ ft}$$

Compute single-mode factors α, β, γ (AASHTO Division I-A 4.4):

$$\alpha = \int_0^L v_s(x)dx = v_s L = \left(5.54 \times 10^{-6} \text{ ft}\right)(29.0 \text{ ft}) = 1.61 \times 10^{-4} \text{ ft}^2$$

$$\beta = \int_0^L w(x)v_s(x)dx = \alpha \cdot w = \left(1.61 \times 10^{-4} \text{ ft}^2\right)(21.74 \text{ k/ft})$$
$$= 3.50 \times 10^{-3} \text{ ft} \cdot \text{k}$$

$$\gamma = \int_0^L w(x)v_s(x)^2 dx = \beta \cdot v_s = \left(3.50 \times 10^{-3} \text{ ft} \cdot \text{k}\right)\left(5.54 \times 10^{-6} \text{ ft}\right)$$
$$= 1.94 \times 10^{-8} \text{ ft}^2 \cdot \text{k}$$

(Step 7: Continued on Next Sheet)

DESIGN EXAMPLE 4.1
STEP 7: EARTHQUAKE LOAD ON ABUTMENT

Recall that, in our force diagram shown earlier in Step 4, a horizontal force of V_Y was applied at the stringer support point. This is the load caused by longitudinal earthquake motion. Since we already have determined our seismic criteria (Step 1) and abutment stiffness (Step 6), we are now ready to compute this force.

The first step is to calculate the static displacement v_s based on a unit load of $P_o = 1$. Recall that the length of the end span was earlier given to be 29 ft and the unit weight of superstructure as 21.74 k/ft.

The bridge is made of 3 simply supported spans. The end spans are fixed at abutments, and have expansion bearings at piers. Therefore, we assume abutment will carry all longitudinal earthquake force from the end span.

Once the static displacement is known, we can compute the three single-mode factors which were defined earlier in Section 3.5.3, Part 2 (Equations 3.1 through 3.3). The integrals are solved from x equals 0 to L, where L is the length of the end span, v_s is the static displacement, and w is the unit weight of deck.

As before, we again have the term in the denominator, which here is:

$$\psi = \left[1 + \sqrt{\frac{\sin(\phi + \delta) \cdot \sin(\phi - \theta - i)}{\cos(\delta + \beta + \theta) \cdot \cos(i - \beta)}}\right]^2 \qquad \text{(Eq. 4.15)}$$

where i = backfill slope angle

The passive pressure, like the active pressure, is modified by the inclusion of the seismic internal angle and acceleration coefficients. In this case, the passive earth pressure equation, which was presented earlier in Equation 4.4, is modified to become:

$$P_{PE} = \frac{1}{2} \cdot \gamma \cdot H^2 \cdot (1 - k_v) \cdot K_{PE} \qquad \text{(Eq. 4.16)}$$

The passive pressure, like the active pressure, is modified by the inclusion of the seismic internal angle and acceleration coefficients.

where γ = unit weight of soil
H = height of soil face
K_{PE} = passive pressure coefficient

The passive pressure coefficient is in turn defined by the following expression:

$$K_{PE} = \frac{\cos^2(\phi - \theta + \beta)}{\Gamma \cdot \cos\theta \cdot \cos^2\beta \cdot \cos(\delta - \beta + \theta)} \qquad \text{(Eq. 4.17)}$$

where, for the seismically induced passive pressure, we use a denominator multiplier defined by the following:

$$\Gamma = \left[1 + \sqrt{\frac{\sin(\phi + \delta) \cdot \sin(\phi - \theta + i)}{\cos(\delta - \beta + \theta) \cdot \cos(i - \beta)}} \right]^2 \qquad \text{(Eq. 4.18)}$$

From the above, it can be seen that, as the seismic internal angle, θ, increases, the seismic active and passive pressure coefficients K_{AE} and K_{PE} approach each other. Also, for vertical backfill, the coefficients become equal when $\theta = \phi$.

5. Applying Active Earth Pressure. Using conventional analysis (i.e., nonseismic) the active earth pressure is typically placed at a distance of:

$$b = \frac{H}{3} \qquad \text{(Eq. 4.19)}$$

from the bottom of the abutment for this static condition. Tests have indicated, however, that the dynamic earthquake pressure acts at a greater distance from the bottom of the abutment. Under earthquake loading conditions, this distance can be taken as:

$$b = 0.60H \qquad \text{(Eq. 4.20)}$$

So that, in analyzing an abutment, two active earth pressures can be computed: one for the static condition and the other for the dynamic one. Each pressure is then applied by the corresponding offsets as defined by Equations 4.19 and 4.20.

In order to more easily compute the earthquake effects, a normalized pressure can be calculated through use of a *thrust factor*, F_T, which correlates the two pressures and allows for use of a single, equivalent pressure to be used. The thrust factor can be defined as:

> **S**o that, in analyzing an abutment, two active earth pressures can be computed: one for the static condition and the other for the dynamic one.

$$F_T = \frac{K_{AE}}{K_A} \qquad \text{(Eq. 4.21)}$$

| EXAMPLE 4.1 | DESIGN OF A STUB ABUTMENT WITH SEISMIC DESIGN CODE—LFD | DET | 10/14 |

STEP 7: Compute Earthquake Load on Abutment (Continued)

Compute period of oscillation:

$$T = 2\pi\sqrt{\frac{\gamma}{P_0 g \alpha}} = 2\pi\sqrt{\frac{1.94\times10^{-8}\ ft^2 \cdot k}{(1k)(32.2\ ft/sec^2)(1.61\times10^{-4}\ ft^2)}}$$

$$= 1.215\times10^{-2}\ sec$$

Compute elastic seismic response coefficient:

A = Acceleration Coefficient = 0.19 (Given)
S = Site Coefficient = 1.2 (Step 1)

$$C_S = \frac{1.2AS}{T^{2/3}} = \frac{(1.2)(0.19)(1.2)}{(1.215\times10^{-2}\ sec)^{2/3}} = 5.18$$

AASHTO Division I-A 3.6.1 states that C_s need not exceed 2.5A:

C_s = 2.5A = (2.5)(0.19) = 0.475 < 5.08 ✔ Use: C_s = 0.475

Compute equivalent static earthquake loading:

$$p_e(x) = \frac{\beta \cdot C_S}{\gamma}w(x)v_S(x)$$

$$= \frac{(3.50\times10^{-3}\ ft \cdot k)(0.475)}{(1.94\times10^{-8}\ ft^2 \cdot k)} \cdot (21.74\ k/ft)(5.54\times10^{-6}\ ft)$$

$$= 10.32\ k/ft$$

Compute force acting on abutment:

$$V_Y = \frac{p_e(x)\cdot L}{R_{STEM}} = \frac{(10.32\ k/ft)(29\ ft)}{2.0} = 149.64\ k$$

DESIGN EXAMPLE 4.1
STEP 7: EARTHQUAKE LOAD ON ABUTMENT (CONTINUED)

Next, as defined earlier in Equation 3.4, we calculate the period of oscillation again using a unit load of 1.0. This is used in turn to calculate the seismic response coefficient. To compute this value we need the acceleration factor which was given based on the bridge location and the site coefficient determined earlier in Step 1.

The seismic response coefficient, however, is not to exceed 2.5A, where A is the acceleration factor (if a Soil Profile Type III were present where A > 0.30, the not to exceed value would be 2.0A).

This is the last value needed to calculate the equivalent static earthquake loading acting on the bridge. This is a unit load acting over the entire length of the end span.

To compute the actual force acting on the abutment we multiply this unit loading by the length of the span. This value is reduced by the response modification factor, R, determined earlier in Step 1. This value in specified by AASHTO Division I-A 3.7 with a table of values presented in Section 3.5.3.

and is based on the dynamic and static active earth pressure coefficients, respectively.

To simplify the calculation, AASHTO allows to combine the static earth pressure with the seismic earth pressure, and assume the combined force will act on H/2. The combined earth pressure can be applied as a uniformly distributed pressure.

6. Caveats. The Mononobe-Okabe analysis method does not take into account the effects of abutment inertia [Ref. 4.4]. While many analysis methods also neglect the effects of inertia when considering seismic behavior and design, this assumption is not a conservative one.

AASHTO indicates in their commentary that for abutments which rely on "their mass for stability it is also an unreasonable assumption, in that to neglect the mass is to neglect a major aspect of their behavior." This means that for substructure components, such as a gravity retaining wall, wall inertia forces should not be neglected.

7. Superstructure Loads. In addition to the earth pressure loading, the designer must also account for earthquake loads from the superstructure. These loads, resulting from longitudinal and transverse earthquake motion, are transferred to and must be accommodated by the abutment.

To calculate these loads, the procedure as outlined in Section 3.5.3, Part 2 is utilized in order to determine an equivalent static earthquake loading, $p_e(x)$. Depending on the type of structure present, this is accomplished through use of either the single mode spectral analysis method or the multimode spectral analysis method. Factors which influence the magnitude of the applied loads are the soil type present, acceleration coefficient at the project site, length of the span at the abutment, and unit weight of the bridge deck.

This loading condition, together with the superstructure dead load and earth pressure loads discussed above, represent the three major loading conditions influencing the design of an abutment.

4.1.8 Rehabilitation and Maintenance

Like any other component of a highway bridge, abutments are susceptible to the ravages of deterioration. Particularly in structures with a deck joint located over the abutment support point, a bridge abutment can undergo some of the most severe damage in a highway bridge caused by exposure to the elements and harmful agents.

Some of the major types of deterioration and maintenance problems which can occur in an abutment are [Ref. 4.6]:

❏ Settlement or movement
❏ Vertical cracking
❏ Surface deterioration
❏ Deterioration at the water line
❏ Spalling under bearing masonry plates
❏ Backwall undermining
❏ Rotting of timber elements (if present)

The following discussion covers some of the principal forms of deterioration in bridge abutments, as well as some of the remedial methods which can be taken to correct them. Attention is also given to some of the situations which can lead to abutment deterioration so that potential preventive maintenance measures can be taken to correct them.

1. Cracking. Cracks in abutments can develop as a result of a wide variety of situations. Vertical cracking in an abutment stem can often be initiated by differential (i.e., uneven) settlement of the abutment. Cracks can also be induced by deformational loads such as shrinkage.

If proper drainage is not provided for the abutment backfill, a situation can arise where the backfill side of an abutment stem is continually moist,

In addition to the earth pressure loading, the designer must also account for earthquake loads from the superstructure.

Vertical cracking in an abutment backwall can often be initiated by differential (i.e., uneven) settlement of the abutment.

| EXAMPLE 4.1 | DESIGN OF A STUB ABUTMENT WITH SEISMIC DESIGN CODE—LFD | DET | 11/14 |

STEP 8: Compute Shears and Moments

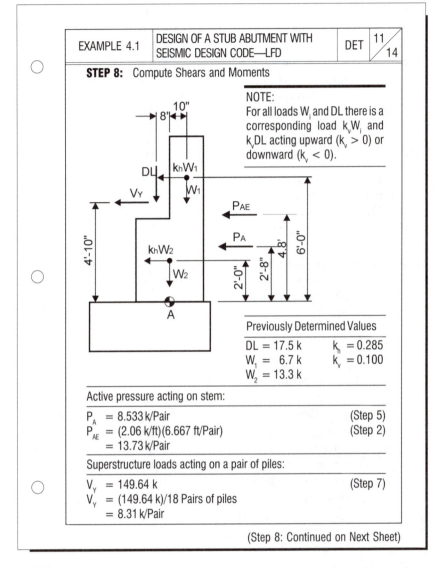

NOTE:
For all loads W_i and DL there is a corresponding load $k_v W_i$ and $k_v DL$ acting upward ($k_v > 0$) or downward ($k_v < 0$).

Previously Determined Values

DL = 17.5 k	k_h = 0.285
W_1 = 6.7 k	k_v = 0.100
W_2 = 13.3 k	

Active pressure acting on stem:

P_A = 8.533 k/Pair   (Step 5)
P_{AE} = (2.06 k/ft)(6.667 ft/Pair)   (Step 2)
     = 13.73 k/Pair

Superstructure loads acting on a pair of piles:

V_Y = 149.64 k   (Step 7)
V_Y = (149.64 k)/18 Pairs of piles
     = 8.31 k/Pair

(Step 8: Continued on Next Sheet)

We are now ready to calculate the shears and moments acting on the abutment. In this calculation sheet, we present a free body diagram of the loads acting on the stem only.

The abutment stem will be designed based on a "strip" of abutment defined by the distance between two pairs of piles (6'-8").

Prior to actually calculating the forces and moments, however, we must compute the equivalent active earth pressure acting on the abutment. Note that we separate the static earth pressure with the seismic earth pressure because they act at different heights. AASHTO does allow to combine both forces. The combined force act at H/2. We did not combine them in this example.

Finally, the load from the superstructure due to longitudinal earthquake motion, which was determined in the previous step, must be reduced to the value acting over a strip of abutment with a pair of piles.

while the exposed face of the wall becomes wet and then dries. This differential between the two faces of the stem can lead to the formation of shrinkage cracks, and the concrete may also be damaged by freeze-and-thaw actions.

One obvious solution to this problem is to provide adequate drainage of the abutment. This can be facilitated by the incorporation of an underdrain system which takes runoff and channels it away from the abutment. The underdrain conduit is typically made of a PVC pipe which is perforated to facilitate drainage. The size of the pipe used will depend on the amount of runoff at the site (see also Section 3.9.8, Part 4).

Weep tubes can be placed into the abutment stem at specified intervals to assist in draining the backfill material. A problem with this approach, however, is that the weep tubes themselves can become damaged, either through deterioration or vandalism. This can further exacerbate the problem by allowing moisture to collect directly upon the face of a abutment. The backfill material itself should be of a composition that facilitates proper drainage. Gravel and sand are backfill materials which are well suited for this. The applicability of any method will vary depending on the specifics of the project site and the owner's preferences.

Another cause of cracking, particularly in older structures, is the use of a poor concrete mix or inadequate reinforcement. When such a situation occurs, replacement rather than rehabilitation may be the only solution. Many older abutments, however, are aided by their large size. Even structures that were constructed as late as the 1950's are equipped with wingwalls that, by any standard, would be considered massive.

The type of rehabilitation selected to repair cracks will obviously vary depending on the size and magnitude of the cracks present. Some shrinkage cracks, for example, can be relatively fine and therefore will not require extensive rehabilitation.

> **E**ven structures that were constructed as late as the 1950's are equipped with wingwalls that, by any standard, would be considered massive.

2. Surface Deterioration. Like any other exposed concrete element, abutments can suffer from surface deterioration problems which are indicated by the presence of:

- ❏ Spalling
- ❏ Scaling
- ❏ Pop-outs
- ❏ Sloughing off corners

A variety of factors can lead to any of the above situations occurring. Chief among contributing causes is, of course, chemical attacks; either through deicing agents or other corrosive materials being sprayed onto exposed concrete. When reinforcing steel corrodes, it increases its volume, which causes concrete to crack. Other potential causes for surface deterioration are the use of a poor concrete mix, poor aggregates, or thermal expansion and contraction.

> **O**ther potential causes for surface deterioration are the use of a poor concrete mix, poor aggregates, or thermal expansion and contraction.

Repair of abutments damaged by surface deterioration is very similar to that described earlier for concrete decks. First, the deteriorated concrete must be removed to a depth where sound concrete is present. Generally this is to a point beneath the reinforcing steel (see Figure 3.27). This surface should be clean and free from debris so that new concrete may be bonded into the void. Bonding is typically made with some form of epoxy bonding compound, although mechanical bonding is also sometimes used.

3. Stability Problems. In Part 1 above, it was mentioned that vertical cracking can result from differential settlement of the abutment. Stability problems such as this can arise from situations ranging from changes in soil characteristics to poor design. Some of the major stability problems for an abutment which could potentially arise as a result of these adverse conditions, or other reasons are:

- ❏ Differential settlement or other vertical movement
- ❏ Lateral movement (sliding)
- ❏ Rotational movement (tipping, overturning)

EXAMPLE 4.1	DESIGN OF A STUB ABUTMENT WITH SEISMIC DESIGN CODE—LFD	DET	12/14

STEP 8: Compute Shears and Moments (Continued)

$\sum V = 0$: $-(DL + W_1 + W_2)(1 - k_v)$ $[k_v > 0]$

$= -(17.5\ k + 6.7\ k + 13.3\ k)(1 - 0.10)$ ⟫ $-33.75\ k$

$\sum V = 0$: $-(DL + W_1 + W_2)(1 + k_v)$ $[k_v < 0]$

$= -(17.5\ k + 6.7\ k + 13.3\ k)(1 + 0.10)$ ⟫ $-41.25\ k$

$\sum H = 0$: $k_h DL + k_h W_1 + k_h W_2 + V_y + P_{AE} + P_A$

$= (0.285)(17.5k + 6.7k + 13.3k) + 8.31 + 13.73 + 8.53k$ ⟫ $41.26\ k$

Axial Force:

$F_A = \dfrac{V_{MAX}}{\text{Dist. Between Piles}} = \dfrac{41.25\ k}{6.667\ ft}$ ⟫ $F_A = 6.19\ k/ft$

Shear Force:

$V = \dfrac{H}{\text{Dist. Between Piles}} = \dfrac{41.26\ k}{6.667\ ft}$ ⟫ $V = 6.19\ k/ft$

$\sum M_A = 0$: $[k_h < 0]\ [k_v < 0]$

$4.83V_y + 0.67DL(1 + k_v) + 4.8P_{AE} + 2.67P_A + 6W_1 k_h + 2W_2 k_h - 0.83W_1(1 + k_v)$

$(4.83)(8.31)$	$=$	40.14 ft-k
$(0.67)(17.5)(1 + 0.1)$	$=$	12.90 ft-k
$(4.8)(13.73)$	$=$	65.90 ft-k
$(2.67)(8.53)$	$=$	22.78 ft-k
$(6.0)(6.7)(0.285)$	$=$	11.46 ft-k
$(2.0)(13.3)(0.285)$	$=$	7.58 ft-k
$(-0.83)(6.7)(1 + 0.1)$	$=$	-6.12 ft-k
TOTAL	$=$	154.64 ft-k

Controlling Moment:

$M = \dfrac{\text{Worst Case Moment}}{\text{Dist. Between Piles}}$

$= \dfrac{154.68\ ft \cdot k}{6.667\ ft}$

⟫ $M = 23.19$ ft-k/ft

Since the direction of earthquake motion can vary, the values of k_h and k_v will also vary (i.e., from positive to negative). First we compute shear occurring in both the vertical and horizontal planes.

These values act over a distance of 6.667 ft (i.e., distance between piles) so we must divide the shears (and moments) by the amount to get a value per foot of abutment.

From the computation of vertical shear it can be seen that there is no uplift. The axial force per foot of abutment is computed using the maximum value.

The calculation for moment shown is the worst case (i.e., $k_h < 0$ and $k_v < 0$). When performing a seismic design, the engineer should check all combinations of sign for k_h and k_v to determine which produces the worst case. For the sake of brevity, we have shown only the worst case situation. Like the shear values above, the moment is divided by the distance between piles to get a moment per foot of abutment.

Differential settlement can arise from problems with the soil such as consolidation or soil bearing failure. Lateral movement or sliding of the abutment can be caused by changes in the soil characteristics, consolidation, seepage, or failure of the slope. Rotational movement can result from the backfill material becoming saturated with water or erosion of the side slopes.

Another factor which can initiate any of the above referenced stability problems is scour. When a bridge abutment is subjected to potential scour damages, it should be supported by deep foundations (piles), unless the spread footing is supported by the solid rock. If piles are shorter than 15 feet, they should be socketed into rock by drilling a hole in the rock, and be cast in the rock with concrete.

When an abutment is fully exposed to underpass traffic, either vehicular or marine, the potential also exists for impact damage. Generally, this is more of a problem for piers than it is for abutments; however, some site geometries necessitate the exposure of abutment elements to traffic.

If such a situation occurs, the abutment (like piers) should be equipped with a protective barrier system to ensure that the stability of the abutment is not compromised by accidental impact. This is particularly a problem for abutments which are supported by exposed piles. Such a configuration is often used in bridges present in marine environments. When piles are exposed in such a fashion, collision with marine traffic can result not only in possible damage to the abutment itself, but failure of the end span.

To protect the abutment, a fender or dolphin system should be installed. A dolphin is a collection of piles, equipped with protective caps which are positioned in a circle around a center pile with their upper ends joined together. Dolphins can be constructed out of timber, steel tubes, or sheet piling.

A fender is a protective system which can be composed of driven piles, rubber, spring elements, or hydraulic-pneumatic components, designed to absorb the impact from a vehicle and thereby protect the bridge element behind it. Fender systems come in a variety of sizes and can be specified to withstand loads which range from the very small to the very large.

4. Bridge Seat Deterioration. As discussed earlier in Section 2.3.3, Part 2, extreme deterioration of a bridge seat can severely compromise the integrity of a structure. Damage to bridge seats, whether they be in the form of individual pedestals or a single bench (e.g., breastwall) is evidenced by spalling, scaling, pop-outs, and/or sloughing off at corners (as we saw for general surface deterioration).

Some of the potential causes of deterioration to an abutment's bridge seats are [Ref. 4.6]:

- ❑ Chemical attack
- ❑ Poor aggregates
- ❑ Poor concrete
- ❑ Thermal expansion and contraction
- ❑ Inadequate reinforcement

Once again, the principal culprit is a leaking joint. Therefore, the first line of defense that a maintenance department has in protecting an abutment's bridge seats is to ensure that the joint over the abutment is functioning properly. If a structure is due for rehabilitation, serious consideration should be given to eliminating joints whenever and wherever possible. This is not always an option because of obvious economic reasons. If pursued, however, the elimination of joints will greatly enhance the longevity of a bridge. If eliminating joints is not possible, an effective way to protect bridge seats is to install neoprene trough under the expansion joint, between the backwall and the superstructure. Another form of preventive maintenance which can be taken is to apply an epoxy protective coating to pedestals to guard against deterioration due to moisture. For new bridge design, epoxy coated reinforcing steel should be used at the bridge seat area.

Repair of damaged bridge seats may require jacking of the superstructure to correct the problem. The level of repair will naturally vary depending on the extent of deterioration present. At one end of the spectrum, repair could consist of simply removing to sound concrete and

> **W**hen piles are exposed... collision with marine traffic can result not only in possible damage to the abutment itself, but failure of the end span.

> **I**f a structure is due for rehabilitation, serious consideration should be given to eliminating joints whenever and wherever possible.

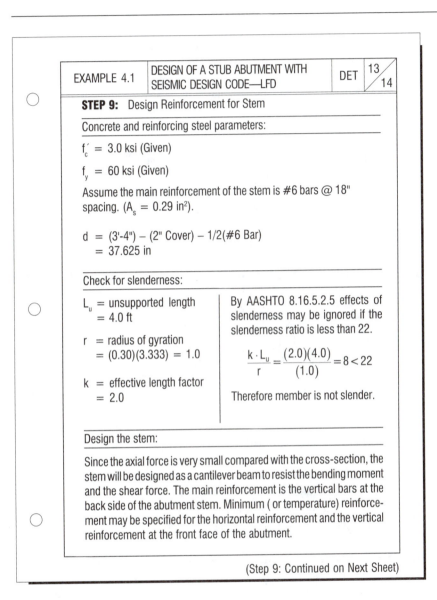

(Step 9: Continued on Next Sheet)

DESIGN EXAMPLE 4.1
STEP 9: DESIGN REINFORCE-MENT FOR STEM

Prior to beginning the actual design of reinforcement, we must first define all of the required concrete and reinforcing steel parameters. In Step 6 of Design Example 3.1 we conducted similar calculations. For references to the specific AASHTO and ACI specifications, the reader is referred to the bending moment capacity for reinforced concrete beams.

We must check the stem to see if the effects of slenderness must be considered (AASHTO 8.16.5.2). The unsupported length of the stem is 4.0 ft. The effective length factor can be determined by referencing Figure 4.13. The computed slenderness ratio value must be less than 22 in order to ignore the effects of slenderness. Since our value of 8 falls well below this limit, the member is not considered to be slender. The stem will be designed as a cantilever beam, and axial force will be ignored.

At this point, we can assume the main reinforcement to be #6 bars spacing at 18 inches.

patching the deteriorated area. If inadequate reinforcement was specified in the original design, supplementary reinforcement should be added.

Another problem which can lead to deterioration of bridge seats is the incorrect location of bearings. If a bearing is not placed properly, it can lead to an eccentric loading which may lead to cracking at the face of a bridge seat. The most economical solution to this problem is to extend the pedestal.

If a bridge seat suffers from so much deterioration, however, that remedial patches will not create an adequate bearing surface, then complete removal and replacement of the bridge seat will be required. The existing bridge seat is razed to the top of footing elevation and a new one constructed. If at all possible, it is desirable to preserve the existing vertical reinforcement to the footing (provided that it is cleaned properly and in good condition). It may also be desirous to supplement the vertical reinforcement with additional dowels. This can be accomplished by drilling and grouting new reinforcement into the existing footing. If, however, the existing reinforcement is in such bad condition that it can not be salvaged, then new reinforcing steel must be used entirely.

Whenever possible, the rehabilitation of any component in a highway bridge should be made to conform to the current details and practices used by a transportation department. Using the example of a deteriorated bridge seat that is to be completely replaced, if the current detail used by an agency is to utilize a breastwall rather than a set of freestanding pedestals, then this alternate should be investigated.

With an eye toward aesthetics, however, any *partial* replacement work performed should be detailed to reflect other components of a structure (e.g., both abutments should either use freestanding pedestals or breastwalls, not a mix of the two).

> Whenever possible, the rehabilitation of any component in a highway bridge should be made to conform to the current details and practices used by a transportation department.

5. Sheet Piling Abutments. An abutment constructed with steel sheet piling was shown earlier in Figure 1.8. Steel sheeting is also sometimes used as an abutment material in marine environments. When placed in such an environment, steel sheeting is susceptible to deterioration through the presence of high water or varying wet-dry cycles. When placed close to underpass traffic, like the steel sheeting abutment in Figure 1.8, accidental collision with traffic is another potential problem.

An obvious remedial measure which can be taken is to remove and replace any damaged or deteriorated sheeting. Another option is to drive new sheet piling around the existing abutment, filling the void between the two with new backing material [Ref. 4.6]. Like other abutments, the material behind a steel sheet piling abutment must be kept free from water. To enhance the longevity of this type of abutment a coating or waterproofing material (e.g., synthetic resin, linseed oil, etc.) should be used. Areas on steel sheet piling abutments which are continually exposed to wet-dry cycles should receive a protective coating.

> Stone masonry abutments need to be maintained so that cracks are not allowed to develop, especially at mortared joints.

6. Stone Masonry Abutments. Stone masonry abutments need to be maintained so that cracks are not allowed to develop, especially at mortared joints. While stone does not deteriorate as fast as concrete, its tensile strength is generally less than that of concrete [Ref. 4.6]. This can lead to problems, particularly when differential settlement occurs. Since deterioration in stone masonry abutments can propagate quickly, it is important that any cracks which are present be immediately sealed with mortar to prevent the intrusion of moisture. Defective joints should be raked out and then rejointed. This can be accomplished with pressure injection with epoxy. Also, any vegetation which has begun to grow into cracks should be removed.

7. MSE Systems. MSE (mechanically stabilized earth) systems were discussed earlier in Section 4.1.1, Part 10. These systems consist of three basic components:

- ❏ The precast concrete facing units or *skin*
- ❏ The metal or polymetric reinforcement
- ❏ The soil

| EXAMPLE 4.1 | DESIGN OF A STUB ABUTMENT WITH SEISMIC DESIGN CODE—LFD | DET | 14/14 |

STEP 9: Design Reinforcement for Stem (Continued)

Compute design moment strength (AASHTO 8.16.3.2):

$$\phi \cdot M_n = \phi\left[A_s f_y\left(d - \frac{a}{2}\right)\right]$$

$$a = \frac{A_s f_y}{0.85 f'_c b} \quad \text{so:} \quad a = \frac{(0.29\ \text{in}^2)(60\ \text{k/in}^2)}{(0.85)(3.0\ \text{k/in}^2)(12\ \text{in})} = 0.5686\ \text{in}$$

$$M_u = \phi \cdot M_n = 0.9\left[(0.29\ \text{in})(60\ \text{k/in}^2)\left(37.625\ \text{in} - \frac{0.5686\ \text{in}}{2}\right)\right]$$

$$= 584.7\ \text{in} \cdot \text{k} = 48.73\ \text{ft} \cdot \text{k} > 23.19\ \text{ft} \cdot \text{k}$$

Design for shear-friction (AASHTO 8.16.6.4):

$$A_{vf} = \text{Required Shear-Friction Reinforcement} = \frac{V_n}{f_y \mu}$$

$V_n = V_u/\phi = 6.19/0.85 = 7.28\ \text{k}$ (Step 8)

$f_y = 60\ \text{ksi}$ (Given)

$\mu = 0.6\lambda$ (AASHTO 8.16.6.4.4) $= (0.60)(1.0) = 0.60$

$$A_{vf} = \frac{7.28\ \text{k/ft}}{(60\ \text{ksi})(0.60)} = 0.20\ \text{in}^2/\text{ft of wall}$$

➥ #6 Bars @ 18 inch Spacing
($A_s = 0.29\ \text{in}^2$)

Temperature steel:

➥ #5 Bars @ 18 inch Spacing
($A_s = 0.21\ \text{in}^2$)

DESIGN EXAMPLE 4.1

STEP 9:   DESIGN REINFORCEMENT FOR STEM (CONTINUED)

Now we will check the strength of the section to see if it can accommodate our controlling moment. The strength is computed in accordance with AASHTO 8.16.3.2. The strength reduction factor ϕ used is 0.90 for flexure (AASHTO 8.16.1.2.2). We see that our section is well within range.

Next shear-friction must be accounted for and the temperature steel specified. With regard to the former, AASHTO 8.16.6.4 specifies the required shear-friction reinforcement to be used. The coefficient of friction μ is based on concrete placed against hardened concrete not intentionally roughened. The value of $\lambda = 1.0$ is used for normal weight concrete. The strength reduction factor $\phi = 0.85$ is used for shear-friction.

This concludes the abutment design example. To be sure, there are many steps still to be completed for both the design and detailing of the abutment. As with all examples in this text, however, the purpose is to provide the reader with an understanding of the fundamental principles rather than a complete design.

The metal reinforcement is generally galvanized to prevent deterioration; however, extreme moisture conditions could potentially lead to deterioration of the reinforcement. Therefore, polymetric reinforcement becomes more popular than metal one. Another potential difficulty is erosion of the backfill material which could destabilize the wall.

When such situations arise, the failed sections will require replacement. If the problem occurs at the lower portion of the abutment, then a large segment of the reinforced earth wall will need to be removed in order to conduct repairs. It is important that, when repairs are made, friction be maintained. This means that backfill should be placed in lifts no greater than 15 in (381 mm) and then compacted prior to placing new material [Ref. 4.6].

8. Footings. A general difficulty with maintaining and rehabilitating footings (and piles) is the difficulty in inspecting them. Unless the footing

> A general difficulty with maintaining and rehabilitating footings (and piles) is the difficulty in inspecting them.

or piles are exposed (as in a pile bent) these elements are buried under several feet of earth. There are, however, indicators of footing problems which can be evidenced by associated problems in the portion of the abutment which is above ground.

We have already discussed the problems which are associated with settlement of an abutment. The presence of excessive vertical cracking could indicate foundation problems below the surface of the earth. Therefore, inspectors should look for cracks which run straight up the abutment stem.

If the footing is exposed (i.e., located above grade), either by design or through erosion and/or scour, spalling and other forms of deterioration of the concrete should be investigated. To repair this damage, it may be necessary to construct a cofferdam around the footing either through the use of steel sheet piling or sandbags.

9. Piles. Piles are used when the soil under a footing cannot provide adequate support for the substructure (see Section 1.1.1 and Figure 1.7). Piles can often be found in areas that are highly susceptible to erosion and scour. This implies that many piles will be used in environments which can be considered as harsh.

As mentioned for footings above, if a pile is exposed, then it is important to ensure that the pile does not lose section properties to deterioration. Concrete piles are susceptible to all of the adverse deterioration other concrete elements are subjected to (e.g., spalling, scaling, etc.). Other types of piles include timber piles which can rot and metal piles which can corrode.

With regard to the latter, timber piles can suffer from attack by vermin which burrow and tunnel their way to the buried member [Ref. 4.6]. In most instances, the vermin will use timber piles for shelter, food, or both (see also Section 2.3.3, Part 5). This is of particular concern in marine environments where they are waterborne and can damage timber piles well below the mud line. One method of protecting timber piles is to have them pressure treated with wood preservatives in accordance with AASHTO M133 standard.

Like columns, severely deteriorated piles can be rehabilitated by jacketing the pile using steel plates. This jacketing does not necessarily have to extend the full length of the pile. A recommended approach is to jacket a pile approximately 2 ft (0.61 m) above to 2 ft below the area which has deteriorated [Ref. 4.6].

When steel piles are used (e.g., steel H piles), it is possible to repair deterioration by adding a section to the deteriorated portions. This is generally recommended for less severe deterioration with losses of section up to 50 percent in smaller and fewer area. Alternatively, the deteriorated steel pile can be encased. When steel piles extend underwater, encasement in usually the preferred method of rehabilitation. If the deteriorated segment of steel pile is located in a dry area or aboveground, another method of repair is to splice a piece of new section to the existing pile. Like any steel member, when exposed to moisture, the steel should be provided with a protective coating to prevent corrosion.

When steel piles extend underwater, encasement in usually the preferred method of rehabilitation.

For concrete piles, repair of deteriorated sections is undertaken using techniques which are very similar to those for other concrete elements. The damaged concrete is removed to a distance below the reinforcing steel. Any damaged reinforcing is replaced and the existing steel remaining is cleaned. The surface of the exposed concrete into which the patch is to be made should be cleaned and coated with a bonding compound. The concrete used to patch the section should be nonshrink or quick setting, so that the propagation of cracks is minimized at the patch location.

Some cracking in concrete piles can occur as a result of the driving process itself. These cracks are tension related and occur when stresses are greater than the concrete's modulus of rupture. When this has occurred, the cracks should be sealed to prevent the intrusion of silt, debris, and moisture. Further deterioration could be initiated by the formation of ice in cracks [Ref. 4.6].

Like footings described in Part 8 above, repair of piles may require the construction of a cofferdam around the deteriorated pile or piles. The driving of sheet piling to create the cofferdam can be somewhat complicated in an existing bridge site because of potential interference with the bridge superstructure above. In some cases, the only option is to remove a segment of the superstructure temporarily so that the sheeting can be driven.

To prevent future deterioration to piles (and footings for that matter), it is important to provide for proper site drainage and eliminate any potential sources of erosion of the earth which surrounds, and protects, the piles. If the piles are located in an area which is susceptible to scour, it may be necessary to place additional riprap or other protective material. When placing the fill material back around the foundation, once work is completed, the fill should be compacted as much as possible.

4.2 PIERS

The development of bridge piers parallels the growth of the modern highway system. Previously, the use of bridge piers was confined to structures crossing rivers or railways. With the development of massive transportation networks, like the U.S. Interstate (see Section 1.2), the need for land piers to facilitate grade-separated highways increased dramatically [Ref. 4.8].

A pier is a substructure which provides the basic function of supporting spans at intermediate points between end supports (abutments). Piers are predominately constructed using concrete, although steel and, to a lesser degree, timber are also used. The concrete is generally conventionally reinforced. Prestressed concrete, however, is sometimes used as a pier material for special structures.

The basic design functions of a highway bridge pier can be summarized by the following list. In general, a pier is designed to:

❑ Carry its own weight
❑ Sustain superstructure dead loads, live loads, and lateral loads
❑ Transmit all loads to the foundation

DID YOU KNOW THAT ancient Roman engineers impregnated their structural timber with oils and resins? In addition to this, they also selected the type of timber based on the intended use. For underwater pile foundations at piers, the Romans preferred oak and ash because of their high durability [Ref. 4.7].

If the piles are located in an area which is susceptible to scour, it may be necessary to place additional riprap or other protective material.

PIERS CAN MAKE the difference between a good looking structure and an unattractive one. Simplicity is often the rule when designing a pier. The piers in Figure 4.7 incorporate elastomeric bearings upon which the prestressed concrete superstructure rests. These relatively thin bearings provide for a visually smooth transition from pier to superstructure. For most structures, including steel and timber bridges, concrete is the material of choice for substructure components. However, steel, and to a lesser degree, timber, are also used to construct piers (e.g., a steel frame pier or timber trestle support structure).

Figure 4.7 A series of single column piers support a prestressed concrete bridge. *(Photograph courtesy of D. S. Brown Company, North Baltimore, Ohio.)*

A s with abutments ... the reader must keep in mind that there are numerous permutations of the general forms of piers in use.

In addition to providing the structural functions detailed above, a properly designed pier should also be aesthetically pleasing and economize the use of materials as much as possible. Also, piers should be located so that they provide minimal interference with traffic passing underneath the structure.

Like abutments, piers come in a variety of configurations, shapes, and sizes. The type of pier selected will depend greatly on the form of superstructure present. Figure 4.7 provides an excellent example of this. The single column piers chosen for this prestressed concrete superstructure work well with this type of structure but would not be applicable for a composite steel structure composed of several primary members and a concrete deck.

Presented below are some of the major types of piers utilized today in modern bridge construction. As with abutments discussed in Section 4.1, the reader must keep in mind that there are numerous permutations of the general forms of piers in use.

4.2.1 Types of Piers

In the sidebar accompanying Figure 1.5, a schematic of some basic types of bridge piers was presented. Like an abutment, a pier has a bridge seat upon which the superstructure rests. In Figure 4.8, this bridge seat consists of a hammerhead shaped pier cap on top of which are placed individual pedestals. The bearings are in turn placed on top of the pedestals on top of which rests the superstructure. It can be seen then, that in Figure 4.8 the pier is intended to support a superstructure composed of five primary members.

The bridge seat can be supported by a single column, multiple columns, a solid wall, or a group of piles. These supporting elements are in turn connected to the pier foundation which could be composed of footings, piles, or a combination thereof.

HAMMERHEAD PIERS are a popular style of pier used in many highway bridges. It was mentioned back in Section 1 that hammerheads are generally used on structures requiring relatively high piers. The reason for this is that a short column height with a hammerhead cap will look too top heavy.

Some transportation departments maintain standards which describe span to vertical clearance ratios that determine whether or not a hammerhead pier can be used. Hammerheads can either be used in conjunction with a single or multiple columns, like the one shown in Figure 4.8.

The columns can be constructed with a rectangular (or square) cross section or even with a circular cross section. When two columns are utilized in conjunction with a cap beam, like the pier shown in Figure 4.8, the pier is sometimes known as a *portal frame* pier.

Figure 4.8 A two column, concrete hammerhead pier under construction.

1. Hammerhead. A hammerhead pier utilizes one or more columns with a pier cap in the shape of a hammer. Figures 1.5, 4.8, and 4.9 show various types of hammerhead piers. Hammerhead piers, like the one shown in Figure 4.9, are constructed out of conventionally reinforced concrete. The supporting columns can be either rectangular (or other polygonal shape) or circular in shape and extend down to a supporting foundation.

Hammerhead piers are predominately found in urban settings because they are both attractive and occupy a minimum of space, thereby providing room for underpass traffic. As mentioned before, hammerhead piers are most attractive when placed on structures with relatively large clearance requirements (although they have been incorporated with shorter clearances). Standards as to the use of hammerheads are often maintained by individual transportation departments.

Hammerhead piers are also attractive solutions when the structure is located on a skew, thereby creating tight alignment constraints for the underpass traffic. When contrasted with a column bent pier (see below) the single column hammerhead offers a solution which provides for a more open and free-flowing look, especially in high traffic, multiple structure environments.

> **H**ammerhead piers are predominately found in urban settings because they are both attractive and occupy a minimum of space, thereby providing room for underpass traffic.

A REINFORCING STEEL cage for a hammerhead pier cap can be seen in the foreground of Figure 4.9. The hammerhead pier in the background still has the formwork in place on the hammerhead cap.

Where the abutment shown earlier in Figure 4.4 utilized wooden formwork, the pier in this photograph makes use of metal forms. Scaffolding has also been erected to provide workers with convenient access to the pier.

Forms must be adequately rigid so that the concrete can fulfill its intended structural function as well as provide a pleasing appearance. The forms used, whether wood or metal, must be fabricated so that they are *mortar-tight* and of sound material which is strong enough so that distortion does not occur when placing and curing the concrete. Generally the construction and removal of formwork is planned in advance of general construction by the contractor [Ref. 4.9].

Figure 4.9 This hammerhead pier still has its cap beam formwork in place.

> In dense urban interchanges ... extensive use of column bent piers can lead to a cluttered image producing a "concrete jungle" effect.

2. Column Bent. A column bent pier, as its name would imply, consists of a cap beam and supporting columns in a frame-type structure. Column bent piers represent one of the most popular forms of piers in use in highway bridges. This popularity is an outgrowth of the extensive use of column bent piers during the nascent development of the U.S. Interstate system.

The column bent pier is supported on either spread footing or pile foundations and is made of conventionally reinforced concrete. Like hammerhead piers, the supporting columns can be either circular or rectangular in cross section, although the former is by far more prevalent.

The use of column bent piers, like that of hammerheads, should be somewhat judicious. For moderate clearance structures with plenty of room for underpass traffic, the column bent pier provides a very attractive solution. In dense urban interchanges, however, extensive use of column bent piers can lead to a cluttered image producing a "concrete jungle" effect [Ref. 4.8].

3. Pile Bent. The pile bent pier is a variation on the column bent pier with the supporting columns and footing replaced with individual supporting piles. The end piles are generally equipped with a batter in the transverse direction. In addition to concrete, timber is also a popular material for this type of pier.

Pile bent piers are extremely popular in marine environments where multiple, simple span structures cross relatively shallow water channels.

Some maintenance problems generally associated with this type of pier, however, are deterioration to exposed piles, impact with marine traffic, and accumulation of debris. When provided with adequate protection against these adverse conditions, however, pile bent piers represent an economical solution for many bridges.

4. Solid Wall. A solid wall pier (also known as a continuous wall pier) as its name would imply, consists of a solid wall which extends up from a foundation consisting of a footing or piles. The top of the wall is equipped with individual pedestals upon which the superstructure rests. For aesthetic reasons, the sides of the wall are often tapered (i.e., the wall is wider at the top than at the base) to create a more pleasing and less imposing support structure.

With regard to the latter issue, it is not desirable to utilize solid wall piers on excessively wide superstructures. Incorporation of solid wall piers under very wide superstructures can lead to a "tunnel effect" for motorists passing under the structure and may require the placement of a special lighting system under the structure.

Solid wall piers are often used at water crossings since they can be constructed to proportions that are both slender and streamlined [Ref. 4.8]. These features lend themselves well toward providing a minimal resistance to flood flows (see Figure 4.11).

> Incorporation of solid wall piers under very wide superstructures can lead to a "tunnel effect" for motorists passing under the structure ...

5. Integral. An integral pier has a pier cap to which the superstructure's primary members are rigidly connected. This type of pier is not altogether common and is generally confined to special structures, particularly when tight vertical clearance constraints pose a problem.

Figure 4.10 Besides the rather unique pier design, what else is different in this picture?

THERE IS SOMETHING a little different in Figure 4.10 besides the rather unique pier design. If you look closely, it can be seen that while the center span is made of steel girders, the end span comprises prestressed concrete girders. In the sidebar accompanying Figure 3.54, the possibility of steel and prestressed concrete being used as primary members in the same structure was mentioned. In this particular structure, the steel girders are provided with a protective coating which is grey in color making the difference in materials extremely subtle to the average motorist passing under the bridge. In the continuing debate over which material, steel or concrete, is better for bridges, structures like this have found a unique answer: both.

6. Single Column. A single-column pier was shown earlier in Figure 4.7. An obvious advantage of these types of piers is that they occupy a minimal amount of space. Single-column piers, like solid wall piers, are often tapered or provide with a flare so that the top of the column is wider than the base. This type of pier is extremely attractive when combined with prestressed concrete box type superstructures by providing an open and free-flowing appearance to traffic passing underneath the structure.

4.2.2 Behavior and Loading of Piers

When viewed in section, a pier comprises a stem or column which is rigidly attached to a base. In such a configuration, a bridge pier behaves either as a cantilever beam or a pin-ended strut depending on the connection with the footing and superstructure.

> **I**f a pier is cantilevered from the footing, it will generally require a much wider foundation in order to offer resistance to overturning moments.

If a pier is cantilevered from the footing, it will generally require a much wider foundation in order to offer resistance to overturning moments. When a pier is pinned at the foundation, the footing usually can be designed with a relatively narrow base since axial to near axial loads are generated on the foundation [Ref. 4.8].

Of particular concern when designing a pier are the horizontal loads which result from live load transmitted from the superstructure, wind loads, any stream flow loads which may be present, and seismic loading conditions. The wind loads, live load centrifugal force, and seismic loads can also contribute transverse loads to be applied to the pier.

The magnitude of these horizontal loads can be reduced through the incorporation of expansion bearings at pier support points. Additional horizontal loads, however, can be contributed by friction and temperature expansion in the expansion bearings. Wind loads acting on the pier as well as possible collision from marine vessels should also be accounted for.

SOLID PIERS are well suited for placement in stream crossings. Their slender and streamlined proportions provide a minimal resistance to flood flows. Another advantage of using solid wall piers in stream or river crossings is that they are not as prone to accumulating debris as multiple column piers. The solid wall pier shown in Figure 4.11 is in obvious need of rehabilitation. The repair work being conducted on this particular structure is being performed using staged construction. This way work can be performed on half of the structure while traffic is maintained over the other half. Upon completion, traffic is opened on the rehabilitated half and work begun on the remaining half of the structure.

Figure 4.11 It's time for this solid wall pier, located in a stream crossing, to be replaced.

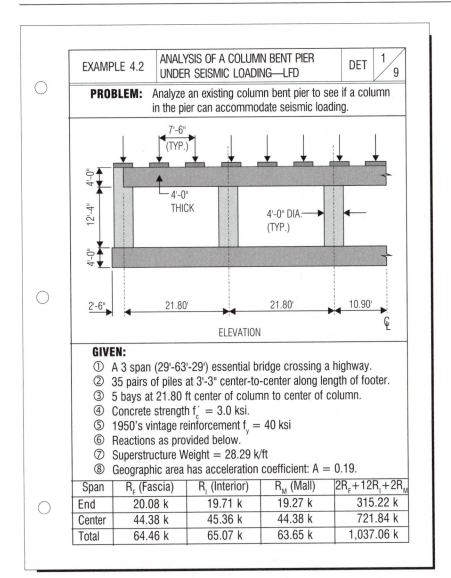

EXAMPLE 4.2	ANALYSIS OF A COLUMN BENT PIER UNDER SEISMIC LOADING—LFD	DET	1/9

PROBLEM: Analyze an existing column bent pier to see if a column in the pier can accommodate seismic loading.

ELEVATION

GIVEN:

① A 3 span (29'-63'-29') essential bridge crossing a highway.
② 35 pairs of piles at 3'-3" center-to-center along length of footer.
③ 5 bays at 21.80 ft center of column to center of column.
④ Concrete strength f'_c = 3.0 ksi.
⑤ 1950's vintage reinforcement f_y = 40 ksi
⑥ Reactions as provided below.
⑦ Superstructure Weight = 28.29 k/ft
⑧ Geographic area has acceleration coefficient: A = 0.19.

Span	R_F (Fascia)	R_I (Interior)	R_M (Mall)	$2R_F+12R_I+2R_M$
End	20.08 k	19.71 k	19.27 k	315.22 k
Center	44.38 k	45.36 k	44.38 k	721.84 k
Total	64.46 k	65.07 k	63.65 k	1,037.06 k

This example is an extension of Design Example 4.1. In this case, however, we will perform the analysis of an existing column bent pier to see if it can accommodate seismic loading. Load Factor Design method will be used.

For the sake of brevity, we will forego the moment distribution analysis of the pier frame. The site parameters (e.g., acceleration coefficient) given in the last design example apply to the pier analysis as well.

The total end span reaction of 315 k still applies. For the piers, however, both the end and middle span must be supported. The total center span reaction is given as 722 k. The breakdown by stringer is also presented for loading of the pier. Other parameters, concerning the amount of reinforcement present in the pier, loading conditions, etc., will be presented throughout the calculation and designated as "given."

As shown in Sheet 9 of Example 4.1, the 3 spans are all simply supported. The pier to be designed supports the end span with expansion bearings, and the center span with fixed bearings.

When applying loads to a pier, the designer should apply the appropriate group loadings as outlined in Section 3.5.5, Table 3.2, and Table 3.4. The group loads used should be those which create the worse case scenario.

4.2.3 Design Criteria

Like the design of any structural component, the design of a pier is conducted to fulfill basic strength and safety criteria. In general, the design of a highway bridge pier should address:

❑ Safety against overturning
❑ Safety against sliding
❑ Safety against bearing failure of the soil
❑ Safety against excessive or differential settlement

> **L**ike the design of any structural component, the design of a pier is conducted to fulfill basic strength and safety criteria.

Another factor which bridge designers are becoming increasingly aware of is the adverse effects of scour at pier (and even abutment) locations. When designing a structure, the potential depth of scour must be accounted for and appropriate scour protection (e.g., riprap) provided to protect against undermining of the pier foundation during floods and excessive flows (see also Section 2.3.6).

When analyzing a multiple column bent pier, an analysis technique such as moment distribution must be employed (see Section 3.12.3). The designer should keep in mind, however, that the distance between joints in this type of pier is generally very large. Because of this, a modified method of moment distribution which takes into account the effects of stiff jointed frames should be employed.

In today's design environment, however, there are usually computer aided methods available to perform the frame analysis of a multiple column bent pier. Many of these programs can trace their origin back to the 1960's and are still in use today, albeit in somewhat modified forms. Most general purpose finite element packages currently on the market should be able to perform the analysis of these types of piers. Using these systems, a model of the subject pier is created consisting of members and joints with output provided detailing moments and shears along each member. Some system may even provide reinforcement design for pier columns and cap beam.

Although the geometry of each pier will be different due to site specific constraints, the design of piers will generally follow specific standards of a given transportation department. Examples of this would be in the use of the same diameter column in column bent piers. This greatly aids the construction process by allowing for the use of reusable formwork. As we have discussed previously, similar designs also aid in the future maintenance of a structure by providing a common point of reference for all structures in a highway system.

The reader will also notice the importance given to aesthetics in this particular section. While civil engineers typically leave such issues to their counterparts in the architectural field, aesthetics of bridges in general, and piers in particular, is an important issue. States such as California, through their

> **I**n today's design environment, however, there are usually computer aided methods available to perform the frame analysis of a multiple column bent pier.

PROTECTING PIERS is an important issue. Whether the pier is a major component located in a body of water, like the pier shown in Figure 4.12 supporting the Tappan Zee bridge, or a small column bent pier located on a secondary road. Piers located in areas with heavy marine traffic must be equipped with a fender or similar protection system to ensure that the integrity of the support is never threatened. When a pier is exposed to regular highway traffic, it too must be protected. This is usually accomplished with the incorporation of a Jersey style barrier placed in front of the pier. These barriers are usually equipped with tapered end sections designed to direct a straying vehicle away from the pier.

Figure 4.12   A two column bent pier helps support the Tappan Zee bridge.

EXAMPLE 4.2	ANALYSIS OF A COLUMN BENT PIER UNDER SEISMIC LOADING—LFD	DET	2 / 9

STEP 1: Determine Type of Seismic Analysis and Other Criteria

For an "essential bridge" by AASHTO 3.3 I-A we have:

IC = Importance Classification = I

With an importance classification of "I" by AASHTO 3.4 I-A for:

0.09 < A < 0.19 and IC = I

SPC = Seismic Performance Category = B

The bridge has an unchanging cross section, with similar supports, and a uniform mass and stiffness, so it is considered to be:

Regular (By AASHTO 4.2 I-A)

For a Regular Bridge, SPC = B, and 2 to 6 spans, we choose to use:

Method 2 = Single-Mode Spectral Analysis (AASHTO 4.2 I-A)

For stiff clay, by AASHTO 3.5 I-A:

Soil Profile Type II: S = Site Coefficient = 1.2

Response Modification Factor (AASHTO 3.7 I-A)

Multiple Column Bent: R = 5

Pier Footing: R = One-Half R for Multiple Column Bent
              = R/2 = 5/2 = 2.25 (AASHTO 6.2.2 I-A)

Combination of Seismic Forces (AASHTO 3.9 I-A):

Case I: $|$100% Longitudinal Motion$|$ + $|$30% Transverse Motion$|$

Case II: $|$30% Longitudinal Motion$|$ + $|$100% Transverse Motion$|$

Load Grouping (AASHTO 6.2.1 I-A):

1.0(DL + Buoyancy + Stream Flow + Earth Pressure + Earthquake)
        (N/A)   (N/A)

DESIGN EXAMPLE 4.2
STEP 1: DETERMINE SEISMIC ANALYSIS AND CRITERIA

In Section 3.5.3, Part 2 we discussed the nature of temporary loads in general, and seismic loads in particular. Prior to beginning design, we need to determine the seismic criteria which will determine which type of analysis will be required: either the more straight forward single-mode spectral analysis or the more complex multimode spectral analysis.

The type of analysis used is dependent on the geometry of the structure (i.e., is the cross-section uniform or not) and the location of the bridge in the transportation network (i.e., acceleration coefficient). Based on our given parameters for the structure, we choose to use the single-mode spectral analysis method (Method 1 - uniform load method can also be used here).

Other seismic criteria which need to be calculated are the response modification factors which will be used to determine seismic design forces for individual members by dividing elastic forces by the R Factors. Finally, the load combinations and groupings are defined. Since the bridge crosses a highway, we don't need to consider buoyancy and stream flow pressure loads.

---

department of transportation, have undertaken an aggressive program to ensure that their structures are not only functional, but pleasing to the eye. Particularly in the design of piers, a well placed chamfer can go a long way toward making a highway bridge more pleasing to look at.

4.2.4 Design of Compression Members

A critical aspect of the design of highway bridge piers is the design of compression members (e.g., columns in a column bent pier). In general, the design of reinforced concrete elements is covered by Section 8 of the AASHTO Standard Specifications. It is beyond the scope of this text to offer a detailed analysis of all the aspects of the AASHTO code which applies to the design of pier components. We shall, however, focus on the design of compression members as set forth in AASHTO 8.15.4, 8.16.4 and 8.16.5, and AASHTO LRFD 5.7.4, because of its particular relevance to pier design.

> **S**tates such as California ... have undertaken an aggressive program to ensure that their structures are not only functional, but pleasing to the eye.

The following discussion offers an overview of some of the major criteria governing the design of compression members. For most equations, the reader is referred to the section of the design code given in the associated text.

1. **Load Factor Design Considerations.** In AASHTO Standard Specifications, a compression member is based on the equations set forth in AASHTO 8.16.4 and 8.16.5 for load factor design. These specifications define the axial load strength of compression members. The axial load strength will vary depending on the type of reinforcement present (e.g., spiral or tie) and the type of loading the member is subjected to (e.g., pure compression or pure flexure). If the effects of slenderness apply to the member (see Part 3 below), then the maximum factored moment, M_u, is *magnified* to account for these effects. The axial load strength of a compression member is based, in large part, on the following parameters:

> ❑ The strength of concrete used
> ❑ The yield strength of reinforcement present
> ❑ The gross section area of the member
> ❑ The total area of longitudinal reinforcement
> ❑ The confinement provided by lateral reinforcement

The general requirements for the design of compression members are given in AASHTO 8.16.4.1.2. The criteria governing the design of compression members under pure compression are given in AASHTO 8.16.4.2.1. For those members under pure flexure, the reader is referred to AASHTO 8.16.4.2.2.

2. **Load and Resistance Factor Design Considerations.** In AASHTO LRFD Specifications, the equations for computing the compression member strength are the same as these in the AASHTO LFD provisions. Refer to AASHTO LRFD 5.7.4.4 for axial resistance, and 5.7.4.5 for biaxial flexure strength.

The transverse reinforcement in the pier columns should meet the minimum requirements of AASHTO LRFD 5.7.4.6 to ensure that sufficient confinement is provided for the concrete. In Seismic Zone 2 and higher areas, additional transverse reinforcement is required to enhance the columns' ductilities.

3. **Slenderness Effects.** When a compression member's cross-section dimensions are small in comparison to its length, the member is said to be slender. Whether or not a member can be considered slender is dependent of the magnitude of the member's *slenderness ratio*. The slenderness ratio of a compression member is defined by the following expression:

$$\frac{k \cdot L_u}{r} \qquad \text{(Eq. 4.22)}$$

where k = effective length factor for compression members
L_u = unsupported length of compression member
r = radius of gyration

> **I**f the effects of slenderness apply to the member ... then the maximum factored moment, M_u, is *magnified* to account for these effects.

> **W**hen a compression member's cross-section dimensions are small in comparison to its length, the member is said to be slender.

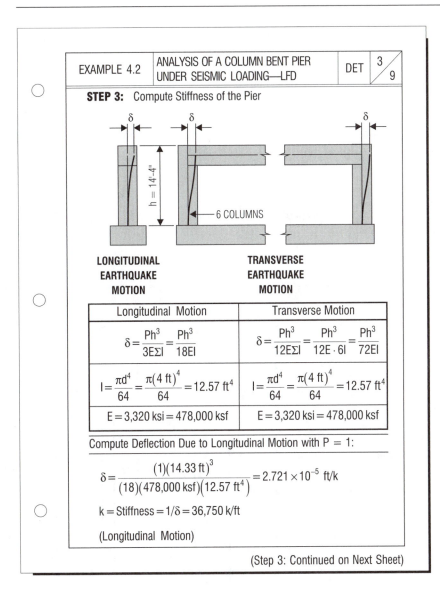

| EXAMPLE 4.2 | ANALYSIS OF A COLUMN BENT PIER UNDER SEISMIC LOADING—LFD | DET | 3/9 |

STEP 3: Compute Stiffness of the Pier

h = 14'-4"

6 COLUMNS

δ   δ   δ

LONGITUDINAL
EARTHQUAKE
MOTION

TRANSVERSE
EARTHQUAKE
MOTION

Longitudinal Motion	Transverse Motion
$\delta = \dfrac{Ph^3}{3E\Sigma I} = \dfrac{Ph^3}{18EI}$	$\delta = \dfrac{Ph^3}{12E\Sigma I} = \dfrac{Ph^3}{12E \cdot 6I} = \dfrac{Ph^3}{72EI}$
$I = \dfrac{\pi d^4}{64} = \dfrac{\pi(4\text{ ft})^4}{64} = 12.57\text{ ft}^4$	$I = \dfrac{\pi d^4}{64} = \dfrac{\pi(4\text{ ft})^4}{64} = 12.57\text{ ft}^4$
E = 3,320 ksi = 478,000 ksf	E = 3,320 ksi = 478,000 ksf

Compute Deflection Due to Longitudinal Motion with P = 1:

$$\delta = \frac{(1)(14.33\text{ ft})^3}{(18)(478,000\text{ ksf})(12.57\text{ ft}^4)} = 2.721 \times 10^{-5}\text{ ft/k}$$

k = Stiffness = 1/δ = 36,750 k/ft

(Longitudinal Motion)

(Step 3: Continued on Next Sheet)

DESIGN EXAMPLE 4.2
STEP 3: COMPUTE STIFFNESS OF THE PIER

In a process similar to that performed for the abutment in Design Example 4.1, Step 6, we will compute the stiffness of the pier. This stiffness will be computed for the pier subjected to earthquake motion in both the longitudinal and transverse directions.

The reader should keep in mind that it is the transverse section of the pier (with respect to the bridge proper) which resists longitudinal earthquake motion and the longitudinal section (with respect to the bridge proper) that resists transverse earthquake motion.

As we saw before in the abutment, a unit load of one is applied to determine the deflection of the resisting section. The inverse of this value yields the stiffness. The calculation for the modulus of elasticity for the concrete used (3,000 psi strength) was shown earlier in Step 6 of Design Example 4.1.

Once the deflection under the unit load is calculated, the inverse of the deflection is the stiffness resisting longitudinal earthquake motion.

Figure 4.13 presents theoretical values of the effective length factor, *k*, for various idealized column end conditions.

When a compression member is braced against sidesway, however, the effective length factor, *k*, is taken as 1.0. A lower value of *k* may be used if further analysis demonstrates that a lower value is applicable (AASHTO 8.16.5.2.3). If the compression member is not braced against sidesway, then a value greater than 1.0 is used which takes into account the effects of cracking and reinforcement on the member's relative stiffness.

The unsupported length of a compression member, L_u, is defined as the clear distance between slabs, girders, or other members which is capable of providing lateral support for the compression member. If haunches are present, then the unsupported length is taken from the lower extremity of the haunch in the plane considered (AASHTO 8.16.5.2.1).

T he unsupported length of a compression member ... is defined as the clear distance between ... members which is capable of providing lateral support for the compression member.

The general equation for the radius of gyration of a member was given earlier in Equation 3.172. This equation is applicable to a member of any cross-sectional geometry. For the evaluation of slenderness effects, however, the radius of gyration, r, may be taken as:

$$r = ql_s \qquad \text{(Eq. 4.23)}$$

where $q = 0.30$ for rectangular compression members

$\quad\quad = 0.25$ for circular compression members

$\quad l_s =$ overall dimension in direction in which stability is being considered

For other geometric cross-sectional shapes, the radius of gyration is determined for the gross concrete section (AASHTO 8.16.5.2.2).

THE EFFECTIVE LENGTH of a column is defined by the product kL and is used to determine the allowable compression in a column. The effective length factor, k, is the ratio of the effective length of an idealized pin-ended column to the actual length of a column with various end conditions. The product kL represents the length between inflection points of a buckled column. Restraint against rotation and translation of column ends influences the position of the inflection points in a column. Theoretical values of the effective length factor, k, are presented in Figure 4.13. Because the column end conditions rarely comply fully with idealized restraint against rotation and translation, the recommended values are higher than the idealized values. Columns in continuous frames which are unbraced by adequate attachment to shear walls, diagonal bracing, or adjacent structures depend on the bending stiffness of the rigidly connected beams for lateral stability. The effective length factor, k, is dependent on the amount of bending stiffness supplied by the beams at the column ends. If the amount of stiffness supplied by the beams is small, the value of k could exceed 2.0. The design values of k for riveted and bolted truss members (partially restrained) is 0.75. For pinned connections in truss members the design value is 0.875 (pin friction) [Ref. 4.4].

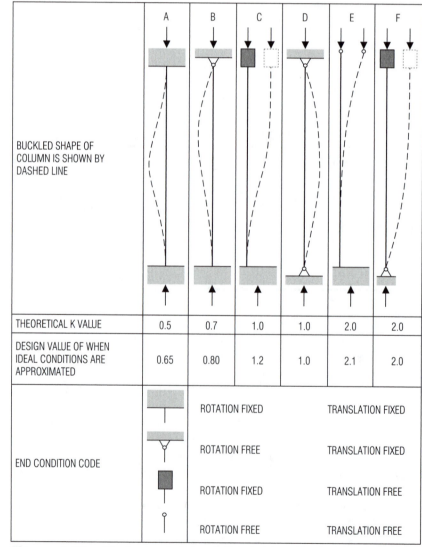

	A	B	C	D	E	F
THEORETICAL K VALUE	0.5	0.7	1.0	1.0	2.0	2.0
DESIGN VALUE OF WHEN IDEAL CONDITIONS ARE APPROXIMATED	0.65	0.80	1.2	1.0	2.1	2.0

BUCKLED SHAPE OF COLUMN IS SHOWN BY DASHED LINE

END CONDITION CODE

ROTATION FIXED   TRANSLATION FIXED

ROTATION FREE   TRANSLATION FIXED

ROTATION FIXED   TRANSLATION FREE

ROTATION FREE   TRANSLATION FREE

Figure 4.13 Effective length factors k *(Adapted from Standard Specifications for Highway Bridges, 17th Ed., Ref. 4.4.)*

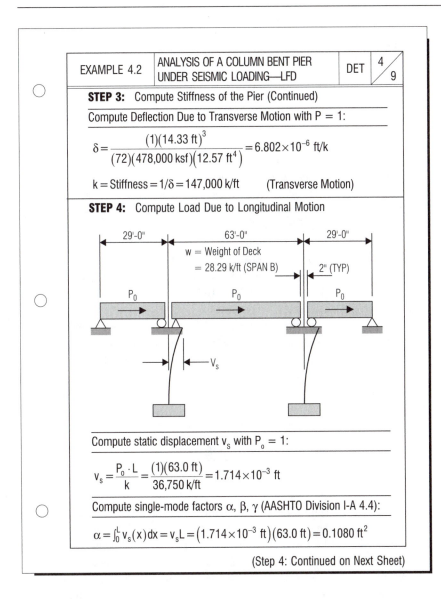

| EXAMPLE 4.2 | ANALYSIS OF A COLUMN BENT PIER UNDER SEISMIC LOADING—LFD | DET | 4/9 |

STEP 3: Compute Stiffness of the Pier (Continued)

Compute Deflection Due to Transverse Motion with P = 1:

$$\delta = \frac{(1)(14.33 \text{ ft})^3}{(72)(478,000 \text{ ksf})(12.57 \text{ ft}^4)} = 6.802 \times 10^{-6} \text{ ft/k}$$

$$k = \text{Stiffness} = 1/\delta = 147,000 \text{ k/ft} \qquad \text{(Transverse Motion)}$$

STEP 4: Compute Load Due to Longitudinal Motion

Compute static displacement v_s with $P_0 = 1$:

$$v_s = \frac{P_0 \cdot L}{k} = \frac{(1)(63.0 \text{ ft})}{36,750 \text{ k/ft}} = 1.714 \times 10^{-3} \text{ ft}$$

Compute single-mode factors α, β, γ (AASHTO Division I-A 4.4):

$$\alpha = \int_0^L v_s(x)\,dx = v_s L = (1.714 \times 10^{-3} \text{ ft})(63.0 \text{ ft}) = 0.1080 \text{ ft}^2$$

(Step 4: Continued on Next Sheet)

DESIGN EXAMPLE 4.2
STEP 3: COMPUTE STIFFNESS OF THE PIER (CONTINUED)

The deflection under a unit load is then computed for the section resisting transverse earthquake motion with the stiffness being the inverse of this value.

STEP 4: COMPUTE LOAD DUE TO LONGITUDINAL MOTION

Similar to the operation performed in Step 7 of Design Example 4.1, we now compute the load acting on the pier as a result of longitudinal earthquake motion. Here, however, we take the properties of the center 63.0 ft span in loading the piers (i.e., the length variable L and unit weight of deck w will be different from before).

Note that earthquake force from superstructure is transferred only to the fixed bearings. In this case, only center span load is transferred to the pier in the longitudinal direction. In the transverse direction, however, we assume all bearings are restricted (guided bearings).

The diagram in the accompanying calculation sheet illustrates the bridge under longitudinal earthquake loading with the static displacement depicted at the pier location. In this calculation sheet, we determine the value of the alpha single-mode factor.

If a compression member is braced against sidesway, then the effects of slenderness may be ignored as long as the following condition is met (AASHTO 8.16.5.2.4):

$$\frac{kL_u}{r} < 34 - \left(\frac{12 \cdot M_{1b}}{M_{2b}} \right) \qquad \text{(Eq. 4.24)}$$

where M_{1b} = smaller end moment on compression member
(positive if member is bent in single curvature;
negative if member is bent in double curvature)

M_{2b} = larger end moment on compression member
(always positive)

The two moments, M_{1b} and M_{2b}, are due to gravity loads which result in no appreciable sidesway. These moments are to be calculated using conventional elastic frame analysis.

If a compression member is *not* braced against sidesway, then the effects of slenderness may be ignored as long as the following condition is met (AASHTO 8.16.5.2.5):

$$\frac{kL_u}{r} < 22 \qquad \text{(Eq. 4.25)}$$

If the effects of slenderness need to be considered as a result of either Equations 4.24 or 4.25 exceeding their specified limits, then the effects can be approximated through use of a moment magnification factor and other criteria. If the slenderness ratio of kL_u/r exceeds 100, however, a more detailed analysis will be required.

This detailed analysis should include "the influence of axial loads and variable moment of inertia on member stiffness and fixed-end moments, the effect of deflections on the moments and forces, and the effect of the duration of the loads" (AASHTO 8.16.5.1.1). Otherwise, the approximate method detailed below may be utilized.

The design of compression members is made using a factored axial load, P_c, which specifies the point at which a member will fail as a result of buckling at the critical load. The method used to calculate this factored axial load (also known as the critical load) is based on the principles first developed by Euler for concentrically loaded slender columns. The critical load is given as:

$$P_c = \frac{\pi^2 EI}{\left(kL_u\right)^2} \qquad \text{(Eq. 4.26)}$$

> **T**he design of compression members is made using a factored axial load ... which specifies the point at which a member will fail as a result of buckling at the critical load.

so that for the simple case of a column hinged at both ends and made of an elastic material, kL_u is the length of the column and E is the modulus of elasticity of the material. If the buckling stress P_c/A is greater than the proportion limit (or yield stress), then instead of the standard Young's modulus, a *tangent modulus* is used. By tangent modulus, we imply a modulus defined by the slope of the tangent to the stress-strain curve of the material used.

> **T**he method used to calculate this factored axial load ... is based on the principles first developed by Euler for concentrically loaded slender columns.

A quick review of the buckled shapes illustrated in Figure 4.13 is helpful to demonstrate some of the basic physical principles behind Equation 4.26. When a member is fixed against rotation at both ends as shown in Figure 4.13(A), the distance between the inflection points is defined by $kL_u = L_u/2$. Therefore, by Equation 4.26, a column which is fixed at both ends will carry four times as much load as when it is hinged (see Figure 4.13).

> **T**herefore ... a column which is fixed at both ends will carry four times as much load as when it is hinged.

To compute the flexural rigidity EI, AASHTO offers two possible solutions with the first being:

$$EI = \frac{\dfrac{E_c I_g}{5} + E_s I_s}{1 + \beta_d} \qquad \text{(Eq. 4.27)}$$

| EXAMPLE 4.2 | ANALYSIS OF A COLUMN BENT PIER UNDER SEISMIC LOADING—LFD | DET | 5/9 |

STEP 4: Compute Load Due To Longitudinal Motion (Continued)

Compute single-mode factors α, β, γ (AASHTO Division I-A 4.4):

$$\beta = \int_0^L w(x)v_s(x)\,dx = \alpha w = \left(0.1080\ \text{ft}^2\right)(28.29\ \text{k/ft}) = 3.055\ \text{ft} \cdot \text{k}$$

$$\gamma = \int_0^L w(x)v_s(x)^2\,dx = \beta \cdot v_s = (3.055\ \text{ft} \cdot \text{k})\left(1.714 \times 10^{-3}\ \text{ft}\right)$$
$$= 0.005236\ \text{ft}^2 \cdot \text{k}$$

Compute period of oscillation:

$$T = 2\pi\sqrt{\frac{\gamma}{P_0 g \alpha}} = 2\pi\sqrt{\frac{0.005236\ \text{ft}^2 \cdot \text{k}}{(1\text{k})\left(32.2\ \text{ft/sec}^2\right)\left(0.1080\ \text{ft}^2\right)}} = 0.244\ \text{sec}$$

Compute elastic seismic response coefficient:

A = Acceleration Coefficient = 0.19 (Given)
S = Site Coefficient = 1.2 (Step 1)

$$C_S = \frac{1.2 AS}{T^{2/3}} = \frac{(1.2)(0.19)(1.2)}{(0.244\ \text{sec})^{2/3}} = 0.701$$

AASHTO Division I-A 3.6.1 states that C_s need not exceed 2.5A:

$C_s = 2.5A = (2.5)(0.19) = 0.475 < 0.701$ ✔ Use: $C_s = 0.475$

Compute equivalent static earthquake loading:

$$p_e(x) = \frac{\beta \cdot C_s}{\gamma} w(x)v_s(x)$$
$$= \frac{(3.055\ \text{ft} \cdot \text{k})(0.475)}{\left(0.005236\ \text{ft}^2 \cdot \text{k}\right)} \cdot (28.29\ \text{k/ft})\left(1.714 \times 10^{-3}\ \text{ft}\right) = 13.44\ \text{k/ft}$$

(Step 4: Continued on Next Sheet)

DESIGN EXAMPLE 4.2
STEP 4: LONGITUDINAL MOTION LOAD (CONTINUED)

The last two single-mode factors, beta and gamma, are computed.

Next, as defined earlier in Equation 3.4, we calculate the period of oscillation again using a unit load of 1.0. This is used in turn to calculate the seismic response coefficient. To compute this value we need the acceleration factor which was given based on the bridge location and the site coefficient determined earlier in Step 1.

The seismic response coefficient, however, is not to exceed 2.5A where A is the acceleration coefficient (if a Soil Profile Type III were present where A $\geq$ 0.30, not to exceed value would be 2.0A).

This is the last value needed to calculate the equivalent static earthquake loading acting on the bridge. This is a unit load acting over the entire length of the center span.

The equation for the equivalent static earthquake loading was first seen in Section 3.5.3, Part 2, Equation 3.6. This value will be used to compute the actual load acting on the pier.

and the second, more conservative solution being:

$$EI = \frac{\dfrac{E_c I_g}{2.5}}{1 + \beta_d} \qquad \text{(Eq. 4.28)}$$

where E_c = modulus of elasticity of concrete, psi
E_s = modulus of elasticity of reinforcement, psi
I_g = moment of inertia of gross concrete section about centroidal axis neglecting reinforcement, in^4

and:

$$\beta_d = \frac{\text{Maximum Dead Load Moment}}{\text{Maximum Total Load Moment}} \qquad \text{(Eq. 4.29)}$$

The β_d factor defined in Equation 4.29 is an approximation of the effects of creep, so that when larger moments are induced by loads sustained over a long period of time, the creep deformation and associated curvature will also increase.

It was stated above that Equation 4.28 is more conservative than the flexural rigidity presented in Equation 4.27. Since, however, reinforcing steel is typically not subjected to the adverse effects of creep, it would seem that the creep parameter $1 + \beta_d$ should be applied only to the concrete portion of the equation (i.e., $E_c I_g / 5$) and not to the reinforcing steel component (i.e., $E_s I_y$). Such an approach would produce a greater economy of materials, especially for columns which are heavily reinforced and for composite columns which are reinforced with structural steel shapes [Ref. 4.10]. When deciding whether to use Equation 4.27 or 4.28, the general rule of thumb is that for heavily reinforced members, Equation 4.27 should be used since it takes into account the contribution of reinforcing steel in the column. If the column is lightly reinforced, however, the more conservative Equation 4.28 should be used. Note that in AASHTO LRFD (5.7.4.3), the greater value of the two equations is used for design.

Once the critical load is computed, the magnified factored moment can be computed using the following expression:

$$M_c = \delta_b M_{2b} + \delta_s M_{2s}$$ (Eq. 4.30)

where M_{2b} = larger end moment on compression member due to gravity loads (always positive)

M_{2s} = larger end moment on compression member due to lateral or gravity loads (always positive)

The two moments, M_{2b} and M_{2s}, are due to loads which result in no appreciable sidesway. The latter, M_{2s}, defines appreciable sidesway by a deflection, Δ, which is defined by the following:

$$\Delta > \frac{L_u}{1,500}$$ (Eq. 4.31)

These moments are to be calculated using conventional elastic frame analysis and both are always positive.

Applied to these moments are moment magnification factors which are defined by the following expressions. For members braced against sidesway the value is:

$$\delta_b = \frac{C_m}{1 - \dfrac{P_u}{\phi \cdot P_c}} \geq 1.0$$ (Eq. 4.32)

> **S**ince ... reinforcing steel is typically not subjected to the adverse effects of creep, it would seem that the creep parameter $1+\beta_d$ should be applied only to the concrete portion of the equation.

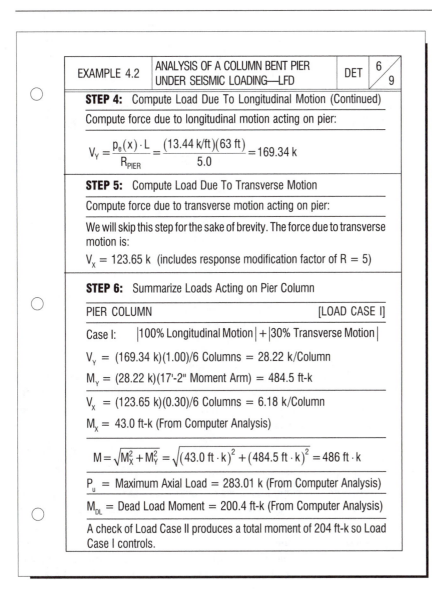

DESIGN EXAMPLE 4.2

STEP 4: LONGITUDINAL MOTION LOAD (CONTINUED)

To compute the actual force acting on the pier we multiply this unit loading by the length of the span. This value is reduced by the response modification factor, R, determined earlier in Step 1. This value in specified by AASHTO Division I-A 3.7 with a table of values presented in Section 3.5.3.

STEP 5: COMPUTE LOAD DUE TO TRANSVERSE MOTION

The computation of the load due to transverse motion is similar, so for the sake of brevity, we will skip the hand computation of this value. Note that half of the force from the end span and half of the force from the center span will act on the pier (assume all bearings are fixed transversely).

STEP 6: SUMMARIZE LOADS ACTING ON PIER COLUMN

The part of the moment acting on the column contributed by longitudinal earthquake motion is shown. The moment resulting from transverse earthquake motion and the worse case axial load on a single column (Column Number 6) were determined using a computer structural analysis software package. A check of Load Case II produced a lower value so Load Case I controls.

and for members not braced against sidesway:

$$\delta_s = \frac{1}{1 - \dfrac{\sum P_u}{\phi \cdot \sum P_c}} \geq 1.0 \qquad \text{(Eq. 4.33)}$$

where P_u = factored axial load at given eccentricity

P_c = critical load (see Equation 4.26)

C_m = factor relating the actual moment diagram to an equivalent uniform moment diagram

ϕ = strength reduction factor (resistance factor)

For members which are braced against sidesway, δ_s is taken to be 1.0. If the member is not braced against sidesway, the moment magnification factor δ_b is evaluated for a braced member and δ_s for an unbraced member (AASHTO 8.16.5.2.7).

The factor which relates the actual moment diagram to an equivalent uniform moment diagram, C_m, is typically taken as 1.0. However, in the case where the member is braced against sidesway and without transverse loads between supports, it may be taken by the following expression:

$$C_m = 0.60 + 0.40 \cdot \left(\frac{M_{1b}}{M_{2b}} \right)$$

(Eq. 4.34)

where M_{1b} = smaller end moment on compression member
   (positive if member is bent in single curvature;
   negative if member is bent in double curvature)
M_{2b} = larger end moment on compression member
   (always positive)

The value resulting from Equation 4.34, however, is not to be less than 0.40. Designers utilizing the service load design method (i.e., working stress) should remember to increase the axial load by a factor of 2.5 and use a strength reduction factor of 1.0 when computing the moment magnification factor.

It is sometimes possible that slender columns which are subjected to axial or near axial loading will have little or no end moments. This does not mean, however, that slenderness has no impact on the strength for this type of compression member. To account for such a situation, AASHTO provides a minimum eccentricity which is dependent upon the cross-section geometry of the compression member for calculating the end moment M_{b2} as well as the associated moment magnification factor (AASHTO 8.16.5.2.8). This minimum eccentricity is defined by the expression (in inches):

$$0.60 + 0.03h$$

(Eq. 4.35)

where h = thickness of section in the direction perpendicular to the pertinent principal axis, in

This minimum eccentricity is used to account for the effects of slenderness on axially or near axially loaded compression members. It is also accounted for imperfection of construction. For a detailed description of this limiting criteria, the reader is referred to AASHTO 8.16.5.2.8 as well as ACI 318 Building Code.

It is sometimes possible that slender columns which are subjected to axial or near axial loading will have little or no end moments.

This minimum eccentricity is used to account for the effects of slenderness on axially or near axially loaded compression members.

4. Interaction Diagrams. The determination of the strength of a compression member subjected to both compression and bending offers

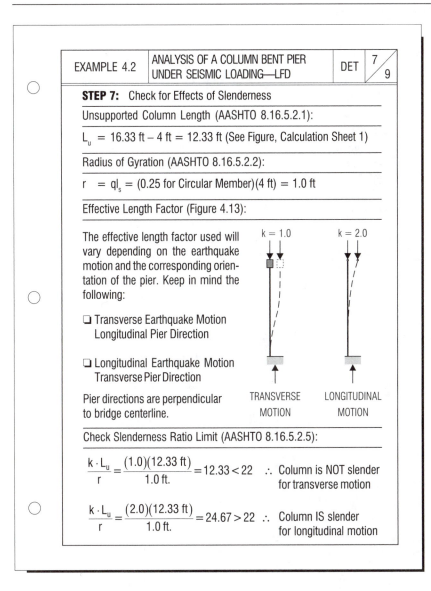

| EXAMPLE 4.2 | ANALYSIS OF A COLUMN BENT PIER UNDER SEISMIC LOADING—LFD | DET | 7/9 |

STEP 7: Check for Effects of Slenderness

Unsupported Column Length (AASHTO 8.16.5.2.1):

L_u = 16.33 ft – 4 ft = 12.33 ft (See Figure, Calculation Sheet 1)

Radius of Gyration (AASHTO 8.16.5.2.2):

r = ql_s = (0.25 for Circular Member)(4 ft) = 1.0 ft

Effective Length Factor (Figure 4.13):

The effective length factor used will vary depending on the earthquake motion and the corresponding orientation of the pier. Keep in mind the following:

❏ Transverse Earthquake Motion
  Longitudinal Pier Direction

❏ Longitudinal Earthquake Motion
  Transverse Pier Direction

Pier directions are perpendicular to bridge centerline.

k = 1.0   k = 2.0

TRANSVERSE MOTION   LONGITUDINAL MOTION

Check Slenderness Ratio Limit (AASHTO 8.16.5.2.5):

$$\frac{k \cdot L_u}{r} = \frac{(1.0)(12.33 \text{ ft})}{1.0 \text{ ft.}} = 12.33 < 22 \quad \therefore \text{ Column is NOT slender for transverse motion}$$

$$\frac{k \cdot L_u}{r} = \frac{(2.0)(12.33 \text{ ft})}{1.0 \text{ ft.}} = 24.67 > 22 \quad \therefore \text{ Column IS slender for longitudinal motion}$$

DESIGN EXAMPLE 4.2
STEP 7: CHECK FOR EFFECTS OF SLENDERNESS

We need to determine whether slenderness effects need to be taken into account for the pier columns. A check needs to be performed for a column subjected to both transverse and longitudinal earthquake motion.

First the unsupported length of the column is determined and the radius of gyration calculated. Recall from Section 4.2.4, Part 3, Equation 4.23, the radius of gyration various for members with circular and rectangular cross sections.

The difference between the response of the pier under the two loading conditions will be defined by the effective length factor k used. Under transverse earthquake motion (longitudinal pier direction) the column is free to translate but fixed against rotation. Under longitudinal earthquake motion (transverse pier direction) the column end is free to rotate and translate (see figure on Calculation Sheet 3). By Equation 4.25, the limit for the slenderness ratio of a compression member not braced against sidesway is 22. We need to consider slenderness under longitudinal earthquake motion.

a great deal of complexity. Failure of the member can be induced by the condition where:

$$P = P_{n0} \quad \text{and} \quad M = 0 \qquad \text{(Eq. 4.36)}$$

When such a situation occurs the compression member will fail by crushing of the concrete. Alternatively, the member can fail when subjected to the loading condition where:

$$P = 0 \quad \text{and} \quad M = M_{n0} \qquad \text{(Eq. 4.37)}$$

In this case, the compression member will fail by exceeding the yield strength of the reinforcing steel like a beam.

Figure 4.14 shows a typical *interaction diagram* for a reinforced concrete column. For any given curve in an interaction diagram, the intersection of the curve with the *y*-axis represents the situation defined by Equation 4.36. The intersection with the curve with the *x*-axis describes the situation given by Equation 4.37.

Interaction diagrams make useful design aids in calculating the required strength of a compression member. The values of P and M which are obtained from interaction diagrams are unreduced so that the designer must multiply these values by the appropriate strength reduction factor ϕ.

Interaction diagrams, such as the ones depicted in Figures 4.14 and 4.15, are based on the compression member's:

❏ Cross-section type (e.g., circular, rectangular)
❏ Cross-section geometry
❏ Strength of concrete used
❏ Reinforcing steel yield point

The use of interaction diagrams is limited to concretes with concrete strength up to and including 4,000 psi [Ref. 4.10]. This limitation is due to parameters which define the equivalent rectangular stress block no longer being constant, but rather decreasing with increasing values of the concrete strength f_c'. Interaction diagrams are published in handbooks issued by the

> Interaction diagrams make useful design aids in calculating the required strength of a compression member.

> If computer software solutions are not available to the designer, design aids like interaction diagrams can be considered an absolute necessity.

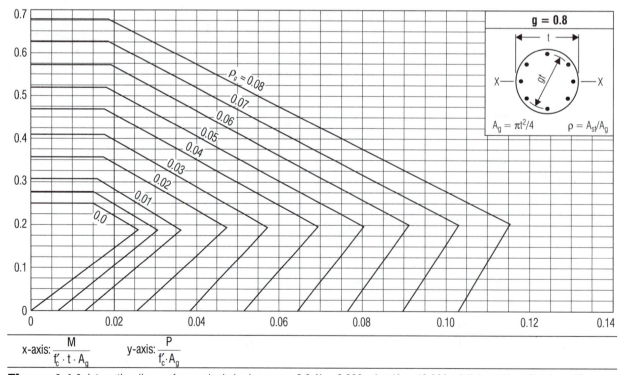

x-axis: $\dfrac{M}{f_c' \cdot t \cdot A_g}$ y-axis: $\dfrac{P}{f_c' \cdot A_g}$

Figure 4.14 Interaction diagram for round spiral columns g = 0.8, f_c' = 3,000 psi and f_y = 40,000 psi *(Adapted from Reinforced Concrete Design Handbook, ACI-SP-3, American Concrete Institute.)*

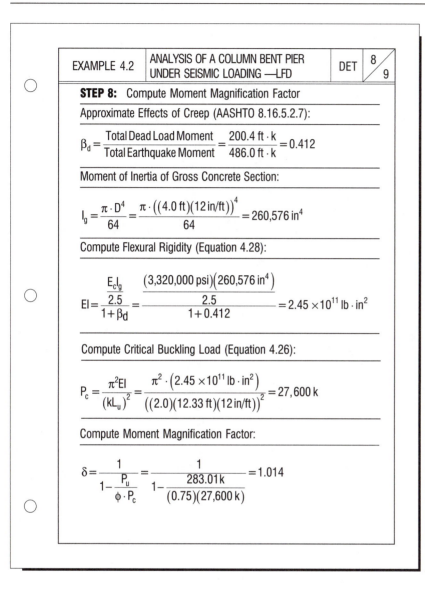

DESIGN EXAMPLE 4.2
STEP 8: COMPUTE MOMENT MAGNIFICATION

To compute the moment magnification factor we first need to compute several parameters. The first is the beta factor defined to take into account the effects of creep. The total dead load moment was given earlier in Step 6. Its value was determined from a computer analysis of the pier frame.

Next we need to determine the gross concrete section moment of inertia. This value is used to determine the flexural rigidity of the column. We will use the more conservative equation for this.

The critical buckling load is computed using the effective length factor of 2.0 found earlier in Step 7. This value is based on the pier being subjected to longitudinal earthquake motion.

Finally the moment magnification factor is computed using the criteria defined in AASHTO 8.16.5.2.7 (see also Equation 4.33). The pier columns are not braced against sidesway in the longitudinal direction.

American Concrete Institute. If computer software solutions are not available to the designer, design aids like interaction diagrams can be considered an absolute necessity.

4.2.5 Rehabilitation and Maintenance

The principal causes of deterioration to a bridge pier are very similar to that of an abutment. Piers suffer from many of the same types of problems which plague their counterparts at the ends of a bridge. Cracking, surface deterioration, and stability problems compounded by the adverse effects of such physical conditions as differential settlement and scour are factors which are common to any substructure component; be it a pier or an abutment.

Piers suffer from many of the same types of problems which plague their counterparts at the ends of a bridge.

A pier, however, because of its location at intermediate support points, is often more prone to some of the problems listed above than an abutment. Some examples of this can be found in:

❑   Scour
❑   Collision with underpass traffic
❑   Collision with ice floes

Piers are also more susceptible to overstressing than abutments because a pier must support two spans rather than one span. While there are differences between the two substructure components in terms of deterioration magnitude, many of the problems faced by piers and abutments are the same.

Because of this commonality in modes of deterioration and methods of repair, the reader is referred to Section 4.1.8 for a description of some of the rehabilitation and maintenance methods used for both abutment and pier components. The reader, however, should keep in mind the differences between these two components. An example of this would be in the use of steel as a pier material. While steel is rarely seen in bridge abutments, the use of steel frame piers is not uncommon. Another difference is that, because of the more likely use of bents as piers, either in the form of column bents or pile bents, the collection of debris and its associated adverse effects presents more of a concern for piers than abutments.

The issue of scour, mentioned above, receives much more intense scrutiny at pier locations. Damage to piers from scour has cost the transportation

> **D**amage to piers from scour has cost the transportation department hundreds of millions of dollars in the United States alone.

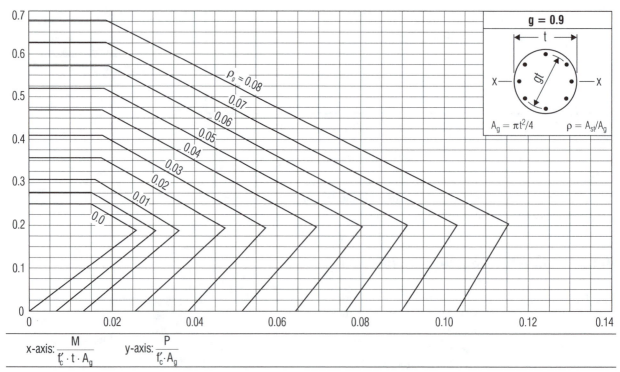

$$\text{x-axis: } \frac{M}{f'_c \cdot t \cdot A_g} \qquad \text{y-axis: } \frac{P}{f'_c \cdot A_g}$$

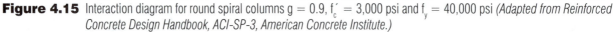

Figure 4.15 Interaction diagram for round spiral columns g = 0.9, f'_c = 3,000 psi and f_y = 40,000 psi *(Adapted from Reinforced Concrete Design Handbook, ACI-SP-3, American Concrete Institute.)*

| EXAMPLE 4.2 | ANALYSIS OF A COLUMN BENT PIER UNDER SEISMIC LOADING—LFD | DET | 9/9 |

STEP 9: Determine Required Reinforcing Steel

Compute Properties for Interaction Diagrams

$P_u = 283.01$ k

$M = (486 + 200.4)(1.014) = 696.0$ ft-k

$$A_g = \frac{\pi \cdot t^2}{4} = \frac{\pi \cdot (48\ in)^2}{4} = 1809.56\ in^2$$

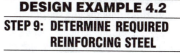

$A_s = 18.17\ in^2$
$gt = 40\ in$
$t = 48"$
$3"$

$$\frac{P}{f'_c \cdot A_g} = \frac{283.01\,k}{(3.0\ ksi)(1,809.56\ in^2)}$$

$$= 5.21 \times 10^{-2}$$

$$\frac{M}{f'_c \cdot t \cdot A_g} = \frac{(696.0\ ft \cdot k)(12\ in/ft)}{(3.0\ ksi)(48\ in)(1,809.56\ in^2)} = 3.21 \times 10^{-2}$$

$gt = 40\ in$ so: $g = 40\ in/48\ in = 0.833$ (must interpolate)

Enter into Figure 4.14 with x = 0.032 and y = 0.052   [g = 0.8]
$\rho_g = 0.021$

Enter into Figure 4.15 with x = 0.032 and y = 0.052   [g = 0.9]
$\rho_g = 0.020$

Interpolate for g = 0.833   [g = 0.833]

$$\rho_g = 0.021 - \left(\frac{0.8 - 0.833}{0.8 - 0.9}\right)(0.021 - 0.020) = 0.022$$

$$\rho_g = \frac{A_s}{A_g} \quad or : \quad A_s = \rho_g \cdot A_g = (0.021)(1809.56) = 38.0\ in^2$$

Since 38.0 in² (Required) > 18.17 in² (Available) ✗ NO GOOD!

DESIGN EXAMPLE 4.2

STEP 9: DETERMINE REQUIRED REINFORCING STEEL

To compute the amount of required reinforcing steel needed we will need to use the interaction diagrams presented in Figures 4.14 and 4.15. These diagrams are used to determine the effects of combined compression and bending acting on the column.

Recall that in Step 6 we identified the moment and axial force acting on a column. In the diagram shown in the accompanying calculation sheet, the given geometry of the existing column is presented along with the area of reinforcing steel currently in place.

Since the value of g is 0.833 we must interpolate between values found in the g=0.8 diagram and the g=0.9 diagram. The x-axis of the diagram takes into account the effects of bending on the column and the y-axis the effects of compression.

Once we have interpolated a value, we can calculate the area of reinforcing steel required by multiplying the resulting ratio value by the gross column area. In doing so we see that the existing reinforcement cannot sustain an earthquake based on the 0.19 acceleration coefficient.

---

department hundreds of millions of dollars in the United States alone. Two of the more famous scour related failures of U.S. bridges occurred in 1987 and 1989. The former saw scour bring down the bridge carrying the New York State Thruway over Schoharie Creek and the latter the failure due to scour of the U.S. Route 51 bridge crossing the Hatachie River in Tennessee. With this in mind, the discussion below will focus on some of the general maintenance and rehabilitation issues concerning scour.

4.2.6   Scour

We have already touched on some of the factors which lead to scour and the methods associated with inspecting a highway bridge for potential scour in Section 2.3.6. Because of the importance of this issue, however, we will touch briefly on some of the remedial and preventive maintenance measures which can be taken to correct scour related damage to a bridge pier (or abutment for that matter).

[4.2.6]

UNDERMINING is the removal of material from underneath a substructure foundation. This phenomenon, generally attributed to scour, is also known as undercutting. When a pier footing, like the one shown in Figure 4.16, is exposed to stream flows, the integrity of not only the pier, but the entire structure can be compromised. Situations like this require immediate attention by maintenance personnel so that adequate protection, either in the form of riprap or other protective measures, can be taken to protect the pier foundations. In most instances, the evidence of scour is obscured by the pier foundation being submerged under several feet of water, requiring underwater inspection to check for possible undermining.

Figure 4.16 An exposed pier footing shows evidence of undermining.

1. Overview. Recall that, in Section 2.3.6, we defined scour as the washing away of stream bed material by water channel flow. The removal of material from under a pier's foundation, often associated with scour, is known as undermining or undercutting. Obviously when such a situation occurs, the stability of a pier and the bridge proper, is compromised. As material is removed from under a substructure's foundation, the entire component will begin to settle.

Scour is usually associated with abnormally fast flowing water which occurs during a heavy storm and/or flood. The term *abnormally* is used because the design of a pier located in a body of water should be accompanied by a detailed hydrologic/hydraulic analysis of the water channel and its associated flows. Such an analysis is typically performed using computer software, an example of which are the HEC programs developed by the U.S. Army Corps of Engineers. The analysis is made using site specific data defining maximum flood conditions.

Scour generally takes place because one or a combination of the following conditions occurs:

❑ Natural conditions in the channel
❑ A constriction in the channel
❑ The bridge itself being a constriction

When scour occurs at a specific localized point in the channel, such as a pier, abutment, drainage structure, or some other obstruction, it is known as *local scour*. Local scour is evidenced by turbulence around piers which erodes material from under the foundation. If scour takes place over a large area of the channel it is known as *general scour*. General scour occurs over a long period of time and is initiated by an alteration in channel flow patterns. General scour is not caused by man made constrictions but rather results from a change in the supply of sediment to a large area. Scour which results from a reduction in the cross-sectional area of a channel due to the placement of an obstruction such as a highway bridge or drainage structure is known as *constriction scour*. Since the cross-sectional area is decreased by the constriction, a higher water velocity results. This higher velocity will typically occur at the bridge location, increasing the potential for scour damage.

The reader only has to recall the massive flooding which overtook the banks of the Mississippi River in 1993 to fully appreciate the magnitude and potential impact flooding can have on a highway bridge structure. During this flood, it was not uncommon to see entire highway bridges completely submerged beneath the flood waters.

2. Rehabilitation and Maintenance. If a pier is found to be suffering from adverse scour conditions, the problem can be corrected by either:

❏ Changing the structure
❏ Replacing the material which has been washed away

The first solution typically involves altering the foundation. This can be accomplished by enlarging the footer, strengthening or adding piles, or providing a sheet piling barrier around the pier foundation. Replacement of material generally involves the placement of erosion resistant material such as riprap or broken concrete around the pier (or abutment) to offer a barrier of sorts to scour.

Obviously the solution selected will depend greatly on the scope of the problem (i.e., how severe is the scour) as well as available funds and material availability. Due to limited resources, it may be feasible to only provide temporary protection to a pier. When this is the case, replacement of the washed away material is the generally accepted solution. For temporary repairs, the soundness of the stone used is generally not important [Ref. 4.6]. Another factor which could affect the method used is the size of the water channel and other environmental considerations (i.e., impact on downstream conditions, etc.).

Discussed below are methods for either replacing washed away material or changing the structure to account for current water channel conditions. To be sure, there are a variety of approaches which transportation departments utilize in addressing the important issue of scour. It is the intent of the following discussion, however, to present the reader new to bridge design with an overview of some of the general forms of rehabilitation and maintenance methods in use.

3. Replacement of Material. As mentioned above, the replacement of washed away material can be made with broken stone or concrete. The size of stone used to protect against scour is dependent upon the characteristics of the bridge site. Some features which are used to determine the size of stone used to protect piers are:

❏ Type and orientation of pier or abutment
❏ Geometry and physical properties of stream
❏ Size and location of scour hole

The reader only has to recall the massive flooding which overtook the banks of the Mississippi River in 1993 to fully appreciate the magnitude and potential impact flooding can have on a highway bridge structure.

Replacement of material generally involves the placement of erosion resistant material such as riprap or broken concrete around the pier ... to offer a barrier of sorts to scour.

❏ Local climate and environment
❏ Material and vegetation of stream bed and banks

The bridge crossing a stream, shown earlier in Figure 4.11, should give the reader a feeling for the type of stone used to protect substructures from scour. Because of the relatively large size of some of these stones, care must be taken by the maintenance personnel in placing them around a pier. Careless dumping of riprap can often damage the pier itself. Another concern is an uneven placement of riprap which can lead to stability problems (see also Section 2.3.6). For this reason, riprap should be placed in uniform lifts.

If concrete is being used as a repair material for scour, it will require either underwater placement or dewatering at the pier location. The latter method requires that water be removed from the pier location so that the concrete can be placed. This method has the inherent advantage of providing a dry environment for placement of the concrete.

Dewatering can be accomplished through the construction of a coffer-dam around a pier using sheet piling. As mentioned earlier in Section 4.1.8, Part 9, the driving of sheet piling under a bridge is difficult because of potential interference with the bridge superstructure overhead. Placement of the cofferdam may only be possible by removing a span. Another method for dewatering a pier is to divert channel flow away from the bridge. This method, however, could potentially create adverse effects at other points along the channel and will require a thorough investigation and analysis to ensure that no associated damage takes place as a result of the diversion.

There are a variety of methods available for underwater placement of concrete. Some of the more popular methods include:

❏ Tremie
❏ Pumping
❏ Underwater bucket
❏ Bagged concrete

A tremie utilizes gravity flow to place concrete underwater. A tremie is a tube which is equipped with a discharge gate at one end and a hopper at the other. With the discharge gate closed, the tremie is filled with concrete and then submerged beneath the water to the location requiring repair. The hopper must be continually filled with concrete and the discharge end submerged during the pour so that the tremie does not become filled with water. Pumping uses the same basic concept except the concrete is pumped through the tube. This provides for greater control in placing the concrete.

Underwater buckets, as the name would imply, consist of lowering buckets of concrete to the location requiring repair. The bucket may be covered or uncovered; however, if it is uncovered, care must be taken during the placement operation. Bagged concrete consists of concrete, wrapped in a burlap bag, which is then placed around the repair location. A certain degree of bonding between adjacent bags takes place as a result of concrete seeping through the pores in the burlap bags. Some bagged concrete consists of dry concrete which is placed and then wetted.

> **C**areless dumping of riprap can often damage the pier itself. Another concern is an uneven placement of riprap which can lead to stability problems ...

4. **Changing the Structure.** The other type of repair method involves physically altering the form and function of the pier. Severely deteriorated piers, like the one shown earlier in Figure 4.11, are sometimes repaired by jacketing the pier with a new layer of concrete. The foundation itself can be deepened and then jacketed to provide added protection and repair deteriorated portions.

Another solution is to drive additional, deeper piles for the pier foundation or repair existing piles which have been damaged. Both operations are complicated by having to work underwater. If the bridge is susceptible to high flood waters which can result in overtopping of the channel (i.e., flood waters exceeding the height of the structure) any solid parapet type barriers should be replaced with open railings to allow the water to pass through. As a protective measure, steel sheeting can be installed around the pier.

5. **Replacing the Structure.** If the scour problem is so severe that none of the methods described in Part 3 or Part 4 above will rectify the situation, the only feasible alternative may be to completely replace the structure. The design of a more scour resistant structure should be performed with the following considerations in mind:

- ❏ The vertical clearance should be as large as possible
- ❏ Deep, pile foundations should be used
- ❏ Socket piles into rock if piles are short
- ❏ The piers should be oriented so as to limit scour
- ❏ The largest possible channel width under the bridge should be provided for

It may also be possible to alter the channel alignment and provide for the incorporation of relief culverts so as to minimize the effect of excessive flows passing under a bridge. By providing for the largest possible channel width, the cross-sectional area becomes larger and thereby decreases the velocity of water passing under the structure. Any major bridge rehabilitation work should also include the removal of any debris located in the channel that could be acting as a constriction to channel flow. While these general guidelines are offered with regard to the replacement of an existing structure, the reader should keep in mind their applicability to the design of a new one.

> **B**y providing for the largest possible channel width, the cross-sectional area becomes larger and thereby decreases the velocity of water passing under the structure.

4.3 BEARINGS

Bearings are mechanical systems which transmit loads from the superstructure to the substructure. In a way, bearings can be thought of as the interface between the superstructure and the substructure. In addition to transmitting vertical loads to the substructure component (i.e., pier or abutment) a bearing also provides for movement due to thermal expansion and contraction as well as rotational movement associated with deflection of primary members.

The importance of bearings cannot be understated. Bearings which become frozen due to corrosion, clogged with debris, or fail to function as originally designed can induce high stresses and potentially lead to failure of an individual span or an entire structure. The importance of bearings in a bridge design is often paid little (or no) attention because many bridge designers rely on manufacturers for the design of individual bearing units. In many cases, a bridge engineer will merely specify the loading conditions and movement that the bearing must accommodate and leave the detailed design of the individual units to the manufacturer of the bearing. This practice, however, is changing and bridge engineers are becoming increasingly aware of some of the nuances associated with design of bearings for highway bridges.

4.3.1 Forces Acting on a Bearing

As mentioned above, bridge bearings are designed to accommodate the transmittal of forces and movement of the structure. The forces applied to a bridge bearing can be identified as:

- ❏ Reactions
- ❏ Longitudinal forces
- ❏ Transverse forces
- ❏ Uplift forces

Reactions acting on a bearing are produced by the end reaction of a primary member acting directly on the center of the bearing/structure interface.

Figure 4.17 Workers assemble a 12,000,000 pound capacity pot bearing for the State of Florida. *(Photograph courtesy of D. S. Brown Company, North Baltimore, Ohio.)*

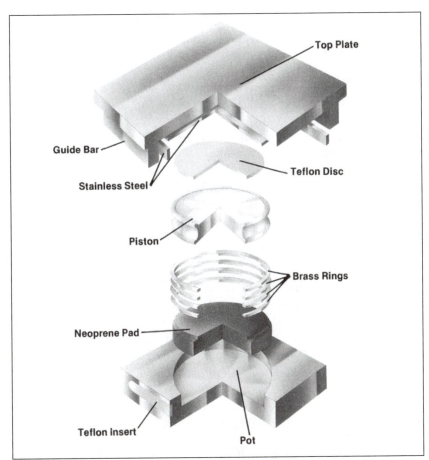

Figure 4.18 Components of a typical guided pot bearing assembly. *(Illustration courtesy of D. S. Brown Company, North Baltimore, Ohio.)*

A POT BEARING consists of a shallow steel cylinder, or pot, on a vertical axis with a neoprene disk which is slightly thinner than the cylinder and fitted tightly inside. A steel piston fits inside the cylinder and bears on the neoprene. Flat brass rings are used to seal the rubber between the piston and the pot. The rubber behaves like a viscous fluid flowing as rotation may occur. Since the bearing will not resist bending moments, it must be provided with an even bridge seat. On the support, the bearing is typically set on a grout, lead, or fabric pad. It is possible to erect formwork around the bearing and pour concrete over the unit as long as care is taken not to contaminate the bearing with concrete. Since pot bearings can accommodate large concentrated loads, special attention must be given to the reinforcing steel and concrete used in the vicinity of the bearing. To help meet concrete pressure limits, masonry plates may be required. Because of the possibility of creating large local stresses, the use of metal shims or blocks at odd points to adjust seat elevations should be avoided.

Reactions resulting from dead and live loads acting on a structure are determined as discussed in Section 3. Longitudinal and transverse forces acting on a bearing, as we have seen in Sections 4.1 and 4.2, can arise from live load, wind and earthquake motion. In addition to seismic loading conditions, wind loading, thermal expansion and contraction, and other miscellaneous loading conditions can contribute part or all of their loads in the form of transverse or longitudinal forces acting on the bearing.

Transverse forces are generally resisted by the bearing's anchor bolts. Transverse forces will also create a moment acting on the bearing equal to the magnitude of the force times the height of the bearing. This can result in large moments for bearings which are very tall (see Figure 4.19). Longitudinal forces act in a direction which is parallel to the centerline of the structure. An example of a longitudinal force acting on a bearing would be a force resulting from vehicular braking force.

4.3.2 Movement of Bearings

Details of typical fixed and expansion bearings are provided in Figure 4.20. While the form and size of the bearing can vary greatly from bridge to bridge

In addition to seismic loading conditions, wind loading, thermal expansion and contraction, and other ... loading conditions can contribute part or all of their loads in the form of transverse or longitudinal forces.

While the form and size of the bearing can vary greatly from bridge to bridge (e.g., steel rocker bearings vs. elastomeric bearings), the intended function is pretty much the same.

(e.g., steel rocker bearings vs. elastomeric bearings), the intended function is pretty much the same. In general, the movement accommodated by fixed and expansion bearings can be classified by the following:

❑ Fixed bearings allow for rotation only
❑ Guided expansion bearings allow for rotation and longitudinal translation only
❑ Multi-directional expansion bearings allow for rotation and translation in any direction

A fixed bearing will allow for rotation resulting from superstructure deflection, and offer restraint against translation. A fixed bearing may be fixed in one direction, or may be fixed in both directions. An expansion bearing, however, allows both rotation and translation, although they may be restricted in transverse direction (guided bearings). For very short span lengths, end rotation may be ignored [Ref. 4.6].

Movement in bearings can be initiated by any one of the deformational loading conditions discussed earlier in Section 3.5.4. This loading condition includes movement due to creep, shrinkage, settlement, uplift, and thermal forces. In addition to movement due to deformational loading, some temporary loading conditions, as discussed in Section 3.5.3, can also initiate movement in bearings. An example of this would be movement resulting from the application of earthquake forces.

4.3.3 Types of Bearings

Like any other bridge component we have seen in the text thus far, bearings come in a variety of shapes and sizes. The applicability of certain types of bearings will vary depending on the loads and movement the bearing is required

TRANSVERSE FORCES acting on a bearing will induce a moment within the bearing itself. The magnitude of this moment is defined as the force times the height of the bearing. This moment may be negligible for relatively thin bearings. However, large bearings possessing a substantial height, like the one shown in Figure 4.19, can have correspondingly large moments acting on them. Uplift acting on bearings is also a concern if the bridge is horizontally curved or even located in an area of high seismic activity. The bearing in Figure 4.19 should illustrate that the "simple" bearing can be a rather substantial design effort in its own right.

Figure 4.19 Some bearings, like the one shown above, can be quite massive in size.

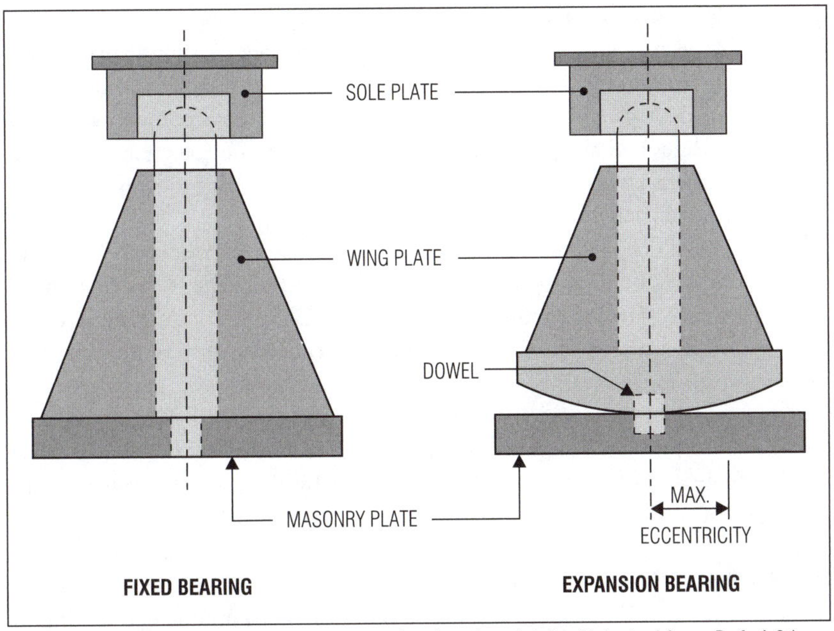

Figure 4.20 Typical fixed and expansion bearing details *(Adapted from Ref. 4.6.)*

A FIXED BEARING, like the one shown in Figure 4.20, transmits vertical loads to the substructure. In addition to this functionality, fixed bearings also serve to restrain the superstructure from longitudinal translation (see Did You Know? sidebar at the top of this section). Fixed bearings can rotate, but cannot translate. Expansion bearings, like the rocker bearing shown in Figure 4.20, are provided with an extra degree of freedom so that they can accommodate both rotation and translation. Rocker type expansion bearings are typically used when a large vertical load and/or large amount of superstructure translation is expected, a situation representative of large span lengths.

to sustain. Originally, steel mechanical bearing assemblies were the standard for most highway bridges. Within the past half century, however, the use of bearings made of a synthetic, elastomeric material has become increasingly popular. Indeed, the AASHTO specification for the design of elastomeric bearings did not first appear until 1961 [Ref. 4.11].

Discussed below are some of the principal types of bridge bearings currently in use. The reader should keep in mind that there are a variety of permutations of each general class of bearings with different manufacturers designing and fabricating bearing systems according to their own in-house standards and methods.

> **W**ithin the past half century, however, the use of bearings made of a synthetic, elastomeric material have become increasingly popular.

1. Rocker Bearings. A rocker bearing is a type of *pinned bearing* which is used to accommodate large live load deflections (as well as large vertical loads). Typically this type of bearing is used for span lengths of 50 ft (15.2 m) and up. The bearing, typically made of steel, is connected to the substructure through use of a steel masonry plate. Connection to the primary member is made using a steel sole plate which is either welded or bolted to the bottom flange of the primary member overhead.

To prevent the rocker in a bearing from *walking*, pintles are used which resist transverse forces that could potentially create such a situation. A pintle is a trapezoidal extrusion which extends upward from the masonry plate. A recess is made in the rocker which in turn fits over the top of the pintle. The fabrication of rocker bearings requires the maintaining of extremely tight tolerances. Rotation in both fixed and expansion bearings is facilitated through the use of a solid circular pin. This pin acts as a hinge which allows for translation and rotation in expansion bearings and rotation in fixed bearings.

2. **Roller Bearings.** A roller bearing, like a rocker bearing, is a form of pinned bearing and therefore is similar to a rocker bearing in many ways (see Figure 4.24). In this type of bearing, translation is facilitated by the use of a roller or group (nest) of rollers. Rotation can be accommodated by a pin, as described above for rocker bearings, or by the rolling action of the rollers themselves. Roller bearings, however, are intended only for spans of moderate length.

AASHTO requires that expansion rollers be equipped with "substantial side bars" and be guided by gearing or other means to prevent lateral movement, skewing, and creeping (AASHTO 10.29.3). A general drawback to this type of bearing is its tendency to collect dust and debris. This can result in the bearing becoming frozen and ceasing to operate as it was designed to. Because of this, AASHTO requires that the rollers and bearing plates be protected as much as possible to prevent the intrusion of water and debris. This protection is complicated by the need for rollers to be easily accessible for maintenance cleaning and inspection.

3. **Sliding Plate Bearings.** A sliding bearing, as its name would imply, utilizes one plate sliding against another to accommodate translational movement. Whether or not rotation is accommodated by this type of bearing is dependent on the magnitude of anticipated rotation. For spans less than 50 ft (15.2 m) in length, AASHTO allows the designer to ignore deflection (AASHTO 10.29.1.1). This provision makes sliding bearings better suited to small structures with span lengths within this range. Sliding bearings can be fabricated out of steel, although other materials such as Teflon and bronze are also used (see Figure 4.21).

4. **Pot Bearings.** Like rocker bearings, pot bearings can accommodate large translations and vertical loads. Figure 4.17 shows a large capacity pot bearing being assembled and Figure 4.18 shows the representative components of a pot bearing assembly. A pot bearing comprises a shallow steel cylinder, or pot, which lies on a vertical axis along with a neoprene disk. This neoprene disk is slightly thinner than the cylinder and is fitted tightly inside. The cylinder confines and seals elastomer so that an isotropic stress state, also referred to as a hydrostatic stress state, is created. An isotropic stress state is a state of stress with equal stresses in any direction, and with zero shear stress. Some bearing manufacturers promote that the elastomer is in a "fluid" state, which is not true. This containment of the elastomeric material allows the bearing to handle much larger loads than if it were not contained since, if not contained, the elastomeric material would deform in an uncontrollable fashion.

It is possible, however, for the elastomer to extrude out from between the cylinder and the piston. This could be caused by excessive clearance between the piston and the cylinder. Another source of this problem could be plastic deformation of the sealing ring. To avoid this problem, the manufacturer needs to maintain a tight tolerance with regard to clearance between the piston and cylinder.

An expansion pot bearing is also equipped with sliding plates made of Teflon, stainless steel, or other material. These plates are designed to allow for translation at the support. A general concern with any bearing designed

> The cylinder confines and seals elastomer so that an isotropic stress state, also referred to as a hydrostatic stress state, is created.

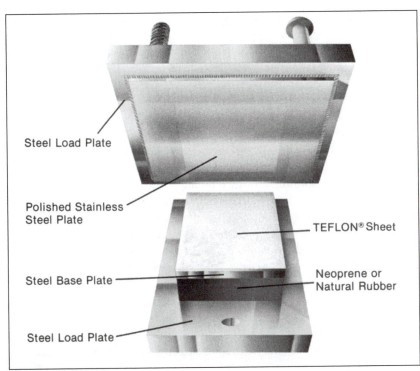

Figure 4.21 Components of a typical sliding bearing assembly. *(Illustration courtesy of D. S. Brown Company, North Baltimore, Ohio.)*

A SLIDING BEARING consists of two components. The top component incorporates a steel load plate with a polished stainless steel plate welded to it. The top plate is welded or bolted to the girder during installation. The bottom component consists of a Teflon sheet which is $1/16$ to $3/32$ in thick.

This sheet is bonded to a stainless steel backing plate, which is bonded to an elastomeric bearing, that is in turn bonded to a steel load plate. All bonding is accomplished through vulcanization during the molding process.

Sliding bearings may be guided or free to move and are custom made to individual project requirements for material types and performance (i.e., expansion, rotation).

to accommodate large loads is the quality of the substructure support element below it (i.e., pedestal or other bridge seat element). Like the bearing, a concrete pedestal must be designed with concrete and reinforcing steel of sufficient strength to handle the large reaction. It is also advisable to avoid the use of metal shims or other devices which are used to adjust the final bridge seat elevation. Such devices can induce large local stresses and should be avoided.

> Like the bearing, a concrete pedestal must be designed with concrete and reinforcing steel of sufficient strength to handle the large reaction.

5. Spherical Bearings. A spherical bearing accommodates rotation through use of a curved bottom plate located at the lower portion of the bearing. This curved plate marries to a matching plate above it. Translation is achieved through use of a flat plate located at the upper portion of the bearing. The curved surfaces of the bearing which allow for rotation are fabricated out of stainless steel, lubricated bronze, or other material. The flat upper surfaces, designed for translation, are equipped with a layer of stainless steel and Teflon.

6. Elastomeric Bearings. An elastomeric bearing can be made up of an unreinforced elastomeric pad or a reinforced elastomeric bearing. A reinforced elastomeric bearing is fabricated by bonding together alternate laminates of rubber (either natural or synthetic) and steel. The rubber and steel are molded together into a solid mass which is free of voids. As the bearing is loaded, the elastomeric material will tend to deform or *bulge*. An illustration of unreinforced and reinforced elastomeric bearings is provided

> A reinforced elastomeric bearing is fabricated by bonding together alternate laminates of rubber (either natural or synthetic) and steel.

in Figure 4.22. It is also possible that the elastomeric bearing is reinforced with fabric rather than steel.

The steel laminates in an elastomeric bearing provide bulging restraint under large compressive loads. In unreinforced pads, bulging restraint is provided by friction between the pad itself and the bearing surface [Ref. 4.11]. Movement in an elastomeric bearing is accommodated by distortion of the bearing material. An elastomeric expansion bearing is designed to handle both horizontal and vertical movement. A fixed elastomeric bearing is restrained against horizontal movement through the use of anchoring dowels which extend from the superstructure, through the bearing, and are then anchored into the substructure bridge seat. A load plate may also be provided at the top of the bearing and underneath it in order to distribute loads and hold the bearing in place [Ref. 4.6].

As mentioned earlier, in terms of highway bridges, elastomeric bearings are a relatively new invention. Since elastomeric bearings have no moving parts, they present an attractive alternative to traditional steel mechanical bearing systems in terms of both functionality and maintenance considerations. As we have seen earlier with weathering steel and prestressed concrete, however, no system can be considered maintenance free. The elastomeric material can become excessively deformed, split, or even cracked; all of which will demand attention by maintenance personnel.

> **A**s we have seen earlier with weathering steel and prestressed concrete ... no system can be considered maintenance free.

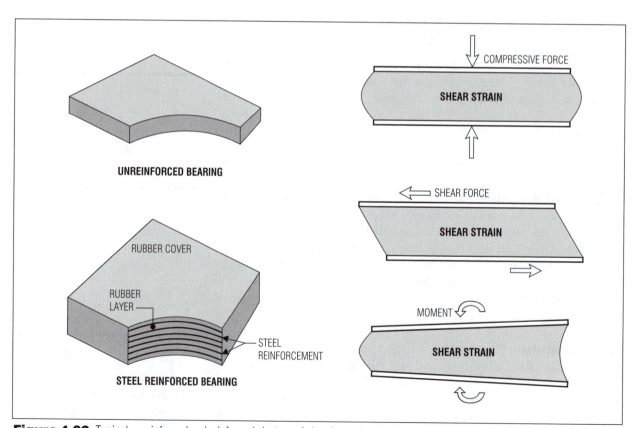

Figure 4.22 Typical unreinforced and reinforced elastomeric bearings along with strains and deformations for compression, shear, and rotation *(Adapted from "State-of-the-Art Elastomeric Bridge Bearing Design," Ref. 4.11.)*

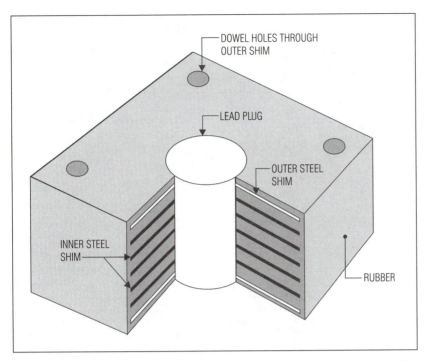

Figure 4.23 Components of a typical lead rubber bearing assembly *(Adapted from "Seismic Design of Bridges on Lead-Rubber Bearings," Ref. 4.12.)*

LEAD RUBBER BEARINGS consist of a laminated elastomeric bearing equipped with a lead cylinder at the center of the bearing. The lead cylinder extends throughout the full depth of the bearing. The function of the rubber-steel laminated portion of the bearing is to carry the weight of the structure and provide post-yield elasticity. The lead core is designed to deform plastically, thereby providing damping energy dissipation. This has the effect of changing the stiffness of the structure and the damping properties. Lead rubber bearings are used in seismically active areas because of their performance under earthquake loads. Under seismic loading, lead rubber bearings offer better performance than traditional elastomeric bearings by reducing the displacement response and the number of cycles at the maximum response [Ref. 4.12].

Deterioration to an elastomeric bearing can be caused by a variety of factors, some of which include:

- ❏ Poor fabrication
- ❏ Insufficient reinforcement
- ❏ Insufficient size
- ❏ Rounding of elastomeric material edges
- ❏ Exposure to corrosive agents
- ❏ Failure of bond between elastomeric material and load plate
- ❏ Variation in material properties over time
- ❏ Excessive loading conditions

In general, synthetic materials like neoprene perform better under hostile environmental conditions than natural rubbers. An analogy can be drawn between reinforced concrete and elastomeric bearings in that, if the elastomeric bearing is provided with sufficient cover (i.e., material thickness beyond the steel laminates), then it should resist corrosion well, just as reinforcing steel should if provided with adequate concrete cover.

7. Lead Rubber Bearings. A lead rubber bridge bearing is essentially an elastomeric bearing equipped with a lead core which extends throughout the height of the bearing. The components of a typical lead rubber bearing are shown in Figure 4.23.

Lead rubber bearings are generally used in structures which are exposed to a high degree of seismic activity. The elastomeric material and

THE ROLLERS USED in roller bearings are usually not completely circular in shape since this can result in a poor economy of materials. Since only the upper and lower portions of the roller are in contact with the bearing surface, the extra material required to make the roller perfectly circular is inefficient. Therefore, the extra material on the sides of the extended circular shape was eliminated to yield the truncated shape depicted in Figure 4.24.

A major problem associated with roller bearings is the accumulation of dirt, debris and moisture in the rollers, thereby hindering performance. In a state of advanced deterioration, roller bearings can become rusted and eventually frozen. When using this type of bearing, it is important to ensure that drainage facilities are detailed to channel all runoff away from the bearing. The bearing itself should be shielded for protection but must also be accessible for inspection and maintenance operations.

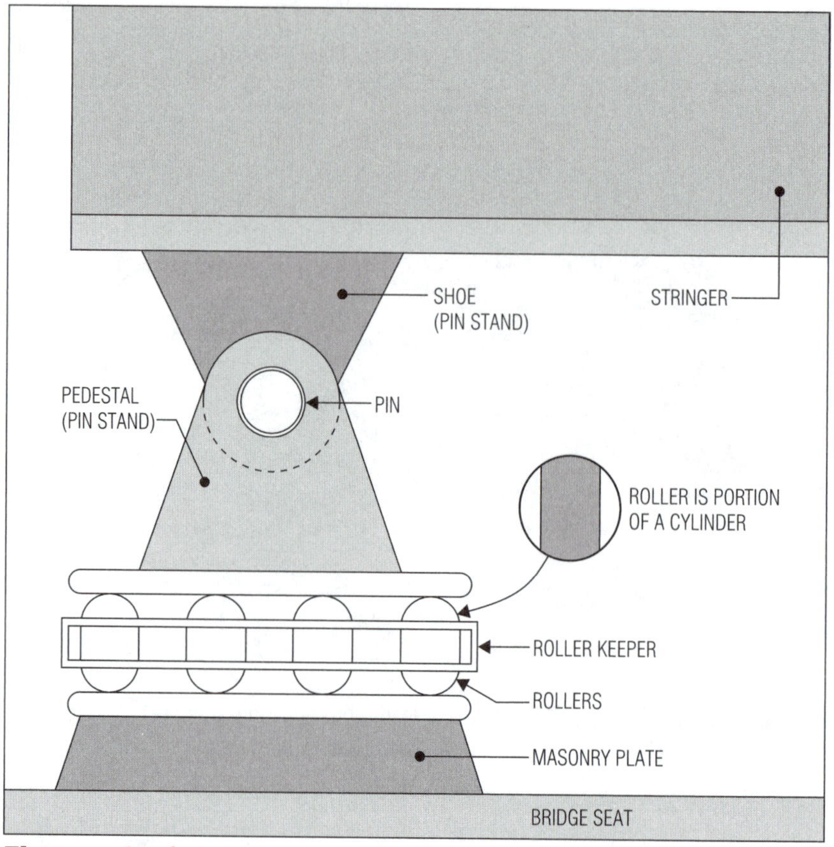

Figure 4.24 Components of a typical roller expansion bearing assembly *(Adapted from Ref. 4.6.)*

steel laminates carry the weight of the structure and provide post-yield elasticity and the lead core provides damping energy dissipation [Ref. 4.12]. Under normal loading conditions, the lead core resists lateral loads. Under seismically induced dynamic loads, however, the lead core yields and assists the elastomeric material in resisting loads while at the same time accommodating lateral flexibility.

4.3.4 Rehabilitation and Maintenance

Like bridge expansion joints, it is important to keep bridge bearings, regardless of their type, free from dirt, debris, and excessive moisture. Corrosion in a bridge bearing can cause it to become locked or frozen. This can result in the creation of abnormally large stresses at the support points as well as inhibiting the natural movement of a structure. It is therefore important that any maintenance program undertaken include constant inspection and cleaning of bearing elements on a bridge. As we saw earlier with some bearing types, this can be complicated by bearing housing units which obstruct both visual inspection and maintenance.

Once again, a prime culprit in bearing deterioration is the presence of faulty joints overhead. If deterioration to a bearing is evident, the inspector must identify the causes for deterioration, be it a leaking joint or poor drainage

Like bridge expansion joints, it is important to keep bridge bearings, regardless of their type, free from dirt, debris, and excessive moisture.

facilities. In steel bearings, particular attention should be given to the condition of the bearing anchor bolts to ensure that excessive rusting has not compromised their integrity.

Another potential problem spot is deterioration of the bearing surface. Corrosion to the masonry plate and/or concrete substructure can present stability problems. When design and detailing a bearing assembly, it is important to maintain adequate edge distance from the face of the masonry plate to the face of the supporting pedestal. Many states maintain strict design criteria governing the placement of the bearing footprint on a pedestal or other bridge seat which the designer should take care to adhere to.

Like any other steel element, steel bearing assemblies should be provided with some form of protective system designed to limit corrosion. This can take the form of paint or galvanizing. As part of an on-going maintenance program, steel bearings will also require periodic lubrication of their working elements.

As mentioned in Section 4.3.3, Part 6, elastomeric bearings will also require periodic inspection and maintenance. Elastomeric bearings should be inspected for an accumulation of dirt and debris. The integrity of the elastomeric material should also be checked in an effort to detect excessive deformation or ozone cracking. In certain instances, it may be necessary to jack the superstructure in order to replace elastomeric material which has been damaged.

Rocker and roller steel bearings are especially susceptible to a build-up of debris in their moving elements. Roller nests, like the one shown in Figure 4.24, are extremely susceptible to collecting debris. The underside of rocker bearings is also a potential collection point for movement-inhibiting debris. In addition to limiting the intended movement of a bearing, dirt and debris will pit and corrode the surface of the bearing elements, which can also impede functionality.

Other potential sources for bearing problems can be identified by the following:

- ❏ Corrosion from chemical agents
- ❏ Settlement of the substructure
- ❏ Excessive deformational loads

Bearings, like any other element in a cold environment, will deteriorate as a result of coming in contact with deicing agents. Settlement of the abutments or piers can result in a bearing becoming destabilizing and undergoing loading conditions which the element was not designed for. Another potential source for this problem is the presence of excessive deformational loads such as creep and shrinkage. While the first problem listed is difficult to control, the latter two can certainly be addressed by a proper and thorough design.

> **B**earings, like any other element in a cold environment, will deteriorate as a result of coming in contact with deicing agents.

REFERENCES

4.1 Starzewski, K., "Earth Retaining Structures and Culverts," *The Design and Construction of Engineering Foundations,* Edited by Henry, F.D.C., Chapman and Hall, New York, 1986.

4.2 Bowles, Joseph E., *Foundation Analysis and Design,* 2nd ed., McGraw-Hill, New York, 1977.

4.3 Peck, Ralph B., Hanson, Walter E., and Thornburn, Thomas H., *Foundation Engineering,* John Wiley & Sons, New York, 1974.

4.4 *Standard Specifications for Highway Bridges,* 17th ed., American Association of State Highway and Transportation Officials, Washington, D.C., 2002.

4.5 *AASHTO LRFD Bridge Design Specifications,* 3rd ed., American Association of State Highway and Transportation Officials, Washington, D.C., 2004.

4.6 *Manual for Bridge Condition Evaluation, 2nd ed.,* American Association of State Highway and Transportation Officials, Washington, D.C., 2003.

4.7 Wittfoht, Hans, *Building Bridges: History, Technology, Construction,* p. 16, Beton-Verlag, Düsseldorf, December, 1984.

4.8 Walley, W. J., and Purkiss, J. A., "Bridge Abutments and Piers," pp. 821–884, *The Design and Construction of Engineering Foundations,* Edited by Henry, F.D.C., Chapman and Hall, New York, 1986.

4.9 Bordner, Randolph H., Chairman, ACI Committee 347, "Guide to Formwork for Concrete," *ACI Structural Journal,* vol. 85, September-October, 1988.

4.10 Winter, George, and Nilson, Arthur H., *Design of Concrete Structures,* 9th ed., McGraw-Hill, New York, 1979.

4.11 Roeder, Charles W. and Stanton, John F., "State-of-the-Art Elastomeric Bridge Bearing Design," *ACI Structural Journal,* vol. 88, January-February, 1991.

4.12 Turkington, D. H., Carr, A. J., Cooke, N., and Moss, P. J., "Seismic Design of Bridges on Lead-Rubber Bearings," *Journal of Structural Engineering,* American Society of Civil Engineers, vol. 115, no. 12, pp. 3000-3016, December, 1989.

5

Implementation and Management

Section Overview

We conclude the text with a discussion of the implementation and management of a bridge in a transportation network. Specifically, this section touches on some of the more general themes and issues behind key bridge related highway concerns, the preparation of final contract documents, and the development and implementation of computer assisted Bridge Management Systems.

A bridge is not a discrete component which is designed, built, and then forgotten about. At the onset of the text, it was stated that "the common highway bridge structure ... is one of the most integral components in any transportation network." It is fitting that we end the text with this same thought in mind, for it is the downfall of many design engineers to view their work in discrete terms. As we have seen in the preceding sections, the ideas of design, rehabilitation, and maintenance are closely interwoven to form a cohesive fabric. Rather than being independent topics, these issues impact one another and, in many ways, influence the performance of a highway bridge throughout its life. In this section, we will touch on some important issues concerning the final implementation and eventual management of highway bridges.

These implementation and management issues specifically concern the incorporation of a bridge into the highway itself. Another topic discussed is the preparation of final contract documents which act as the manuscript of a bridge engineer's efforts. Finally we will briefly touch on a subject which is gaining increased importance in the profession: the management of groups of bridges in a highway network.

Figure 5.1 Whether a bridge is large or small, it is still just one component in a highway network.

Section 5

Implementation & Management

5.1 THE HIGHWAY

A highway bridge carries a highway over an obstruction. The functionality and performance of a bridge is therefore defined by the associated highway it is intended to carry. In a way, the highway can be thought of as another component in the structure; just as the superstructure, piers, and abutments are components. Major highways, like The New York State Thruway shown in Figure 5.2, depend on bridges to carry the roadway along a logical alignment. While the bridge engineer, with respect to a given design project, is not terribly interested in the hundreds and hundreds of miles which the highway may encompass, he or she should be quite interested in the few hundred feet of highway which resides to each side of the structure's approaches.

The following discussion is intended to provide an overview of highway design fundamentals for the structural engineer who may be unfamiliar with these basic concepts. Also provided is a discussion of pertinent highway related issues which significantly impact the design of a highway bridge. Finally a short overview of the important issues of traffic safety and maintenance of traffic during construction is offered.

5.1.1 Design Elements of a Highway

Although it is not the intent of this section to provide a complete discourse on highway design, it is important that the basic nomenclature and highway related design elements be presented for the structural engineer who may not be familiar with them. Designers who have had an active involvement in highway design may wish to skip this section. For a complete discussion of highway design, the reader is referred to a general purpose text on the subject.

A HIGHWAY BRIDGE carries a "highway" over an obstruction. The integration of a bridge into a highway is not a trivial affair. The interface of the structure with the approach roadway often requires the design of a reinforced concrete approach slab. The elevations of a bridge are all impacted by the overpass roadway vertical alignment. Likewise, the geometry of the structure in plan is influenced by the horizontal alignment of the overpass roadway. Bridges constructed to facilitate the implementation of grade separated roadways must meet the needs of not only an overpass alignment, but an underpass alignment as well. As we have seen earlier, this affects the size and shape of piers as well as a host of other bridge related issues.

Figure 5.2 Bridges are an integral component of any transportation network.

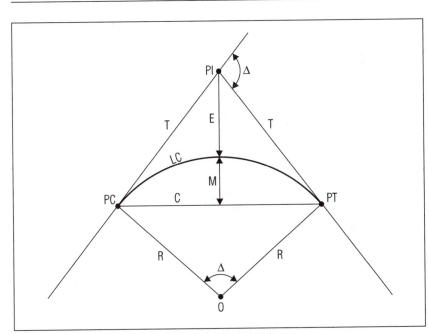

Figure 5.3 Constituent elements of a horizontal highway curve.

HORIZONTAL CURVE ELEMENTS AND NOMENCLATURE

Figure 5.3 shows the constituent elements of a horizontal highway curve. The following is a detailed description of the variables used to describe a horizontal curve:

Δ = Interior Angle
E = External Distance
M = Middle Ordinate
T = Tangent Distance from PC/PT to PI
C = Chord Length from PC to PT
R = Radius of Curve
O = Center of Curve
LC = Length of Arc from PC to PT
PC = Point of Curvature (curve begins)
PT = Point of Tangency (curve ends)
PI = Point of Intersection

1. **Horizontal Alignment.** A horizontal alignment is the path which defines the geometry of a highway in plan. This alignment can be represented by a:

❑ Straight tangent
❑ Circular curve
❑ Spiral

Obviously, the first type of horizontal alignment is the simplest to deal with in terms of establishing the location and orientation of a highway bridge. Things become somewhat more complicated when either of the latter two types of alignments is present. A circular curve and its constituent elements is presented in Figure 5.3. We shall discuss the geometric parameters of this type of curve shortly. A spiral is a curve with a constantly changing radius. A spiral curve is used in highway alignments to provide a gradual change in curvature. The definition of the geometry of a spiral curve is beyond the scope of this text. The reader is referred to a general purpose highway design book for more on this subject. A classic book on route design in general is Hickerson's text on this subject [Ref. 5.1]. Although this text was originally published some time ago, it remains relevant and useful today.

Distance along any horizontal alignment is defined by a unit of measurement known as a *station*. A full station is defined as 100 ft and, therefore, a half station is equal to 50 ft. If the start of a horizontal alignment is taken as 0, a point 1,355.56 ft from the beginning of the alignment would be denoted as 13+55.56. (i.e., 13 stations (1300 ft) plus 56.56 ft). This value represents the distance from the start point (0+00) *along the path of the horizontal alignment*, be it a tangent, curve, or a combination thereof.

> **A** spiral is a curve with a constantly changing radius ... used in highway alignments to provide a gradual change in curvature.

A simple curve consists of a circular curve which is formed by two tangents. In Figure 5.3, the elements which make up a horizontal curve are defined. From this diagram, we can see that the curve begins at a point designated as the PC or *Point of Curvature*. This represents the first tangent point on the alignment. The second and last tangent point is known as the PT or *Point of Tangency*. Which is *first* and *last* is determined by the direction of stationing (i.e., either increasing or decreasing) along the alignment. The angle formed by the intersection of the two tangents is known as the *interior angle*. This angle is also sometimes known as the *intersection angle*.

The curvature of a horizontal alignment can either be defined by its radius or the so-called *degree of curve*. The degree of curve is defined by the central angle which:

❑ Subtends a 100 ft arc
❑ Subtends a 100 ft chord

When the former is used, this is known as *arc definition* and the latter as *chord definition*. In highway design arc definition is the norm. The use of chord definition is predominately confined to the definition of railroad alignments and will not be covered in this text. With regard to arc definition, however, the degree of curve, *D*, is defined by the following expression:

> The use of chord definition is predominately confined to the definition of railroad alignments and will not be covered in this text.

$$D = \frac{5,729.58}{R}$$ (Eq. 5.1)

where D = degree of curve
R = radius of curve

Using basic trigonometry, it is possible to define the components of a horizontal curve by the following expressions:

$$T = R \cdot \tan(\Delta/2)$$ (Eq. 5.2)

$$E = R \cdot (\sec(\Delta/2) - 1)$$ (Eq. 5.3)

$$M = R \cdot (1 - \cos(\Delta/2))$$ (Eq. 5.4)

$$C = 2R \cdot (\sin(\Delta/2)) = 2T \cdot (\cos(\Delta/2))$$ (Eq. 5.5)

$$LC = 100 \cdot \Delta/D$$ (Eq. 5.6)

For a description of the variables used in Equations 5.2 through 5.6, consult the sidebar accompanying Figure 5.3. While in many instances a horizontal alignment will coincide with the centerline of the roadway, in certain instances it may be offset from the centerline.

2. Vertical Alignment. A vertical alignment is the path which defines the geometry of a highway in elevation. A vertical alignment can be represented by a single tangent at a given grade, a vertical curve, or a combination thereof. Although a vertical curve can be represented by a circular curve, in the United States the common practice is to use a parabolic curve. Figure 5.4 shows a typical vertical curve and its constituent elements. A vertical alignment is married to a corresponding horizontal alignment with each alignment tied together by a common stationing.

A curve pointing up, as the one shown in Figure 5.4, is known as a *crest vertical curve*. If the curve points downward, it is known as a *sag vertical curve*. In highway bridge design, the vertical alignment of the overpass roadway, in conjunction with its horizontal alignment, is used to define elevations at key points on a structure. An example of this would be the elevation of bridge seats or the top of an abutment wingwall or backwall.

In addition to this, a vertical curve greatly affects the vertical clearance of the bridge (i.e., the minimum distance between the underside of the superstructure and the feature crossed). As stated earlier in Section 1.1.1, Part 4, AASHTO specifies an absolute minimum clearance of 14 ft (4.27 m) and design clearance of 16 ft (4.88 m). The stopping sight distance is another feature controlled by the vertical alignment of a roadway which is of importance to highways in general and bridges in particular. Especially for structures located on crest vertical curves, the stopping sight distance becomes a critical variable in ensuring safety for traffic passing over a structure.

An important variable in determining the properties of a parabolic vertical curve is the *rate of grade change* per station which is defined by the following expression:

$$r = \frac{g_2 - g_1}{L} \qquad \text{(Eq. 5.7)}$$

where g_1 = grade from which stationing starts, percent
g_2 = grade toward direction of stationing, percent
L = vertical curve length, stations

> **A**lthough a vertical curve can be represented by a circular curve, in the United States the common practice is to use a parabolic curve.

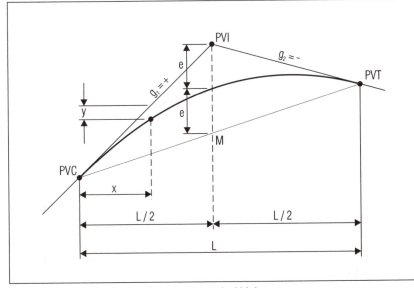

Figure 5.4 Constituent elements of a vertical highway curve.

In Equation 5.7, if the vertical curve length were 700 ft, the value of L used in the expression would be 7. Also note that the grades are entered into the equation in percents so that if a grade was equal to 2.25 percent, it would be entered into the expression as 2.25 *not* 0.0225. Grades that slope downward are negative (like g_2 in Figure 5.4) and those that slope upward are positive (like g_1 in Figure 5.4).

Another key point on a vertical curve is the so called *turning point*. The turning point represents the location of minimum or maximum elevation on a vertical curve. To determine the location (i.e., station value) of the turning point the following expression is used:

$$x_{TP} = \frac{-g_1}{r}$$

(Eq. 5.8)

where g_1 = grade from which stationing starts, percent
r = rate of grade change

> **T**he turning point represents the location of minimum or maximum elevation on a vertical curve.

In Figure 5.4, we see that the middle ordinate distance, e, is defined as the vertical distance from the PVI (Point of Vertical Intersection) to the vertical curve below. This distance is given as:

$$e = \frac{(g_1 - g_2) \cdot L}{8}$$

(Eq. 5.9)

where g_1 = grade from which stationing starts, percent
g_2 = grade toward direction of stationing, percent
L = vertical curve length, stations

Using basic trigonometry, it is also possible to determine the elevation at any point along the curve. Given a point x referenced from the start of the vertical curve (PVC) in stations, the elevation on the curve at that point is given by:

$$EL_x = \left(\frac{r}{2}\right) \cdot x^2 + g_1 x + EL_{PVC}$$

(Eq. 5.10)

where EL_x = elevation at point x on curve, ft
g_1 = grade from which stationing starts, percent
EL_{PVC} = elevation at start of curve, ft
r = rate of grade change

> **I**n today's design environment, horizontal and vertical alignment problems are generally solved using computer aided methods ...

Design Example 5.1 provides a short presentation of some of the principles outlined above. In this particular example, a new bridge is being located above a new highway. The designer is asked to define an appropriate vertical curve for the underpass roadway.

In today's design environment, horizontal and vertical alignment problems are generally solved using computer aided methods, either in the form of batch oriented programs or interactive graphic systems. As we will

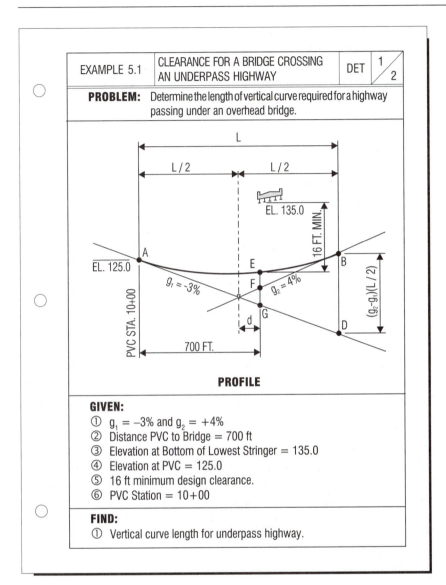

| EXAMPLE 5.1 | CLEARANCE FOR A BRIDGE CROSSING AN UNDERPASS HIGHWAY | DET | 1 / 2 |

PROBLEM: Determine the length of vertical curve required for a highway passing under an overhead bridge.

PROFILE

GIVEN:
① $g_1 = -3\%$ and $g_2 = +4\%$
② Distance PVC to Bridge = 700 ft
③ Elevation at Bottom of Lowest Stringer = 135.0
④ Elevation at PVC = 125.0
⑤ 16 ft minimum design clearance.
⑥ PVC Station = 10+00

FIND:
① Vertical curve length for underpass highway.

DESIGN EXAMPLE 5.1
GIVEN PARAMETERS

In this example, we are presented with a structure to be placed over a new highway. Given a specified minimum clearance of 16 ft, we are asked to determine the required length of vertical curve for the underpass alignment.

We are given the elevation and station of the vertical alignment's PVC. We also know that the low point on the bridge is 700 ft from the PVC of the underpass vertical curve. The elevation of the low point on the bridge superstructure is also known.

The forward and back grades for the underpass alignment are given and cannot be changed.

The main purpose of this example is to demonstrate some of the manual techniques utilized in computing vertical alignment properties. As we will see, the required curve length is eventually computed using similar triangles. Problems of this nature, in today's design environment, are easily solved using computer aided techniques. The manual solution of such problems, however, can be readily found in professional engineering examinations.

see in the section discussing contract documents, it is possible to make the step from engineering design of vertical alignments and other bridge related design information (in a computer environment) to the final details and drawings.

3. Stopping Sight Distance. A key parameter which determines the safety of any highway is the stopping sight distance. Figure 5.5 shows the parameters governing the definition of stopping sight distance for a crest vertical curve. As its name would imply, the stopping sight distance is the length of roadway needed between a vehicle and an arbitrary object (at some point down the road) which allows a driver to safely stop a vehicle before reaching the obstruction. This is not to be confused with *sight distance* in general, which is simply the "length of roadway ahead visible to the driver" [Ref. 5.2].

AASHTO specifies that the minimum stopping sight distance should be computed using a height of eye (i.e., driver eye height) of 3.50 ft (1.0 m) and a height of object (i.e., obstruction in roadway) of 2.0 ft (600 mm) [Ref. 5.2]. The stopping sight distance is actually the sum of two distances. These distances are defined as the travelling distance required for:

❏ The driver to apply the brakes
❏ The vehicle to come to a complete stop after the brakes are applied

The first parameter is quantified by the *brake reaction time* and the latter by the *braking distance*. AASHTO provides a table of stopping sight distances based on this approach to defining stopping sight distance. The values are presented in Table 5.1. The stopping sight distances provided in Table 5.1 are for various design speeds and wet pavement conditions. Actual and rounded design values are given.

A general rule of thumb is that longer vertical curve lengths produce larger stopping sight distances. Quite naturally, this will have an impact on the design of a highway bridge, particularly those located on relatively short vertical curves. A variety of factors will influence the final profile established for the bridge, which can range from the camber of primary members to the thickness of the wearing surface provided. When rehabilitating a bridge, the stopping sight distance can become a concern, especially for older structures which are being brought up to current specifications. In many instances there may simply be very little that the design team can do to boost the stopping sight distance on a structure. In such a situation, the structure will have to be posted with a reduced speed limit which corresponds to the allowable value which the bridge can support.

In new bridge projects or major rehabilitations, where the designers have room to adjust the vertical alignments of the roads involved, an effort can be made to increase the length of vertical curve to help increase

A general rule of thumb is that longer vertical curve lengths produce larger stopping sight distances.

When rehabilitating a bridge, the stopping sight distance can become a concern, especially for older structures which are being brought up to current specifications.

STOPPING SIGHT DIS-TANCE criteria vary depending on whether the vertical curve is a crest or sag curve. The situation presented in Figure 5.5 is for a crest vertical curve. Two key geometric criteria are the height of the driver's eye, represented by the variable H₁, and the height of an object, represented by the variable H₂. The magnitude of the stopping sight distance will vary depending on the speed for which the road is designed. Obviously, the faster a vehicle is traveling, the larger the stopping sight distance required. Current AASHTO criteria places the driver's eye at 3.5 ft and the height of roadway object at only 2.0 ft.

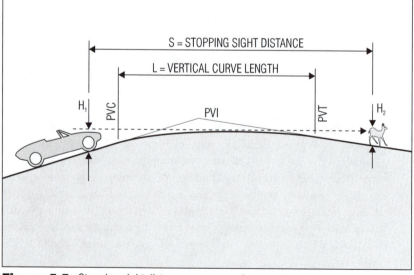
Figure 5.5 Stopping sight distance parameters for a crest vertical curve.

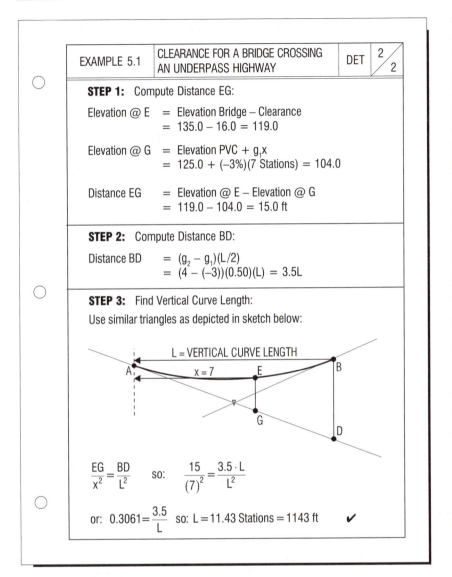

EXAMPLE 5.1	CLEARANCE FOR A BRIDGE CROSSING AN UNDERPASS HIGHWAY	DET	2/2

STEP 1: Compute Distance EG:

Elevation @ E = Elevation Bridge − Clearance
= 135.0 − 16.0 = 119.0

Elevation @ G = Elevation PVC + $g_1 x$
= 125.0 + (−3%)(7 Stations) = 104.0

Distance EG = Elevation @ E − Elevation @ G
= 119.0 − 104.0 = 15.0 ft

STEP 2: Compute Distance BD:

Distance BD = $(g_2 − g_1)(L/2)$
= (4 − (−3))(0.50)(L) = 3.5L

STEP 3: Find Vertical Curve Length:

Use similar triangles as depicted in sketch below:

L = VERTICAL CURVE LENGTH

x = 7

$$\frac{EG}{x^2} = \frac{BD}{L^2} \quad \text{so:} \quad \frac{15}{(7)^2} = \frac{3.5 \cdot L}{L^2}$$

or: $0.3061 = \dfrac{3.5}{L}$ so: L = 11.43 Stations = 1143 ft ✔

DESIGN EXAMPLE 5.1
STEP 1: COMPUTE DISTANCE FROM E TO G

From the illustration at the bottom of the accompanying calculation sheet, we see that we will need to determine the two vertical legs of similar triangles: EG and BD. To compute the first we simple take the difference in elevations at each point. The elevation of the first point, E, is simply the elevation at the bottom of the super-structure minus the design clearance; both of which were given. The elevation at point G is found by proceeding from the PVC elevation straight along the tangent grade of -3 percent.

STEP 2: COMPUTE DISTANCE FROM B TO D

The distance from the PVT of a vertical alignment to the first tangent is easily computed using the equation which was provided in the illustration on Calculation Sheet 1. When computing values, remember to keep a consistent unit of measure. In the text and this design example we utilize stations not feet. As is the case when dealing with any units, consistency is the key to eliminating potential error.

Once the two distances are known, then it is a simple matter to determine the required vertical curve length.

stopping sight distance. This adjustment, however, does not come without an associated price.

Constructing very long vertical curves, naturally, can prove costly in many situations. Therefore, a balance must be reached which reconciles economy with safety. For *crest* vertical curves, AASHTO provides the following expressions for determining the minimum length of crest vertical curve based on a required sight distance:

$$L_{min} = \frac{A \cdot S^2}{100 \cdot \left(\sqrt{2 \cdot H_1} + \sqrt{2 \cdot H_2}\right)^2} \quad \text{for } S \leq L \qquad \text{(Eq. 5.11)}$$

and
$$L_{min} = 2S - \frac{200 \cdot \left(\sqrt{H_1} + \sqrt{H_2}\right)^2}{A} \quad \text{for } S > L \qquad \text{(Eq. 5.12)}$$

Au: Tables have been renumbered in order to text citation, ok.

In Equations 5.11 and 5.12, the variable A represents the algebraic difference in grades of the vertical curve in percent. When the height of the eye is taken as 3.5 ft and the height of the object as 2 ft, as when computing the *stopping* sight distance, these expressions become:

$$L_{min} = \frac{AS^2}{2,158} \quad \text{for } S < L \qquad \text{(Eq. 5.13)}$$

and

$$L_{min} = 2S - \frac{2,158}{A} \quad \text{for } S > L \qquad \text{(Eq. 5.14)}$$

AASHTO offers a simple and straightforward method for establishing design controls for vertical curves based on stopping sight distance. Tables 5.2 and 5.3 present K values for crest and sag curves, respectively. This K term is defined as the ratio of:

$$K = \frac{L}{A} \qquad \text{(Eq. 5.15)}$$

Design Speed, mph	Brake Reaction		Deceleration Rate, ft/s²	Braking Distance on Level, ft	Stopping Sight Distance	
	Time, sec	Distance, ft			Computed, ft	Rounded for Design, ft
20	2.5	73.5	11.2	38.4	111.9	115
25	2.5	91.9	11.2	60.0	151.9	155
30	2.5	110.3	11.2	86.4	196.7	200
35	2.5	128.6	11.2	117.6	246.2	250
40	2.5	147.0	11.2	153.6	300.6	305
45	2.5	165.4	11.2	194.4	359.8	360
50	2.5	183.8	11.2	240.0	423.8	425
55	2.5	202.1	11.2	290.3	492.4	495
60	2.5	220.5	11.2	345.5	566.0	570
65	2.5	238.9	11.2	405.5	644.4	645
70	2.5	257.3	11.2	470.3	727.6	730

Table 5.1 Stopping Sight Distance Values for Various Design Speeds *(Adapted from Ref. 5.2.)*

where L = vertical curve length, ft
A = algebraic difference in grades, percent
S = sight distance, ft

This value is particularly useful in determining the horizontal distance from the PVC of a vertical curve to its turning point (i.e., maximum point on a crest curve and minimum on a sag). To put it another way, the point where the slope is zero occurs at a distance from the PVC which is equal to K times the approach gradient [Ref. 5.2].

For a sag vertical curve, the length may also be controlled by headlight sight distance or by passenger comfort. Therefore, a longer curve may be required than the stop sight distance required in Table 5.2. Refer to Table 5.3 for details.

4. Roadway Width. Another highway related safety concern is the width of the roadway which a bridge carries. A prime location for accidents on a bridge is at the structure's approaches where, in many cases, the width of the highway narrows. One obvious way to enhance safety is to provide adequate width for the traffic lanes as they come onto a bridge. AASHTO provides various criteria governing the minimum roadway width of a bridge. These widths depend on the type of loading the structure is

> A prime location for accidents on a bridge is at the structure's approaches where, in many cases, the width of the highway narrows.

Design Speed, mph	Stopping Sight Distance, ft	Rate of Vertical Curvature, K (length (ft) per percent of A)	
		Computed	Rounded for Design
20	115	6.1	7
25	155	11.1	12
30	200	18.5	19
3	250	29.0	29
40	305	43.1	44
45	360	60.1	61
50	425	83.7	84
55	495	113.5	114
60	570	150.6	151
65	645	192.8	193
70	730	246.9	247

Table 5.2 Design Controls for Crest and Sag Vertical Curves Based on Stopping Sight Distance *(Adapted from Ref. 5.2.)*

subjected to (e.g., HS20, HS15) and the amount of traffic passing over the structure (i.e., ADT, DHV).

For new and reconstructed bridges, the values for various traffic conditions are presented in Table 5.4. For bridges over 100 feet in length, and having design volume over 2000 vehicles per day, the travelled way width plus 3 feet on each side may be used as the minimum bridge width. For existing bridges with load restrictions of HS15, narrower bridge widths are allowed by AASHTO.

Quite naturally, there will be some debate as to what exactly constitutes a "narrow bridge." The criteria applied to define narrowness must vary depending on whether the bridge is designed to carry one or two lanes. To define narrowness, one study used the following criteria [Ref. 5.4]:

❑ For one lane a total width of 18 ft (5.5 m) or less and
❑ For two lanes, a combined total width of 24 ft (7.3 m) or less.

This particular study came to the conclusion that bridges "are more dangerous than the highway system as a whole, and narrow bridges can be a safety problem" [Ref. 5.4]. There was, however, no strong correlation made between accidents and any particular physical feature at the bridge site. As with any enhancement to a bridge constructed during rehabilitation, there has to be a trade-off between functionality and cost considerations. Widening of a structure or adjustment of an approach

Design Speed, mph	Stopping Sight Distance, ft	Rate of Vertical Curvature, K (length (ft) per percent of A)	
		Computed	Rounded for Design
20	115	16.5	17
25	155	25.5	26
30	200	36.4	37
35	250	49.0	49
40	305	63.4	64
45	360	78.1	79
50	425	95.7	96
55	495	114.9	115
60	570	135.7	136
65	645	156.5	157
70	730	180.3	181

Table 5.3 Design Controls for Sag Vertical Curves *(Adapted from Ref. 5.2.)*

alignment is by no means an inexpensive enterprise. A first goal should be to at least meet the minimum width requirements put forth by AASHTO and outlined in Table 5.4.

In addition to providing adequate width, a bridge must be equipped with appropriate traffic protection devices at the approach-bridge interface. This is typically accomplished through use of a transition which connects the approach protective system with the bridge system. This *protective system* could consist of guard railing, solid barrier, or a combination thereof. Most transportation departments maintain their own standards with regard to the specific form of transition which must be incorporated into the final design.

It has been found that impacts at the ends of bridge railings and parapets represent the most severe type of bridge-related accident [Ref. 5.4]. If any alteration is made to either the bridge or approach railing or barrier systems, then the other should also be upgraded at the same time to ensure a smooth transition of the protective system from approach to bridge.

5.1.2 Maintenance of Traffic

To some engineers the term *maintenance of traffic* may imply simply throwing up some signs and traffic cones. In this age of bridge rehabilitation, however, the proper design and planning for maintenance of traffic is a crucial aspect of the design process. Not only is maintenance of traffic one of the more important issues in a rehabilitation design, it is also one of the more expensive ones. It is not uncommon for transportation departments to develop two alternates for a design: one in which the bridge is closed to traffic completely, and another where traffic is maintained over the bridge through the use of *staged construction*.

Staged construction is a process where one portion of a bridge is closed to traffic and worked on while the other remains open. In general, staged construction imposes the following limitations:

❑ Traffic lanes must be constricted.
❑ Vehicle speed may be reduced.
❑ Protective devices need to be installed to protect workers.
❑ A construction joint must be placed parallel to the longitudinal centerline of the structure.
❑ Shoring may be required for cantilevered elements.
❑ Design and construction costs increase.

DID YOU KNOW

THAT in the early part of the 1970's, bridge-related accidents in the States of Virginia and Kentucky not only represented a high percentage of all accidents, but also accounted for a disproportionate number of fatalities and injuries? Narrow bridges are often a prime culprit in these accidents [Ref. 5.4].

In addition to providing adequate width, a bridge must be equipped with appropriate traffic protection devices at the approach-bridge interface.

In this age of bridge rehabilitation ... the proper design and planning for maintenance of traffic is a crucial aspect of the design process.

Design Volume veh/day	Roadway Width of Bridge
Under 400	Width of traveled way plus 2 ft each side
400 – 2000	Width of traveled way plus 3 ft each side
Over 2000	Approach roadway width

Table 5.4 Minimum Roadway Widths for Bridges *(Adapted from Ref. 5.2.)*

With regard to the latter item, the design of a bridge which is staged is significantly more complicated than one which is not. It is possible to even make the statement that design of a staged bridge is a little like conducting the design of two bridges. The detailing of everything from concrete decks to abutment backwalls is conducted in pairs; one set for the first stage and another for the second. In certain cases, there may be even more than two stages used!

In some instances, it may even be necessary to maintain traffic other than motor vehicles over (and under) a structure. On the right side of Figure 5.6, the presence of a pedestrian walkway is visible. Other situations may call for the maintenance of railroad or marine traffic. This brings to light that bridge rehabilitation also impacts underpass traffic as well. Depending on the geometry of the structure, extensive work to substructure components can require maintenance of traffic operations as intense as those on the overpass.

In developing a complete traffic control plan, the bridge design team needs to shed their focus on the particular confines of the bridge site and look beyond each approach several hundred feet. Vehicles approaching a bridge construction site need to be alerted to the presence of a work site ahead and a corresponding reduction in speed. Also, it is highly likely that the path of the oncoming vehicles will be altered, switching them from the normal alignment of the traffic lane, to one adjusted for the staged construction. All of this information must be communicated with proper signing located at appropriate distances from each approach on the overpass, and to each side of the bridge on the underpass. In addition to signage, other safety devices, like flashing arrow boards (see Figure 3.57) are also used. As traffic closes in on the work site, signage is supplemented with traffic cones and barrels. Even closer, more robust protective devices such as break-away barricades, and precast Jersey barriers are provided. The precast concrete

> **I**n developing a complete traffic control plan, the bridge design team needs to shed their focus on the particular confines of the bridge site and look beyond each approach several hundred feet.

PROPER MAINTENANCE of traffic at a bridge construction or rehabilitation site is a critical aspect of the design process which should not be treated lightly by the designers. Particularly in staged construction, like that shown in Figure 5.6, maintaining traffic over one part of the bridge while work is performed on the other impacts the location of construction joints, reinforcing steel lap splices in the concrete deck, and a host of other details. The planning for maintenance of traffic in staged construction must take place at the onset of design to ensure that adequate lane widths are maintained and any possible structural requirements (e.g., shoring of cantilevered slabs) is provided for.

Figure 5.6 Maintenance of traffic devices include drums and break-away barricades.

barriers should be bolted to the concrete deck to ensure the safety of the travelling motorists.

Obviously the most limiting factor in all of this is space. At times, it may even be necessary to bring traffic to a standstill, and allow one lane of traffic only to pass over the structure; simply because there is no room for anything else. On small, local roads this can usually be done without much difficulty. On major highways, however, where motorists are used to traveling at 55 mph (and often much faster) the necessity of providing adequate signing and protection for workers is paramount.

Most transportation departments provide their own in-house standards for traffic control plans. These plans generally specify:

- ❏ Appropriate signing
- ❏ Setback distances from the work site
- ❏ Appropriate lane widths depending on the design speed

In many instances, the design team will be required to develop a new, albeit temporary, horizontal alignment which is used to carry traffic over the portion of the structure which remains open. In doing so, the appropriate AASHTO criteria must be utilized *for the reduced speed* at the project site. If significant changes are being made to the vertical alignment of the structure, the change in elevation must be accounted for so that a smooth transition is made from the approach. Like the transitional horizontal alignment mentioned above, this adjustment is usually temporary in nature. To provide for extra lane width, it may be necessary to utilize a portion of the shoulder (if one is present). In such an event, the designers should ensure that the shoulder is sufficiently stabilized to support the traffic. When properly designed, a traffic control plan will provide for safety to both workers and motorists. If not given adequate attention, however, maintenance of traffic can become a headache that few can afford.

5.2 CONTRACT DOCUMENTS

The contract documents of any engineering project act as the manuscript detailing the design team's findings. No matter how good the design, final plans which do not accurately and effectively convey the final engineering design can potentially lead to a poorly constructed project. For a highway bridge, be it a new structure or an existing one undergoing rehabilitation, the preparation of the final contract documents is a time consuming affair. A common acronym used for contract documents is that of PS&E, which translates into a three volume submission of:

- ❏ Plans
- ❏ Specifications
- ❏ Estimate

Rather than being a discrete operation which takes place after an engineering team has finished its design, the preparation of contract documents runs parallel with the design effort. If this preparation is not properly

> Rather than being a discrete operation which takes place after an engineering team has finished its design, the preparation of contract documents runs parallel with the design effort.

managed, a bridge design project can quickly become a chaotic and expensive enterprise.

Although the final goal in a bridge design project is to submit contract documents, which will eventually lead to the construction and implementation of the engineer's design, it is incorrect to view the final PS&E submission as an end in and of itself. Contract documents, like a design, grow in stages throughout the course of design as a result of intermediate submissions. The discussion below outlines the various phases of submission of contract documents and provides an overview of some of the latest trends and techniques available for producing contract documents, most of which are computer related.

5.2.1 Design Submissions

Obviously for a project of substantial size, a design team is not going to simply turn over a set of plans after completing work. Sometimes, especially in text books, it is easy to forget that designs are performed for *someone else,* not merely as an exercise to solve some abstract problem. In the bridge design world this "someone else" is generally a transportation department (owner). When a project begins, there is (hopefully) a general consensus on project scope and the nature of work to be done. This consensus, however, is not the final word on what will eventually result from an engineering design.

Engineering design is an iterative process and therefore requires constant refinement from the onset of design to its eventual conclusion. Therefore, the design process itself demands several check points where an owner and designer can discuss the progress of work and make decisions which further refine and define the design. Perhaps an owner originally intended to utilize a certain type of pier but the designer later determines that the desired form of pier is not feasible. Somehow this change in scope has to be communicated and the vehicle used to communicate the engineer's thoughts are interim submissions.

Naturally, these submissions have to be scheduled at logical points in the design process. While many transportation departments maintain their own standards as to when and how design submissions should take place, a generally accepted format is to make four separate submissions which are designated by the following:

- ❑ Alternative Study
- ❑ Preliminary
- ❑ Advanced detail
- ❑ Final design

Discussed below is the level of detail which goes into each submission and what products should be produced by the design team at a given stage in the design process.

1. Alternative Study. Before any design is started, the design team usually first performs an engineering study that focus on selecting the best option for the proposed structure. Typically three alternatives are studied.

Before any design is started, the design team usually first performs an engineering study that focus on selecting the best option for the proposed structure. Typically three alternatives are studied.

Depending on the individual situation, different materials (i.e., steel, concrete), different type of structures (i.e., slab-on-girder, box-girder, adjacent slab), different span arrangements (i.e., single span bridge, three-span bridge), or combination of these mentioned, may be chosen as alternatives. Based on the engineer's judgment and the owner's preference, the three best options are selected for the detailed study.

Preliminary structural analyses are then performed for each alternative. If the bridge is over a stream, a hydrological and hydraulic study also needs to be performed to make sure that the proposed bridges will have sufficient opening so that they will not cause flooding on the upstream. The structural analyses should provide enough information such as the sizes of the preliminary members. Normally, a typical cross-section for each bridge alternative is provided in the report, and a preliminary cost estimate is also provided for each alternative. The cost estimates are based on the previous project costs of the same material and of the similar structural type and size.

The most important part of the study is to offer recommendations on which alternative should be chosen for the final design. That is usually done using a decision matrix, taking consideration of the major factors that have significant impact on the project. These factors include:

- ❏ Initial construction cost
- ❏ Maintenance
- ❏ Constructability
- ❏ Environmental impact
- ❏ Aesthetics

How these factors are weighted depends on the location and the importance of the bridge. For the vast majority of highway bridges, the initial construction cost should be weighted over 50%, followed by maintenance. The most cost-effective option usually wins. For a major bridge, especially in a urban setting, engineers may give more weight to aesthetics and constructability.

The final deliverable (the product) of the study is an engineering report. Once the owner approves the recommendations, the recommended option will be advanced to the second phase of the design process.

2. Preliminary Submission. A preliminary design should function like the working lines in an artist's painting. A preliminary submission is used to flesh out the design process, provide a schematic to the owner on how the engineer sees the problems associated with the design, and describe intended measures to be taken in order to complete the design. All of this may sound well and good, but the preliminary submission of any engineering project can often be one of the most difficult.

To the new engineer, this may seem somewhat strange. After all, if the preliminary submission is only a schematic, how severe could the problems be at this early stage? The answer to this question is that problems arise from preliminary submissions because they are extremely difficult to review.

> **A** preliminary design should function like the working lines in an artist's painting.

A typical preliminary submission of a bridge design project consists of the following products:

❏ A short set of plans (typically no more than four or five sheets)
❏ A preliminary engineer's estimate of project costs

It is relatively straightforward to look at a set of *final* plans and follow the proposed work to be done. Preliminary plans, however, are a cartoon of what the final plans will look like. This means that there are a lot of things left out. The absence of material, in and of itself, often leads to questions.

For engineers placed in the position of reviewing preliminary plans, it is important to recognize that much of the real design work has yet to be done. The preliminary submission should focus on the scope of work for which design measures are to be taken *and nothing else.* At the preliminary stage of a project it is not important to see reinforcing in a pier if it has yet to be decided what type of pier is to be used in the first place. This may seem rather obvious, but engineers, by nature, like to see things in their completed form to understand all aspects of what it is that they are reviewing. The cost associated with providing this, however, places an extreme burden on the designer.

The request to see an overabundance of information in preliminary submissions is not a feature of bridge or transportation projects alone. The preliminary submission checklist for site development projects in many municipalities looks more like a final design submission than a preliminary one. Both owner and designer, however, have to view the preliminary submission as a chance to set the design process down a common road. Serious problems can arise if this is not achieved at the end of the preliminary submission stage.

Because almost all preliminary plans are prepared through the use of Computer Aided Design and Drafting (CADD) techniques, there is no need to view the preliminary plans as "disposable." By using a careful and thoughtful CADD approach, the preliminary plans can lay the foundation for the final plans to follow. The preliminary plans should include:

❏ Bridge plan, elevation and typical section
❏ General notes
❏ Vertical and horizontal roadway profile
❏ Type of foundation
❏ Type of abutment and pier

The preliminary estimate, like the plans, is a rough sketch of the final costs associated with the bridge. While specific construction item prices are used to develop the final estimate, preliminary estimates are best developed using costs from previous projects on a more gross scale. It is a good idea to include a certain amount for contingencies to cover items missed or ignored when developing the estimate.

A geotechnical report, and a hydrological and hydraulic report should also be included as a part of this submission.

> **P**reliminary plans, however, are a cartoon of what the final plans will look like. This means that there are a lot of things left out. The absence of material, in and of itself, often leads to questions.

3. Advanced Detail Submission. Once the preliminary submission has been accepted by the owner, work can begin on preparation of the advanced detail submission. At the advanced detail stage, the plans are almost at the level of being ready to be used in the field. The design and detailing of the major components of the structure have been, by the end of this stage, completed and transferred to the drawings. Ancillary (although essential) information such as reinforcing bar schedules and traffic control plans may or may not be included with this submission.

We have spoken extensively on the owner's need to review preliminary plans as preliminary, not final plans. Likewise, it is important for the design engineers to respect the process as well. At times, designers may submit plans that look more like advanced detail plans rather than preliminary and are then faced with major reworking of the drawings when a change has to be made.

The function of the advanced detail submission is to provide the owner with a hard look at what the final product is going to look like. It is at this stage that detail oriented problems are usually addressed. An example of this would be correcting of a drainage appurtenance or selection of a different expansion joint seal. It is also not at all uncommon for more significant changes to take place at this stage and designers should make allowances for such alterations in their schedules. In general, however, the advanced detail set of plans should look pretty much like the final plans in both shape and form. Although a detailed estimate is usually submitted at this stage along with the advanced detail plans, contract specifications may or may not be included.

> The function of the advanced detail submission is to provide the owner with a hard look at what the final product is going to look like. It is at this stage that detail oriented problems are usually addressed.

4. Final Submission. As its name would imply, the final submission is generally that: final. The submission of the plans is usually made on a form of permanent medium (e.g., Mylar) and is accompanied by a final estimate with associated workup sheets, and detailed contract specifications. Design calculation sheets may or may not be required to be submitted, but engineers should always keep a copy as a permanent record, and as a reference for the future design. With regard to design calculations, if computer software was used to perform the design, a copy of the input used and the associated output should also be included. Since the use of CADD in preparing plans is becoming so prevalent, many agencies are also requesting that the final plans be accompanied by the computer version on a CD or DVD.

5.2.2 Computer Aided Design and Drafting

In reviewing older texts, it is often humorous to read the sections describing the "latest advances" in computer technology to aid the profession. In the rapidly changing world of computer technology, texts can become obsolete just months after hitting the shelves. Two things that do not vary that much, however, are common sense and organization skills; and these are two of the most important ingredients to implementing a successful CADD operation.

For many years, designers shied away from using CADD in bridge design because of the extremely variable nature of highway bridges in general [Ref. 5.5]. Even in the relatively homogeneous world of a local state transportation network, no two bridges are alike. Since one of the principal advantages of

CADD is speed through repetition, and no two bridges are alike, why then should an engineering office use computer rather than manual methods?

Since the late 1980's, this argument has essentially become moot. The speed of today's computer hardware makes the skilled CADD technician several times faster than a manual draftsperson. Only 25 years ago, however, this statement could not be so easily made. While it now costs a relatively small amount of money to set up a single CADD workstation, the cost in 1985, for example, represented a significant amount of money, which could literally make or break an engineering firm.

Fast hardware and slick software, though, do not by themselves imply a successful implementation of CADD. Bridge design projects offer particular challenges which can only be addressed through use of common sense and organization.

Discussed below are some basic techniques which can be utilized to more effectively manage a bridge project through use of computer assisted methods. The goal of using any computer system is to maximize the inherent benefits of speed through repetition whenever and wherever possible.

> **F**ast hardware and slick software, though, do not by themselves imply a successful implementation of CADD.

> **O**ne of the most basic problems to befall any computerized operation is a disorganized method of storing data files on a computer's mass storage device.

1. **File Organization.** One of the most basic problems to befall any computerized operation is a disorganized method of storing data files on a computer's mass storage device (i.e., hard drive). Many engineers would laugh at the idea of dumping all of their drawings into a single flat file and labeling them as "Drawings." When it comes to storing computerized data, however, many take the same approach.

It is now a common practice to have all computers in an engineering office networked. All CADD files should be stored on the server, rather than individual personal computers, so that everybody working on the project have access to the files. That way also ensures that the files people have access to are the latest version. The worst thing could happen to the CADD file management is that different people make modifications to the same files saved on different computers, so that there are different versions of the "latest files" with the same file names.

In order to successfully use CADD in producing final drawings, however, a consistent and orderly naming convention must be implemented. The simplest approach is to adopt a sequential numbering system for all details (e.g., det-001, det-002, and so on). A separate index must be maintained identifying what each drawing file corresponds to. For miscellaneous details like expansion joints, appurtenances, and the like, this may be the only approach.

Major structural elements, such as abutments, decks, and piers can be stored a little differently. In a set of bridge plans, elements like these will appear in a multitude of locations. A sectional view of an abutment, for example, may be used in the detailing of reinforcing in the backwall of the abutment, excavation details, in the longitudinal section of the entire structure, and other places throughout the plans. In addition to this, if the detail is drawn to scale and the facilities are present within the CADD software used, it is also possible to retrieve quantities from the CADD generated geometry of the detail (e.g., area of backwall, area of pedestals). Some packages even have the capability of going from the graphic image of the element (e.g., pier elevation) to an analysis module (frame analysis program) to generate the design.

Therefore, since these major components can serve several different functions, they should be easily identifiable and stored as discrete, logical components, so that how the detail is defined is as important as what it is called. A logical way to break a bridge component down is according to *views*. By a view, we imply the orientation of the detail which is identified as either:

❑ Plan
❑ Elevation
❑ Section

A set of drawings for a bridge project is essentially used to describe a three dimensional structure in two dimensions. This is accomplished by presenting the various elements and components of a structure in one of the three views listed above. Therefore, in describing the major components, each one should have a representation in one of the three listed orientations. It should be noted that this approach is designed for conventional two-dimensional CADD systems and may not be applicable to more advanced three-dimensional modeling systems.

The next item used to describe the element is the name of the component the element is derived from. Recall that we describe a component as a major structural feature such as an abutment, deck, or pier. This list can be expanded to include major elements from a component which are typically depicted in one of the three views listed above. These include wingwalls, backwalls, and approach slabs to name only a few. Some

Short Name	Long Name	Description
abut_pln	abutment_plan	Plan view of backwall and pedestals.
abut_elv	abutment_elev	Elevation of backwall and pedestals.
abut_xsc	abutment_xscn	Cross section of backwall and footing.
brig_pln	bridge_plan	Plan view of entire bridge.
brig_elv	bridge_elev	Elevation of entire bridge.
brig_xsc	bridge_xscn	Cross section of entire bridge.
pier_pln	pier_plan	Plan view of pier.
pier_elv	pier_elev	Elevation of pier.
pier_xsc	pier_xscn	Cross section of pier
wing_pln	wingwall_plan	Plan view of abutment wingwall.
wing_elv	wingwall_elev	Elevation of abutment wingwall.
wing_xsc	wingwall_xscn	Cross section of abutment wingwall.

Table 5.5 Sample File Naming Convention for Geometric Source Files.

THE NAMING OF CADD files at first glance may seem somewhat innocuous. Proper organization of drawing files, however, can make the difference between a successful CADD implementation and a disastrous one. If everyone is left to his or her own devices, a plethora of naming conventions and storage schemes will be used, the impact of which is usually never fully appreciated until the time a submission is due. A sound file organization scheme also means proper use of the main advantage of CADD: speed through repetition. It should be the goal of any CADD shop to create a readily accessible library of details which can be accessed and used for everything from quantity workups, to design, to preparation of the final drawings. The naming convention shown in Table 5.5 offers one such approach. Note that the short file name column is for operating systems which place a limit on the number of characters in a filename.

sample names for drawings and their associated meanings are depicted in Table 5.5.

2. Geometric Source Files. So we see that to describe a major element in the bridge, we use a two-part name which indicates the view and the particular element being described. However, what exactly is in these drawing files? As mentioned above, each major component should be drawn to scale, meaning that the details should be generated at a scale of 1:1. This allows for distances, areas, and other geometric properties to be taken right off the screen without having to worry about applying scale factors (e.g., $1/4$ in = 1 ft). To ensure accuracy in generating the geometry of elements, CADD software which is capable of double precision accuracy is highly recommended.

> To ensure accuracy in generating the geometry of elements, CADD software which is capable of double precision accuracy is highly recommended.

These actual scale source files should also be free from annotation (i.e., notes, dimensioning, etc.). Since the major elements are referenced in so many different locations, the source files (as we will call them) act as a template upon which we can base the final, annotated details. Since we are using a 1:1 scale, the details in the source file can be transformed to any desired scale. Taking the abutment section example again, the scale used for a longitudinal scale will be much different than that used to detail backwall reinforcement. By maintaining one actual scale source file we can utilize the same template in two separate locations without having to "reinvent the wheel."

A tool which many CADD packages possess that greatly facilitates this process is called *parametric modeling*. Using this approach, a general model of the element is created whose dimensions are variable. This means a generic parametric model of a stub abutment can be created once, and for each project, the technician simply enters the height and depth of backwall, depth of footing, etc. and the generic shape will be drawn to the appropriate dimensions. Such a feature, quite naturally, greatly speeds the process of creating the base geometry of an element.

3. The Forgotten D in CADD. One of the worst things an engineering organization can do is to utilize CADD as an overglorified technical pen, by which we imply a process where the CADD system is employed to generate drawings through a pure brute force method. Each sheet is created one at a time in a process similar to manual methods. Such an approach fails to take advantage of the inherit benefits of CADD.

> One of the worst things an engineering organization can do is to utilize CADD as an overglorified technical pen.

In the discussion above we have touched upon only a few of the natural extensions of the geometric information which goes into the final drawings. Anyone who has had to sit down and compute the area of a complicated abutment geometry to determine the amount of sealer needed can testify to the tedious nature of the process. Designers and technicians alike need to be aware of the potential uses of the information they are dealing with in an effort to derive the maximum benefits from the CADD system.

We have only briefly touched on the design aspect of CADD which can appropriately be called "the forgotten D in CADD." For many people, CADD has become a misnomer for drafting only. True CADD, however, incorporates design as an essential aspect of the entire process. Under a true

CADD approach, design software should be capable of producing the majority of the drawing sheets *automatically*. If a structural analysis system is used to generate the size of column needed in a pier, its height, and required reinforcement it should also be capable of producing a graphic representation of this information. This detail will more than likely require refinement and editing, but the design software should be performing the majority of the work. Although drafting software has done much to bring automation to the forefront in the engineering world, it has also served to adversely diminish the importance of design software in the drawing preparation process.

4. Graphic Standards and Quality Control. Like the organization of details and drawings, the standards used in preparing the final drawings also need to be established *and rigorously enforced*. Items which require standardization are:

- ❏ Line thicknesses
- ❏ Text sizes
- ❏ Dimensioning criteria (arrow sizes, text offset, etc.)
- ❏ Annotation of notes

On most bridge projects of a significant size, several individuals will be involved in the preparation of the final drawings. Some may like big arrows, other smaller ones. If each is left to his or her own devices, individual tastes and preferences will permeate each detail, creating final drawing sheets which are dissimilar, unattractive, and difficult to follow.

Prior to beginning a project, standards should be documented and issued to all technicians working on the project. Periodic checks of work should be made to ensure that conformity with the standards exists. These checks should be conducted more frequently at the onset of the project and can taper off toward the middle. For established CADD departments, new individuals joining the staff should be monitored more closely.

This is not to say that standards should be cast in stone and never revised. On the contrary, there is always room for improvement and enhancement in the preparation of contract documents; however, it should not take place in the middle of a project. A key to ensuring that standards are adhered to is to document them in written form. Each technician should be provided with a key that describes all pertinent graphic standards so that there is little room left for doubt. It will be difficult to envision all possible permutations when first developing this key, so it should be updated from time to time.

One problem associated with CADD is the ability of errors to propagate throughout a set of drawings. We have already mentioned the advantages of speed through repetition. A CADD department must always be on guard, however, for error through repetition. Using the abutment backwall section as an example again, if the source geometry file is incorrect, then it will be wrong everywhere it has been referenced in the drawings. Therefore, it is essential that quality control procedures be implemented to catch potentially far-reaching errors at the beginning rather than end of a project.

> We have already mentioned the advantages of speed through repetition. A CADD department must always be on guard, however, for error through repetition.

Check plots of all major geometric components should be made with dimensions scaled by hand to ensure accuracy. As the project progresses, check plots are also beneficial to catch potential annotation problems as they happen. This periodic checking "spreads the pain" so to speak, and provides for a more fluid drawing preparation process. A helpful tool which can be used to achieve this level of quality control is to supplement submissions to the owner with in-house submission dates, giving everyone a deadline to meet. This will ensure that the design team members themselves are pleased with quality of work.

5.2.3 Conclusions

From the above, it should be evident that the preparation of contract documents is not a trivial affair. Indeed, an entire volume could be written on this process alone. The above has been offered, however, as a guide to the potential pitfalls that may occur during this crucial part of a bridge design project. As engineers, we tend to focus so intently on the design aspect of our work that we can easily lose sight of the management component. Because we are trained to design, our natural impulse is to become mired within the design, which inevitably leads to losing sight of the overall picture. Engineers need to produce a set of documents that will lead to the eventual construction of the project. It is always nice to know that a column can sustain a certain amount of loading, but if the column is never built there is not much point to the analysis.

With the advent and proliferation of CADD systems in the design environment, the traditional methods of producing contract documents has changed considerably in some areas, and not so much in others. Maintaining graphic standards, for example, is not a new idea. Whether a drawing is generated by hand or with a computer, consistency must still be maintained. As mentioned at the beginning of this section, most of the information provided above is more common sense than anything else. Common sense, however, is a valuable commodity when performing the design of a highway bridge.

The design of a structure has also undergone extensive changes in the past thirty years. It was mentioned earlier in the text that many designers avoided continuous span structures because of the complexity involved in the analysis. It is difficult for today's engineers to understand a time when a mechanical calculator was a luxury. In fact, when the word "calculator" was used by the engineers who designed many of the bridges in our infrastructure, it was in reference to a technician who sat at the side of a designer crunching out calculations by hand and with log tables.

Today the use of design software in the workplace is not only the fact but also a necessity. In preparing contract documents, it is essential that a *paper trail* be maintained of all computer derived solutions and made part of the final documentation. It is all too easy to accept computer generated analysis as an "answer" that requires no justification. We have already touched upon the importance of augmenting computer calculations with a hand check. This does not mean that the entire design needs to be completed twice. It does mean, however, that certain key parameters of the design should be checked to ensure that answers are in the right ballpark. These hand checks should also be

> In fact, when the word "calculator" was used by the engineers who designed many of the bridges in our infrastructure, it was in reference to a technician who sat at the side of a designer crunching out calculations by hand ...

incorporated into the final analysis documents. This can make for an imposing document when completed, but it is all part of the final record of the design process.

It should also be noted that many transportation departments maintain their own preferences on all of the issues discussed in this section. Whether it is the size of arrowheads on a dimension or the information to be included in the final design submission, each owner has their own standards which a designer is obliged to comply with. As we have stated all along, with proper organization and common sense, the preparation of contract documents will lead to the construction of a lasting project.

5.3 BRIDGE MANAGEMENT SYSTEMS

Throughout the course of this text we have discussed the nature of highway bridges, the allocation of funds for their construction, the design of their major components, and preparation of the final contract documents which lead to their construction. In addition to these topics, we have also covered the important issues of bridge maintenance and rehabilitation as they pertain to the bridge as a whole and specific elements. The focus, however, has always been on the individual bridge. We have, though, consistently mentioned that the highway bridge is but one component itself in an expansive transportation network. The task of dealing with hundreds and even thousands of highway bridges at once is one which, over the past decade, has gained increased prominence and importance.

In essence, this problem of coping with deficient bridges is one of *management*. How does an owner manage a host of structures in a network given the omnipresent restrictions of a limited availability of finances and resources? It is one thing to say that a certain bridge's piers are in bad shape and another one has a poor deck, but if funds are only available to fix one or the other, which one should be rehabilitated first? If a group of certain bridges all have bearings in deteriorated condition, why has this deterioration taken place? Is it because of faulty bearings? Maybe a certain type of expansion joint above the bearings is especially prone to failure? These are all questions which maintenance personnel at transportation departments ask. They are just samples of the type of questions that are supposed to be answered by a Bridge Management System (BMS).

In the present environment a BMS is almost always taken to mean a computerized management system which is used to track the condition of a group of bridges in a highway network and assist in the determination of remedial measures to be taken. A BMS, however, does not necessarily have to be a computer based system. To be sure, when dealing with thousands of bridges, the practical management of such a massive amount of data demands computer assisted methods. This, however, belies the fact that transportation departments have had Bridge Management Systems in place for a number of years, even if they were not called that. A BMS is nothing more than an organizational and decision assisting system. Whether that system is based on 3" × 5" index cards and monthly meetings or through the use of a relational database system, it is still a BMS. In recent years, with the bridges that were born out of the development of the U.S. Interstate system reaching fifty years in age,

> **❝**The traveling public expects bridges, a vital segment of the U. S. surface transportation system, to be unfailingly safe and durable.**❞**
>
> CHARLES F. GALAMBOS
> [Ref. 5.6]

> **T**his, however, belies the fact that transportation departments have had Bridge Management Systems in place for a number of years, even if they were not called that.

the need for quickly and efficiently managing the maintenance and rehabilitation of highway bridges has increased dramatically.

Although much work has been performed in developing working, computerized BMSs, there is still a great deal that remains to be done toward maximizing the potential usefulness of these systems. In this section we will offer a short background on the basic parameters which define what a BMS needs to address, some of the major difficulties associated with developing a working and *accurate* system, and lastly the potential link of such systems to the design phase of a bridge project. Since the focus of a BMS is typically on maintenance, this last important application of BMS is often forgotten.

5.3.1 Background and History

The difficulties associated with bridge management in the United States can be traced back to the development of the U.S. Interstate. The construction of major portions of the Interstate at such a rapid pace resulted in a majority of highway bridges being built in roughly the same era. While this had the effect of spurring an economic boom through readily accessible transportation from one coast to the other, it has also resulted in many bridges growing old and deficient *at the same time*. Another period of extensive bridge construction, albeit to a lesser degree, occurred during the Depression years of the 1930's. The result of this expansion has had an effect similar to that of the Interstate development which took place from the 1950's to 1970's. The effects of "growing old at the same time" has increased both the magnitude of the problem and the burden placed on maintenance departments in addressing these deficiencies.

In the preceding sections, the reader has been provided with a sampling of some of the more persistent problems associated with highway bridges. These problems can range from a leaking deck joint, to fatigue damage to steel primary members, to scour at substructure footings. It is the goal of a BMS to provide a maintenance department with the ability to determine:

- ❏ The overall condition of any bridge in the network
- ❏ The condition of specific components of a particular bridge

In addition to this basic *condition assessment* of a structure or group of structures, a BMS should be equipped with analytical and/or statistical methods which aid the user in determining:

- ❏ Potential maintenance and rehabilitation plans
- ❏ Associated costs of such plans

> **T**wo factors which complicate the development of a BMS are the expansiveness of the database required to describe the condition of a structure ... and the variable nature of highway bridges themselves.

To meet these four goals is no small task. Two factors which complicate the development of a BMS are the expansiveness of the database required to describe the condition of a structure (see below) and the variable nature of highway bridges themselves. In this book alone we have talked about dozens of different types of bridges, numerous forms of components which can make up each type of structure, and the many permutations of element types within each component and element class. This variable nature is much more than just defining whether the bridge is steel or concrete. If it is a steel bridge, what kind of deck is used, concrete or orthotropic plate? Is there a separate asphalt wearing surface or is it integrated? Are the piers column bent, hammerhead, or even a steel frame? All of this information must be known and accurate in order for any of the four goals listed above to be met.

To address these questions, in previous years, transportation departments relied on manual methods in their efforts to maintain the bridges in their network. To a great degree, based on the excellent record of durability of highway bridges, these methods have worked with remarkable success. The aging of the infrastructure, particularly with many bridges coming of age for rehabilitation at the same time, has made manual methods incapable of meeting the challenges faced by maintenance departments. To address the management of highway bridge maintenance and rehabilitation, computerized methods present the only reasonable method for dealing with such a large amount of information.

5.3.2 Inventory Database

The foundation of any BMS is the *inventory database*. An inventory database contains record information on the type of elements in a highway bridge and their associated condition. In Section 2.3 we discussed the process of inspecting highway bridges and the associated task of recording the inspection. The core of an inventory database is built around this inspection data. In a manual system, maintenance personnel can pull the inspection report for a given bridge from the file and peruse through the various pages to determine the condition of various elements. In a computerized system, the inspection information is stored in a database. The concept of the inventory database has its roots in the creation of the National Bridge Inventory (NBI) in the 1970's [Ref. 5.7]. Many state transportation departments, however, maintain their own scheme of rating individual elements (see Section 2.3.3). There is also a corresponding variation in the *level of detail* of each state's inventory database.

The "level of detail" of an inventory database basically concerns the amount of information stored for each bridge. For any given structure there can be hundreds and hundreds of different attributes stored which describe everything from deck condition to drainage facilities. The process of sorting through and disseminating all of this data is one of the core challenges in creating a working BMS. If logging and sorting through all of this data is such a challenge, applying it to the decision making process of selecting and scheduling bridges for maintenance and rehabilitation is even more of one. Without the inventory database, however, the building of a BMS would be impossible. The inventory database, in essence, represents a picture of a highway bridge. How fine or blurry that picture is can be directly linked to the quality and integrity of the inventory database.

While field inspection data, like that described earlier in Section 2.3, forms the nucleus of the inventory database, it is by no means the only source of information which can be incorporated. Using present computer automation methods, everything from photographs of a bridge to its referenced location on a topographic map can be built into the database and accessed by the user. Another potential source of information which is beginning to make its way into BMS inventory databases is record plan information. As we will discuss in

The inventory database, in essence, represents a picture of a highway bridge. How fine or blurry that picture is can be directly linked to the quality and integrity of the inventory database.

more detail later, once the geometric properties of an element are known (e.g., primary member section properties, column diameter), it is possible to make the step from management decisions to design decisions; all from the single repository of information that is in the inventory database.

It should be noted, however, that more is not necessarily better. If a wealth of information is stored in a database, yet never utilized, it simply adds overhead to the system performance. Building a large database requires significant resources, both in terms of manpower and money, and the creation of massive amounts of data that will never be used drains these resources from the meaningful work of applying the data.

5.3.3 Maintenance Database

Where the inventory database maintains a record of the elements comprising a bridge and its relative condition, a maintenance database contains a description of the work that has been done to date on a structure as well as the work that is presently scheduled to be done. This information is referenced against the inventory data to determine remedial measures to be taken in correcting deficiencies, meaning that if a bridge is slated to have new deck joints installed, then possibly major rehabilitation work can be deferred for another year or two while work is performed on structures with more pressing needs.

5.3.4 Project and Network Level Analysis

A BMS can either function using a project and/or network level analysis approach. *Project level analysis* concerns itself with individual structures and the remedial measures that are to be taken to correct any deficiencies. Associated costing and predicted ramifications of various measures can be performed in an effort to determine which method of repair offers the best solution, both in terms of economy and safety.

Network level analysis concerns itself with a group of bridges and makes its decisions based not only on the needs of an individual bridge, but that of the network as a whole. An example of this would be in one bridge requiring deck repair and another suffering extensive scour damage. With finite funds available, the BMS could assist in the decision making process which identifies correcting the scour problem, with the ultimate impact of structure failure, to be more pressing than fixing the deck, which should not be ignored but at least can be deferred until later. This is but one example of a network level decision making scenario.

A well rounded BMS provides the functionality of examining bridges using both of the methods described above. Although the theoretical image of a BMS is one that produces a list of bridges with appropriate measures to be taken, the reality is much different. A BMS is not so much a decision making tool as it is a decision *assisting* tool. Engineers must absorb this information and with the aid of the BMS arrive at a logical plan of attack for maintaining a network's structures. There are simply too many factors outside of the BMS analysis process that influence project selection for the system to function as a "black box." It is difficult to imagine the coding of a routine in a BMS which accounts for the political pressure employed by a legislator with a deteriorating bridge in his or her community.

A BMS is not so much a decision making tool as it is a decision *assisting* tool. Engineers must absorb this information and with the aid of the BMS arrive at a logical plan of attack for maintaining a network's structures.

A way to view the network level–project level relationship is that of the macroscopic database to the microscopic one. The macroscopic database provides a view of the entire set of bridges, in essence acting as a bird's-eye view from far away. From such a view, maintenance personnel can gain an appreciation of the magnitude and scope of the problems they are facing. This can be called the pie chart view. For example, a typical network analysis product is to show the percentage of bridges which can be classified as poor, good, or excellent. A well established BMS can perform network level optimization analysis—determining the optimal time to take improvement actions on various bridges in the network, under the constraints of the limited budget.

The microscopic project level analysis provides a detailed snapshot of an individual structure. This snapshot includes information on specific elements, the present condition, and possible ramifications if left untouched. The project level view of a bridge can be used to refine the selection process and weed out final candidates for various levels of repair. Where the network analysis methods can be used to determine which bridges make the final round of consideration, a project level approach can be used to select the winning candidates, and be used to define the rehabilitation scope. This two-step approach provides a coherent basis for project selection which takes advantage of both methodologies.

5.3.5 Predicting the Condition of Bridges

Predicting the future condition of a highway bridge is an important factor in determining the type and scope of repair a bridge should receive. This prediction is usually made based on one of the following possible scenarios where:

❑ No work is performed
❑ Partial, interim measures are taken
❑ Full repair to correct all deficiencies is made

> Where the network analysis methods can be used to determine which bridges make the final round of consideration, a project level approach can be used to select the winning candidates.

A basic tool in making these predictions is the so-called *deterioration model*. A deterioration model takes the present condition of an element and extrapolates the condition of an element based on certain remedial measures. The following is an example of how a deterioration model can work. A structure's bearings and pedestals show evidence of corrosion and deterioration causing them to rate a 3 out of a possible 7. If no work is performed, a deterioration model may indicate that the bearings could fall to a 1 in 2 years. If partial work is done to correct failing deck joints and provide surface repair to the pedestals, the rating may hold at a 3 for 3 more years. If the structure is jacked and the deteriorated bearings replaced, the resulting rating would be a 7. The resulting rating is then used to determine an overall rating for the entire structure, so that the picture becomes a little bit more complicated when weighting all of the various alternatives. Maybe the bearings will be repaired and an existing pier problem left alone, or vice versa. These are the type of questions which a deterioration model is supposed to address.

The answers produced by a deterioration model are based in large part on the wealth of knowledge already present in a transportation department and then incorporated into the model. These projections should take into account

DID YOU KNOW

THAT the U.S. spends approximately $1 trillion on transportation services (1993 dollars)? This translates into roughly 17 percent of the nation's total output. The transportation systems included in this expenditure include roads and bridges, rail and waterways, airports, transit lines, and other transportation systems [Ref. 5.8].

historical data on bridges in the same geographic region and of a similar type. Variations in geography, climate, and structure type will obviously have a great impact on the answers generated by a deterioration model. For example, if a structure is in a marine environment or constantly exposed to deicing agents, the corresponding effects on concrete components should be accounted for in the model. In a way, building a deterioration model can be considered more of an art than a science. Because there are so many factors that may affect a bridge's future condition, most BMSs use probabilistic models to give future deterioration predictions.

5.3.6 Miscellaneous Decision Assisting Criteria

In conjunction with the results generated by the deterioration modeling of a structure, there are a variety of decision assisting criteria which are used to arrive at a general recommendation for work to be done. One such criterion is the *level of service criterion*. The level of service criterion is similar in concept to the Importance Classification (IC) used in determining the effects of earthquake loading on a structure (see Section 3.5.3, Part 2). In essence, the level of service criterion defines whether or not a structure can be considered *essential*. Examples of essential bridges would be structures that carry emergency vehicles and school buses. This model should relate structure functionality to various characteristics of the structure such as deck width, vertical clearance, and load carrying capacity [Ref. 5.7].

Other decision assisting criteria are used to account for the impact of factors ranging from future traffic conditions to deterioration of a structure. These models are used to optimize the expenditure of a transportation department's resources to address conditions that may exist several years into the future.

5.3.7 Costing Models

Quite naturally, the costing of various treatments and alternatives plays an important role in a BMS. As we discussed earlier in the preparation of an engineer's estimate (see Section 5.2.1), the basis of any estimate is historical costing from previous work performed. Incorporated into any BMS should be the ability to track cost expenditures which correspond to various levels of work *and detail*. Meaning that, a BMS should maintain in its database the cost of projects on a gross scale (e.g., the cost for a complete rehabilitation of a conventional overhead bridge in the system) and on a more refined scale (e.g., the cost of retrofitting deck joints).

In addition to these basic work cost schedules, a BMS must also take into account various budgetary and funding considerations and limitations (e.g., federal matching funds, allocation of funds to various geographic regions). Costing models must also account for inflation and other economic parameters which influence the cost of a project which is deferred for work at a later time.

I n addition to these basic work cost schedules, a BMS must also take into account various budgetary and funding considerations and limitations.

A BMS should also take consideration of the user cost savings for travelling time, fuel, safety, and serviceability improvements. That is the reason why a BMS always give preference to the heavily travelled bridges when deciding which bridges should be rehabilitated first.

These are just some of the basic criteria which go into making a costing model for a BMS. Given the complex nature of project funding in the transportation industry (see Section 2.1), a wide variety of factors can influence the cost of specific remedial measures to be taken. This complexity can lead to making the development of a costing model one of the most difficult tasks in creating a BMS. The accuracy of results produced by these models must also be taken in light of the wide variety of factors which influence them. There is always a tendency, however, to view rough costing numbers derived from a BMS in the same way as one would review an engineer's final estimate.

Like any other feature in a BMS, the answers produced are more general indications rather than actual conditions. It is the responsibility of the owner to sift through the information generated and distill it into a thoughtful, and hopefully accurate, maintenance plan.

5.3.8 Optimization Models

Optimization analyses may be performed on both network level and project level. A mathematical approach called "Liner Programming" is used for the analyses. The objective function of the optimization is to "minimize the life-cycle cost". The life-cycle cost is the total cost from present to the indefinite future, including maintenance, rehabilitation, and user costs. All future costs are converted into present values.

BMS optimization determines the least-cost strategies for maintenance and rehabilitation for the entire network, based on the results of deterioration and cost analyses. Life-cycle cost analysis is used for the optimization model. It also considers the desired level of service that any bridge should accommodate. For example, if a small bridge is unsafe to the public, it will be rehabilitated even though widening a major Interstate highway bridge may make more economical sense. The optimization is performed under the constraints of the available budget.

The optimization is usually a top-down approach. It first determines which bridges need to be repaired/rehabilitated under the budget constraint, and then determines what actions should be taken for these selected bridges by performing optimization on the project level.

For small bridge populations, the bottom-up approach may be used. Although it takes more computing time, the bottom-up approach provides a more accurate result than the top-down approach.

5.3.9 Building the Database

Building a BMS database is a formidable, and often awe-inspiring task. There is simply an overwhelming abundance of information required to develop accurate models, predictions, and recommendations. This can lead to the development of a BMS becoming mired in the creation of a database alone. This is not a characteristic of BMS alone but in the construction of any similar system, such as a Geographic Information System (GIS). What is needed in building a database of this size is patience and a logical implementation plan.

One method in creating such a massive repository of information is for an agency to *bootstrap its way up the database*. The "bootstrap" approach calls for the creation of a core database, which in the case of a BMS is the inventory database. Because of the push started with the creation of the NBI, many

> It is the responsibility of the owner to sift through the information generated and distill it into a thoughtful, and hopefully accurate, maintenance plan.

> In general, development of a BMS is predicated on the existence of a sound inspection program, without which there can be no description of a structure.

transportation departments are well developed in this respect. In general, development of a BMS is predicated on the existence of a sound inspection program, without which there can be no description of a structure. It is important to emphasize that the goal of a BMS, like that of a design system, is to create a model of a structure in the field. Where a frame analysis package needs to know the dimensions and material properties of columns and cap beams in order to perform its analysis, a BMS needs to know their general type and condition so it too can perform an analysis.

No agency, however sophisticated in its automation methods, will be able to design and implement a BMS with the required database completely in place. There is simply too much information for this to occur. Development of a BMS needs to begin with a core database which is built upon over the course of time. With such an approach the basic functionality of various modules within the system can be developed, tested, and implemented as the database grows and *matures* over time. Using this approach, a transportation department can begin to realize immediate benefits from the system and still pursue the development of a BMS in its "final" form.

We put "final" in quotations because a BMS is truly never final but rather continually evolving. Indeed, the methods of funding, designing, and constructing bridges themselves are not static, so therefore a system developed to manage them can in no way be static itself. Throughout the development of a BMS, however, there are a variety of immediate benefits which can be realized which fall significantly short of an ultimate system implementation.

For example, simply being able to quickly access and view structure inventory and inspection data is a benefit in and of itself, particularly when many transportation departments rely on retrieving hardcopy versions of inspection data from a file cabinet. In the development of a BMS, the first goal should be the accessing and retrieval of data that already exists. If inspection data is present in digital form, it should immediately be made available to maintenance and even design personnel at the earliest opportunity. Like any other computer system, once the actual end users get their hands on the data, an explosion of potential uses of that data will occur that no developer of a system could ever imagine on his or her own. Therefore, it can be said that immediate access to data by the end users of that data is not only important for the users themselves, but is also a critical step in the development of a BMS.

5.3.10 Managing Small and Large Structures

An important issue in the development of a BMS is how small and large structures are handled within a single database. Quite naturally, the maintenance operations for a three span structure are significantly different in magnitude and scope when compared with a hundred span structure. Difficulties arise, however, when a hundred span structure is treated in the same way as a three span bridge, and vice versa.

One method of addressing this discrepancy is to treat a large structure as a group of bridges by itself. This is done by performing all of the BMS analysis methods on a span by span basis, so that in essence, a hundred span bridge is turned into a mini-network of a hundred structures which traverse from support to support. This so-called span-based approach is even sometimes applied to a network of bridges as a whole (i.e., both large and small bridges).

It should be remembered, however, that rehabilitation for the majority of bridges in any network rarely occurs on a span by span basis but rather on a structure by structure basis. For example, if the second span of a three span structure has a deck which requires replacement, it is highly unlikely that only the second span deck alone would be replaced. This is because many bridges constructed in the first half of last century utilized different material properties (e.g., strength of concrete and reinforcing steel) and different geometries (e.g., thickness of deck, curb, and sidewalk width) than are customary today, making a span based rehabilitation infeasible. A transportation agency, for example, would not reconstruct a single span to 1950's era standards.

As a method of determining overall network costs, however, the span-based approach offers some benefits. When actual predictions and recommendations are generated by the BMS, though, they should take into account the probable structure-wide application of remedial measures (i.e., replacement of the second span deck will necessitate replacement of the first and third span deck as well).

> It should be remembered, however, that rehabilitation for the majority of bridges in any network rarely occurs on a span by span basis but rather on a structure by structure basis.

5.3.11 Current Bridge Management Systems

As we have discussed, a BMS is a very complicated system, which requires a significant amount of resources to develop. Most transportation departments in the U.S. do not even have sufficient funds for the routine maintenance, so it is not practical for each DOT to develop its own BMS. Most DOTs adopt one of the two popular bridge management systems—"Points" and "BRIDGIT."

Points is a BMS developed by FHWA in conjunction with six states, and some private consultants. In its database, a bridge is divided into individual elements. These elements with the same materials and can be expected to deteriorate in the same manner are grouped into sections. The condition of each element is reported on a scale of 1 to 5, based on the inspection report.

> Most DOTs adopt one of the two popular bridge management systems—"Points" and "BRIDGIT."

Points uses probabilistic approach for predicting future deterioration. Its cost models have the ability to estimate user costs such as accidents, travel time and fuel costs, etc. For optimization, it uses top-down approach by optimizing the overall network before selecting individual projects.

BRIDGIT is a BMS developed jointly by NCHRP and National Engineering Technology Corporation. BRIDGIT is very similar to Points in terms of modeling and capacities. Their database, the deterioration prediction models, and the cost models are all similar. The primary difference between BRIDGIT and Points lies in the optimization approach. BRIDGIT adopted the bottom-up approach for the optimization. It can also perform "what if" delaying action analysis on a particular bridge. It can tell if delaying a particular project will save or cost more money for the entire bridge life.

BRIDGIT is slower than Points, so it is better suited for small networks.

5.3.12 BMS Link to Design of Bridges

In most discussions of BMS development there is usually an ancillary mention of the potential link to CADD facilities present at a transportation department. This important component to a working BMS, however, is often ignored. The need for a strong link between maintenance and design operations in a transportation department, both in terms of computer software and day-to-day operations, will not only make for better constructed projects but will also reduce much duplication of effort.

At first glance, the potential link between BMS and CADD applications may seem somewhat tenuous. True, they both address bridge needs, but where a BMS analyzes remedial measures and budgetary considerations, a CADD system focuses on the design and eventual preparation of final contract documents. There exists, however, a common ground between these two systems which can be exploited to their mutual advantage.

Figure 5.7 illustrates how the link between BMS and CADD is as natural as the cycle of planning, designing, building, and maintaining a structure is itself. The common ground shared by both BMS and CADD applications is the bridge database. At first glance, the information required by each system may seem to be very different. While there are certainly many differences in the information required by each system, there is also quite a bit of commonality which cannot be ignored.

> **T**he common ground shared by both BMS and CADD applications is the bridge database.

THE CYCLE OF DESIGN and maintenance of a highway bridge also includes the planning (and budgeting) of resources and the physical construction of the structure. This cycle demands a line of communication between the maintenance and design bureaus of a transportation department to ensure that a structure can fulfill its safety and serviceability requirements. In a similar fashion, BMS and CADD need to work together in an effort to avoid a duplication of effort. While BMS and CADD offer functionality which is in many ways very different, they share a common link: the bridge database. As inventory databases become more and more detailed, the extension of these databases to include information relevant to CADD operations is a very real possibility. For example, an inventory database of a BMS often stores the length of spans and the type of primary member used. If the sectional properties of the primary member and deck are also included (e.g., W36x150 stringer and 8 in deck), then a load rating analysis of the structure can be performed within the CADD environment. This data can then be passed back to the BMS for producing an analysis of whether rehabilitation should be conducted or not. This is but one example of how BMS and CADD can work together to achieve common goals.

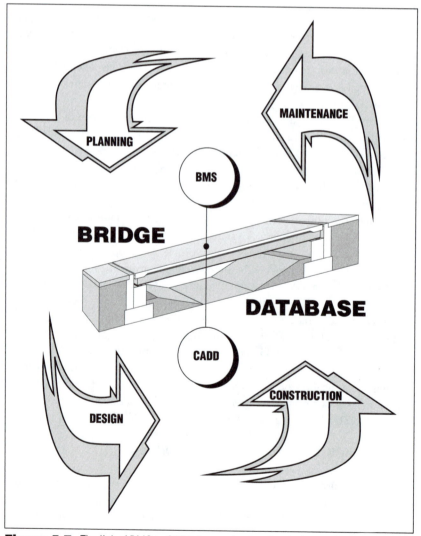

Figure 5.7 The link of BMS to CADD is as natural as the design-maintenance cycle.

A basic example of how BMS and CADD can work together is in the load rating of a structure. A BMS needs to know the load carrying capacity of a structure in order to determine what the course of maintenance should be on a structure. A functionality present in most CADD systems (tailored for bridge design) is the ability to prepare a load rating analysis. In a disparate environment where BMS and CADD work separately, this information would have to be determined by the design department using whatever means are at their disposal (CADD or manual) and then provided for hardwiring or computer spread sheets into the BMS database.

An integrated approach, however, utilizes an expanded inventory database. Most BMS inventory databases already store the length of spans in a structure as well as the type of primary members used (e.g., rolled section, prestressed concrete). The database would need to also include the section properties of the primary member (e.g., W36x150, AASHTO-PCI Type III prestressed concrete girder), deck thickness, and other relevant geometric data. Working off of *the same database,* the CADD system could access the required information, perform a load rating analysis, and pass the information back to the BMS for future analysis in determining potential remedial measures to be taken.

The same type of link can be applied to a wide variety of structural components. The application of this link does not merely apply to structural analysis of bridge components. In the section on the use of CADD in contract document preparation (Section 5.2.2) we discussed the functionality of parametric modeling. If detailed geometric information is also maintained, then the automated production of drawing sheets can also be facilitated. This data can be further applied to the computation of rough quantities (e.g., area required for application of concrete epoxy protective coating, volume of concrete to be removed for component replacement, etc.) which can again be passed back to the BMS for a more refined estimate of proposed work to be performed on a structure selected for repair. To be sure, such detailed interaction would not be performed on a network level analysis, but on the more detailed project level analysis where significant questions can arise. The potential for obtaining a more refined answer in short order is a very real possibility.

Obviously, there is a great deal of work required to build such an integrated system. Like the development of a BMS, however, such an integration is not going to be achieved overnight. The process is also facilitated by the fact that many of the pieces, both on the BMS and CADD end, are already developed. What remains to be done is the integration between them. While the task is certainly formidable, it is by no means impossible. The load rating example given above is an excellent first step to be made toward integrating BMS and CADD applications. From there, cross-links between the systems can be cobbled together.

Another obvious concern for such integration is the massive size of the database involved and the time required to build it. With respect to database size, there is no need to maintain all information in a single database. Separate databases can be established as long as links and the ability to cross-update the databases is accounted for in their design. As far as building the database is concerned, the same bootstrap approach which is recommended for the creation of a BMS database applies to the development of a design or CADD database.

> A basic example of how BMS and CADD can work together is in the load rating of a structure.

> **T**he data needed for most CADD application level analysis can be obtained from record plans and/or field measurements.

The data needed for most CADD application level analysis can be obtained from record plans and/or field measurements. As an activity which can be performed in conjunction with the inspection of a structure, field verification of key CADD related data can be achieved. Again, the information required would be small at first and gradually built upon as the need presented itself. Slowly, one structure at a time, the database will grow and along with this growth will be a corresponding growth in functionality and usefulness.

5.3.13 BMS Link to Pavement Management Systems

A Pavement Management System (PMS) performs much of the same functionality as a BMS, with the emphasis on sections of highway rather than bridge structures. As the bridge is but one component in an overall highway network, the link between pavement and bridge management systems is an important one. The principal benefit of such an integration would be a more unified and logical expenditure of funds. Rather than treating the maintenance of highways and bridges as discrete and independent operations, a link of PMS and BMS applications provides the foundation upon which a transportation department can more judiciously and efficiently allocate funds.

> ...**a** link of PMS and BMS applications provides the foundation upon which a transportation department can more judiciously and efficiently allocate funds.

It is not at all uncommon to have a section of highway receive maintenance work (e.g., resurfacing) and then have structures in the same vicinity undergo rehabilitation. If a combined highway-bridge work schedule is anticipated through the use of an integrated pavement and bridge management system, then consolidation of resources could be made, thereby reducing the overall cost to each project. Such an integration has to be undertaken in a fashion similar to that described for the link between BMS and CADD applications. Like the BMS-CADD integration, the integration of a PMS with a BMS can be made utilizing a common database.

The common link between PMS and BMS is the geography which both highways and bridges share. Where maintenance work in a PMS is analyzed over large lengths of highway (e.g., several miles) the work for a bridge occurs at a specific point, so that an integrated PMS-BMS system could identify locations where bridge and pavement work coincide.

5.3.14 GIS and Imaging Technologies

Another technology which can enhance the functionality of both BMS and PMS is that of a GIS. The ability to view both bridge and pavement data within the context of the geography which they share provides an excellent tool for both visualizing and presenting the work a transportation department is undertaking. Another technology which can be exploited in the development of a BMS is that of imaging. Imaging technology allows for the scanning and automated access of plans, inspection reports, and other pertinent information in a digital environment, so that if a BMS arrives at a certain recommendation, and it is desirable to view the inspector's original remarks in the inspection report, a user can simply access the actual inspection report from within the BMS without having to look at the actual hardcopy report.

Both GIS and imaging technologies serve to illustrate the rapid changes that have taken place in the development of bridge management systems. The creation of a sound database, however, like the creation of a solid foundation, provides the basis which makes the extension to these and other emerging technologies possible. Over the next several decades, these systems will mature and grow to the point where it will be difficult to imagine maintaining structures without them; just as it is difficult to imagine the design of highway bridges without the aid of a personal computer.

REFERENCES

5.1 Hickerson, Thomas F., *Route Surveys and Design,* 4th ed., McGraw-Hill, New York, 1959.

5.2 *A Policy on Geometric Design of Highways and Streets,* 4th ed. American Association of State Highway and Transportation Officials, Washington, D.C., 2001.

5.3 Oglesby, Clarkson H., and Hicks, R. Gary, *Highway Engineering,* 4th ed., p. 445, John Wiley & Sons, New York, 1982.

5.4 Brinkman, Charles P. and Mak, King K., "Accident Analysis of Highway Narrow Bridge Sites," *Public Roads*, vol. 49, no. 4, pp. 127–133, March, 1986.

5.5 Tonias, Demetrios E., et al., "CADD as a Production Tool in Bridge Design," *Public Works*, pp. 34–37, April, 1988.

5.6 Galambos, Charles F., "Bridge Design, Maintenance, and Management," *Public Roads*, pp. 109–115, vol. 50, March, 1987.

5.7 *Guidelines for Bridge Management Systems,* American Association of State Highway and Transportation Officials, Washington, D.C., 1993.

5.8 *The National Highway System: The Backbone of America's Intermodal Transportation Network,* U.S. Department of Transportation, Federal Highway Administration, Washington, D.C., December, 1993.

Appendix

Item	Multiply	By	To Produce
Acceleration	foot per square second (ft/sec²)	0.3048	meter per square second (m/sec²)
Area	square inch (in²)	645.2	square millimeter (mm²)
Density	pound-mass per cubic inch	27,680	kilogram per cubic meter (kg/m³)
	pound-mass per cubic foot	16.02	kilogram per cubic meter (kg/m³)
Energy	British thermal unit (Btu)	1055	joule (J)
Energy/area/time	Btu/ft²/hr	3.152	watt per square meter (W/m²)
Force	pound (lb)	4.448	newton (N)
	kilopound (kip)	4.448	kilonewton (kN)
	ton (2000 lb)	8.896	kilonewton (kN)
Length	inch (in)	25.40	millimeter (mm)
	foot (ft)	0.3048	meter (m)
	mile (mi)	1.609	kilometer (km)
Mass	pound (av.) (lb)	0.4536	kilogram (kg)
	kilopound (kip)	453.6	kilogram (kg)
	ton (2000 lb)	907.2	kilogram (kg)
Power	Btu/hr	0.2929	watt (W)
	horsepower (hp)	0.7457	kilowatt (kW)
Pressure, stress	pound-force/in² (psi)	6.895	kilopascal (kPa)
	kip-force/in² (ksi)	6895	kilopascal (kPa)
	pound-force/ft² (psf)	992.9	kilopascal (kPa)
	inches of mercury (at 32°F)	3.386	kilopascal (kPa)
	feet of water (at 39.2°F)	2.989	kilopascal (kPa)
Speed	miles/hr (mph)	0.447	meters/second (m/s)
Temperature	degree Fahrenheit (°F)	(°t-32)/1.8	degree Celsius (°C)
Volume/time	gallon per minute (gal/min)	0.2271	cubic meter per hour (m³/hr)

Table A.1 SI Conversion Factors

Bar Size Number	Nominal Dia., in	Spacing of Bars, in													
		2	2½	3	3½	4	4½	5	5½	6	7	8	9	10	12
3	0.375	0.66	0.53	0.44	0.38	0.33	0.29	0.26	0.24	0.22	0.19	0.17	0.15	0.13	0.11
4	0.500	1.20	0.96	0.80	0.69	0.60	0.53	0.48	0.44	0.40	0.34	0.30	0.27	0.24	0.2
5	0.625	1.86	1.49	1.24	1.06	0.93	0.83	0.74	0.68	0.62	0.53	0.47	0.41	0.37	0.31
6	0.750	2.64	2.11	1.76	1.51	1.32	1.17	1.06	0.96	0.88	0.75	0.66	0.59	0.53	0.44
7	0.875	3.60	2.88	2.40	2.06	1.80	1.60	1.44	1.31	1.20	1.03	0.90	0.80	0.72	0.6
8	1.000		3.79	3.16	2.71	2.37	2.11	1.90	1.72	1.58	1.35	1.19	1.05	0.95	0.79
9	1.128		4.80	4.00	3.43	3.00	2.67	2.40	2.18	2.00	1.71	1.50	1.33	1.20	1
10	1.270			5.08	4.35	3.81	3.39	3.05	2.77	2.54	2.18	1.91	1.69	1.52	1.27
11	1.410			6.24	5.35	4.68	4.16	3.74	3.40	3.12	2.67	2.34	2.08	1.87	1.56

Table A.2 Average Area per Foot of Width for Various Reinforcing Bar Spacings

Bar Size Number	Nominal Dia., in	Weight, lb/ft	Number of Bars									
			1	2	3	4	5	6	7	8	9	10
3	0.375	0.376	0.11	0.22	0.33	0.44	0.55	0.66	0.77	0.88	0.99	1.10
4	0.500	0.668	0.20	0.40	0.60	0.80	1.00	1.20	1.40	1.60	1.80	2.00
5	0.625	1.043	0.31	0.62	0.93	1.24	1.55	1.86	2.17	2.48	2.79	3.10
6	0.750	1.502	0.44	0.88	1.32	1.76	2.20	2.64	3.08	3.52	3.96	4.40
7	0.875	2.044	0.60	1.20	1.80	2.40	3.00	3.60	4.20	4.80	5.40	6.00
8	1.000	2.670	0.79	1.58	2.37	3.16	3.95	4.74	5.53	6.32	7.11	7.90
9	1.128	3.400	1.00	2.00	3.00	4.00	5.00	6.00	7.00	8.00	9.00	10.00
10	1.270	4.303	1.27	2.54	3.81	5.08	6.35	7.62	8.89	10.16	11.43	12.70
11	1.410	5.313	1.56	3.12	4.68	6.24	7.80	9.36	10.92	12.48	14.04	15.60

Table A.3 Total Areas for Various Numbers of Reinforcing Bars

Acknowledgments

The authors would like to acknowledge the input and commentary received from the many people who spent time perusing through draft copies of this edition. Specifically, the authors thank the principal reviewers of this book, listed below, for their time and effort:

❑ Jack Hu, P.E.   California Department of Transportation
❑ Cris Moen. P.E.   Johns Hopkins University

The authors would also like to express his appreciation to the D.S. Brown Company of North Baltimore, Ohio, Hammer Graphics Inc. of Piqua, Ohio and Dr. Paul Bradford of Watson Brwman Acme Corp., New York for the assistance in providing graphics depicting various deck joint and bearing details. The authors also wishes to thank Robert C. Donnaruma, P.E., and The New York State Thruway Authority for providing various photographs which were used throughout the text.

Also, the author would like to acknowledge the help and assistance put forth by Larry S. Hager, senior editor for this book, who has provided invaluable support during the process of preparing this manuscript. The authors would also like to thank the many other individuals at McGraw-Hill responsible for bringing this book to press, including David Zielonka, Margaret Webster-Shapiro, David Fogarty, and Rick Ruzycka. Thanks also to Shashi Bhushan at International Typesetting and Composition for help in coordinating the layout and final presentation of the page layout.

Lastly, the authors wish to extend their sincerest thanks and appreciation to their families, whose patience and fortitudes throughout the preparation of this book made it all possible.

Illustration Credits

All photographs and illustrations were prepared by the authors, except those figures listed below.

Item	Page	Source
Figure 1.1	1	MTA Bridges and Tunnels, Special Archive
Sir Henry Bessemer	4	The Institute of Materials, London, United Kingdom
Figure 1.11	14	Benaim International Ltd (Owner: Kowloon-Canton Railway Corporation,Hong Kong; Designer: Benaim; Engineer: Arup & Maunsell; Contractor: Maeda-Chun Wo JV)
Figure 1.12	15	Benaim International Ltd (Owner: Railway Procurement Agency, Dublin, Ireland; Designer: Benaim; Engineer: Roughan & O'Donovan; Contractor: GRAHAM)
Figure 1.14	16	Jack Hu
Formwork	28	Maryann Tonias
Modular Joint	31	Paul Bradford
Secondary Member	33	New York State Thruway Authority
Strip Seal Joint	35	Paul Bradford
London Bridge	40	Lake Havasu Area Visitor and Convention Bureau
Interstate Sign	57	Maryann Tonias
Figure 3.4	80	Allan L. McClimans & Martin Stancampiano
Figure 3.8	91	D. S. Brown Company
Figure 3.9	92	D. S. Brown Company
Figure 3.50	324	Pauline E. Tonias
Figure 3.54	338	Pamela Garrabrant
Figure 3.56	353	Pamela Garrabrant
Figure 3.57	357	New York State Thruway Authority
Figure 4.2	370	Pamela Garrabrant
Figure 4.4	372	Maryann Tonias
Figure 4.7	402	D. S. Brown Company
Figure 4.10	405	Pamela Garrabrant
Figure 4.12	408	Richard Garrabrant
Figure 4.16	424	New York State Thruway Authority
Figure 4.17	428	D. S. Brown Company
Figure 4.18	429	D. S. Brown Company
Figure 4.19	430	Richard Garrabrant
Figure 5.1	439	Richard Garrabrant
Figure 5.2	440	New York State Thruway Authority

Index